HALFBREED

HALFBREED

*The Remarkable True Story
of George Bent—Caught Between
the Worlds of the Indian
and the White Man*

DAVID FRIDTJOF HALAAS

ANDREW E. MASICH

DA CAPO PRESS
A Member of the Perseus Books Group

To George Bent

and

Cheyenne Memories

Maps by Bookcomp, Inc.

Cataloging-in-Publication data for this book is available from the Library of Congress.

First Da Capo Press edition 2004

ISBN 0-306-81320-3

Published by Da Capo Press
A Member of the Perseus Books Group
http://www.dacapopress.com

Da Capo Press books are available at special discounts for bulk purchases in the U.S. by corporations, institutions, and other organizations. For more information, please contact the Special Markets Department at the Perseus Books Group, 11 Cambridge Center, Cambridge, MA 02142, or call (800) 255-1514 or (617) 252-5298, or e-mail specialmarkets@perseusbooks.com.

1 2 3 4 5 6 7 8 9—07 06 05 04 03

Contents

Maps

Acknowledgments

We have pursued the George Bent story for over a decade. In 1993, Robert M. Utley, who knows a good story when he sees one, began work on his own Bent book only to discover that we were already on the trail. He immediately abandoned his project to clear the way for ours. Later, he not only critiqued our manuscript but helped guide it to publication. Bob is more than just the American West's premier historian. He is a man of uncommon graciousness and goodwill.

In Oklahoma, Laird Cometsevah, president of the Southern Cheyenne Sand Creek Descendants and a chief of the Council of Forty-Four, and his wife Colleen spent many hours with us explaining the intricacies of Cheyenne language, culture, and history. Arleigh Rhoades, a Dog Soldier headman, shared his vast knowledge of the George Bent family and led us on a tour of the Bent country of west-central Oklahoma, including Colony's Indian cemetery. We were fortunate to have interviewed the late Lucille Bent, George Bent's granddaughter. Joe Big Medicine, Alonzo Sanky, and Lee Pedro, NAGPRA representatives for the Cheyenne and Arapaho Tribes of Oklahoma, offered support and counsel, as did Linda DeCarlo.

In Montana, Steve Brady, president of the Northern Cheyenne Sand Creek Descendants and headman of the Crazy Dog Society, and Otto Braided Hair, coordinator of the Northern Cheyenne Sand Creek Office, shared with us their great knowledge of Cheyenne life. Ray Brady, the late Luke Brady, Martin Brady, Barbara Braided Hair, Mildred Red Cherries, Lee Lonebear, Reginald Killsnight Sr., Holda Roundstone, Joe Walks Along, William Walks Along, Norma Gourneau, Roger Old Mouse, and Douglas Spotted Eagle, participated with us in the Sand Creek Massacre site location hearings in Montana, Denver, and Washington, D.C.

We thank our old friend David N. Wetzel, director of publications at the Colorado Historical Society, who read portions of the manuscript and helped in many other ways, from tracking down illusive archival and photographic sources to solving vexing computer problems. Clark Secrest, our own curmudgeon and confidant, spurred us on when the going got tough. We owe much to other Society staff as well, especially Chris Geddes, Mary Ann McNair, Marghi Aguiar, Jennifer Adams, Peggy Hermann, Larry Borowsky, Rebecca Lintz, and Barbara Foley. The Society's board of directors provided financial support during a critical phase of the project. Board Vice Chairman Joe Halpern gave constant support and guidance, as did Board Chairman Frank Kugeler. Walter A. Koelbel and William F. Wilbur recognized from the beginning the importance of the project. We thank them for their confidence and wise counsel.

We thank the Colorado Endowment for the Humanities for a grant that supported the early research phase.

Our gratitude to Father Peter Powell and Donald Berthrong, both true masters of Cheyenne history. Dr. Lincoln Faller provided letter-perfect and definitive transcriptions of the Bent–Hyde correspondence located at the Beinecke Library, Yale. Rancher William F. Dawson not only read portions of the manuscript but allowed us and our Cheyenne friends full access to his property at the Sand Creek Massacre site. The late John C. Ewers offered encouragement and support. Lee Scamehorn, professor of history at the University of Colorado, alerted us to valuable Bent–A. E. Reynolds correspondence.

We thank our friends and colleagues at the Smithsonian National Anthropological Archives, Smithsonian Institution, Library of Congress, Southwest Museum, National Archives, Oklahoma Historical Society, Kansas Historical Society, Missouri Historical Society, Kansas City Public Library, Denver Public Library, Sedgwick County Historical Society, Missouri State Historical Society, Pioneer Museum, Shawnee Mission, Newberry Library, National Archives–Chicago Branch, Dull Knife Community College, National Park Service–Bent's Fort, National Park Service–Fort Laramie, Beinecke Library–Yale, and the University of Oklahoma Library and Archives.

A tip of the hat and best bow to Jean Afton, Everett Burch, Steven H. Chestnut, Margaret Coel, Mindy Elswick, Mark Gardner, Jim Hutchins, Dick Kreck, Dietmar and Helga Kuegler, Robert W. Larson, Ben Lawless, Dianna Litvak and Brian Winn, Susan and Craig Miner,

Acknowledgments

Rick Manzanares, Craig Moore, Eli Paul, Ramon Powers, Jim Richardson, Alexa Roberts, Gary Roberts, Rodney Staab, Al and Carol Stine, Colin Taylor, Janet Vaughan, Kim Walters, Bill Welge, Ray Werner, Chris Wheeler, Dallas Williams, and George Williams.

The staff of the Senator John Heinz Pittsburgh Regional History Center gave its support, praise, and criticism—in equal measure at the right time. Betty Arenth, Audrey Brourman, the museum division, and the rest of the gang deserve more thanks than we can express.

For their expert opinion and steadfast support, our deep appreciation to Robert Pigeon, editor at Da Capo Press; and our agent Jim Donovan of Dallas, Texas.

We owe the most to our families. Debbie, Matt, Molly, Max Masich, and Mom were Andy's support team and source of inspiration. David Halaas lovingly thanks his wife Kathleen Brown and children, Kristine, Jenny, Bryan, and Keith; and Richard H. Shay, Virginia Shay, and Susan Langhorne.

Finally, the authors would like to thank each other. It's been an extraordinary collaboration—and we're still talking to each other.

Prologue

In west-central Oklahoma, about twelve miles south of Weatherford, the town of Colony huddles in a small valley thick with trees,
a shaded oasis in endless grasslands. A visitor driving through sees first
a row of comfortable brick ranch-style homes, complete with expansive, well-groomed lawns, patio barbecues, and minivans parked in
two-car driveways. A short way down the road is the old town center.
An American flag waves above the post office, parked cars point
toward a five-table cafe, and here and there stand turn-of-the-century
frame houses, some well kept, others abandoned.

Nothing unusual. Just a small Oklahoma town.

Across the road from the town center a broken sign, lettered in peel-
ing paint, announces *Cheyenne and Arapaho Tribes of Oklahoma*.
Bleachers, pole-and-brush arbors, and ceremonial grounds stand in a
field of weeds and spreading bur oaks, their twisted, lopsided branches
marking the faint traces of long-forgotten roadways. Beyond is a brick
foundation, topped by a crumbling water tower, a remnant of the once
lively Seger Indian School. Vines and brambles overrun the broken
remains. Insects are thick here, the sound of cicadas loud in the silence
of the trees.

Leaving Colony, the road rises. Not far from town, a country lane
crosses the main highway. Most travelers ignore it and continue on,
but those who turn south notice, within a few hundred yards, a dirt
driveway leading up a hill. There is no sign, but cracked and fallen
grave markers identify a cemetery.

A man works a small riding mower through dusty dry grass, carefully steering around hidden stones and rotted wood headboards. One
section of ground is fairly open; mounded earth and withered flowers

indicate recent burials. Ignoring this area, the man aims his machine at an eight-foot wall of thick-stalked Johnsongrass. Smoke belches from the mower, the engine sputters, then dies. The man shrugs, pushes the mower up the trailer ramp hitched to his pickup truck, and drives off.

At the edge of the tangled bramble stands a small stone marker. *Standing Out Bent—Our Mother* reads the inscription. Not far away, another stone: *Mary Washee Bent*. A small opening leads into the thicket. Here in the green maze, one loses all sense of distance and direction. Mosquitoes and chiggers assault the intruder. A few feet, a hundred feet—it is impossible to judge—stands a waist-high Colorado rose-red granite stone, its size and quality unique in this place. Parting the stalks it is possible to read the inscription: *George Bent, 1843–1918.* Nothing more. Nothing to indicate that buried here is a great Cheyenne warrior and frontiersman, the son of William Bent, builder of Bent's Fort, and his Cheyenne wife, Owl Woman, the daughter of the Keeper of the Sacred Arrows.

George Bent stood on the stoop of his three-room frame house, overlooking the town of Colony. He squinted into the hot sun hoping to catch a glimpse of Willie's buckboard as it crested the rise west of the valley, but the road lay empty. His eyes drifted toward the red-bricked Seger Indian School, shaded and cooled by the groves of cottonwoods and oaks lining Cobb Creek. Canvas tipis dotted the grassy clearing nearby. Before parents took their children home for the summer, they would camp here for a few weeks, visiting with friends.

Movement on cemetery hill east of the school caught his eye. A burial had taken place that day, another of the old-timers gone. He would think on that later. Above the cemetery, a rainbow arced across the sky, interrupted only by thin streaky clouds—mare's tails, his mother had called them. Bent returned his gaze to the west road. That morning his son had taken the wagon over to Weatherford to meet the train and pick up George Bird Grinnell. It had been five years since Bent last saw the world-famed historian and Indian authority, and so he wore his gray wool suit—his only suit—even though the day was hot and humid. Earlier, rain had drenched the valley, and now heat rose in shimmering waves carrying with it the pungent smell of wet sage and grass.[1]

Then he saw it. The buckboard descended into the valley and rattled past the hotel and the Colony Mercantile Co., then turned up the road to Bent's house. Grinnell stepped down from the buckboard to greet the man he had traveled more than two thousand miles to see. Bent stood nearly six feet tall and weighed over 250 pounds. In his broad-brimmed hat and store-bought clothes, and smiling behind a white man's gray walrus mustache, he looked like a prosperous Oklahoma rancher.[2]

But Grinnell knew better. This was no white man—the fold of his eyes, the bronzed face and jutting cheekbones, said otherwise. This was George Bent, the mixed-blood son of the legendary William Bent and Owl Woman, the daughter of White Thunder, the Cheyenne's most revered holy man.

During his long life, Bent had brushed against the edges of greatness, always in the center of controversy and danger, always a survivor, but a man who moved uneasily between Cheyenne and white worlds, never gaining full acceptance in either. Raised a Cheyenne by his father's three wives—sisters all—then sent East to be educated in white schools, Bent fought as a Confederate cavalryman during the Civil War; joined the Cheyennes as a Crooked Lance warrior and fought their Indian enemies—Pawnees, Delawares, and Crows; experienced the horrors of Colonel John M. Chivington's massacre of Chief Black Kettle's village at Sand Creek; rode with the Cheyenne Dog Soldiers in revenge raids against the whites; interpreted for Chief Red Cloud during General Connor's Powder River campaign; fell in love with and married Magpie Woman, daughter of Black Kettle; negotiated the pivotal Medicine Lodge Treaty as U.S. interpreter and advisor to tribal leaders; played a central role in the creation of the Cheyenne-Arapaho Reservation in Oklahoma; hobnobbed with Kit Carson, Buffalo Bill, Wild Bill Hickok, and George Armstrong Custer, and fought beside Crazy Horse, Tall Bull, and Roman Nose; battled alcoholism; suffered broken marriages and the alienation of his children; and powerfully influenced Cheyenne leaders during the tribe's agonizing transition from the free life to reservation confinement.

Now, in his final years, Bent felt a passionate need to set the historical record straight and to preserve the memory of the Cheyennes as a free people. "Whites never get it right,"[3] he would say. And so the world's greatest historians and ethnologists sought him out, to learn from him—and that's why Grinnell was here. People thought of him, the blue-blood New Yorker, as "the Indian Authority," but Grinnell knew in his heart that without George Bent, he knew nothing.[4] Yet Bent was a hard man to know. Like most Indians, he almost never spoke of himself. But Grinnell understood that the stories Bent told about his people helped define the storyteller and revealed much about the man who stood before him. Even more, he knew that Bent was the product of two great families; in fact, the two most powerful and influential families on the high plains during the formative years of the American West. These families—one white, the other Cheyenne— shaped Bent's character and imprinted on him the values of two very different worlds. His father, steely-eyed, tenacious, and controlling, a man who willingly took risks and built an empire, yet a man vulnerable and naïve in love and family affairs, endued his son with his indomitable spirit but little of his enterprise. After a decade and more of interviews and correspondence with Bent, however, only now did Grinnell realize that White Thunder, Keeper of the Cheyennes' Sacred Arrows, influenced his grandson's life more than any other man. Stoic, stubborn, starry-eyed, dogged by bad luck but a man of courage and principle, White Thunder's omnipresence inevitably drew Bent into the very heart of Cheyenne spiritual and political life. So together these two men and their families—coming from worlds apart—created the mixed-blood George Bent.

Bent seemed not to notice Grinnell's obvious fatigue from the long journey. Taking the historian by the arm, he led him to the brush arbor behind the house, for he had an urgent need to begin. There was so little time left; the old ones were dying, and without them no one, not his children, not his grandchildren, not the whites, would know the truth of what it was to be Tsistsistas—Cheyenne. He would use this

white man to preserve the history of his people and his own family.[5]
*The two men sat down. Grinnell pulled a small notebook from his coat
pocket, licked the tip of his pencil, and wrote June 3, 1912. Bent began
to talk.*

"My father, William W. Bent, was born in St. Louis in 1809 . . . "

George Bent's Country

Chapter 1

WORLDS APART

William Bent was one of eleven children of Silas Bent, a prominent and well-connected judge, and Martha Kerr, a highborn Virginian. The Bent farm sprawled on a high bluff overlooking the Mississippi River; a post-and-rail fence defined the property and prevented stray animals and roaming children from a precipitous descent into the roiling Mississippi waters. Towering oaks and sycamores shaded the rambling two-story frame house, and a barn and adjoining shed gave further evidence of the family's affluence.[1] Here, at the gateway to the West, the Bent children heard the stories of great explorers such as Lewis and Clark, the first Americans to trek overland to the Pacific, and Zebulon Pike, who had recently ascended the Mississippi River itself. The children absorbed, too, the tales of the explorers' guides—Indians such as the legendary Shoshone woman Sacagawea, who took Lewis and Clark over the passes and into the great unknown.

Later, the boys read the advertisement in the *St. Louis Missouri Republican* calling for one hundred "enterprising young men" to fill William Henry Ashley's 1822 fur expedition to the distant reaches of the Missouri, a mysterious land said to be jealously guarded by Blackfeet Indians. Charles, the oldest of the Bent brothers and first to answer the call, trapped beaver in Sioux country as early as 1823 as a hired hand for the Missouri Fur Company. When the company reorganized two years later, twenty-five-year-old Charles earned full partnership, joining such veteran fur men as Lucien Fontennelle, William Vanderburgh, Andrew Drips, and Joshua Pilcher. In a few years, seventeen-year-old William joined him, while the younger brothers, George and Robert, tugged hard at the bonds that tied them to the family farm, eager to go west and share a trapper's life with their wandering brothers.

1

During the 1827–28 season, Charles and William experienced the exuberance and despair characteristic of the fur trade. The Missouri Fur Company trapping expedition, headed by Joshua Pilcher, started badly. In September the party of forty-five men had set out with high hopes from Council Bluffs, working up the Platte River. Disaster struck when the trappers reached the Wind River Mountains near the confluence of the Platte and the Sweetwater. As the men made their night camp, Crow warriors charged the horse herd, blankets waving, and captured all but a few of the one hundred riding horses and pack animals.

Pilcher ordered the men to cache the company's trade merchandise. These goods would be needed at the summer rendezvous on Bear Lake, 150 miles west over South Pass. The only hope now was to continue on toward the Green River, establish a winter camp, and persuade friendly Indians to sell them horses. With pack animals they could retrieve the cached merchandise and return in time to be competitive at the summer rendezvous.[2]

But the winter was hard. The men worked the Green and its tributaries, finding precious few beaver. Most of their energies were expended in staying alive, building rude log and brush shelters, and hunting what game they could find. Charles and William saw firsthand that a mountain man's life was not all romantic adventure.

One of the partners acquired horses from the Shoshones and with a few of the company's men returned to the Sweetwater cache. Here they discovered that the merchandise, so carefully buried the previous fall, was wet and damaged. They salvaged what they could, carrying the rotted and mildewed goods over South Pass to link up with the rest of the company at the annual rendezvous.

Back on the Green, the Bents and their associates departed the dismal winter camp and made their way to Bear Lake, where they joined the great trade fair with its promise of fun and profit.

This was the second consecutive year that the mountain men had chosen Bear Lake as the rendezvous site. It furnished the requisite needs: grass and water, food and fuel. More than that, it was beautiful, even by mountain man standards. The rendezvous point hugged the south shore of the spectacularly blue waters, and as more of the mountaineers arrived, the gathering resembled a small village. At the lake's bank stood shelters fashioned of bulrushes; sweet pine smoke rose above the tipis, and even from a distance the scene pulsed with activity and excitement: foot and pony races, target shooting, gambling, unpacking of plews and trade goods, constant arrivals of newcomers—sometimes joyously punctuated by booming cannon fire—and the sounds of shouts and songs of hard men freely imbibing from jugs of hard liquor. The excitement continued into the night, different perhaps, but with the same recklessness.

But it was not an all-male gathering. Women were everywhere present, scraping hides, cooking, mending, and some next to their men fully participating in the camp's abandon. Children, too, ran about, unrestrained in their joy, for the rendezvous was the stuff of dreams. These youngsters were the sons and daughters of the fur trade, the progeny of European men and native women. They were the embodiment of the merging of races and cultures, and here they were in their glory, accepted for who they were, in a haven far from questioning worlds, both Indian and white.[3]

Into this swirl of sights and sounds the Bents arrived with Pilcher's main band. The great names of the fur trade were already there. Jim Bridger, tall, sinewy, and tough, and already a legend, held court spinning gaudy yarns. Jim Beckwourth, the son of a Virginia planter and an African slave, his intimidating presence contrasting with his lively wit, regaled his own wide-eyed followers.

Some were not there, however—the indefatigable Jedediah Smith, up in Hudson's Bay country fighting hostile Umpquas; Tom Smith, recently peg-legged by Indians on the North Platte River; and Sylvestre Pratte, felled by disease in the great North Park of the Central Rocky Mountains. Even for the best of men, death in these mountains could come cruelly and without warning. Few were remembered, their graves unmarked and lost forever.

Thus the rendezvous, a reunion of survivors.

Right now the camp buzzed with the recent exploits of these indomitables. Just days before, Blackfeet warriors had attacked Bridger and Robert Campbell's thirty-one-man company six miles from the lake. Beckwourth and a companion named Calhoun chanced to be with the party. The fight turned ugly as more and more warriors appeared. Beckwourth wheeled his horse and turned back to assist a straggler, an old man who had shouted out, "Oh, God, I am wounded!" Beckwourth found an arrow "trembling" in the man's back. "I jerked it out, and gave his horse several blows to quicken his pace; but the poor old man reeled and fell from his steed, and the Indians were upon him in a moment to tear off his scalp."[4] The besieged men were now dangerously low on powder and ball. Campbell called out for volunteers to ride for help. Though suffering from a head wound and his horse shot down, Beckwourth responded. Taking Calhoun with him, the mountain man rode through the Blackfeet warriors, quickly outdistancing his pursuers. He soon returned with sixteen well-armed men, others streaming behind—all with their blood up and spoiling for a fight. Hawken rifles cracked, driving the warriors from their cover, and soon the battle became a rout. Beckwourth claimed the mountaineers took seventeen scalps, while Campbell lost only four men killed and seven wounded.[5]

That evening the rendezvous erupted in wild celebration. The camp's "halfbreeds and women" danced over the scalps, many of the mountain men joining in.[6] The women and their mixed-blood children, said Beckwourth, treated the victors as heroes, "knowing that we had preserved them from a captivity to which death were preferable."[7]

Meanwhile, Pilcher and the Bents anxiously awaited word of the Sweetwater party and the cached goods. At last an advance rider came in announcing the pack train's approach. The Bents joined the mad rush out of camp to see what goods remained, for news of the damaged cache had already swept the company. Reaching the party, the partners tore open the packs. What they saw assaulted their senses: rusted axes and trade muskets; molded tobacco, coffee, and spices; soaked gunpowder caked in damaged canisters; mildewed and blackened Hudson's Bay blankets, trade cloth, and yard goods. Nothing to trade now, the expedition—and the company—faced total ruin.

Back in camp, the partners confronted an uncertain future. The beleaguered company could claim only eighteen packs of beaver, a profound disappointment for nearly a year of hard work in icy streams and snowbound camps. Every day, the rendezvous' lively trade of goods and plews contrasted with their own poverty. There was nothing more to do except retreat back over South Pass and head down the familiar Sweetwater–Platte river route to Council Bluffs and St. Louis.[8]

Bad luck dogged the brothers and their companions. Joined by the renowned William Sublette and his strong party of seventy-five veteran trappers, they should have expected better. Near Independence Rock in present-day Wyoming, a Crow war party shadowed the slow-moving pack train. As the fur men crossed the broad waters of the Platte, the warriors attacked, killing two trappers and wounding several others. The Crows also captured a large quantity of horses and furs.

Shortly thereafter, one of the company, Hiram Scott, fell ill and could ride no farther. While the rest of the party proceeded overland, two men were ordered to take Scott downriver in a bull-hide boat. They would join up where great bluffs rose above the river. But during the dangerous river descent, the boat overturned, and with weapons and food lost, the two guardians abandoned their charge and pushed on night and day until they overtook the company. The trappers, however, reasoned that their own dire straits—starving and exhausted men, jaded horses and pack animals, depleted lead and powder—made Scott's rescue impossible. Meanwhile, the forlorn man, feverish and alone, crawled sixty torturous miles to the rendezvous point, waiting for his comrades to return. The next year, Scott's bleached bones were discovered beneath the bluffs that would forever bear his name.[9]

For the Bents it was a fitting end to a disastrous expedition.

When the buckskinned brothers limped into Council Bluffs with pockets and packs empty, more bad news awaited them. Their father, Silas, had died the winter before. Finally home in St. Louis, twenty-nine-year-old Charles considered the family's new circumstances. His two sisters were married, and brother John, a lawyer and state legislator, needed no help. Young Silas, age nine, would remain with his mother. But the other brothers, William, Robert, and George, struck by the Bent wanderlust, naturally turned to Charles for guidance.

The Bents had learned well the lessons of their recent mountain ordeal. Trapping the high country dominated by the great British and American fur companies was at best chancy and certainly dangerous. They would never forget the ruthless and ruinous competition, hostile Indians, hard winters, and punishing treks across vast distances.

Most of all they questioned the inner workings and process of the fur trade itself. Trappers labored at the end of a long economic chain that stretched from the icy beaver ponds of the Rocky Mountains to the bustling fur-trading centers of Santa Fe and St. Louis, from the sweaty hat factories of Cincinnati and Philadelphia to the capricious markets of New York and Boston, London and Paris, where fickle fashion governed demand. They had to buy traps and supplies at exorbitant prices and sell pelts and furs for paltry sums. To be sure, they traveled far and saw wondrous things—but their freedom was an illusion. The brothers now knew this life. There had to be a better way, one with less risk and greater profit. And so in the spring of 1829, forty miles from Westport, Missouri, at a place called Round Grove, Charles and William joined independent traders bound for Santa Fe.

This season the traders were nervous. Hostile Indians, dry water holes, bandits, inept guides—all had brought financial loss the year before. Perhaps there was safety in numbers. Not seasoned trail bosses themselves, the merchants looked elsewhere for leadership. The name *Bent* came forward. David Waldo, a Santa Fe trader, thought Charles the right man and urged him to accept the train's captaincy. Bent's experience and solid character impressed the others, who elected him without a dissenting vote.[10]

In June, the thirty-eight-wagon outfit rolled out of Round Grove, the great 775-mile journey before them. The merchants packed the wagons with an abundance of manufactured goods: domestic cottons, silks, calicoes, velvets, drillings, shirtings, black bottles, Galena lead, powder, patent medicines, cookware, everything an isolated frontier community needed. The traders expected to bring home a treasure in gold and silver, furs, mules, and raw wool.[11]

Twenty-year-old William stood at his brother's side as the older Bent took command of this loose alliance of independent-minded traders, teamsters, and frontiersmen. A captain's responsibilities would challenge any man. Besides selecting campsites, settling disputes, and assigning daily duties, the captain must anticipate danger of any kind—and there was danger enough on the Santa Fe Trail.

A detachment of U.S. infantry under command of Major Bennett Riley, authorized by President Andrew Jackson himself, escorted the caravan. However, the soldiers pulled back when the train reached Chouteau's Island on the Arkansas River some four hundred miles out; they had strict orders not to cross the Mexican border. The island also marked the site where the merchants, besieged by Comanches the year before, had cached rawhide bags filled with Spanish silver.

Before taking leave of the troops, Captain Bent negotiated for the use of a few of the army's oxen, for he had noticed on the trip that these draft animals seemed to endure the trail's rigors and scarcity of water better than the mules. Oxen better than mules? It was an idea worth testing.[12]

With their escort left behind, the merchants again expressed their fear. They saw phantom Indians lurking behind every sand hill and tumbleweed, and it was only through Bent's steady hand that the wagons moved at all. Suddenly, the traders' worst nightmare became frightening reality. Out of hidden ravines charged hundreds of Kiowa and Comanche warriors. They seemed to be everywhere. The traders panicked, reaching for their untested guns and fumbling with their priming horns, scarcely able to take aim. One of the merchants recalled the scene: "I saw Charles Bent charge alone and check fifty Indians that had killed one man and were in close pursuit of another. It was in this surprise that this heroic act occurred. I can see him now as plainly as I saw him then, mounted on a large black horse, I think bare-headed, with his long black hair floating in the wind; and I distinctly remember his words of defiance when he made the charge."[13] This checked the enemy long enough for the wagoners to bring up a small cannon. Although the inexpert gunners fired wildly, the cannon's shattering report and blast of white smoke sent the Indians racing for the protection of the ravines.

Mounted on a split-eared Indian mule, William rode at his brother's side, furiously ramming charges down the barrel of his flintlock rifle—no easy task on a frightened animal.[14] Charles ordered the wagons corralled and rifle pits dug. At the same time, scouts galloped off in a desperate attempt to bring back the soldier escort, now camped on the Arkansas River nine miles distant.

Later that night, at about one o'clock, three companies of foot-sore troops straggled into the wagon circle. Phillip St. George Cooke, a second lieutenant with the escort, noticed that the Indians had attacked where the wagons would be most vulnerable. The caravan was corralled in a "natural amphitheater of sand-hills," he said, "about fifty feet high, and within gun-shot all around. There was the narrowest practicable entrance and outlet."[15] When dawn broke, the soldiers accompanied the shaken merchants deeper into the sand hills. Charles directed the men to roll the body of one of the company's traders, killed the day before, into an abandoned rifle pit. The reinforced caravan plodded through the sand until it reached a wide plain dotted with a scanty and dwarfish growth of dried grass, which afforded little protection against the swirling winds that whipped through the wagons.[16] Here, the army once again turned back to its camp at Chouteau's Island, there to await the traders who were expected to return in October.

The loss of the escort again caused anxiety. It was all Charles could do to keep the company together. Many of the men wanted to return with the soldiers to the Arkansas bivouac. To make matters worse, a band of poorly armed Mexican buffalo hunters, as panicked as the traders themselves, joined the expedition. Meanwhile, the Comanches continued their sporadic attacks, running off mules and horses, keeping the men awake and constantly on edge.

Word reached Taos that the caravan was under siege. Ewing Young—known in the mountains for his fighting prowess—and forty well-armed men came out to help. Joined by another strong party of fifty-five frontiersmen, the combined force pushed its way to the endangered train. Among the rescuers was Kit Carson, a youth of twenty but already an experienced mountain man. The Kiowas and Comanches disappeared before this veteran force, and Bent's outfit, confidence restored, rolled on, passing through Taos on its way to Santa Fe.[17]

It was a journey to be remembered, not only for its dangers but also for its success. When at last the traders returned to St. Louis later that year, they sold their New Mexican goods for enormous profits.

It was a good beginning for the Bents. Charles quickly refitted for a return trip to Santa Fe. By the next year he had forged a business relationship with Santa Fe trader and former mountain man Ceran St. Vrain. It was a partnership that would transform the fur trade in the Southwest and make both men wealthy as well as legends on the Santa Fe Trail.

William, however, was not yet done with the mountains. After the successful Santa Fe Trail expedition, the brothers separated, William off with a band of free trappers, working his way north, always keeping the shining mountains to the west, trapping the clear waters of the Upper Arkansas and its tributaries.

The trappers chose their winter camp carefully. Many tribes—Utes, Cheyennes, Arapahos, Comanches, Kiowas, Apaches—contested this rich hunting ground, an advantage to the company for it would bring a variety of trading partners into the region. But the trappers greatly underestimated the dangers. The Utes claimed the mountains to the west; the allied Cheyennes and Arapahos regularly raided the Kiowa, Comanche, and Apache horse herds to the south. It was an explosive mix, no one controlling the region, no one willing to give it up. But all were sure to seek out these white strangers, sample their goods, and test their resolve. On a stream the French named *Fontaine-qui-bouille* and known to the Bents as Fountain Creek, William and his party built a stockade of cottonwood pickets where they stored their merchandise and furs, carrying on a lively trade with passing Indians.[18]

Here, Cheyenne Chief Yellow Wolf stopped to investigate these curious newcomers. He and a strong force of warriors were returning from a successful horse raid against Bull Hump's band of Comanches on the Red River. The warriors were in a celebratory mood and stayed a few days at the stockade, trading and learning more of these bearded men in buckskin. Yellow Wolf and most of his party eventually rode off, anxious to return to their villages on the South Platte. But two young Cheyennes, who had not yet had their fill of the treasure of novelties brought by the traders, remained behind.

Without warning, a band of Comanches, led by Bull Hump himself, rode toward the stockade. Alone, Bent strode out to meet them, knowing that the discovery of Cheyennes hiding within the stockade might bring death to them all. Using sign language, Bent learned that Bull Hump was indeed in search of the Cheyenne horse raiders. Looking straight at the Cheyenne moccasin prints plainly in view, Bull Hump demanded to know if his enemies were about. There was no time to think. Bent signed that the Cheyennes had all gone north to their villages on the Platte. Bull Hump signed again—no Cheyennes here? No. Bull Hump consulted with his warriors, turned back to stare into the steel-gray eyes of the white man, then abruptly rode off. The two Cheyennes understood how close they had come to capture and death. When they returned to the villages they told everyone how Bent had refused Bull Hump's demand for their surrender.[19]

William's split-second decision began his lifelong bond and partnership with the Cheyennes. There was money to be made in the mountains, not the mountain man way of endless work in icy streams, but trading with native peoples, who were expert in fur and hide hunting, as well as capturing horses for trade. By establishing a fixed trading post, the Indians would come to him with their furs and hides and horses. In return he would provide them guns, powder and ball, red cloth, trade beads, tobacco, brass wire for bracelets, hoop iron for arrow points, butcher knives, small axes and tomahawks, vermilion, abalone shell for ear drops, and—increasingly—whiskey.[20]

Over the next eighteen months, these ideas crystalized as he waded the waters of the southern Rockies. On his trips to Santa Fe, where he resupplied for renewed assaults on the mountains, he met brother Charles and his Santa Fe Trail partner Ceran St. Vrain, who were intrigued by William's idea of fixed trading posts. Particularly, the entrepreneurs liked the concept of eliminating the trade's middlemen, who took for themselves a large percentage of the profits. By 1832 the Charles Bent–St. Vrain partnership hit full stride. With a trading store in Taos, another planned for Santa Fe, and with merchandise and other assets exceeding one hundred thousand dollars, the partners looked for new opportunities.[21]

Meanwhile, William tested his idea at a large post located near the junction of Fountain Creek and the Arkansas River. Here, he packed in supplies and goods for trade with his Cheyenne friends, as well as other passing Indians. To this makeshift picket-post came brother Charles and his ox-drawn wagons—by now Charles was convinced of their superiority over horses and mules—the first wheeled vehicles in the Upper Arkansas country. Now old enough to help their elder brothers in the western fur business came George, age eighteen, and Robert, age sixteen.

That summer Cheyenne chiefs Yellow Wolf, Little Wolf, Wolf Chief, High Back Wolf, and Standing on Hill met the Bents at the Purgatoire River where it spills into the Arkansas. At this council William served as interpreter, supplementing his broken Cheyenne with quick hand gestures. After smoking and the exchange of gifts, Yellow Wolf explained that his tribe was wholly dependent on the buffalo, which ranged in great numbers on the southern plains. But generally, he said, they were scarce along the foothills of the Rockies, where the Bents, unfortunately, had located their post. In contrast, the chief said, the grass country farther down the Arkansas near the Big Timbers was rich in buffalo. Even better, there were no Utes, longtime enemies of the Cheyennes. The Cheyennes usually wintered at the Big Timbers, and enemies—especially the Utes, Comanches, Kiowas, and Apaches—dared not attack their villages.

It was an extraordinary proposal, for Yellow Wolf's meaning was unmistakable. If the Bents would move their operations to Big Timbers, the Cheyennes would partner with the brothers in their expanding trade empire. William and Charles immediately understood and with their new partners smoked on the pact. From the wagons came salted pork and beef, while the Indians provided antelope meat, along with buffalo berries, chokecherries, and ripe plums.[22]

The chiefs took the occasion to give Cheyenne names to their new friends. William, short-statured and slim, they already knew as *Schivehoe*, "Little White Man." Charles they gave the name, *Pe-ki-ree*, "White Hat." George became *Ho-my-ike*, "Little Beaver." And young Robert, the handsomest of the brothers, they called *Otatavi-wee-his*, "Green Bird."[23] The feast over, the Bents' heavily loaded wagons rolled off for St. Louis, where the brothers would again exchange prairie produce for specie and bank notes.

Next year, in the spring of 1832, the brothers returned, this time with Mexican laborers and tools—pulleys, adzes, shovels, hammers, iron spikes, sheet iron, hinges, bolts, and construction materials of all kinds. The partners would construct what they were already calling Fort William. But they did not return to Big Timbers. For whatever reasons, the Bents selected a site in a bend of the Arkansas, some forty miles west of the spot designated by Yellow Wolf. True, grass was plentiful here, and William found the soil ideal for the manufacture of adobe bricks, but it was not Big Timbers.

The workers dug great borrow pits down by the river, mixing the soil with prairie grass and water. Then they pressed the sticky compound into wooden molds, their fingerprints embedded in the adobe surface. Thousands of unbaked bricks, set on end, dried in the sun, all laid out on the river's bank as far as the eye could see. Slowly, the fort took form and substance. When it was completed, it made a stunning appearance. A Santa Fe Trail traveler who saw the fort described it with some wonder:

William Bent and his enterprising brothers commenced and completed this remarkable stronghold, far away upon the banks of the Arkansas, four hundred miles from an American settlement, and in the very heart of the great wilderness of the West. Although built of the simple prairie soil, made to hold together by a rude mixture with straw and the plain grass itself, the strength and durability of the walls is surprising and extraordinary. Though Indians should come in swarms as numerous as the buffalo, Fort William would prove impregnable, for the Red Devils would never dream of scaling the walls, and if they should their sure destruction would follow, for the building is constructed with all the defensive capacities of a complete fortification. Round towers, pierced for cannon, command the sweep all around the building, the walls are not less than fifteen feet high, and the conveniences to launch destruction through and from above them are numerous as need be. Two hundred men might be garrisoned conveniently in the fort, and three or four hundred animals can be shut up in the corral. Then there are the store rooms, the extensive wagon houses, in which to keep the enormous, heavy wagons used twice a year to bring merchandise from the States, and to carry back the skins of the buffalo and beaver, besides which the great wall encloses numerous separations for domestic cattle, poultry, creatures of the prairie, caught and tamed, blacksmith and carpenter shops, etc., etc. Then the dwellings, kitchens, the arrangements for comfort are all such as to strike the wanderer with the liveliest surprise, as though an "air built castle" had dropped to earth before him in the midst of the vast desert.[24]

The brothers Bent presided over this great adobe castle. Their personal attire and power impressed travelers. One early visitor observed that the brothers "dressed like chiefs, in moccasins thoroughly garnished with beads and porcupine quills; in trousers of deer skin, with long fringes of the same extending along the outer seam from the ankle to the hip; in the splendid hunting-shirt of the same material, with sleeves fringed on the elbow seam from the wrist to the shoulder, and ornamented with figures of porcupine quills of various colours, and leathern fringe around the lower edge of the body. And chiefs they were in the authority exercised in their wild and lonely fortress."[25] The Bent–St. Vrain partnership with the Cheyennes, Arapahos, and other tribes proved a success from the beginning. William managed affairs at the fort, quickly learning Indian languages and customs. Charles handled the business from St. Louis and bossed the annual caravans to Santa Fe and back. In Taos, St. Vrain, who had received Mexican citizenship, shrewdly worked government officials in Santa Fe. Both Charles and St. Vrain married into prominent Mexican families, received generous land grants from Governor Manuel Armijo, and built elaborate haciendas near Taos.

At the fort itself, Indian affairs occupied William. Good relations with the Cheyennes were imperative, but William went beyond that—his connection with the tribe developed into a personal bond. As the representative of Bent, St. Vrain & Company, he met all the great Cheyenne leaders, for the Cheyennes made good on their promise to live near the fort. With the fort built, the southern bands moved to Big Timbers country on the Arkansas River.

Shortly after the fort's completion in November 1833, a great meteor shower lit up the sky. The Cheyennes forever remembered it as the Night the Stars Fell, for they thought the world had ended. Warriors donned their finest clothing, as if readying for battle. As they ran for their horses, they sang their death songs, sure that this war against the stars would be their last. From the fort's rooftops, women, too, sang, and the dogs for miles around howled against the sky. The Cheyennes had every reason to expect the worst. The summer before, in battle against the Pawnees, the Sacred Arrows—the very heart and soul of Cheyenne life—had been lost.

Now, a few months later, the sky was falling.

William, too, watched the heavens from the fort's parapets. Through the night he talked with the chiefs, and especially White Thunder, the Keeper of the Sacred Arrows and the most venerated and influential of all Cheyenne men.

The world did not end; dawn broke at last. William Bent and White Thunder shared the wonder and terror of that night, a night they would never forget. 26

White Thunder, W*o-pi-no-no-mie*, was in his seventieth year the Night the Stars Fell.[27] As Keeper of the Sacred Medicine Arrows, *Mahuts*, he occupied the very center of Cheyenne life, for he was the successor of Sweet Root, the Prophet, who delivered the Medicine Arrows to the *Tsistsistas*, the Cheyenne people.[28] It is said that the power of the Creator, the Great-grandfather, flowed to the Cheyennes through the Arrows. And it is also said that the Keeper of the Arrows held the Cheyenne people in the palm of his right hand, that he owned the people.[29]

When Sweet Root lived is unknown; surely, it was before 1750 when the Cheyennes began their migration out of the lake country of Minnesota and entered the plains region west of the Missouri River, where they acquired Spanish horses and hunted the buffalo. But whenever it was that Sweet Root lived, he went to Sacred Mountain, an eminence east of the Black Hills favored by plains people for its pipestones.[30] Here, he and his wife entered the heart of the mountain, where they lived for four years. When they emerged they carried with them four arrows sheathed in coyote skin.[31] Sweet Root explained to the people that the beautifully crafted arrows—each fletched with eagle-tail feathers, painted red and dark blue, and tipped with stone points—carried great power. Two of the shafts, "Man Arrows," ensured Cheyenne victories over all enemies. The other two, "Buffalo Arrows," guaranteed successful hunts and a plentiful supply of meat. It is said Sweet Root lived the life span of four old men, perhaps four hundred years, during which time he once took the form of a sweet root, used by nursing mothers to increase the flow of milk. Finally, after growing old then young again, Sweet Root left the earth forever, passing on guardianship of the Arrows to his successors, among them Medicine Bear, Feathers, and—White Thunder.[32]

Born in 1763, White Thunder lived through the pressures of hostile neighbors and disease, and with his people was forced ever westward, abandoning one home after another. The farther west they migrated, the more horses they acquired through a complex trade network with plains peoples. The more horses, the more mobile the Cheyennes became. Out on the plains the people abandoned their earthen lodges and took to living in tipis, shelters made from buffalo skins stretched over a conical framework of poles. These relatively light, mobile homes were transported, as was other gear, on travois, horse drags fashioned from lodge poles.

Living on the vastness of the plains, the Cheyennes followed the migrating buffalo herds and soon became entirely dependent on these huge animals for virtually every need, from food and clothing, to shelter, tools, even sacred objects.

White Thunder remembered some of the old ways—the fortified villages, the cornfields, the sedentary life—but the younger generation knew only the way of the plains and the horse and the buffalo. He could also remember encounters with the *Suhtai*, strangers from the north speaking an Algonquin language similar to Cheyenne. At first the two tribes viewed one another with suspicion, but when White Thunder became Arrow Keeper, about 1820, the *Suhtai* and *Tsistsistas*, together with other like-speaking bands, merged to form the Cheyenne nation.[33]

Rich as the plains country was in buffalo, competition for hunting grounds was fierce. Many tribes vied for dominance. In the north the Cheyennes competed with Crows, Shoshones, Crees, Blackfeet, and the powerful Sioux confederation. Some Cheyenne bands remained near the Black Hills, forming a lasting alliance with the Sioux. These bands, steeped in the *Suhtai* tradition, drew strength and protection from *Issiwun*—the Sacred Medicine Hat made from the scalp of a buffalo with the horns still attached—brought to the people by Erect Horn, another of the Cheyennes' great culture heroes.[34] Other Cheyenne bands moved south, following the southern buffalo herds, and drawn, too, by the promise of horses and new trade opportunities. The power and prestige of these southern bands were immeasurably bolstered by the presence among them of the Medicine Arrows and the Arrow Keeper. It was as if the heart and soul of the Cheyennes went south.

By White Thunder's time, the Southern Cheyennes anchored their villages on the South Platte River, while their warriors drove deep into Comanche, Kiowa, and Apache country as far south as the forks of the Canadian and Cimarron Rivers, raiding the herds of their horse-rich enemies.

With the southern bands and sharing in the success and trials of the move south came the Cloud People—the Arapahos—the Cheyennes' greatest allies and truest friends. Indeed, wherever the Cheyennes went, the Arapahos usually followed. The Cheyenne-Arapaho alliance was important for several reasons. It helped the tribes control the great buffalo range between the Platte and Arkansas Rivers against threats posed by the Utes and Shoshones on the west, the Crows and Lakota Sioux on the north, the Pawnees on the east, and the Kiowas, Comanches, and Apaches on the south. It also permitted the Cheyennes and Arapahos to dominate the north-south trade corridor through which flowed guns from the north and horses from the south.

By occupying this middle position—between the competing powers north and south, east and west—the Cheyennes and Arapahos acquired wealth beyond anything they had ever known. Their tipis were large and well furnished, metal kettles and knives replaced traditional cookware, their horse herds ever expanded, and their warriors earned the respect and fear of enemies.

Truly, they occupied the right place at the right time.[35]

In numbers, however, the Cheyennes and Arapahos were relatively few. Combined, they could count perhaps a thousand fighting men, far fewer than the allied Comanches and Kiowas. Thus, the migration south stalled at the muddy waters of the Arkansas River. South of the river, the Comanches, Kiowas, and Plains Apaches—with nearly four thousand warriors—claimed the grasslands that stretched across Texas and into Mexico. These tribes effectively blocked the Cheyennes, who could only make fleeting incursions into these southern plains rich in booty and trade possibilities. But the Arkansas River Valley itself, with its game and timber and grass, remained a no-man's land ripe for the taking by any tribe strong enough to hold it.

In 1821, Mexico gained independence from Spain. Now, for the first time, American goods and traders were welcomed into the country. Soon, trade caravans plied the Santa Fe Trail, a great highway of commerce between Santa Fe and St. Louis. Comanche and Kiowa raiders saw opportunity and attacked the merchant trains, particularly near Chouteau's Island on the Arkansas River, which marked the trail's midway point.

Yet the wagon trains kept coming.

Unlike their enemies to the south, the Cheyennes and Arapahos looked at the caravans not as targets but as potential suppliers of goods. Rather than fight the newcomers, they would partner with them, thereby gaining the guns, powder, lead, cloth, metal tools, horses and mules, and all the other desired goods while, at the same time, bypassing their Indian trade partners, north and south. In short, they would cut out the middleman and go straight to the source. The Santa Fe traders sought furs and hides, which the Cheyennes and Arapahos had in abundance. It was a perfect match.

Precisely at this moment, in the summer of 1830, William Bent met up with Cheyenne chief Yellow Wolf at the Fountain Creek trading post. When Bent protected the two Cheyenne warriors from Bull Hump's angry Comanche war party, the timing could not have been better, for it resulted in a partnership that would alter the course of Indian-white relations on the southern plains.

The Cheyennes, as they had promised the Bents, moved from their villages on the South Platte to Big Timbers on the Arkansas. Now, with their new allies and in the shadow of Bent's Fort, they faced their enemies with the confidence born of superior resources—Hawken rifles instead of cast-off trade muskets, fine horses, an abundance of food and supplies.

And so it was time to test their new power.

In 1832 a small Cheyenne war party rode east to attack the Pawnees—the hated "Wolf Men." When the raiders arrived at the earthen villages on the Lower Platte River, they were discovered and quickly cut down by the Pawnees. This was not all. To discourage further raids, the Wolf Men dismembered the bodies of the slain enemies and dumped them in a shallow creek to be ravaged by wolves. Later that year, a Cheyenne war party came upon the massacre site. Despite the mutilations they could still recognize their kinsmen by their clothing and hair adornment. When news of the disaster reached the Cheyennes, all the camps went into mourning. Grieving mothers and wives slashed their arms and legs and cut off fingers.

Such a terrible loss must be avenged.

The next year, just as the wild cherries ripened in late August, the council chiefs, forty-four great leaders representing all the Cheyenne bands, agreed to an attack on the Pawnees. All signs pointed toward victory. Joining the Cheyennes were their allies, the Arapahos and Oglala Sioux. Even more heartening, White Thunder, the Keeper of the Arrows, would lead the people in this war on the Wolf Men.

The camp criers, the old men who announced news, called out for the women to pack up everything—lodges, furnishings, food—and to prepare the children for the long journey to come. Quickly, hundreds of loaded travois headed northeast toward the Platte River, carving great gashes into the dry earth and throwing up clouds of dust that could be seen for miles. In advance of the procession rode the scouts, searching for signs of the enemy. But such a great village could not travel unnoticed. Pawnee and Oto warriors ambushed the Cheyenne advance party, forcing a battle.

White Thunder and his wife rode at the head of the warriors; the women and children followed behind. Before them lay a grassy lowland. Those who could not fight ran to the high bluffs bordering the river valley where there was an unobstructed view of the battleground.

18

A long line of Pawnee and Oto warriors suddenly appeared. Never before had the enemy been seen in such strength. But the Cheyennes rode forward with confidence, the Medicine Arrows leading the way.

White Thunder, his body painted red, stepped out in front of the Cheyenne line. From the coyote skin quiver he withdrew one of the four Medicine Arrows. The women on the bluffs turned their backs, for they were not allowed to see the Arrows uncovered. White Thunder took the arrowhead between the fingers of his left hand, pointing it at the enemy. With his right hand he drew back an invisible bowstring, as if firing an arrow. At the same time, he chewed a sweet root, spitting the juice at the Pawnees, an ancient ceremony calculated to blind and confuse the enemy. Finally, he raised his left foot and stamped it, causing the Cheyennes to shout their approval. The Arrow Keeper repeated this ritual four times. Then Bull, the bravest of the Cheyenne warriors, rode to the Arrow Keeper, his lance pointing toward the ground. White Thunder tied all four of the Medicine Arrows to Bull's lance, entrusting to his care the fate of the people.

Suddenly, the young warriors, by now worked into a battle frenzy and eager to touch the enemy and count the first coup, surged ahead of Bull and the Medicine Arrows. White Thunder looked up in horror. The Medicine Arrows must lead in the attack; otherwise, their power would be lost. Bull, the Medicine Arrows tied to his lance, quirted his fleet warhorse, frantic to overtake the charging warriors. But it was too late. The Cheyenne and Oglala warriors crashed into the enemy. Dust blinded everyone as war cries filled the air. Warriors counted coup and many men on both sides fell. At last catching up, Bull glimpsed a Pawnee on the ground and heard the high-pitched wail of his death song. Leaning over his horse's neck, Bull aimed his lance toward the Pawnee. The enemy warrior dodged the thrust, and with unexpected quickness, reached out and wrested the lance from Bull's grasp.

The unthinkable had happened: the enemy had captured the sacred Medicine Arrows. The Cheyennes charged the Pawnees and Otos again and again, but their confidence had been shaken by the loss of *Mahuts*. As the Cheyennes grew disheartened, so too did their allies. Despite White Thunder's pleadings, the warriors drew off, the wails of the women and children following their retreat.[36]

The loss of the Medicine Arrows and the defeat were staggering blows not only to the Cheyenne way of life but also to White Thunder's prestige and influence. Even before the loss of the Arrows many had questioned his selection as Arrow Keeper. Some said he was *Suhtai*, a descendant of those "strangers from the north," and thus not *Tsistsistas*. Many believed that no *Suhtai* could be a successor to Sweet Root. True, the previous Arrow Keeper had befriended White Thunder; it was also true that White Thunder's wife was *Tsistsistas*. Still, his selection as Arrow Keeper was suspect and controversial. Indeed, those opposed to him had once caused the Arrows to be taken from him. True, they were returned, but only reluctantly and after anguished debate.[37]

Now the Pawnees possessed the Medicine Arrows.

Then the stars fell, surely a portent of doom. Fear and agitation stalked the villages. The Arrows must be retrieved. Yet without them and their power, any attack on the Pawnees would surely fail. Perhaps White Thunder could make new ones. The council chiefs ordered it so, and it was done.

White Thunder and the four Arrow Priests worked with the utmost care and ceremony, laboring four days over the task. The Arrow Keeper assembled the necessary materials—straight shoots of currant wood, white downy eagle feathers, red and dark blue pigments, and flint points. The Medicine Arrows were like no others. The half-inch-diameter shafts measured thirty-six inches in length and were almost perfectly straight. The flint points were securely lashed into place with buffalo sinew and covered with a shroud of downy eagle feathers. The fletching at the tail end of each arrow was fashioned from the split feathers of a mature eagle.[38] The shafts and the fletching were painted red for mother earth, and over this the priests added blue figures representing the sun, moon, stars, and animal life.[39]

The results of the painstaking work and rituals pleased the council chiefs and most of the elders. The Arrow Renewal ceremony had been followed according to Sweet Root's instructions, and the arrows themselves looked identical to the originals. Nevertheless, White Thunder was uneasy. His many critics—especially those who had opposed his selection as Arrow Keeper—continued to blame him for losing the Arrows in the fight against the Pawnees. White Thunder himself feared that the power of the Arrows could not be re-created or transferred, no matter how careful the ceremonies or the work.[40]

Although he kept these doubts to himself, a nagging uneasiness forced him to act. In the winter of 1833–34,[41] not long after the Medicine Arrows were duplicated, the Arrow Keeper and his wife quietly gathered a few trusted friends—Old Bark and his wife, and Doll Man—and together they set off for the Skidi Pawnees' earthen village on the Loup River.[42] His plan was as bold as it was improbable. In fact, it was almost a suicide mission. He would go to the Pawnees unarmed and on foot and plead for the return of the Sacred Arrows. In return, he would pledge peace between the longtime enemies.

Reaching the Pawnee village, White Thunder led his small party to the lodge of Big Axe, the Skidi chief.[43] Once in the chief's lodge, the Cheyennes were safe. No one would attack them here. After food and drink, the Arrow Keeper disclosed his purpose. But Big Axe explained that the arrows had already been dispersed among the four Pawnee villages. He possessed only one. White Thunder's resolve impressed him, however, and he allowed that he was willing to exchange the arrow for a permanent peace between the tribes.[44] White Thunder offered the pipe he carried, and the two men smoked.

Big Axe quickly spread the news among the villagers. White Thunder, he said, had invited the Skidis to visit the Cheyenne villages on the Arkansas River at Big Timbers, where the Cheyennes and Pawnees would make peace and exchange presents. Of course, whenever the two tribes met there was potential for violence. But the Arrow Keeper pledged that he himself would side with the Pawnees if the Cheyennes and their allies made trouble.[45]

White Thunder had been responsible for the Arrows and the people naturally blamed him for their loss. By making peace with the Pawnees, the Arrows would be restored and with them the blessings and power of Great-grandfather and Sweet Root. Thus, White Thunder's prestige and power would be restored—and his critics silenced.

White Thunder returned to the Cheyenne villages, taking with him a few Pawnees, Big Axe's brother among them. The Arrow Keeper entered the village triumphantly, carrying the recovered Medicine Arrow. He explained that the three other Arrows were dispersed among the several Pawnee bands. Only if peace prevailed, he warned, would it be possible to reunite all the Sacred Arrows and restore *Mahuts* to the people.

White Thunder's hopes for the restoration of *Mahuts* soared the next year when, on August 6, 1835, Colonel Henry Dodge and three companies of U.S. Dragoons arrived at Bent's Fort. The Cheyennes erupted in joy when they discovered that with the white soldiers came Big Axe's brother. Perhaps the Pawnees had come to give them news of the three missing arrows. White Thunder asked Dodge to help restore the Arrows to the Cheyennes. Despite William Bent's best efforts to translate the urgency of the occasion and the intricacies of Cheyenne-Pawnee politics, Dodge understood nothing.[46]

Dodge thought he had accomplished at Bent's Fort what he had set out to do—to forge peace between the Cheyennes and Pawnees. But in reality he had blundered into the Cheyennes' desperate attempt to recover the Arrows and had interpreted the "exchange of arrows" as some sort of quaint custom among plains Indians—"it is customary among these wild Indians to exchange arrows in making peace; these are medicine arrows," he said. Dodge blithely departed Bent's Fort confident that his dragoon diplomacy had caused the warring tribes to smoke the pipe of peace.[47]

Before leaving the Arkansas and the Cheyennes, Dodge decided to appoint "chiefs" to negotiate treaties and conduct business with the U.S. government. Accordingly, he bestowed silver peace medals on four reluctant Cheyennes, who accepted the mantle of authority only because the strange officer insisted. When an army clerk asked William Bent to translate the name of one of these honorees, he was told simply, "White Man's Chief."[48] Bent, of course, understood the sarcasm. He not only knew and used the Indian sign language, the lingua franca of the plains, but he also spoke Cheyenne and Arapaho like a native. He could also communicate effectively in Comanche, Kiowa, and Apache. As the principal representative of Bent, St. Vrain & Company, he had gained the trust and respect of the tribes. He also had developed a special bond with White Thunder and the Cheyennes, essential if the Bent–St. Vrain trade empire was to expand and prosper.

Thus far the relationship had been beneficial. The company had already realized significant returns on its investment, even considering the enormous expense of constructing the fort and stocking it with trade goods. But competition was keen. Bent, St. Vrain & Company needed an edge, something that would give it an advantage over the competition.

White Thunder's thoughts also turned to trade alliances and political power. His bold decision to strike out alone and retrieve one of the Medicine Arrows from the Pawnees did much to restore the people's confidence in him. But popular approval could be fleeting, some other calamity might befall him—and he was still, after all, *Suhtai* and therefore in the eyes of many, a false prophet. His critics were quiet now, but he knew their voices could be raised against him at any time.

Now, the two most powerful men on the Arkansas—one white, the other Indian—saw the potential of an alliance. Already they were friends and knew each other's power and prestige. Perhaps a union of families would create an unbreakable bond between them that would benefit not only the two men personally but also the Cheyenne tribe and the Bent trade empire.

White Thunder had much to gain by a marriage alliance. William Bent offered direct access to the goods of Bent, St. Vrain & Company. Moreover, he was a man of great influence among whites and Indians, friends and foes. He was a man of consequence and power. Finally, Bent had a genuine respect for Cheyenne ways and was fluent in the language. Could White Thunder do better than bring this man into his family and tribe?

William, too, carefully weighed the implications of marriage. Brother Charles and Ceran St. Vrain had married highborn Mexican women. These connections were critical to the success of the Bents' trade negotiations in the New Mexican capital of Santa Fe. Charles had encouraged William to think of the strategic consequences of marriage. It was not a matter to be entered into lightly; this was business, not just an affair of the heart.

Mis-stan-sta, Owl Woman, daughter of the Arrow Keeper, represented the highest in caste and class among the Cheyennes. Politically, William could do no better. But what would friends and family back home think? What would Mother think? And what of love? How much these considerations influenced his decision will never be known—William did not put his thoughts to paper. What is known is that among white frontiersmen—trappers, traders, military men—Cheyenne women had an unmatched reputation for intelligence, beauty, and grace.[49]

William was not the first white man to contemplate marriage with an Indian woman. In fact, in the fur trade, there was a long tradition of Indian-white unions. Mountain men typically took Indian wives but abandoned them once they returned to white society. Indian women and their families, likewise, saw these liaisons as opportunities for short-term economic gain. Trappers and traders could supply them with the trade goods they coveted and that only white men could provide. True, their hairy faces offended Cheyenne sensibilities—the women knew them as "dog-faced men"—and their lousy clothing and dirty appearance made them less than perfect companions. Yet, for many Indian women the promise of wealth and an easier life for their families made marriage to such men acceptable.

William was not a lowly mountain man. He was a trader, and not just any trader but the master of the largest fur trading post on the southern plains.

It is unknown whether White Thunder first broached the possibility of marriage, or whether William approached him. Perhaps the idea struck both men at the same time. Owl Woman was White Thunder's eldest, but any of his four daughters might be a suitable companion for *Schi-vehoe*, Little White Man. William, now twenty-six, had never been married. The western mountains and plains had been his home for eight years; newly constructed Bent's Fort would likely be his home for years to come, maybe forever. St. Louis and its society seemed far away just now. In any case, he reasoned, Owl Woman would be a good match.

As to her appearance, Lieutenant James W. Abert of the United States Topographical Engineers on a visit to Bent's Fort was so struck by her beauty that he asked her to pose for a watercolor portrait and described her in his journal:

"Mis-stan-star [sic]," a Shieene [*sic*] squaw . . . [is] a remarkably handsome woman . . . [and] has not been obliged to work; therefore her hands are in all their native beauty, small, delicately formed, and with tapering fingers. Her wavy hair, unlike the Indians' generally, was fine and of silken softness. She put on her handsomest dress in order to sit for me. Her cape and undergarment were bordered with bands of beads, and her beautiful leggins, which extended only to the knee, were so nicely joined with the moccasin that the connection could not be perceived, and looked as neat as the stockings of our eastern belles; and the modest attitude in which she sits is characteristic, but will be best conceived by the sketch.[50]

Marriage to such a desirable woman would honor any man.

The precise location of the wedding ceremony is not recorded. Owl Woman's sister, Island, said it was in a village near "some trading post,"[51] undoubtedly Bent's Fort, William's adobe castle. And it was a momentous occasion, a great celebration uniting two singularly important families. The marriage of William Bent and *Mis-stan-sta* was like no other.

The Cheyennes did not insist on William's participation in the elaborate rituals required of a Cheyenne man. But *Mis-stan-sta*, in keeping with her rank and social position, followed prescribed rituals precisely and fully. Village women dressed her in the finest garments decorated with elk teeth and porcupine quills; her hair was carefully combed and braided; and her face was painted with vermillion. Everything was prepared for her. When she rode, her horse was led by the women; when not on a horse, she was carried on a blanket, her feet never allowed to touch the ground; meat was cut for her and she was hand-fed; her lodge, specially made for her, was supplied with bedding, backrests, cooking and eating utensils—all furnished by relatives and friends. The lodge itself was placed near her father's. She still wore the protective chastity rope, which she would continue to wear for ten days, or until she and her husband felt comfortable with their new relationship.[52]

Central to the day's events was the distribution of gifts. Now it was William's turn to shine, for his gifts and generosity were wondrous indeed. White Thunder was the principal recipient of this largesse, but everyone shared in William's fabulous giveaway. Horses, guns, kettles, blankets, knives, tobacco, beads, trade cloth, mirrors, silver ornaments, hard candy, bridles and other horse equipment—all this and more was offered to the astounded villagers. Such gifts and in such quantity had never been seen before. By day's end, Owl Woman and William, husband and wife, retired to the privacy of their new lodge. She was now a Bent and he a Cheyenne, the son of the Arrow Keeper.

If William Bent had been born a Cheyenne, he would have moved into his wife's village, sharing the life and traditions of her family circle. But his union to Owl Woman was no common marriage. She was the daughter of the Arrow Keeper, and he ruled the Bent trade empire from Bent's Fort, the great force that held the Southern Cheyennes on the Upper Arkansas River.

Owl Woman's village often encamped close to the fort's walls, enjoying a preferred trade relationship with Bent, St. Vrain & Company. More than any other band, these Southern Cheyennes increasingly depended on the fort's trade goods, for this is what gave them power and prestige among their own people and the tribes of the southern plains.

And so, the newlyweds moved between two worlds: the white world of the adobe-walled fort and the Cheyenne world of the buffalo-hide lodge. Though William modified his ground-floor apartment to accommodate Owl Woman, she softened the hard dirt floor, covering it with blankets and furs and arranging backrests and other furnishings against the whitewashed walls. Even so, the single-windowed corner apartment remained closed-in and dark. Further, it was noisy and malodorous. The blacksmith's hammer and anvil clanked incessantly, and the forge's acrid, sulfurous smoke filled the air. Cooking fires partially took the edge off the corral smells, but nothing could be done to quiet the loud bellows and brays of overburdened draft and pack animals. In the courtyard, wagons and carts rumbled day and night. All in all, the fort was more a place of business than a home.

Owl Woman greatly preferred her lodge in the nearby village. Pitched near White Thunder's tipi, it was roomy and airy, and welcome light filtered through the parchmentlike lodge cover. Outside, the sounds of the village seldom intruded. Horses grazed on far hills, the smoke of small cooking fires spiraled skyward through adjustable tipi flaps, and children played under the watchful eyes of elders or older children. Inside the tipi, everything had its place and was arranged for comfort. As was Cheyenne custom, the small flap-entry faced east. Religious and sacred objects hung in the rear of the lodge, a place of honor. The family's possessions and supplies—food, cooking utensils, clothing, bedding, riding gear, weapons—were stored out of the way to allow easy movement. In summer, the tipi's skirt could be rolled up to take advantage of cooling breezes; in winter, buffalo robes and the tipi liner provided insulation against the cold.

William and Owl Woman slipped between these worlds. She generally stayed in the village but frequently visited the fort, attracted by the multicultured excitement. Mexican traders, American soldiers and explorers, African slaves, mixed-blood scouts, mountain men and fur trappers, and the many tribes of the southern plains—the fort was alive with foreign languages and customs. William presided over all, acting as peacemaker, magistrate, negotiator, benefactor, and counselor. Business success depended on maintaining good relations among all his customers. Nothing so disrupted trade relationships as war, so he became a powerful advocate for peace.

Though he conducted business with all the tribes of the plains, he was closest to the Cheyennes, for he had married the Arrow Keeper's daughter and this assured him a special place in the life of the tribe. But William earned respect as well. In 1836 Yellow Wolf led a successful horse raid against Chief Bull Hump's Comanches on the North Fork of the Red River. The enemy warriors followed Yellow Wolf's trail directly to Bent's Fort. Unaware of his pursuers, Yellow Wolf generously presented William with a magnificent Comanche buffalo horse. After resupplying, Yellow Wolf and his men galloped off to their camp on the South Platte. But runners from White Thunder's village soon appeared at the fort, shouting that Bull Hump's warriors were nearing the fort and riding hard. This was not good. White Thunder's lodge with the Sacred Arrows stood immediately outside the fort's main gate. There was no time to dismantle it. So as the sentries scanned the southern horizon, William and fifteen men lifted the lodge and wedged it through the fort's main gate. The Sacred Arrows themselves were hung in William's apartment, just minutes before the Comanches came riding up. The scene was strikingly similar to the encounter of nearly a decade before. Then, too, Bull Hump chased Yellow Wolf and his horse raiders. But this time, Bent negotiated safely behind the thick walls and iron doors of his fort, his men armed and ready with swords, rifles, and pistols. Still, it was a tense moment. Bull Hump demanded the surrender of the horse thieves, but Bent claimed no knowledge of Yellow Wolf's raiders. He had no intention of letting these angry Comanches inside the fort, where they might find the stolen horse and White Thunder's lodge. By this time, Bull Hump's warriors had discovered Yellow Wolf's trail leading north, and the Comanches wheeled their lathered ponies around and rode off.[53]

William Bent, the Arrows hanging above his own bed, had saved White Thunder and the sacred *Mahuts*.

In the summer of 1837, a party of Bowstrings, the most reckless of the Cheyenne warrior societies, called on White Thunder, his lodge restored to its place of honor outside the gates of Bent's Fort. The Bowstrings—young men all—asked the Arrow Keeper to perform the traditional Arrow Renewal ceremony to ensure a successful horse raid against the Kiowas and Comanches. White Thunder agreed, for the Arrows needed renewal. Only the year before a Cheyenne had murdered a fellow tribesman, and, as Sweet Root had taught, such a crime stained the Arrows with blood. But the holy man refused to be hurried; the time was not propitious for the cleansing ceremony. The headstrong Bowstrings insisted. They wanted Kiowa horses and needed the blessing of the Arrows. The Arrow Keeper warned them that if the Arrows were renewed now—against his wishes—the Bowstrings' raid would surely fail. The hotheaded warriors would not be denied. They raised their quirts and lashed the old man until he agreed to perform the sacred ceremony.

William was away when the Bowstrings came calling. Had he been at the fort, he would have seen to White Thunder's protection.

The old man gathered his arrow priests and reluctantly renewed the Arrows. After the four-day ceremony, he dutifully listened for Sweet Root's approval and guidance. But the Prophet was silent. The Bowstring raid was doomed and White Thunder knew it. Nevertheless, forty-two warriors set out on foot for the Kiowa and Comanche camps on the Washita River, confident they would return riding captured horses.[54]

As White Thunder had presaged, the raid was a disaster. Not one of the Bowstrings returned alive. Word reached the Cheyennes through a Kiowa man married to an Arapaho. The Kiowa reported that the Bowstrings had died bravely, singing their death songs after their ammunition had run out.[55] The news of the tragic defeat was mitigated by the jubilant announcement that the Brule Sioux had won a great victory over the Pawnees and had recaptured one of the Sacred Arrows—a Man Arrow. Soon and with great ceremony the Sioux returned it to White Thunder.[56] Still, the pain of the Bowstring disaster ran deep and affected nearly every Cheyenne family. In time, the tribe's grief turned to anger.

Porcupine Bear, the headman of the Dog Soldier warrior society, met with White Thunder, his father-in-law, and the two men agreed that the Sacred Arrows should be moved against the Kiowas.[57] This was an extraordinary and historic decision. In the memory of the *Tsistsistas*, the Arrows had been moved against an enemy only two or three times. With his father-in-law's support, the charismatic Dog Soldier leader boldly announced that he himself would take the war pipe to all the allied camps—Cheyenne, Sioux, Arapaho—and urge them to join in a great war of revenge.[58]

Armed with two of Sweet Root's arrows and with Porcupine Bear taking the lead, White Thunder now believed that the war against the Kiowas could not fail. There would be no hurry. This time ancient protocol and traditions would be observed. To demonstrate the proper humility and respect, Porcupine Bear would approach each allied camp on foot. He would smoke in council with chiefs and headmen, and food and gifts would be exchanged. Of course, he would make time for visits with friends and relatives. Everything would be done according to tribal law and with the Arrow Keeper's guidance and approval.

All seemed well. White Thunder had recovered two of Sweet Root's original arrows, he enjoyed the support and good will of William Bent, his son-in-law, and he had formed an alliance with Porcupine Bear—

another son-in-law—and the leader of the Dog Soldiers, the most powerful of the Cheyenne military societies.

Then disaster.

During the winter of 1837–38 Porcupine Bear made the rounds, visiting the camps and smoking with chiefs and leaders. Finally, on the South Platte River, he arrived at the large *Omissis* —Eaters—village of Northern Cheyennes. By now, Porcupine Bear was an experienced emissary of White Thunder. But before he could make his appeal to the Northern leaders, American Fur Company traders working out of Fort Laramie rolled into camp with a large stock of trade goods—including barrels of whiskey.

Whiskey. Sweet-tasting, irresistible, and deadly.

William Bent always warned of its insidious power, but the Cheyennes like other plains tribes would have it, and at any cost. For a cupful they would give away their most prized possessions, and the traders knew it.

By evening, the camp was reduced to drunken chaos. The few who abstained cowered in their lodges, afraid to venture outside. Porcupine Bear, too, drank his fill. In the lodge of his cousins, Little Creek and Around, he sat by himself singing Dog Soldier society songs, mindless of his mission, lost to the power of the whiskey. As he sang, Little Creek and Around began a playful pushing match that quickly turned serious. When Little Creek drew a knife, Around called out to Porcupine Bear for help. The Dog Man responded instinctively. Drawing his own butcher knife, he drove his weapon deep into Little Creek's chest. As his cousin fell, Porcupine Bear—instantly sober—pressed the knife into Around's hand and ordered him to finish the job, then called on other relatives who were present to take the knife and add their own cuts.[59]

News of the killing swept through the camp. No greater crime could be committed than for a Cheyenne to kill a tribesman. It was, of course, a personal tragedy for Porcupine Bear and his family. But it was also a great tragedy for White Thunder and the Cheyenne people. Cheyenne law was very specific about such a crime. The assailant must be exiled from the people. Now banished, Porcupine Bear, his relatives, and all the Dog Soldiers who accompanied him, were outlaws.[60]

Again, blood had stained the Sacred Arrows. The alliance between White Thunder and Porcupine Bear, once so full of promise, had been smashed in an instant of drunken violence. Who would carry the war pipe for White Thunder? Who would lead the movement of the Arrows against the Kiowas? Old Little Wolf, the oldest surviving Bowstring, stepped forward. Young men rallied to his call and the Bowstrings, now reorganized, took up the war pipe and vowed to protect *Mahuts* in White Thunder's move against the Kiowas.[61] The great war of revenge would go forward—White Thunder really had no choice—but its outcome was now in doubt. Porcupine Bear and the Dog Men were disgraced, and White Thunder no longer controlled the war's course. At the critical moment, leadership had devolved upon the shoulders of younger and less experienced men.

In the spring of 1838, the Cheyennes and a small party of Lakota Sioux allies gathered on the Arkansas River just below Bent's Fort,[62] where the warriors prepared themselves for the battle to come. The Cheyennes took advantage of their preferred trade status with William Bent, exchanging buffalo robes for guns, powder, flint, and lead bullets. The criers circulated through the camps instructing the people to make ready for a move to the sand hills on the south side of the Arkansas River near Chouteau's Island. Here, the people would rendezvous with the Arapahos, then move directly on the Kiowas.

The great village set out. At the sand hills, where the Arapahos joined the village, the allied chiefs met in council. The Cheyennes said to the Arapahos, "Friends, we have made this road—come to this decision—that no prisoners shall be taken. These people have killed many of our young men, Bowstring soldiers, and that is the road that we have made—to take no one alive."[63]

The chiefs sent out scouts, chosen for their bravery and swiftness, for they would go on foot. They must not alert the Kiowas of their presence; success depended on surprise, and men on horseback might be heard and draw enemy eyes. As the village moved south, the wolves continually searched for the enemy. Finally, one party returned waving a wolf skin, an indication they had discovered the main Kiowa village. The scouts entered the Cheyenne camp, and, howling like wolves, twisted their heads from side to side as if in search of prey. They ran to the chiefs, who stood in the center of a crowd of people. In single file, the scouts circled the chiefs, then stopped and told them what they had found.

The warriors jumped on their horses, brandishing lances and coups sticks, and charged the center of the camp with their sacred shields uncovered. For those who had not heard for themselves, the criers told the people that the final push against the Kiowas would begin the next day.[64]

The people moved in columns, surrounded by organized bands of society men—Bowstrings, Kit Foxes, Red Shields, Dog Soldiers, Crooked Lances, and the Chiefs, who rode out ahead screened by selected scouts. Still shunned by the people and regarded as outlaws, Porcupine Bear's Dog Soldiers rode separately, more than a mile from the main body. The renegades numbered only seven—an unlucky number for a Cheyenne war party, but these outcasts consistently disregarded tradition and made their own rules.[65]

The Dog Men actually opened the battle of Wolf Creek. As the outriders neared the Kiowas, now encamped with their friends the Comanches and Apaches, they sighted a party of thirty Kiowa buffalo hunters and their women cresting a distant hill. Motioning to his six men to hide in a nearby ravine, Porcupine Bear whispered, "Keep down, keep down out of sight. I will deceive them." Then he rode back and forth, hand shading his eyes, signaling to the Kiowas to come on, buffalo were in sight. The unsuspecting hunters rode forward, their women close behind leading the men's swift warhorses. As Porcupine Bear gazed toward the imaginary buffalo herd, always keeping his back to the enemy, he again whispered to his men, "Be ready now; they are getting close. We must not give them time to prepare for us."[66]

The enemy came so close that the Cheyennes could plainly hear their voices. The Dog Men rose up and attacked. The surprise was complete. The Kiowas had no chance to draw their bows from their cases or to mount their warhorses. With their eagle-bone whistles screaming and their shields held high, the Cheyennes tore through the Kiowas.

Porcupine Bear fought with unmatched ferocity, for he had much to prove and his honor was at stake. He lanced one enemy with such force that he lifted him clear out of his saddle. The Kiowa's wife, dressed in a fine elk tooth dress, quirted her horse and galloped off. The Dog Man ignored her and rushed on, charging the enemy with abandon. Enemies fell to his lance—twelve in all. Close behind him, Crooked Neck, one of his relatives, cut down eight more. Within minutes, all the Kiowas, men and women, lay dead.

The sun stood high in the sky when the main Cheyenne column, unaware of the Dog Soldiers' fight, attacked the Kiowa village on Wolf Creek. White Thunder and the chiefs had ordered the women and children to the safety of the surrounding hills, while they directed the battle from a small hillock on the valley floor. Although the Cheyenne warriors fought with bravery and skill, their attacks were uncoordinated and they could not capture the village or strike a decisive blow. Protected by the mature men of the Red Shields society, White Thunder watched the battle, pacing nervously. Some believed him despondent, almost suicidal. Many saw him walk dangerously near the fighting, exposing himself needlessly. Several of the Red Shields heard him say, "I will now give the people a chance to get a smarter man to guide them. They have been calling me a fool."[67]

At times the fighting was hand-to-hand, and in the dust and smoke it was impossible to follow the ebb and flow of battle. Suddenly, the tide turned. Kiowa and Comanche horsemen broke through the thin line of Red Shields and swept over White Thunder and the chiefs. The Arrow Keeper fell beneath the enemy's charging horses, lost in clouds of dust.

The Cheyennes claimed victory at Wolf Creek, yet the people did not rejoice. Although the Kiowas, Comanches, and Apaches lost between fifty and sixty killed and many more wounded, the Cheyennes and their allies also suffered heavy losses. Chiefs, headmen, and some of the bravest warriors had fallen. But the greatest loss was White Thunder himself, the only Arrow Keeper in Cheyenne history to be slain in battle.

Porcupine Bear was held responsible for the stain on the Sacred Arrows, for he and his Dog Soldiers had been exiled for the crime of murder. Despite their heroic fighting at Wolf Creek, Porcupine Bear's detractors insisted that he had attacked prematurely. By preceding the Arrows in battle, he had in fact negated their holy power and prevented the total victory that could have been won that day. Although he had counted the first coup, this honor was kept from him because of his outlaw status. White Thunder's son-in-law had disgraced himself and his family. The Little Creek tragedy would be remembered for years, and the stigma attached to it would haunt the family for generations. In time, perhaps, memory of the disgrace might fade, but whenever a tribal dispute arose, the crime would surely surface and be used against family members.[68]

Silently lashing their wounded to the travois, the people withdrew from Wolf Creek, the Medicine Arrows carefully guarded by Tail Woman, White Thunder's widow.[69]

With Tail Woman leading, *Mahuts* securely wrapped in the coyote bundle on her back, the Cheyennes made their way back to the Arkansas River. The people were in a somber mood as they went into camp just above Bent's Fort. There would be no scalp dances; too many brave men had fallen at Wolf Creek.

At the fort, the Bents comforted Tail Woman, Owl Woman's mother, while Kit Carson and other Bent men cast watchful eyes toward the south; Kiowas and Comanches could be expected to avenge the deaths of so many of their people.[70] No one had questioned Tail Woman's right to care for the Arrows temporarily, but now a permanent keeper must be chosen, a *Tsistsistas* man above reproach. The Council of Forty-four chiefs, with the concurrence of the society headmen, would choose White Thunder's successor. The previous Arrow Keeper had selected White Thunder, but many saw this break with tradition as the cause of the recent troubles. Following the great migration south to the Arkansas, the Cheyennes had suffered defeat in battle, loss of the Sacred Arrows, tribal murders and banishments, the Bowstring disaster, and the violent deaths of chiefs and warriors and the Arrow Keeper himself.

At their village near Bent's Fort, the Forty-four chiefs gathered in a double lodge erected in the camp's center. After much smoking and deliberation, they announced their decision: Lame Medicine Man, a wise and popular chief of the Hill Band, possessed the requisite skills and temperament to be the tribe's spiritual leader. He was even-handed and known for his generosity, but most important of all, he was *Tsist-sistas*, a suitable and proper successor to Sweet Root.[71]

The expected Kiowa retaliation never came, even though Cheyenne war parties continued to raid the horse herds of their southern enemies. In 1840, a party led by Seven Bulls visited an Arapaho village on the Arkansas and learned that the Kiowas and Comanches wanted to make peace with the Cheyennes. The Kiowas would bring back the scalps of the Bowstring warriors massacred on the Washita in 1837, and would even compensate the Bowstring families with horses and other gifts.[72]

When Seven Bulls returned to the Cheyenne village, the council chiefs decided the Dog Soldiers should have the honor of making peace with the Kiowas, Comanches, and Apaches. The Dog Soldiers were still the strongest of the warrior societies, although Porcupine Bear's defectors had diminished their numbers. The chiefs called for White Antelope and other headmen to speak for their society. This was important business. After much discussion the Dog Soldiers agreed to negotiate the peace. To this the council chiefs shouted: "*Ha ho, ha ho, Hotami-taniu*, Thank you, thank you, Dog Soldiers!"[73]

The Cheyennes concluded the peace with the Kiowas, Comanches, and Apaches at Two Buttes Creek in the summer of 1840. True to their word, the Kiowas and Comanches brought with them the forty-two Bowstring scalps. Bull Hump and Shavehead of the Comanches, and Little Mountain, Satank, Yellow Hair, and Eagle Feather of the Kiowas presented these trophies, carefully wrapped in a fine Navajo blanket. High Backed Wolf expressed appreciation for the gesture, but told his former enemies, "Friends, these things if shown and talked about will only make bad feeling. The peace is made now; take the heads [scalps] away with you and use them as you think best; do not let us see them or hear of them."[74]

After smoking on the peace and exchanging gifts, Little Mountain said to the Cheyennes, "Now, friends, choose the place where we shall come to meet you; it must be a wide place, for we have large camps and many horses."

The Cheyenne chiefs suggested Bent's Fort: "Just below the fort is a big place on both sides of the river. We will camp on the north side and you people on the south side. Let us meet there." This was agreeable to the Kiowa and Comanche chiefs. Little Mountain spoke for all of them: "There we will make a strong friendship which shall last forever. We will give you horses, and you shall give us presents. Now, in the morning we will go back, and when we get to our camp we will send you a runner and let you know when we shall be there."[75]

The Cheyennes had been in camp just below Bent's Fort for only three days when they saw dust rise on the horizon to the south. Soon, the Kiowas, Comanches, and Apaches pitched their camps on the flats south of the Arkansas River, directly across from the Cheyenne and Arapaho villages. White-topped tipis flooded the valley, smoke hung heavy over the cottonwoods, while enormous herds grazed on the surrounding hills.

When all the tribes had arrived and settled in, High Backed Wolf invited the Kiowas and Comanches to the Cheyenne village for a great feast. Exotic delicacies from Bent's Fort—rice, dried apples, cornmeal, and molasses—supplemented the boiled meat and roots prepared by the women. No one went hungry. The feasting lasted through the night and into the next day. All the while, the Cheyennes offered their new friends a bounty of gifts—blankets, cloth, beads, brass kettles, butcher knives, and most appreciated of all, guns. High Backed Wolf worried about this last item, for he knew this fragile peace could be broken at the slightest provocation. He shouted out to his people, "Those of you who are bringing guns must fire them in front of the lodges; not here close to these people." He gestured to the guests, who were acknowledged to be the best of the sign talkers: "Do not be frightened if you hear shots; it is our custom when we are going to give a gun to anyone to fire it in the air."[76] The *pop, pop* of sporadic gunfire soon sounded like the roar of a full-blown battle. William Bent added to the din by firing one of the fort's new cannons, causing some guests to leap to their horses, ready to flee, until reassured by their new friends. There was talk in camp about opening kegs of liquor, but Bent wisely kept his stores locked and closely guarded. The villages were peaceful now, and he intended to keep them that way. The Kiowas, Comanches, and Apaches were important new customers. Peace was good for business.[77]

The next day, the Cheyennes and Arapahos forded the river to the Kiowa, Comanche, and Apache camps. Now, the Cheyennes and Arapahos would see just how generous their southern neighbors could be. Horses—hundreds upon hundreds—were trotted in from the hills and presented with great ceremony. So many gift horses were given away that the Cheyennes had not enough halters and rope to lead them all away.

It was time to celebrate. The tribes joined in horse and foot races, feasts, shooting matches, dances, ball games, and games of chance. At the fort, William and Charles Bent, Kit Carson, former Comanche captive Jim Hobbs, and Tom "Peg-leg" Smith looked on and participated in the celebration. Another Smith, John Simpson, a Bent trader married to a Cheyenne woman, regaled tribesmen with his tall tales as he led tours through the fort, taking visitors from storeroom to parapet.

For fifteen days men and women crossed and recrossed the river, visiting and trading. Former enemies sat smoking together, recalling brave coups, asking for details of friends and loved ones killed in past battles. Some of these stories would find their way into hide paintings, to be retold by warriors over and over again.

As the great celebration neared its end, Cheyenne Bowstring warriors rode over to the Kiowa camp to honor their new allies. In the ensuing dance, the Cheyennes respectfully recounted their coups on the Kiowas and Comanches at the Battle of Wolf Creek

Suddenly, Porcupine Bear, riding a fine horse, broke through the dance circle. Boldly, angrily, he began to pantomime twenty coups he counted at Wolf Creek, coups denied by his own people for his crime of killing Little Creek, his cousin. He was an outlaw, and by attacking prematurely at Wolf Creek he had ruined the chance for total victory. Nevertheless, Porcupine Bear rode up to the Kiowa men and, looking directly into their eyes, thrust his lance into their faces, one by one recounting his coups. The Bowstrings were as shocked as the Kiowas by this brazen and disrespectful display, magnificent as it was. But rules seemed not to apply to this renegade. Outlawed or not, no one doubted his bravery and skill. When Porcupine Bear finished his dramatic performance, the Kiowas invited him into the chief's lodge, there plying him with questions about Wolf Creek. How did the Kiowa hunters fight? What happened to the woman wearing the elk tooth dress? And so it went. Direct questions, honest answers, mutual respect. Despite the pain of the retelling, rancor drifted away. It was better to *know* the truth than to be burdened forever with unanswered questions.

Finally the great peace concluded. It was time to move on. Women struck the lodges, and the tribes rode off, each going separate ways. But they rode off as friends and allies. For the first time in memory, peace prevailed in the Upper Arkansas River country. William welcomed this, for now he could expand his business and raise a family.[78]

Chapter 2

GROWING UP CHEYENNE

In the third year of the peace, George Bent—*Ho-my-ike*, or "Beaver"—the third child of William and Owl Woman, was born July 7, 1843, in his mother's lodge near Bent's Fort.[1] Although a mixed blood, he looked like any Cheyenne boy—long black braided hair, dark eyes, prominent cheekbones, and long straight nose. His dark skin was a shade lighter than most boys but in dress and behavior he was Cheyenne. His father had named all of his children after his own brothers and sisters. But his mother made certain they had proper Cheyenne names as well. Mary—*Ho-ka*, or "Little Woman"—the oldest, was born in 1838, three years after William and Owl Woman married. Robert—*Octavi-wee-his,* or "Bird"—came in 1841, and Julia—*Um-ah*, or "Talking Woman"—in 1847. Sometime in the mid-1840s, William took two of Owl Woman's younger sisters, Island and Yellow Woman, into his lodge, a common practice among Cheyennes, especially when a husband possessed wealth and status. Yellow Woman bore him another son, Charley—*Pe-ki-ree*, or "White Hat"—in 1845. When Owl Woman died suddenly in 1847 of complications from Julia's difficult birth, the sisters shared responsibility for raising the mixed-blood brood.[2]

George was raised Cheyenne. Strapped securely to a cradleboard in the lodge circle, the fire in the center, the sky blinked at him through the crossed tipi poles of the smoke hole high above. The soft sounds of the Cheyenne language mingled with the harsher tones spoken by his northern *Suhtai* relatives and of his father's English. As he grew older, Tail Woman, his grandmother, taught him respect for his elders, to always speak quietly in their presence, never to interrupt or contradict. As was Cheyenne custom, he was almost never punished. His mother and aunts—he made little distinction between them—taught by example and reacted to unruly behavior with stern glances and wagging fingers, never resorting to physical discipline. But George was not an unruly child. He loved attention and generally got it by his charm and quick wit. From an early age he demonstrated uncommon intelligence and a facility for languages. He grew up speaking Cheyenne and English, but also quickly picked up Spanish, Comanche, Kiowa, and Arapaho. He could speak six languages, and swear like a trapper in a half-dozen more.

He and his brothers received special treatment, for like all Cheyennes they were the future defenders of the people, the hunters and providers. Men were at high risk for early death—who knew when they might fall to an enemy arrow or bullet, or be gored by an enraged buffalo bull? George spent his childhood learning about horses, hunting, and battle. No woman would ever ask him to gather firewood, pick berries, fetch water, or perform other camp chores. Girls did this work. For him horses became his most familiar companions. He learned to ride even as he learned to walk, suffering inevitable falls, climbing back on, not fearing this animal he called *nathoze*, or "my pet."[3] He watched the men nurture and gentle their horses, always mounting from the right side, using voice commands and quirts to control their animals. He and the other boys seldom used saddles, but rode bareback or cinched a blanket to the horse's back. A horsehair rope looped around the animal's lower jaw sufficed for bridle and reins. He learned to identify individual horses instantly, even in the dark, by their physical characteristics and personalities.[4]

Living near the fort, he also had occasion to study white horsemanship, so different from Cheyenne practices. He remembered the fort's resident broncobuster, an old Mexican named One-Eyed Juan. George marveled at his strangeness. Juan always mounted from the left side; rode a heavy silver-mounted saddle, complete with leather skirt, which he called a *mochila*; and placed his feet in massive hooded stirrups. He controlled his mount with a silver bridle that had an iron curb bit and jangling spurs with cruel barbs. That Juan was a fine rider George could see, but he looked on in horror as Juan branded the animals with red-hot irons and drove nails into their hooves, attaching iron shoes.

Sometimes old Juan showed off for the Bent boys. Saddling up a fierce mustang, he placed a Mexican silver dollar under his foot in each of the wooden stirrups, then rode this wild bucking beast until it hung its head in submission, its spirit broken. Juan then dismounted and proudly withdrew the silver coins, still in the wooden stirrups exactly where he had put them. This display always delighted George, but the cruelty of it disturbed him, too. It was not the way Cheyennes gentled and rode horses.[5]

Other white practices puzzled him as well. He often saw trader Uncle John Smith, married to a Cheyenne, discipline his mixed-blood son, Jack. Once the old man dumped a bucket of ice-cold water over young Jack just to stop his crying. The boy squalled all night, and all night Uncle John poured water on him to shut him up. Finally, Jack fell asleep, too exhausted to cry any more.[6] Such scenes frightened George. He was glad his father accepted the Cheyenne way, deferring to his stepmothers in matters of discipline and education.[7]

Island and her sisters preferred to guide and instruct their children, encouraging them to play games that mimicked adult behavior. As soon as George could walk, he was presented with a bow and arrows, while his sisters, Mollie and Julie, received deerskin dolls that they carried everywhere. Together, the Bent children established tiny villages. The girls modeled their behavior after their mother's and erected lodges, gathered firewood, and cooked meals. The boys hunted, went out on mock war parties, and defended the village. When enemies threatened, the girls struck the tipis and loaded toy possessions on dog travois; the boys, astride stick horses, rode out to cover the retreat, then met the attackers, bravely counting many coups. The victorious boy warriors returned to camp carrying buffalo hair "scalps" attached to willow poles. The girls were properly impressed by the boys' prowess, praising them effusively at a great "scalp dance." George liked the girls, for they often singled him out as worthy of special attention. They admired his good looks and easy charm, as well as his skill with bow and arrow.

George spent endless hours shooting arrows at moving and stationary targets, creeping up on small game animals, roping horses, competing in foot races and wrestling matches—essentials in perfecting the skills of a warrior and hunter.[8]

After Owl Woman's death, George and the other children lived with their stepmother, Island, and Charley's mother, Yellow Woman. Their father might be with them, or he might be at the fort, or he might be trading among the Indians in some remote village. When his trade business took him to Cheyenne villages, George usually traveled with him. During winter, William brought the whole family to Big Timbers. While their father traded, the children played in the snow near the lodge, often going to their grandmother's tipi nearby. Tail Woman regaled them with stories of their grandfather White Thunder, the Arrow Keeper who had died in battle against the Kiowas.[9]

Wherever they might be, when friends rode by the Bent women were gracious hosts, never failing to invite travelers in for a meal of dried, pounded cherries, mixed with buffalo marrow and sweet roots. George and the children watched from behind the piles of trade goods as the men sucked on long-stemmed pipes, the smoke hanging heavy in the cramped space of the lodge.[10]

Such was the rhythm of village life. Always movement—sometimes to Big Timbers close to the buffalo herds, sometimes to the fort, but always someplace where grass was thick, wood plentiful, and water fresh and sweet.

Wherever streams and rivers flowed, George enjoyed the water. He and his brothers were strong swimmers and spent hours in the Arkansas, playing and laughing. Streams were important gathering places. Not only did women go there to fetch water, wash clothes, and bathe, younger women found the privacy of the dark, tree-lined banks ideal for meeting young men and courting. Of course, it would be inappropriate for young people to meet alone and unchaperoned, but "chance" encounters at the water's edge would not draw disapproving eyes.[11]

While playing in the water, children delighted in catching fish. They would form lines, beating the water and making noise, forcing the fish toward a barrier where they could be stabbed or thrown flopping on the banks. George never forgot the old *Suhtaio*, the people of the north who had merged with the *Tsistsistas* before the buffalo days, who still remembered how to make seines for catching fish. Some children laughed at them, but George stayed away, fearing their strange ways.[12]

George loved games of chance, which took many forms, from pure gambling to horse and foot races. In the game of Hands—*No-o-its-in-is-ta*, "they are hiding"—a player held bones behind his back, one marked, the other plain. The opposing player attempted to guess which hand held the marked bone, and players and onlookers bet on the outcome.[13] But he was most passionate about horse racing. He always knew the swiftest horses, which the men marked by cutting notches in the animals' ears. These racehorses were treated with the greatest care and respect and ridden only on special occasions. They were separated from the general herd during the day and safely picketed close to the lodges at night. The boys who guarded them got up before dawn and stayed with them throughout the day. Never did they let them out of sight, for to lose such a horse would be disastrous for the warrior who depended on it and a great disgrace for the boy. George never missed an opportunity to watch or participate in a horse race.

Cheyenne men also engaged in foot races. One of George's most vivid childhood memories was of a twenty-mile race between Crossing Over, a Kit Fox Society man, and Four Horns, a Bowstring warrior. The race started at Sand Creek, coursed over to the head of Short Timber Creek, and followed that stream until it emptied into the Arkansas River six miles below Bent's Fort. It was rough country, broken by sand hills, cactus, and sage. At the finish line, only ten feet separated the exhausted runners, with Crossing Over declared the winner. Spectators wagered their personal property, but the highest stake was the honor of the two warrior societies. In this case, the Kit Foxes prevailed. Fifty years later Cheyennes still remembered the event.[14]

Shortly after the great race, young George took sick and the family sent for a doctor named Lone Bear. William explained how this same man had saved his life years before when he had suffered a severe throat infection that prevented him from swallowing, or even talking. To feed William, George's mother had taken broth into her own mouth and squirted it into her husband's swollen throat through a goose quill.

He grew so thin she feared he would die, so she summoned old Lone Bear, who William knew as One Eye, for he had been gouged protecting the trader from a knife-wielding Kiowa. Using a large spoon handle, the medicine man depressed Bent's tongue and instantly diagnosed the problem. He left the lodge shaking his head and returned a short time later with a handful of small, prickly sandburs, each about the size of a pea and with barbs sharp enough to pierce skin. He asked Owl Woman to bring him a length of sinew and a lump of marrow fat. One Eye divided the sinew into six strands, knotting the end of each. Then, using an awl, he made a hole in each sandbur and strung them like beads on the knotted threads. After lubricating the sandburs with the thick marrow grease, he took a notched stick and pushed the combined burs—now a barbed ball—down Bent's throat. When the stick was completely inserted, One Eye steadily drew the sinew back. With the ball came the putrid mass that had clogged Bent's throat. He repeated this procedure several times until the passage was sufficiently clear to allow the patient to swallow soup. Within a few days, William was well enough to sit up and talk. Thereafter, whenever Bent resided at the fort, he would allow no other doctor, Indian or white, to treat his family.[15]

Now William naturally turned to One Eye when a similar ailment struck his son George, even though the fort contained well-stocked stores of medicine and patent remedies. One Eye examined George, prescribed treatment, and the youngster quickly recovered.[16]

During the day, Cheyenne children had the run of Bent's Fort. George and his friends roamed everywhere—the shops and stores, the sentry lookouts, the roofs. They had strict instructions to touch nothing and not to interfere with the fort's business, but being children they sometimes explored forbidden places such as the icehouse and billiard room. The billiard table, brought to the fort in 1836 by William's brothers, George and Robert, was the only one of its kind in the whole Upper Arkansas River country. The brothers also brought exotic peacocks, whose gay plumage and piercing shrieks astonished and alarmed the Cheyennes, who called them thunderbirds. Candies, imported Chinese ginger, New Orleans molasses—all delighted fort visitors, especially George and his playmates.[17]

The fort's only goat, a gift of Ceran St. Vrain, caused great wonder among the Cheyennes, who had never seen this strange creature before. George and the children often harnessed it to a miniature cart, also the gift of St. Vrain, then trotted about the fort and nearby village, entertaining everyone, young and old.[18] As the goat aged, it became increasingly cross and took cruel pleasure in scattering little groups of Indian children and chasing them everywhere.[19]

Food always attracted the children. The smell of flapjacks and pumpkin pie, and occasionally taffy, lured them to the kitchens. Bent's slaves, Andrew and Dick Green, known to the Cheyennes as "black white men," cooked for the fort's company, as did Charlotte—who described herself as "de onlee lady in the dam Injun country"—and later Chipita, the housekeeper and laundress.[20] In the winter months, Chipita presided over the taffy pulls. A large, good-natured French-Mexican woman married to a Bent employee, Chipita boiled the molasses, then invited the children to a "candy-pulling frolic." George remembered that even the fort's hard-drinking laborers and teamsters joined in the fun.[21]

Candles particularly fascinated the children. Tallow candles provided the fort's main source of light. George spent many hours watching Chipita fix the wicks and pour a molten mixture of tallow and beeswax into tin molds, perhaps a dozen candles in a set. The molds were then dipped in a barrel of cold water until the candles hardened and could be separated from the tin.[22]

George looked forward to fort celebrations, especially scalp dances and the annual Fourth of July extravaganza. When he was young, the Cheyennes celebrated a victory over the Pawnees with a scalp dance held within the fort's adobe walls. A great bonfire lit the courtyard. Cheyenne women painted their faces black and red and wrapped themselves in expensive Navajo blankets. Their finest necklaces and earrings jingled as they danced in unison to the men's drumbeats and their own tambourines. Together men and women sang and danced, their shadows large against the fort's walls. "I never in my life saw a happier set," said one observer. "The women laughed and jumped in rapturous delight, whilst their husbands and lovers were grouped around on the roofs of the fort looking on most complacently."[23]

Enemy scalps stretched on willow hoops were exhibited on long poles, held high for all to see. Warriors recounted their battle honors—their coups—in the light of the fire. They celebrated life itself and Cheyenne superiority over all enemies. It was a supremely joyous moment, a not-to-be-missed opportunity for young men to court young women, for married couples to reaffirm their devotion and pride in one another. Children, too, celebrated as they proudly watched their elders rejoice in the victory over the hated Pawnees. It was a time for the Cheyennes, individually and as a people, to declare their greatness.[24]

The Bents greeted Independence Day with booming cannons and a giant American flag hoisted over the fort's main portal. Several days before the holiday, William dispatched berry pickers up the Arkansas to the Purgatoire River to gather chokecherries and especially wild mint for a frontier version of mint juleps. Mixed with ice from the icehouse, Bent called the powerful drink a "hail storm." On this day, George and the children munched and sucked on ice until their lips numbed from the cold. Again, there was dancing and singing, this time the Americans—soldiers, trappers, travelers, traders—celebrating *their* nation's greatness.[25] Here at Bent's Fort, so distant from the states, the Fourth of July held special meaning. Standing alone, here on the edge of Mexico and in the heart of Indian country, the fort always evoked strong feelings of patriotism. Frederick Ruxton, who visited in 1845, remarked that the "solitary stranger passing this lone fort, feels proudly secure when he comes within sight of the 'stars and stripes' which float above the walls."[26]

The Bents also boomed cannons when Colonel Stephen Watts Kearny and his Army of the West arrived in late July 1846. On this occasion, William rolled out the fort's brass six-pounder and fired a salute. Unfortunately, the enthusiastic but inexperienced gun crew charged the piece with too much powder and the cannon blew up. The burst barrel was too heavy to move, so for years it lay on the ground in plain sight. George remembered it as a favored plaything, and it always invited comment from visitors.[27]

General Kearny's soldiers camped just outside the fort's walls. The officers found accommodations inside, as did Susan Magoffin, a married woman traveling alone on the Santa Fe Trail. She thought the fort

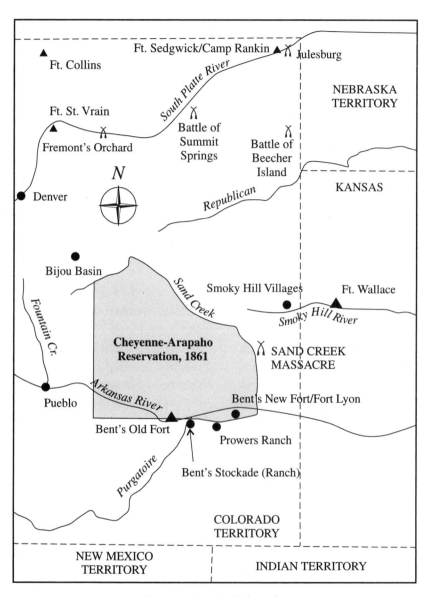

George Bent's Colorado

"crowded to overflowing. Col. [*sic*] Kearny has arrived and it seems the world is coming with him."[28] With the outbreak of the Mexican War, Kearny had been ordered to Santa Fe, there to show the American flag and demand the surrender of the military forces commanded by New Mexican governor Manuel Armijo. Many other U.S. volunteer and regular troops rested and resupplied at Bent's Fort that year.

George's father knew all the old army officers—Kearny, Fremont, Dodge, Doniphan, Cooke, Price, and Sumner—who stopped at the fort for information and supplies. The old man was especially proud of his service as scout and guide to Kearny's Army of the West and Colonel Sterling Price's regiment of Missouri Volunteer Cavalry. Along with brother George, William formed a "spy" company, composed of old mountain men, ordered to scout the mountain passes and keep an eye out for Armijo's troops. For this service, William acquired the title of colonel, an honorific that remained with him the rest of his life.[29]

While George's father and Uncle George assisted Kearny in military operations, Charles Bent remained in Taos, preparing the way for Kearny's invasion. Following the Americans' bloodless victory over Armijo, Kearny appointed Charles the territory's first U.S. governor. The choice was logical. Charles had married into a prominent Mexican family and was exceptionally well connected in Santa Fe and Taos. New Mexican businessmen approved of the appointment, for the war had disturbed trade relations and brought economic chaos. His connections with Bent, St. Vrain & Company and the Bent trade empire made his name known to political leaders, army officers, traders, and merchants everywhere. With civil affairs in New Mexico now under Bent's capable direction, Kearny, guided by Kit Carson, marched off for California, anxious to engage Mexican troops in that distant land.[30]

But the peace in New Mexico was fragile. True, Colonel Sterling Price and his Missouri Volunteers, guided by William Bent, arrived in Santa Fe and occupied the town. But in Taos, Governor Charles Bent faced trouble. Pueblo Indians and Mexican insurgents, seething at the imposition of American rule and Price's army of occupation, plotted to overthrow the new government and assassinate military and civil leaders, including Price and Governor Bent.

On January 19, 1847, the attack came with deadly swiftness. A frenzied mob assaulted the governor's house, smashed the door, and riddled Charles with bullets and arrows. Unseen by the attackers, Charles's wife, Ignacia, along with Josefa Jaramillo Carson, Kit's wife, and Rumalda Luna Boggs escaped with their children and servants by hacking a hole through an adobe wall using a poker and an iron spoon.[31]

Charlie Autobees, one of Bent's traders, also escaped the massacre and brought news of the tragedy to William Bent's camp at Big Timbers. Here George and the other children heard the terrible details. Uncle Charles had been scalped—not with a knife but a taut bowstring—the grisly trophy tacked to a board and paraded through the streets of Taos, and his head had been severed from his body. The Bent store had been looted and burned to the ground. William could hardly contain his fury. When word of the disaster reached the Cheyenne camps, Yellow Wolf and other chiefs offered to lead a war party down to Taos and wipe out the Pueblo Indians. But a company of sixty volunteers, traders and mountain men, including Ceran St. Vrain and Jim Beckwourth, had already joined Sterling Price's troops from Santa Fe in a vengeful slaughter of more than three hundred rebels.[32]

Back at Big Timbers, William, grief-stricken, set off for Bent's Fort. On the way he encountered a suspicious-looking Mexican, riding at a gallop. Cocking his rifle, Bent shouted for the man to stop, then asked the stranger what he knew of the Taos revolt. The man pleaded ignorance, but his eyes shifted uneasily. William believed he knew more than he told. Lewis Garrard, who accompanied Bent, thought his friend would surely shoot the Mexican. Instead, Bent shouted, "Vamos, pronto!" But as the man rode off, Bent expressed regret that he had not killed him.[33]

Grief seemed to hang over the fort that year. Charles, age forty-six, the oldest of the Bent brothers, dead in Taos, his headless body buried near the church in Santa Fe. Robert, age twenty-five, the youngest and perhaps the most handsome of the Bents—admiring Cheyennes called him Green Bird—had also suffered violent death, killed and scalped in 1841 by Comanches near Chouteau's Island while escorting a Bent train. Now he lay in a grave outside the fort's northeastern bastion.[34]

Only William and George remained of the westering Bent brothers. George, like his brother Charles, had married a Mexican woman and taken up residence in Taos. Lucky to have escaped the violence, he served as foreman of the grand jury convened to indict the conspirators and murderers of brother Charles. The members of the jury—all Bent friends and employees—included Lucien Maxwell, Asa Estes, Antoine LeRoux, Charley Towne, and Charlie Autobees. For fifteen days, Ignacia Bent, Josefa Carson, and Rumalda Boggs recounted the awful details of the governor's death. Shortly after, a court found the accused guilty of all charges. Judge Carlos Beaubien, another Bent trader, pronounced the sentence: "*Muerto, Muerto, Muerto.*" Fifteen rebels were hanged at Taos that April.[35]

And six months later, Uncle George Bent, age thirty-three, died. After a lingering illness, probably consumption, and after a battery of white and Indian remedies, George succumbed on October 23, 1847. His friends remembered him as "highly esteemed and respected and possessed of almost unbounded influence with the various Indian tribes." The Cheyennes had honored him with the name Beaver—*Ho-my-ike*—an animal they admired for its energy and intelligence.[36]

Now, young George—also *Ho-my-ike*—had lost three uncles, two buried in cactus-covered graves in the cemetery outside Bent's Fort. George sometimes rode out to the cemetery on a two-wheeled *carreta* with the red-haired Irish caretaker, who planted prickly pear on the mounded earth near the Bent stones as protection against scavangning wolves and coyotes. His mother, Owl Woman, was dead, too, her body not covered with dirt as was customary among whites but placed on a scaffold exposed to animals and birds so that she might return to the earth.[37]

His father was the last of the brothers and now the sole heir of the Bent trade empire. More than one hundred fort employees and their mixed-blood families depended on him for their livelihood. And thousands of southern plains people—Arapahos, Kiowas, Comanches, Apaches—relied on him for guidance and trade. But of all, the Southern Cheyennes were most dependent. Bent's Fort dominated their lives. They had purposely come to the Arkansas River to be near the fort. They had told the Bents where to build the post, then gathered around it, always moving but never very far away. And Bent was their friend and protector. He was one of them, married to the Arrow Keeper's daughter, with children and family ties. William—and his family—could no more leave them than they him, their lives conjoined and inseparable.

Death seemed to hover over the southern plains and Upper Arkansas River country in the summer of 1849. Since the earliest contact with Europeans, strange and deadly diseases had periodically ravaged Indian camps. Sweet Root had warned the people that whites "will try always to give you things, but do not take them . . . this will bring sickness to you. These people do not follow the way of our great-grandfather. They follow another way."[38]

In 1832, as Bent's Fort was under construction, Mexican adobemakers brought smallpox to the Arkansas. William understood the dangers and warned off the Cheyennes, attempting to isolate the disease. The smallpox epidemic temporarily halted the fort's construction, striking down many of Bent's workers. William himself was poxed and confined to his bed. He recovered, but his face forever bore the scars.[39]

In 1849 another disease struck—cholera.

A Cheyenne war party, nearly two hundred strong including women, had raided the Pawnees and were returning to their village on the Smoky Hill when they struck an immigrant train circled on the banks of the Platte River. The warriors investigated, for there was no movement or sound, everything deathly quiet. As the men pulled back the white-topped wagon covers they discovered to their horror dead and dying white men, some doubled over in agony. Older Cheyennes voiced a warning: the white men were dying of the deadly "cramps."

In panic they wheeled their horses, running from the invisible enemy. When they returned to the main body, they shouted for the people to turn back, and together they raced for One Eye's camp on the Smoky Hill. But before they had gone far, half their number fell to the disease.[40]

Earlier that year, in April, William had taken son Robert on the annual trek east. The train of twenty ox-drawn wagons packed with buffalo robes would bring a good price in St. Louis. William thought it time to bring along eight-year-old Robert, the oldest of the boys, and show him the business of the trade. Left behind with their stepmother Island were Mary, age eleven, George, now six, Charley, four, and Julia, age two.

When the cramps struck, Island, Yellow Woman, and the children were on Bluff Creek, a tributary of the Cimarron, where the Kiowas had invited Feathered Bear's Cheyennes and Bull Head's Arapahos, as well as Comanches, Apaches, and Osages, to a great Sun Dance. The Osage camp was the center of much activity. These people lived among white settlements and were renowned traders who supplied other plains tribes with kettles and other goods. Island herself traded for a small iron kettle.

Just as the ceremonies began, a Kiowa dancer collapsed. Within moments, an Osage spectator outside the dance circle also doubled over. Chief White Face Bull of the Scabby Band went over to the stricken man and then cried out for the people to run and get away. The signs were clear: the man had the cramps. Panic seized the villagers. The Osages escaped northeast, while the Cheyennes fled in the opposite direction. Feathered Bear, White Face Bull, and Yellow Wolf blamed the Osages for bringing the cramps into their villages and took their people southwest toward the Cimarron.[41]

Island and Yellow Woman, with Feathered Bear's *Hevhaitanio* Band, placed George and Charley on a travois loaded with kegged water, cooked meat, and bread. All night they traveled, the mule straining at the travois. By noon the next day, they reached the Cimarron. Here, the sisters carried their mother, Tail Woman, now weakened by the sickness, to the shade of a large cottonwood tree. George saw people fall down, clutching their stomachs, unable to stand. And he watched his grandmother die in the shade of the tree. The boy helped his mother build a scaffold high in the cottonwood and saw her gently place Tail Woman on it. There was no time for ceremony.

Nearby, Little Old Man, a great Cheyenne warrior, mounted his favorite warhorse that he had adorned with a stuffed mole skin necklace, a charm he used to ward off enemy bullets and arrows. Dressed in his scalp shirt and headdress and holding aloft a shield and lance, he shouted, "If I could see this thing, if I knew where it was, I would go there and kill it!" Then he fell from his horse into his wife's arms and died. The bravest warrior struck down by the invisible enemy. No one, not Feathered Bear, not Yellow Wolf, not White Face Bull, no one could control their fear. Terror gripped every person, every family. The village disintegrated in mad flight.

Island and Yellow Woman put the children back on the travois and set out alone for Bent's Fort, whipping the already lathered mule to greater speed. Perhaps they could outrun the disease. Once at the fort, surely the great walls would protect them.

By the time William and young Robert returned from their long journey east, his wives and the children were already there—and nearly half of the Southern Cheyennes lay dead.

Death stalked the Cheyenne camps. On the Arkansas River, the Smoky Hill, Cimarron, and even on the Platte, it was all the same. Death touched every family. George lost not only his grandmother, but aunts and uncles as well.

With death in the fort and all around it, William saw no other choice. He packed his wagons with family belongings and all his trade goods and fled north for Fort St. Vrain, the northernmost outpost of the Bent trade empire. Here, on the South Platte, perhaps there was a chance for life.[42]

Ox yokes creaked as the wagon train carrying George and his family rolled westward along the Arkansas River trail, the teamsters' cracking whips breaking the quiet of the sagebrush prairie. His father led the wagons toward Fort St. Vrain, riding in his recently purchased St. Louis spring carriage. George, Bob, Charley, and baby Julie traveled with Island and Yellow Woman in the slow-moving wagons. Island, who loved to ride bareback on fast horses, found it unbearable. George's stepmother desperately wanted to leave the cramping death behind them as quickly as possible, but the plodding oxen could not be hurried.

The slow pace wore on the entire party. Signs everywhere reminded them of the sickness that had taken nearly half the population of the Southern Cheyennes. Never had such so much death and tragedy befallen the *Tsistsistas*. George was frightened by the sight of funeral scaffolds in trees, empty lodges, belongings dropped on the trail—

shields, bows, dresses, dolls, cooking ware—and here and there, corpses of men, women, and children abandoned by the living who were too exhausted and too terrified to care for the dead. It seemed that all the world had changed and that life as they had known it could never be the same.

And so they made their way past El Pueblo, the adobe settlement at the confluence of the Arkansas River and Fountain Creek, not far from where William had established the first Bent trading post back in 1829. The train then headed north along the Trappers Trail, skirting the Front Range of the Rocky Mountains, the rolling grasslands now greening from spring rains, the snowcapped peaks shining brilliantly white against the sky. On the far horizon, Longs Peak, known to the Cheyennes and Arapahos as Twin Guides, pointed the way north.

As they neared the South Platte River, the party halted at Scout Creek.[43] Here, his father pointed to the site where Kiowas and Cheyennes had fought a great battle before the children were even born and told the story of the brave Kiowa warrior who wore a dog rope, a rawhide sash similar to those worn by the four bravest Cheyenne Dog Soldiers. The great Kiowa again and again charged the Cheyennes, who, fearful of his power, retreated, then drew their bows and shot him full of arrows. Meanwhile, the Kiowa women had dug defensive pits near the cotton-wood trees, where they had tied their horses.

George would always remember this story, told by his father during the terror of the flight from death. For a brief moment, he forgot his fear and jumped into the Kiowa pits, which were clearly visible, and with his brothers wildly reenacted the battle, each of them taking turns playing the role of the brave Kiowa rope-wearer. This respite was short-lived. All too soon, his father called for the children to rejoin the wagons—they must keep moving.[44]

When the wagons reached the South Platte River, George saw the ruins of several abandoned adobe forts, victims of the cutthroat competition forced by the Bent–St. Vrain traders. Forts Lupton, Jackson, and

Vasquez—all had challenged the Bents for trade dominance on the high plains. All had failed. Their great gates now lay open, ghostly reminders of the heyday of the Trappers Trail.

At last, the weary family reached Fort St. Vrain, not as grand as the adobe castle his father had built on the Arkansas, but to George it seemed a fortress. Its imposing adobe walls measured 130 feet long by 60 feet wide, and at the corners were loopholed bastions 19 feet across. A large double gate swung open on the fort's east side, and bleached lodge poles of Indian camps still stood down by the river. The fort itself sprawled on the high ground, dominating the tree-filled valley of the South Platte.[45] William had originally named the fort in honor of George's uncle and namesake, but most people now knew it as Fort St. Vrain. After driving out the competition, his father had relocated his main trade operations south to the Arkansas, allowing this fort to fall into disrepair.

As the men unloaded the trade goods, George explored his new home and met trader Tim Goodale and his Sioux wife, who lived at the fort and would become his companions over the next three years. His father had determined to use Fort St. Vrain as the headquarters of his trade business—a bit of irony, for Bent and Ceran St. Vrain had dissolved their partnership in February 1849, shortly before the cholera attack. St. Vrain had believed the fur and hide business was in decline and strongly urged his friend to move to Taos, forget his Indian partnerships, and tap the lucrative Mexican side of the Santa Fe trade.

Ceran may have terminated his partnership with the company, but George retained a memory of him as a man riding a mule, dressed in a white blanket coat with a "sugar loaf" hood. The Cheyennes knew him as "Blackbeard," while Lewis Garrard, who traveled with him in 1846, described him as a "gentleman in the true sense of the term, his French descent imparting an exquisite, indefinable degree of politeness . . . combined with the frankness of an ingenuous mountain man."[46]

George remembered stories of Ceran's brother Marcellin, too. Five-and-a-half feet tall and weighing only 115 pounds, his extraordinary wrestling skills impressed his Cheyenne friends, that is until he pulled down and accidentally killed an Indian opponent during a rough-and-tumble match at Bent's Fort early in 1849. After that, he made himself scarce in Indian country, abandoning his Sioux wife, "Red," whom he had married at Fort St. Vrain. Also left behind were his mixed-blood children, two sons and a daughter. He sent for his children two years later and raised them with his white wife in their St. Louis home. Meanwhile, every day Red climbed a hill and maintained a vigil, staring eastward, looking in vain for the return of her husband.[47]

George knew that his father would never abandon Island or force the children to live in St. Louis with white people. But still the story bothered him—he thought of Island standing on the hill, searching the eastern horizon waiting for him to return. It was almost too terrible to think about.

But George's days at Fort St. Vrain were happy ones. He remembered little of the decline of the hide business and the awful devastation caused by the cramp sickness. William had journeyed to Fort St. Vrain not just to escape the disease but to rebuild the Bent empire by going among his clients and partners, now including the Northern Arapahos, Sioux, and Northern Cheyennes. George met his father's traders, men such as Goodale, Lucas "Goddamn" Murray, and others, who used Fort St. Vrain as headquarters. These tough frontiersmen fanned out in all directions, trading with the Indians, constructing double log cabins, and always keeping William apprised of their success and new trade opportunities. George remembered especially the log trading post constructed on Scout Creek, the site of the Cheyenne-Kiowa fight, where he again explored the battlefield and its pits.[48]

William took the family with him when he trekked toward Fort Laramie, 150 miles north of Fort St. Vrain. The fort stood on the Oregon Trail, now crowded with California-bound gold seekers, and in the summer of 1851 it would be the site of a great gathering of plains people, summoned by Thomas "Broken Hand" Fitzpatrick, Indian agent for the Upper Arkansas and Platte.[49] The federal government had appropriated one hundred thousand dollars for gifts to be distributed among the tribes at Fort Laramie. Now that gold had been discovered in California and thousands of argonauts traveled the Oregon-California Trail, it was imperative that a new agreement with the plains tribes be concluded, one that allowed safe passage for overland travelers and ensured peace among warring tribes.

William sought to take advantage of the new trade opportunities north of the Platte River, a region beyond the traditional boundaries of the Bent domain. Now with family in tow, he arrived at Fort Laramie well before September 1, 1851, the date set for the opening of the conference. All that summer the tribes gathered. By September more than ten thousand Cheyennes, Arapahos, Shoshones, Lakotas, and even some Crows camped at the great council grounds. Among these were a handful of U.S. dragoons under the command of Colonel Edwin V. Sumner, sent there to protect the trade goods and preserve the peace.[50]

Inevitably there were misunderstandings and confrontations between the tribes. More than once, William, along with Kit Carson, Jim Bridger, and Fitzpatrick, helped cool hot tempers. Finally, on September 8, the soldier cannon boomed, signaling the opening of the talks. The chiefs gathered around the great flagstaff fashioned from three lodge poles lashed end to end, the Stars and Stripes waving at its top.

While tribal representatives and federal agents debated the terms of the treaty, Father Pierre-Jean De Smet, a famed Jesuit priest—called "Black Robe" by the Indians—went among the tribes seeking converts. The Indians were willing. Under the cover of a specially erected buffalo-hide sanctuary, Black Robe baptized more than three hundred Cheyenne children, including George and twenty-seven other mixed-bloods. George trembled as the white priest approached him. Then the Black Robe made the sign of the cross and sprinkled holy water on his forehead, all the while intoning Latin chants, a language foreign to his ears.[51]

The Cheyennes matched Father De Smet's Christian proselytizing with pageantry of their own. Cheyenne holy men organized an ear-piercing ceremony for the children, a fact the Jesuit himself recorded. The good priest allowed that this ritual was common among all the tribes of the Upper Missouri. In the Cheyenne ceremony, the mother selected a prominent man to pierce the designated child's ear; the father then announced the choice of the piercer to the villagers. The mother placed the child on a carefully prepared and painted animal skin. Then, while a chosen friend or relative held the child still, up to six incisions were cut in the rim of each ear, which would receive and carry eardrops and other ornaments. As each cut was made, the piercer recounted one of his own coups or brave deeds. The proud parents paid the honored man with the gift of a fine horse.[52]

While William accepted Christian baptism—he himself had been raised a Roman Catholic—he would not permit his children to be scarred in the Cheyenne ceremony. George and the other children would always move between two cultures. William knew that such disfigurement would brand them as Indians and make their acceptance into white society more difficult. But Island wanted the children to go through this rite of passage, for it was customary, even expected, among her people. Indeed, for a man of her husband's wealth and stature not to allow the ritual would be scandalous. In this test of wills, William won. George would have liked to wear the dangling shell eardrops of a warrior, but he was glad his father prevailed. He feared the cutting ceremony, for he knew he might grow faint at the sight of his own blood and thus embarrass his family.[53]

Even now, in childhood, George, Mary, Robert, Charley, and Julia were caught between their father and mother. All the Bent children would have to find their own paths between white and Indian worlds.

Back on the Arkansas River, Bent's flat-nosed Irish trader Goddamn Murray forwarded promising reports from his log quarters at Big Timbers. The Cheyennes, although vastly reduced in numbers by cholera, still looked to Bent traders for powder and ball, kettles and knives, sugar, and other essentials.

By 1852, in the north, new competitors vied for a piece of the Indian trade along the overland trails. The return on investments, once so promising, in reality proved pitifully small. William looked again to the Arkansas River and his old Cheyenne partners. It was time to return.

Once again, the Bent wagons followed the Trappers Trail, this time south, along the South Platte River, the Rocky Mountains always to the west, the buffalo-rich grasslands to the east. George, now age nine, picked out the familiar landmarks: the Kiowa-Cheyenne battleground on Scout Creek;[54] farther south, Pikes Peak in snowy splendor; then along Fountain Creek and on to the Arkansas. South of the river, marking the gateway to Santa Fe and Taos, loomed *Wah-To-Yah*, the Utes' Breasts of the World, known to American explorers as the Spanish Peaks.

Finally, as the wagons wound along the banks of the Arkansas, George saw, shimmering on the horizon, the adobe walls of Bent's Fort. From a distance it still looked like a majestic castle on the plains. But as the Bents drew nearer, the cracked walls prepared them for the scene within. The old fort was returning to the earth—melting and crumbling walls, missing ladders, broken wooden steps, the once busy plaza choked with weeds.[55]

The fort could be repaired, of course, but William had decided to abandon it. Two years before he had almost negotiated its sale to the army. But the War Department would not meet his price then, and certainly, with the fort in disrepair, would not meet his price now. Better to strip it than to sell it for an unacceptable price, or allow squatters to claim it.

As Island drove George and the children to the Cheyenne camps at Big Timbers, William remained behind with his most trusted employees to dismantle the fort and salvage what they could—the timbers, iron hardware, fur presses, wagons, harness, anything that could be used at his new outpost at Big Timbers.

About six miles below the fort, at Short Timber Creek, George looked back and saw a plume of black smoke spiraling skyward. He asked his stepmother what it meant. She replied that the smoke came from the fort. His father had stayed behind to destroy it, for it was a sad place. Too many people had died there. Island went on to explain that his father had planned to blow up the fort, and with it all the bad memories. George recalled later that "four of [my father's] brothers had died that had lived at this fort and our mother died there. . . . He was disgusted on account of this. Whenever he looked around where they used to live in rooms, it made him feel bad and this is why he blowed the fort up."[56]

No doubt Island and the children believed this, but for William, the fort had outlived its usefulness. He was too good a businessman to wantonly destroy his principal asset. He had good reasons to abandon the fort and move to Big Timbers. The Cheyennes had always wanted his trade headquarters located there. Big Timbers was closer to the buffalo range, and it was a favored winter camping location, with plenty of wood, water, and grass.

However, by the early 1850s the Arkansas River country was overrun by competing traders, unscrupulous men who offered cheap goods and whiskey to the Cheyennes and neighboring tribes. These itinerant traders had no great fort to maintain with all of its retainers, appurtenances, equipment, and hangers-on. They operated with almost no overhead.

A few years before, during the war with Mexico, U.S. troops had taken advantage of William's good nature and strong patriotism by using the fort not only as a way station but as a supply depot. He had never been compensated for his generous support of the war effort. Later, he offered the fort to the government at what he thought was a fair price, sixteen thousand dollars; the army, however, countered with an insultingly low bid.

Giving up the fort made sound business sense. And so William joined his family on the road to Big Timbers, where Goddamn Murray awaited their return at the log trading post.

Among the great tangle of cottonwood trees—Big Timbers stretched over forty miles on the north side of the Arkansas—the traders erect a U-shaped cluster of log and mud-brick buildings on the river's low banks. Cheyenne and Arapaho lodges completely encircled the compound, and on the south side of the river sprawled the Kiowa, Comanche, and Apache camps.[57]

Later, George wrote of that winter of 1852–53:

I remember so well of that winter. Cheyennes killed war party of Pawnees on Smoky Hill River that had stolen some horses from Thunder Bull's band of Arapahoes on Crooked Creek. There was 9 Pawnees in this party. Cheyenne war party took up their trail and over took them and killed them all. I remember the Cheyennes had all of their scalps in this scalp dance as other parties had big scalp dance in front of building. My father give them presents.[58]

That same winter, sister Mary and brother Robert attended school in Westport, Missouri, under the watchful eye of their guardian, Albert G. Boone, grandson of famed frontiersman Daniel Boone.

George and his younger brother Charley and little Julie now had the trading post and the surrounding Indian camps to themselves. The children traveled from village to village with their father or with trusted Bent traders, including John Hatcher, a Kentuckian known as "Freckled Hand" and perhaps the best man of all; Lucas Murray, who George remembered as both "Goddamn" and "Flat Nose," was his father's second in command; Robert Fisher, known inevitably as "Fish"; Tim Goodale, from Fort St. Vrain and one of George's favorites; and Tom Boggs, of St. Louis and a close Bent family friend, called "White Horse."

These traders were "squawmen" all, and the fathers of mixed-blood children, George's playmates. "These men were good men," George said later, "they all spoke Spanish and made fine signs with their hands, and talked to Indians in this way."[59] In the camps, he loved to handle the traders' wares, especially the brightly colored Mexican blankets and shining silver jewelry. He learned how the traders bargained for the best price and watched in amazement as Cheyenne men traded ten buffalo robes for one Mexican blanket, just to please their wives and daughters.[60]

Yet these were not happy days for the Bents. The trade had lost its luster. Epidemics had decimated the Southern Cheyennes; many of George's childhood friends had died. The trade itself was in transition, with small, independent operators plying their goods up and down the Arkansas River villages. Of necessity, his father had consolidated the business, shutting down far-flung posts such as Fort St. Vrain, Adobe Walls on the Canadian River, and Bent's Fort itself. Friends advised him to get out of the business. But how could he? The Cheyennes were his own people now; his children were born of Cheyenne women. For almost thirty years the Cheyenne villages had been his home. Beyond the necessity of business, St. Louis and Westport attracted him not at all. Neither did society in Taos and Santa Fe.

But George knew his father was troubled. So many Cheyennes had died, and it was impossible for young men and women to find suitable partners. A new morality had taken hold as the old clan system broke down. Now cousins married cousins, and the old rules of courtship, marriage, and social interaction no longer applied. The people were hungry and impoverished. White travelers and traders reported that sexual favors could be purchased from a Cheyenne woman for a cup of sugar or a dram of whiskey, something unheard of just a few years before. Once the most chaste of people, the Cheyennes struggled to survive in this frightening new world.

William, too, struggled to find his way. When Owl Woman died in 1847, his life changed. She had been more than a convenience, more than an entrée into the Cheyenne trade network. He had loved her. She had been his center, the mother of his children. She had taught him the language and ways of the Cheyennes. He depended on her. Now she was gone. True, he had taken her sisters, Island and Yellow Woman, into his lodge, but he had done so out of respect for Cheyenne tradition. These were less than loving relationships. The sisters needed a provider, and William needed a mother for his children. Though Yellow Woman, the youngest sister, bore him a son, Charley, she was seldom in the lodge and George never considered her his stepmother. She was young, headstrong, and lived apart from the family circle. Island, however, devoted herself fully to William and the children's needs. She was the only mother that George ever knew.[61]

Life at the Big Timbers camp had none of the order or formality of Bent's Fort. By living in the stockaded post, among his traders, William was less the master and more the first among equals. At the old fort he had had his own quarters and some physical separation from the Bent–St. Vrain employees. No one questioned his authority. He was counselor, chief trader, magistrate—in short, master of his domain. But at Big Timbers, traders and their mixed-blood families lived in cramped quarters among their Indian customers. It was no different for William and his children. George lived with Island in a nearby lodge, or in one of the crowded rooms of the log trading post, constantly surrounded by noise and people and the turbulent movement of wagons and travois. And there was the disruptive influence of incessant gossip and rumor. The old rules seemed not to apply.

Into this upside-down world, in the fall of 1853, rode explorer John C. Fremont, leading his fifth assault on the Rockies, this time to find a central route for a transcontinental railroad. With him came James F. Milligan, not one of the typical starry-eyed adventurers who tended to follow the swashbuckling explorer but a native Missourian and hardened veteran of the recent war between the United States and Mexico. An educated man, he chaffed at Fremont's monumental ego and dictatorial ways. When the expedition reached Big Timbers, he and Fremont argued and parted company. Milligan wintered at the trading post to care for the expedition's lame mules and surplus equipment, remaining at Big Timbers until Fremont returned in May.

Milligan found life at Big Timbers more exciting than he had anticipated. As a later traveler remarked: "The manner of living among the Squaws is rather looser than civilized people generally permit."[62] Milligan devoted more than half of his own journal to the intimate details of life at the Bent camp. On December 6, 1853, he reported the innocent pleasure of a candy-pulling frolic with English nobleman Lord Charles William Wentworth Fitzwilliam.

But there was a seamier side to life at Big Timbers, and Milligan quickly found it. Almost before Fremont had departed for the mountains, the young Missourian had taken a Cheyenne "wife," an arrangement he instantly regretted, for with her also came her entire family and dependents. It was far cheaper, he found, to "hire" a Cheyenne woman for the night than to "marry" one and live as husband and wife.

The Big Timber camps seethed with sexual tension and lawlessness. Milligan recorded in his journal nightmarish tales of prostitution, murder, and an adulterous affair with Goddamn Murray's wife. On January 19, 1854, Milligan lent his Indian "wife" to the son of the Arrow Keeper in return for an Arapaho woman. The two couples then spent the night in the Arrow Keeper's lodge.[63]

Such was life on the Arkansas.

George lived in this environment. And it must have affected him, for his father participated in some of these scandalous affairs. He seemed no longer to be in control and had taken to thrashing his

Mexican employees with a stick whenever they displeased him or carelessly allowed stock to stray.[64] George traveled with his father to Indian camps on trading trips and knew that he bedded women other than his stepmother and aunt and that he suffered from the disease common to men who frequented the lodges of promiscuous women.[65]

But George never doubted his father's love for him and the other children. He had seen how his father patiently instructed older brother Bob in the workings of the family business. And he had seen Mary go off to school in Westport, Missouri, to live and be educated among the whites. He was glad, however, that his father had not forced him to go to so distant a place, far from home and family.

In the fall of 1853, William began construction of a new trading post— one entirely of stone. It would be located on the high bluffs just east of the log stockade at Big Timbers. The chaos of life at the camps had convinced him that he needed an imposing headquarters to separate himself and family from his own traders and to impress his Indian partners of his power and influence. The old fort may have been an unacceptable financial encumbrance but it had at least provided him with a place where he was the undisputed master. He understood this now. The new fort would be built to last, a castle befitting the king of traders.

If he had thought about it, the idea made little sense, for of all people he should have known that nothing on the plains lasted forever. The buffalo herds were fast moving away from Big Timbers, and grass and wood supplies—once so abundant—were dwindling. William knew through experience that fixed locations for trade were bad business. But he would not return to St. Louis to take up a new life. He had long ago made his choice—he would remain on the Arkansas with the Cheyennes. The new stone fort, he believed, was his family's only hope for the future.

William's freight wagons now hauled stone quarried near the new fort site.[66] George saw the masons lay out the fort and shape the stone. His father watched, too, but he worried about George and the younger children. What would become of them, here at Big Timbers? He could see they were growing up unsupervised—wild, really—for following the deaths of Owl Woman and Tail Woman, Island had been hard-pressed to care for the children. Yellow Woman, away much of the time, was of little help, and he knew he could not watch them himself, preoccupied as he was with the construction of the new fort.

On February 19, 1854, Milligan, who was still at the fort, wrote, "All hands at work covering the new fort and hauling wood. . . . Bent trading fast. Having run the opposition out of goods he has it all his own way." A few days later, on February 21, this entry: "Bent's Squaw traded her horse 'Pigeon Toe' for two fine mules. Bent trading robes fast, it being the close of the season. Boys dubing & chinking the new fort." And the next day: "Boys at work on the new fort which is very nearly completed. Bent intends moving in it as soon as done. The rats are eating up all his goods here."[67]

On February 23, 1854, William ordered Island's lodge dismantled and erected anew just outside the stone fort. His wife would never confine herself within the walls of a white man's house. Nor would she allow the children to live in such a place. While he was with his step-mother George always lived in a buffalo-hide lodge. He never lived at the stone fort, for within a week of its completion he was off with his father, bound for Westport—and school.[68]

The following week, William's attendants greased the axles of his personal carriage and loaded fourteen wagons with robes and trade goods. As the caravan headed east, William purchased another buffalo-hide lodge, this one for Island's use on the trail and when she was at Westport.[69]

When the wagons reached Pawnee Rock, a famed camping place on the Santa Fe Trail, George noticed rows of bleached-white ox skulls just below big stone bluffs. His father told him the story. Years earlier, two big ox trains had been caught in a terrible blizzard. Under the bluffs the animals had frozen to death. Later, passing Indians noticed the bleached bones and arranged the long-horned skulls in neat rows. George was both fascinated and terrified by the sight of these hollow-eyed heads watching the Bent train pass.[70]

While George played among the skulls, the men went out and killed several buffalo cows, capturing a young calf. Then, Milligan reported in disgust, "Bent's Semi-Barbarian Children killed it in mere wantonness while my back was turned."[71]

George showed no remorse for the act, no respect for an animal that sustained the Cheyennes and all peoples of the plains. The brutality offended William's sensibilities. It was time someone took charge of his children before they reverted to savagery.

Perhaps there was hope for them in Westport, now only two hundred miles distant.

Chapter 3

IN THE WHITE WORLD

The Santa Fe Trail was alive with prairie schooners and freight wagons of every type and description. East-bound wagons were laden with trade goods from Santa Fe, Taos, Old Mexico—buffalo hides, bales of pelts, colorful Mexican blankets, finely worked silver. Enormous herds of mules and ponies, only recently acquired through trade, followed in the wake of the lumbering freight wagons. West-bound wagons were heavy with manufactured goods—canned foods, tools, firearms, ammunition, kettles, packed barrels of trade goods, all manner of necessities and luxuries not found on the frontier.

The great trains, traveling in opposite directions, passed like ships at sea, their white-canvas tops billowing in the wind. The road was really three, sometimes four roads, parallel ruts cut deep into the raw earth and sandstone outcrops. The independent trains, each consisting of twenty to thirty wagons, seldom lost sight of one another. They snaked from horizon to horizon, the dust rising high in enormous plumes. Dust devils darted in the wind, sometimes lifting the white canopies, tormenting the teamsters and trail-weary animals. The pace was excruciatingly slow. A well-bossed train might make twenty miles in a day, but most ox-pulled wagons usually rolled half that distance. A landmark such as Pawnee Rock stayed in view for hours, even days at a time. Travelers called this area the Pawnee Rock Country, for they could see the butte for hundreds of miles. When it disappeared from view, they entered what they called another "country," this time perhaps "Plum Buttes." Chouteau Island Country particularly impressed itself on young George:

I seen the sticks of the Chouteau's picket house or ranch. It had been burnt some time before. Chouteau's Island was great place for war parties to stop and paint their buffalo scalp robes when ever they had scalps. Near the Island they also got white clay to paint their robes to make them look white. The way they made black paint was this: They dug little holes in ground and fill this with buffalo blood and charcoal willow. The blood acted as glue. I seen these holes in 1854 where this black paint was made.[1]

And so they rolled on, one "country" after another, each distinctive, each with its special feature, a river or bluff or prairie.

In the spring of 1854 William Bent's train moved as just one more on the great trail of commerce. No one, however, had traveled this route more or knew it better. His herders and bullwhackers were the most experienced in the business, and the best paid. George, ten years old, big for his age, always curious and wide-eyed, absorbed all that passed around him. For the rest of his life, even as an old man, he remembered this trip in all its swirling detail.

Ox trains started from Bent's Fort in spring and returned in August. It took 3 or 4 months to make the round trips. My father sent 25 to 30 wagons, 6 yoke of oxen to each wagon, or 12 oxen. The horses, mules and loose oxen were driven behind this train by two Mexican herders. They had 4 herders, 2 night herders. These 2 slept in wagons during the day while the train was on the road. The wagons were used as corral. The herders drove the cattle or oxen into this corral early in the morning just at daylight. These oxen were yoked in the corral then led to the wagons to their places. The object was to be on the road before it got too hot. The men had no breakfast until the train stopped at 10. o'clock. Then men had breakfast. They didn't start again until 2 or 3 o'clock in evening and did not stop until night. If the men wanted to they could have their supper, but they generally got big dinner before starting out in afternoon. The wagon masters knew all the camping places and they knew when to start the train to make these places. The herders also knew watering places for the stock and good grazing grounds. They always hired herders that knew these places and they always hired good ox drivers also.[2]

At night, George recalled, after the wagons had been corralled, the men divided into separate messes, each with its own cook. The white and Mexican herders and teamsters ate together, as did the Shawnee and Delaware hunters. George and his family and any guests dined apart from the rest of the company.[3] Unless the hunters were successful in knocking down a buffalo or antelope, the usual fare was beef, bread, boiled dried apples, rice, and coffee sweetened with sugar or molasses. Whatever the fare, after a long, hard day the men brought huge appetites, and quantity rather than quality ruled the cook-fires.[4]

William always kept an eye out for mess guests. Not only would they help break the monotony, but they often carried with them not only news from the states but also important intelligence concerning wood, water, and grass ahead; war parties; buffalo herds; and perhaps most important of all, sickness on the trail. This last bore special relevance this spring. Just before the family had started out from Big Timbers, smallpox struck a nearby Cheyenne camp. This disease had not yet ravaged the Cheyennes as it had other plains tribes, but Bent immediately recognized the danger and acted decisively. He ordered the village quarantined and burned the infected blankets, only recently received in trade from the Kiowas. This saved his friends from a full-scale outbreak.

Now on the trail this sickness seemed far behind, but he knew how quickly epidemics could be spread by west-bound trains. The white trade wagons carried more than just goods; they brought death and suffering as well. Within William's memory whole tribes—the Mandans and Blackfeet among them—had nearly been wiped out. And just five years before, the Southern Cheyennes had lost half their number to cholera.

William's interest in visitors and trail news extended beyond social nicety; it was essential to the well-being of his family and the men who worked for him. It was the reason so many people, Indian and white, depended on his counsel and leadership.[5]

As the train rolled ever eastward, the terrain slowly changed. Trees, high grass, and streams cut the trail, and then the rolling green hills of the Big Blue River Country came into view. Soon William recognized the pasturage six miles southwest of Westport on the Kansas-Missouri border. Here, wagon masters of in- and outbound trains took advantage of the rich grass, grazing their animals until they were ready to move.

George had never witnessed such a gathering of wagons, men, and animals. He had experienced great gatherings of traders and Indians at Bent's Fort, but never before had he seen so much canvas on wheels. Thirty trains comprising six hundred wagons, seventy-two hundred oxen, and horses and mules—too many to count—all grazed at the Westport pasturage. And the crowds of people—Mexicans, Americans, French, Shawnees, Delawares, Pawnees, these and more—busied themselves at countless tasks. As William went on to the steamboat landing on the Missouri River near Westport to make arrangements for transshipping his goods to St. Louis, George explored the fringes of this wide-open boomtown. Not far away from the pastures, at the Last Chance Saloon, bullwhackers and herders washed the trail dust from their throats and spent the night, George remembered, "dancing with low down women."[6]

But Westport beckoned. After William had transacted his business on the steamboat docks, he returned to the pasturage for Island and the children. It was time for George, Charley, and Julia to meet Albert· Gallatin Boone, who had already taken in Robert and Mary. William had determined that the children would live at Westport and receive the blessings of the white world and white education. The children had seen enough of the wilds of the Big Timbers Country. Island raised no objection, but the white world crowded her senses. Her world lay back with her people, far from the hard sounds and sour smells of the city, with its strange people of unintelligible words. Her home would always be of shining mountains and buffalo plains, where you could see forever.

Albert Gallatin Boone, the grandson of the legendary Daniel Boone, towered over George and the children. Impressive in his own right, he stood nearly six feet tall, weighed over two hundred pounds, and sported a full, gray-streaked beard. Affable, literate, an avid Bible reader, a slave owner and proslavery advocate, Boone had long been associated with William Bent. They were related by marriage, had frequent business dealings with one another, and were intimate friends.[7]

Boone's store in Westport was more than a place to outfit wagons and buy sundries. It was a gathering place for traders and trappers and, increasingly, a hub for proslavery radicals and border ruffians.[8] It stood in the heart of Westport's growing industrial and trade district. Surrounding it were manufactories of all kinds—harness, saddle, tentage and wagon covers, yokes and bows, guns and gun furnishings, candles, wheels, wagons, and other goods. The town of two thousand people included blacksmiths, wheelwrights, millers, masons, carpenters, boilermakers, shipbuilders, and roustabouts, as well as doctors, lawyers, teachers, clergy, and merchants.[9] On Westport's streets every type of man of the West was represented.[10]

In a small frame house, three blocks from the store, George, Charley, and Julie Bent joined their siblings Bob and Mary, who had already been under Boone's care for more than a year. The entire family now crowded into the limited space. Except Island. She erected her tipi nearby, living alone, for William and Boone had agreed that the children must be taught white ways; they would have to give up the comfort of their mother's lodge and their comfortable frontier clothes. Out West, a French tailor in William's employ had made clothing for the children modeled after the buckskin garb preferred by trappers and traders. Now, for the first time, George would wear shoes instead of moccasins, underwear—a novelty for him—and coats and trousers of linen and wool. His sisters would wear dresses with full skirts and petticoats.[11]

The striking mixed-blood Bents attracted attention wherever they went. George had his mother's thick black hair—now cropped short—dark eyes, and prominent cheekbones. From his father he inherited a narrow, straight nose, square jaw, and light bronze complexion. He was tall for his age and strong, his chest and shoulders already well-muscled for a boy of eleven, but like his father he had small feet and hands. Where older brother Bob was quiet and methodical, George sometimes acted impulsively, unable to control his curiosity and youthful enthusiasm. As the second son, he seemed to get along with everyone, and laughter came easy to him. Charley, just a little younger than George but much smaller—even for his age—was watchful and bright but given to outbursts of temper. Mary, the oldest of the Bent children, heavy-boned and dark, her open gaze friendly and without guile, was always protective of her younger brothers and sisters. Julie, fair-skinned and delicate, even now showed signs of the beauty that would later attract the attention of men.

Island remained only a few weeks in Westport, just long enough for William to conduct business in St. Louis. She never moved into the Boone house—or any other house in Westport. She stayed in her tipi and would have nothing to do the frilly petticoats offered by the white women. With William gone, Island had time on her hands.

She caused quite a stir.

The Westport women were intrigued and came in great numbers to view Colonel Bent's "tipi wife." Although Island did not try to draw attention to herself, her horsemanship impressed the ladies, who even years later remembered the strange Cheyenne woman who rode astride in her split buckskin skirt, causing sparks to fly from the hooves of her galloping saddle mule as it pounded down Westport's cobblestone streets. She was, recalled one dazzled witness, a "veritable centaur."[12]

When not riding bareback, Island often harnessed her finely matched mules to William's light carriage and expertly trotted her team through town, to the amazement of onlookers. The gossip of the town women annoyed Boone, who morally opposed mixed marriages, but William seemed not to mind. Unlike many traders and mountain men, he made no distinction between "Indian" and "white" wives; indeed, he only married Indian women and was not afraid of the social consequences in white society. On many occasions he brought his Indian wives back to Westport, and his friends in St. Louis knew of his western marriages by "Indian custom." He made no secret of his personal life, and offered no apology. [13]

Moreover, he demonstrated fatherly pride in his mixed-blood children, taking them wherever he went, even introducing them to high society in St. Louis, where he was born and where the Bent name was well known. And he insisted on providing them with the best that money could buy and saw to their every need. Before he and Island left for the Arkansas, he arranged for the children to see Dr. John W. Parker, a respected Westport physician. The doctor treated the family and its servants for an assortment of ailments, prescribing suction cupping to draw out sickly humors and to relieve internal congestion, all-purpose patent "bitters," and other medications. William himself received treatment for his gonorrhea.[14]

This done, William turned to the children's educational needs. In 1854 Westport was not just a town of commerce and industry, it also boasted five churches and three schools. The community's foremost institution of learning was the Shawnee Indian Mission, three miles west of town in "Indian Country." Here, in August 1848, Reverend Nathan Scarritt had founded the Western Academy, a coeducational school intended for the children of affluent Westport families. It was very much an experimental school, for Reverend Scarritt opened it to both Indian and white students, who studied side by side. In December 1853, when Scarritt was reassigned to the new Methodist Episcopal Church in Westport, the Western Academy moved with him. William Bent chose Scarritt's school as the place where his children would receive instruction not only in reading, writing, and arithmetic, but in the classics as well. Upon Scarritt's departure, Chris Huffaker became schoolmaster and the two-story frame building was renamed Mr. Huffaker's Classical Academy.[15]

Both Scarritt and Huffaker were progressive educators who believed Indians, whites, and mixed-bloods were intellectual equals and could be taught in the same classroom. Years later Scarritt explained:

A score or more of young gentlemen and young ladies from across the [Kansas-Missouri] line, and some, indeed, from more distant parts of Missouri, were admitted into this department. This brought the whites and Indians into close competition in the race for knowledge, and I must say that those Indian scholars whose previous knowledge had been equal to their competitors were not a whit behind them in the contest for the laurels of scholarship.[16]

Thirty-three-year-old Scarritt, with his intense dark eyes, chiseled features, and lantern jaw, must have terrified George and the other mixed-bloods, but they soon learned that while he was a hard disciplinarian he was a man of kindly disposition, a man who genuinely cared for their welfare. Huffaker, too, favorably impressed the children. He stressed the fundamentals of grammar, reading, penmanship, and arithmetic, carefully watching over his charges, testing and scoring their progress.

When William and Island left with their train bound for the Arkansas River, the children settled into a school routine. Clutching their blue Webster spellers, they participated in weekly spelling bees, recited lessons, and moved their pencils and quills over paper, practicing their serifs and scrolling their flourishes. First the pupils were taught to write all the small letters, then the capitals. Then Scarritt or Huffaker would write out some fact or sentiment, which the students dutifully copied in their composition books. Perhaps they penned such pronouncements as "Romulus founded the City of Rome," or "Heaven, from all creation, hides the book of fate."

On a typical day, the pupils were taught two lessons, which had to be recited to perfection before the class could be dismissed. Failure to complete the lesson might result in some harsh punishment—a slap on the hand, a hickory switch well applied, or exile to the dunce corner. Posture and bearing were as much a part of the curriculum as academic subjects. The children were taught to hold "correct posture" and to fill their lungs "with atmosphere" while enunciating correctly such phrases as "Marry you! Marry you, you pestiferous little pygmy!" George no doubt thrilled to the impassioned recitation delivered by his classmate Stephen B. Elkins, later U.S. senator from West Virginia, in which he quoted Patrick Henry's defiant declaration, "*Give me Liberty or give me death.*" George may not have understood all the implications of American Revolutionary rhetoric, but he understood the defiance of it and the need for people to live free or die.[17]

How different all this was from the unstructured education of a Cheyenne boy or girl. A whipping for an infraction of the rules? A slap on the hand for talking out of turn? Was this any way to learn? Back on the Arkansas River, George learned by example. Oral tradition—the stories told by elders around the campfire—and the recounting of coups and brave deeds, for George *this* was the stuff of education. These stories taught life's lessons. George absorbed them, practiced them every day. But in Westport, structure and discipline forged learning. He competed with other boys and girls in spelling bees, was graded on his progress, and was judged daily. He heard *No!* more often than *Yes!* His teachers insisted there was only one way; only one civilization and culture worthy of study and emulation—the Christian way, one with a strict moral code, one that brooked no deviation from prescribed behavior and thought. Out in Indian Country, George had learned that *his* people, the Cheyennes, were the Chosen Ones. Only the *Tsistsistas* followed the way of the Grandfather and the prophet Sweet Root. His culture was rich in tradition and truth; Cheyenne men were stronger and fleeter; Cheyenne women more pleasing to the eye and better mothers. His tribe was superior to all others.

Now, George was taught that the whites were the Chosen Ones, that their Christian God and his prophet were all-knowing and all-powerful, that nations and peoples without Christ were unworthy and pagan, that whites, with their history and books and technology, were superior to all others. Beauty meant straight noses, light skin, fair hair, and delicate features—an aesthetic entirely foreign to his experience.

And so, George and all the young Bents grappled with these contradictions. Their difficulties were compounded on the docks and streets when they were sneered down as halfbreeds—not white, not Indian, but mixed-bloods, inferior to all. In the classroom Scarritt and Huffaker treated them as equals. But George quickly learned that he would have to conform to this new world—a world that would shape his destiny.

George whooped a Cheyenne war cry when his father's train rolled into the Westport pasturage in the spring of 1855. After a year of confinement, he and his brothers and sisters were now to return to their roots and a summer's vacation on the Arkansas.

After weeks on the trail George first viewed the new stone fort as the caravan turned at the bend of the river. There, a mile distant, the freshly cut stones gleamed white in the sunlight. George jumped from the slow-moving wagons and raced ahead, eager to explore the new fort and see his friends. Clucking chickens scattered before him as ran through the recently hung gates. This fort did not compare in size to the old one, measuring little more than one hundred feet square, but it was impressive nonetheless, with its eighteen-foot-high stone walls, twelve neatly plastered rooms arrayed around a central court, and a great warehouse standing just outside the east wall. He recognized the old fort's cannons mounted on the parapets, but he was surprised to find that no bastions guarded the corners.[18]

Traveler O. A. Nixon, visiting the fort when the Bents arrived, recorded in his journal on July 31, 1855, "A Warm, windy day. Col. Bent arrived at the Fort to-day with his family." A few days later, on August 5, Nixon wrote, "Went down to the Room (Office) to see Mrs. Bent, to-day. She's pretty much Indian."[19] The fort impressed Nixon, not just for its appearance but also as a symbol of the culture and society he had left behind in the states. "It is a very good Fort and a safe refuge to the emigrants or for who-ever seeks one; nice rooms, plastered walls, &c . . . remind me of HOME and it seems that I am in a Civilized Country again."[20]

And that was William's intention all along. The new fort, with its imposing walls, clean white-plastered rooms, warehouses and shops, and comfortable accommodations, reflected the order he needed. It symbolized his authority and power. Never again would he be just one man among equals, living shoulder to shoulder with his clients and employees. Although he understood and respected the free ways of the Cheyennes, he wanted for himself and his children the familiar social structure of his youth, one that was defined by a clear hierarchy. Now, with the new fort, William was again the master of his domain; his world was secure.

When George returned to Westport for school in September, he did not know it would be seven years before he saw the fort again.

Although he missed home, George enjoyed life at the Boone house, and he made friends with the other mixed-blood children. The children of Louis Vasquez, Ceran St. Vrain, William Guerrier, Thomas Fitzpatrick, Jim Bridger, and Kit Carson were his intimate friends and would remain so for the rest of his life.

The Panic of 1857 jolted the Boone household. Money was scarce and Boone, like other investors, was hard-pressed to make payment on his debts. When George completed his course of studies at Mr. Huffaker's Classical Academy, his father entrusted him to the care of his longtime friend, Robert Campbell, in St. Louis.

In 1824, a St. Louis physician, Dr. Bernard G. Farrar, had diagnosed Campbell with consumption and advised him to go West to clear up his lungs. Campbell followed the doctor's orders and ended up as one of the leading figures of the Missouri River fur trade. In the West he met William Bent and the two became fast friends. Even though William had brothers, sisters, and cousins in St. Louis—prominent citizens all—he turned to his old friend Campbell to take in his mixed-blood son, George. Campbell had already assisted the sons and daughters of other mountain men, Bridger's and Fritzpatrick's children among them, as they attempted to adapt to St. Louis society and schools.[21]

George remembered his first meeting with Campbell, "He was very old man then. He was guardian also for several Mexicans attending school in St. Louis. He was big man among all the Western men those old days. He was fine old gentleman and stood away up in St. Louis."[22] George found him more tolerant and accepting of mixed-bloods and people of color than his Westport guardian Boone, more tolerant even than his St. Louis aunts and uncles. Shortly before George moved to St. Louis, he read in the papers that Campbell had created a sensation by emancipating his slave Eliza and her two children.[23]

Campbell's unusual action must have been news to create a stir in a city like St. Louis. It was now one of the nation's most populous and prosperous industrial and trade centers. Even Westport, which had so impressed George, paled by comparison. When his father was a boy, St. Louis had a population of 3,500. By 1854, when George first saw it, it had grown to over 78,000, and within ten years it would soar to 170,000—more than half recent immigrants from Germany and Ireland. Indeed, the city seemed destined to replace Pittsburgh as the gateway to the American West.[24]

Bustling St. Louis, with its strange peoples and babble of foreign languages, intimidated even older brother Bob, who visited in April 1857. Bent cousin Bud Boggs, the son of Dr. J. O. Boggs, chanced to encounter Bob on the street. Bud wrote his father:

As I was walking along the street the other day someone tapped me on the shoulder and on looking up who should I see but Bob Bent. I was very much surprised I could hardly speak at first, and I tell you I was extremely glad to see him. He is afraid to go out by himself in the city for fear of getting lost. I took him around to see all the sights (that is, all I knew of) and quite astonished him. He was down here at the Drugstore and after looking around a while said that it wasn't half as fine as ours [in Westport]. I then took him round to A. Leitchson and we got a glass of soda. He starts home tomorrow I believe and Col. Boone and wife this evening.[25]

William enrolled George in St. Louis's Academy of the Christian Brothers. Located in a swank residential neighborhood, this institution enjoyed a reputation for the highest scholastic standards. Granted a state charter in 1855, the Catholic boarding school appealed to young men interested in pursuing an ecclesiastical career. By 1857 Brother Ambrose served as president, and under his leadership school enrollment quickly grew. Priests and other church functionaries were in great demand, not only in St. Louis but also on the western frontier.

George's Westport education did not at all prepare him for the brothers. Their brand of religious indoctrination, high academic standards, and monkish discipline fell on the boy like a blacksmith's anvil, and he did not last long in this environment—within the year he was gone. Robert Campbell came to the rescue, as he had for other mixedblood boys who had been sent to the Christian Brothers. Trader Seth Ward's two children had also gotten into trouble at the college. Campbell successfully negotiated the reinstatement of one boy, but the other was expelled and forced to matriculate at a more liberal school.[26]

Webster College for Boys was more to George's liking. It was an institution well known to the Bent family. Relatives offered it financial support, and one uncle created a scholarship for boarding students. Another, Joseph K. Bent, a prosperous St. Louis contractor, played a major role in the actual construction of the school. Perhaps more important to George, it was not strictly a religious school, as was Christian Brothers.[27] The college sprawled over a hillside ten miles from the city's heart and comprised 150 acres of scenic woodlands, complete with walking paths and recreational fields. The school administration touted this natural environment as "eminently healthy, enjoying almost entire immunity from the diseases peculiar to the Mississippi Valley . . . its atmosphere is pure and invigorating; it is subject to no miasmatic influences."

The course of instruction was not as rigorous as at Christian Brothers, but school officials maintained that its curriculum "is similar to that pursued in the best Institutions in the country, varying only in some minor particulars." Students received "an extensive course of instruction in practical and scientific knowledge," a solid grounding in the classics, and course work in Latin, Greek, and German languages. All were expected to perform daily recitations and were graded on the results. A perfect score was 4.0. Whether George ever attained such excellence is unknown; however, what he learned here served him well in later life.

The school year was divided into two sessions of twenty weeks each, beginning on the first Monday in September and the last Monday in January. Holidays were generous: Thanksgiving and Fast days, Washington's birthday, May Day and a whole week at Christmas. Summer vacation began on June 19.

Like Christian Brothers it was a boarding school. George was allowed to visit his St. Louis home the first Saturday of every month— no doubt a welcomed respite from the drudgery of academic work and the rules of the college. After all, the school's catalogue warned: "The DISCIPLINE in the *Family* [boarding students] and the *School* will be strict." The "REGULATIONS" detailed the school's high expectations:

Boys will not be permitted to occupy their rooms except as sleeping and dressing rooms; nor can they visit each others' rooms without express permission.

Every member of the Family is required to attend Morning and Evening Family Worship, and also Public Worship on the Sabbath with the Principal.

No immoral or ungentlemanly conduct on the part of any boy can be tolerated. The penalty is expulsion.

The use of tobacco, in any form, upon the premises is strictly forbidden.

Each pupil must furnish towels, napkins, napkin ring, slippers, and umbrella, and *each article of clothing must be distinctly marked.*[28]

When George first arrived in St. Louis, he stayed with Robert Campbell, now his legal guardian. The Campbell house stood in the heart of the city, ten miles distant from the school, a difficult commute even after the Missouri Pacific Railroad established a station at Webster.[29] Aunt Dorcus Bent Carr lived closer to the campus, and it is likely that George lived with her during some of his Webster College years. Dorcus, William Bent's closest sister, was a widow with six children. Even so, she took in George's older sister Mary. Mary delighted the household with her mastery of the piano and easily fit into the family.

George, however, now a strapping seventeen-year-old with jet-black hair and a wispy mustache, needed masculine guidance. His visits were brief and confined largely to holidays. Robert Campbell watched over him, whether on campus, at the Campbell home, or at Clarkson's, a boardinghouse near Webster College catering to young mixed-blood boys. By 1861, when his younger brother Charley matriculated at Webster College, George had found accommodations at Clarkson House. The boys felt welcome here. For the boarding-house was a haven for other mixed-blood children, friends like Felix St. Vrain, who, like the Bents, struggled to survive in the unfamiliar city and the strict academic discipline of the college.[30]

Summer vacations, of course, freed George from the confining routine of the school year. He usually returned to his father's newly built Westport farm, by 1860 a rambling, two-story brick home located on four hundred acres of rolling hills and pasturage overlooking Brush Creek, near the Big Blue River.

The summer of 1860 was special to George. Back in April, Mary, now age twenty-two, had married a twenty-seven-year-old Westport saloonkeeper, Robison M. Moore. The wedding had been an extravagant affair, drawing traders, trappers, and dignitaries from St. Louis, Westport, and the frontier. The *Kansas City Journal of Commerce* reported that William gathered his old friends around him in an "Indian Council and passed around the pipe of peace," and the wedding "was such a one as could be given only on the Western frontier and at the mansion of Col. Bent."[31] This was George's first opportunity to visit his sister and new brother-in-law, who lived at the farm and managed the property. He knew that his father had at first opposed the marriage, fearing that the handsome barkeeper was out for Mary's fortune and might mistreat his plump, dark-skinned, half-breed daughter. Further, rumor had it that the bridegroom liked his liquor. But over time, Moore proved himself to be honest, sober, and hardworking, winning over the suspicious father-in-law. That summer, George had ample occasion to take full measure of the man and the marriage. What he saw he liked, so much so that he gladly spent the summer at the farm, where a U.S. census taker included him as a dependent of his sister and brother-in-law.[32]

But marriage was not the only excitement that summer. George's former guardian, Uncle Boone, had suffered financial ruin following the Panic of 1857. Once worth more than one hundred thousand dollars, he had spent a fortune on proslavery causes. Now he was broke and casting about for a job. William Bent quickly secured his old friend a position as federal Indian agent for the Upper Arkansas Agency, headquartered at Fort Wise. Fort Wise was actually William's new stone fort, which the army had leased the year before and named for Virginia governor Henry A. Wise. William had been appointed Indian agent in 1859, but within a year found the responsibilities onerous and a distraction from his trading business. He had performed his duties well; both the government and his Cheyenne and Arapaho charges considered him an agent without peer. This well-deserved reputation—after all, no white man could match his knowledge of Indian people—lent special weight to his efforts to secure Boone's appointment as his successor.[33]

The following summer George again returned to the Westport farm. But by this time, much had changed, not only in Westport but on the national scene as well. Abraham Lincoln had been elected president, triggering the secession of the southern states from the Union. In April 1861, Confederate batteries fired on Fort Sumter, South Carolina, prompting Lincoln's call for seventy-five thousand federal volunteers to suppress the rebellion.

Closer to home, Missouri's secessionist governor Claibourne F. Jackson declared that not a single soldier from his state would respond to Lincoln's call. He mobilized the militia and entreated the men to "rise . . . and drive out . . . the invaders who have dared desecrate the soil which your labors have made fruitful, and which is consecrated by your homes."[34] Pro-Union Captain Nathaniel Lyon rushed to secure the sixty thousand muskets housed in St. Louis at the U.S. Arsenal, now threatened by proslavery insurgents mustering at nearby Camp Jackson. After sneaking the weapons off to safety in Illinois, Lyon, now a brigadier general, turned his attention to the thousand rebel militiamen at Camp Jackson. His four volunteer regiments, most of them German-speaking recruits, bolstered by a battalion of steady regular troops, quickly captured and disarmed the Confederates.

On May 10, 1861, Lyon marched the prisoners through the streets of St. Louis, intending to confine them at the arsenal. Along the way, angry crowds of Southern sympathizers pelted the Union men with stones and coarse epithets especially aimed at the Damned Dutchmen. Tensions mounted and a single shot rang out. The volunteer troops, jittery, untrained, and near panic, opened fire, killing onlookers. The slaughter was indiscriminate—men, women, even a baby in its mother's arms. In one place, fifteen dead lay heaped on the street, the blood coursing through the cobblestones. Lyon's command reached the arsenal, but not before twenty-eight citizens were shot dead and many more wounded. Church bells tolled all night; bonfires lit the sky; and angry mobs, inflamed by stump-thumping oratory, crowded the streets.

In Jefferson City, the pro-Southerner state legislature met and granted Governor Jackson near-dictatorial powers. Jackson acted quickly. Calling for fifty thousand volunteers, he commissioned former governor and Mexican War hero Sterling Price a major general and ordered him to organize a militia force to defend the Missouri government from the Unionists.

The boys at Webster College witnessed the events of May 10, 1861. The Camp Jackson "massacre" burned in their minds and filled them with rage. When school recessed on June 19, George and Charley hurried home to Westport, where they shared what they knew of the tragedy, sprinkling their stories liberally with "Damn Yankees" and war talk. Secessionists rallied at Boone's store, roaring their anger and vowing vengeance. Caught in the war hysteria, George, Charley, and other mixed-bloods joined the secessionist State Guard. George brought his own horse and saddle. Already an expert horseman—after all, he had been raised a Cheyenne and practically born to a horse—he hoped to serve in the ranks of the cavalry. The warfare he knew, consisted of mounted charges, hand-to-hand combat, and displays of personal bravery.

When he reached the capital city of Springfield in late June only days before his eighteenth birthday, George's Ranger company formally enrolled in Colonel Martin E. Green's Missouri Cavalry, a regiment of Sterling Price's newly formed army.

Sterling Price. The same Price with whom his father had served during the Mexican War. William had always spoken highly of Price and cherished the honorific title of colonel that he himself had won during those heady days. Now it was George's turn to serve Price and win his own battle honors.

Like many recruits rushing to Springfield, George carried his own weapons, perhaps a shotgun or Hawken rifle. Others who joined up were burdened with pikes, bowie knives, dueling pistols, and antique flintlock muskets; some had no weapons at all. Within weeks his ranger outfit, a motley group of one-hundred-day volunteers, began to take shape. Training was rigorous, for Price knew it was difficult enough to turn a farmer or schoolboy into a foot soldier, but transforming raw recruits into efficient horse soldiers seemed impossible given the few days remaining before they must fight Nathaniel Lyon's federal force, which even then marched toward Springfield.

Charley, however, barely sixteen and small for his age, contrasted in appearance to his older brother George. Short and small-boned like his father, light-skinned for a Cheyenne with no hint of facial hair, and boyish in bearing, he was sent packing by a recruiting sergeant, who judged him too young to pass muster even in this army of young men. Stung by the rejection, Charley returned to Westport, then set off for the Arkansas River Country to join his mother's village.[35]

So George—without brother Charley—learned cavalry tactics as set forth in the manual written by one of his father's old friends, Philip St. George Cooke. There was much to learn. He had always mounted a horse like a Cheyenne, from the right. Saber-wielding white men, however, mounted from the left. Linear formations of horsemen aligned in precise ranks—Cheyenne sign language identified white horse soldiers with a series of taps of the forearm, indicating men in a row—was a new concept, too. The army also emphasized coordinated action and obedience. In the State Guard, men fought under a rigid command structure: noncommissioned officers led a ten-man squad; captains officered fifty-man companies; colonels commanded six to eight companies, or about five hundred men. Despite the discipline and the imperative of obedience, this uniquely democratic volunteer army elected its own officers, from sergeants to brigadier generals.[36]

Bugle calls now ruled George's life: Reveille . . . Stable Call . . . Mess Call . . . Boots and Saddles . . . and Retreat. And on mounted drills, the bugles directed their every movement: *squads right . . . squads left . . . by squads into line . . . right wheel . . . left wheel . . . trot . . . gallop . . . Charge!* At first, the bugle calls all sounded alike to him. But he worked hard to distinguish the notes, and in a short time he almost thought in bugle tunes. The sergeants drilled into him that in war the varied bugle blares must be instantly recognized, instantly obeyed.[37]

In Price's army, cavalry made up nearly two-thirds of the total force, an advantage in the western theater where troops maneuvered over vast distances. But the cavalry was poorly armed and ill equipped. And three weeks of training hardly sufficed for the men and their horses to master the complexities of mounted combat.

All too soon, on August 10, 1861, at Wilson's Creek, located just southwest of Springfield, Missouri, Confederate and Union forces joined battle. The rebel force, some ten thousand strong, was completely surprised by General Lyon's determined assault. Union batteries fired directly into the white tents of the Confederate encampment. Blue-coated troops surged forward in regular line of battle, while Confederate soldiers milled about in utter confusion. Incredibly, the federals failed to press their advantage. Confederate commanders quickly rallied their men and counterattacked. Many of George's comrades still had no weapons—they had none of their own and the army had not yet issued them muskets—yet these boys bravely followed George and the other front-rank men, who shouted Indian war cries as they charged. In the face of this furious attack, the Union men wavered and then fell back, leaving General Lyon mortally wounded. The Confederates had won a stunning victory at Wilson's Creek. Yet the day ended with staggering losses for both sides; nearly 20 percent of the twenty thousand men engaged were killed, wounded, or missing.[38]

Wilson's Creek was George's baptism of fire. He could not help but be impressed by the enormous numbers of men engaged, by the thunder of artillery and crash of musketry. He had seen men killed and wounded, thousands of men, more than all the Cheyennes on the Arkansas River. He began to understand the importance of tactics and strategy, discipline and obedience, the imperative of coordinated action and adequate military intelligence. As a horse soldier, he saw the futility of mounted charges against waiting lines of foot soldiers armed with bayonets and long-range rifle muskets.

But he had survived, and he had survived unscathed. It was war more terrible than he had ever imagined. It was not war as the Cheyennes knew it, but still, he was now a veteran soldier.

George fought in other battles: Lexington, Missouri (September 20, 1861), a Confederate victory where George's unit took cover behind movable breastworks constructed of hemp bales; then the great Union victory at Pea Ridge, Arkansas (March 7–8, 1862), the largest battle fought west of the Mississippi River, where rebel Indian auxiliaries committed fearful atrocities and brought condemnation from both Confederate and Union leaders. By this time, George's State Guard unit had been recommissioned as the First Missouri Cavalry, now in General Martin E. Greene's brigade of Price's division. The bitter fighting had taken its toll not only on men but horses as well. The attrition was so great that Confederate authorities converted entire cavalry regiments into infantry, rearming the men with long rifle muskets and training them to fight on foot.

But George chose not to fight on foot. Rather than surrender his horse and slog through the mud of Arkansas and Mississippi, he joined Captain John C. Landis's horse artillery, a crack unit attached to Greene's Missouri Brigade. At first, George was drawn to Landis. He reminded him of his father—short, shrewd, and, at times, quick to anger. Captain Landis was a West Point dropout—rumor had it that he detested military discipline—but he turned out to be a no-nonsense professional and a natural-born soldier, steady and cool under fire. His sixty-two-man battery fought from the Battle of Pea Ridge to the end of the war, suffering unusually high casualties. But Landis made up in meanness what he lacked in stature. His men loved him and hated him for his hard-charging combativeness.

During the siege and Confederate retreat from Corinth, Mississippi (April–June 1862), the Missouri Brigade time and again distinguished itself, and Landis's cannoneers, always in close support, gained a reputation for recklessly exposing themselves to enemy fire while manning the battery's two twelve-pounder Napoleons and two twenty-four-pounder howitzers.[39]

George refused to be a foot soldier, but service in the horse artillery was no light duty. In fact, the life of an artilleryman was often brutally short. Exposed to enemy sharpshooters and counterbattery fire, George and the gunners performed perhaps the most dangerous duty in the service. To be effective, they had to be able to *see* their targets and then advance their guns to the most forward and exposed positions. They were, then, themselves visible targets. Shells exploded above them, sometimes bursting ammunition chests on the caissons. Dead horses and mules had to be cut from their traces so that the guns could be advanced or retired, all in the enemy's view. Charging enemy infantry and cavalry sometimes overran their positions, forcing the gunners to fire canister and grapeshot at point-blank range. Hand-to-hand fighting often followed. In battle, George and the batterymen worked the guns, sponging the hot bores, ramming charges, priming, aiming, and firing every thirty seconds. Casualties were appallingly high. During the Corinth campaign in the summer of 1862, Landis's battery suffered losses of more than 20 percent.

The fighting around Corinth would be George's last combat in a Confederate uniform. In late May 1862 the Union commander, Henry "Old Brains" Halleck, slowly pushed forward his one hundred thousand-man army—cautiously entrenching after each day's march—against Confederate General P. G. T. Beauregard's rebel force of sixty-six thousand.

Halleck's advance was glacial. Twenty miles in thirty days. But slow as it was, Beauregard realized he could not stop the weight of this grinding war machine. He had no choice but to retreat.

Just before first light on May 27, a signal rocket shot out of the woods from Landis's battery and arced over the lines of Beauregard's army, momentarily lighting the sky and the faces of thousands of waiting Confederates. As the men silently shouldered their muskets and began the ordered withdrawal, a Union battery of heavy thirty-pounder Parrott rifles let loose on the retreating rebels, concentrating on Landis's artillerymen. Landis instantly replied with his large-bore bronze guns. George and his fellow batterymen brought up the heavy twenty-four-pounder howitzer shells, then loaded and fired with measured sureness to cover the retreat. One of George's comrades, hunkered behind the fieldworks, described the day-long artillery duel:

> Most of [the enemy] shells were thrown high, and, when they were considerably spent, could be distinctly seen whizzing over—or, beginning to turn, would fall rapidly, and occasionally burst in or near our lines. We could always see them in time to get out of the way, and they did no damage, only disturbing our position under the shade of the trees, and causing us to make room, when one of these visitors came crashing down through the limbs.

General Beauregard selected Landis's battery as his observation post during the day. He stood beside the Captain, both officers peering at the enemy lines through their field glasses. Beauregard. Pierre Gustave Toutant Beauregard. The man who opened fire—and the war—at Fort Sumter. The man who routed the Yankees at Bull Run. The man who designed the cross-shaped Confederate battle flag, the very symbol of the rebellion. Beauregard was a legend. As George approached him, he saw a man of just medium height, yet he seemed to tower over the feisty little Landis. The general was remarkable—a Louisiana Creole, olive-skinned and exotic looking, an impeccably dressed Southern gentleman with broad shoulders, large dark eyes, black hair, and a heavy jaw framed by a heavy moustache. To George, he looked almost Indian and had the air of a chief. Throughout the bombardment, his steady nerves and clear orders calmed the men. That day, Landis's battery and the Missourians allowed Beauregard's army to disengage from Corinth virtually unscathed. The men would never forget their rearguard stand against overwhelming odds.[40]

By July General John Pope and his Army of the Mississippi replaced the plodding Halleck. In August, Pope ordered General Philip Sheridan's cavalry division to press Beauregard and his retreating Confederates. Landis's battery again covered the withdrawal until the rebels reached the Tuscumbia River, where the battle lines stalled in the sweltering Mississippi heat. Here, the monotonous routine of guard duty and stable call was punctuated by sudden combat and terror. The morale of the Missouri men fell as food supplies dwindled and casualty lists grew long. But Landis kept the guns firing, barking orders and risking the command almost to the point of insanity. George and his ragged fellows fought on and, despite their weariness, were instrumental in keeping Sheridan's troopers from overrunning the strung-out rebel lines.

But on August 26, Union cavalry slashed behind the retreating rebels, and George, with other Missourians, found himself cut off. He later remembered that while on a "scouting expedition . . . we were forced to fall back, and during the evacuation of [Corinth] I fell into the hands of the Union cavalry . . . with two hundred other Confederate[s]."[41]

But was he on a "scouting expedition?" In the confusion of battle and unaware of George's capture, the company clerk of Landis's battery dutifully recorded that Private Bent had *deserted*.[42] And perhaps he had. Perhaps he *had* lost his taste for fighting. Landis was a hard man, uncompromising. Staying with the battery could get a man killed. Like his father, George's survival instinct was strong. When he found himself cut off by the blue riders, he made a decision—he surrendered. In truth, Price's army was falling apart and men were deserting by squads and companies. Four days after his capture, George appeared before Provost Marshal D. C. Anthony and signed an "Oath of Allegiance":

I Solemnly Swear, That I will bear true allegiance to the United States of America, and support the Constitution and Laws thereof; that I will oppose Secession and Rebellion; that I denounce the so-called Confederate States, and pledge my honor, property, and life, to the sacred fulfillment of this oath, here freely taken, admitting that its violation will be illegal and infamous. Sworn to and Subscribed before me [D.C. Anthony] this 30th day of August 1862.[43]

On September 3, 1862, the riverboat *Rowena* steamed up the Mississippi River and docked at St. Louis, disgorging wounded soldiers and Confederate prisoners. Among the latter was George Bent.[44] Union officials judged these prisoners to be deserters and therefore remanded them not to an ordinary prisoner-of-war camp but to the custody of the district provost marshal, who confined political dissidents in a special prison.

Prodded along by blue-coated soldiers with bayoneted muskets, George made his way through the familiar streets of St. Louis. From dockside to city center, sympathetic citizens gathered at curbside, offering words of encouragement. Hoopskirted ladies, staunch secessionists all, waved their handkerchiefs and smiled admiringly, often stepping into the streets to avoid walking beneath federal flags hanging over the sidewalks.

The column of prisoners came to an abrupt halt at the corner of Eighth and Gratiot Streets. George looked up. He knew this place. He could never forget the majestic three-story octagonal tower, flanked by wings of red brick. In a strange twist of fate, he had arrived at McDowell Medical College and the adjoining classrooms and dormitories of Christian Brothers Academy, the very institution he had escaped from only five years earlier when he was a student there. In December 1861, the entire complex had been confiscated by the federal government and renamed Gratiot Street Military Prison.[45]

For an hour George stood in the street, sweating in his hot, battle-worn wool uniform, waiting to be searched by the tough prison guards. These men missed nothing. They took money, knives, papers—everything of value and anything that might be used as a weapon. Only then did they take the prisoners inside.

As the guards escorted George to his cell, the prison vibrated with the exciting news of an escape attempt. Only the day before, the *St. Louis Daily Missouri Democrat* had reported:

Escaped from the Gratiot Street Prison—Five prisoners effected an escape from Gratiot street prison at about 7 o'clock Sunday evening, by digging through the wall of the basement into a privy in the yard of the Academy of Christian Brothers, adjoining the prison on the north. The fugitives were discovered in a few minutes after their exit, and chased, but soon disappeared, and are missing.[46]

The *Democrat* also took notice of the arrival of the "rebel deserters liable to suspicion."[47] George's St. Louis friends may have read about his capture in the newspaper, and George remembered "while being marched through the streets with the other prisoners, I was lucky enough to be recognized by a young fellow who had attended the academy with me. He went straight away to my brother Robert, who was in the city purchasing Indian goods, and told him that I was among the Corinth prisoners."[48] Robert Bent immediately went to George's guardian, Robert Campbell, and pleaded for help. The well-connected Campbell knew exactly what to do. He went to District Provost Marshal Bernard G. Farrar, the son of Dr. Bernard G. Farrar, the physician who years before had recommended that Campbell go west for his health. George never forgot Campbell's intervention on his behalf: "He was fine old gentleman. . . . He was the one that got me out from prison in St. Louis."[49] Without hesitation or question, Colonel Farrar acted on Campbell's entreaties. On September 5, 1862, he signed George's release: "George Bent, prisoner, will be released to report at this office for final discharge on oath and bond."[50]

But to George it had not been that simple. For forty-eight hours he had laid on the straw-covered floor of his dungeonlike room, along with hundreds of other prisoners, wondering what would happen next. Would his captors treat him as a white soldier, or would they see only his dark skin and treat him as an Indian? Would they shoot him? Hang him? He didn't know. But each hour as he lay there, the more terrible his future seemed. He had arrived at the prison ravenously hungry, but so far he had gotten little to eat. Another Gratiot Street prisoner described the daily fare:

We are allowed only two meals a day, and it keeps the cooks busy to get through with them by dark. Some two or three hundred eat at a time, and the tin plates and cups are never washed from the first to the last table. For breakfast we have one-fifth of a loaf of baker's bread, a small portion of bacon, and a tip cup of stuff they call coffee. For dinner the same amount of bread, a hunk of beef, and a pint

of the water the beef was boiled in, which is called soup, and sometimes a couple of boiled potatoes—all dished up and portioned out
with the hands; knives, forks and spoons not being allowed. Many
leave the table as hungry as they went to it.[51]

On the afternoon of the second day, the wooden door of the great
hall creaked open and an officer, followed by two wary enlisted men,
bellowed, "George Bent!" His worst fears were realized. Certainly,
this was his final moment—the firing squad had arrived. The escort
led him through the courtyard and up steps to an office on the upper
floor. George shuffled in, his head bowed. When he lifted his eyes he
saw seated behind a large desk an officer who displayed two rows of
gold buttons on his dark blue uniform. The man pitched into him right
away. Why had he forsaken the Union and joined the rebel army?
George said nothing. All he could think about was the hangman's rope
tightening around his neck. Then, unexpectedly, Colonel Farrar identified himself as a family friend and asked if he would like to go home.
With inexpressible relief, George choked out, "You bet I do!"

Once again the power of William Bent and the Bent name. Colonel
Farrar released George to the custody of brother Robert, known to be
a loyal Union man, and within hours the brothers were packed and
riding for the Arkansas River country.

George was going home, a free man.[52]

Chapter 4

BETWEEN TWO WORLDS

R iding with his brother Bob at the head of the Bent train, George could see his father's stone fort high on the bluff. Below it, partially hidden by a hazy pall of wood-smoke, stood the new buildings of Fort Lyon. The sight of so many blue-coated soldiers made him uneasy. They were everywhere, plastering adobe walls, chinking stone quarters, shingling leaky roofs. Sharp-eyed sentinels looked toward the Bent train as it passed by.

George had last seen his father's new fort in the summer of 1855. Then it had the look of freshness. The great cottonwoods of Big Timbers towered above the river. Grass provided forage in abundance for horses and livestock. The Santa Fe Trail rutted the land, but it was still a freighters' road, a trail of commerce.

But now in October 1862, the trail was a deep scar on the landscape.[1] Since 1859, hordes of gold seekers—the Pikes Peakers—had rushed across the plains, casting aside refuse and abandoning equipment in their mad scramble for instant wealth. Their animals had cropped the lush prairie grasses to clumps of dried stubble. And the valley of the Arkansas was now a soldiers' camp.[2] Enemies lurked there. George had seen many such places during his year of service in the Confederate Army. Open sewers with their flies and stench, the barren parade ground, broken wagons and discarded equipment, outbuildings dug into the hillside, jutting chimneys, the noise of hammers on anvils and of bugles and drums—all proclaimed a military encampment. And flying at the center of this raw frontier post, a giant garrison flag—not the flag of the Confederacy but the banner of the enemy.

Bob told how the soldiers had come to occupy the fort.

In September 1860 their father had offered the stone trading post to the government. Once again the army balked at the idea of purchasing his property. After all, the old frontiersman did not hold clear title to the land, and his asking price of twelve thousand dollars seemed high. But Major John Sedgwick, whose dragoons had spent the summer futilely chasing elusive Comanches and Kiowas, reported to the quartermaster general that "the use of the fort for storing our supplies for this winter was absolutely necessary and I think will save the government more than the value of it. We could not build such a work for a less sum, but we could build one that would answer the purpose for much less." The quartermaster agreed that the property would be valuable as a warehouse and contracted to lease it for sixty-five dollars a month.[3]

A good bargain. But the army still needed a regular fort, one that would house troops. Accordingly, the quartermaster took Sedgwick at his word and ordered him to build a new fort "for much less." Sedgwick had hoped the government would hire civilian contractors to do the work, but the burden of construction fell on his weary soldiers, who wanted nothing more than to return to Fort Leavenworth and comfortable winter quarters. It was a matter of economics. Extra duty pay for soldiers working as laborers and mechanics was twenty-five cents and forty cents a day, respectively.[4] Civilian contractors would demand from one to two dollars a day.

So the troops grumbled as they set to the task of building a post on the bottoms one-half mile above Bent's stone fort. With winter's chill already in the air, Sedgwick set his men to work erecting rude shelters. Yet the expected snows never came that year, and the work expanded to include stables, a guardhouse, a hospital, and stone corrals. By November 1860 most of the labor had been completed, a remarkable achievement considering that the troops, suffering from malnutrition and scurvy, used only the crudest tools—broken axes and hatchets, crowbars fashioned from wagon tires, and trowels made from wood and old camp kettles. Robert had been amazed by the progress. But the men worked with a will because they faced the dismal prospect of spending a high plains winter in canvas tents.[5]

So now Union troops occupied the Arkansas River country, not twenty miles downstream from their father's new ranch at the mouth of Purgatoire Creek. Bob had grown accustomed to the soldiers; indeed, they were among the Bents' best customers. As for George, even though he had signed the oath of allegiance to the United States, he still recoiled at the sight of the enemy he had fought from Wilson's Creek to Corinth.

This was no place to tarry. The brothers rode on.

At the mouth of the Purgatoire, they splashed across the shallow ford of the Arkansas, just below the Bent stockade. The ranch was larger than George had imagined—and more formidable. Cotton-wood pickets defined the one-hundred-foot square compound, which enclosed living quarters for his father and employees. Also inside were stables, a blacksmith shop, and a storehouse for trade goods. On the northern and western sides, George noticed deep trenches, probably not for defense but rather borrow pits excavated for the dirt needed to cover the flat-roofed adobe buildings. On its southern side, a great gate opened to a plaza. As the brothers rode in, Bob pointed out their father's private quarters, located directly across the central court. In the middle of the yard stood the familiar hide press, buffalo robes piled high beside it waiting to be compressed into bales of ten robes each.[6]

George was surprised, too, by the ranch's activity. The familiar faces were there, Mexicans and mixed-bloods mingling with mountain men and white traders. His brother had told him that the buffalo had dis-appeared from the valley and that the Cheyennes seldom came down from their villages on the Smoky Hill, Republican, Solomon, and Saline Rivers. Bent's traders, as in the old days, traveled great distances to exchange their wares in the Indian camps. Tanned buffalo robes and green hides could be gotten there. The Cheyennes and Arapahos, the Kiowas and Comanches, and Plains Apaches still coveted the white man's things, still needed guns, ammunition, kettles, and knives.

So the baling press kept creaking.

Bob and George had wasted no time in getting out of St. Louis, and the old man never expected to see his rebel son ride through the gates. He had heard George was fighting Yankees in Mississippi but he knew nothing about his capture or release from prison. He had last seen George on a visit to Webster College in St. Louis, more than two years before. The schoolboy was now a man, a veteran of great battles. He was tall, a head taller than his father, with powerful shoulders, his body lean and tough from a year of hard campaigning. A black mustache set off his bronzed face and made him look older than his nineteen years. His father had changed as well. The lines and creases of his sunburned face had grown deeper, his hair had turned gray, and the white stubble of his beard revealed an aging man plainly in his fifties.

They had much to talk about. That night in William's quarters, sister Mary and her husband Robison Moore joined them. Charley and Julia were away with Yellow Woman and Island, in the Cheyenne villages on the Republican River, a hundred miles and more distant. George told of his life in Sterling Price's army, the battles he had fought, and his recent imprisonment and timely rescue.

In turn, William explained that much had changed on the Arkansas since George had gone off to school in Westport and St. Louis. When he had left in 1855, the Cheyennes and Arapahos were at peace with the whites, and trains traveled the Santa Fe Trail unmolested. Traders had free access to the Cheyenne camps and offered their goods without worry of theft or danger.

Those days of peace were long gone. White overland roads had encroached on Cheyenne country. In 1857 the army sent Colonel Edwin V. Sumner west to chastise tribes that had recently attacked white travelers. He particularly sought the Cheyennes, whose young men had practically stopped the movement of all wagon trains along the central route. Even Santa Fe traders along the Arkansas were sometimes attacked. William tried to warn the Cheyennes that Sumner was hunting them. As George remembered it, "My father notified the Cheyennes to look out for the troops, that they were coming from Platte Rivers to fight them. He wanted them to move south of Arkansas River. Northern Cheyennes were the ones that were raiding on Platte Rivers and not the Southern Cheyennes. Good many Cheyennes were camped around my father's fort at same time. My father and Agent [Robert C.] Miller told Cheyennes and Arapahos not to move away from the fort. As long as they were camped near the fort, Miller would take care of them."[7] Yellow Wolf's Hairy Band followed William's advice, camping one mile east of the fort. A band of Arapahos camped one mile west.[8]

As Sumner's command pressed the search between the Platte and Arkansas Rivers, Agent Miller, eager to safeguard the government's annuity goods until Sumner had humbled the Cheyennes, asked William for permission to store the goods at the fort. William refused because if Summer's troops attacked the Cheyennes, the Indians would retaliate. Not only would they take the government goods but they also would clean him out and probably massacre everyone at the fort. But late on the night of July 19, William changed his mind. He simply could not abandon his friend to the fury of the Cheyennes. George remembered Agent Miller as a good-looking, longhaired man with a sailor's tattoo on his arm.[9] By a formal contract signed the next morning, William turned over the fort for the agent's use in exchange for a rental and storage fee.[10] William threw a few belongings into a wagon and the next day headed for St. Louis with his family.

Meanwhile, near the forks of the Solomon River, a great village of Northern and Southern Cheyennes had gathered. All the important chiefs were there: for the southern bands, Black Kettle, White Antelope, Old Whirlwind, and Rock Forehead, the Arrow Keeper himself; and for the northern bands, Brave Wolf, Little Gray Hair, Dull Knife, and Spotted Wolf.

Two charismatic warriors, Ice, a northerner, and Dark, from the south, rallied the warriors with promises of victory against the white soldiers, whom the scouts reported were even now riding hard for the village. Ice and Dark shared a dream vision, a plan for success. They claimed they could render the warriors bulletproof and lure the soldiers into a trap. But as William told George, these two warriors were only "playing Medicine Men." They had no holy power, yet their talk had nonetheless excited the young men who had never fought white troops before and wanted holy protection against the soldiers' bullets. Ice and Dark selected a lake nearby, pronounced it magic, and told the warriors to dip their hands into the waters. When the enemy approached, the Cheyennes had only to raise their hands to cause the rifle balls to roll harmlessly from the muzzles of the soldiers' guns.[11]

On July 29, 1857, Sumner's First Cavalry, leaving the slow-moving artillery and infantry behind, moved toward the Cheyenne village. Sumner's Delaware scout, Fall Leaf, spotted a fleeing band of warriors and reported the Indians in fast retreat. Fearful that the Cheyennes might slip through his hands, Sumner ordered his six companies to pursue. But the Cheyennes were not in retreat. They stood in regular line of battle, singing war songs, then slowly advanced toward the troops, their arms outstretched, palms forward, eager to engage the enemy. Quickly, the Cheyennes flanked the soldiers and pressed forward. It seemed the warriors would overwhelm the soldiers. Suddenly, Sumner—known as "Old Bull" for his booming voice—rose in his stirrups and shouted: *"Sling Carbines! . . . Draw Sabers!"* As one, the cavalrymen drew their blades from iron scabbards and brought them to their shoulders. A scraping clank echoed across the valley. Steel flashed in the sunlight. Sumner roared, *"Trot! . . . Gallop! . . . Charge!"*

The saber charge completely confused the warriors. Where were the bullets? They were prepared for those. But Ice and Dark had told them nothing about slashing sabers. The warriors scattered. Fortunately, the soldiers' horses, tired and winded, were unable to follow the fleet ponies of the retreating Cheyennes. Even so, the bluecoats hacked four warriors down and wounded many others. But the Cheyennes had not suffered a total defeat. They used their bows and arrows with good effect, killing two soldiers and wounding nine, among them a young lieutenant named J. E. B. Stuart. George knew of Stuart, who now fought with Confederate general Robert E. Lee. William told the story as he had heard it. Stuart "came up with a Cheyenne man and attacked him with the sabre, but was shot in the breast and badly wounded."[12] Of the soldiers killed and wounded, Stuart was one of only a few who suffered gunshot wounds.

The Cheyennes had been so certain of victory that they had left their village unprotected. Caught up in the mad retreat, the women and children abandoned their lodges and joined the headlong rush south toward the Arkansas River and safety.

The ignominious defeat at Solomon Forks forever disgraced the would-be medicine men, Ice and Dark. The proud Cheyennes never forgave them; never again would their names be spoken or passed on to the children of the tribe.[13]

War now visited the valley of the Arkansas. The Cheyennes may have been defeated at Solomon Forks, but they were by no means ready to surrender to Colonel Sumner—or anyone else. The young men spread across the prairie, attacking wagontrains, travelers, and isolated settlements. Sumner tracked the Cheyennes to the Arkansas, where the trail disappeared. He moved over to Bent's stone fort, where he confiscated the Cheyennes' annuities. When Agent Miller arrived, Sumner agreed to distribute some of the annuities to the peaceful Cheyennes and Arapahos camped near the fort. But he threw the lead, powder, and flint into the muddy Arkansas.[14]

William recounted these things at the family reunion that night. The war, of course, adversely affected his trade. Bent's business depended on peace, so in 1859 he had agreed to serve as U.S. Indian agent to the Cheyennes and Arapahos and use his influence to stop the fighting.

As George listened he grew more agitated. His father was convinced that the white tide of immigrants could not be stopped. "Unless prompt measures were taken," he warned, "a desperate war of starvation and extinction is imminent." And he predicted that a massacre of Indians would inevitably result unless the tribes gave up the hunt and became farmers. George could not believe his ears. His father had advised the Cheyennes to accept the government's offer of a worthless tract of land in southeastern Colorado. He was asking them to renounce not only their way of life but also the land guaranteed to them by the 1851 Fort Laramie Treaty. Had the old man forsaken the people and his own children?

William resented the implication. What he had done as agent he had done for the good of the Cheyennes—and his own mixed-blood children.

As William related the circumstances of his government service, he recalled a letter he had written while in a Cheyenne village at the junction of Beaver Creek and the South Platte River in the summer of 1859. Here, among his longtime friends and relatives, he felt confident that he could influence them and bring a lasting peace:

> The Cheyans and Arrapahos have took my advice to them last Winter and this last Spring. I am proud to say they have behaved themselves exceedingly well. . . . Theair will be no troble settling them down and start farming. They tell me they . . . have passed theair laws amongst themselves that they will do anything I may advize. It is a pitty that the Department can't send Some farming implements

and other necessarys this fall Sow as they could commence farming this Coming Spring. . . .

After I deliver the Indians theair goods I intend . . . to have a conversation with the Kioways and Commanches. I suppose that [they] will be purtay saucy—but as I have bin appointed agent I feel it my dutay to see all of the Indians under my Agency—if they sculp me.

I am compelled to visit St. Louis abought the last of August as I left some of my business unsettled which must be settled this fall. I received Commissioner Mixes letter ordering me to remain with the Indians but my business unsettled in the States Amounts to more than three time the Amt of my Salary. I dont think the Department will blame me for going to St. Louis and Staying 8 or 10 days and return this fall to the uppur Arkinsas. I have mutch more to say but the Indians bother me so that I shall have to close you Must excuse my bad Spelling as I have bin so long in the Wild Waste I have almost forgotten how to Spell.[15]

When George was last on the Arkansas, buffalo still roamed the region. True, the great herds were much reduced from when his father had built his first fort, but even in 1855 the Cheyennes could subsist on buffalo. But now, the great white migrations had split the herds. Ever since the 1859 gold rush, no buffalo could be found along the Arkansas River, even at Big Timbers where his father had built his new fort.

Back then, George, like most Cheyennes, believed the buffalo would always be there for them. How could they disappear? It was not possible. But now, his father told the family that if the Cheyennes did not confine themselves to reservations and take up farming and the white man's ways, they were doomed. William wished it were not so, but he saw no alternative. When he got his ten-day furlough in St. Louis, he—with the assistance of a clerk—penned a report setting out in detail his course for the preservation of the peace and the final disposition of the tribes:

A smothered passion for revenge agitates these Indians, perpetually fomented by the failure of food, the encircling encroachments of the white population, and the exasperating sense of decay and impending extinction with which they are surrounded. . . .

I estimate the number of whites traversing the plains across the center belt to have exceeded 60,000 during the present season. The trains of vehicles and cattle are frequent and valuable in proportion; post lines and private expresses are in constant motion. The explorations of this season have established the existence of the precious metals in absolutely infinite abundance. . . .

The concourse of whites is therefore constantly swelling, and incapable of control or restraint by the government. This suggests the policy of promptly rescuing the indians, and withdrawing them from management as may anticipate and prevent difficulties and massacre. I repeat, then, as the suggestion of my best judgment, that immediate and sufficient steps be taken to assemble and finally dispose of these particular tribes of Indians, viz: The Kiowa and Comanches, the Cheyennes, and the Arapahoes, by reducing them, under treaties and arrangements, to become agricultural and pastoral people, located within specific districts, judiciously selected and liberally endowed, to which they shall be restricted, and the white men excluded from among them. These numerous and warlike Indians, pressed upon all around by the Texans, by the settlers of the gold region, by the advancing people of Kansas, and from the Platte, are already compressed into a small circle of territory, destitute of food, and itself bisected athwart by a constantly marching line of emigrants. A desperate war of starvation and extinction is therefore imminent and inevitable, unless prompt measures shall prevent it.[16]

But it was not just the Cheyennes William was worried about. Another subject more personal agitated him—the fate of the mixed-bloods. "There are in each of these tribes," he said, "a few halfbreeds, the children of white men intermarried with the Cheyennes and Arapahoes, for whom these tribes desire to make suitable reservations and provisions."[17] Whether the plight of the halfbreeds weighed heavily on the minds of tribal leaders is unknown, but certainly it concerned William. His five children were halfbreeds, and as their father, he felt it his duty to see to their future. The surest way to protect them was to get them land—land with boundaries and titles guaranteed by the federal government. But this he would leave to others, for he had already determined to resign as agent to return to his own pressing business affairs. Who better to replace him than his best friend and the former guardian of his children, Albert G. Boone?

Boone had fallen on hard times. The Panic of 1857 had taken his fortune and left him a ruined man. He desperately needed a job, and William seized the opportunity. Using his considerable influence, he secured Boone's appointment as agent for the Upper Arkansas. The Cheyennes, Arapahos, and the mixed-bloods would be under Boone's care and supervision.

Boone set to the task as soon as he arrived out West. Building on the tentative agreement forged by William and Commissioner A. B. Greenwood in September 1860, he gathered tribal leaders to finalize the treaty. On February 18, 1861, at William's stone fort—recently renamed Fort Wise by the army—Cheyenne and Arapaho leaders affixed their marks to the document. Unfortunately, only a few of the Southern Cheyenne chiefs had come in. Black Kettle and White Antelope were there, as was Lean Bear, all respected leaders of the Southern Cheyennes. But they represented only the peace faction. The war faction stayed away, as did the Cheyenne Dog Soldiers, who remained defiant in their camps on the Smoky Hill. Without the participation and agreement of these bands, the Fort Wise Treaty was doomed from the start. Boone should have known this. William had given careful instructions, and Bob Bent served as one of the official U.S. interpreters during the treaty's proceedings.

The agreement signed that day was stunning in its scope. The 1851 Treaty of Fort Laramie had given the Cheyennes and Arapahos ownership of all the lands between the North Platte and Arkansas Rivers, and from the Rocky Mountains to a point some three hundred miles east. The Fort Wise Treaty stripped the tribes of this vast domain and restricted them to a small triangular tract of land anchored on the Arkansas River in south-central Colorado Territory. This small reservation, only a fraction of the Cheyennes' former holdings, was dry and unsuited to agriculture and, perhaps of more importance to the tribes, almost entirely devoid of buffalo. In return for this wild waste, the tribes would receive $450,000 over a period of fifteen years and some additional money for the construction of sawmills, gristmills, and mechanic shops. The government expected the Indians to use the money to buy all of the farming implements necessary to begin their lives as an agricultural people.

Boone may not have concluded a workable treaty—those chiefs who stayed away were sure to object—but he lived up to his promise to look after the mixed-bloods. Not all mixed-bloods, but at least Robert Bent and John Smith's son, Jack. Both Robert and Jack Smith were included by name in the treaty:

It is further understood, before signing the above treaty, that it was the particular request and wish of the chiefs and councillors in general convention, in consideration of Robert Bent being one of their halfbreed tribe, that he should have, as a gift of the nation, six hundred and forty acres of land, covering the valley and what is called the Sulphur Spring, lying on the north side of the Arkansas River and about five miles below the Pawnee Hills, and they wish the general government to recognize and confirm the same; and that Jack Smith, son of John S. Smith, who is also a halfbreed of said nation, shall have six hundred and forty acres of land, lying seven miles above Bent's Old Fort, on the north side of the Arkansas River, including the valley and point of rock, and respectfully recommend the general government to confirm and recognize the same.[18]

Conflict of interest? Robert had interpreted the treaty provisions to the chiefs and translated their responses to the commissioner. Boone, his guardian, was the agent in charge, and his father, the former agent, had framed the entire document. Certainly, these conflicts and connections must have raised eyebrows in Washington. Nevertheless, the Senate ratified the treaty and President Abraham Lincoln signed the document on December 15, 1861. For the government this was a deal too good to pass up. Title to the goldfields—mines rich enough to fund the war effort against the seceded southern states—was now free and clear. Any irregularities could be overlooked.[19]

Even with the treaty, however, tensions ran high along the Arkansas. Isolated acts of violence sometimes broke the peace, and it only seemed a question of time before a wider conflict erupted. So William urged George to stay at the ranch. The Cheyenne villages were dangerous— no telling when open war might break out. White settlements were also a dangerous place, especially for a recently released Confederate prisoner, and a halfbreed to boot. Fort Lyon was garrisoned by Colorado troops still flushed with the great victory at Glorieta Pass, near Santa Fe. There, in March 1862, the Coloradans stopped an invading army of Texans and pushed them back down the Rio Grande. These First Colorado foot soldiers had just recently been reequipped and mounted as cavalry, under the command of the acclaimed hero of Glorieta, the Indian-hater John M. Chivington.[20] They were full of themselves and eager for a fight, rebels or redskins.

George knew for the time being it would be best to stay clear of Fort Lyon.

Sometime that winter, William went to Denver on a shopping trip. He outfitted George in a suit of new clothes, knowing full well his son could not wear his Confederate butternut in this Union country. George also received a "fine fieldglass," and, even more to his liking, a five-hundred-dollar sorrel racehorse.[21] Now, well mounted and dressed as a civilian, George accompanied his father on business trips to Fort Lyon, only twenty miles away from the Purgatoire ranch. He enjoyed visiting Boone, whose Upper Arkansas Agency was head-quartered at the fort. He found other friends there, too, including Uncle John Smith and his son Jack, George's childhood playmate. Fort Lyon offered the only sizable community on the Arkansas, the only place a young man could find entertainment.

The post sutler's store was the center of social activity. A man could get a drink here, bet on a horse race, play cards, and exchange tall tales. It was also an easy place to get into trouble. Harsh words often resulted in fistfights or worse. Talk in this place naturally turned to the war in the East. George had much to say, especially about Fort Lyon, which had been renamed for Union general Nathaniel E. Lyon. Lyon, the first general officer killed in the war, had fallen at Wilson's Creek. George had fought there with the Confederates under the command of Sterling Price. Talk quickly spread about George's rebel leanings. One Union officer reported to the post commander that the halfbreed Bent had been served liquor at the sutler's store. "If this young Bent comes around," he wrote, "it will be well to take charge of him until you are satisfied. If he has been in the Confederate service and still talks in this way, it won't do him any harm or injustice to be put in the guard-house or in irons awhile anyhow." Another officer agreed but thought young Bent deserved harsher treatment. "George Bent, a son of old Bent by a Cheyenne woman, was educated in the East. . . . He is a noted Rebel and ought to have been killed long ago."

George was not one to take such abuse. He was a proud man. If pushed he would push back.[22]

It was long past time for George to leave the Arkansas. Union men would not tolerate a red rebel among them. His life was in danger—and his temper would sooner or later get the best of him. He decided to return to his Cheyenne family. In the spring of 1863, leading his prized sorrel, George made for the Republican River and the Cheyenne villages.

When he reached the sprawling village on the Republican River he created quite a stir. Sporting a mustache, dressed in white man's clothes, and leading a magnificent racehorse, he did not go unnoticed. Who was this white man? He spoke perfect Cheyenne, but the words came haltingly, as if he was trying to remember them. George had not seen a large Cheyenne village for seven years, and the sounds and smells flooded his mind with memories. He had been born in such a village, but strangers now surrounded him. He looked for familiar faces, hoping to see someone he knew. Curious children grabbed at him, exploring buttons, pockets, even the rowels on his spurs. George surprised everybody by asking for his mother's lodge. His mother? Women covered their mouths in amazement. George persisted. Where was Island?

Yellow Woman? What of Charley? Julia? Now the people understood. They told him that his family was with Chief Black Kettle's Eaters and the Ridge people, over on Beaver Creek.

The reunion there was much different. His family embraced him, eager to hear of his travels and the news he brought from his father. George quickly settled in. This was home. Mixed-blood friend Edmund Guerrier came by, anxious to hear the latest news of the white man's war in the East. These stories of combat soon drew other young men. George told them all of his great battles against the bluecoats: the synchronized marching of uniformed men, the thunder of cannon fire and crash of musketry, bands playing as battles roared—the mysterious ways in which whites made war. His name *Ho-my-ike*— Beaver—seemed not to suit him anymore. They began calling him *Do-ha-eno*, from the Spanish *Tejano* or "Texan," because to the Cheyennes all rebels were Texans. George's Southern drawl confirmed their belief that he had become a Texan.[23]

Do-ha-eno attracted a following of young men and warriors—and particularly the society men, members of the Cheyenne soldier bands who hunted together, fought together, sang together, prayed together, and died together. The societies—there were six in all—took turns in policing hunts, village moves, and dances and in leading war parties. Each society had its unique customs, regalia, and songs. Each was fiercely proud and competitive. The Bowstrings, *Him-a-tano-his*, also known as Wolf Soldiers, cloaked themselves in wolfskin; Crazy Dogs, *Hota-mi-massau*, wore distinctive short robes cut into strings and bonnets ornamented with antelope horns and eagle feathers; Dog Soldiers or Dog Men, *Hota-mita-niu*, camped apart and were considered outlaws by many of the tribe and known for their boldness and for *Ho-tam-tsit*, the Dog Rope carried by their bravest warriors; Kit Foxes, *Wohkseh-hetaniu*, commonly called Fox Soldiers, painted their bodies black and always carried the skin of a kit-fox; Red Shields, *Mahohe-was*, also known as Bull Soldiers, attracted mostly seasoned warriors and older men; Crooked Lances, *Him-oweyuhk-is*, known in the north as Elk Horn Scrapers, often wore captured army uniforms and became known as the Blue Soldiers; and finally the Chiefs, *Wihiu-nut-kiu*, a select group of men who had been chosen as chiefs and gave up allegiance to their former societies.[24]

The societies composed of mostly young men were interested in *Do-ha-eno*. He was a man of impressive physical stature who had been tested in battle. He carried the Bent name, and the famed Arrow Keeper, White Thunder, was his grandfather. George would add prestige to any military society, and all vied for his membership.

That spring and into the summer the people moved from place to place visiting other bands and hunting buffalo. As a child among the Cheyennes, George had watched the men run buffalo but he had never been allowed to join the chase. Now a man, he was expected to bring meat and hides to his mother's lodge. His inexperience showed. In one hunt, as he rode at full gallop alongside a bull buffalo, his horse stumbled and as it rolled a hoof crashed down on his elbow, causing a severe injury that would bother him for the rest of his life.[25]

During this time, George gradually took on a more Cheyenne appearance. First a pair of moccasins replaced his boots and spurs; then a breechclout and leggings, far more comfortable than woolen trousers. But like most mixed-bloods, he kept his mustache, a sign that he was a breed apart, not wholly Indian and not quite white.

In June, the village moved back to the Republican River. Here, the Cheyennes and Lakotas joined in celebrating one of the largest Sun Dances ever held on the plains. The combined village spread out in two great circles and numbered twelve hundred Lakota lodges and six hundred Cheyenne. Slow Bull hosted the Cheyenne dance, inviting Lakota bands under Spotted Tail, Pawnee Killer, Bad Yellow Eyes, Black Feet, and Two Strikes. The Lakotas responded by holding a dance of their own, to which they invited the Cheyennes.

The Sun Dance was held every summer. It was both a solemn occasion and a time of celebration. Participants—all men—gazed at the sun and the moon, seeking help and guidance. Typically, the dancers endured self-torture by piercing their breasts or shoulders with wooden skewers three to four inches long to which buffalo skulls were tied. Some men moved freely about the dance circle dragging the heavy bones until the skewers tore from their flesh. Others were suspended from poles until the weight of the skulls tore the skewers from their pierced bodies, allowing them to fall to the ground unconscious. Some men made offerings of their own flesh, cutting strips from their arms, chests, and legs. The scars left by the torture testified to a warrior's bravery and spirituality. Gift-giving and dances followed the four-day ceremony. The sufferers paid the piercers, generally with a horse; sometimes they offered the sexual favors of their sisters as payment.[26]

Another Sun Dance followed Slow Bull's. The outcast Dog Soldiers hosted this one at their camp on Beaver Creek, a tributary of the Republican just a few miles upstream from the great village. Again the ceremony attracted thousands of Cheyennes and Lakotas. The Sun Dances of that summer were, George remembered, the "best Medicine Lodge I ever seen." He did not participate in the ceremony but held deep respect for the men who did, perhaps wondering if he could endure such pain.[27]

While the people gathered for these great ceremonies, the council chiefs had occasion to discuss issues of importance. For hours they sat, smoking their red stone pipes, talking among themselves. Always respectful of one another, the younger always deferring to elder chiefs, they pondered the disappearance of the buffalo from the Arkansas River valley. William Bent—Little Chief—had counseled them to give up the hunt and become tillers of the soil. This was preposterous, of course; the buffalo would last another hundred years.[28] But coming from Bent, the proposal deserved serious consideration. The treaty Boone and Greenwood had them sign back in February 1861 was a swindle. Some of them had signed it, but these had little idea of what the papers meant. Black Kettle, recently chosen by the tribe as one of the six head chiefs of the Southern Cheyennes,[29] had affixed his mark to the Fort Wise treaty, but now he asserted he never would have signed a paper that exchanged Cheyenne lands for seeds and plows. Whether or not the respected Black Kettle signed the treaty was of great interest to the Cheyennes, but to the whites it meant everything, for they considered him the leader of all Cheyennes. Whites never quite understood. No single chief commanded the entire nation. Most of the chiefs gathered here near Beaver Creek had never seen the treaty and had not signed it. They would continue to hunt and live on their traditional lands.

This talk of whites drifted to the great war between the "Texans" and the Great White Father. Lean Bear, who had just returned from Washington and proudly wore around his neck the peace medal given to him by Abraham Lincoln, spoke of the great guns he had seen and the power of the United States. President Lincoln had urged the Cheyennes and other tribes to stay out of the war; already too many young men had died in battle. But Black Kettle told of Indian runners, sent by the Confederate general Albert Pike, who were even then in the camps calling for the Cheyennes to join the South in attacks on Fort Larned and Fort Lyon. The chiefs had listened to these overtures, but before Black Kettle made up his mind he would speak to *Do-ha-eno*, old Bent's son just returned from the war.[30]

Black Kettle had known *Do-ha-eno* when he was *Ho-my-ike,* the son of his friend William Bent. It would be good to talk to this young man who had so much experience in the ways of the whites. He spoke their language, had fought in their war, and could offer advice. In fact, *Do-ha-eno* had fought at Pea Ridge, Arkansas, where General Pike's Indian allies had played a major role in the battle. George had fought beside these Indians. He told Black Kettle that the Indians there had not understood the white way of warfare. They had scalped their enemies, horrifying the white people North and South. It was not a good thing, George said, for Indians to fight in this war.

As they talked, a bond grew between them. George was honored that such a great man would seek him out. And soon it was clear to everyone that Black Kettle not only liked this son of Bent but had taken him into his lodge to guide him as he would his own son. George had much to learn about the ways of the Cheyennes. He had been away for so long. Who better to teach him than Black Kettle?

Born in 1801 to the *Hii-vai-ta-nu,* the Hairy People Clan, Black Kettle was descended from the northern *Suhtai,* as was George's grandfather, White Thunder. He had married twice. Utes captured his first wife, Little Sage Woman, in a bloody fight at the head of the Cimarron River in 1848. For many years he searched for her but to no avail. Time and again he proved himself in battle, first as a Bowstring warrior, then as a Crooked Lance. He took a second wife, Medicine Woman Later, and though he loved children and helped raise his nieces and nephews, he had no children of his own. Shortly after his second marriage, in 1855, he was recognized as the leader of the *Wu-ta-pi-u* (Eaters) band and chosen a council chief. And in 1861, he was honored to be selected as one of the Southern Cheyenne's six head chiefs. Once he joined the society of chiefs, of course, he gave up his affilia-

tion with the Crooked Lances, for chiefs were peacemakers, negotia-
tors, and trusted counselors. Although his days as a warrior were past,
he could teach young George the ways of the Crooked Lances.[31]

According to Black Kettle, the Crooked Lances were the boldest of the
Cheyenne warrior societies. Only they and the venerable Red Shields
had the right to fire guns during their ceremonial dances. The society's
name came from its four sacred crooked lances (in the north, only two
were crooked), which were carried by the four bravest men. Black Kettle explained that the shafts of these lances were wrapped with otter
skin and at four points along the shaft eagle feathers were tied. An elk
horn carved in the shape of a snake—a blue-racer sent from the sun—
was attached to the head of each lance. At society dances, another elk
horn carved in the shape of a lizard two feet long was placed on a bed
of sage in the center of the drummers' circle. The lizard's head always
faced the center of the lodge. A society man scraped a smaller notched
bone along the spine of the lizard, thus giving the society the name of
Elkhorn Scrapers among the Northern Cheyennes.

As part of George's education, Black Kettle repeated the ancient
story of how the Crooked Lances first scraped the elk horn:

> Once there was a very beautiful girl in the camp, and all the young
> men wanted to marry her, but she would have none of them. The
> Dog Soldiers and the Kit Fox Soldiers had a dance, and each young
> man tried to do his best, but the girl would look at none of them.
> Then it came the turn of the [Crooked Lances], and they felt dis-
> couraged, because they thought they could do no better than the
> other societies had done. But a man who possessed spiritual power
> spoke to them, saying: "That girl will be here to see you dance, and
> she will fall in love with one of you, and he will get her. Now go and
> bring me the horn of an elk—a yearling—one that has no prongs on
> it, and the shank-bone of an antelope." The young men brought him
> what he had asked for. He carved the elkhorn in the shape of a snake,
> and on it cut forty-five notches. Then he made from the shank-bone
> of the antelope an implement to rub over the horn; and this device

was used in the dance. The girl was there to see the dance, and fell in love with and married one of the young men.[32]

These and other stories captivated George. Black Kettle's narration of the society's mysteries was compelling. That summer George joined the Crooked Lances. Now it was time to test his fighting skills, not as a white soldier but as a Cheyenne warrior.

That winter on the Smoky Hill, George rode out toward the Solomon River on his first war party. He had been prepared by the older warriors, especially Hawk Nose, who had taken him aside and warned, "If they kill the badger, don't go near it." George wondered why. Hawk Nose explained that if a war party came across a badger they might club it to death in order to foresee the future. The warriors would line up and one at a time look into the dead animal's pooled blood. Hawk Nose said, "If a warrior saw in the reflection a gray-bearded man, he knew that he would grow old. If he saw himself scalped, he knew he would die in battle." Each man who looked into the blood was required to tell what he saw. Hawk Nose had participated in such a ceremony just the year before. He saw himself in the blood as an old man and felt great relief. But he cautioned George, "If you see yourself with eyes shut or scalped you will always feel badly." Therefore, he advised George not to gaze into the badger's blood but to hang back. No one would question the reason or think less of him.[33]

When the warriors reached the Solomon at the mouth of Asher Creek they encountered a small group of Delaware Indians who had been out trapping beaver and otter. The chance meeting began friendly enough. The two groups sat down and talked and agreed to meet again the next day. But the Delawares feared the more numerous Cheyennes. Suspecting treachery, the Delawares gathered up their traps and packs and rode off down the Solomon toward the Smoky Hill. The next day, the Cheyennes, angered by the Delaware's breach of faith, attacked. George remembered that the Delawares started firing their long-barreled rifles, "and right there I saw my first Indian fight. The Cheyennes killed two Delawares and captured all the party's horses and packs of beaver and otter fur. One Cheyenne, Big Head, was killed."[34] George never looked favorably on this fight. There was no reason for it. The Cheyennes did not want to kill the Delawares, whom they respected as warriors. Besides, there were only a few of them and many Cheyennes. The fact that Big Head was killed meant the Crooked Lances must throw away the Delaware scalps. There would be no scalp dances in the Cheyenne village when the war party returned.[35]

Following the Delaware fight on the Solomon, George spent the winter with the Ridge band on the Smoky Hill. Black Kettle was nearby with his band of *Wu-ta-pi-u,* Eaters, and together the people settled in, far from the Arkansas River and the white immigrant roads. All the troubles of the past year seemed distant. No harm would come to the Cheyennes here where the buffalo were plenty.

Chapter 5

MASSACRE AT SAND CREEK

Spring finally came and with it green grass. As the horses fattened and gained strength, the young men grew restless, anxious to join war and hunting parties. Some wanted to head west and engage their mountain enemies, the Utes; others talked of raids against the Crows, far to the north; and the Crooked Lances looked east, eager to renew battle with the hated Pawnees. But one day in late April of 1864, camp criers announced the arrival of the Dog Soldiers, one hundred lodges strong. As the newcomers rode into the center of the circled tipis, the villagers gathered round. The Dog Men carried three wounded warriors and news of a war that would change the Cheyenne world forever.

One of the wounded, Mad Wolf, called for *Do-ha-eno*. Pushing his way through the crowd, George Bent reached the injured man's travois and knelt beside him. Who had done this?

Mad Wolf tapped his forearm, the sign for white soldiers lined all in a row. Bluecoats had attacked his war party on the South Platte River near a place the whites called Fremont's Orchard. There had been no provocation. After spending a quiet winter on Beaver Creek, Mad Wolf, along with Little Chief, Bull Telling Tales, Wolf Coming Out, Bear Man, and ten others, started north to raid in Crow country. As they neared the South Platte they rounded up four mules that had strayed from a white man's herd. Whites were trespassers, unwelcome strangers in this land. The Dog Men thought nothing of appropriating the animals for their own use; the whites owed them this much. That same evening, however, an angry rancher entered their camp, motioning that the mules belonged to him and he wanted them back. The Dog Men made him understand that although they were willing to return the lost animals, they expected a reward for their trouble.

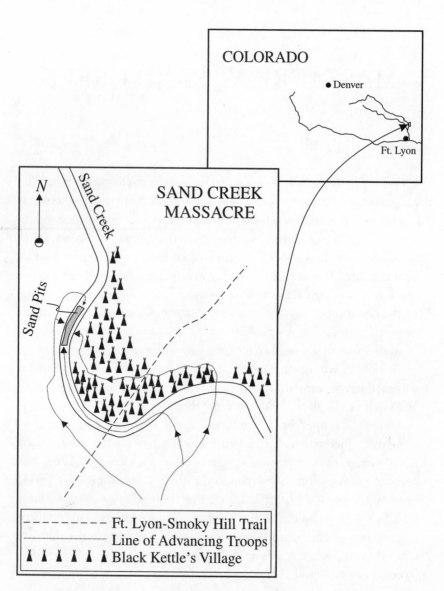

Sand Creek Massacre

Then they sent the white man away, telling him to return the next day with suitable presents.

Early the next morning, April 12, the Cheyennes slowly approached the South Platte River. Suddenly, one of them shouted out: "*Ve-ho-e*! Soldiers coming!" Riding hard, fifteen or twenty bluecoats, their pistols drawn, formed in line of battle. The warriors jumped off their slow pack animals and quickly mounted their fleet war ponies, then turned to face the soldiers. A trooper shouted to them, but none of the Cheyennes could understand him. Finally, an officer rode forward, signing that the Indians should throw down their weapons. But before the Dog Men could respond, the soldiers opened fire. Three warriors fell: Mad Wolf, wounded in the hip; Bear Man, shot twice; and Wolf Coming Out, hit in the leg. The lead soldier leveled his revolver and charged Bull Telling Tales, who shot an arrow straight through the man's body, the iron point protruding from his back. As the soldier lay on the ground, Bull Telling Tales sent a second arrow through his heart, then dismounted and cut off his head. At this, the soldiers stampeded in wild retreat. The warriors shot down another man whose horse lagged behind the others.

Mad Wolf told George that they could easily have killed all the soldiers, who had "acted very foolishly," but the Cheyennes were not at war with the whites and so the young men broke off the engagement. As proof of the fight and his coup, Bull Telling Tales passed around a blood-stained uniform coat, as well as a pocket watch, pistol, and fieldglass.[1]

The chiefs knew that George had fought in the white man's wars. Would the whites seek revenge for this fight at Fremont's Orchard? After all, they had suffered two dead and several wounded in the engagement. What course should the Cheyennes follow?

The warriors, George answered, should not ride the main-traveled roads. Back in Missouri in 1861 he had watched bluecoats shoot down innocent whites simply because they were suspected of being Rebels. Stay away from the soldiers, he warned; they were dangerous and unpredictable and could not be trusted.[2]

The chiefs agreed. The people would be safer in the country south of the Arkansas River, a place where there were no soldier roads.

Only days after the Dog Soldiers arrived in camp, Crow Chief and his entire band straggled in. There was more bad news. On April 15, soldiers had attacked Crow Chief's village of seventy lodges on the Republican fork, east of Denver.[3] That day, a man named Antelope Skin had ridden out of camp at dawn to hunt buffalo. Before he had gone far he saw soldiers trotting toward the village. Antelope Skin raced back to the sleeping camp, where he shouted the alarm. Fortunately, the horse herd was near the village, and the women and children mounted and rode off just as the soldiers charged. All the people escaped, and Antelope Skin, who had concealed himself in some bushes, even managed to shoot several arrows at the troopers, wounding one of them. Nevertheless, the soldiers looted and burned the village; nothing remained but ashes.

Raccoon, a Southern Cheyenne chief, also arrived with his band, bringing news of an attack on his small village. The soldiers had overtaken his people as they moved down Beaver Creek toward the Republican. Although no one had been killed, the people had lost all of their lodges and most of their belongings.

The whites, it seemed, had declared war on the Cheyennes. Why?

The Dog Soldier chiefs—Tall Bull, Bull Bear, and White Horse—surprised everyone by asking the young, half-white warrior, *Do-ha-eno*, to lead a party of "wolves" to locate the soldiers and report on their movements. George flushed with pride. He had been singled out by the boldest of the Cheyenne warriors. Of course, most Cheyennes still regarded the Dog Soldiers as renegades, outlaws from the tribe ever since Porcupine Bear's exile in 1837. But George knew he had been honored. Through the years, the Dog Soldiers had gained a reputation for their fighting abilities. Many young men of all bands and warrior societies admired them and joined them in raids on Indian enemies and, occasionally, on whites. Young men also admired the Dog Soldiers for their fierce independence. Everyone knew that the Dog Men stayed away from white traders and forts, often throwing annuity goods into the fire rather than accept gifts with conditions attached.[4] They would not even trade at Bent's Fort for goods; what they wanted from the white men they took. Now the famed Dog Soldier leaders had asked George to help them, surely a sign of acceptance and respect for this son of a white man. But the chiefs saw to it that this young halfbreed would not go alone. They selected three experienced warriors to accompany him: High Back Bear, Spotted Wolf, and Elk River.

On the first day out, they met Antelope Skin, who had been tracking the soldiers ever since the destruction of Crow Chief's village. Antelope Skin told the scouts that he had seen the soldiers turn back toward Denver. George and his party quickly returned to the village and reported to the chiefs.[5]

On May 15, the Cheyenne leaders met in council to discuss Bent's report. As expected, the Dog Soldiers argued for war. These attacks by the whites must be avenged. Crow Chief and Raccoon urged restraint, even though their people had suffered most. White Antelope and Old Little Wolf agreed—it was better to negotiate a peace than subject the people to a long war with the soldiers. The wisest course would be to move to the Arkansas and join Black Kettle's Eaters and Lean Bear's Southern Hill people.

That day, the Dog Soldiers broke off from the main camp and moved north toward the Platte River Road. Whatever the others decided, the Dog Men would attack whites wherever they found them.

George stayed with the Hill band, along with the refugees from Crow Chief and Raccoon's bands, and moved south, away from the soldiers.[6]

But hardly had the combined bands begun their journey when news came that Chief Lean Bear, brother of the renowned Dog Soldier chief Bull Bear, had been shot down and killed by bluecoats on Ash Creek. Runners provided the details:

On May 16, the villages of Lean Bear and Black Kettle, 250 lodges in all, had been camped on Ash Creek, only thirty miles south of the Hill people on the Smoky Hill River. That morning Cheyenne hunters reported the approach of one hundred horse soldiers pulling two cannons. Lean Bear and Black Kettle urged their people to remain calm. After all, Lean Bear had led a peace delegation to Washington in 1863 and received a medal from the Great Father, Abraham Lincoln. And both Lean Bear and Black Kettle had wintered near Fort Larned and enjoyed friendly relations with the traders and soldiers. True, they had heard of the fight at Fremont's Orchard, but the Dog Soldiers were known for their warlike ways and for getting into trouble. Surely the whites knew that the Dog Soldiers were an independent band exiled from the Cheyenne nation. There was no good reason for the army to attack peaceful villages.

Lean Bear, his silver medal prominent around his neck, rode out to meet the soldiers. He warned his excited warriors to stay back; a show of force might frighten the whites and start a fight. Alone, he rode forward to shake hands with the officer and show him the papers given to him during his peace trip to Washington. As he neared the soldiers, now in line of battle, the officer shouted to his men. Suddenly, the troops opened fire. Lean Bear fell to the ground wounded. While he was on his back, bluecoats swarmed around him, firing. The chief never had a chance. Another Cheyenne leader, Star, also fell wounded. Soldiers rode over him, too, riddling his body with bullets. Then came the heavy boom of cannons. Canister shot kicked up dust in front of the mounted warriors, though the ricocheting balls did little damage. The warriors returned the fire, arcing arrows into the soldier line. Dust and smoke shrouded the battle, allowing small parties of warriors to charge and harass the bunched and confused soldiers. Two bluecoats fell with arrow wounds; five other were killed by pistol and rifle fire.

In the chaos of battle, Black Kettle rode in, shouting, "Don't make war with the whites!" But the fighting went on for hours, until finally the soldiers broke off and retreated to Fort Larned. Besides Lean Bear and Star, one other warrior died in the fighting and many more were wounded. Despite these losses, the Cheyennes had managed to capture fifteen army horses, complete with saddles, bridles, and saddlebags.[7]

Joined now by the Black Kettle–Lean Bear bands, George found himself in a combined village of more than 450 lodges, moving south toward Medicine Lodge Creek, where the Kiowas, Comanches, Apaches, and Arapahos had already gathered to fatten their horses on the rich grass along the banks of the creek.

As the great procession moved, George learned that Black Kettle had wintered on the Arkansas River west of Fort Larned. Even though he had remained in close contact with the Indian agent and officers at the fort, Black Kettle had not received the annuities promised him by

Boone's 1861 Fort Wise Treaty. Discouraged by these broken promises and alarmed by rumors of the Fremont Orchard and Beaver Creek fights, Black Kettle and Lean Bear had determined to head north and link up with bands on the Smoky Hill River. The soldiers intercepted them on Ash Creek, only a few days' travel from Fort Larned.

The village moved slowly, the warrior societies protecting the rear and flanks, always alert for enemies. Finally, the people reached the Salt Plains of Medicine Lodge Creek. The Kiowas and Plains Apaches were camped in a great circle, preparing for a sun dance, while the Comanches camped apart, staking their lodges on both sides of Medicine Lodge Creek. The Arapahos camped north of the village on Coon Creek, twenty-five miles south of Fort Larned. The tribes felt safe here. George had never seen so many Indians assembled in one place. No enemy—not even the soldiers—would attack such a concentration of strength.[8]

From here, in camp on the Salt Plains, Black Kettle sent a scout to his old friend William Bent, whom he supposed would be at his ranch on the Purgatoire River. Few Cheyennes dared travel the roads or approach troops after Lean Bear's murder—and especially now after the Dog Soldiers' retaliation on the Platte River settlements had closed the roads to Denver and created hysteria among the whites.[9] It was a dangerous mission, but Black Kettle desperately needed Bent's counsel; perhaps he could use his influence to stop the war.

The messenger found the old trader on the road, just east of Fort Lyon, riding at the head of his wagon train bound for Westport and St. Louis. Black Kettle's news of the recent attacks did not take Bent by surprise. Only the day before, he had learned of the fight on Ash Creek from Lieutenant George S. Eayre of the First Colorado Cavalry, the very officer who had led the attack on Black Kettle and Lean Bear. Eayre had been on his way to Fort Lyon to explain his actions to the district commander when he came upon Bent's train. Alarmed by the young officer's report, Bent understood the urgency of meeting with Black Kettle and other Cheyenne leaders. He immediately changed his plans, sending Robert on with the caravan. Bent told the messenger that he would meet Black Kettle in seven days at the Arapaho camp on Coon Creek.

About June 5, William reached the rendezvous point. Black Kettle was already there—and so was George. With the Indian leaders

William discussed the war. He was convinced that Lieutenant Eayre had exceeded his authority and operated beyond the bounds of his military district when he attacked Lean Bear and Black Kettle at Ash Creek. In fact, he was confident the lieutenant would be arrested and cashiered from the service.[10] The Cheyennes, he said, should hold back and not retaliate for at least twenty days. During that time, William would travel to Fort Leavenworth, two hundred miles east, and lay the facts before departmental commander Major General Samuel Curtis.

When the meeting with the chiefs ended, William left George and rode to nearby Fort Larned, only to discover that Colonel John M. Chivington, commander of the Colorado Military District, had been ordered to Fort Lyon and would soon be in the field against the Cheyennes. This unexpected news altered his plans. Now he would go to Fort Lyon and see Chivington. Fort Lyon was closer than Fort Leavenworth, and perhaps he could make the colonel understand that the Cheyennes had not started the war, that Black Kettle and the Southern Cheyennes earnestly desired peace. Quickly, William returned to Coon Creek, picked up George, and together father and son rode for Fort Lyon.[11]

After five days of hard travel, the Bents sighted the familiar stone fort atop the bluff overlooking the Arkansas. George, still dressed as a Cheyenne warrior, rode for the relative safety of the Purgatoire ranch, staying clear of the main road and army patrols. William headed for the fort and a meeting with Colonel Chivington.

Chivington. William knew him. The hellfire-and-brimstone preacher had arrived in Denver in 1860 as the presiding elder of the Methodist Episcopal Church for the Rocky Mountain District. Draped in lion skins and with Colt revolvers strapped to his waist, he quickly gained a reputation, even among frontier toughs, for his peculiar brand of "muscular Christianity." When the Civil War broke out, Chivington requested— and received—a fighting commission as major of the First Colorado Volunteer regiment. In March 1862, the Coloradans fought Texans near Santa Fe. In a narrow defile called Apache Canyon during the Battle of Glorieta Pass, he charged the Confederate guns and turned back the Rebel advance on the Colorado goldfields. Although most

Coloradans hailed the preacher-turned-soldier as a hero, Chivington's raid rise to glory had won him detractors, whom he dismissed as so many "*Secessionists* and *Bummers*, and in my very soul I am glad *they* don't like me."[12] Following the Union victory at Glorieta Pass, Chivington, backed by a few fiercely loyal officers, forced out regimental commander John P. Slough and succeeded to the command of the regiment and the Colorado Military District.[13] Now his ambition knew no bounds. Acting in concert with Colorado territorial governor John Evans, he headed the Republican Party's effort to gain Colorado statehood, seeking for himself election to the high office of U.S. representative. A brigadier general's star would lend prestige to the statehood movement and help advance his candidacy to political office. "If I can get this appointment now," he wrote to a supporter, "after the war is over I can go to Congress or U.S. Senate easy."[14] But he needed another military success—any victory, whether against Rebels or redskins.

Yes, William knew Chivington well. For the sake of his mixed-blood children and the Cheyenne people, he somehow had to convince this man that the war the army now waged against the Cheyennes was wrong and must be stopped.

The meeting did not go well. William argued the case for peace. He told Chivington that Black Kettle opposed war, and that in any conflict both whites and Indians would suffer. Government trains would be targets and civilian losses would be enormous, both in life and property. No settlement, not in New Mexico, Colorado, Kansas, Dakota, or Nebraska, would be safe. There were not soldiers enough, he argued, to guard all the roads, stage and telegraph stations, ranches, and military posts.

Chivington, full-bearded, barrel-chested, and more than a foot taller than old Bent, would have none of it. "I'm on the warpath," he growled. Besides, he said, he had no authority to make peace, and "citizens would have to protect themselves."[15]

William saw the futility of further conversation. This man Chivington was beyond reason. Disgusted, William left him and rode to his ranch, twenty miles up the Arkansas.

Here, he quickly told the family of his confrontation with Chivington, for it was clear the ex-preacher was not only an enemy of the Cheyennes but of the Bents. The colonel had vehemently voiced his opposition to racial mixing and said that Bent was nothing but a lowly "squawman." George he considered a halfbreed Rebel who had violated the oath of allegiance sworn at the time of his parole by leading Cheyenne war parties against white soldiers and settlers. Chivington had warned his officers that young Bent posed a special threat, for he had been educated in white schools and was by "all appearances a white man." He further told his officers that "I have been reliably informed that this halfbreed Bent, in order to incite the Indians against the Whites, told them that the Great Father in Washington having all he could do to fight his children at the south, they could now regain their country."[16]

Chivington was a dangerous enemy. Not only did he command all troops in the Colorado Military District, he also saw himself as the hand and sword of God. Killing Indians was God's work. "So Mote it be," he would say.[17] And by killing George Bent—a halfbreed—he would strike a blow against both the Confederacy and the Cheyennes. In one stroke, Chivington would smite the enemies of the state, red and white, and go a long way toward realizing his personal ambition of wearing a brigadier's star and the top hat of a congressman.

William warned George to stay far away from this man and his troops. If Chivington caught him, he would kill him on the spot.

Though William and George both knew it had been a mistake to treat with Chivington, the respite at the Purgatoire ranch was good for them. They had traveled long and hard and badly needed rest. Over the next few weeks, Mary and her husband Robison Moore, now living at the ranch, joined William and George in discussions about the war that now had drawn perilously close to the Bent ranch. Older brother Robert was in Westport, of course, with the Bent train; George had just missed him. Charley, too, was away, thought to be on the Republican River with his mother Yellow Woman, raiding with the Dog Soldiers. This was a sore point with William, but he had no control over Yellow Woman, who had left him several years before, nor could he control his youngest son. George was glad to see his stepmother, Island, but he noticed she was strangely distant and quiet in William's presence.

At the ranch, George read the Denver papers, which were filled with news of the Indian war and the panic that had swept the border settlements. William hardly knew what to believe. But he did know that his business had suffered. No wagon train was safe, not even his. He complained bitterly about his business losses, telling the family that the government had failed to pay him the promised lease on his new fort.[18] And his trade with the Cheyennes and Arapahos had sharply declined, partly because the Indians were constantly on the move and could not be located. He also blamed competition from the corrupt agent Samuel Colley and his son, Dexter. These two, in cahoots with old Uncle John Smith, had accepted bribes and sold the Cheyennes annuity goods already set aside for the tribe's use. William knew how the cheat worked: Colley received the annuity goods but withheld them from the tribes, then invited the chiefs to pay for their government treaty goods with presents—ponies, mules, buffalo robes. At the same time, Dexter Colley traveled the camps, using the Indians' own annuities as trade for hides and other goods. William figured that the Colleys and Smith had earned some thirty thousand dollars in two years of illegal trade with the Cheyennes, Arapahos, Kiowas, and Comanches. Once, when William was trading in the same camp as Dexter Colley, he discovered a box stamped "U.S. Upper Arkansas Agency." Colley's trade goods were the government annuities. William lamented that "the Indians knew they were purchasing their own goods, but did not complain about it." He sympathized with Black Kettle, who had removed his people from the agency for this very reason.[19]

About July 1, Agent Colley sent an urgent message to the ranch. He wanted to meet with William as soon as possible. Putting aside his personal distaste for the agent, William went over to Fort Lyon to see what he wanted. Colley showed him a proclamation issued by Governor Evans on June 27, 1864:

To the friendly Indians of the plains:
Agents, interpreters, and traders will inform the friendly Indians of the plains, that some members of their tribes have gone to war with the white people. They steal stock and run it off, hoping to escape detection and punishment. In some instances they have attacked and killed soldiers, and murdered peaceable citizens. For this the Great Father is angry, and will certainly hunt them out, and punish them. But he does not want to injure those who remain friendly to the

whites. He desires to protect and take care of them. For this purpose, I direct that all friendly Indians keep away from those who are at war, and go to places of safety.

Friendly Arapahoes and Cheyennes belonging on the Arkansas river will go to Major Colley, United States Indian agent at Fort Lyon, who will give them provisions and show them a place of safety.

Friendly Kiowas and Camanches [*sic*] will go to Fort Larned, where they will be cared for in the same way.

Friendly Sioux will go to their agent at Fort Laramie for directions. Friendly Arapahoes and Cheyennes of the Upper Platte will go to Camp Collins, on the Cache la Poudre, where they will be assigned a place of safety, and provisions will be given them.

The object of this is to prevent friendly Indians from being killed through mistake. None but those who intend to be friendly with the whites must come to these places. The families of those who have gone to war with the whites must be kept away from among the friendly Indians. The war on hostile Indians will be continued until they are all effectually subdued.[20]

Colley asked William to carry the proclamation to the Cheyennes and Arapahos. William thought the proclamation was a good thing, for it clearly separated the warring bands from friendly ones such as Black Kettle's.

Considering all the tales of Indian uprisings that had swept the territory over the last month, Governor Evans had shown restraint. Denver itself was in a panic over the killings on Isaac P. Van Wormer's ranch, twenty-five miles southeast of the city. On June 11, 1864, ranch foreman Nathan Ward Hungate, his wife, and two children had been brutally murdered. Rumor had it that the Cheyennes had committed the crime.[21] Several days later, the Hungates' mutilated bodies were propped in a wagon box and exhibited to the people of Denver. The Hungate children, an infant son and a four-year-old daughter, were displayed between the scalped and mutilated bodies of their parents.[22]

The city went wild. People believed that an "army of Indians" was marching on Denver. When a Mexican horse herder drove his animals into the city, the cloud of dust raised by the herd incited a riot, for residents believed it was evidence of the long-feared attack had finally come. Church bells rang the alarm, and everyone in the city rushed terror-stricken to the town armory in search of safety. Even Governor Evans was convinced that the Plains Indians were combining to clean out all white settlements. Chivington, who knew better, encouraged these fears.

Given the circumstances, the governor's proclamation was the best deal the Cheyennes and Arapahos could hope for. William returned to his ranch, then with George rode for the Arapaho camp on Coon Creek and Black Kettle's people on Medicine Lodge.[23]

By the second week in July, William and George had explained the governor's proclamation to the Cheyennes and Arapahos. When their leaders expressed satisfaction with the governor's terms, William led them to Fort Larned, where he had arranged a meeting with Captain J. W. Parmetar, the post's commander.

Parmetar was an embarrassment to the army and a danger to the Indians in his district. One officer described him as a "habitual, beastly, debased, demoralsed [sic], and brutalized, drunkard" who openly consorted with prostitutes and paid them with commissary stores, fell drunk on parade, and antagonized friendly tribes.[24]

Although the drunken Parmeter treated the Cheyennes with contempt and angered the chiefs, William left Fort Larned feeling that "everything was settled satisfactory on both sides."[25] George, of course, stayed away from the meeting. The soldiers were nervous, their commander unpredictable and trigger-happy. It was best for the young mixed-blood to remain hidden in the Indian villages for the time being.

When the meeting was over, the Bents returned to the Purgatoire stockade only to find that all was not well on the home front. George's stepmother Island, his father's second wife, had run off with Joe Barraldo, a mixed-blood who occasionally worked as a Bent trader. The old trader could scarcely contain his anger. In a letter to Samuel Colley, he fumed: "I am not in a very good humor, as my old squaw ran off a few days ago, or rather went off with Jo. Barraldo, as she like him better than she did me. If I ever get sight of the young man, it will go hard with him."[26] William believed the runaways were headed for the Cheyenne village on the Solomon River.

Other news was equally disturbing. Cheyenne and Arapaho war parties had attacked ranches, stages, and wagons on a wide front, ranging from the South Platte River in Colorado to the Little Blue in Nebraska. The army had again closed the road to Denver, allowing only strongly armed caravans to proceed. For weeks, neither wagons nor mail could get through.

The raiders were not just Cheyennes—the Lakotas, Arapahos, and Kiowas also were at war. Only days after William and George returned to the ranch, the Kiowa leader Satanta appeared outside the stockade at the head of a war party. Satanta said he had come in peace, but the Bents sensed trouble. The chief said he wanted Agent Colley. William and George believed Satanta wanted blood, and although the Bents bore no love for the corrupt official, they refused to divulge his whereabouts and kept the gates to the compound securely barred. The Kiowas angrily quirted their horses and rode off. Later, the Bents learned that these same Kiowas had recently run off horses at Fort Larned and killed a sentinel. The incident reminded George that his was a family caught between two worlds. A misstep either way could mean death.[27]

George heard these reports of raids and war with growing excitement. His Crooked Lance society friends were in the thick of things, counting coups and gaining prestige while he languished at the ranch under the restraints imposed by his father.

The pull of battle proved too strong, however. Despite his father's advice, in early August, *Do-ha-eno* packed his gear, rounded up his best horses, and, in company with his young friend Howling Wolf, headed north for the Solomon River camps, where Black Kettle had moved his people.

Three days out, they cut Black Kettle's trail and followed it north. As they approached the forks of the Solomon, they saw low on the horizon a bank of smoke suspended over not one village but many stretching along the river as far as the eye could see. Village after village greeted them with the beat of drums and singing. In the center of the camp circles, men and women, young and old, danced and celebrated. Tipis overflowed with a profusion of wealth, everything piled together: heaps of fine silks; groceries of all kinds, including canned oysters, sides of bacon, and bags of coffee and sugar; bolts of the highest quality cloth; boots and shoes. They looked about and saw old men wearing ladies' bonnets and veils, and young men paraded in striped shirts of bright colors, made for them by their sweethearts and wives from captured bolts of silk. Friends pressed upon them gold rings, pocketknives, fancy top hats, and enough silk to make a dozen shirts. All the while, George and Howling Wolf watched returning war parties carry in plunder taken from wagon trains and settlements.[28]

The raids seemed appropriate retaliation for the unprovoked attack on the Dog Soldiers at Fremont's Orchard and Lieutenant Eayre's murder of Lean Bear.

But George had not been in camp long before he received news of the combined Dog Soldier–Lakota attacks along the Platte and Little Blue. In just ten days, August 7–16, the raiders had killed fifty-one whites and wounded nine.[29] They had also captured seven women and children. These prisoners might be adopted into the tribes, as was done with such traditional enemies as the Crows and Utes, or traded for food or goods—or, if the war continued, exchanged for Cheyenne prisoners held in the soldier forts.

In any case, George knew that the conflict had entered a new phase. The raids were more than plunder and ponies; they had now widened to an indiscriminate war on all whites, not just the soldiers. Like other society men, he sought the honor, status, riches, and, important to a young Cheyenne, attention of women that came to a brave and successful warrior. The scalp dances were opportunities for young men to meet women, and George longed to participate in these celebrations. He was ready, even eager, to fight the Pawnees, Crows, and Utes. But warring on whites was another matter. He had lived with them, gone to school and church with them, shared their lives in Westport and St. Louis. His father was white, as were his guardians back East. Was he now to kill these people, to treat them as enemies?

Younger brother Charley, now in the camps with his mother Yellow Woman, seemed to have resolved these conflicting loyalties. He had joined the Dog Soldiers in the raids on the Platte and Little Blue, and his aggressiveness had drawn attention. The Dog Soldiers spoke of his courage, for he attacked white enemies with a vengeance born of hate. Perhaps this was Charley's way of gaining acceptance by the warrior societies. George wondered, however, whether the older men used his brother to get liquor. But the whites had noticed him, too. Newspapers had singled him out as a "renegade halfbreed" and the "leader" of the Dog Soldiers.[30] That Charley would have been selected to lead a Dog Soldier war party was pure nonsense—he was too young and inexperienced for that. Nevertheless, Charley had renounced his whiteness.

The choice was not so clear to George. His father and Black Kettle had always worked for peace. This summer William had traveled among the tribes carrying Governor Evans's peace proclamation. He had pledged his word to military authorities that Black Kettle's Southern Cheyennes had not participated in any raids against the whites. And of course, the Bent family was identified with the Southern Cheyennes in countless ways. William had married the Arrow Keeper's daughters and had spent years in the Cheyenne villages; his children were half Cheyenne. For any Bent—Charley or George or Robert—to be seen riding with the raiders would undermine William's lifelong efforts to secure peace on the Arkansas River. It would also indict Black Kettle and his people, for the army associated the Bent children with the Southern Cheyennes. If a Bent joined the raiders, then it might be supposed that Black Kettle, too, condoned war.

And there was Island. She had left his father for Joe Barraldo, and Barraldo had been seen with the Dog Soldiers during the Little Blue raids. Island may have severed her relationship with William, but her name was still linked to the Bents. Worse, news came to George that Barraldo had actually talked to Laura Roper, a sixteen-year-old captive taken with Lucinda Eubank on August 7 near the Little Blue Station. The first night after the raid, Barraldo saw the Roper girl and asked if she feared for her life. With surprising calmness, Laura indicated that she did not. If the Cheyennes had intended to kill her, she said, they would have done so already. Barraldo agreed. She would probably be returned to her people soon.[31]

Laura Roper and Lucinda Eubank were in the camps now, along with another white woman, Nancy Jane Morton, taken August 8 near

Plum Creek Station on the Platte River. George could imagine their fear. The warriors sometimes passed captive women among themselves, raping them repeatedly, then exchanged them for horses or plunder. But the Roper girl had not been molested. George thought she seemed happy, for she often smiled and played games with the Indian children. The Cheyenne women, too, treated her well, and delighted in dressing her and combing her hair.[32]

Lucinda Eubank, however, remained disconsolate. George learned that her husband had been killed during the raid and she feared for her two children, Isabelle, age three, and Willie, not yet a year old. Isabelle had been in Laura Roper's arms at the time of the raid and the Cheyennes thought her the mother. Only when the raiders reached the Republican camps did they allow Lucinda to see her little girl.[33]

Unlike Laura Roper and Lucinda Eubank, Nancy Morton had been seriously wounded at the time of her capture and was still confined to a Sioux lodge, unable to walk. George decided to see her, even though this was risky. He knew he should stay away; when the white women were released, they might single him out as one of the raiders. That Charley and Joe Barraldo had been seen during the raids no doubt already had made life difficult for his father. There was Chivington, too—he had identified George as a renegade halfbreed and Confederate agent. If Nancy Morton or Lucinda Eubank or Laura Roper pointed to him as one of the raiders, the soldiers would turn on all the Bents.

But George went to see Nancy Morton anyway.

Her appearance shocked him. Her eyes were swollen shut, and she suffered from two arrow wounds, one in her left side just under her armpit, the other in her thigh. Quietly, he asked how she had been taken. She said that she and her husband had been traveling the trail just west of Fort Kearney, Nebraska. Nancy was driving the wagon and saw distant riders. She woke her husband and asked him to look, but he could see nothing and told her not to worry. Shortly, though, the riders neared and Nancy saw they were Indians. Her husband now understood the danger. He grabbed the reins and shouted, "They won't kill you!"[34] But Nancy panicked and threw herself from the wagon. As she fell, her husband asked, "Oh my dear, where are you going?"[35] When she hit the ground, a following wagon smashed against her, but she got up and ran for the river, where she saw her cousin, John Fletcher. As she approached him, he screamed, "We're all going to be killed!" Just then an arrow thudded into his chest, knocking him down. Blood gushed from his wound, forming a great pool at Nancy's feet; then he shuddered and died. Her brother, William Fletcher, was nearby, hiding in the tall grass. He said they should run for the wagons, but as he got up three arrows struck him simultaneously. He whispered, "Tell my wife Susan I am killed. Good-bye, my dear sister."[36] Two arrows hit Nancy, although in her panic she hardly felt the pain. Suddenly, Indians rose up all around her. They held another captive, nine-year-old Danny Marble, who had been traveling with his father just behind the Morton wagon. One warrior pulled Nancy up on to a horse, and they all rode away.

The story came out disjointedly, but George had heard enough. Her wounds showed signs of infection. If they were not treated, she would die. He left the lodge and in moments returned with a Cheyenne doctor. The old man bound raw liver around her eyes, rubbed roots and herbs into her wounds, and had her drink a pungent broth. When the doctor finished his ministrations, George brought in Laura Roper and Lucinda Eubank. Even years later, Nancy remembered the joy: "We all began to cry for we all knew each others sorrow."[37] The reunion was short, and again the Sioux separated the captives. The next day, George returned. "How delighted I was to see him as he was so very kind to me," Nancy recalled, "but he didn't stop long as he said Mrs. Eubanks babe was quite ill and he was going over to see if it had proper care. He called on Mrs. Eubanks and found that the child was improving."[38]

In a few days, Nancy was strong enough to walk. One night, George brought her to his lodge to meet Island, for his stepmother knew a few words of English. Nancy never forgot the evening: "Their tepee was decorated with many gorgeous decorations which looked to me very grotesque. The old squaw took me on her lap and kissed me and told me she was so sorry the Indians had killed my husband and friends, then she would caress me and tell me not to worry for she thought I would get home some day. She combed my hair and tried to comfort me all she could in her grotesque way."[39]

George had done all he could. He had insisted a Cheyenne doctor treat Nancy Morton's wounds, reunited the captives, and had his stepmother and other Indian women make the prisoners as comfortable as possible. He would not be a part of this war on white women and children.

Meanwhile, army and government officials in Denver and at Fort Lyon also weighed the matter of war and reached their own conclusions. Agent Colley thought the Cheyennes needed a dose of army steel to force them to comply with treaty provisions. Colonel Chivington ordered officers in his district to fire on any Indians they encountered and not to encumber "your command with prisoner Indians."[40] In Denver, the *Rocky Mountain News* published a second proclamation issued by Governor Evans. This one authorized "all citizens of Colorado, either individually or in such parties as they may organize, to go in pursuit of all hostile Indians on the plains, scrupulously avoiding those who have responded to my call to rendezvous at the points indicated; also to kill and destroy as enemies of the country wherever they may be found, all such hostile Indians."[41] On August 12, the War Department granted approval for Evans to raise a regiment of one-hundred-day U.S. volunteers to put down the Indian uprising. The following day, the call to arms rang through Denver City and mountain mining camps. The war would be carried to every Indian village outside the zones of safety prescribed by Evans's June 27 proclamation.[42]

In mid-August, the war that George wanted to avoid came to him. Captain Edward B. Murphy of the Seventh Iowa Cavalry intercepted a party of Lakota buffalo hunters on Elk Creek. The running fight brought the soldiers to the outskirts of the great Solomon River camps. George heard the gunfire. Over the hill he saw his friend Hawk signal that soldiers were approaching. George and fifty other warriors ran for the pony herd. Clutching his bridle and blanket, he jumped the first horse he found, then galloped toward the enemy. As he crested the hill, he saw other warriors converging on the troops. The frightened soldiers bunched up, then retreated in confusion. Now it was the soldiers' turn to run, but two bluecoats fell behind, futilely slapping the flanks of their exhausted horses with the barrels of their carbines. The warriors easily caught up to them and cut them down. George thrilled to the excitement of the chase. It was like running buffalo. With the others he pursued the cavalrymen for miles until his pony finally tired. George rode back to camp, flushed with his first real victory as a Cheyenne warrior.[43]

He could not help but think how different this fight was from the battles he had experienced as a Confederate cavalryman. In the East, he had fought as one man in a disciplined unit. Here, every warrior fought individually. No one gave orders, and there seemed to be no obvious strategy; yet everyone attacked, some striking the enemy's flanks, others jabbing at the front and rear, always looking for points of weakness. Shrill war cries and the scream of eagle-bone whistles pierced the air, causing panic among the troopers and their mounts. Burdened by heavy saddles and equipment, the soldiers were easy targets for the bareback-riding warriors, armed with bows, lances, pistols, and cut-down rifles. Warriors closed to count coup, darted away, and attacked again to capture a horse or wrest a weapon from a soldier's hand.

In Civil War battles, armies struggled for territory or to capture or kill the enemy. Here, the objective was less to kill than to demonstrate superiority. Each warrior sought personal battle honors—coups, horses, scalps—for these brought honor within the tribe. At the same time, victory reaffirmed Cheyenne superiority.

A few days after the Elk Creek fight a letter arrived from William Bent. The chiefs asked *Do-ha-eno* and Ed Guerrier to translate. Bent wanted the chiefs to come to Fort Lyon and negotiate a peace. On pages torn out of a ledger book, George and Ed scribbled the chiefs' response. One letter was addressed to Agent Colley, the other to the commander at Fort Lyon:

Cheyenne Village Aug. 29th/64
Maj. Colley.
Sir

We received a letter from Bent wishing us to make peace. We held a consel in regard to it & all came to the conclusion to make peace with you providing you make peace with the Kiowas, Commenches [*sic*], Arrapahoes, Apaches and Siouxs.

We are going to send a messenger to the Kiowas and to the other nations about our going to make [peace] with you. We heard that you [have] some prisoners in Denver. We have seven prisoners of you which we are willing to give up providing you give up yours.

There are three war parties out yet and two of Arraphoes. They have been out some time and expect now soon.

When we held this counsel there were few Arraphoes and Siouxs present; we want true news from you in return, that is a letter.

Black Kettle & other Chieves[44]

The letter was skillfully composed, at once conciliatory and demanding. The Cheyennes offered to exert their influence with the other tribes to bring about peace. They also admitted to holding seven white prisoners and noted that three Cheyenne and two Arapaho war parties were still out on raids. The chiefs demanded, as a condition of peace, that the whites must negotiate with all Cheyenne allies— Kiowas, Comanches, Apaches, Arapahos, and Sioux. Further, before the Cheyennes freed their white captives, the Indian prisoners held in Denver must be released.

Black Kettle dictated the letter from a position of strength. The Cheyennes had just routed Captain Murphy's troops, war parties had closed most roads to Denver, and the tribes held white women and children prisoners. Further, five war parties were still out and would not be recalled unless a peace agreement was negotiated.

George and Ed were obvious choices to carry the letters to Fort Lyon, but Black Kettle feared they would be shot down on sight. Soldiers had seen Ed in the Indian camps, and George was thought to be a Confederate agent. Besides, they were mixed-bloods and regarded by most whites as renegades. So Black Kettle decided to send full-bloods. The aged Lone Bear, who had lost an eye defending William Bent from a Kiowa assailant, seemed a good choice. He knew many white officers at Fort Lyon, and his daughter was married to trader John Prowers. His wife would accompany him as a sign to the soldiers that he had come in peace. Black Kettle also selected Eagle Head, an experienced warrior and father of George's friend, Howling Wolf. He would be the party's scout and protector.[45]

On the morning of September 4, near Fort Lyon, Lieutenant George Hawkins of Company A, First Colorado Cavalry, intercepted Lone Bear's party. Lieutenant Hawkins had strict orders to shoot on sight any Indians he encountered. But these Indians showed no warlike intent as they walked toward him, their uplifted hands holding sheets of paper. Hawkins took them prisoner and escorted them to the Fort Lyon commander, Major Edward W. Wynkoop.

Wynkoop was at first furious when Hawkins presented his captives. District and department orders were clear: all Indians should be deemed hostile and shot on sight. But these "hostiles" carried two letters, one addressed to him, the other to Agent Colley. In them, Black Kettle himself outlined a peace plan that provided for the release of white captives. Wynkoop quickly sent for Colley, and together they questioned the Cheyennes. Wynkoop asked Lone Bear whether he knew that he could have been shot for approaching the fort. Lone Bear replied, "I thought I would be killed, but I knew that paper would be found upon my dead body, that you would see it, and it might give peace to my people once more." Eagle Head, too, indicated his willingness to sacrifice himself to restore the peace. Wynkoop later wrote, "I was bewildered with an exhibition of such patriotism on the part of two savages, and felt myself in the presence of superior beings." He had not expected such courage and nobility from a "race that I had heretofore looked upon without exception as being cruel, treacherous, and blood-thirsty, without feeling or affection for friend or kindred."[46]

The Cheyennes offered to help Wynkoop recover the white captives held in Black Kettle's village on the Smoky Hill. Wynkoop felt compelled to act. If the captives were to be saved, we had to get to them quickly. Troops were already in the field and might at any moment attack the Cheyennes. In any fighting, captives would surely be killed. He quickly penned an explanatory letter to Colonel Chivington, then on September 6 marched for the Smoky Hill with two mountain howitzers and 127 troopers.

Guided by Lone Bear, Wynkoop reached Black Kettle's village on September 9. Here, he was greeted by about seven hundred warriors "drawn up in line of battle and prepared to fight,"[47] the largest concentration of plains Indians ever to confront U.S. troops. It was a chilling sight. One of Wynkoop's officers, Captain Silas S. Soule, remarked that the warriors "closed around us as though they meant to gobble us up."[48] Armed Dog Soldiers pushed against the soldiers, thrusting their hands into the soldiers' pockets searching for tobacco. Others stuck grapes into the vents of the howitzers.[49] Surrounded, outnumbered, and thoroughly intimidated, Wynkoop thought his small force would be wiped out. But before a shot was fired, Lone Bear arranged a parlay between Wynkoop and the chiefs. The major had brought old John Smith with him to translate. But the chiefs pushed George Bent forward. He could be trusted to accurately interpret the words of this tall white officer. George was willing. After all, his father's letter had prompted this peace effort. As the council progressed, George became the center of attention, for even Wynkoop turned to him to confirm the accuracy of Smith's translations.[50]

Bull Bear, the Dog Soldier chief, spoke first. He angrily recounted how at Ash Creek his brother Lean Bear had held aloft his peace medal as the soldiers shot him down. The whites, he said, were "foxes, and no peace could be brought about with them." Arapaho chief Little Raven spoke next. He allowed that he had always lived in peace with the whites and had "loved them," but now he agreed with Bull Bear: there could be no peace with the treacherous whites.[51]

Lone Bear stood up to say that the words spoken by Bull Bear and Little Raven shamed him. The chiefs had sent him to Fort Lyon to offer peace. Would they now break that promise and attack the soldiers who had only responded to their call? Black Kettle should stand by his promises—if he did not, then Lone Bear would join the soldiers and fight his own people. He even offered Bull Bear two of his finest horses if the Dog Man would stop threatening the soldiers and say no more in council. Bull Bear took the horses and fell silent, his brooding presence menace enough.[52]

Black Kettle—George at his side—stepped forward. He agreed with Lone Bear. The Cheyennes would not break their word. He had dictated the letters that had brought the Tall Chief to the village. He would now return to the Indian camp and work to secure the release of the white captives. In the meantime, Wynkoop should withdraw to a safe place some twelve miles distant.

Three days later, the Cheyenne chiefs arrived in Wynkoop's camp, bringing with them four white captives: Laura Roper, Isabelle Eubank, Danny Marble, and Ambrose Asher. The other captives, Lucinda and Willie Eubank and Nancy Morton, were in distant camps and it would take some time to recover them. Black Kettle revealed that another prisoner, a Mrs. Snyder, was dead. She had hanged herself in the lodge of her Arapaho captor.[53]

Still, Black Kettle and the other Cheyenne and Arapaho chiefs were determined to accompany Wynkoop to Denver, where they hoped to meet with the governor and military authorities and sue for peace. With this good news, Wynkoop hurried to Fort Lyon. Here, the officers' wives took charge of the released captives. Then Wynkoop loaded the chiefs in army escort wagons and headed for Denver and Camp Weld for a meeting with Governor Evans and Colonel Chivington. Black Kettle and White Antelope represented the Southern Cheyennes; Bull Bear, the Dog Soldiers; and *Neva*, *Bosse*, Heaps-of-Buffalo, and *Notanee* would speak for Arapaho chief Left Hand. Wynkoop brought along John Smith as his interpreter.[54]

George did not accompany the chiefs on their journey to Denver. He was known there and his presence might disrupt the proceedings. But he did not lay idle in the Cheyenne village. For some months he had wanted to join his Crooked Lance brothers in raids against the Pawnees.[55] Now that the chiefs had left for Denver, the young society men saw an opportunity to strike their old enemies, the Wolf Men. Lakota allies had told them that the Pawnees were on the Republican River hunting buffalo.[56]

Rock Forehead, the Arrow Keeper, offered to make *Do-ha-eno* a special shield, one like those he had made for Big Wolf, High Wolf, Crow Neck, and his own son, Fox Tail. This was a great honor. It was a sign of Rock Forehead's affection and marked *Do-ha-eno* as a promising young warrior. George wanted such a shield to take on the raid, but before accepting the gift, he talked with Charley's mother, Yellow Woman. She knew about such things, for she had recently spent time with the raiders on the South Platte River. To George's surprise, she advised that he not accept the sacred shield—although it possessed powerful medicine, many obligations and responsibilities came with it. George would have to care for it, perform daily ceremonies, and obey strict rules. If he failed to observe these rituals, he might die, either in battle or by accident. This convinced George that the risk was just too great. He declined Rock Forehead's offer, but he still went on the raid.[57]

Several raiding parties set out for the Pawnee hunting camps. George's party of five warriors, led by Big Horse, left on September 21. But when George and his companions reached the Republican, they found that the Pawnees had already gone. Dejected, the warriors headed home.

When they arrived back at the Smoky Hill village, all was confusion. Shortly after they had departed, the people had moved slowly toward Fort Larned. While they were camped on Walnut Creek, warriors came tearing into camp, shouting, "Soldiers are coming!" The men rushed out to meet two companies of Colorado cavalry, led by Major Scott Anthony. The Cheyennes quickly pushed back Anthony's men, who dug in on a hillside, fighting for their lives. Just then, a larger force of soldiers, commanded by Major General James G. Blunt, appeared. The tide of battle suddenly turned, and the entire Cheyenne-Arapaho village retreated toward their old Smoky Hill camp. Over the next three days, the warriors successfully protected the people as they moved away from the soldiers.[58]

George rejoined the village just as it returned to the Smoky Hill. A few days later, Black Kettle and the chiefs came in with news of their meeting in Denver with Evans and Chivington.[59] Black Kettle could hardly contain his excitement. The whites had agreed to call off the war if his people moved over to Fort Lyon and surrendered to the fort's commander, Major Edward Wynkoop, whom the Cheyennes knew as Tall Chief. He had promised that no troops would harm them there.

Bull Bear was not convinced, especially since the great village had been attacked even as the chiefs were negotiating peace. In Denver, Bull Bear had offered to join the soldiers and fight the Lakotas or anyone else who had "no ears to listen" to peace. He had said, "I am young and can fight. I have given my word to fight with the whites. My brother (Lean Bear) died in trying to keep peace with the whites. I am willing to die in the same way, and expect to do so."[60]

But now Bull Bear felt betrayed; the white foxes could not be trusted. The Dog Soldiers would never submit to military authority.

They would rather take their chances living free in their buffalo-rich home between the Smoky Hill and the Republican. Let the troops try to run the Dog Men like they did the peace bands.

Black Kettle continued to speak for peace, just as he had at Camp Weld. His opening statement there had impressed everyone:

> We have come with our eyes shut, following [Wynkoop's] handful of men, like coming through the fire. All we ask is that we may have peace with the whites; we want to hold you by the hand. You are our father; we have been travelling through a cloud; the sky has been dark ever since the war began. These braves who are with me are all willing to do as I say. We want to take good tidings home to our people, that they may sleep in peace. I want you to give all the chiefs of the soldiers here to understand that we are for peace, and that we have made peace, that we may not be mistaken by them for enemies. I have not come here with a little wolf's bark, but have come to talk plain with you. We must live near the buffalo or starve. When we came here we came free, without any apprehension, to see you, and when I go home and tell my people and have taken your hand and the hands of all the chiefs here in Denver, they will feel well, and so will all the different tribes of Indians on the plains, after we have eaten and drunk with them.[61]

Even Chivington seemed swayed by the chief's strong words. At the end of the conference the colonel had said: "I am not a big war chief but all the soldiers in this country are at my command. My rule of fighting white men or Indians, is to fight them until they lay down their arms and submit to military authority. You are nearer Major Wynkoop than anyone else, and you can go to him when you are ready to do that."[62]

By late October, Black Kettle had convinced his people that they would be safe at Fort Lyon. With six hundred Cheyennes he moved south. About the same number of Arapahos, under Little Raven and Left Hand, also determined to surrender to the soldiers. But two thousand Cheyennes, including Bull Bear's Dog Soldiers, chose to remain on the

Smoky Hill. Here, they would wait until word came from Black Kettle that peace was certain.[63]

When Black Kettle reached Dry Creek—the Big Sandy, or Sand Creek to the whites—forty miles northeast of Fort Lyon, he called for the people to go into camp. Runners soon brought news that the Arapaho surrender at Fort Lyon had gone well. The Tall Chief had distributed rations in exchange for weapons.

Meanwhile, George rode over to his father's ranch. While there, news came from Fort Lyon that Black Kettle's meeting with Wynkoop had not gone as planned. The Tall Chief had relinquished command to Major Scott Anthony, the same "Red-eyed Chief" who had attacked the Cheyennes a month before on Walnut Creek. Anthony was not sympathetic to the plight of Black Kettle's people. He told them that he would not "permit them to come in, even as prisoners, for the reason that if I do, I shall have to subsist them upon prisoner's rations."[64] He ordered Black Kettle to stay on Sand Creek, where the Cheyennes might find buffalo and fend for themselves. When Anthony received new orders from headquarters, he would contact Black Kettle and let him know where to take his people.[65]

During George's stay at the ranch, William kept in constant contact with military authorities and civilian traders at Fort Lyon. He was convinced that peace was certain. The Camp Weld negotiations had been a good sign. The chiefs had shaken hands with Evans and Chivington, and all concerned—Wynkoop, Anthony, Colley, Black Kettle, White Antelope, Left Hand, and Little Raven—believed that any tribe that surrendered in good faith would be protected.

Now that Anthony had assured Black Kettle he would be safe on Sand Creek, William saw no reason why George should not join the Cheyennes. Island was there, Julia and Charley, too, along with other family and friends, Ed Guerrier and Jack Smith, old Uncle John's son, among them. The peace chiefs were there: Yellow Wolf, White Antelope, Lone Bear, and, of course, Black Kettle.

George left the ranch and arrived at the Sand Creek village on November 26.[66] He followed a well-rutted lodgepole trail northeast to the village, now located below high bluffs on the big bend of Sand Creek.

More than one hundred Cheyenne lodges stretched for over a mile along the northeast bank.[67] George easily identified the distinctive circles of the Cheyenne bands, each with its own uniquely decorated lodges. As he crossed the sandy creek bed, he saw a large American flag flying from a tall lodge pole placed in front of Black Kettle's tipi. Surrounding Black Kettle were the lodges of the *Wu-ta-pi-u* clan.[68] Just west of these he saw the sun-colored lodge of his father's old friend, Chief Yellow Wolf. Around it were gathered the *He-va-tan-i-u*, the Hairy Rope people. North of Black Kettle were White Antelope's *Hissi-o-me-tan-i-u*, the Hill band. Still farther north and a little upstream were a few *Suhtaio* clustered around Lone Bear, whom the whites called One-Eye. At the upper end, near the bend of the creek, George could see War Bonnet's lodge and his *Ho-iv-i-ma-nah*, the Scabby band. Bear Tongue's followers were nearby. Strangely, Sand Hill's people chose to camp downstream a short distance apart from the main village.[69] A few Arapaho lodges huddled outside the Cheyenne camp circles, near Lone Bear.[70]

High bluffs on the creek's west bank sheltered the village; nearby springs provided clear water; pools in the creek bed offered water for the horses; and buffalo ranged east of the village. Timber was in short supply, but deadfall and buffalo chips fueled campfires.

All in all, it was a good place.

People moved about the village. Women scraped hides, eager to finish the robes before winter's chill set in; children played in the pockets of snow left by an early storm; and small hunting parties rode in and out, some with travois loaded with fresh meat.

On November 27, the day after George arrived, John Smith came in with a wagon of trade goods owned by Dexter Colley. With him came Private David Louderback of the First Colorado Cavalry and civilian teamster Watson Clark. Smith made War Bonnet's lodge his trading headquarters, exchanging the usual trade goods—probably the Cheyennes' own annuities—for mules, ponies, and buffalo robes.[71] Louderback, who had never been in an Indian village before, marveled at the sights and sounds around him, while teamster Clark assisted Smith.[72] The next day's trade garnered Smith more than one hundred first-rate robes, along with three ponies and a mule.[73]

Night came and the village settled. It was quiet this evening, but cold. Wind snapped at loose tipi flaps, and, occasionally, a dog barked at a prowling coyote. Nothing unusual, for this was a place of safety. No need for camp guards—just sleepy boys watching the herds.

The next morning, November 29, just at sunrise, George stirred, still wrapped in a thick buffalo robe. Suddenly, he felt the rumble of hooves. Someone shouted, "Buffalo!" But other voices cried out, "Soldiers!" He jumped up and ran outside, wearing only his breechclout. The cold morning air bit into his bare flesh, and the frost-covered sand stung his feet. The still half-hidden sun raked a deep orange light across the tipis, casting jagged shadows pointing toward the bluffs west of the village. Fully awake now, George looked southward down the dry creek bed and saw soldiers trotting in columns of four heading straight for the village. The troopers' blue-gray overcoats matched the pale morning sky. They were so close he could see the steam blowing from the horses' nostrils. More soldiers appeared on the bluffs and on the flats to the east. He looked toward Black Kettle's tipi and saw the garrison flag fluttering over his lodge, a small white flag tied beneath it. The chief shouted, "Don't be afraid! There is no danger! The soldiers will not hurt you!" George saw women and children running toward Black Kettle, as if the power of his presence would protect them from the approaching soldiers.[74]

At the same time White Antelope attempted to quiet the frightened women and children, urging them not to run away. Then White Antelope advanced toward the troops, his arms outstretched. He and Black Kettle had brought the Cheyennes to Sand Creek, the people had trusted their judgment, and both had given their word that this was a safe place.

The troops dismounted—and opened fire. Bullets ripped through the tipis with a staccato thumping like the sound of hailstones against lodgeskins.

George looked toward White Antelope. The chief shouted, "Soldiers no hurt me—soldiers my friends."[75] Then he folded his arms across his chest and began singing his death song:

141

Nothing Lives forever,
Only the Earth and the Mountains

The troops fired a crashing volley, and White Antelope fell, cut down in a storm of lead.[76]

George grabbed his weapons and ran for the high bluffs to the west of the village. Anger welled up in him. Black Kettle and White Antelope were peace chiefs. But White Antelope lay dead and Black Kettle stood directly in the path of the soldiers' charge. George thought him as good as dead.[77]

Not far away, John Smith and son Jack sat in their lodge eating breakfast with David Louderback and Watson Clark. A woman cried out, "Soldiers coming!" Uncle John looked out the tipi to see a column of soldiers less than a mile away. He thought they might be Blunt's troops from Fort Riley, Kansas, so he ran toward them, hoping to make his presence known. As he neared the soldiers' line, he saw they were not Blunt's men but Lieutenant Luther Wilson's company of the First Colorado from nearby Fort Lyon. Louderback was at his side and recognized men from his own unit. He stuck a white handkerchief on a stick and waved it over his head. Both men shouted and gestured to the soldiers. But when they got to within one hundred yards of the blue line, dismounted troopers fired three volleys in their direction. Several soldiers fired at Smith, yelling, "Shoot the old son of a bitch!" At the same time, one of Lieutenant Joseph A. Cramer's men of the First Colorado veterans galloped out to rescue the old man. But troopers of the Third Regiment—the hundred-day men—shot him off his horse. Terrified, Smith and Louderback ran back toward the village.[78]

As the two men ran back, teamster Clark jumped into Smith's trade wagon, where he found a tanned buffalo hide. This he tied to a lodge pole and frantically waved it back and forth, hoping the soldiers would recognize him. But the troops fired on him, too, their bullets splintering the wagon box and wheels. When Smith and Louderback reached the wagon, Uncle John and Clark dove for cover in the lodge where baled buffalo robes and piled trade goods offered some protection. Louderback, however, remained outside. Standing on the wagon's tongue, he peered over the box to watch the troops as they began encircling the village. Suddenly, from the south, two cannons boomed. Hundreds of lead canister balls sprayed the ground; overhead, shells exploded, filling the air with hot iron fragments. Louderback ducked into the lodge, where he found not only Smith and Clark but Charley Bent as well.[79]

Ed Guerrier, who had joined Smith's group, realized there was no use in talking to the soldiers. As soon as the shooting started, he ran northeast in search of horses, for the soldiers had already captured the herds to the south and west. After running about five miles he met his cousin, one of White Antelope's daughters, driving a herd of fifteen ponies. Together, they rode for the safety of the Smoky Hill camps, fifty miles to the northeast.[80]

When the troops first opened fire, Jack Smith had gone for horses. Unable to find any, he joined the crowds of people running for the upper end of the village. The soldiers now occupied both banks of the creek, laying down a murderous crossfire. Jack ran for about a mile, but the fleeing Cheyennes could offer little resistance. A few of the warriors had been able to retrieve their weapons before they ran from their lodges, and these men slowed the troops some. Women and children and old ones hugged the creek's ravines and banks for protection; some furiously dug pits in the sand. A few desperate mothers even hid their infants, covering them with sand and dry leaves.[81] There was no use fighting. With soldiers all around them, Jack saw escape to the north was impossible. He turned around and made his way back to the village and entered his father's lodge. Here, as the fighting and killing raged around him, he sat quietly, not knowing what to do.[82]

As George ran west toward the bluffs, he joined up with ten men who hoped to find horses on the high ground. They scrambled up the bluffs and headed for the sand hills beyond. From this high point, George looked back toward the village. What he saw and heard horrified him. Soldiers galloped through the camp firing indiscriminately at women and children and those too old to run. Friends and family members ran upstream, many falling from exhaustion or wounds. Others burrowed into the soft sand to protect themselves from the soldiers' bullets. Shells burst above clumps of huddled people. Women screamed, soldiers shouted, bugles sounded, and over all roared the deafening crash of rifle fire and artillery.

Just then he saw soldiers riding hard toward him from the south. Here, on the open prairie away from the creek, there was no cover except for tufts of grass and sage. With the soldiers bearing down on them, his group split. George went with Little Bear, Spotted Horse, Big Bear, and Bear Shield and ran in a northeast direction back toward Dry Creek. There they might make a stand in the ravines and behind the high banks. Running hard, they made the creek just before the soldiers could ride them down. Sheltered by five-foot banks, the warriors turned their guns and bows on the enemy. The soldiers reined in their horses and drew back out of range.

George heard someone shouting. Not far downstream, he saw his friend Red Owl and a group of people digging into the sand. Red Owl called for George and the others to come over and join them; together they might hold off the soldiers. When George reached the trench carved into the creek bed at the base of the bank, he counted nineteen men, women, and children. Only the strongest and fastest had made it this far above the village. Many others, he could see, lay downstream in the sand, dead or wounded. Next to George a man bravely defended his wife and two daughters. George remembered: "He jumped out of the hole and ran towards the troops that were coming upon us, and as he came back into the hole he told me and his wife that he was killed." Blood gushed from the man's mouth and he fell face forward into the pit.[83]

Spotted Horse realized they were all in a death trap. Soldiers were even now approaching from the opposite bank and would soon be in position to fire directly into their pit. George, too, recognized the danger. With Spotted Horse and Bear Shield, he scrambled from the hole. The others remained behind, too frightened to move.

The three men ran downstream, dodging bullets as they went. George looked back to see soldiers on the bank pouring a steady fire into the position he had just left. He could hear the screams of the women and children and knew they would be slaughtered.[84]

Then he saw Black Kettle. It seemed impossible, but the old chief was alive. Beneath an overhanging bluff he and others had dug a long trench. It was a strong defensive position. They had used their bare hands to form a protective mound of sand on the exposed side of the dugout.

George ran toward Black Kettle and safety. A few yards from the pit, however, a bullet slammed into his hip, knocking him forward and down into the trench. Stunned, he lay motionless in the dampness of the sand, pain shooting through his leg.[85]

On the high bluff overlooking the village Colonel John Milton Chivington sat his black horse. Next to him, watching the carnage below, stood Robert Bent. From this vantage point they could plainly see a six-by-twelve-foot American flag above Black Kettle's lodge. Even through the din of battle, Robert could hear the chief shouting for the people to gather around the flag. Then, as the soldiers charged toward the village, he heard Chivington yell, "Remember our wives and children murdered on the Platte and Arkansas!"[86]

Only the day before, Robert and his father had been at the Purgatoire stockade. In mid-afternoon, Chivington and his command surprised and surrounded the ranch. Chivington herded the Bents—Mary and Rob Moore, William, and Robert—into the ranch house and placed them under arrest. An armed guard was posted at the doors and around the corral. The Bents were ordered to stay inside; anyone who attempted to leave would be shot. Presently, Chivington called Robert outside. His command needed a guide, one who knew the location of the Cheyenne village on Sand Creek. He had already pressed Jim Beckwourth into service, but now the old mountain man, reluctant to attack peaceful Cheyennes, claimed not to know the way. Chivington did not trust this black man who had lived among the Crows. Robert had no choice. He was already on the Fort Lyon payroll as a guide and interpreter. Chivington would brook no argument. The implication was unmistakable: Robert would guide or he would die.[87]

Now here he was, on a bluff overlooking the village, watching as the soldiers attacked his mother's people and his brothers and sister. Chivington rode off toward the village. He ordered Robert to stay close by. The twenty-five-year-old Bent witnessed horrors he would never forget.

He saw five women run out and tear their clothes off to show their sex. As they begged for mercy the soldiers shot them down. He saw a woman whose leg had been shattered by a shell fragment hold up her arm as protection from a saber-wielding soldier. The saber blow broke her arm. The woman rolled over and raised her other arm. The saber came down again, breaking that one, too. As she moaned in pain, the soldier looked down impassively, then rode off. He saw a group of women, huddled in a sandpit, send a six-year-old girl with a white flag toward the soldiers. The child had only walked a short way when the soldiers shot her. Then they turned their guns on the women and killed them all. He saw men, women, and children scalped and mutilated. He saw an unborn child cut from her mother's womb and deliberately laid beside her body. He saw infants killed in their mother's arms. He saw two soldiers stumble upon a baby hidden in a mound of sand. They drew their pistols and fired, then, dragging the child by an arm, yanked her out of the hole. He saw White Antelope dead, his genitals and ears cut off, and heard a soldier brag that he would make a tobacco pouch out of his scrotum. And he saw Charley taken prisoner, the soldiers looking for an excuse to shoot him. [88]

Like Jack Smith, Charley found no escape from the soldiers. The fighting at the pits above the village seemed hopeless, so he made his way back to Uncle John Smith's lodge. Somewhere along the way he met men of Company H of the Third Colorado, and a good thing, too. These Mexican scouts, under Lieutenant Mariano Autobee, recognized him as William Bent's son and brought him to Captain Silas S. Soule, one of the few company commanders who retained control over his men. Soule had strictly forbidden his company of First Colorado veterans from engaging in any of the day's atrocities. In fact, he had ordered the troopers to hold their fire during much of the morning's fighting. He also knew the Bents well and was sure that Charley would be killed once the Thirdsters—the self-styled "Hungate avengers"— discovered his presence. Soule escorted Charley to Smith's lodge, where soldiers guarded Jack, four captive children, and the Cheyenne wife of Charlie Windsor, the sutler at Fort Lyon.[89]

About two o'clock that afternoon Captain Soule saw a grim-faced Lieutenant Cramer of Company G, First Colorado. Cramer looked Soule in the eye, shook his head, and said, "I am ashamed of this." Sickened by the killings, Soule approached Chivington and asked the commander for permission to take Charley back to Fort Lyon with the wounded. Chivington had been outraged by Soule's conduct on the field that day and at first refused the captain's request. But he wanted the insubordinate Soule out of the way; his actions at Sand Creek had clearly proven him an enemy and a threat. The dark-faced colonel finally relented.

An hour later, Charley shared an ambulance with wounded Captain Presley Talbot of Company M, Third Colorado Cavalry, bound for Fort Lyon. During the jarring ride, Charley heard Captain Soule angrily denounce the Thirdsters as a "perfect mob—every man on his own hook." Soule made no secret of his disgust: "White Antelope, War Bonnet and a number of others had Ears and Privates cut off. Squaws snatches were cut out for trophies. You would think it impossible for white men to butcher and mutilate human beings as they did."[90]

At the fort, the provost confined Charley to the guardhouse, but Soule had saved his life. Locked in irons, the youngest Bent pulled at his chains and raged against his jailers. But at least, as a mixed-blood, he had had a chance. His full-blood friends and relatives had been shot on sight, for Chivington had ordered that no prisoners be taken. Even so, it had been a close call. In a few days, he was released to his father's custody.[91]

Jack Smith was not so lucky. Placed under guard at about the same time as Charley, he stayed in Smith's lodge to await his fate. With him through that afternoon and through the long night were his stepmother and father, along with Louderback and Clark. In the morning, soldiers pushed their way into the lodge and helped themselves to the baled buffalo robes, blankets, and other trade goods that belonged to John Smith. They took everything, claiming these "supplies" were needed for the two field hospitals located nearby. When Smith and Louderback protested, the soldiers threatened to shoot or hang them both.[92]

When news of the disturbance reached George Shoup, colonel of the Third Regiment, he posted a guard and ordered Jim Beckwourth to keep an eye on things. By noon, the guard had disappeared, but Beckwourth remained. John Smith would remember what happened next:

A soldier came up outside of the lodge and called me by name. I got up and went out; he took me by the arm and walked towards Colonel Chivington's camp, which was about sixty yards from my camp. Said he, "I am sorry to tell you, but they are going to kill your son Jack." I knew the feeling towards the whole camp of Indians, and that there was no use to make any resistance. I said, "I can't help it." I then walked on towards where Colonel Chivington was standing by his camp-fire; when I had got within a few feet of him and heard a gun fired, and saw a crowd run to my lodge, and they told me that Jack was dead.[93]

Beckwourth was in the lodge when the shooting occurred. He remembered that a group of ten or more soldiers forced their way into the lodge. When John Smith was called outside, Beckwourth was sitting across the fire from Jack, just six feet away. Then someone thrust a revolver through a hole in the lodgeskin and fired.

The bullet entered below his right breast. He sprung forward and fell dead, and the lodge scattered, soldiers, squaws, and everything else. I went out myself; as I went out I met a man with a pistol in his hand. He made this remark to me: he said, "I am afraid the damn son of a bitch is not dead, and I will finish him." Says I, "Let him go to rest; he is dead."[94]

When Chivington heard the shot, he feigned surprise: "Halloo; I wonder what that is?" Louderback, who was standing next to Chivington, mumbled under his breath, "No matter what a man has done, they ought to give him a show for his life." An officer heard the remark

148

and warned Louderback not to shoot "his mouth off around there about killing Indians."[95]

Teamster Clark was there, too. He remembered that when Jack was shot he "raised up and fell in the fire and I pulled him out." Clark remembered, too, that the naked and scalped bodies of White Antelope and his wife lay just outside the lodge. Whether the soldiers meant this as a grisly warning to "halfbreeds and Indian lovers,"[96] as Clark believed, the troopers made plain their hatred for mixed-bloods. Hal Sayre, a major of the Third Regiment, said no one mourned Jack's death. "As a matter of fact," he said, "some of the boys dragged the body out onto the prairie and hauled it about for a considerable time."[97]

When the shooting started early that morning, Little Bear, one of George's close friends, ran from the village to the upper sandpits, where George and Black Kettle had already found refuge. He later told George:

> After leaving the others, I started to run up the creek bed in the direction taken by most of the fleeing people, but I had not gone far when a party of about twenty cavalrymen got into the dry bed of the stream behind me. They chased me up the creek for about two miles, very close behind me and firing on me all the time. Nearly all the feathers were shot out of my war bonnet, and some balls passed through my shield; but I was not touched. I passed many women and children, dead and dying, lying in the creek bed. The soldiers had not scalped them yet, as they were busy chasing those that were yet alive. . . . I ran up the creek about two miles and came to the place where a large party of the people had taken refuge in holes dug in the sand up against the sides of the high banks.[98]

George looked up to see Little Bear jump into the pit. His friend looked frightful, his war bonnet in shreds and his shield riddled with bullet holes. But Little Bear had survived. Directly above Black Kettle's trench, soldiers thrust their guns over the bank and fired blindly into the creek bed. Warriors responded by arcing arrows up over the bank.

The soldiers were so close George could hear their orders, even their conversations. God he hated them, laughing as if they were on a hunting party and had cornered the game. All his life he had felt white arrogance, that smug superiority. But these soldiers were treating his people like animals. A bullet plowed into the sand just inches from his face. Enraged and numb to the awful pain in his hip, he jumped up and shouted in English, *"Come on, you goddamn white sons of bitches, and kill me if you are a brave man."*[99]

Suddenly, high above them, an artillery shell exploded, raining lead balls and shell fragments. The soldiers had moved their cannons upstream. Two mountain howitzers were positioned on the east bank; two more were moved onto the bluffs to the west. George understood this new danger, as he himself had served such guns in the Confederate army. The soldiers, he knew, would now fire spherical case shot, hollow iron balls filled with lead musket balls and a bursting charge of gunpowder. Case shot was designed to inflict fearful damage on people, not things. Fired properly, the balls would burst directly above their targets and shower death below. The soldiers might also fire canister, tin cans filled with more than a hundred lead musket balls.[100] At close range it was deadly. But here, beneath the bluffs and hidden in their trench with its sandy parapet, he thought his group was relatively safe from these shotgunlike charges. He worried more about the bursting shells and case shot. But these horse soldiers, pressed into service as artillerymen, were not well trained. He could see that their shots went wild and they cut their fuses too short. The sun now burned low in the western sky. If the people could hold out until dark, they might survive.

For those who were not well protected by deeply dug pits or who panicked and ran, death was certain. George could see around him the mangled bodies of men, women, and children who had taken shelter in shallow pits or who ran from their positions only to be struck down by the gauntlet of fire coming from both banks.

As night fell, the soldiers drew off. Only a few shots here and there broke the silence. Black Kettle looked about the trench. He could see most of his family. Nine nieces, ten sisters, and many cousins had been with him in the village. Some of them were here with him now, but his wife, *Ar-no-ho-wok*, Woman Here After, was not.[101] She lay somewhere back toward the village, dead. He would go back for her. George wanted to accompany him, but the stiffness in his hip was too great. Black Kettle would have to go alone.

Cautiously, the chief moved downstream. Finding his way by starlight alone, his steps made no sound in the soft sand. He went among the frozen bodies, turning them and feeling their faces. The bodies had been stripped, and many had been scalped and mutilated. The soldiers had cut off fingers and ears to remove rings and other silver ornaments.[102] He went on. As he approached the village, he saw more dark objects on the sand. His hands again moved across the corpses. Near where *Ar-no-ho-wok* fell, he saw movement. And then he heard a moan and recognized his wife. She was alive. Blood from nine wounds stained her clothing and body. He gently picked her up and carried her on his back, working his way upstream.[103]

George was waiting for him when he returned. It was time to leave. Black Kettle had seen the soldiers encamped at the village. They had formed a hollow square and built bonfires. Occasionally, nervous sentries fired blindly at sounds in the creek, fearing a counterattack by Cheyenne warriors. But the noises came mostly from Cheyenne rescue parties in search of the wounded. Scavenging coyotes, camp dogs, and wolves also frightened the soldiers, touching off flashes of gunfire.[104]

The survivors slowly moved out of the pits and headed upstream. About half the people were wounded, and many were nearly naked, their clothing left behind as they fled the soldiers. George could walk, for no bones were broken, but he was stiff and sore. After a few miles, they began to meet men who had managed to reach the horse herds at the beginning of the attack. They had driven all the loose horses upstream, away from the fighting, and waited there until the shooting stopped. Then they had moved downstream until they met George and the other survivors. George's cousin was among the herders. The boy apologized for bringing only one horse but said that he had only one lariat. George gladly accepted the pony, but his hip was so painful he could not mount. Several men lifted him onto the animal's back.

The party straggled northeast toward the headwaters of the Smoky Hill, where the Dog Soldiers and other Cheyennes who had not surrendered were encamped. Finally, after about ten miles, they reached a sheltering ravine. They could go no farther. Women and children suffered terribly from their wounds and the cold. George would remember this place and that night:

That was the worst night I ever went through. There we were . . . without any shelter whatever and not a stick of wood to build a fire with. Most of us were wounded and half naked; even those who had had time to dress when the attack came, had lost their buffalo robes and blankets during the fight. The men and women who were not wounded worked all through the night, trying to keep the children and the wounded from freezing to death. They gathered grass by the handful, feeding little fires around which the wounded and the children lay; they stripped off their own blankets and clothes to keep us warm, and some of the wounded who could not be provided with other covering were buried under piles of grass which their friends gathered, a handful at a time, and heaped up over them. That night will never be forgotten as long as any of us who went through it are alive. It was bitter cold, the wind had a full sweep over the ground on which we lay, and in spite of everything that was done, no one could keep warm. All through the night the Indians kept hallooing to attract the attention of those who had escaped from the village to the open plain and were wandering about in the dark, lost and freezing. Many who had lost wives, husbands, children, or friends, went back down the creek and crept over the battleground among the naked and mutilated bodies of the dead. Few were found alive, for the soldiers had done their work thoroughly; but now and then during that endless night some man or woman would stagger in among us, carrying some wounded person on their back.[105]

George's group now numbered nearly a hundred. The wounded ones, especially the children, were too weak to even cry. All the people were hungry and cold. At last, with no one able to sleep, Black Kettle gave the word to move on. But some warriors mumbled that the old chief had no right to lead anymore. Still, the people stirred and finally climbed out of the ravine, even though dawn was hours away.

At daybreak, the sun struck their faces, bringing warmth and hope, the endless night finally over. Soon riders came from the Smoky Hill camps, men who had picketed their finest horses near their lodges in Black Kettle's village and had ridden for help soon after the first shots rang out. Now they brought horses loaded with blankets, buffalo robes, and food.[106] George remembered that "people began to join us in little groups and parties. Before long we were all mounted, clothed, and fed, and then we moved at a better pace and with revived hope."[107]

Late in the day, the people saw the first smoke of the Cheyenne villages, their long, tortured journey nearly at an end. As they entered the camps, frantic villagers besieged them, searching for loved ones. Some were joyously reunited. Others had their worst fears confirmed. George later described the terrible scene:

> As we rode into that camp . . . everyone was crying, even the warriors and the women and children screaming and wailing. Nearly everyone present had lost some relations or friends, many of them in their grief were gashing themselves with their knives until the blood flowed in streams.[108]

All the camp was weeping. And George would never forget. Never.

Chapter 6

RIDING WITH THE
DOG SOLDIERS

The Dog Soldiers had camped at the head of the Smoky Hill River where the cottonwoods grew thick, a place the Cheyennes knew as "Bunch of Timbers." The trees dwarfed the tipis and heavy smoke hung low in the branches, for the women had built great bonfires as beacons. Sand Creek survivors streamed into the village, and George wondered at this. Given the fury of cannon and gunfire at Sand Creek, he thought it impossible that any of Black Kettle's people could have escaped. But every day more people came into the village, some afoot, some on horseback, many dragged on travois, too wounded or weak to walk. Within a week of the massacre, nearly 400 had found refuge among the renegade Dog Soldiers. No one knew with certainty how many had died, but, after speaking with other survivors, George reckoned the dead at 53 men and 110 women and children. He could learn nothing of Island and Charley, who were still missing.[1]

His childhood friend, Ed Guerrier, unwounded and leading a small party of relatives, had come in the day after George's arrival. Guerrier found George recuperating on a soft bed of buffalo robes, tended by women who had applied a poultice to the ugly gunshot wound in his hip. Luckily, the bullet had missed the bone and George would be able to stand in a matter of days. The friends reviewed the nightmarish events of the massacre, and with other eyewitnesses pieced together the awful reality of Sand Creek. Many tribal leaders had fallen, among them chiefs White Antelope, Standing Water, Lone Bear, War Bonnet, Spotted Crow, Two Thighs, Bear Man, Bear Robe, Yellow Shield, old Yellow Wolf, and the Arapaho Left Hand.[2]

The attack at Sand Creek decimated the Southern Cheyenne clans. Black Kettle's people suffered the most; only a few men survived. In contrast, most of Sand Hill's group, which had camped downstream away from Chivington's main path of attack, escaped with relatively few casualties. But Yellow Wolf's band was cut in half, including the eighty-five-year-old chief, the very man who had introduced William Bent to the Cheyennes thirty years before. Yellow Wolf's brother, Big Man, also fell. Most of War Bonnet's band lay dead on the frozen ground at Sand Creek. The Ridge Men, too, lost many people after their chief, White Antelope, was shot down early in the fighting. Chief Lone Bear, who lost an eye defending George's father in the old days, was killed, but most of his *Suhtaio* managed to escape. The Arapahos, always near to the Cheyennes, had also suffered. Not only had Chief Left Hand been killed, but of the fifty or so Arapahos present only four survived. The *Masikota* clan and several of the Cheyenne bands that had remained on the Smoky Hill with the Dog Soldiers were the only ones not directly affected by the slaughter at Sand Creek. But all Cheyennes had lost friends and relatives.[3]

Even those who had escaped unwounded faced hardship. The troops had stolen or destroyed everything: horses, lodges, clothing, camp kettles and utensils, and the entire winter store of food. Now, the survival of Black Kettle's destitute people depended on the charity of the Dog Men and Lakota and Arapaho friends.

George worried that the war faction would now question Black Kettle's leadership. The chief had been the leading proponent of peace. He had gone to Camp Weld and returned to persuade the people to trust the whites—and he had led them to Sand Creek. Even as the soldiers attacked and the bullets tore through the lodges, he had urged his people to remain calm and not fight back. George loved the old man but wondered how one so wise could have been so taken in by the whites. How could he have trusted them? George felt shame for the white man's blood that flowed through his veins, but his anxiety lessened when he learned that the council chiefs were urging the grieving and angry people not to cast Black Kettle aside. Such a great leader should not be shunned for one lapse of judgment, they said, and many still regarded him as the strongest of the Cheyenne Council of Forty-four.

And so, when the chiefs gathered to decide what the people should do, Black Kettle took his usual place among them. Everyone agreed Sand Creek must be avenged. But there were questions. Why had the soldiers attacked with such viciousness? Why had they killed and mutilated women and children? It seemed that the conflict with the whites had somehow changed. No longer was it just a war over land and buffalo. Now, the soldiers were destroying everything Cheyenne—the land, the buffalo, and the people themselves.

Why? George thought he knew. He had lived among the whites and had fought in their war. He knew their greed for land and possessions—their appetite for these things was boundless. But they also obeyed rules of warfare peculiar to them. They waged war on men, and only on recognized fields of battle. In the great life-and-death struggle between North and South even then raging in the East, prisoners were routinely paroled and released or held in guarded camps, where they were fed and cared for. And the whites never warred on women and children, who were protected by law and by an unshakable code of honor.

George would not presume to interrupt the council and tell the chiefs why the whites fought the Cheyennes differently than their own people. But he knew that the answer to this question was as startling as it was brutal. Men like Chivington did not see the Cheyennes as people but as vermin to be exterminated, adults and children. Chivington had said: "kill all—little and big—nits make lice."[4] But how was he to explain this to the Cheyennes and the Dog Soldiers, who believed themselves to be superior to all others? That anyone would think the Cheyennes inferior would be beyond their comprehension. It was useless to try and explain. But he could at least go to Black Kettle and help him understand that the coming war would be for the very survival of the Cheyennes and their way of life.

Still, Black Kettle counseled peace. A war with the whites, he said, could not be won. The newcomers were too numerous, their weapons too strong. Besides, they had the ability to fight even in winter when Cheyenne horses were weak and food was scarce. Endless lines of army and civilian wagons, filled with food and supplies, rolled the trails and split the great buffalo herds. There was no escape from these people. For Black Kettle, Cheyenne survival depended on peace. War would only bring more Sand Creeks, more deaths, more sorrow.

But his powers of persuasion failed him. One by one the council chiefs smoked the red stone war pipe, each recognizing the importance of his decision. When the pipe reached Black Kettle, he passed it on, refusing to smoke. But the others took it up, indicating they would fight. The chiefs sent leading warriors to carry the war pipe to the Lakotas on the Solomon River and to the Northern Arapahos on the Republican. George agreed with Black Kettle's assessment of the soldiers' capacity to make war, but like most other Cheyenne men, he felt the need to blood his lance and exact revenge for Sand Creek. Caught up in the war fever, he and Guerrier accompanied the pipe bearers and watched the allied chiefs, each in his own camp, take up the pipe and smoke.

After the Lakota chiefs had smoked and agreed to join the war, George hurried home to see his father at the Purgatoire River ranch. He needed to tell him about Sand Creek and of the war that would soon engulf Colorado and the Great Plains. Ed agreed to go with him. As they went about securing horses, old Chief Grey Beard told them that the allied villages would soon move and consolidate on Cherry Creek, a branch of the Republican. Just as they left the camp, fifteen-year-old Howling Wolf, another Sand Creek survivor, joined them. The three rode slowly, never pushing their horses, for George's hip wound still bothered him, especially after his long ride with the pipe bearers.[5]

The weather turned cold, but the sky remained clear. The riders reached the Arkansas a few miles above Fort Lyon and climbed a high bluff overlooking the river. Below them sprawled a military camp, the busy bluecoats silhouetted against the white canvas of their tipi-shaped Sibley tents. Surprisingly, the soldiers were singing. George could hear the cheery strains of familiar carols that took him to his childhood at Bent's Fort. Then he remembered. It was Christmas Eve. He turned to Guerrier to share his discovery but saw only fear in his friend's dark eyes. Guerrier was in no mood for reminiscing. The sight of so many soldiers panicked him. He was sure that if they continued on to the Bent stockade, still fifteen miles upriver, the soldier patrols would cut their trail and track them down. The only hope lay in surrender. George thought this was madness. Surrender would be suicide. But Guerrier refused to listen, and the two friends separated.

George watched anxiously as Ed turned his pony toward the soldier camp. Ed had always been a good talker and had a knack for getting out of tough spots. Besides, with his command of languages he could pass himself off as Mexican, or even white. But George knew that he himself could not go down to the fort, parley with the soldiers, and keep his temper in check. Those bluecoats were murderers. He would not lick their boots, nor would he again let himself be confined in a Yankee jail. Without waiting to see how Guerrier fared, he jabbed his heels into his horse's flanks, and with Howling Wolf following, headed west for the Purgatoire stockade.

After a long night and a day of avoiding soldier patrols, the tired riders arrived just as the Bents were sitting down to enjoy their Christmas dinner. The dinner stopped abruptly when the two Indians stepped into the candlelit dining hall. At first no one recognized them, dressed as they were in the clothes they had gotten from the Dog Soldiers. But George spoke up, perhaps even wished them "Merry Christmas," and the family rushed to greet him.

The unexpected reunion held surprises for everyone. The family had thought George dead, and George was amazed to find that his stepmother Island, along with two other women and three children, had been taken prisoner at Sand Creek and released to his father's custody. Bob was at the ranch as well. He had survived his ordeal and now revealed to George that Charley had also escaped death. Captain Silas S. Soule, who had refused to allow his company to fire on the peaceful village, had rescued Charley and escorted him to Fort Lyon. After nearly a week in irons, the youngest Bent had been released from the guardhouse and immediately rode for the Dog Soldier camps on the Smoky Hill.[6] Mary was safe at the ranch with her husband Robison Moore. George reported that Julia, too, was in the Dog Soldier villages; somehow, she had survived the massacre without a scratch.

The next day, William took George aside. There were things about Sand Creek he should know. Bob had no choice but to lead the troops to the village. Chivington's Thirdsters had surrounded the house and were threatening to kill the whole family. If it had not been for Colonel Tappan's sudden appearance, there would have been a massacre at the stockade as well. When Tappan rode in, he had with him twenty men of the First Colorado Cavalry—the Veteran Battalion. These were the men who had whipped the Texans at Glorieta Pass in New Mexico in 1862. They were tough soldiers who had seen real combat, and they had no stomach for killing women and children. When they pulled in to the ranch they unslung their carbines, formed a skirmish line, and faced Chivington's recruits, who had their weapons leveled on the Bents. This was too much for the Thirdsters, who backed down in a hurry—they were afraid to buck so many real soldiers. William also wanted him to understand that Captain Soule and Lieutenant Joe Cramer were friends of the Bents and the Cheyennes. He said that these men had not burned powder at Sand Creek. Soule had even called the Thirdsters "cowardly Sons of Bitches" for attacking and butchering defenseless people. Now, Chivington and Major Jacob Downing were gunning for both of them. Cramer and Soule were no safer than the Bents.[7]

George asked about the fight itself. He had been dug in and never had a clear view of the slaughter around him, and neither did the other survivors. The old man recounted the horror as he had heard it from Cramer. The lieutenant had told him that "women and children were scalped, fingers cut off to get the rings on them, and this as much with Officers as men, and one of those officers a Major; and a Lt. Col. Cut off Ears of all he came across—squaw ripped open and a child taken from her, little children shot, while begging for their lives, women shot while on their knees, and with their arms around soldiers a begging for their lives, and all the indignities shown their bodies that ever was heard of, things that Indians would be ashamed to do." Captain Soule had witnessed how the bodies "were all scalped, and as high as half a dozen taken from one head. They were all horribly mutilated. One woman was cut open, and a child taken out of her, and scalped."[8] William wanted his son to understand that he and Bob were doing all they could to stop Chivington. Along with Soule, Cramer, Wynkoop, and Tappan, they would testify before specially convened congressional committees and tell what they knew—they would tell them everything.

For George, it was not enough.

George rested at the ranch for almost a week, the gash on his hip healing rapidly. Cavalry patrols rode by every day, an ominous reminder that the army continued to view the family with suspicion. Colonel Bent was a squaw man whose first loyalty was not to the government but to his halfbreed children and the Cheyennes. Even though William posted lookouts at all the approaches to the stockade, George knew he could not remain long; his presence put them all at risk. On New Year's Day 1865, he led Howling Wolf, Island, and the other Cheyenne captives north to join the Dog Soldiers on Cherry Creek, where the boundaries of Kansas, Colorado, and Nebraska came together.[9]

After four days of hard travel, George's party entered a village of nearly five thousand people, the scattered lodge circles stretching in every direction as far as the eye could see. All the Southern Cheyenne bands were here, including Black Kettle's. Camped nearby were Spotted Tail's Brule Lakotas and Pawnee Killer's Oglalas.

Here, too, were the Dog Soldiers, once reviled by the Cheyennes as renegades, now revered as war leaders and the tribe's best hope for survival. The elders had explained to George that through the years, ever since the exile of Porcupine Bear and his followers, the Dog Soldiers had grown and developed into a separate division of the Cheyenne Nation. Intermarriage with Lakotas had changed not only their dress and traditions but their language as well. Chief Tall Bull— *Tatanka Haska*—himself was half Sioux and fluent in both Cheyenne and Lakota.

George was drawn to the Dog Men and their Northern Cheyenne and Lakota allies. He thought them "wild Indians." Their hide clothing, unusual feathered headdresses, and warlike ways held a strange fascination for him.[10] The Dog Soldiers had always resisted white encroachment—they had no choice—located as they were along the Platte and Smoky Hill River trails. Conflict with westering emigrants and soldiers was inevitable. The Overland route, favored by the whites, had divided the great herds of buffalo and antelope, which fled from the newcomers' wagons and guns. Early on, the whites had shown themselves to be unpredictable and not worthy of trust, for their wagons brought disease and death. The Dog Men shunned them, even refusing offers of peaceful trade, and attacked the intruders on sight. Many believed the disaster at Sand Creek had proved their wisdom. Now, in the war to come, the allied tribes turned to Tall Bull, Bull Bear, and White Horse for leadership.[11]

While George had been away, several small war parties raided ranches along the South Platte. But now the whole village buzzed with talk of a great coordinated attack on the white settlement at Julesburg and nearby Camp Rankin on the Overland Trail in northeast Colorado. Chiefs assigned warrior societies to guard the village, not against enemy attack but to prevent impetuous young men from joining war parties and attacking the enemy prematurely. They cautioned the warriors that the move on Julesburg must be a surprise. If all went according to plan, decoys would draw the soldiers out of the fort, while the allied warriors, nearly a thousand strong, would remain hidden in the sand hills to the south. When the soldiers followed the decoys into the hills, the trap would spring shut.

George had already made his decision: he would ride with the warriors in their war against the bluecoats. In doing this, he was going against both Black Kettle and his father. The old man had reminded him that he had signed an oath of allegiance and sworn not to take up arms against the United States. But George argued that he had signed as a Confederate soldier, not as a Cheyenne warrior. The murder and betrayal of Sand Creek had changed everything—he would join the Dog Soldiers to avenge his people. Rearmed at his father's ranch and now well mounted, he was ready to kill bluecoats wherever he found them. Twenty-one years old, in the prime of life, tall and muscular, he exuded a confidence born of combat experience. An expert horseman and familiar with all weaponry—Indian and white—he was respected by his Crooked Lance brothers and their new Dog Soldier allies.[12]

Charley, now nineteen, leaner than George and not as tall, was already with the Dog Men, raiding ranches along the South Platte River. He had been humiliated by his capture and confinement at Fort Lyon, where he had been shackled like a dog, held prisoner with women and children, and tormented by his guards. Only the power of the Bent name had saved him. These memories haunted him. Now he burned for revenge. To prove himself he would fight with the Dog Soldiers and show his enemies no mercy.[13]

The brothers rode side by side as the allied warriors left the Cherry Creek camp on January 6, 1865. Trusted society men guarded the front, rear, and flanks of the column. At the head rode the Dog Soldier and Lakota chiefs, for they knew the way and had been the first

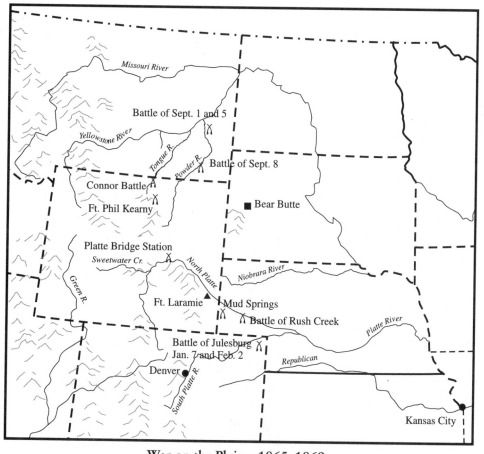

War on the Plains, 1865–1869

to take up the war pipe. The Arapaho and Cheyenne chiefs followed. Then came the main body of warriors, and behind them a number of boys and women, who had come along to lead pack ponies.[14]

The chiefs led this force northwest toward Julesburg. There was no straggling, and the order of it all impressed George. This was not a mob bent on revenge but a disciplined body of men moving with a unity of purpose. Never before had the tribes gone to war on such a grand scale. Every warrior—George and Charley included—knew he was a part of something unprecedented. The tragedy at Sand Creek had brought three great tribes together, for they now understood that no one tribe alone could defeat the white invaders. The survival of the plains tribes and their very way of life depended on cooperation and discipline.

Before the chiefs and the great host of Indians arrived on the South Platte, Dog Soldier wolves scouted the Julesburg area. Near the river in the broad, flat valley stood a crudely fashioned earthen breastwork, roughly square, surrounding a cluster of sod and adobe buildings. A flag fluttered atop a pole in the center of the compound, marking this as Camp Rankin, garrisoned by a company of the Seventh Iowa Cavalry. Less than a mile to the east, about two hundred yards from the riverbank, the Cheyenne scouts spied the Overland Stage Station, sutler's store, and large government warehouses, which together made Julesburg an important supply depot. Drooping lengths of iron wire connected the rough-hewn telegraph poles, which ran parallel to the road. The valley itself had been stripped of every stick of wood. The grass and all but the prickliest cacti had long since been cropped and consumed by the voracious animals of gold seekers, emigrants, and soldiers. Cattle, horses, and mules had been herded into large, well-constructed adobe corrals. The scouts reported that the bounty of the storehouses and the size of the herds were just as the Lakotas had earlier indicated. And the whites suspected nothing.

That night George hid himself with the other warriors in the sand hills overlooking the stage station. Thinking back on his war experience in the East, he marveled that so many men and horses could be so near the enemy and not be discovered.

The excitement among the warriors ran high. The night was clear and cold, and few could sleep. Long before daylight, whispered instructions passed from man to man and everyone began preparing for battle. George painted his face as the Crooked Lance elders had taught him. He dressed in his finest clothes, ready for victory or death. Around him, some of the warriors carefully removed war bonnets from rawhide cases and presented them to the four directions; others placed horned buffalo caps on their heads; still others adorned themselves with feathers and stuffed birds. Most parted their hair in long braids into which they wove otter fur or red and blue woolen trade cloth. George gathered the hair on the top of his head and braided it into a short scalp lock. He had decided to let his hair grow like the other warriors, and hoped that soon it would be long enough to decorate with disks of hammered silver. Many of the Cheyennes wore fringed and painted war shirts, over which they placed breastplates made from bone and beads. Stroud cloth breechclouts and buckskin or cloth leggings protected their legs, and beaded moccasins with colorful geometric designs covered their feet. Moonlight reflected from their polished silver pectorals and armbands, and from their abalone shell eardrops.

Their weapons were as varied as their dress. They carried lances, shields, bows and arrows, tomahawks, and knives. He saw only a few guns and counted himself lucky to have his father's fine carbine when others had only cut-down muskets, obsolete rifles, and short-ranged pistols.

Shields, war bonnets, and lances required special attention and sacred rituals peculiar to each warrior society. The men carefully prepared their warhorses, painting them with vividly colored handprints, circles, and slashes to enhance the animal's performance and to show off battle coups and honors. They had notched the ears of their fleetest horses and now clubbed, braided, or cropped their tails, sometimes adding eagle feathers and trade cloth. Medicine bundles bearing roots, stones, and other sacred objects were tied to the horses' necks or carried on the warriors' bodies, but George could not help but wonder whether these rituals, so earnestly applied, would protect his friends when the soldiers got them in their sights. Some men also tied human scalps to the ornamented bridles, a time-honored ritual calculated to terrify enemies. The warriors preferred to ride into combat unencumbered by saddles, but George still preferred his father's Mexican saddle. Though he was an excellent horseman, he knew some of the young men around him could put the most talented circus riders to shame. The Cheyennes were born to the horse—light cavalry like the world had never seen.[15]

The chiefs selected Big Crow to lead the decoy party. George knew him well, for he was the headman of George's own warrior society, the Crooked Lances. At daybreak, Big Crow and ten picked men, most no older than George, slowly worked their way down a draw that snaked out of the sand hills toward the river and Camp Rankin. Using this cover, they approached to within pistol shot of the fort, then rose out of the gully and charged the unsuspecting sentinels, shooting and yelling as they went. George heard the soldiers' return fire and the familiar notes of a bugle sounding "Boots and Saddles." Then he saw thirty-seven troopers in sky-blue greatcoats lead their horses from behind the fort's walls, mount, and ride directly toward Big Crow and the decoys.

His excitement grew. How could these foolish soldiers be tricked by such an obvious ruse? But Big Crow and his men were superb, employing subtle deceptions to lead the inexperienced soldiers on. The chiefs signaled the criers to alert the gathered warriors to be ready to charge, but this was unnecessary. Everyone could see the soldiers gain on the decoys, who again checked their horses, expertly feigning fatigue, to encourage the bluecoats. Once the soldiers galloped past the stage station, they were beyond the protection of the fort's guns. Within minutes the riders approached the edge of the sand hills and the impatient warriors.

Suddenly, a group of eager young men bolted from the sand hills and charged the distant troopers. The trap so carefully laid was ruined. The soldiers reined in their mounts and stared in disbelief at the sand hills. The horizon erupted with the charge of nearly a thousand warriors. Terror-stricken, the soldiers wheeled their horses and madly dashed for the safety of Camp Rankin. George heard another bugle blast. Incredibly, the frightened cavalrymen dismounted to fight on foot. This may have been an accepted tactic in the East, but here it was madness—George knew the Cheyennes would immediately close in for the kill.

The decoys now turned on their pursuers, smashing into the confused knot of men just three hundred yards from the fort. One of the dismounted soldiers was a bugler, a tall, young sergeant. Starving Elk, a well-known Crooked Lance, rode in and counted first coup on him. Then Old Crow, his face painted red and mounted on a big bay, struck the man with a saber and fired a bullet into his right cheek. Blood gushed from the soldier's mouth, splattering his uniform coat. Medicine Water followed Old Crow and grabbed the reins of the bugler's horse, taking it as a prize.[16]

George joined the running fight. He saw Whirlwind, a green stripe painted across his broad nose, carrying his distinctive bear-paw shield as he bore down on a group of retreating cavalrymen. Whirlwind lanced one soldier in the back, then drew his revolver and fired at another, eager to capture the bluecoat's fine Appaloosa. The fleeing soldiers returned fire, but their bullets hissed harmlessly over Whirlwind's head.[17]

George rode past other warriors engaged in hand-to-hand fights and joined Charley in the charge on the stage station. As they galloped in, George saw the passengers tumble out of the station house, the tails of their frock coats flying and as they ran, clutching their hats, for the fort. He could see the full-bearded express messenger, wearing a yellow sack coat, jump on the back of a big buckskin, which he had just unhitched from the stage. The white man grabbed the horse's lead rope and, clutching its mane, drove his heels into the animal's flanks and rode for his life toward the fort's stockade. At that moment, Big Crow veered off from the main body of warriors to take up the chase. Wearing a red-speckled war shirt and swinging his rawhide quirt over his head, he closed on the stage man as civilians and soldiers at the fort offered covering fire. Just as the man reached the walls of the stockade, Big Crow brought his quirt down hard on the fleeing man's back, a brilliant coup.[18]

George recognized the bravery of the act but still could not understand why Big Crow had let the enemy live. He and all the warriors had been told that this fight was to the death—a fight for the survival of the people. Yet, Big Crow seemed satisfied to humiliate the white man by lashing him with his whip but allowing him to live. For the Indians, this was the time-honored way of fighting. But George knew that the Cheyennes would have to learn the white way of war. Killing the enemy was more important than counting coup.

The Indians killed fifteen soldiers in the running fight; several civilians, caught in the open, fell as well. A number of warriors were wounded, but no one was killed. It was a victory, but not the victory hoped for. More than half the soldiers who had been drawn out of the fort made it back and now lobbed exploding howitzer shells toward the Indians who were ransacking the Julesburg stage station, sutler store, and government warehouses. The crash of the cannons frightened many of the warriors at first, but artillery held no mystery for George, who reassured his companions, instructing them to stay out of range of the small twelve-pounder mountain guns.

At the station, George found that "breakfast had just been put on the table and was still hot. I sat down with several Indians and ate a good meal. It was the first meal I had eaten at a table for a long time."[19] He stuffed himself with hot buttered biscuits and laughed as an old warrior with a sweet tooth tied a large bowl of sugar to his belt and awkwardly mounted his horse. Meanwhile, in the adjoining warehouses, warriors plundered sacks of cornmeal, sides of bacon, and barrels of syrup and molasses. The mountain of canned goods, however, mystified them. When they cut through the tin, the stink of sardines, corn oysters, and tomatoes repulsed them. But during a lull in the fighting, George explained that these delicacies were quite edible and slurped an oyster as proof—to the amazement and disgust of his friends.[20]

As George searched the station, he discovered an express package addressed to a soldier. He slashed it open and found inside a new frock coat with nine brass buttons and piping on the sleeves. He tried it on for size. It fit perfectly. Then and there he resolved to wear it in the fighting to come. He had captured this Yankee officer's uniform, and now, as a Cheyenne warrior, he would use its power against his enemies. But as a former Rebel, he would also wear it to humiliate the hateful bluecoats. He would wear it proudly and defiantly.[21]

George heard the boom of a distant cannon, followed seconds later by the deafening crack of a bursting shell just above the station. He ran outside and saw that the troops were deliberately firing high, hoping to scare the Indians away from the storehouses without destroying government property. He warned his friends to stay near the buildings; they would be safe there. And so the riot of looting went on. Years later he recalled:

Some of the warriors found a big tin box and knocked the lock off. It was full of pieces of green paper. The Indians handled the paper but did not know what it was. One man took a big bundle of paper, chopped it into three or four pieces with his tomahawk, and then threw it up in the air, laughing as the wind blew the fragments across the valley.[22]

But George knew the value of the money, and he figured it might come in handy if he once again found himself in the white world. He jumped off his horse and madly chased the paper, stuffing as many of the greenbacks as he could grab into the pockets of his frock coat. As he said later, "I secured a good deal of the money, but the Indians had already emptied the paymaster's box."[23]

He felt no pity as the warriors went among the dead troopers, scalping the bodies and stripping them of weapons and clothing. When they came to the bugler, killed by Starving Elk and Old Crow, they left behind his blood-soaked shirt—it was of no use to them now.[24]

They continued to plunder the warehouses as the boys and women came up with the packhorses and busied themselves lashing barrels and sacks to the animals' backs. A few Cheyennes lassoed wagons and attempted to pull them with their war ponies, an effort they soon abandoned. Some of the men got ready to burn the warehouses, but the chiefs stopped them, pointing out that if the buildings were left standing the Indians could return when the whites had refilled them.[25]

As the soldiers peered cautiously from behind the fort's walls, the warriors finally rode off, driving before them herds of captured horses, mules, and cattle. The pack animals were so heavily burdened that it took three days to reach the main encampment on Cherry Creek.

By the time the last of the pack-weary ponies stumbled into the village, scalp dances were already in progress. Not a single warrior had been killed in the fighting, a cause for great rejoicing. George danced with the others and later described the scene:

Ever since Sand Creek the Cheyennes had been mourning for the dead, but now that the first blow had been struck in revenge, everyone began to feel better, and that night the young men and young women held scalp dances in all the camps, for all the soldiers who had been killed at Julesburg had been scalped by the warriors, and the young people kept up the dances and drumming until after daylight.[26]

The allied warriors stayed on Cherry Creek for three days. During this time the chiefs met in council to decide what should be done next. Their first concern was for the safety of the women and children and the elderly. They decided to move north, away from the Platte River Road toward Powder River country and the Black Hills. All the while, the celebrations continued. George realized that the Indians had never consumed so much "white man's food"; the variety and quantity were unprecedented. Tomahawks and knives were put to new uses prying open tinned wonders, for which the people soon acquired a taste.

The women had never prepared this new food and came to George with many questions. They were particularly intrigued with the red catsup, corked tight in octagonal glass bottles, that they had found in large quantities. George explained that catsup made anything taste good. So the women mixed together candied fruits, imported cheese, olives, oysters, covering all with catsup—bottle upon bottle. The concoction sickened scores of people, including many warriors. Although no one directly blamed George for the stomach cramps, some in camp whispered about him. He was, after all, *vehoe*, a white man. Many remembered, too, that his own brother had led the bluecoats to Sand Creek. Could any halfbreed be trusted? George learned of the whispers from friends and knew he would have to be more careful about sharing his knowledge of white ways. This knowledge was power— but he had to use it carefully. His influence depended on trust. If he made mistakes, his whiteness would be used against him and the whisperers could become dangerous. He recalled stories his mother had told him of how his grandfather, White Thunder, had been criticized by men jealous of his power. They attempted to discredit him, circulating rumors about his northern *Suhtai* heritage. He was not truly *Tsistsistas*—pure Cheyenne—they said and not worthy to carry the Sacred Arrows. Like his grandfather, George knew what it was to be an outsider and resolved to be more careful in the future and to seek opportunities to prove himself.[27]

In mid-January 1865 the great village moved northwest to a well-known camping site at White Butte Creek. George had seen the place identified on maps as Summit Springs. Here, in the middle of the high, dry plains of northeastern Colorado, the village reassembled, each tribe camping in its own circle of tipis. Cheyenne scouts brought news that a large force of horse soldiers with cannons had searched the Republican River and had discovered the recently abandoned village site on Cherry Creek. George learned that these Nebraska volunteer troops were under the command of General Robert B. Mitchell. But the bluecoats headed east, away from the encampment. Mitchell's incompetence amazed George. How could this officer, not more than a day's march away from the great village, have missed the Indian trail? But it was probably for the best. If the soldiers had found the allied tribes, George believed there would have been a terrible battle, for the warriors would have fought to the death to protect their women and children, the nightmare of Sand Creek still fresh.[28]

At White Buttes the chiefs had another council, agreeing to continue the trek north to the Black Hills and the northern tribes. As the village moved, the warriors made coordinated assaults on the South Platte Road along a one hundred-mile front. The plan called for a three-pronged attack in which the Cheyennes would strike west of Julesburg toward Denver, the Arapahos would raid the Julesburg area, and the Lakotas would hit wagons, stations, and ranches along the Platte River Road east of Julesburg.[29]

Black Kettle opposed the decision and continued to urge peace, arguing that the young men had sufficiently avenged Sand Creek. More attacks would only bring soldiers and trouble. But the chiefs and headmen rejected his counsel. And so Black Kettle announced he would lead eighty lodges of his loyal followers south to the Arkansas, where he would meet up with the Southern Arapahos, Kiowas, and Comanches.[30]

Although Black Kettle was his mentor and friend, George could not go with him. He thought the chief right in his belief that the Indians could not win this war, but it was too soon to forgive the whites and make peace—they had not paid enough for Sand Creek. He would ride and fight with the Dog Soldiers.

The day before the village moved north, he went over to Black Kettle's camp to bid the old man farewell. While there he went around to the lodges to grasp the hands of his friends Little Robe, Bear Tongue, Red Moon, and others who had been with him at Sand Creek. Some of these men had families, and he could understand their reluctance to expose them to the dangers of war, especially in winter when the people needed to conserve their scant supplies of food and forage.[31]

As the allied village crossed the South Platte, the three war parties went their separate ways. George rode with one hundred warriors up the Platte toward Valley Station, twenty-five miles west. On January 28, the party struck American Ranch, a way station three miles east of Valley Station, running off more than five hundred head of fat cattle and burning one hundred tons of government hay. Then the warriors herded the cattle downstream, crossed on the ice to the north side of the river, and made camp, making no effort to hide their fires or their position.

The next morning, a company of cavalry found them and attempted to recover the stolen stock, but George's companions knew exactly what to do. Selecting a few of the lean and sick animals, they drove them away from the main herd. The strays distracted the troops, who immediately broke off the pursuit to round them up. The warriors then drove the remaining cattle to a place of safety on the north bluffs, while a scouting party recrossed the ice and followed the soldiers toward Denver, skirmishing all the way. In the day's action, the Indians killed two soldiers while suffering no casualties themselves.[32]

Over the next few days, the war parties attacked every ranch, every station, every outpost, and anything that moved on the South Platte River Road. Years later, George relived the excitement of these great raids:

> I did not see a tenth of the things that happened along the South Platte during those stirring days, but I saw many strange things. At night the whole valley was lighted up with the flames of burning ranches and stage stations, but these places were soon all destroyed and darkness fell on the valley. Our big village strung along the north bank of the river for some distance, the Cheyennes, Sioux [Lakotas], and Northern Arapahos camped separately, but all the camps near together. In every camp the fires were burned all night, and until daylight feasting and dancing and drumming went on. I

remember that, when I was out with raiding parties at night, we used to halt and look for the campfires to tell which way the village lay, and when we could not see the fires we would listen for the drums. On a still night you could hear them for miles and miles along the valley.[33]

On the January 29, 1865, George reached the main village on the north side of the South Platte, just opposite Harlow's Ranch west of Julesburg. The women killed and butchered the fattest cattle and everyone ate their fill of fresh beef, not as tasty as buffalo but acceptable given the season. Other parties brought in captured food and goods—bacon, hams, flour, sugar, rice, cornmeal, shelled corn, molasses, canned meat and fruits, hardware, silk, dress goods, clothing, boots, shoes, bolts of cloth, and many strange and wonderful household items and personal effects.

The celebration was justified. The raids had been well coordinated, and few men had been wounded. But then came disturbing news. George learned that the day before Cheyenne and Arapaho warriors had crossed the river and killed the ranchmen at Harlow's and captured a woman. While plundering the station, the warriors uncovered a cache of whiskey and many of them quickly got drunk. A young Cheyenne crazed with liquor accidentally shot one of the Arapahos, killing him instantly. This cast a sobering pall over the entire village.[34]

Another incident made an even deeper impression on George. A group of nine recently discharged Colorado volunteers had blundered into a Cheyenne war party on the South Platte Road. The warriors killed all the men without hesitation or mercy. But as they went through the troopers' baggage, they made a horrifying discovery— Cheyenne scalps taken at Sand Creek. The warriors instinctively recoiled from the unlucky reminders of death. In battle they would take scalps, but these were the remains of Cheyennes. Only women and holy men could safely handle the dead without bringing misfortune to themselves and their families. One scalp they identified as belonging to Little Coyote by the small seashell tied to the tightly braided scalp lock; another they identified as White Leaf by the scalp's unusually light color. Both men had been at Sand Creek, and neither had been seen since. These grisly trophies had not been cleaned and stretched on willow hoops, Cheyenne fashion, but were crusted with dried blood and appeared to have been clumsily cut and torn from the skulls. In a frenzy of revenge, the warriors split open the breast of one of the soldiers and ripped out his heart, then scalped the other white men and hacked their bodies to pieces. The discovery of the scalps reopened the wound of Sand Creek.[35]

The raiders now swept all the ranches and stations east and west of Julesburg, carrying off everything. George's party moved up the Platte to Gillette's ranch, nine miles west of Julesburg, destroying telegraph poles as it went. At Gillette's they stripped the station and fired everything, even the surrounding grass. But they could not destroy the iron machinery that they found loaded on an abandoned caravan of heavy freight wagons, equipment George knew was headed for the Colorado mines.[36] He looked closely at the machinery, especially a huge cast iron flywheel, and suddenly realized that its smooth, finished rim was the perfect place to leave a message. He grabbed a lump of charcoal from a nearby fire pit, then in large, clear script—one that would have made his old teacher Reverend Scarritt proud—scrawled, "Go to Hell." George rode on to rejoin the war party, satisfied that any whites who chanced to pass would know the Bent boys were among the Sand Creek avengers.[37]

On the morning of February 2, the big village again moved north, the Lakotas in the lead. Before the warriors left the South Platte Valley the chiefs had decided to again attack Julesburg, for they believed the soldiers and stage men would have had enough time to restock the warehouses. A thousand Cheyenne, Arapaho, and Lakota horsemen descended on the outpost. Again, decoys tried to draw the bluecoats from the fort, but this time the tactic failed. So the warriors charged, circled the stockade, and taunted the soldiers with shouts and obscene gestures. But nothing could draw the white men out. The chiefs devised a new strategy. The warriors would plunder the storehouses in plain view of the fort, and then burn the buildings one by one. Perhaps this would prompt a reaction. First they fired the stage station and telegraph office, then one after the other, the sutler's store, warehouses, and stables. Great columns of smoke billowed into the air visible up and down the valley for miles, but the soldiers remained huddled behind the fort's breastworks.

George again advised the chiefs to pull down the telegraph poles and cut the wire, explaining that the whites could signal each other over great distances through the talking wire. This was done. The Indians destroyed more than fifty miles of line, the wire either left tangled on the ground or dragged into the river. The poles fueled bonfires around which the people sang and feasted, celebrating the great victory. One such gathering took place directly across the river from Camp Rankin. The thumping drums and the high-pitched nasal singing kept the troops awake and at their posts through the long night.[38]

Following the sack of Julesburg, George joined a war party and rode west. After a few miles, he saw a detachment of the Seventh Iowa Cavalry riding the opposite way headed for Julesburg on the other side of the wide river. Through his father's field glasses he watched an officer ride to the riverbank, aim his rifle, and fire directly at him. George could scarcely believe it. The Cheyennes had just destroyed Julesburg and forced the soldiers to cower behind breastworks, but here this ignorant white man seemed not to care. George galloped down to the willows at the river's edge, pulled out two revolvers, and though he knew he was far out of range emptied them in the direction of the officer, the lead balls skipping across the ice or flying high and wide. All the while, he shouted a stream of obscenities that could be heard plainly by all the bluecoats. Captain Eugene F. Ware of the Seventh Iowa Cavalry was on the receiving end of George's futile demonstration and later wrote that "he began to fire a lot of good American words at me, and they were shot in such good English that I became satisfied that the Indian was not a Cheyenne or a Sioux."[39]

On February 5, after a hard march over the dry ridge between Lodgepole Creek and the North Platte, the people camped near Mud Springs, an abandoned stop on the Overland Stage route, where a small detachment of the Eleventh Ohio Cavalry operated a telegraph station. With a war party George rode over to the outpost, hoping to find the patrol on open ground, but the soldiers were already pinned down, firing from loopholes chopped chest high at regular intervals in the log buildings.

There was no way for the warriors to get at the well-hidden whites or at the horses, which were protected by a strong corral. But in the afternoon, almost as tribute, the soldiers released their horses and mules, hoping the Indians would take the animals and leave. The ploy worked. The Indians dashed after the stock, counting coup on them by touching them with arrows, quirts, or bows. If a man touched an animal, it was his. When George reined in, just out of rifle range, he noticed that the telegraph wire, strung on low posts, was still intact. Certain the soldiers had signaled for help, he advised the headmen to order a withdrawal, for reinforcements were likely on the way.[40]

The war party rejoined the village just as the people were crossing the frozen North Platte River, the men sanding the ice so the plunder-heavy ponies could cross without slipping. On the high bluff four miles north of the river, the camp criers shouted, "Camp here—Four Sleeps!" That night George and other young people celebrated. "I was up all that night," he remembered, "dancing with a party of young men and women. It was full moonlight and not very cold, and scalp dances were going on around the fires in all parts of the big village, the drums beating and the echoes coming back from the high bluffs."[41]

The next afternoon, he noticed a Lakota man on the bluffs south of the village maneuvering his horse and holding a buffalo robe on one side of his head, a signal that enemies were coming. George rushed for his horse anxious to be the first to win battle honors. When he reached the heights he saw spread before him a panoramic view of the Platte Valley. To the west, far in the distance, stood Chimney Rock, with its nearby companions, Jail and Courthouse Rocks. His father had described these places to him when he was young, and it seemed almost as if he had been here before. He remembered his father's story of Hiram Scott, the trapper who had been abandoned at this place in 1828 and left to die. But there was no time to reflect on those olden days. For on the other side of the river, he could just make out white-topped army wagons coming straight toward him. And he could see Indians like so many ants charging across the ice toward the soldiers. George pulled out his field glasses and scanned the scene below. The four companies escorting the wagons pulled one piece of artillery. These must be the soldiers coming to relieve the besieged command at

Mud Springs Station. The officer in charge was Colonel William O. Collins of the Eleventh Ohio Cavalry, commanding at Fort Laramie.

But even as George reported this news to the chiefs, the bluecoats corralled their wagons near the mouth of Rush Creek and prepared to fight. The first Indians to cross the river charged right up to the soldiers' guns, hoping to stampede the horses, but the troopers' rapid-fire repeating rifles and a blast from the howitzer drove them back to the cover of the surrounding hills. The fighting now became a siege, the soldiers and Indians sniping at one another. As the warriors maneuvered for better position, the bluecoats dug rifle pits deep into the sand. One group of Cheyennes crawled along the ice, using the cover of the riverbank to approach within a hundred yards of the soldiers. From here they poured arrows and bullets into the rear of the enemy position. One warrior approached near enough to shoot two arrows into the back of a trooper who had hidden himself under a wagon.[42] At this, Colonel Collins ordered a counterattack. George watched sixteen men lead their horses out of the wagon corral, mount, and with revolvers drawn, charge the Cheyenne sharpshooters. In the fighting, George's young friend, Yellow Nose, small for his age and unable to mount his plunging horse, was shot in the chest.[43] Just then, a large party of warriors swept around a sand hill, checking the advance of the soldiers. In the hand-to-hand struggle, two soldiers fell dead and nine others were wounded as the bluecoats retreated to the corral. One of the soldiers, mounted on a fast roan, broke through the Indians and raced up the Laramie Road, frantically whipping his horse. Several warriors pursued and finally overtook him. When the soldier fell, the warriors cut his heart out and then shot his body full of arrows. In his saddlebags they found a dispatch, which George translated. Colonel Collins had written to the commanding officer at Camp Mitchell, reporting that he had corralled his wagons and faced a thousand Indians. The situation was desperate and he needed reinforcement immediately.[44]

The Cheyennes could not dislodge the soldiers, who fought for their lives. George reasoned that a relief column would eventually come to Collins's aid and advised the chiefs against a long siege. On the morning of February 9, the warriors withdrew from Rush Creek, leaving the soldiers hiding in their burrows like so many prairie dogs. The village once again moved north.

For three days the people traveled hard, attempting to put as much distance as they could between themselves and the pursuing cavalrymen. Within a week the Black Hills loomed on the horizon, and here the combined village divided. The Arapahos headed west for Powder River country and Spotted Tail's Brule Lakotas turned east, while the Cheyennes waited for word from their runners, who had been sent to locate the Northern Cheyenne camps. Here in the Black Hills buffalo were scarce, so the people hunted antelope and elk. Old Grey Beard directed George and the other young hunters to dig antelope pits and organized a drive that corralled many animals. George never forgot this. It was the first time he and many of the Southern Cheyennes had depended solely on game other than buffalo.[45]

Finally, the runners returned with news that the Northern Cheyennes and Red Cloud's Oglalas were on Powder River only three days distant and urged the tired villagers to press on and join the other tribes—buffalo were abundant, they reported, and a big dance was already being planned to celebrate the arrival of the Southern *Tsistsistas*.

As they approached the Northerners' village, George saw hundreds of beautifully painted buffalo-hide lodges. The Southerners had long used lightweight canvas tipi covers acquired through government annuities and trade at Bent's Fort. But much more separated the Southern Cheyennes from their Northern cousins. In the early 1830s, when his father and uncles first established trading posts on the Arkansas River, a portion of the tribe went south and remained. These people hunted the southern buffalo herds and entered into a trade partnership with the Bents. In less than forty years, the two divisions of the Cheyenne people had grown apart and evolved in their own way, a fact George always remembered:

> Our southern Indians all wore cloth blankets, cloth leggings, and other things made by the whites, but these northern Indians all wore buffalo robes and buckskin leggings; they had their braided hair wrapped in strips of buckskin painted red, and they had crow feathers on their

heads with the ends of the feathers cut off in a peculiar manner. They looked much wilder than any of the southern Indians, and kept up all the old customs, not having come much in contact with the whites. . . . They were growing more like the Sioux in habits and appearance every year. They did not dress like us at all, and their language was changing. They used many words that were strange to us.[46]

Together, the reunited Cheyennes spent the winter. Confident that the soldiers would never venture this far north, war parties now turned their attention to traditional Crow enemies. But as it turned out, the Crows found the Cheyennes first. On a dark March evening, nine Crow warriors raided the Cheyenne horse herds, running off a dozen or more ponies. A light snow fell during the night, allowing George and the other men to easily track the raiders. On the trail they found evidence that one of the Crows had been bucked from an unbroken Cheyenne pony and in the fall had lost his bow and quiver. This discovery encouraged the trackers, who quirted their horses nearly to exhaustion overtaking and trapping the enemies in a box canyon. After a short hand-to-hand fight, four Crows lay dead; the other five escaped by releasing their captured horses and hiding in the boulder-strewn hills. George arrived just as the Cheyennes were scalping the dead. The Crows wore their hair so long that the victorious warriors saw no harm in splitting the four scalps, making eight in all.

George remembered their triumphant return: "When we got back to camp one of the biggest scalp dances I have ever seen was started. These northern Indians were great scalp dancers, both men and women, and the way they kept up the dancing, drumming, and singing beat anything I have ever seen."[47]

The dancing and singing went on for three weeks, so long in fact that the drumming scared away the buffalo, forcing the village to move southeast to Little Powder River. The Crazy Dogs, the Northern Cheyenne society appointed by the chiefs to oversee the move, ordered the drumming stopped and threatened to whip anyone who even touched a drum.[48]

The initial excitement of the tribal reunion began to wear thin. Besides, Crow hunting seemed a diversion from the Cheyennes real purpose of punishing whites for the crime of Sand Creek. The Northerners, too, wanted the whites punished. They had heard the stories of Sand Creek and shared the Southern Cheyennes' outrage.

In mid-May, on the Tongue River, the allied tribes came together once again. Here, the chiefs and headmen—Dull Knife, Old Man Afraid of His Horses, Little Wolf, Tall Bull, Bull Bear, and White Horse for the Cheyennes; Spotted Tail, Lame White Man, and Red Cloud for the Lakotas; Black Bear for the Arapahos—sat in council to de-cide where the united tribes should strike. They settled on the Platte River Bridge, a vital crossing on the Oregon Trail 250 miles north of Denver.

The army had concentrated men and supplies at this point, and the chiefs believed a victory there might stop gold seekers and emigrants from crossing the northern plains. To celebrate the decision and honor those Cheyennes who had suffered at Sand Creek, the Indians built an enormous bonfire in the center of the Cheyenne camp circle, and all three tribes participated in dances hosted by the military societies— the Northern Elk Horn Scrapers, Southern Crooked Lances, Crazy Dogs, Dog Soldiers, Red Shields, Kit Foxes, and Bowstring Men. The glow of the fire lit thousands of faces. The Cheyennes felt safe and strong here among their allies.[49]

George, however, could not wait for the warriors to organize the attack. Shortly after the dances, he joined a small war party of young men and headed for the Oregon Trail and Fort Laramie, two hundred miles south. For weeks he raided along the wagon road, attacking ranches, stage stations, and army outposts, killing and looting as he went. Near Sweetwater Station, Captain James E. Greer of the Eleventh Kansas Cavalry reported seeing a white man with the Indians. He noted that all the warriors were "well mounted and carried shields."[50] When George returned with scalps, he told others he had gone "clean to Fort Laramie." His break with the white world was now complete—there could be no turning back.[51]

He had developed a taste for fighting, eagerly taking his place with the other men. On July 25, 1865, the Cheyennes led the movement of the allied warriors to Platte River Bridge, the Crazy Dogs scouting the way and covering the flanks, while the disciplined Dog Soldiers as usual guarded the rear and prevented straggling. To keep dust clouds from rising, the society men allowed no one to ride faster than a walk.

As the warriors neared the high ground surrounding Platte River Bridge, the chiefs called on George and others who carried field glasses to climb the bluffs and scout the enemy position below. As George scanned the bridge and the soldiers' log fort, the main body of men took cover behind the sand hills and prepared for battle. Turning to look into the valley behind him, George saw the experienced warriors pull their feathered headdresses from their rawhide cases, each man raising his to the four directions, finally lifting it high to the sun and placing it on his head. Men grasped their bull-hide shields with their right hands and removed the protective buckskin covers, exposing sacred charms and ornaments. Quickly, they dipped the shields to the ground four times, then held them up to the sun and shook them four times. After this, they shifted the shields to their left arms, leaving their right hands free for their weapons—war clubs, bows, lances, sabers, pistols, and rifles.[52]

The chiefs directed a small party of well-mounted decoys to draw the bluecoats away from the building guarding the bridge. From his place on the hill, George followed the progress of ten warriors, including a young Lakota named Crazy Horse, as they rode toward the bridge.

The soldiers, however, did not take the bait. They were experienced men—Ohio and Kansas troopers reinforced by a detachment of U.S. Volunteers, Confederate prisoners who had recently taken an oath of allegiance to the United States. These "galvanized Yankees" had agreed to wear Union blue on the condition that they would only fight Indians and not their fellow Southerners.

All morning the chiefs had struggled to maintain discipline, but when the eager young warriors heard the boom of cannon fire, they rushed the camp guards, desperate to push their way through. The watchful Crazy Dogs whipped them back. If the young men had charged into the valley then, the decoy strategy and the attack would have failed. But they had made noise. Unsure whether the soldiers had discovered the warriors' presence, the chiefs pulled back the decoys, determined to wait until tomorrow. That night, George, Charley, and other excited warriors went into camp, their enthusiasm only slightly dampened by the strict discipline enforced by the Crazy Dogs, who forbade singing or talking.[53]

The next day, July 26, Charley left the camp at dawn with a few scouts. Before the sun had cleared the mountains on the eastern horizon, the chiefs divided the warriors into three main groups. One party cautiously probed down the Platte, while the largest contingent stayed concealed behind the bluffs northwest of the bridge. George joined the third group, which snaked silently behind the bluffs directly north of the bridge. This time the Crazy Dogs allowed the warriors hiding behind the bluffs to peer over the rocky outcrops and see for themselves what was happening in the valley below. This way they would better understand the need to stay out of sight until it was time to spring the trap.

At about nine o'clock in the morning, George watched twenty-five cavalrymen pound across the planked bridge and turn west along the road running between the river and the line of bluffs that masked the Indians. These men of the Eleventh Kansas had been assigned to meet and escort a wagon train approaching from the west. Leading the detachment was Caspar Collins, a twenty-year-old lieutenant of the Eleventh Ohio Cavalry and son of Colonel William O. Collins, the very man who had fought the Cheyennes at Rush Creek the winter before. Unaware of the danger, the soldiers advanced in column toward the main Indian position. George could hardly believe it. Surely they would see the Indians, many in full regalia, looking down on them from the hills. As the bluecoats trotted past George's hiding place, the Indians charged and George heard Collins shout, "Retreat to the bridge!"[54] The troopers wheeled, spurred their mounts, and rode for their lives. But before they had covered much ground, a band of Dog Soldiers, Charley among them, swept in to cut them off. Seeing the danger, a company of soldiers ran across the bridge, hauling behind them a mountain howitzer, its polished bronze barrel gleaming in the bright sun. When they reached the end of the span, the men immediately brought the gun into action, firing point blank into the mass of onrushing warriors. They continued firing until Collins's men and the Indians became so intermingled that the cannoneers feared killing their own men.

Just as the cannon blasts ceased, George and his group struck the left flank of the retreating column. He rushed in among the soldiers. Dust and gun smoke filled the air, reducing visibility to less than a dozen yards. Through the din of shots and war cries, he heard an unhorsed soldier scream to his comrades, "Help me! Help me! Don't leave me!" Then George saw Collins rein in his powerful gray, pulling the animal's head back toward the fallen soldier. As George rode for the bridge, Collins came right at him. They passed within a few feet of one another. As their eyes met, an arrow struck the young officer's forehead. George could have touched him, he was so close. Blood poured down Collins's face, and his eyes glazed. The young officer dropped his reins, and his out-of-control horse ran straight for the massed warriors. Collins reeled in his saddle and fell just as a warrior grabbed the animal's bridle.[55]

The fight did not last long. Soon, dead bluecoats lay along the road in ones and twos for over a mile, but many were clustered just where George and his party had attacked. Nearly all the soldiers who ventured out with Collins were killed or wounded.

In full view of the Platte Bridge station, warriors went among the dead, stripping them of their clothes and weapons. Others hoped to lure the soldiers from the station by mutilating the fallen. They paid special attention to the body of Lieutenant Collins, for George had identified him as an officer by his shoulder straps and the yellow stripes on his trousers. With grim efficiency, the Indians slit his belly and drew out his intestines, then bashed in the back of his skull and scooped out his brains. Using their tomahawks, they hacked off his hands and feet and then wrapped his body in the hated telegraph wire. The Cheyenne war leaders fully understood the use of the "talking wire." Now the warriors used it to drag the disfigured body along the road. If the bluecoats wanted the wire, they could wind it off the body of their dead leader. But their calculated provocations failed. The soldiers refused to leave the protection of their station.

Even though the soldiers would not venture far, they were still dangerous. Sharpshooters fired from behind fortifications, and cannon shells reached out nearly a mile. After pulling down telegraph poles to fashion travois for their wounded, the Indians returned to positions on the surrounding hills, there to recount their coups and taunt the soldiers from a safe distance.

Later in the afternoon, George learned that more soldiers were coming, this time from the hills to the west. "We all jumped on our horses and rode up the road in plain view of soldiers at the bridge. This must have been a grand sight for them as all the Indians were running up the river toward the government train."[56] In less than a mile they came upon army wagons bunched in a small hollow not far from the river. Now George understood why Collins had made his foolish advance. He had ridden out to support this wagon train bound for the Platte Bridge station. Surrounded, the newly arrived bluecoats fired from behind the protection of piled bed sacks and boxes. Some took cover under the wagons, while others fired from the wagon boxes through slits cut in the canvas tops.

At first, the Indian attack was scattered and uncoordinated. None of the society headmen or chiefs had arrived yet, and the warriors fought individually, each man looking for an opportunity to strike a coup or capture a horse. Two teamsters ran for the river, but only a few Indians followed them. As the white men splashed across the slow-moving water, one held his pistol belt over his head. Left Hand, Roman Nose's brother, followed close behind, but when the teamster reached the far bank, he suddenly turned and fired a shot into Left Hand's face, killing him instantly.

Shortly after this, Roman Nose himself arrived and quickly organized the attack. He motioned for the warriors to hold their fire and shouted, "We are going to empty the soldiers' guns."[57] Roman Nose and a few other experienced men galloped around the wagons, drawing enemy fire. Although bullets cut the feathers of their headdresses, not one soldier bullet found its mark. The power of Roman Nose's medicine impressed all the Indians, who had found cover behind clumps of sagebrush or in shallow, hand-dug depressions. After circling the wagons two or three times, the great warrior signaled for everyone to charge. The Indians rose up and with high-pitched war cries rushed forward on foot.

George joined them, but by the time he reached the wagons most of the soldiers had been slain. However, a few determined bluecoats still fired from under the wagons. These men were hard to kill. George and several others with guns charged the position, firing blindly at the hidden soldiers. When these bluecoats were silenced, the warriors found still more crouching in the wagon boxes. Using clubs and knives, they cut down three of them. Then Tomahawk, an old Suhtai warrior, dragged a fourth man from the wagon with his bare hands and threw him on the ground, thus counting the bravest coup of the day.

Many warriors had been killed in the assault, and more were wounded. Filled with anger for the loss of their friends, the Cheyennes plunged their lances and knives into the bodies of the dead soldiers, pinning them to the ground. Then they fired the wagons, using the red-hot iron hoops from the wagon wheel hubs to torture Tomahawk's captive. As George examined the killing ground, smoke still filled the hollow. He counted twenty-two dead soldiers. These men, he suspected, were only dismounted cavalry returning from some distant post. They had not expected a fight, and their wagons contained nothing of use—only bed sacks and mess chests—certainly nothing worthy of the eight Cheyennes killed. So the disgusted warriors threw away the white men's scalps, leaving them on the battleground.[58]

At dawn the next morning, war parties set off in all directions to attack anything that moved on the roads. George headed north with the main body of Cheyennes and Lakotas. These men moved deliberately and with confidence. Their power was great—no force on the plains, Indian or white, could match their strength.

Finally, they reached the stream called Crazy Woman's Fork, where it empties into Powder River, one hundred miles north of Platte Bridge. Here, they found the Cheyenne-Lakota-Arapaho village. Dull Knife's Northern Cheyennes and Bull Bear's Dog Soldiers camped near Red Cloud's Oglalas. Not far downstream, Black Bear's Arapahos pitched their village. For weeks, celebrations and ceremonies continued without interruption. The Sun Dance as performed by the northerners fascinated George, for he and the Southern Cheyennes noticed many subtle differences in the ancient ceremony. The Sacred Arrow Renewal, carried out by the Southerners, drew the attention of the Northern Cheyennes, many of whom had never witnessed the mystery of *Mahuts*.

But George was most interested in the scalp dances, for these were opportunities to meet young women. He moved from camp to camp, dancing, courting, and recounting coups.[59] *Hee-man-eh*, whom George referred to as "half men–half women," orchestrated the scalp dances. These special Cheyennes, with their gentle ways and feminine dress, were honored among the people as great love-talkers and matchmakers. They saw to every detail of the celebrations, which were always held at night by the light of a huge tipi-shaped bonfire. The *Hee-man-eh* led young men and women through a series of four line dances—the Sweetheart Dance, Matchmaker Dance, Slippery Dance, and Galloping Buffalo Bull Dance. These gatherings allowed men and women to meet, touch, and look longingly at one another—all with the approval of parents and elders.

The *Hee-man-eh* encouraged the young people to choose partners. During the all-night celebration, couples covered themselves in blankets, caressing one another and whispering of love.[60] George had participated in many fights and had accumulated battle honors, and the *Hee-man-eh* had little trouble matching him with attractive young women, who eagerly sought his company. This life seemed natural and logical to him, as he huddled under a warm wool trade blanket whispering with beautiful Cheyenne and Lakota girls, who shyly hid their smiles and avoided his direct gaze. The girls were at the same time curiously bold, never breaking his grasp or leaving the blanket that protected them from prying eyes. When George finally raised the blanket, the smell of the sweet, clean air mingled with the smoke of the fire. And overhead, the sky itself seemed ablaze with countless stars, more than he had ever seen before, and he wondered whether they too were celebrating.[61]

The great village was too large to remain intact for long. Soon the Arapahos moved toward the Big Horn Mountains in search of game and fresh grass for their horses. Lakota and Cheyenne hunters traveled farther and farther from the village to find buffalo. Small war parties also set out to renew the attacks on the white man's roads to the south.

As George danced and hunted, Island, never one to sit idle, joined a raiding party of twenty-three warriors. A married Cheyenne woman traveling with a war party that did not include her husband was scandalous. But Island's companion, Joe Barraldo, fearing old Bent's wrath, had long since abandoned her. Cheyenne custom allowed a spurned husband to exact a measure of revenge, ranging from demanding payment for the lost wife to taking the life of the other man.[62] Barraldo had reason to be nervous. Colonel Bent's temper was well known, and the young man probably figured the cuckolded trader would not settle for horses. Yet Island was still a young woman and attractive, and once Barraldo was out of the picture she had taken up with another man. George was happy for her. He loved her like a mother. His father certainly had many faults, any one of which might have driven her away. Among the Cheyennes, when a woman no longer wanted a husband, she would pile his belongings outside the tipi and he would shuffle off humiliated. Island had taken the only course open to her when Barraldo came around—she could not, after all, have shoved Bent out of his stockade.

After successful raids on the Upper Platte, Island and the Cheyenne war party made their way north to Powder River country. She and four of the men led packhorses and a travois heavily loaded with plunder. Behind them, other warriors drove a herd of captured stock taken from army posts and stage stations. On August 16, only a few miles from the great Cheyenne village, Pawnee scouts under the command of Major Frank North accompanied by a detachment of the Seventh Iowa Cavalry overtook Island's party. She saw the enemy first, thinking them Cheyennes or friendly Lakotas. The strangers waved a blanket, signaling that it was safe to approach. Then she heard the shrill tones of the Pawnee war cry: "*Ki-de-de-de-de!*" She quickly shouted a warning, "*Pani, Pani!*" But it was too late. Island and her four companions, slowed by the travois, were overrun and cut down almost immediately. A short distance away, the rest of the Cheyenne raiders abandoned the captured herd and by cutting loose their pack animals soon outdistanced the Pawnees, whose winded horses were unable to keep up.[63]

Not far away, at Gourd Buttes, Lakota buffalo hunters discovered a column of eighty-one covered wagons moving northwest toward Powder River. Soldier escorts flanked the train of civilian and military wagons. The Lakotas had stumbled onto Colonel James A. Sawyers's road-building expedition to the Montana goldfields. Captain G. W. Williford, commanding two infantry companies of the Fifth U.S. Volunteers—more "galvanized Yankees"—accompanied Sawyers and his civilian contractors. A detachment of Dakota Cavalry under Lieutenant J. R. Wood augmented the military force.[64]

The Lakotas rode into the big Powder River village shouting, "White soldiers!" Bull Bear jumped on his warhorse and rode among the Dog Soldier lodges urging the warriors to gather their weapons. Red Cloud did the same in the Lakota camps, while Dull Knife rallied the Northern Cheyennes. The village erupted. Women pulled children into the lodges as the men ran for their ponies. George grabbed his lariat and caught his warhorse.[65]

Riding up Powder River about fifteen miles, the warriors intercepted Sawyers's expedition and George quickly sized up the situation. The teamsters had corralled the wagons for their midday break and had turned out the oxen to graze and water. The warriors immediately charged the herd, riding swiftly across the open grassland, hoping to cut it off from the wagon corral. But the long rifles of the foot soldiers and rapid-fire cavalry carbines drove the Indians back. Bull Bear and Red Cloud cautioned their men to stay out of rifle range, but some, eager for honors, rode in groups of five and ten, circling the wagons. George proudly watched warriors ride bareback, hanging low behind the necks of their ponies. The bravest warriors charged close to the wagons, taunting the soldiers with a string of English obscenities. The Cheyennes spoke little English, but they were quite fluent in the white man's profanity—the Bent brothers had taught them well. He noticed that the taunting had the desired effect, as red-faced white men jumped up from behind their cover, shouting back and firing wildly. But the whites could not be drawn out of the corral, not even when the warriors sounded cavalry calls on captured bugles. Firing continued until dark, when George and the others finally withdrew.[66]

At noon the next day, August 15, 1865, a Mexican emerged from the corral, signaling that the whites wished to parley. Red Cloud, Bull Bear, and Dull Knife turned to George, for if they were going to talk with the whites they wanted him to interpret. George was willing but warned them not to advance without a white flag. The four men rode toward the wagons, George dressed in his captured frock coat and the chiefs in full war regalia. As they moved forward, George waved a white flag, which he had attached to a lance. The soldiers held their fire. When the chiefs reached a point midway between the Indian and white positions, George thrust the lance into the ground. Presently, four white men rode out to meet them: Sawyers, Lieutenant Wood, Captain Willison, and the Mexican interpreter.[67]

The chiefs asked why the soldiers had come to this country. George quickly translated, but the English words he voiced sounded strange to his ears, so long had he been among the Cheyennes. Sawyers answered that his was not a military expedition; he had not come to fight but only wanted to build a road to the Montana goldfields. He promised to be clear of the region as quickly as possible and wanted permission to continue. Red Cloud peremptorily refused the request and told Sawyers to find another route. Dull Knife said the whites should go west around the Big Horn Mountains, far beyond Cheyenne territory. Sawyers protested. The suggested route was too long; his horses and men would never survive such a journey. Contemptuously, Bull Bear said the condition of Sawyers's horses and men did not concern him. If the whites were too weak to make the journey, they should turn around and go back. Besides, the Cheyennes were strong and welcomed a fight. Winter was coming on, and the army would soon have to withdraw anyway.

In frustration Sawyers directly addressed George, asking what it would take to get permission to cross Indian land. Without consulting the chiefs, George shot back: "You can hang Colonel Chivington!"[68] The officers recoiled at this sudden flash of anger. But George had more to say. The present war was the result of Chivington's slaughter of women and children at Sand Creek. Somewhat unnerved, Sawyers noticed that this "son of Bent" used American slang and sprinkled his Southern drawl with phrases such as "damn Yankees." George concluded his verbal assault with a threat to "clean out" all the whites in Indian Territory. Sawyers asked whether the Indians feared General Connor, the new district commander, who had killed so many Shoshones on Bear River, Utah Territory, in 1863. George bluffed, saying that he knew all about Connor, and the allied tribes were even now concentrating and were more than a match for anything the general could throw at them. Looking at the hundreds of splendidly mounted warriors on the hills around him, Sawyers saw there was truth in George's words.

The young halfbreed's appearance marked him as a man apart, not entirely Indian, and not quite white. His intelligence and command of

English and Cheyenne, combined with his fabulous dress—staff officer's uniform, red breechclout hanging nearly to the ground, leggings, beaded moccasins—impressed Sawyers and the officers. Bent was dark-skinned with piercing black eyes. He wore his hair shorter than other Cheyennes, and a mustache of fine black hair curled around the corners of his mouth. Tall and ruggedly handsome, he was a man of obvious physical strength—bull neck, square jaw, broad shoulders, and a massive chest that stretched the seams of his blue frock coat. Even in the company of chiefs, this halfbreed Bent was an intimidating presence, a man to be reckoned with in both Indian and white worlds.[69]

After a pause, Sawyers proposed to pay for safe passage. Would the Indians accept a wagonload of supplies? George discussed this offer with the chiefs. Dull Knife told George to tell Sawyers that they would accept the payment, provided the whites delivered the goods here, at the parley point. And so the deal was struck, much to Sawyers's relief and Captain Williford's disgust. Williford believed that the poorly armed warriors were no match for the soldiers' long-range rifle muskets and six-pounder howitzer.

Sawyers returned to the corral and immediately ordered a wagon loaded with three thousand pounds of supplies, including bacon, flour, hardtack, sugar, coffee, dried apples, cornmeal, and tobacco. At the same time, he ordered the teamsters to hitch their wagons and prepare to move fast, for he knew the column must gain a more defensible position closer to water. He directed that the wagons make for the high ground as soon as the Indians began dividing the supplies among themselves.

When the supply wagon rolled from the corral and reached the meeting place, the chiefs rode out. This time George asked Charley to accompany them. He had learned from Sawyers that newspapers and trail rumor had identified George as the head of the Cheyenne Dog Soldiers and that the authorities considered him personally responsible for depredations. So he would hang back and wait with the warriors this time while Charley played the role of interpreter. Charley agreed, for he cared little what the whites thought of him. He had renounced their world. George had not, and while he still considered himself Cheyenne he did not want to completely disconnect from the white world.

From a nearby hill, George saw Bull Bear and Red Cloud shake hands with Sawyers. He saw Charley and other warriors push through the officers and crowd around the wagons, eager to get a share of the spoils. Suddenly, shots and war cries rang out. Lakota warriors swept in on the wagon train, which was already moving toward the high ground. All was confusion. The chiefs, officers, and warriors still mingled near the tribute wagon. Now, they all scrambled for their horses and rode for safety.

George looked on in disbelief. He had given his word that the Cheyennes would guarantee the soldiers' safety, and now the Lakotas had made a liar of him. Sawyers and the other officers would remember George Bent as the man who had deceived them. He left the battleground angered by the Lakota charge and breach of faith. For him, this fight was over. Dull Knife felt the same way. The two men rode back to the village. The Cheyenne-Lakota alliance had always been fragile, but now it seemed on the verge of collapse.

Charley stayed and fought, however, cursing and taunting the bluecoats in their new corral on the banks of the Powder. Later, he tried to arrange another meeting with the soldiers, but they no longer trusted any Indian, especially one named Bent. During a long-distance shouting conference the soldiers said they only wanted to move peacefully northwest toward the mountains. Running low on ammunition, Charley pressed them to trade for powder and ball, even offering a wad of captured greenbacks as payment. But Captain Williford stopped the exchange by ordering his cannon crew to open fire. Close to Charley's position, an exploding shell struck a horse, blowing it apart.[70] Armed only with bows and smoothbore muskets, the Lakotas soon tired of the long-range shooting. Siege warfare was not their style, and they realized that the soldiers were too dug in and too cautious to be drawn out. Gathering their booty, the Lakotas followed the Cheyennes back to the village.[71]

When Charley returned, George told him the terrible news of Island's death. Cheyenne warriors had found her body and brought it to the village. The Pawnees had scalped and stripped her, even taking her cherished belt, the one she had carefully decorated with silver and brass buttons.[72] All through the night the brothers talked of the old days and their life with the daughters of White Thunder—Owl Woman, George's mother; Yellow Woman, Charley's mother; and Island, the woman who had raised them both.

As they talked they shared the supplies Charley had retrieved from Sawyers's wagon. For the first time in many months, the brothers drank sugared coffee, ate dried apples, and smoked white man's tobacco. George surprised Charley with the news that the Civil War was over. Mary Fletcher, a sixteen-year-old white captive taken by Sand Hill's band on the North Platte River near Fort Laramie, had recently told him that General Lee had surrendered to General Grant at a place called Appomattox, Virginia. Both Bents knew the end of the rebellion would seriously affect the army's war on the Cheyennes. Troops and supplies would soon reinforce the scattered volunteers now stationed at isolated outposts. For the people of the plains, the real fighting had only begun.[73]

George told the chiefs that the war between the whites had ended and explained what this would mean to the Cheyennes, but war parties continued to hunt traditional enemies, especially the Crows. Even though he knew the real danger came from the whites, George was still eager to prove himself as a warrior. At the end of August he joined a party of eight Dog Soldiers, led by his friend Red Lance, and headed for the Yellowstone River country one hundred miles north. Armed as a Cheyenne warrior with bow, arrows, and a plain bull-hide shield decorated with eagle feathers, he still wore his captured army frock coat—the one he had taken at Julesburg in January—its brass buttons now tarnished by eight months of camp life. He felt almost naked without the fine rifle his father had given him back on the Arkansas, but without the proper ammunition it was useless now. So he would fight the Cheyennes' traditional enemy in the traditional way.

On the rolling high plains they soon encountered a strong body of Crows. Outnumbered, the Cheyennes retreated. This was the first time George had fought Crows out in the open, and their appearance startled him. They were magnificent, riding as one through the grass, their faces painted red, their hair spiked straight up in front but long and flowing behind. George saw with sudden clarity that these Crows, who knew the land, knew every hill and ravine, would soon overtake his war party. He looked over his shoulder and saw seven well-mounted warriors gaining fast and now so close he could make out the braided horsehair rope of their war bridles.

He signed to Red Lance and the others to ride on, then impulsively reined in his powerful thoroughbred. His horse, he knew, was one of the fastest on the plains, for he had raced it often against the finest horses and had never lost. He was sure that no Crow pony could catch him. Jerking the animal's head around to face the enemy, George shouted a war cry and then charged, at the same time drawing his bow and shooting an arrow toward the bunched-up warriors. The Crows halted, drew their own bows, and loosed a hail of arrows in return. Now, in front of his enemies, George raised his bow, shaking it defiantly, daring them to fight. With war cries of their own, the Crows surged forward. George hugged his horse's neck as more arrows whipped close to his ear. He looked toward the Dog Men and saw they had gotten safely away. He dug his heels into the thoroughbred's flanks and the horse leapt forward, its powerful body stretched full-length. The Crows quickly fell behind, their war cries now distant.

When he came up to the Dog Men, they greeted him with shouts of approval. They had seen him charge the enemy and draw them off so that they might escape. George had earned his place among them— they would never forget his bravery in this fight against the Crows.

When the war party reached the Cheyenne village on Powder River, Red Lance honored George by depicting his brave deed in a ledger-book captured during the raid on Julesburg. The book was a plain army account book with lined and numbered pages, and the warriors had used colored pencils and crayons to record their bravest coups. As George flipped through the book, he recognized that the events recorded—all battles and coups—had occurred in the last year, most of them since the Sand Creek Massacre in November 1864. One colorful drawing depicted two great Dog Soldier warriors—Wolf With Plenty of Hair and Chief Tall Bull. With his sacred buffalo hide Dog Rope flying from his shoulder, Wolf gallops in to rescue a dismounted Tall Bull as Pawnees close in for the kill. Another page captured his attention: Whirlwind riding hard at Julesburg in pursuit of blue-coated soldiers, who are lanced and shot from their saddles. All the

great deeds—of the Dog Soldiers and other society men—were represented, and now his own coup against the Crows would be recorded.[74]

Red Lance sat cross-legged, the book in his lap, and as George
recounted his fight with the Crows, his friend drew the scene, using
the whittled stub of a pencil. George's coup was recorded in the center of the ledgerbook. With consummate skill, the artist deftly outlined
George's powerful warhorse. The pencil scratched unerringly, and Red
Lance did not lift it from the paper until he had finished a figure. Other
Dog Men who had witnessed the coup gathered around and offered
further description and details, which Red Lance carefully included in
the picture. The action flowed from right to left, and enemy arrows fill
the air as George, dressed in his uniform coat, turns to face the enemy,
holding his bow high, taunting the Crows. The artist finished the
drawing by penciling the sign of a beaver—*Ho-my-ike*—above
George's head. He was proud of his inclusion in the tribal history but
secretly wished a white artist had also been on hand. Whites would
never comprehend the full meaning of Red Lance's drawing. They
would think it childlike and overlook the amazing accuracy of its lit-
eral detail and the hidden meaning of its symbols.[75]

Every day camp criers reported fights with army patrols. Particularly
troublesome were the Pawnee and Omaha Indian scouts, who now
fought alongside the white soldiers. The army had equipped them with
the latest firearms, while the allied tribes still relied heavily on bows and
lances. True, they had captured many guns since the Sand Creek revenge
raids began in January, but finding ammunition posed an insurmount-
able problem. The white man's firearms required a bewildering variety
of cartridges that were nearly impossible to acquire, either in trade or
by capture. Many warriors possessed old-style flintlock muskets and
molded their own bullets, but these weapons were inferior to the rapid-
fire breechloaders carried by the troops and their Indian allies.[76]

Then came news of a major fight. Black Bear's Arapaho village on
Tongue River had been attacked and burned by troops under the
command of General Patrick E. Connor. The Cheyennes now knew of
Connor. George had learned from Sawyers that Connor's California Volunteers had surprised a village of Shoshones camped on Bear River in

Utah Territory, killing 278 people, many of them women and children. Colonel Chivington had regarded Connor as his principal rival in the quest for scalps, glory, and a brigadier's star. Connor had bested Chivington in this grisly contest and had been given command of all troops in the newly formed District of the Plains, headquartered in Denver.

The energetic Connor wasted little time. He organized a three-pronged army that would converge on Powder River, the homeland of the Northern Cheyennes and their Arapaho and Lakota allies. Colonel Nelson Cole commanded the right column, with nearly 1,400 men and a train of 140 wagons; Lieutenant Colonel Samuel Walker led the center column, comprising 600 men and a large train of pack mules; Connor himself accompanied the left column, about 1,000 men, including 800 soldiers and teamsters, and 200 Pawnee and Omaha scouts. Old mountain man Jim Bridger guided Connor's column, grousing incessantly about "damned paper-collared soldiers," who were obviously out of their element in the wilds of the West.[77] Artillery supported all three commands. Connor's army represented the largest force ever to take the field against the western tribes.[78]

As George feared, the reinforcements freed up by the end of the Civil War had already arrived.

Connor made no secret of his intentions. On Independence Day 1865, at Fort Laramie, he issued standing orders to all commanders: "You will not receive overtures of peace or submission from Indians, but will attack and kill every male Indian over twelve years of age."[79]

But the campaign did not go well. From the beginning, the volunteer troops made it clear they wanted to go home. The Civil War was over, and they had not signed on to fight Indians in the western wilderness. In some cases entire companies mutinied. Even the officers grumbled. Most of them had never been on the plains, and none of them had ever fought Indians. While Connor occupied his column by building a fortified camp at the head of Powder River, Cole and Walker got lost, wandering about until they stumbled into one another by chance and joined forces. As they vainly searched for Connor and his supply depot, Lakota bands—Minniconjous, Sans Arcs, Hunkpapas, and Blackfeet Sioux—tracked them from the Missouri River country.[80] Cole and Walker had no idea where they were, and, to make matters worse, their grain-fed horses were hungry and dying by the score.

Then the weather turned. On September 1 and 2, the columns struggled through scorching heat. But on the evening of September 2, the temperature plunged below freezing. Snow, rain, and sleet pelted the troops. Company commanders marched their men in circles to prevent crippling frostbite. The soldiers lit bonfires and fed the horses grass and cottonwood bark in a desperate attempt to keep the animals alive. But by morning, 414 horses lay dead and frozen on the picket line.[81]

The Lakotas surrounded the soldiers' positions, probing the lines and looking for opportunities to capture stock. On September 3, the troops burned their supply wagons to prevent their capture, for there were not enough teams to pull them. The following day, the Indians struck the remaining horses, but the animals were too weak to be run off. Lakota messengers then rode for the Cheyenne village, carrying news that the exhausted soldiers were vulnerable. If the Cheyennes came at once, perhaps the tribes could achieve a great victory. George, Charley, and the other warriors responded quickly, arriving at the soldier camp on the morning of September 5.

As George approached Powder River, he looked down and saw the whole valley. The stream looped between high bluffs, and the river bends choked with dense tangles of scrub brush and trees. He knew the warriors would have a difficult time pushing their way through the thickets, but the soldiers were there—weakened but still dangerous. With hundreds of others he galloped into the valley, dressed in full battle regalia. War cries and the shrill sound of eagle-bone whistles combined with the pounding of the war ponies echoed eerily against the steep bluffs. Once he was down in the thickets, George could see little, but he heard firing in front of him and smelled the sulphurous gun smoke. He was so close to the soldiers he could hear the shouts of battery commanders as they directed howitzer fire against the Indians gathered on the hills.[82]

As he felt his way through the heavy underbrush, two companies of cavalry suddenly appeared in front of him, trapped between the river and the Cheyennes. With a shout he joined the charge on the soldiers, straining to cut them off before they could escape across the river and find safety behind the wagon corral on the opposite bank. The army horses stopped abruptly at the steep bank, so the troopers abandoned their animals and swam for their lives, throwing themselves into the river and holding their rifles and cartridge boxes above their heads. George whooped and fired a last shot at the splashing bluecoats, then turned his attention to the eighty army horses left behind. He tore open the saddlebags filled with provisions and ammunition. The Cheyennes valued these things, but they had no use for the starved and gaunt horses. The Northern and Southern Cheyennes, along with Lakota warriors, pushed and shoved in the rush for the saddlebags. George stood apart, not wanting to get involved in the "fierce wrangle" over the plunder.[83] He had never seen such greed and rivalry among the tribes before and worried that their bond was beginning to unravel. If that happened they would not stand a chance against the whites, even such disorganized and desperate ones as these.

One of the scouts soon located a ford, and George crossed the icy waters, coming up on the soldiers' wagon corral and hasty entrenchments. Just then, the mighty Roman Nose rode in, mounted on a fine white pony and wearing his famous one-horned war bonnet with trailing feathers that swept the ground. George looked on proudly, for the war leader was one of his own Crooked Lance society men. All eyes turned to Roman Nose. George remembered:

He called out to the warriors to form a line and get ready for a charge, as he was going to empty the soldiers' guns. The Indians formed a long line from the river nearly to the bluffs and sat on their ponies facing the troops. Roman Nose then put his pony into a run and rode straight out toward one end of the line of troops. When he was quite close he turned and rode at top speed straight along the front, from the river clear to the bluffs, the troops firing at him at close range all the way. Reaching the bluffs, he turned and rode back along the line again. In this way he made three, or perhaps four, rushes from one end of the line to the other; and then his pony was shot and fell under him. On seeing this, the warriors set up a yell and charged. They attacked the troops all along the line, but could not break through anywhere.[84]

George believed that if the Cheyennes had been better armed they might have broken the bluecoat line. But they had been fighting for nearly a year now and had not more than a handful of serviceable guns among them. They were desperately short of powder, lead, caps, and flint. Resupply was impossible, and the soldiers had been careful to burn all the stores and provisions they could not carry with them.[85]

Although this battle—known to the Cheyennes as the "Roman Nose Fight"—failed to destroy Connor's army, the Indians had demonstrated their superiority and forced the bluecoats to huddle in defensive positions. The Lakotas and Cheyennes drew back to the tree-covered hilltops only when the troops opened fire with their artillery. At long range, the cannons were little more than an irritant, but George's spirits fell when he heard that a stray shell had killed Black Whetstone, a very old man who had been guarding horses and smoking behind the hills.[86]

George took some satisfaction in the knowledge that General Connor's grand campaign had failed miserably. The Cheyennes and their allies had successfully contained the soldiers, who no longer threatened the main village. The chiefs ordered the people to move east toward the Black Hills, where scouts reported large herds of buffalo. On the way, George and a few friends rode over to Bear Butte, for these Southern Cheyennes had never seen the tribe's holiest place. Here, generations before, the prophet Sweet Root had delivered the Sacred Arrows to the people and had enriched their lives with the laws that now governed them. When the sacred mountain loomed before them, the older men dismounted, filled their pipes, and, holding the stems toward the mountain, prayed to the Creator. Then they smoked and told the others of Sweet Root and the importance of Bear Butte to all Cheyennes.[87]

Later that same day, the hunters found the buffalo herds, but the chase did not go well. As the Cheyennes carefully approached the herd, Lakota hunters suddenly charged into the animals, spoiling the surprise. The buffalo stampeded, and the organized hunt turned into a dangerous free-for-all. Warriors shot wildly into the herd, while the women, who were nearby ready to skin and butcher the carcasses, rushed to get out of the way. Both tribes blamed the other for the failed hunt, and heated quarrels threatened to turn deadly. The chiefs interceded in time to avoid bloodshed, but the incident reminded the Southern Cheyennes that they were far from home. This was not the first trouble between Cheyennes and Lakotas. The two tribes had been together for nearly a year now; if they were to remain allies and friends, it was time for the Southern Cheyennes to return home to the Arkansas.[88]

In late September, the Bent brothers joined Southern Cheyenne chief Little Wolf, their father's old friend, and with several bands of Dog Soldiers set off for the south.

By October 20, George and Charley reached the Platte River. Here the brothers and the Dog Soldiers once again raided the Platte Road, capturing wagon trains loaded with goods bound for Denver. In early November, the raiders moved south to the Solomon Fork and went into camp. But the Bents and a few Dog Men rode along with Little Wolf's homesick Southerners as they continued the journey south.[89]

November 19, 1865, dawned cold and clear. One year had passed since the massacre at Sand Creek. George and Charley rode with a war party led by Fat Bear and headed for the Smoky Hill River. The brothers knew this territory, for home was not far away. As they looked toward the river they saw among the trees loose cattle grazing on the short grass. The war party galloped down a slope to round up the strays but suddenly came upon a stage station. White men were everywhere, some herding stock, some planking the new station house, and one man unhitched lathered horses from a coach that had recently arrived. The startled warriors were just as surprised as the whites, for the last time they had crossed the river at this place, no stage line ran along the Smoky Hill.

The station hands stopped their work and dove for their guns as the Cheyennes attacked. The whites forted up in a nearby adobe hut—a nearly impregnable structure embedded in the hillside—that the warriors surrounded. George counted eight white men, including a black man, who had run from the smithy's shack.

An hour after the siege began, George noted that the firing from the dugout slackened. Suddenly, a white man dashed for the stagecoach to retrieve ammunition. Gunfire again erupted, forcing George and the other warriors to duck for cover. Obviously, the white men were short of ammunition, but they had shored up their position and George thought there was little purpose in continuing the siege. He told Fat

Bear he would talk to these whites and see if a treaty had been signed ending the Indian war, for he had heard such rumors through white captives. Maybe the stage men had newspapers and useful information.

Behind the safety of piled boards, George yelled to the white men, "Has the treaty been signed?" One shouted back, "Yes!" The man identified himself as Perrin, and then asked who among the Indians could speak such good English. George cautiously walked out from behind the stacked lumber, answering, "I'm the son of Bill Bent." This long-range conversation continued for a few minutes, then George suggested everyone lay down his weapon, come out and shake hands, and talk. Perrin agreed, and so the two sides met at the station house. Cautiously, the whites emerged from the dugout and walked toward the stagecoach.

George opened the conversation by saying that he and the Cheyennes had expected to find Pawnees here, not a stage station. But he was glad to hear a treaty had been signed. This was good. The war had gone on long enough. As a sign of friendship, he offered to help the white men gather their scattered animals. Both sides still eyed the other suspiciously, but George stayed at the coach with Fat Bear and a few other warriors, talking with the stagehands as they hitched up the horses. Perrin said the Butterfield Overland Despatch Company had just opened operations in the spring and this Kansas station was known as Downer's, located some 250 miles out from Denver.

Suddenly a shot rang out and an arrow thudded into the stagecoach. Charley and the Dog Men—with no warning to anyone—had renewed the fight. The Indians at the coach, including Fat Bear and George, took cover behind an earthen bank. The whites, too, hit the dirt. Hugging the ground, George looked up and saw bullets riddle the stage messenger and the man next to him, killing both instantly. Charley's renegades captured one of the stockmen, but the other stage men, after a brief stand at the coach, ran for the bluffs only a short distance from the station. Charley and two Cheyennes mounted and pursued.

George and Fat Bear looked on in horror. They knew the whites would never reach the safety of the bluffs. But at that moment, the fleeing men jumped into a buffalo wallow and turned their rifles on the Cheyennes. Charley and the Dog Men shouted their war cries and galloped past the shallow depression. As they turned and circled, the black white man rose up to get better aim. One of the warriors shot first, the bullet glancing off the black man's head, knocking him backward into the pit. The Cheyennes saw the white men push the black man's limp but still breathing body back up to the rim, using it as a breastwork.

Charley drew back, furious that the men in the hole had wounded two of his friends. While several warriors kept the whites pinned down, Charley rushed back to the station. With the help of others, he grabbed the captive stock tender and stripped him. Then—in plain sight of the wallow—staked him to the ground. The man screamed as the warriors cut out his tongue and replaced it with his severed penis, then built a fire on his belly hoping to lure the whites out. But there was no movement in the hole. By nightfall Charley gave it up and left for Little Wolf's camp, located a few miles north.

George did not witness the torture inflicted on the white herder. He and Fat Bear had already left, shocked and disgusted by Charley's treachery. That night, in the village, the brothers argued. George had pledged to lay down his weapons and talk in peace, but Charley's actions had threatened the lives of Fat Bear and the other Cheyennes who had agreed to the truce.[90]

The halfbreed brothers, once so close, decided to go their separate ways. Charley rode for the Dog Soldier camps on the Solomon River; George continued south with Little Wolf's band. Charley would war to the death and make no peace with the whites. George, however, had come to believe that Black Kettle had been right. Cheyenne survival depended on accommodation. He was proud he had participated in the retaliation for Sand Creek. The people had won great victories, but they could not sustain their advantage against the awesome power of the whites. He had witnessed that power on eastern battlefields, and he had seen the great cities and steamboats and railroads and the countless people who would soon rush the plains. If Black Kettle had truly signed a treaty ending the war, then George should be at his side, translating the white man's words and guarding against deceit.

Chapter 7

BLACK KETTLE
AND MAGPIE WOMAN

George left Charley and the Dog Soldiers on the Solomon Fork and headed south with Little Wolf's Southern Cheyennes. He was now a battle-hardened warrior, having fought in every engagement from Julesburg to Powder River. The fighting and constant movement had dragged on for nearly a year, far longer than he had expected. Cheyenne war parties rarely stayed out more than a few weeks, but the rules of war had changed. The massacre at Sand Creek demanded retaliation on a scale never before seen on the plains. Three great nations—Cheyenne, Arapaho, and Lakota—had united with common cause against the white killers. Now, this great alliance, once so strong, was weakened by traditional intertribal tensions, food shortages, and, for the Southern Cheyennes, a yearning to return to their home on the Arkansas River.

Little Wolf and his weary band moved cautiously as they neared white settlements. In late December, just north of the Smoky Hill River, George met runners who brought news that Black Kettle's village was camped seventy-five miles south of Fort Dodge on Bluff Creek. But George and the other warriors rode horses so exhausted and broken down that they had to send runners on foot to announce their coming. This confirmed in George's mind the futility of warring against the whites, who could carry their attacks to the Cheyenne villages at any time. Unlike the Indians, they carried provisions for themselves and for their horses and could operate even when winter snows covered the grass. But Indian ponies could not survive a winter campaign.

When Little Wolf's people reached Bluff Creek, Black Kettle's Cheyennes, Little Raven's Arapahos, and Poor Bear's Prairie Apaches greeted them.[1] To George's great surprise, his father and brother were in the village. The old man was doing a brisk business, trading as if nothing had happened. For a year George had been fighting whites, but here his father and two other whites traded among the Indians without fear. Truly the war must be over and a peace treaty signed. He pressed his father for information—they had not been together since those terrible weeks following Sand Creek when George had stayed at the ranch recovering from his hip wound.[2]

George was not surprised to learn that his father had been at the very center of the government's effort to end the war. In October 1865 William had brought Black Kettle and the Southern Cheyenne chiefs to the mouth of the Little Arkansas River to meet with the U.S. peace commissioners. After Sand Creek, Black Kettle and the other chiefs had been suspicious, but they trusted Bent and agreed to attend the peace council. President Andrew Johnson appointed a group of high-ranking civilians and military men—among them Major General John B. Sanborn, Agent Jesse Leavenworth, and Major General William S. Harney—but Secretary of Interior James Harlan and Major General John Pope insisted that Kit Carson and William Bent be included. Their experience and knowledge would be essential to the success of the negotiations.[3] Old John Smith interpreted for the Cheyennes and Margaret Adams for the Arapahos. The Arapahos distrusted Smith and felt that Margaret, the mixed-blood daughter of French-Canadian trader John Poisal and his Arapaho wife, would better plead their case. After all, she had once been married to the respected mountaineer and Indian agent Thomas "Broken Hand" Fitzpatrick.

As the conference opened, the Cheyenne and Arapaho leaders learned that the Great Father, Abraham Lincoln, had been assassinated by one of his own people and that President Johnson had succeeded him. Commissioner Sanborn tried to reassure the agitated Indians by saying that the new Father was aware that "great wrongs have been committed without his knowledge. He has heard that you have been attacked by his soldiers, while you have been at peace with his government; that by this you have met great losses in lives and property, and by this you have been forced to make war. All this he disapproves of, and the people of the whole nation agree with him." He told the chiefs that they would receive compensation for their losses and that "we all feel disgraced and ashamed when we see our officers or soldiers oppressing the weak, or making war on those that are at peace with us."[4]

Black Kettle then rose and solemnly shook hands with the commissioners, looking each man in the eye. He asked, "Is it true that you came here from Washington, and is it true what you say here to-day?" Speaking slowly, deliberately, allowing Smith time to emphasize the words, Black Kettle said, "My shame is as big as the earth. It is hard for me to believe white men any more."[5]

Then the old chief deferred to his friend Bent. William stood and spoke in Cheyenne: "Friends, I would like for you once more to take my advice. I am satisfied that there is no deception. I am well aware that we have both been deceived at prior times in the execution of our treaty by white men in authority, but we must not judge all white men alike." He acknowledged that Governor Evans and Colonel Chivington had lied to him and used him to lure the Indians into the death trap of Sand Creek.[6]

The commissioners agreed that this treaty represented a "turning point in our history." Commissioner James Steele rose to say: "We fully realize that it is hard for any people to leave their homes and graves of their ancestors; but, unfortunately for you, gold has been discovered in your country, and a crowd of white people have gone there to live, and a great many of these people are the worst enemies of the Indians—men who do not care for their interests, and who would not stop at any crime to enrich themselves."[7] He promised that the government would give the Indians a "country that is full of game and good for agricultural purposes, and where the hills and mountains are not full of gold and silver."[8]

The commissioners proposed that the new Cheyenne and Arapaho reservation would be located north of the Platte or south of the Arkansas, far from the central overland routes that carried the whites to the goldfields. Both Little Raven and Black Kettle accepted the inevitability of this decision. The Indians simply could not live in close contact with white people. But the chiefs believed that the "half-breeds"—who were promised their own lands—might well survive along the Arkansas River and Santa Fe Trail.[9]

William, of course, prompted the whole discussion of the mixed-bloods. He firmly believed that the mixed-bloods walked a perilous path between two worlds and were particularly vulnerable to manip-ulation and discrimination by both Indians and whites. The govern-ment must see to their special needs if they were to survive. Besides, he was looking after the interests of his own children. He had never held clear title to any land along the Arkansas, a sore point in all his dealings with the government. This new treaty presented the unique opportunity to guarantee his children an inheritance that he himself could not provide.[10]

Black Kettle and Little Raven would accept the new reservations provided the commissioners made proper arrangements with the Comanches and Lakotas, who already claimed those territories. Still, it would be hard to leave the land of their fathers. Little Raven spoke for both the Cheyennes and Arapahos: "There is something very strong for us—that fool band of soldiers that cleaned out our lodges, and killed our women and children. This is strong on us. There, at Sand creek, is one chief, Left Hand; White Antelope and many other chiefs lie there; our women and children lie there. Our lodges were destroyed there, and our horses were taken from us there, and I do not feel disposed to go right off in a new country and leave them."[11]

Black Kettle agreed but voiced hope for the future: "In broad day-light we talk, and talk the truth; we want nothing bad, and expect nothing but truth. We are different nations, but it seems as if we were but one people, whites and all. We have peace once more, and can sleep soundly, and we can live."[12]

Only months earlier, while fighting the whites on Powder River, George had demanded that Colonel Chivington be hanged for Sand Creek. Now he learned that his father had been called to testify before army and congressional hearings investigating Chivington's conduct. The colonel had resigned his commission, avoiding an army court-martial; nevertheless, a congressional investigation concluded that Chivington and his men had massacred a peaceful village under the protection of military authority.

William told George that Chivington and his supporters remained defiant, however. In the streets of Denver, one of the mad colonel's cronies, Charles W. Squire, gunned down Captain Silas Soule. The captain had been haunted by the scenes of slaughter at Sand Creek and had dared to testify against Chivington. Further, Soule had ordered his men to hold their fire, to spare the fleeing women and children. George already knew that it had been Soule who had saved Charley's life by offering him safe passage to Fort Lyon. Soule's assassination shocked the Bents and confirmed Chivington's brutality.[13] George wondered what would become of the preacher-soldier. This much he did know, Chivington's political and military ambitions were ruined. He could scarcely believe that the army had taken such a strong stand against one of its own and that the government had pledged reparations to chiefs and families who had suffered losses.[14]

Of course, George had a personal interest in reparations, for everything he owned—including four racehorses and some fine Navajo blankets—had been stolen or destroyed at Sand Creek.[15] He consoled himself and took some pride in the knowledge that he had struck back. In fact, the allied tribes had beaten the army, closed the emigrant roads, and forced the U.S. government to take responsibility for the crime of Sand Creek.[16]

For the first time in months, George slept well and soon settled into the routine of village life. No longer fearing soldier attacks, he would remain here on Bluff Creek for the winter.

Just when everything seemed to be going well, I. C. Taylor, the drunken and incompetent agent for the Cheyennes and Arapahos, got it into his head to stop William from trading with the Indians. Envious of the old trader's influence over the tribes, Taylor tried to revoke Bent's license and even requested military assistance to remove him from tribal lands. But the military refused, saying that Bent had Major General Pope's personal endorsement. In fact, Pope had issued orders that military commanders should defer to Bent's counsel in all matters regarding Indian relations. This infuriated the agent, who saw his power undermined by a civilian trader.[17]

In February 1866 George looked on as Taylor rode into the Bluff Creek village—now grown to more than four thousand people with the arrival of the Apaches and Arapahos—escorted by a company of cavalry. Among the soldiers he noticed Major Edward W. Wynkoop. The Department of the Interior had charged Wynkoop with securing the signatures of those Cheyennes who had not participated in the Little Arkansas treaty negotiations. Besides, the Senate had made a number of changes before ratifying the treaty. These had to be explained to the chiefs, and Secretary Harlan had personally selected Wynkoop for this difficult mission.[18]

The Cheyennes knew and trusted Tall Chief Wynkoop. They remembered that he had counciled with them on the Smoky Hill River in September 1864 and had taken the chiefs to Denver to meet with Colonel Chivington and Governor Evans. They had respected his courage for entering the great Dog Soldier village with only a handful of men, and to show their respect they had released white captives to his custody.[19] Once again, here on Bluff Creek, the Cheyennes turned over to Wynkoop a white captive, this time seventeen-year-old Mary Fletcher, who had been taken by Sand Hill's band on the North Platte in August 1865.[20]

George—dressed in blanket and breechclout—sat with Dog Soldier headmen Porcupine Bear and Bull Bear as Wynkoop addressed the chiefs. Also around the council fire were Black Kettle; Little Raven; Rock Forehead, the Cheyenne Arrow Keeper; Big Head; Hairy Wolf; Bear Tongue; Red Iron; and the Apache leader Poor Bear. Black Kettle and Little Raven joined Wynkoop in urging the war factions—especially the Dog Soldiers—to accept the Little Arkansas treaty. But the Dog Men resisted, insisting that the Republican and Smoky Hill country must be preserved as tribal hunting lands. Further, Big Head, angry that he had been attacked on his way south to the Bluff Creek village, demanded that all white roads through this buffalo-rich territory be diverted or closed.

The talks grew tense when Porcupine Bear—the son of the famed Dog Soldier leader of earlier years—said he would kill Wynkoop if the

Later in his life, George Bent was an interpreter at the Seger Indian School in Colony, Oklahoma, when this photograph was taken in 1905. Bent was well known for his knowledge of Cheyenne history and culture and carried on extensive correspondence with the nation's leading ethnologists and historians. *(Courtesy Archives & Manuscripts Division, Oklahoma Historical Society)*

William Bent, frontiersman, trader, Indian agent, married the Arrow Keeper's daughters and tied his future to the Cheyennes. *(Courtesy Colorado Historical Society)*

Bent's Fort, the adobe castle on the Arkansas River, as it appeared when Bent was a boy. Drawn by Lt. James Abert, 1845. *(Courtesy Colorado Historical Society)*

Col. William Bent, Fort Dodge, Kansas, 1867, flanked by Arapaho chief Little Raven, holding his granddaughter, and the chief's sons. *(Courtesy Colorado Historical Society)*

Owl woman (*Mis-stan-sta*), daughter of the Arrow Keeper, White Thunder, married William Bent in 1835 and gave birth to George Bent in 1843. Drawn by Lt. James Abert at Bent's Fort, 1845. *(Courtesy Colorado Historical Society)*

George Bent and his Cheyenne wife Magpie, the niece of Chief Black Kettle, in their wedding dress, c. 1867. Bent is dressed in white man's garb but on his feet—moccasins. *(Courtesy Colorado Historical Society)*

In her later years, Standing Out Woman was known for her singing and extraordinary beadwork. *(Courtesy Smithsonian Institution)*

Standing Out Woman *(May-you-hi)*, married George Bent in 1878, while he was also married to Magpie and Kiowa Woman. *(Courtesy Denver Public Library)*

Smithsonian ethnographer James Mooney photographed Bent's children (left to right Neal, Willie, Mary, Daisy) while conducting interviews on Cheyenne and Arapaho Reservation in 1892. *(Courtesy Smithsonian Institution)*

Camp Weld Conference September 1864 in Denver. Left to right, kneeling, Maj. Edward Wynkoop and Capt. Silas S. Soule; seated, White Antelope, Bull Bear, Black Kettle, Neva, Na-ta-nee; standing, unidentified, unidentified, John Smith, Heap of Buffalo, Bosse, unidentified, unidentified. *(Courtesy Colorado Historical Society)*

Col. John M. Chivington, Methodist Episcopal minister, commanded the Colorado troops that massacred Black Kettle's village at Sand Creek. His military and political ambitions were equaled only by his hatred of Indians. *(Courtesy Colorado Historical Society)*

The Third Colorado Cavalry attacked Black Kettle's peaceful village at Sand Creek on November 29, 1864. The Sand Creek Massacre convinced Bent and the Cheyennes that the whites were determined to exterminate them. Painting by Robert Lindneux;. *(Courtesy Colorado Historical Society)*

Little Bear (c. 1875) and George Bent fought for their lives at Sand Creek. *(Courtesy Smithsonian Institution)*

Private Joseph W. Aldrich, Co. F, First Colorado Cavalry, was among the ten soldiers killed at Sand Creek, November 29, 1864, possibly by friendly fire from the undisciplined "100 daysers" of the Third Colorado Volunteers. *(Courtesy Colorado Historical Society)*

Bent participated in the revenge raids on Julesburg, Colorado, in the months
following the Sand Creek Massacre. *(Courtesy Colorado Historical Society)*

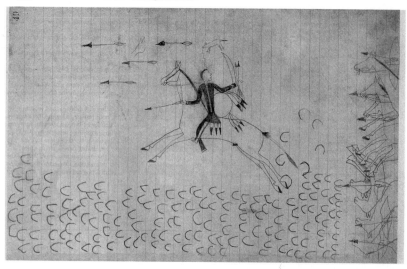

George Bent (*Ho-my-ike*, Beaver) defies the Crows on the Yellowstone River
in 1865 as shown in this sketch taken from the Cheyenne Dog Soldier
ledgerbook. *(Courtesy Colorado Historical Society)*

White Horse, a Pawnee Scout, rode with the army and engaged Cheyennes in Powder River country in 1865. He may have been with a detachment of troops that killed Bent's stepmother Island. *(Courtesy Colorado Historical Society)*

George Bent's half-brother Charley shortly before his violent death in 1867. *(Courtesy Colorado Historical Society)*

William F. "Buffalo Bill" Cody served as chief of scouts for the 5th Cavalry during the summer of 1869. Cody and James "Wild Bill" Hickok asked Bent to scout with them, but Bent refused—he would not "go against" his own people. *(Courtesy Colorado Historical Society)*

Cheyenne chief Stone Calf and his wife, 1877. Bent translated for Stone Calf when he verbally sparred with Gen. Phil Sheridan. The chief told the general to let his soldiers grow their hair long so that the Dog Soldiers could have the honor of killing them like men. *(Courtesy Smithsonian Institution)*

Cheyenne prisoners at Ft. Marion, 1876. *(Courtesy Colorado Historical Society)*

Agent John D. Miles and Sam Whitt (left) with Little Robe and interpreter Ben Clark, c. 1878. *(Courtesy Archives & Manuscripts Division, Oklahoma Historical Society)*

Whirlwind (here pictured in 1877), a formidable warrior and later chief, was a longtime friend of Bent's but was critical of his drinking and business dealings on the Cheyenne and Arapaho Reservation. *(Courtesy Smithsonian Institution)*

Interpreter Phil McCusker supplied George Bent with liquor. Though Agent Miles banned him from the reservation, he married into the Cheyenne tribe and remained Bent's friend. *(Courtesy Archives & Manuscripts Division, Oklahoma Historical Society)*

Cheyenne and Arapaho delegates visited Gettysburg on their way to Washington, D.C., in November 1884. Among those pictured at Devil's Den are (left to right) Black Wolf, Left Hand, Whirlwind, Powder Face, Big Jake, John Williams, Sue and Lina Miles, and Ed Guerrier (in white suit). *(Courtesy Archives & Manuscripts Division, Oklahoma Historical Society)*

Bob Bent with Cheyenne schoolboy Tom "Carlisle," during an 1884 visit to the Carlisle Indian School. George Bent's drinking problem prevented him from accompanying his brother and the Cheyenne and Arapaho delegation to Washington, D.C. *(Courtesy Cumberland County [Pennsylvania] Historical Society)*

Beef issue on the Cheyenne and Arapaho Reservation, 1889. *(Courtesy Archives & Manuscripts Division, Oklahoma Historical Society)*

Ed Guerrier at Carlisle Indian School with Bent's troubled daughter Julia (right) and Laura Standing Elk in 1884. *(Courtesy Cumberland County [Pennsylvania] Historical Society)*

Cheyenne and Arapaho delegation assembled by John D. Miles and Samuel Crawford with Bent's help at Oklahoma City, June 1889. This Miles photo documented the gathering as evidence the delegation was duly selected and represented the will of the Cheyennes and Arapahos. Hunched and unhappy, Bent sits with white hat second from right. *(Courtesy Archives & Manuscripts Division, Oklahoma Historical Society)*

Bent interprets for ethnographer John J. White and Indian school superintendent John Seger, as Big Knee and his wife share Cheyenne stories at Colony, Oklahoma, 1905. (Left to right, Bent, daughter Mary Blind, Big Knee and his wife, Standing Out, Seger, White). *(Courtesy Archives & Manuscripts Division, Oklahoma Historical Society)*

This Cheyene Dog Soldier ledgerbook drawing depicts a scene described by George Bent in his correspondence. *(Courtesy Colorado Historical Society)*

Wooden Leg, a Cheyenne who fought at the Battle of Little Big Horn in 1876, draws scenes of brave warrior deeds in a ledgerbook. *(Courtesy Colorado Historical Society)*

Dog Soldiers were forced to sign the amended treaty. Wynkoop already suspected trouble from Porcupine Bear. When the Dog Men arrived at the conference the day before, the chief had refused to shake hands with him. Wynkoop learned that he had lost relatives at Sand Creek and hated all whites. Now, the major turned for advice to his interpreter, a mixed-blood Arapaho woman he had pressed into service, but she only buried her head in her blanket and wept hysterically, certain that Porcupine Bear would make good on his threat and kill them all.[21]

Wynkoop now sat next to John Smith, who replaced the unnerved woman as his principal interpreter. A wooden box stood in the center of the circle. On it lay the amended treaty, a pen, and an inkwell. On one side of the circle sat Black Kettle and the peace faction who had already made their marks on the treaty paper. Opposite them sat Porcupine Bear, hunched and grim, and to his left, Bull Bear, the hotheaded Dog Soldier chief. On Porcupine Bear's right sat George Bent.

Finally, Wynkoop stood and approached Porcupine Bear, holding out to him the pen. George spoke to the chief in low, soothing tones, urging him to be the first of the Dog Soldiers to sign the treaty. This infuriated Bull Bear, who warned Porcupine Bear not to break with the Dog Men. Other Dog Men shouted their agreement: Porcupine Bear must not sign. Minutes passed. Porcupine Bear sat silently, looking neither right nor left. Suddenly, the chief grunted, rose to his feet, and walked to the box. Without a word, he took the pen and scratched a cross on the paper.[22]

George had won the battle of wills, but the victory had come at a price—his relationship with the Dog Men would never be the same. He had also won a powerful friend. Wynkoop was impressed with young Bent. He reported to his superiors that George was a chief and had used his influence to convince Porcupine Bear and other Dog Men to endorse the treaty.[23]

Wynkoop, however, understood that the agreement was fragile and could be shattered at any moment. During the talks a trader named Boggs cheated four Cheyennes by exchanging eleven one-dollar greenbacks for ten ten-dollar bills. When the warriors learned of the deception, they took revenge by killing and scalping the trader's young son, whom they caught on the open plains, just six miles east of Fort

Dodge. After the talks, Wynkoop and the army investigated the incident but thought it best not to prosecute the Cheyennes, given the circumstances.[24] Some of the Dog Soldier bands, encouraged by Charley Bent, continued to harass isolated settlements and trains.[25] Such incidents threatened the peace, but in the months following the Bluff Creek council, whites traveled the roads in relative safety, and the Indians enjoyed a welcomed respite from war. The Cheyennes could now turn their attention to family and home.[26]

When George walked through the village, people noticed him. He had not only proved himself in battle, but he often stood with the chiefs at important councils. As the son of William Bent and Owl Woman, he was a scion of the best families. This, coupled with his skills as a negotiator and fighter, made him attractive to young women. William saw this, and understanding the importance of a good marriage he approached Black Kettle. The chief had a marriageable niece whom he regarded as a daughter. Her name was Magpie Woman, *Mo-hi-hy-wah*, and George had already noticed her, for in the last year she had grown from a girl into a striking woman.[27] Black braids framed fine angular features, and her lips seemed to pout, except when she smiled at him. Then her face softened and her dark eyes came to life. She carried herself with a haughty pride befitting her family's high standing. In fact, she lived in Black Kettle's lodge, which George had shared on many occasions. By the light of the fire he had watched her mother comb and braid her hair. On mornings, he made certain to be near the stream when she came to draw water. Here, among the willows, they would talk, away from prying eyes and chaperones. Her beauty and station had intimidated some of the young men, but not George. He possessed a confidence and worldliness that appealed to her. One afternoon, when the autumn chill had descended on Bluff Creek, George boldly opened his red-wool blanket and with a sweep of his arm enveloped her in it. Huddled in the blanket's warmth, they whispered to one another and spoke of love.[28]

Black Kettle and William agreed that the marriage would suit both families and were glad that George and Magpie raised no objection. Young people sometimes resisted marriages arranged by their parents. But George could certainly see the advantage of a marriage to Black

Kettle's daughter, and Magpie could not deny her attraction to George and the advantages that such a union would present. The arranged marriage was important not only to Black Kettle and the Bents but to the Cheyennes as well. George represented a political and trade entrée into the white world. For the Bents, Magpie represented a consolidation of their influence in the Cheyenne world.

That spring the two families hosted a marriage ceremony unequalled since William married Owl Woman more than thirty years before. William rolled out fourteen trade wagons and opened them in a grand giveaway. Black Kettle presented George with the magnificent bay horse given to him by General Harney at the Little Arkansas Treaty negotiations in October.[29] Some said the gift would have meant more if the animal had been captured in battle, but all agreed that coming from General Harney, a soldier of strong heart, the gift was appropriate.[30]

Magpie's elaborate dress was suitable for the daughter of a great chief. It was meticulously crafted of dark blue trade cloth, the white selvedge outlining the sleeves. Rows of rare and expensive elk teeth covered the upper part of the garment, while the skirts were intricately quilled and beaded in floral and geometric designs. Around her neck she wore a dentalium choker and long necklace, and from her pierced ears dangled beautifully worked jewelry. Silver rings adorned her fingers, and her beaded moccasins were of the finest white antelope hide.

In deference to his father, George wore a dark three-piece suit of the best broadcloth, complete with a striped shirt and silk cravat. His hair was cut short, combed, and oiled; his mustache was neatly trimmed. But on his feet, he wore finely beaded moccasins.[31]

On this day, everyone expected George to look as a white man; so too, Magpie was to look the part of a highborn Cheyenne, the daughter of a chief. For this was not just a union of two people, or even of two great families. It was a joining of two cultures, each wanting something of value from the other.

The wedding couple posed for a photograph. When they entered the white man's makeshift studio, he guided them through the torturous ritual necessary to make a photographic image. He cautioned them not to smile or move a muscle—any motion would spoil the picture. For half a minute, George and Magpie sat bolt upright, staring at the camera, their faces expressionless. The photographer carefully arranged their clothing, the folds of Magpie's quilled and elk-tooth-studded dress, the lapels of George's coat and his moccasined feet. They were a stunning couple and the white man did not want them to leave. He induced Magpie to pose separately, reclining on a couch like a princess, her Cheyenne nobility evident.

George never forgot the excitement and rituals surrounding his marriage. The celebrated couple slept side by side in a magnificently decorated and furnished lodge, but for ten long days and nights they did not embrace or consummate their union. Custom dictated that they should lie apart and talk, using the time to get to know one another. Magpie wore around her waist a chastity belt or, as George called it, a "safety rope" of tightly braided horsehair. At the end of the ninth day, the women took Magpie away, removed the safety rope, and carefully plucked all the hair from the lower part of her body. Then they bathed her and combed and braided her hair. In time, they brought her back to the lodge and presented her to George, all of them covering their mouths as they giggled and smiled shyly. Black Kettle's wife, *Ar-no-ho-wok*, supervised these proceedings, making sure that the ritual was properly performed. Finally, the women left the lodge, fastening the door flap behind them. Later they returned and painted the bodies of the couple red, signifying that Magpie was no longer a virgin and that the proper rituals had been observed. The newlyweds now began their lives together.

George learned how upper-class Cheyenne married couples were expected to behave. Magpie led him through the customs. When he entered the lodge after hunting, she would wash his hands and remove any clothes that might be stained with blood. At mealtime, Magpie would bring meat prepared in her mother's lodge and offer it to her husband along with drink, holding the wooden cup to his lips.

Husbands also had to observe marital rituals. George combed and flattened Magpie's long hair, and on special occasions he would paint slashes of red on the side of her forehead, indicating the number of coups he had counted.

Only the "better classes of the tribe practiced these customs," George later explained, with "the poorer ones not making so much ceremony."[32]

In May 1866, shortly after the wedding, William left for Washington, where ratification of the treaty had been delayed in the Senate. The old man was miffed. He had put his reputation on the line by promising that the Great Father would soon implement the provisions of the treaty, especially those relating to reparations and annuities. Yet the Cheyennes and Arapahos had received nothing. The chiefs also demanded the immediate return of the children taken captive at Sand Creek. In anger, William wrote to the commissioner of Indian Affairs, D. N. Cooley:

These Indians had, owing to the Sand Creek massacre and other outrages perpetrated upon them, lost faith in the white man, and it was only by the most earnest assurances, added to an acquaintance of nearly forty years with them, that I could last fall while acting as Commissioner for the United States, induce their leading chiefs to sign the treaties, and if the annuity goods provided for in said treaties are promptly sent forward this spring as therein provided, I have no doubt that the stipulations of the Indians will be kept in good faith, but if they are not these Indians will think the government has broken its faith with them, and I candidly believe the result will be a more bloody and terrible Indian war, than has ever before taken place upon the plains.[33]

William's displeasure was heightened by the government's failure to recognize his efforts in bringing the Indians to the Little Arkansas and agreeing to sign the treaty.[34] He felt used by the self-serving officials who now gave him little credit for his role in bringing peace to the plains. Finally, he wanted to make certain that the halfbreeds—including his own children—received the lands guaranteed to them. These details, he feared, might easily fall through the cracks of the infamous Washington bureaucracy.[35] He concluded his work quickly, for he had little taste for the crowded city and formal airs affected by foppish men and dainty ladies in the nation's capital. Before he left, however, he saw to it that the authorities knew of the Indians' displeasure with Agent I. C. Taylor and received assurances that this troublesome agent would soon be replaced.

In August, shortly after his return to the Purgatoire ranch, William received word that special agents of the Bureau of Indian Affairs,

W. R. Irwin and Charles Bogy, had been dispatched to Fort Zarah to settle all claims and ensure compliance with the 1865 treaty. The government contracted William to bring the Cheyenne and Arapaho annuities to the talks. Perhaps the mountain of goods he brought would induce the recalcitrant chiefs to at last sign the treaty. But the councils that followed in late summer and early fall 1866 failed miserably. Only a few chiefs came in, the Dog Soldiers continued raiding on the Smoky Hill route, and the talks themselves were marred by incidents of drunkenness and violence. William pulled out in disgust, selling his stock of goods to trader David Butterfield.[36]

In November he returned to Fort Zarah, this time with sons George and Bob. Things again started badly. Charley, who had been supplying liquor to the Dog Soldiers, got drunk and threatened to kill his father. When George intervened, Charley exploded. He had learned of the role his older brother had played in negotiations between the Dog Soldiers and Wynkoop at Bluff Creek. George had sold out to the whites, Charley told others, and if he saw the chance he would shoot him dead. William knew he had to keep Charley away from the whiskey and pleaded with the military authorities to arrest his renegade son. But they refused, fearing that this action might result in a general uprising.[37]

Then, on November 8, George's friend Fox Tail, a Dog Soldier and the son of Rock Forehead, came to William and boasted that he would kill a white man. Later that day, Fox Tail shot down one of Bent's Mexican herders in front of many witnesses. Everyone knew Fox Tail had committed the crime, but the Dog Soldiers refused to give up the Arrow Keeper's son and withdrew from the conference still opposed to the treaty.

Once the Dog Soldiers had left, Black Kettle and the peace chiefs renewed their commitment to the agreement and accepted the goods and supplies brought to them by Butterfield as full reparation for the loss of the pony herds at Sand Creek. The government hoped to pay all the reparations at Fort Zarah, but the Cheyennes questioned the quality of the presents and vehemently disagreed with the proposed method of distribution. The agents wanted to distribute the goods only to the families of the Sand Creek victims, while the chiefs thought this would foment tribal infighting and proposed instead that the distribution be made to the tribe as a whole, just like annuity payments.[38]

George knew the Fort Zarah councils had produced no real change. The Dog Soldiers continued to oppose any treaty that ceded the Smoky Hill country, the Indian children taken captive at Sand Creek had not been returned, and sporadic raids threatened white roads and outposts. While Wynkoop reported success at Fort Zarah, William headed home, frustrated with Dog Soldier intransigence and government red tape and double talk.

George shared his father's views and was glad to return to the Bluff Creek villages south of Fort Zarah. Magpie waited for him there, living now in Black Kettle's lodge. Here, away from the whites and the complicated and tiring world of treaty negotiations, he could get on with his life as a husband and a Cheyenne warrior.

In December several war parties set out for Pawnee country. George joined a large force of eighty warriors led by Eagle Head, a Bowstring headman and father of Howling Wolf. One afternoon as they rode on the trail, Eagle Head called a halt and announced that every man must offer a flesh sacrifice to ensure the success of the raid. So the men dismounted and built several sweat lodges. Fires were lit and the stones heated. Big Wolf, knife in hand, went before each man, cutting long strips of skin from their upper arms. No one objected, nor did anyone show sign of pain. But when Big Wolf approached George and his friend Red Moon, the young men objected, arguing that they had not been told beforehand that this would be required. But Eagle Head, the pipe bearer, insisted. If the two men did not comply, they would have to return to the village disgraced and the entire war party's medicine would be spoiled. At this, George realized that all eyes had suddenly turned to him. He had not expected his loyalty to be tested in this way and was relieved that he did not stand alone—Red Moon had also refused. But George stood out. His fair skin and mustache marked him as a mixed-blood. As he looked into the eyes of his companions, he recognized some who would welcome his failure, jealous men who saw him as a white man, *vehoe*. Suddenly, he felt uncomfortable. In another place and time, he wore his mustache proudly as a mixed-blood. But here, with sudden clarity, he realized that some Cheyennes still regarded him as a foreigner. To be fully accepted, he must look as they looked and believe as they believed. But did he? Did he believe a flesh sacrifice would bring success? Or was it so much superstitious hokum dreamed up by a holy man? When he had lived among the whites, he had heard them ridicule Indians ways. But he had witnessed miraculous cures and had seen the power of a warrior's medicine when rituals were properly performed. He understood, too, that his failure to participate in the flesh offering would not just threaten the outcome of the raid but would forever brand him a coward and, worse, a white man.

George approached Big Wolf, who still grasped the sacrificial knife. Holding out his arms, he boldly ordered him to cut *two* strips from each. As the knife flashed across his forearms, he neither flinched nor betrayed any sign of fear. Soon it was over, and the warriors nodded their approval as he slowly walked to the sweat lodge, blood streaming from his arms.

After two day of unsuccessful scouting on the Smoky Hill in central Kansas, the Cheyenne wolves sighted a party of Kaws. While these were not the hated Pawnees, Eagle Head decided to attack. He would not return to the village without counting a coup. The warriors rushed in, counting many coups and taking one scalp, then easily ran off the surprised Kaws. This was enough; Eagle Head turned the warriors for home. When they neared the village, the men dismounted and blackened their faces as sign that they had vanquished the enemy without loss to their own party. Then they charged the Cheyenne camp, shouting war cries and shooting their guns into the air. Women rushed from their lodges, trilling as they ran to greet the returning warriors. A grand scalp dance began almost immediately, and the explosion of drums and singing continued long into the night.

This was George's first successful war party since his marriage to Magpie. She touched the scabs on his arms as he painted her face and combed her hair. Later, at the dance, she took the scalp in her hand and held it aloft, thrilling at her husband's prowess as a Cheyenne warrior. Back in the privacy of their lodge, Magpie removed George's clothing and bathed him. Then, with the sounds of drums and singing echoing in the night, they made love.[39]

Chapter 8

CHEYENNE AUTUMN

In January 1867, just a month after his triumphant return to Black Kettle's Bluff Creek village south of Fort Zarah, George moved over to the Kiowa and Prairie Apache camps, twenty miles west. Trader David Butterfield had contracted with George to sell goods to these tribes. Business boomed, especially the trade in arms and ammunition. The subsistence of the Kiowas and Apaches, and all the peoples of the plains, depended on guns—not just for hunting but for survival. Without the rifles manufactured in Pennsylvania and the powder made in Delaware and the lead mined in Illinois, they could not hope to defend themselves against attack. They needed firearms and would do anything to get them. It was a vicious cycle: whites produced weapons, Indians slaughtered more and more buffalo for hides, whites converted the hides into leather drive belts that drove eastern factories and the world's industrial revolution. For a hundred years and more, the plains tribes had depended on the buffalo for food, shelter, clothing, and tools. By increasing the yearly kill, the tribes participated in their own destruction. George and other traders acted as brokers, although they hardly understood their role or the awful consequences of the guns-for-hides exchange.[1]

In January and February, George lodged with Kiowa Chief Kicking Bird, while his good friend Charlie Rath, an old Bent–St. Vrain employee, stayed with Chief Satanta. Both traders had learned from William Bent himself that the only way to successfully conduct business in an Indian village was to move into the lodge of the dominant chief, who then protected the trade goods and the trader.[2]

By March George returned to Black Kettle's village and Magpie. For the next three weeks he continued his trade, filling Butterfield's wagons with Cheyenne buffalo robes and raw hides. But just as the grass began to green, runners brought ominous news: white soldiers—cavalry, infantry, and artillery—nearly fourteen hundred strong were on the march and had reached Fort Larned, only sixty miles north of the Cheyenne winter camps. George knew such a force meant trouble; each night as Black Kettle entered the lodge, George saw the worry in the old man's face. After a council with his chiefs, Black Kettle told George that the village would move south, out of the soldiers' path. Let the Dog Soldiers fight the bluecoats; the southern bands would drag their lodges all the way to Texas and Comanche country to stay out of harm's way.[3]

The Kiowas and Prairie Apaches followed Black Kettle's lead. When the tribes reached the North Fork of the Canadian, they joined the Comanche villages of Ten Bears and Tall Hat. The white traders in Ten Bears' camp quickly learned that the soldiers were on the move and immediately packed their wagons, staying only long enough to supply the Cheyennes with the sugar and coffee that would sustain the people during their flight south.[4]

A few days later, when Black Kettle arrived on the South Fork of the Canadian, he received more troubling news. On April 14, Major General Winfield Scott Hancock, the Union hero of the Battle of Gettysburg and one of the army's most aggressive commanders, had surrounded a combined Dog Soldier–Lakota village on Pawnee Fork, near Fort Larned. Fearing another Sand Creek Massacre, the people had fled, abandoning their lodges and possessions.

Hancock occupied the village for three days, using the time to search the camp and inventory its contents. With so much abandoned, the general had expected the Indians to return and negotiate. Instead, the warriors had attempted to draw the soldiers away from the captured village by attacking stage stations on the Smoky Hill Trail. In retaliation, Hancock torched the village; he would brook no insolence from these red rebels, for his Civil War experience had taught him that only decisive action would suppress rebellion. Taking the war to every Indian lodge would crush resistance and force the Cheyennes to accept government control.

As the flames shot skyward, Hancock ordered his cavalry commander, Lieutenant Colonel George A. Custer of the Seventh Cavalry, to hunt down the Dog Soldiers and their families. At the head of Custer's column rode George's closest friend and soon-to-be brother-in-law, Ed Guerrier. Ed had pledged to marry Julia in the summer of 1865 when she came south with Black Kettle's band.[5] The peace chief had sought to remove his people for the war of retaliation following Sand Creek. Lured by the high pay offered by the army, Guerrier had joined the U.S. service as an interpreter and had been assigned to assist Hancock in the negotiations with the Dog Soldiers and their Lakota allies. He had been with Hancock since arriving at Fort Larned and had witnessed the series of meetings that had led up to the village's burning.

Later, when he returned to Black Kettle's village, Guerrier told George that the talks at Fort Larned had gone badly from the very beginning. On April 12, Hancock had conducted the first meeting at night around a bonfire—offensive to the Dog Soldiers who felt important councils should always be held in the full light of day. Hancock, however, seemed determined to impress the Cheyennes and instructed all of his officers to don their dress uniforms—glittering epaulettes, sashes, and hats and shakos festooned with ostrich plumes and red horse tails. The chiefs dressed in their finery, too. Tall Bull, lean and a head taller than most of the soldiers, wrapped himself in a red trade blanket, and all the chiefs wore dangling eardrops, silver armbands, bone breast-plates, and long trailing scalp locks decorated with silver disks.[6]

Handsome and resplendent in his dress uniform, his goatee neatly trimmed, Hancock lectured the Dog Soldier leaders, particularly insulting Tall Bull, who glared at the arrogant general and tapped his foot impatiently throughout the long harangue. The other chiefs—Bull Bear, White Horse, and Grey Beard—better controlled their tempers, listening impassively to Guerrier's translation. The general ranted on. He said he had been purposely slighted by the absence of the famed Roman Nose, even though Guerrier explained that while the Crooked Lance warrior was a respected fighter, he was not a chief and had no place at such councils. Nevertheless, Hancock took Roman Nose's failure to attend as a sign that the Cheyennes were plotting an attack. If the Cheyennes wanted war, he warned, his army would give it to them in full measure. Before this bewildering council broke up, Hancock made a show of his good faith by returning an Indian boy who had been captured at Sand Creek. But even this gesture backfired; after taking the child on their laps and looking him in the eye, the Cheyenne chiefs shook their heads and said they did not recognize him as one of their own.[7]

Frustrated by the failure of his first meeting with the Indians, Hancock angrily marched toward the Cheyenne village, which he believed to be somewhere on the Pawnee Fork of the Smoky Hill. The next day, emissaries from the Indian camp begged the general not to advance farther, explaining that the people feared a repetition of Sand Creek. But Hancock refused to change his course and told the runners that he would talk only with Roman Nose, whom he still believed to be "head chief" of the Cheyennes. On April 14, as Hancock moved toward the village, armed and painted warriors suddenly appeared across his line of march. Officers barked commands and buglers instantly responded with blaring calls. Cavalrymen drew sabers and galloped into battle formation, while the artillery sped into position and gun crews trained their cannons on the warriors.

Before a shot could be fired, Edward Wynkoop, recently appointed U. S. Indian agent, spurred his horse forward and rode straight for the cluster of chiefs and headmen arrayed behind the warrior line. He soon returned to a point between the opposing forces. With him were the chiefs—and Roman Nose. Hancock confronted the war leader and demanded to know if he wanted war. Roman Nose pointed out that if he had wanted war he would not have ridden up so close to the soldiers' cannons. The general asked why he had not come to Fort Larned to meet in council. Roman Nose explained that his horses were poor and too weak to travel; besides, everyone had told him a different story. No one seemed to know why Hancock had brought his soldiers, not even Guerrier, the general's own interpreter. Abruptly, Hancock declared the parley over and announced that his troops would camp near the village where talks would resume. Roman Nose and the chiefs rode the ten miles to their encampment to warn the people of Hancock's approach. The soldiers followed not far behind.

As soon as he got back to the village, Roman Nose began putting on his war regalia—including his famous one-horned headdress—and told the chiefs that when Hancock arrived he would go out and shoot him in the head with a pistol. The general, he said, was "spoiling for a fight. I will kill him in front of his own men and give them something to fight about."[8] The chiefs feared that if Roman Nose carried out his threat, the soldiers would massacre the women and children. Even now, the women were rounding up the ponies and preparing for flight. Tall Bull and White Horse urged Bull Bear, the only man who had influence over Roman Nose, to ride with the war leader and restrain him if possible.

Roman Nose made quite an impression on Hancock's entourage. A newspaper correspondent described him riding toward Hancock: "I have never seen so fine a specimen of the Indian race as he—quite six feet in height and finely-formed, dressed in the uniform of a United States officer, and provided with a numerous quantity of arms. His carbine, a Spencer, hung at the side of his pony, four heavy revolvers were stuck in his belt, while his left hand grasped a bow and a number of arrows—the bow being strung and ready for instant use."[9]

Ed Guerrier sat his horse next to Hancock when Roman Nose approached. The Crooked Lance warrior acknowledged Guerrier, his friend and relative by marriage. Roman Nose turned to Hancock, looking at him for a long time. He told the general to back off, that the troops were frightening the women and children. Hancock asked why they should be afraid. Roman Nose shot back, "Have you not heard of Sand Creek? Your soldiers look just like those who butchered the women and children there."[10] And with anger rising in his voice he told Guerrier that he was about to kill the general, confident that his friend would not betray his intentions. But at that moment, Bull Bear reached down and grabbed the war leader's bridle, pulled the pony's head around, and led Roman Nose back toward the village. Guerrier later told George that it had been a very close thing. Hancock "the Superb" had almost been shot dead on the plains of Kansas.[11]

After the flight of the village, Custer ordered Guerrier to guide the Seventh Cavalry in pursuit. Custer liked Guerrier, who looked the part of a frontiersmen with his well-groomed, shoulder-length black hair and drooping mustache. Still, the mixed-blood scout was in a difficult spot. Not only did he have friends in the village, but he would soon marry George Bent's sister, Julia. As they rode, Ed could not help but remember that Roman Nose had once courted Julia, but it was he who had won the beautiful mixed-blood Bent girl's affection. For these mixed-blood lovers were a breed apart and possessed a bond that outsiders would never understand. And now she was among the fleeing Cheyennes. Julia, like Ed, had survived the horrors of Sand Creek and he could well imagine her terror at the approach of Hancock's soldiers.[12]

Ed should have followed George's lead and said no to scouting for the army. Now, like Robert Bent at Sand Creek, he found himself at the head of the soldiers leading them against his own people. Custer, who hoped to capture as many villagers as possible, had ordered Guerrier to scout three miles ahead of the column. Ed had no intention of turning over hostages to Custer or any other soldier. When he spotted a young Cheyenne rounding up ponies in a ravine, he signaled for him to make a break—the soldiers were coming up fast. Guerrier told Custer that the Indians had scattered and the trail was nearly impossible to follow, especially since they were not dragging lodge poles. These of course had been left behind in the abandoned village. Inexperienced in Indian warfare, Custer took Guerrier at his word and chose a trail north, away from the fugitives.[13] Thanks to Guerrier's services as "scout," Custer and the Seventh never saw a single Indian during the entire chase. It was, as Custer himself characterized it, a "futile pursuit."[14]

After the runners told the people of the disaster on Pawnee Fork, Black Kettle and the chiefs decided to move down to the Washita, where George and the other men hunted buffalo for three weeks. Then the village moved west to the headwaters of the Washita. Here, other Cheyenne bands joined Black Kettle's people.

The Cheyennes decided to strike back at the whites for Hancock's foolish and unprovoked aggression. The warriors would not allow such an insult to go unanswered. War parties went out in all directions. George joined a party of seventy warriors under a medicine man named Lame Bull. They struck out for Cimarron Crossing, on the trail to Santa Fe. George knew this watering place near Fort Dodge. It was a favorite campsite for large freight trains rich in livestock and trade goods and was a perfect target for the raiders. But there was another reason to go to Cimarron Crossing. The six runners who had brought news of Hancock's attack had themselves been jumped by soldiers there. George knew these men well, for they were of Black Kettle's village. Two of them, Lone Bear and Eagle Nest, were still missing and it was feared they had been killed.

When the war party reached the Cimarron, they found Lone Bear's skeleton on the river bank; Eagle Nest's body was later found in the sand hills south of the river. That evening Lame Bull's party struck a westbound train, running off fifty mules. The next day, George and the Cheyennes rode west and intercepted another train at a water hole. The warriors hid in a ravine, waiting for the teamsters to lead the thirsty animals to drink. But before Lame Bull gave the signal to attack, a few young men rushed the mule herd, ruining the surprise. The frightened bell-mare made a beeline for the corralled wagons. George's friend, Howling Wolf, knew that if he could capture the bell-mare the other mules would follow. In his attempt to cut the animal off, Howling Wolf was shot through the thigh and fell off his horse. Under fire, George galloped forward to help his friend. As he approached Howling Wolf, he reached down and pulled the wounded man up behind him and carried him back to the safety of the ravine. The warriors managed to capture twenty-two mules and four horses. Satisfied with the success of the raid, Lame Bull led the party back to the main Cheyenne camps, which now stood on the North Fork of the Red River in the heart of Comanche country—the farthest south the Cheyennes had ever camped.[15]

The plains were again in flames. Cheyenne and Lakota warriors swept through Kansas, Colorado, and Nebraska, attacking Kansas Pacific railroad trains and construction crews, stage and telegraph stations, ranches, and wagon trains. Dog Soldiers even attacked Custer's headquarters at Fort Wallace. On June 26, as Seventh Cavalry officers watched, several warriors decoyed a detachment of soldiers from the fort. Within sight of the post, a large party of Cheyenne warriors—Charley Bent conspicuous among them—appeared from nowhere and attacked.[16] According to Captain Albert Barnitz, who was leading the detachment, the Cheyennes presented a magnificent sight on their painted ponies:

They turned suddenly upon my line, and came literally *sailing* in, uttering their peculiar *Hi!—Hi!—Hi!* and terminating it with the war-whoop—their ponies, gaily decked with feathers and scalp-locks, tossing their proud little heads high in the air, and looking wildly from side to side, as their riders poured in a rapid fire from their repeating arms, or sending their keen arrows with fearful accuracy and force.[17]

The bodies of the killed troopers were stripped and mutilated within view of their terrified comrades.

So went Hancock's War. For four months the Cheyennes exacted a terrible revenge. The commissioner of Indian Affairs summed up the disastrous summer campaign: "We lost over 300 soldiers and citizens, several millions of dollars in expenses, and an immense amount of public and private property, and killed, it is believed, six Indians, and no more."[18] Further, Custer pushed his Seventh Cavalry to exhaustion, causing demoralized troopers to desert in large numbers. Hancock was relieved of command and Custer court-martialed for abandoning his troops.[19]

In late May, when George and the raiders returned to the Red River camps, Black Kettle sought him out. The chief told him that a Mexican named Sylvestre had arrived several days earlier carrying a dispatch from Colonel Jesse Leavenworth, agent for the Kiowas and Comanches. No one in the village could read the letter, so Black Kettle had impatiently awaited George's return. George read the letter and then informed the old chief that Leavenworth wanted Black Kettle, along with Kiowa, Comanche, and Apache chiefs, to meet with him at the mouth of the Little Arkansas in Kansas to negotiate a peace. Black Kettle consulted with the Cheyenne chiefs, but because the journey would take them through the territory of their Indian enemies—the Wichitas and Osages—none would agree to accompany him. The danger was heightened since Cheyennes had recently attacked a Wichita horse-raiding party and killed one of its number. But Black Kettle was determined to go anyway. His wife, George, and Sylvestre would accompany him, as would his cousin, Lone Bear. Lame Man and his wife agreed to go as well, but only to visit their daughter Jenny, who lived with "Dutch Bill" Griffenstein near the Wichita village.[20]

Ten days from camp, the party struck an immense herd of buffalo. For days they rode through the milling animals, hunting as they went and enjoying fresh meat every night but always keeping a watchful eye out for enemy warriors. One day, they came upon an Osage hunting party. George surprised a chief, who had just made a kill and was stripping the hide from the carcass. The Osage looked up, and George spoke to him in English: "We are Cheyennes, on our way to the Wichita village to see the agent there." The Osage identified himself as *Pawhuska* and was glad the Cheyennes had come in peace. He would do what he could to help them and invited Black Kettle to eat at his brush-and-hide wigwam, which was only a short distance away. After feasting on roasted buffalo ribs, fried bread, and coffee, George translated for the chiefs as they discussed the peace mission. *Pawhuska* warned them they would likely meet the Sac and Foxes—also Cheyenne enemies—the next day. This tribe, he said, was on the way to its new reservation in Indian Territory, recently established by the government. *Pawhuska's* information was accurate.[21]

The next day, Black Kettle and his party met *Keokuk*, chief of the Sac and Foxes, who spoke good English and was surprisingly friendly. He led them to his camp, which consisted of army surplus wall tents instead of traditional tipis. *Keokuk* treated them to another buffalo feast. During the meal, George made a speech in English, fast becoming the lingua franca of the prairie tribes, telling them why Black Kettle was here and of his hopes of making a peace with Agent Leavenworth. The next day the Cheyennes continued their journey toward the Arkansas River, the buffalo still thick around them. When they sighted the Wichita village, Black Kettle sent Sylvestre ahead to notify Leavenworth of their arrival. That afternoon George and the others forded the muddy, flood-high waters of the Arkansas. On the opposite bank, watching them make the dangerous crossing, stood Agent Leavenworth, Dutch Bill Griffenstein, and Cheyenne Jenny, along with a number of white traders well known to George. As they entered the village, they found the chiefs sitting in a circle smoking, while women wailed in mourning for the Wichita horse raider recently killed by the Cheyennes. George and Black Kettle rode by, their faces showing no trace of concern. But both men wondered whether the Wichitas would attack. Once in the village, however, all was peaceful. Black Kettle shook hands with the Wichitas as well as with chiefs Ten Bears and Tall Hat, who had already arrived with a Comanche delegation.

When they met in council the next morning, Leavenworth informed everyone that the commissioner of Indian Affairs and many other important government officials, including the Cheyenne's old adversary, General William S. Harney, were ready to make peace and hold a council with all the tribes. Then Leavenworth stood and read a letter from the commissioner, while George translated for Black Kettle. All the chiefs agreed that it was good, and Ten Bears recommended that Medicine Lodge Creek sixty miles south of Fort Larned would be the ideal place to hold the council. The Kiowas, he said, often held their sun dances there. Black Kettle thought this a good plan but said he needed to return to his village and consult with the other Cheyenne chiefs.

George was ready to accompany him, but Leavenworth asked him to stay. He had been impressed with Black Kettle's mixed-blood protégé and was eager to hire to him to help notify all the tribes of the time and place of the council. But Leavenworth first needed the approval of his superiors in Washington. George agreed to stay over until the agent received his instructions. While Leavenworth went to Fort Larned and Black Kettle returned to his people, George stayed with Dutch Bill and Cheyenne Jenny in Wichita country.

Within a month's time, Leavenworth returned with a letter authorizing George to go out among the tribes and spread the news of the proposed Medicine Lodge Creek council. For the next few weeks, as he traveled from tribe to tribe, he enjoyed the company of Cheyenne Jenny. She was an invalid and was forced to ride in a spring wagon, but her reputation was known far and wide, for she had long worked to foster peaceful relations between plains tribes and whites. At Little Raven's Arapaho camp on the Cimarron, George sent criers to bring the chiefs and headmen of the soldier societies together. Once gathered, George read the commissioner's letter in English, then translated it into Arapaho. The Arapahos agreed to meet at Fort Larned to determine the exact location of the treaty council on nearby Medicine Lodge Creek.

George and Jenny found Black Kettle's camp on Wolf Creek, south of Fort Larned in Indian Territory. The Dog Soldiers had just arrived from the north, and with them Charley. George assembled the chiefs and headmen in a large lodge in the center of the village circle and, with Black Kettle at his side, read the commissioner's letter. When he finished interpreting it, Chief Tall Bull stepped forward and told Charley to read the letter again and translate it for the Dog Soldiers. Charley was one of them now and could be trusted. George had spent too much time with Black Kettle and was too closely identified with the peace faction. Nevertheless, George succeeded in gaining the support of all the chiefs, including the Dog Soldier leaders. From here, George continued to the Kiowa, Comanche, and Apache camps, reading the letter and convincing the tribes to participate.

A few weeks later, George rode into Fort Larned, accompanied not only by Black Kettle and the Cheyenne chiefs, but also by the Arapaho, Kiowa, Comanche, and Prairie Apache leaders. His entrance into the fort filled him with dread. He feared the soldiers would arrest him or shoot him down without warning, for he had been identified in border newspapers and eastern magazines as a renegade leader.[22] But to his great relief, the army officers treated him with respect and the talks went on as planned. All the chiefs agreed on Medicine Lodge Creek, some fifty miles south of Larned, as the location for the council grounds.

Leavenworth's trust in George's abilities had been well placed. Not only had he located all the camps, but he had convinced tribal leaders to go to Fort Larned at the height of Hancock's War. It was an achievement worthy of his father. He had demonstrated his powers of persuasion and the respect he held among the tribes. He had already earned his place among the warrior societies; now he had earned the right to sit with the chiefs at the council fires.[23]

Whites, too, saw George in a new light. While his loyalties always remained with the Cheyennes, he had gained the confidence of government officials. For the next fifty years, in one capacity or another—interpreter, advisor, special agent, school administrator—he would serve the U.S. government.[24]

When George and Black Kettle arrived on Medicine Lodge Creek in early September, hints of red and orange flecked the leaves of the great cottonwoods and elms towering over the hollow that formed the center of the treaty grounds. Even now, a month before the tribes were to assemble here, wagons from Fort Larned rumbled in daily with their loads of provisions and presents. Black Kettle along with twenty-five lodges of his extended family established camp on the south side of the creek, very close to where the chiefs and the commissioners would soon gather. George helped select a fine site for Black Kettle's lodge, which he and Magpie would share with the chief's family. Magpie was nearly eight months pregnant, although she still did small chores and helped entertain the many guests, Indian and white, who came to call on her husband and stepfather.

Most of the Cheyennes, some two hundred lodges, camped forty miles away on the Cimarron, awaiting the return of war parties. They would not move until the Arrow Keeper, Rock Forehead, had begun the four-day Arrow Renewal ceremony, which would purify the tribe and prepare the leaders for the important negotiations to come. This suited the Dog Soldiers, for over the summer the young men among them had raided white outposts and settlements. Tall Bull and Bull Bear had determined they should stay away until it could be shown that the commissioners on Medicine Lodge Creek had indeed come in peace. And they would keep a watchful eye on Black Kettle and his son-in-law, George Bent, who was now his constant companion. The whites had misled the old chief before—Sand Creek was evidence of that. This time the Dog Soldier headmen would see to it that Black Kettle did not exchange Cheyenne lands for a few trinkets and promises of peace.[25]

Over the next several weeks, travois of the other four tribes came from every direction, the chiefs guiding on Black Kettle's circle. Little Raven's Arapahos with 170 lodges set up camp above the council grounds; Ten Bears' Comanches placed 100 lodges in a fine grove just below the Arapahos; next came 150 Kiowa lodges under White Bear, Black Eagle, Sitting Bear, and Kicking Bird; and finally, downstream, Poor Bear located his 85 Apache lodges. By the time the commissioners arrived, more than 5,000 Indians had assembled on Medicine Lodge Creek. On every hill and in every valley for miles around, thousands of ponies grazed on the rich grass.[26]

Whites also crowded the grounds. By the time the commissioners arrived, nearly a thousand teamsters, soldiers, commissioners and aides, cooks, laundresses, interpreters, and camp followers camped across from the army's great corral, located near Black Kettle's lodge.[27]

On the night of September 27, George shared supper with Black Kettle, Little Robe, Superintendent of Indian Affairs Thomas Murphy, and Agent Edward Wynkoop. Suddenly, Apache and Arapaho camp police, assigned to guard the government wagons loaded with presents, pushed into the lodge, shouting the arrival of eight heavily armed Dog Soldiers, led by Grey Beard and Roman Nose. With them came Ed Guerrier. Through the mixed-blood interpreters, Murphy asked Grey Beard whether the Dog Men were going to support the council and work for peace. He told him that the other peace commissioners were expected any day and with them would come even more wagons of presents and provisions. Grey Beard was not impressed: "A dog will rush to eat provisions. The provisions you bring us make us sick, we can live on buffalo but the main articles we need we do not see, powder, lead, & caps. When you bring us these we will believe you are sincere."[28] But he gave Murphy some hope, indicating that no new war parties would be sent out in retaliation for Hancock's attack on the Dog Soldier village on Pawnee Fork. Murphy quickly agreed that Hancock's actions had been wrong and was relieved to hear Grey Beard's parting words: "Keep a strong heart . . . we are only revenging that one thing."[29]

Nevertheless, the meeting was a tense one. As Murphy and Grey Beard spoke through Guerrier and George, Roman Nose held back, silent and gloomy, glaring at Wynkoop, whom he blamed for bringing General Hancock to the Dog Soldier village. Wynkoop was in real danger. The Crooked Lance warrior was known for his volatile temper, and Guerrier knew that Roman Nose had threatened Hancock's life at the talks on Pawnee Fork. Only through Bull Bear's intercession had the general escaped with his life. Wynkoop understood the danger and kept his distance.[30]

The absence of the main body of Cheyennes on the Cimarron bothered not only Murphy but the chiefs of the allied tribes as well. Little Raven and the Arapahos believed that the Cimarron Cheyennes were hostile and planned an attack on the council grounds once the commissioners arrived. Ever since Sand Creek, Little Raven had blamed the Cheyennes for bringing the soldiers down on both tribes. Now, he hoped to separate the Cheyennes and Arapahos and negotiate his own peace with the commissioners. The Arapaho guards who shouted out the arrival of the Grey Beard–Roman Nose party shared Little Raven's fear of the Dog Soldiers, and throughout the council they remained suspicious of the Cheyennes.[31]

As the tribes slowly assembled, an Arapaho warrior paid George a visit. The man arrived at his lodge leading a fine horse and announced that he had brought the animal as a gift. Surprised, George saw that it was Red Bull, the father of Tom White Shirt, the Sand Creek captive the Cheyenne chiefs had not recognized as one of their own during the talk with Hancock at Fort Larned back in April. While Hancock had chased the Dog Soldiers that spring, George and Agent Wynkoop had reunited the boy with his family at the Arapaho camp on Beaver Creek; now Red Bull was repaying that kindness.[32] Even though Cheyenne-Arapaho relations seemed strained, George enjoyed the friendship and respect of both tribes.

On October 14, the peace commissioners arrived at the treaty grounds. Nathaniel G. Taylor, Commissioner of Indian Affairs, served as the president of the commission and was joined by General William S. Harney, General Alfred H. Terry, and, replacing General William T. Sherman, General C. C. Augur. Other commissioners were John B. Henderson, U.S. senator from Missouri and chairman of the Senate Committee on Indian Affairs; Samuel F. Tappan, former lieutenant colonel of the First Colorado Volunteers and president of the army's investigative commission on Sand Creek; and John B. Sanborn, who had represented the Department of Interior at the 1865 Treaty of the Little Arkansas. Accompanying the peace commissioners were Kansas representatives Governor Samuel Crawford, Lieutenant Governor J. B. Root, and U.S. Senator Edward P. Ross. The council attracted a large press corps, representing leading newspapers and magazines in New York, St. Louis, Chicago, Cincinnati, and Atchison.[33]

The commissioners met with the assembled tribes for the first time on October 15, 1867. Although Black Kettle was present with his extended family, the Dog Soldiers and the rest of the tribe still camped on the Cimarron, a day's ride away. This annoyed everyone. Senator Henderson wanted an ultimatum sent over to the Cimarron camps, an action that was hotly opposed by General Harney. Harney advised patience; Hancock's attacks of last April had infuriated the warriors and frightened the women and children. He pointed out that the presence of so many soldiers at the council grounds made the Cheyenne leaders understandably suspicious of the commissioners' intentions.

Black Kettle then spoke. The Cheyennes on the Cimarron, he said, would soon initiate the Arrow Renewal ceremony. When this sacred ritual was completed, it would take still more time for the Cheyennes to move over to Medicine Lodge. He warned that when they did come, they would be hungry; extra rations should be sent to his camp. When the Dog Soldiers arrived, he would see to their needs. Of course, by distributing food Black Kettle would strengthen his position as chief within his own band and perhaps raise his prestige among the Dog Soldiers as well. The chiefs and commissioners then agreed that the official opening of the conference should be on October 19, four days hence. That night, Superintendent Murphy delivered the necessary provisions to Black Kettle's camp.[34]

Just as darkness fell, however, news spread that a strong party of Dog Soldiers, led by Tall Bull, had arrived at the council grounds. The Cheyenne warriors went directly to General Harney's tent. There, with George Bent and John Smith translating, the general had a friendly conversation with Tall Bull and Grey Beard. Harney had known the Cheyennes ever since his 1855 Platte River expedition, when he had proclaimed: "By God, I'm for battle—no peace!"[35] Through the years the Dog Men had come to respect the old dragoon, and now Grey Beard good-naturedly presented him with a worn and tattered paper, a safe conduct pass signed by Harney on July 17, 1858. The two men laughed about it, then embraced. All the while, the warrior escort remained outside the tent, weapons ready.

When Tall Bull and Grey Beard mounted to leave, they agreed to return the next night and talk more. Harney then directed them to Black Kettle's camp, where rations awaited. After they had eaten, the Dog Men left Black Kettle and returned to their own village on the Cimarron.[36]

The following evening, as promised, Tall Bull and Grey Beard returned to meet with the commissioners. After extracting an apology for the Hancock affair, the two men crossed to the south side of Medicine Lodge Creek and again met with Black Kettle. This time they had more than food on their minds. Tall Bull told Black Kettle that he must ride to the Cimarron camp and explain to the people what he expected to gain—or lose—by making peace with the whites. If he refused, the Dog Men would kill his horses.[37]

When George saw Black Kettle later that night, he noticed that the chief was visibly shaken. Black Kettle told George that the Dog Soldiers had threatened him. No one had ever spoken to him in such a disrespectful manner. As the night wore on, the men decided that the only course open to Black Kettle was to go to the Cimarron village and do as the Dog Men demanded. There was no time to lose; the peace conference would begin on the nineteenth, and Black Kettle needed to be there. Without his influence there might be no peace at all.

George and Black Kettle set off for the Cimarron immediately. When they arrived, they saw that Rock Forehead had not yet begun the Arrow Renewal ceremony. After the chiefs and headmen had been summoned, Black Kettle presented his case. Once again he urged peace. But the Dog Men interrupted. Black Kettle had made peace with the whites before, yet the bluecoats had attacked at Sand Creek anyway. Besides, the Dog Soldiers were the aggrieved party, for it was their village that Hancock had destroyed on Pawnee Fork. It was not up to Black Kettle—a leader of the southern bands—to make peace for the Dog Men. Black Kettle should say nothing and promise nothing. Tall Bull, Bull Bear, Little Robe, White Horse, and Grey Beard would lead the negotiations with Harney and the others. Once Rock Forehead had renewed the Sacred Arrows, they would go to Medicine Lodge Creek and speak for themselves. But they would go in their own good time. And they would not come as children to the call of "the white father." The treaty-makers could wait.[38]

Grey Beard accompanied Black Kettle and George back to Medicine Lodge. They arrived just in time for the opening ceremonies. The commissioners had made a clearing among the cottonwoods and erected a lofty brush arbor to shade the assembly. Superintendent Murphy had set up campstools and an odd assortment of folding chairs for the press corps and commissioners. Logs had been arranged for the chiefs and tribal representatives. The Indians faced the commissioners in a great half-circle. Satanta's Kiowas anchored one end, along with Ten Bears's Comanches. With them was interpreter Philip McCusker, a white man fluent in both languages. At the other end sat the Prairie Apaches with Chief Little Bear, and next to them, Little Raven's Arapahos and mixed-blood interpreter Margaret "Broken-hand" Fitzpatrick Adams. In the center of the great crescent of chiefs sat Black Kettle, and beside him, Grey Beard. Between and a little behind the two Cheyenne leaders were the Bent brothers, George and Charley. The younger Bent had been assigned by the Dog Soldiers to keep an eye on his brother and Black Kettle. As long as Charley remained sober and kept quiet, George had no objection to the arrangement.

The attendees—whether white, Indian, or mixed-blood—appeared in a spectacular array of dress. The commissioners wore dark suits or uniforms; the press corps was seen in sack coats, or vests and shirt-sleeves. The Indians, their faces painted, dressed according to tribal customs and individual taste, mostly trade blankets and altered army coats, mixed with traditional breechclouts, buckskin shirts, and moccasins. Seated on a folding chair in the center of the proceedings, Margaret Adams wore a petticoated scarlet dress with matching bonnet.[39]

The participants paid particular attention to their headdress. Commissioner Tappan sported a natty sailor cap of dark blue wool; Commissioner Augur contained his wild hair with a black felt plug hat; General Harney, always presenting a military appearance, donned an old-style dragoon forage cap; reporters wore straw hats, top hats, and bowlers. Indians preferred eagle feathers, in ones, twos, and in some cases, an entire bonnet full. But some deviated from this practice, wearing cast-off black felt army hats. Black Kettle, however, stood out in his tall 1854-pattern blue dragoon shako, topped with a gaudy orange pompon. He wore this despite the Cheyenne belief that a brimmed hat was the very symbol of whiteness. Cheyenne warrior-artists always drew whites wearing hats. When they recorded their coups in captured ledger books or on buffalo robes, surrendering whites were depicted removing their hats, thereby humbling themselves. But here at Medicine Lodge, Black Kettle chose to adopt the headgear of the whites, demonstrating his eagerness to accommodate the commissioners.[40]

George and Charley Bent, always near Black Kettle, also dressed for the occasion. Charley wrapped himself in a red trade blanket and was indistinguishable from others in the Cheyenne delegation. George, however, wore a suit of broadcloth, complete with vest and cravat. Only the moccasins on his feet betrayed his Indianness. Their sister Julia was also present. Now in her late teens and betrothed to Ed Guerrier, reporters were struck by her beauty. One correspondent wrote that she had a charming laugh and her feet were of "the most diminutive size." He went on to observe that "a peep at her trim ankles might drive an anchorite [sailor] insane."[41]

Commission president Taylor welcomed the chiefs and introduced the other commissioners. He announced to the tribes that Senator Henderson would speak for the whites. He is a "great peace man," he lectured. "Listen to him."[42] Unfortunately, the great peace man had not yet arrived at the arbor, an embarrassment to the other commissioners who had selected Henderson as their spokesman. Taylor apologized for the delay, admitting that the whites could not negotiate without him.

Grey Beard seized this opportunity to address the assembly. With George translating, he told the commissioners that the Cheyennes could not negotiate either, for the Dog Soldier chiefs were still on the Cimarron engaged in the Arrow Renewal ceremonies. He said he would listen, but neither he nor Black Kettle could speak for the tribe. Black Kettle remained silent, his grim countenance contrasting sharply with his gaily decorated cap.[43]

George understood better than anyone Grey Beard's meaning. His father-in-law and mentor was locked in a power struggle with the Dog Soldiers that not only threatened his position of leadership but also the future of the Cheyenne people. Tall Bull had earlier threatened to kill Black Kettle's horses, and now Grey Beard announced that no chief was present at the council who could speak for the Cheyennes. George translated this public humiliation, knowing that Charley would report to the Dog Soldiers whether Grey Beard's message had been accurately interpreted.

But on this day, George thought of more than tribal politics and peacemaking. Across Medicine Lodge Creek, in a specially prepared lodge, Magpie was in labor, ready at any moment to give birth to their first child.[44]

Finally, Commissioner Henderson arrived. Foregoing the usual pipe-smoking and expressions of goodwill, he spoke harshly to the chiefs, accusing their warriors of committing depredations against railroad construction crews and white settlements. He acknowledged that the Indians might have grievances as well: "We have come to correct these wrongs," he said.[45] As the other chiefs stood to speak against white encroachment on their lands, Grey Beard and Black Kettle sat in silence.

On the afternoon of October 21, the Comanches and Kiowas signed a treaty presented to them by the commissioners. That night, in a heavy rainstorm, the reporters saw two riders enter Black Kettle's camp. A short time later, four Cheyennes—Black Kettle, Grey Beard, Little Robe, and White Horse—forded Medicine Lodge Creek and rode to the commissioners' compound and said they wanted to talk. Here, they were ushered into a tent, where Taylor, Harney, and a few newspaper men joined them. John Smith and George explained to the whites that the Cimarron Cheyennes needed to confer with Black Kettle before the meeting began. Taylor agreed, since the other commissioners had not yet been summoned from their beds. As the Cheyennes spoke in low tones, the rain pounding loud against the tent, the reporters noticed Black Kettle's obvious nervousness. One of them even thought the chief behaved as if his life were in danger. Finally, Little Robe said the Cheyennes were ready to address the commissioners.

The group of Cheyenne chiefs impressed the correspondents. The Cheyennes were taller than the Comanches and Kiowas, and the reporters thought them the handsomest of the tribes they had yet seen at Medicine Lodge. They carried themselves with a regal authority that commanded respect, and it was obvious they had come to the treaty grounds not as supplicants but as equals.[46]

Little Robe spoke for the chiefs. He said that the Arrow Renewal over on the Cimarron had just begun and that it would take four or five days for the Cheyennes to reach the council grounds. Senator Henderson expressed the opinion that the Arrow Renewal ceremony was all a "humbug." Harney vehemently disagreed: "It is life and death with them," he said, adding that "it is their religion, and they observe all the ceremonies a great deal better than the whites do theirs."[47] Taylor asked Little Robe when the ceremonies would be completed, pointing out that the Kiowas and Comanches had already signed the treaty. Once again the Cheyennes huddled among themselves. This time they asked Black Kettle to speak for them. The chief explained that things had gone wrong with the ceremonies and the Arrow Keeper had had to start over again. But he promised that the Cheyennes genuinely wanted peace. "When I look to my left I see you, and that you intend to do right; and when I look to my right I see my men, and know that they intend to do right. I want you both to touch and shake hands."[48] Black Kettle assured the commissioners that the Cimarron leaders would arrive at the treaty grounds in four days. It was an impressive performance; his sincerity and passion convinced the commissioners to wait four more days.[49] George must have been glad that the old chief had regained some of the respect he had lost since arriving at Medicine Lodge.

While the tribes and the commissioners waited for the Cheyennes, George and Black Kettle received a procession of guests, including military officers and members of the commission entourage. Major Joel Elliott and Captain Louis McLane Hamilton of the Seventh Cavalry visited nightly to smoke and talk, as did agents Wynkoop and Leavenworth. Dr. Remick, one of George's old St. Louis school chums, came by frequently, and commissioners Sanborn and Harney were also received at Black Kettle's lodge during the four-day lull.[50]

When the Cheyennes failed to appear on the appointed day, Black Kettle and George grew anxious. Arapaho chief Little Raven made matters worse. He told the commissioners that he had learned the Cheyennes were planning to attack the Medicine Lodge council grounds and were even then moving into position. This caused a sensation among the reporters. But General Harney kept his cool and assured all that the Cheyennes would keep their word. Just then, Little Robe rode in from the Cimarron with news that the Cheyennes would arrive the next day. He said the Cheyennes would approach riding hard with pistols blazing, but the whites should not be alarmed; the warriors just wanted to celebrate the end of the Arrow Renewal ceremonies and the beginning of peace.[51]

October 27 dawned clear but cool. Captain Barnitz of the Seventh Cavalry awoke to find ice in his water bucket, but as the sun rose the frost melted and the day warmed up. Just before noon, Barnitz saw movement across the creek to his front:

> The Cheyennes arrived, they crossed the creek . . . and emerged from the woods, in line of battle, firing their guns into the air, singing and yelling! One portion of the tribe—about a squadron formed in line in front of my camp, on a little rise of ground about 150 yards distant, and behind them and on their left flank about 200 Arapahos sat on their ponies, with bows strung, and on the other side of camp the Comanches, and Kioways, and Apaches were out in force—and for half an hour or so the intentions of the Indians were at least questionable. I had taken the precaution to have all the horses brought in and tied to the picket line before the arrival of the Cheyennes, and on their approach, I buckled on my pistols, and had all the men quietly retire to their tents, and put on their belts and cartridge boxes, and be ready in an instant in case the Indians should make a charge.[52]

No one who was there ever forgot the Dog Soldiers' entrance into Medicine Lodge.

Late that evening, after the Cheyennes had returned to their camp near Black Kettle's group, sentries reported to General Harney that a party of Cheyennes had just forded Medicine Lodge Creek and wanted to see him. The general, who had been preparing for bed, pulled his coat on and stepped out into the firelight. There, a beautiful Cheyenne woman, her dress decorated with elk teeth and elaborate quillwork, held the lead rope of a magnificent Indian pony. Beside her, an older woman cradled a newborn baby. George approached and greeted Harney. He explained that his wife, Magpie, the daughter of Black Kettle, had given birth to a girl, Ada, on October 19, the opening day of the great peace council. At a sign from George, Magpie moved forward and presented the pony to Harney, placing the horsehair rope in his hand. The general was visibly affected. He could not help but remember that nearly two years ago to the day he had presented Black Kettle with a fine bay horse following the council on the Little Arkansas

River. And George could not help but remember that on the occasion of his marriage to Magpie, Black Kettle had presented that same horse to him. Now it had gone full circle. Here, celebrating the birth of his first child, George had selected his finest horse, and, like a chief, presented it to the soldier chief.[53]

At ten o'clock the next morning, the Cheyennes and Arapahos gathered in front of Commissioner Taylor's tent on the council grounds to negotiate their own treaty.[54] The Kiowas, Comanches, and Prairie Apaches had already signed their own treaties, and many had packed their gifts and had moved away from Medicine Lodge Creek. Still, many of the allied tribes surrounded the treaty grounds to witness the conclusion of the conference and the signing of the Cheyenne and Arapaho treaty.

Commissioner Henderson opened the proceedings and summarized the provisions of the agreement. The Cheyennes and Arapahos promised never to "kill or scalp white men, nor attempt to do them any harm." Further, they promised to stay away from white roads when outside the reservation, and to cede all lands in Kansas given to them by the 1865 Treaty of the Little Arkansas in lieu of a new reservation completely within Indian Territory bounded on the north by the Kansas state border, on the west and the south by the Cimarron, and on the east by the Arkansas River. In return, the government promised to pay the tribes twenty thousand dollars annually and assign a resident agent. The government would also provide clothing, schools, hospitals, and workshops. Each family head was authorized to select 320 acres for private use in hopes of encouraging ranching and farming.[55]

After the Cheyennes politely acknowledged Henderson's remarks, Little Robe rose to propose that Little Raven should have the honor of speaking first, for the Arapahos had patiently waited all through the conference for the arrival of the Cimarron Cheyennes. Taken by surprise, Little Raven hesitated, then stood and delivered a rambling address. Now it was the Cheyennes' turn. Buffalo Chief, tall and handsome, his long braids wrapped in blue and red trade cloth, eagle feathers tied to his scalp lock, spoke for all the southern bands and for the Dog Soldiers as well.[56] His message was clear: The Cheyennes did not want to live in houses or restrict their movements to a reservation.

They wanted to hunt on their traditional lands between the Arkansas and Platte Rivers—that vast territory in Kansas and eastern Colorado. Once the buffalo were gone, the Cheyennes would be willing to consider reservation life. "We are willing, when we desire to live as you do, to take your advice about settling down; but until then, we will take our chances."[57]

Having stated the Cheyenne position—there could be no doubt about his meaning—Buffalo Chief sat down and no Cheyenne stood to take his place. Silence fell over the council ground. The commissioners turned to John Smith and George. Was anybody else going to speak? No. The Cheyennes had said all they wanted to say.

The commissioners spoke among themselves. Buffalo Chief had struck at the very heart of the treaty by insisting on the right to hunt on the Cheyennes' traditional lands. The whole point of the treaty from the government's point of view was to remove the Indians from the main travel arteries in Kansas and Colorado. Henderson knew the entire peace effort was in jeopardy. Unless a deal could be struck, the Cheyennes would refuse to sign and the treaty would be so much worthless paper.

Walking away from the commission table, Henderson motioned for John Smith and George to join him. Together they walked some distance from the brush arbor, talking all the while. No one—not chiefs or commissioners, not even the vigilant reporters—could hear what was said. Finally, George called Buffalo Chief and other Cheyenne leaders to walk with them. He explained to the chiefs that Henderson would allow the Cheyennes to hunt as they had always hunted—between the Platte and Arkansas Rivers—provided they would sign the treaty and agree to all its provisions. Henderson was willing to grant this concession because he believed the buffalo would soon disappear. The Cheyennes, however, thought otherwise. The buffalo were plentiful now and would be forever. And so, Buffalo Chief took Henderson's hand, looked the commissioner in the eye, and with an emphatic "Ha Ho!" agreed to make his mark on the treaty paper. It had been Henderson's idea, but it was George who had convinced the Cheyenne leaders to actually sign.[58]

One by one, the chiefs shook hands with the commissioners, then walked over to the treaty and made their marks as a clerk dutifully recorded the phonetic spelling of their Indian names. Black Kettle, *Moke-tav-a-to*, was given the honor of signing first, an acknowledgment of his leadership over the southern bands. Then in succession came Little Bear, *Nac-co-hah-ket*; Spotted Elk, *Mo-a-vo-va-ast*; Buffalo Chief, *Is-se-von-ne-ve*; Slim Face, *Vip-po-nah*; Grey Beard, *Wo-pah-ah*; Little Rock, *O-ni-hah-ket*; and Curly Hair, *Ma-mo-ki*.

But Bull Bear, Tall Bull, White Horse, and Little Robe—Dog Soldiers all—along with two men, Heap of Birds, a Bowstring headman, and Whirlwind, refused to sign.

Superintendent Murphy watched nervously. Greatly agitated, he ran to Henderson and Taylor and warned that if the Dog Soldiers' signatures did not appear on the treaty, Medicine Lodge would be a failure; the raids and warfare would continue.

Again Henderson and Taylor turned to George and old Smith. George went to the holdouts and demanded an explanation. Little Robe brushed off the question by saying that the treaty had enough marks already. But George insisted, his temper flaring. Without the marks of the Dog Men, he said, the treaty was no good and there would be no peace for the Cheyennes. All the commissioners and the press corps watched the heated exchange. Finally, George led the Dog Men to the treaty table, where each in turn took the "feather" and made their marks. Bull Bear, *O-to-ah-nac-co*, however, signed at the top, above Black Kettle's name. The others signed at the bottom: Tall Bull, *O-to-ah-has-tis*; White Horse, *Wo-po-ham*; Little Robe, *Hah-ket-home-mah*; Whirlwind, *Min-nin-ne-wah*; and Heap of Birds, *Mo-yan-histe-histow*.[59]

George's forceful handling of the chiefs impressed the commissioners and press corps, and the officers, too. They knew that without his intercession, the Treaty of Medicine Lodge would not have been successfully concluded.

The Cheyenne chiefs then led their people to the corralled wagons and the piles of treaty goods: food, bolts of cloth, kettles, axes, firearms—most obsolete or defective—and surplus military stores such as uniform insignia, hats, trousers, and coats. The chiefs carefully managed the distribution of the goods, each family gathering its share only when called by name, the women leading horses dragging travois.

In a very short time, the tribe moved on, the people carrying what they could, but leaving much behind.

George remembered later that he could not bear to see the unclaimed goods rot on the prairie, so he and Smith "hauled away as much of the Stuff as we could handle." They would find an opportunity to trade the goods at a later date.

George remained at Medicine Lodge for several days following the departure of the Cheyennes. He was still on the government payroll as interpreter, and Agent Wynkoop wanted to talk to him about an important assignment with the new Cheyenne and Arapaho Agency.[60]

Chapter 9

DEATH SONGS

For more than a year Agent Edward Wynkoop had observed George's skills as a negotiator. Young Bent's abilities as a translator impressed him, as did his growing influence with the Cheyenne and Arapaho chiefs and leading men. At Medicine Lodge, even the arrogant Dog Soldiers listened to him, and no man had played a larger role in persuading these recalcitrant chiefs to sign the treaty. Wynkoop could use such a man, someone he could trust, who could speak Cheyenne and Arapaho and knew sign talk. Of course, other mixed-bloods and even a few whites spoke Indian languages. Margaret Adams, the Arapaho mixed-blood, was a respected interpreter, as was Ed Guerrier; so were white men such as old John Smith and Philip McCusker. But George Bent stood out. He was well educated—he had attended more years of college than Wynkoop himself—and well connected through his father and mother's families. He mixed easily with army officers, traders, chiefs, and warrior society headmen. He understood politics and treaty matters, and he knew war—he had already demonstrated that he could be a formidable enemy. Wynkoop could use such a man, if only George would agree to serve. Before the encampment at Medicine Lodge had broken up, Wynkoop offered George a permanent position with the Cheyenne and Arapaho Agency as interpreter and as the government's representative in the Indian camps.

The proposition interested George. At Medicine Lodge he had stood at the center of the negotiations and had worked directly with the peace commissioners and the chiefs. It had been a difficult but exhilarating experience. The talks could have fallen apart at any time, given the issues and the volatile personalities involved. The combination of Tall Bull and Harney, Henderson and Bull Bear, Black Kettle

243

and Roman Nose was a dangerous mix, but George had been up to the task and had made a difference. He had persuaded the most obstinate chiefs to sign the treaty document. This, of course, had been his assignment, but he truly believed that the Medicine Lodge Treaty was good for his people, that only through peace could they survive. He was, after all, his father's son. William had always worked for peace, even from his earliest days on the Arkansas. Peace was good for business. But through the years the old man had come to see the Cheyennes as more than trade partners. He had married three Cheyenne women and fathered children by two of them. Since coming among them, the Cheyennes were the only family he knew. Yet, he was not Cheyenne.[1]

For George it was different. He was born Cheyenne, his native language was Cheyenne, he thought in Cheyenne, and the Cheyennes considered him one of the people. The Cheyennes, on the other hand, called William "Little White Man"; they saw him as a man to be respected and consulted but a white man nevertheless. Despite the real bond that had developed between William and the Indians, he never forgot his roots; he always believed that the white way was the right way, that the Indians must inevitably submit to the superior culture, abandon the hunt, and become farmers. George, too, believed whites possessed superior technology and military power, but he never conceded that white ways were superior to Indian ways.

By working for Wynkoop, he would please his father and Black Kettle, both of whom would see the value of such a position. Magpie would approve as well, for her husband would not only bring to the family money and prestige but also traders' goods. Others in the tribe, however, might view his acceptance of Wynkoop's offer as the ultimate treachery. He would be working for the white man, in effect, spying on his own people. The Dog Soldiers might see it that way; certainly his brother Charley would. But Charley had already left Medicine Lodge with the Dog Soldiers. George respected Tall Chief Wynkoop and considered him the best white friend—after his father—the Cheyennes had. He decided to accept the agent's offer.[2]

Even as George considered Wynkoop's proposition, Charley and the Dog Soldiers went looking for the Kaws. At Medicine Lodge the Kaws

had embarrassed and insulted the Cheyennes. In full view of the assembled tribes, raiders had run off a large number of Cheyenne horses.
The young men among the Dog Soldiers wanted to retaliate immediately, but their chiefs and headmen urged restraint. Now with the
treaty signed, the Dog Men went in pursuit of the horse thieves. In
early November, at the mouth of Walnut Creek, Charley's war party
met ten U.S. scouts, who had recently left Fort Harker in western
Kansas, in search of a detachment of lost soldiers. One of the scouts,
Major N. D. McGinley, described the encounter:

These hostiles were the "Dog Soldiers" in full strength. At their head
rode their chief, Charles Bent. It was agreed that Bent, with nine
unarmed companions, should ride forward and meet [scout Charles]
Coridoro with his nine scouts, all of whom should be unarmed.
Coridoro knew that no reliance could be put in any promise made
by Bent, and told his men to slip their Colt's pistols into their boots.
Then they lifted their carbines high above their heads, where they
could be seen by the Indians, and then laid them on the ground. Each
party then rode forward to meet the other. Bent and Coridoro
advanced in front of their men and began powwowing.

Bent was insolent. He said that if the troops would lay down their
arms and surrender, they would be escorted to Fort Harker without
injury. This would have been an achievement that would have
caused laughter and rejoicing in every Indian camp from Canada to
Mexico. Coridoro scorned the proposal. Applying an epithet, Bent
exclaimed "I know who you are, Charlie Coridoro," and wheeled
his horse suddenly to dash away. Coridoro jerked his pistol from his
boot and fired, at considerable distance. The bullet struck Bent just
above the hipbone. He clung to his horse and escaped with his men,
over whom were whistling bullets from the pistols the scouts had
pulled from their boots.[3]

Three weeks later George appeared at Fort Harker and reported
that his brother had died from a fever resulting from his wounds.

George understood why Charley had so terrified white settlements
in Kansas, Colorado, and Nebraska. He was a mixed-blood, a fusion

of Indian and white. To whites he was a "halfbreed," the evil progeny of miscegenation. His white schooling had no civilizing influence but provided him with knowledge that only made him more dangerous. The settlers believed his "white intelligence" and "Indian savagery" made him the frontier's most fearsome foe, a nightmare come true. Tales of his cruelty strengthened this conviction.[4]

Whites on the frontier remembered that after Hancock's attacks on the Cheyennes in the spring of 1867, Charley had led the Dog Soldiers in raids that all but stopped construction of the Kansas Pacific Railroad. He had even attacked Track's End—a wild collection of civilian workers, frontier hangers-on, and soldiers—where his warriors killed the construction crew and repeatedly drove their tomahawks into the skulls of the dead workers. At Plum Creek Station, he had shown the warriors how to derail a train by using levers to pull up the spikes and twist one rail slightly to the side so the engineer would not be alerted to the danger. When the train came chugging down the rails, the engine jumped the track and plowed into the prairie, the cars piling on in a spectacular crash. The following train hit the brakes, and with wheels spinning and sparks flying, the engineer threw the drive-wheels into reverse and backed up before the Dog Soldiers could overtake it. After plundering the wreckage, the warriors set the cars ablaze using hot coals from the engine's firebox.[5]

Frontier newspapers and illustrated magazines spread stories of Charley Bent's savage successes, including his attack on Fort Wallace, the headquarters of Custer's Seventh Cavalry. Riding his distinctive white horse directly in front of the troopers, Charley had taunted them and challenged them to personal combat. The troopers fell for it. When they rode out to meet him, Dog Soldiers swept in and overwhelmed the detachment. Then, the Indians horribly mutilated the bodies of the dead—these soldiers would not trouble the Cheyennes in the afterlife. William A. Bell, a British photographer and newspaper correspondent who witnessed the action, described the body of one soldier in grisly detail:

A portion of the sergeant's scalp lay near him, but the greater part was gone; through his head a rifle-ball had passed, and a blow from the tomahawk had laid his brain open above his left eye; the nose was slit up, and his throat was cut from ear to ear; seven arrows were standing in different parts of his naked body; the breast was laid open, so as to expose the heart; and the arm . . . was hacked to the bone; his legs, from the hip to the knee, lay open with horrible gashes, and from the knee to the foot they had cut the flesh with their knives.[6]

Charley's campaign of terror was so effective that panic-stricken whites reported seeing him at the head of nearly every Cheyenne attack from Nebraska to Texas, whether he was there or not. George's little brother had brought new meaning to the Bent name. Once it had symbolized peace and cooperation; now it evoked fear. George and Robert, and William too, were described variously as renegades, half-breeds, and squawmen. The criticism stung, for each of the Bent men had chosen his own path through the clash of cultures. William had devoted his life to peaceful relations and trade with the Cheyennes; now, frustrated by the government's duplicity in its dealings with the tribes, he had retired to his Purgatoire stockade. Robert, who had always been at his father's side, attempted to work his Arkansas River ranch and occasionally served the army as a guide and scout. George, who had once ridden with Charley and the Dog Soldiers, now saw the futility of fighting and had accepted Wynkoop's offer to work as an interpreter and liaison with the tribes.

Charley had never understood how his family could support the government's efforts to confine the Cheyennes to a reservation, ending their freedom and dooming them to scratching out an existence as farmers. He had come to see his own family as the enemy, as traitors to the Cheyennes, and this sense of betrayal fueled his anger and caused him to threaten to kill not only his father but George as well. Although Mary had married a white man, Charley's hatred did not extend to her. He called her Mollie. She had mothered him during their Westport days when they had lived in the white world. His relationship with her was not Indian. A Cheyenne man would never speak directly to his elder sister, not because he disliked her but because strict tribal incest taboos demanded that younger brothers keep their distance and show respect.

And so, a brother would speak to his sister only through others. She was the *Namhan*, the namer of his children, not a playmate or one to joke with. But Charley had come of age not in the Cheyenne villages but in the Boone household in Westport. His bond with Mollie was strong. He sometimes visited her, looking for the lantern she would place in her window as a sign that it was safe to approach the house.

One night she saw him crouching in the irrigation ditch, waiting for her to light the candle. She ran outside, carrying clean clothes and food, and invited him into the house. "No," he murmured, "I only wanted the old man." Then he uncocked his rifle and slipped into the darkness. Only then did Mary understand that her brother had come to kill their father.[7] William had tried to reclaim his son but in the end referred to him as that "durn'd scoundrel." Charley responded by bragging that one day he would hang his father's scalp on his belt.[8] But it was Charley who died first, a bullet in the back.

In the Cheyenne camps on the Cimarron, south of Fort Larned, George assumed his new duties. At five dollars a day he would be well paid to live in the village and report on Cheyenne activities. Agent Wynkoop, working out of his headquarters at Fort Larned, received regular reports and was pleased with George's work. On February 1, 1868, Wynkoop wrote to Superintendent Thomas Murphy: "The interpreters employed to remain with the different tribes have so far been of no service to me whatever, they being with the exception of George Bent employed by different trading establishments and consequently attending more to the private interests of the traders than looking out for the interests of the government."[9] There was not much for George to report, only that the people were hungry and needed flour, sugar, and coffee. He wrote Wynkoop of the critical shortages and feared that violence might soon erupt. Fortunately, the hunters returned with buffalo meat, and a crisis was averted.

But the buffalo bounty brought a new problem. Rich in hides, Cheyenne men now used their wealth to buy liquor from Fort Dodge merchants. The camps, George reported, reeked with illegal whiskey, and in some cases entire villages lay drunk. It was a dangerous situation, one that required the agent's personal attention. And so, early in the spring of 1868, Wynkoop made his first inspection tour of the Cheyenne and Arapaho villages. He brought wagons filled with long overdue provisions, including beef, flour, bacon, coffee, sugar, and salt. On his visit, Wynkoop learned that the chiefs—even Black Kettle—supported the warrior societies in mounting a war party against the Kaws, who had gotten the best of Cheyenne raiders the past November. The villagers still mourned the five young men cut down by Kaw bullets and arrows. The Cheyennes would not rest until they had bloodied their enemy.[10]

Resigned to the fact that peace between the Kaws and Cheyennes was hopeless at the moment, Wynkoop sent George to northern New Mexico on a peace mission to the Moache Utes and Jicarilla Apaches, traditional enemies of the Cheyennes and Arapahos. Representing Black Kettle, Little Raven, and Wynkoop, George arrived at Cimarron Springs in April and initiated talks with the two tribes. According to Agent E. B. Dennison, the proceedings were "in every aspect satisfactory," with the Utes and Apaches agreeing to meet Wynkoop and conclude the peace.[11]

On his return, George stopped at his father's ranch, where he discovered that the old man had brought from Westport a new bride, a twenty-year-old mixed-blood named Adaline, the daughter of William's old Upper Missouri trade friend Alexander Harvey and his Blackfeet wife. George knew the girl. He had seen her often at Robert Campbell's home in St. Louis, when he was attending Webster College. Campbell had been her guardian, too, but she was five years younger than George, so he had paid her little attention. Now, unbelievably, she was his stepmother. His father had been lonely ever since Island ran off with Joe Baraldo and Yellow Woman had joined the Dog Soldiers. But he was now fifty-nine years old—the Cheyennes had taken to calling him Grey Beard—and his new wife was not only young but pregnant as well. William could give little detail about his whirlwind courtship and wedding, but George learned from his father's trusted black servant, Billy, that the colonel had been dead drunk at the time of the marriage ceremony. The family, of course, suspected that Adaline was only after the old man's money and made no effort to stop her when she announced her intention to return to the Westport house to have her baby.[12]

It was all unsettling. George and brother-in-law Robison Moore needed little excuse to get away from the bizarre family scene and mounted their horses and rode the short distance to Boggsville. Here, Kit Carson had recently settled with his wife Josefa. Carson had resigned his army commission in July 1867. He had earned the rank of colonel during the Civil War and then commanded at Fort Garland in southern Colorado. In January 1868 Carson had accepted an appointment as Colorado's superintendent of Indian Affairs and immediately set off for Washington, D.C., to negotiate a treaty for the Utes.[13] While there, he consulted doctors about his rapidly deteriorating health. On April 13, two days after his return to Boggsville, forty-year-old Josefa gave birth to a daughter. The child was healthy, but the delivery had been difficult. Ten days after the birth, Carson's beloved Josefa died of a fever.

The next day, April 24, George and Moore rode up to the Carson adobe and found the grieving family. The old scout was in a reminiscing mood, and the men listened as Kit spoke of the old days. Among his memories was the fight he had long ago with the Crows when William and his brothers constructed their first stockade on the Arkansas, near the mouth of Fountain Creek. As Carson supervised a woodcutting party, sixty Crows ran off the company's horses. The twenty-year-old Carson set out in pursuit with twelve well-armed white men and two Cheyennes. A heavy snow had recently fallen, and Kit easily tracked the Crow raiders, catching up with them on the open prairie. He and his companions fired their Hawkin rifles with deadly accuracy, killing two Crows and recovering all the stolen stock.

George had heard the tale recounted many times before but listened respectfully as Kit told them of the great 1864 battle against Kiowas, Comanches, and Apaches at Adobe Walls, an old Bent–St. Vrain trading post in the Texas panhandle. On that occasion, only Kit's iron will and the fire from his two twelve-pounder howitzers saved his command. As the old man finished the story, he led the men to his corral and showed them a splendid racehorse, the very one he had ridden at Adobe Walls. Haggard and weary, the sounds of mourning echoing from the adobe house, he offered to sell the animal. George thought the price fair and bought it on the spot, thinking himself lucky to ride away with the famed mountain man's favorite warhorse. Four weeks later, he learned that old Kit, the fast family friend, had died.[14]

Soon after his talk with Kit, George returned to Magpie and baby Ada in Black Kettle's village near Fort Larned. There the chief informed him that two hundred Cheyenne warriors, led by Dog Soldier chief Tall Bull and Little Robe, had struck the Kaws near Council Grove, Kansas. But it was hardly the decisive victory the Cheyennes had hoped for. George's Westport guardian and former Cheyenne agent, Albert G. Boone, had attempted to mediate but to no avail. The Cheyennes had thought the Kaws would plead for peace; instead, they came out shooting. On June 3, the two tribes in full regalia maneuvered, circled, and blustered. Although there was much shooting and yelling, the only casualties were three Cheyennes and one Kaw wounded. Frustrated by their inability to exact revenge on their enemy, the Dog Soldiers turned on nearby whites, raiding farmhouses and businesses for livestock and food.[15]

After spending a few days with his family in Black Kettle's camp, George rode to Fort Larned and reported to Wynkoop, telling him that the Cheyennes were unhappy—they still had not received the firearms and ammunition promised at Medicine Lodge. After listening to George's report from the camps, Wynkoop informed him that General Phil Sheridan had recently taken command of the vast military Department of the Missouri, which encompassed all the territory of the plains tribes. Short, stocky, and possessed of boundless energy, Sheridan emerged from the Civil War as the Union's greatest and most celebrated cavalry leader. George knew his reputation. Sheridan never avoided a fight, and when he attacked he held back nothing. He believed in total war and had shocked the nation in 1864 by his ruthless destruction of the Shenendoah Valley, the Confederacy's breadbasket. The devastation was so complete the soldiers quipped that even a crow flying over the charred valley would have to carry its own provisions.[16]

George again told Wynkoop of the hunger in the Cheyenne camps. The irregular and uncertain food supplies provided by the government made it essential that the promised guns and ammunition be issued at once. The agent understood that the Cheyennes needed firearms for hunting and had petitioned the government repeatedly for permission to issue them. He agreed to broach the subject again when Sheridan arrived at Fort Larned to treat with the chiefs.

When Sheridan arrived at Larned, the Cheyenne, Arapaho, Kiowa, Comanche, and Apache chiefs gathered in council. John Smith and Dick Curtis, who had lived among the Cheyennes, translated for the chiefs, while George stayed at Wynkoop's side as the agent's personal interpreter. The Indians seemed well pleased with the new commander. But as the council came to a close, the talks took a peculiar twist. Wynkoop, who had been silent, now spoke up. At the urging of the chiefs, he asked Sheridan's permission to issue guns and ammunition. Sheridan finally agreed, saying it would be good for the Indians to have guns—that way his soldiers might "kill them as men." George translated this word for word to the Cheyenne chiefs. Stone Calf, a respected Southern Cheyenne council chief and a man known for his humor, quickly rose. Dressed in a frock coat with army officer's shoulder straps and a German silver dragonfly hanging from his neck, the chief said through George: "Then let your soldiers wear long hair so that [our warriors] will have some honor in scalping them." Grinning, Sheridan shot back that he was sorry he could not allow his men to wear their hair long as they would get lousy. Stone Calf smiled and nodded as George translated the general's words.[17]

As Black Kettle's people moved toward Fort Larned in early June to receive their Medicine Lodge annuities—including the firearms—an army detachment led by Lieutenant Frederick Beecher intercepted them. The officer sought George out and closely questioned him. Beecher wanted to know more about the Kaw fight near Council Grove. George explained that only a few boys of Black Kettle's village had joined the Dog Soldiers in the raid. He admitted that these hotheads had stolen eleven head of cattle and taken a few things from houses vacated by settlers. For this, Black Kettle had ordered them whipped. George argued that this public humiliation would be more a deterrent against future raids than any punishment Beecher might impose. He told Beecher how the Cheyennes worried about being cheated at the annuity distribution. The lieutenant asked what the chiefs would do if they were cheated. George talked it over with the chiefs, then turned to Beecher and said, "They will go home and be poor and cry." Satisfied, Beecher rode off and the village continued its movement toward the fort.[18]

The annuity distribution on August 9 went off better than expected, and Wynkoop believed that although the Cheyennes had not received all the arms and ammunition promised, enough had been delivered to satisfy the young men, at least for the moment.

Of course, George had not divulged everything he knew about Cheyenne movements; rather, he told the young lieutenant exactly what he wanted to hear. A week before the annuity distribution, some of Black Kettle's and Little Rock's young men, along with nearly all the Dog Soldiers from the camps of Bull Bear and Rock Forehead—two hundred in all—rode off to avenge a recent attack by the Pawnees. Twenty Lakotas and four Arapahos, Little Raven's son among them, joined the Cheyennes. The war party represented different camps and clans, even tribes, and no one man emerged as undisputed leader. However, five young Cheyennes exerted the most influence: Tall Wolf, George's friend and the Arrow Keeper's oldest son; Man Who Breaks the Marrow Bones, a brother of Chief White Antelope who had been murdered at Sand Creek; Porcupine Bear, George's cousin and son of Big Head, a council chief; Bear That Goes Ahead, brother of Chief Sand Hill; and Red Nose of Black Kettle's village.[19]

When the war party reached the Saline Valley, in central Kansas, Red Nose and Man Who Breaks the Marrow Bones convinced most of the warriors to turn toward the white settlements, where they could secure ammunition and fresh horses. Twenty men, however, refused to join, fearful that any contact with the whites would lead to trouble. These men continued north toward the Pawnee villages in Nebraska, carefully avoiding white roads and settlements. The main body, now numbering about 180 warriors, camped and waited for daylight. During the night, Red Nose and the other young war leaders, along with about 25 of their followers, scouted the trail ahead. The first cabin they encountered belonged to a homesteader named Shaw. The warriors boldly approached the house and spoke to the two men and two women. The Cheyennes demanded coffee and sugar, but when Mrs. Shaw and her sister offered the steaming brew in hot tin cups, they threw it back into the women's faces. When the husbands objected, the warriors beat the men with clubs and chased them from the ranch. The Cheyennes now plundered the cabin and gang-raped the two women, leaving them unconscious but alive. Red Nose's group then moved on to the next ranch, where they killed one white man and captured and raped another woman.

When the raiders returned to the main camp, they were met with shouts of disapproval. Surely the killing and rapes would bring soldiers down on them all. Many thought the captive should be returned immediately. But Red Nose and Man Who Breaks the Marrow Bones refused to give her up. A furious argument erupted, ending only when the warriors forced the troublemakers to release the woman. That evening a small party escorted the frightened captive back to her home.[20]

The leaderless war party had now devolved into feuding factions. Some wanted to continue the raiding, now that it had begun; others wanted to end the entire raid and go home. The group finally resolved to return to the Cheyenne villages by way of the settlements, taking whatever stock they could run off. Red Nose and Man Who Breaks the Marrow Bones again took the lead. A cache of whiskey was discovered at one of the ranches, and soon the war party was completely out of control. The liquor-crazed men attacked isolated ranches in the Saline and Solomon Valleys. Sweeping through the settlements, they killed sixteen white men, shot and wounded two women, seized several other women and their children, burned scores of ranches, and ran off with hundreds of horses and mules. Panicked settlers streamed from the valleys seeking military protection and demanding revenge.

Less than a year after the peace of Medicine Lodge, full-scale war had broken out on the plains.[21]

News of the Cheyenne outbreak reached George in Little Rock's village on the headwaters of Pawnee Fork near Fort Dodge. The chief opposed the raids on the Saline and Solomon and quickly set out to find Wynkoop, taking George with him as interpreter. They arrived at Fort Larned on August 19. George told the agent that the peace chiefs, Black Kettle and Little Rock, had been unable to control their young men. He explained that many had been under the influence of the Dog

Soldiers, who had only reluctantly accepted the Medicine Lodge Treaty and still claimed the government had not entirely fulfilled its promise to supply guns and ammunition to the Cheyennes. Wynkoop understood but reckoned that he was powerless to prevent more bloodshed unless Black Kettle and Little Rock moved their people over to Fort Larned, where their safety could be guaranteed. Wynkoop urged Little Rock to persuade Black Kettle to come in, but Little Rock doubted the peace chief would risk it. After all, it had been only four years since Sand Creek. The Cheyennes would never trust soldiers now that war fever ran high.

Before taking leave of the anxious agent, Little Rock asked Wynkoop if he really thought he could protect the people from the soldiers. Yes, said Wynkoop, but only if Red Nose and Man Who Breaks the Marrow Bones surrendered to military authorities, along with others guilty of the recent crimes. Little Rock vowed he would do his best to persuade the people, saying, "I am here in your service. At the same time I am a Cheyenne, and want to do all I can for the welfare of my nation. If the chiefs and headmen refuse to comply with your demands, I want to know if I can come with my wife and children (whom I love) and place myself and them under your protection, and at the same time act as a runner between you and my people." Wynkoop took the chief by the hand and said, "I will protect you."[22]

Little Rock had been right. Black Kettle's people were already striking their lodges. The chief intended to make a run for Comanche country far to the south, away from the soldiers.

When the people reached the Arkansas River crossing, George and Magpie, with Julia and Ed Guerrier, left Black Kettle and struck westward on the Santa Fe Trail toward William Bent's stockade and home. George did not know how or where the whites might retaliate, but he reasoned that Magpie and the baby would be safer with the old man. He would know what to do. Black Kettle continued south, heading for the Washita River—and safety. This was the last time George saw the great chief.[23]

George and Magpie arrived at the Purgatoire ranch to find that William and his young bride had returned to Westport. George was disappointed that his father would not see his new granddaughter; however, sister Mary with her children, Ada, William, and George,[24] could be depended upon to spoil baby Ada, the newest addition to the Bent clan. Julia comforted Magpie, whose family was with Black Kettle's village on the Washita River. Bob was also at the ranch, although he spent most of his time watching over their father's business interests. It was the first time the siblings had been together since Charley's death the previous November.

Certainly the family discussed the recent fighting, which touched the lives of Cheyennes everywhere. The Dog Soldiers and a few warriors from other bands had been responsible for the Saline and Solomon raids. Man Who Breaks the Marrow Bones still grieved for his father, White Antelope, murdered and mutilated at Sand Creek. Others, such as Red Nose, talked about violations of the Medicine Lodge Treaty, especially the government's refusal to deliver up promised guns and ammunition, and the encroachment of whites on Cheyenne buffalo ranges. George thought these were but excuses for the poorly conceived and executed raids. To be sure, there had been plenty of provocations, but the whole sad affair had been a "bad mistake," and this time he thought the Indians were to blame.[25] He knew the whites would blame the whole nation for the wanton acts of a few.

George was still on Wynkoop's payroll as interpreter, but the agent had taken a leave of absence and had gone to Philadelphia convinced that the Southern Cheyennes and Arapahos had crossed the Arkansas and were now far beyond his jurisdiction. Sometime in late October 1868 George rode over to Fort Lyon, hoping to catch up on news of Black Kettle and the progress of the war. While there he chanced to meet Bob, who had recently signed on as an army scout. A Cheyenne war party had raided a beef herd at Boggsville on September 8, and Bob had led an army patrol in pursuit.[26] The raiders had threatened the Bent ranch, and although he did not like the idea of tracking his own people, he felt he had no choice but to join Captain William H. Penrose's troop of the Seventh Cavalry.[27]

While George was still at the fort, Captain Lewis H. Carpenter with three companies of the Tenth Cavalry—the famed black "Buffalo Soldiers"—and Major Eugene A. Carr of the Fifth Cavalry trotted in. The hard-riding troops brought news of recent fighting. Carpenter's Buffalo Soldiers had been campaigning for the past month. In late September, they had rescued Major George A. Forsyth and his command of fifty civilian scouts, who had been attacked on the Arikaree River by two hundred Cheyennes and their Lakota allies. The scouts had retreated to a sandy island, where they dug in and fought off repeated charges. The warriors withdrew after four days of fighting, but not before they had lost five men killed, including the famed Roman Nose. The scouts had lost four men killed, among them young Lieutenant Beecher. Many more were wounded on both sides.[28]

Shortly after the Beecher Island fight, Carpenter had a fight with these same warriors. His troop had been escorting Major Carr, who was en route to assume command of the Fifth, when on October 17 he was attacked on Beaver Creek. Carpenter corralled his wagons and fought off almost suicidal attacks. Although only three Buffalo Soldiers were wounded, it had been a sharp engagement. Carpenter said that the soldiers shot down five warriors as they circled the wagons on their fleet war ponies. George wondered how much of the officer's story could be believed. He knew the whites never got it right, often embellishing tales of their own bravery and exaggerating Indian losses.[29]

After recounting their narrow escapes, Carr and Carpenter introduced George to two of the frontier's most celebrated scouts, William F. "Buffalo Bill" Cody and James B. "Wild Bill" Hickok. These men were sights to behold. Both dressed in gaudy fringed buckskin shirts and trousers, the likes of which had not been seen since the days of the fur trade when mountain men had brought their pelts into Bent's Old Fort. Both cut dashing figures, with their shoulder-length hair, mustaches, and chin-whiskers. George could not help but be impressed, and he was sorely tempted to accept Major Carr's offer to serve as his chief of scouts at a pay of ten dollars a day, twice what he was making as Wynkoop's interpreter. The prospect of hobnobbing with the likes of Cody and Hickok appealed to his sense of drama and adventure, but he wondered whether the government would be inclined to pay a scout who never found any Indians—for George would never lead the soldiers to his people. Respectfully, he turned down the offer.[30]

George also refused to track down Cheyenne raiders who had stolen mules from Fort Union on the Santa Fe Trail in northern New Mexico. Bob had agreed to hunt Cheyenne stock thieves, but George would not. He would work for the government as an interpreter, he would even work to persuade Cheyenne and Arapaho leaders to sign treaties, but he would not take the field against the Cheyennes. Nothing good could come of it.[31]

General Sheridan now sent out thousands of troops—regulars and volunteers—to track down the elusive Cheyennes, bring them to battle, and destroy them once and for all. Sheridan operated on the principle that "the only good Indians were dead ones,"[32] a philosophy adopted with some zeal by his new field commander, Lieutenant Colonel George Custer of the Seventh Cavalry. Custer had just returned to his regiment after a year's forced absence, during which time he suffered the humiliation of arrest and court-martial for abandoning his command while campaigning in Colorado and Kansas—all for a one-day tryst with wife Libbie at Fort Riley. Custer was back with a vengeance, eager to prove himself to Sheridan and Sherman, who had persuaded President Grant to reinstate him. Dressed in the fringed buckskin of a frontiersman and his face now hidden by a thick reddish beard, he desperately needed a victory. In November 1868 the opportunity presented itself.[33] His Osage scouts reported the trail of a war party heading toward the Washita River, some two hundred miles south of Fort Dodge in Indian Territory.

The Seventh Cavalry followed the tracks in the fresh snow to a sheltered and sleeping village in the river valley. Just before daylight, on November 27, 1868, Custer ordered the attack. The troopers completely surprised the camp, riding in from four directions. At the charge, the band played "Garry Owen" until frozen spit clogged the instruments. In companies, platoons, and squads, the mounted soldiers cut through the village, shooting down everything that moved— men, women, children, even the dogs.

Once again, Black Kettle was targeted by U.S. troops—almost four years to the day after the attack on his village at Sand Creek. This time, the old chief did not waste energy trying to reassure his people. He mounted his horse and pulled his wife, *Ar-no-ho-wok*—Medicine Woman Later—up behind him. When they reached the river's edge, soldiers appeared in front of them. Armed with repeating carbines, the troops let loose a fusillade that cut down the old chief and his wife. The soldiers splashed over their bodies with hardly a downward glance as they galloped toward the women and children now frantically running from the tipis.[34] They showed little mercy. The troopers scalped the dead, occupied and plundered the village, and then, at Custer's orders, burned the lodges and shot and killed more than eight hundred Indian ponies.

Meanwhile, survivors made for the Cheyenne, Arapaho, Kiowa, and Comanche camps located farther down the Washita River. Before the allied warriors could rally and offer battle, Custer escaped the valley with most of his command but left behind Major Joel Elliott's detachment of twenty men, which had continued its pursuit of fleeing women and children well beyond the village. With more warriors coming up from the nearby camps, Custer had shielded his hard-pressed command with more than fifty captured women and children as he hastily retreated.

The news of Black Kettle's death and the destruction of his village on the Washita reached Fort Lyon by the first week in December 1868. At that moment, Magpie's world collapsed. Her mother, *Nis-ta-nah*—Corn Tassle Woman—and her entire family were with Black Kettle.[35] As far as she knew, all her aunts, uncles, and cousins had died there on the Washita River. George did what he could to learn the details of the fight and soon received news that Custer had taken captives, *Nis-ta-nah* among them. The reports from the soldiers, however, were garbled. Some said the woman was Black Kettle's widow; others insisted she was his sister.

The confusion stemmed from the whites' imperfect understanding of George's relationship to Black Kettle. George may have referred to his wife as Black Kettle's daughter, when in fact she was his niece and stepdaughter, because the Cheyennes made no distinction between daughters and nieces. Magpie regarded her uncle Black Kettle as a father, especially after her own father, Cut Lip Bear, was killed at Sand Creek. No wonder the military authorities, in a flurry of dispatches, referred to the captured woman as Black Kettle's widow. Eventually the confusion was sorted out, but not until President Andrew Johnson, responding to reports from Sheridan, Sherman, and Wynkoop, became involved in the matter. Embarrassed by Wynkoop's letters to newspapers in which the agent argued that Washita was another Sand Creek, the army was anxious to return the celebrated *Nis-ta-nah* to George and Magpie. The president ordered that she be released from "military captivity" at Fort Hays, Kansas, and conveyed at government expense "to the home of her daughter in Colorado."[36]

But George and Magpie were not in Colorado. In January 1869 he had reported to Camp Supply, Indian Territory, the new agency headquarters for the Cheyennes and Arapahos as well as Sheridan's base of military operations. The reunion with Magpie's mother occurred here. George now learned that the loss of life at Washita was not nearly the 103 claimed by Custer. Survivors told him that fewer than 30 Cheyenne men, women, and children had been killed, along with several Arapahos. Many, of course, had been wounded, but it appeared that most of these would recover.[37]

While it was true that Black Kettle and thirteen other Cheyenne men had been slain, George also learned that Major Joel Elliott's detachment, which Custer listed as missing, had been wiped out. George had developed a friendship with the handsome, dark-haired major while the Seventh Cavalry had been assigned to guard annuity wagons at Medicine Lodge. They had spent many hours smoking and talking in Black Kettle's lodge. Soldiers at Camp Supply and Cheyenne and Arapaho survivors told him that Elliott's party had ridden two miles down the Washita in pursuit of fleeing villagers. The major's men killed Little Rock as the chief—armed only with bow and arrows—fought to protect the women and children. Suddenly, Cheyennes and Arapahos, with a few Kiowas, surrounded the soldiers. Elliott ordered his men to dismount and form a defensive circle in the tall grass. The warriors soon overwhelmed the soldiers and killed them all, cutting their bodies to pieces with knives and tomahawks.[38]

Hungry and destitute, Cheyenne survivors of Washita sought shelter where they could. Some joined the villages camped near Fort Cobb and Camp Supply. *Mo-nah-see-tah*, Little Rock's daughter, moved in with Custer at Camp Supply, then accompanied him as the Seventh

Cavalry pursued the scattered Cheyennes who had not yet surrendered to military authority. Custer found the young woman useful. He communicated with her through sign language, and she proved helpful in negotiations. By his own account, Custer found the slain chief's daughter vibrant and beautiful, and officers and scouts with the Seventh contended that the commanding officer not only took her into his care but into his bed as well. Cheyenne tradition corroborates this, holding that *Mo-nah-see-tah* bore Custer's child late in 1869.[39]

George and Magpie took *Nis-ta-nah*, Magpie's mother, into their lodge. The two women became inseparable. This disrupted the family circle, for as a Cheyenne man George could not live in the same lodge with his mother-in-law. Custom prohibited him from speaking to *Nis-ta-nah* or even makng eye contact with her. The taboo against contact with his mother-in-law was strong, and soon George was banished from the lodge. So here he was, a respected man, a wealthy leader of his tribe, without a wife to comfort him or lodge to call his own. This would not do. In short order, he moved in with a comely eighteen-year-old named Kiowa Woman, whose parents were killed at Washita.[40] Considering George's high political and financial standing in the tribe, no one would have noticed had the woman been Magpie's sister. Marriage to sisters was commonplace among wealthy Cheyennes. But George's marriage to Kiowa Woman—who was unrelated to his first wife—scandalized some traditional people. Such marriages usually did not work, for the wives inevitably competed for the affection and attention of the husband. Tensions grew between George and Magpie. She still nursed Ada and was not ready to resume an intimate relationship with her husband. Magpie had been taught that several years should pass before a wife had more children. George understood this disciplined abstinence. It was the Cheyenne way, but it was not his way. He loved women; he loved their company. Magpie understood this and accepted that a man of his stature would not live alone. And so, in late 1868, George married Kiowa Woman, who bore him a daughter, Julia, a year later.[41]

Despite his apparent wealth, George was having financial difficulties. As early as January 1869, he had enlisted the help of Superintendent

Thomas Murphy to secure seven months of back pay. As Wynkoop's interpreter, beginning in April 1868, he was entitled to five dollars and one army ration per day, a considerable sum.[42] Murphy contacted Indian Affairs commissioner N. G. Taylor, urging prompt payment not only to George but to John Smith and Margaret Adams as well.[43] Agency records and pay vouchers had been in disarray ever since Wynkoop departed for Philadelphia in August. George believed that because the agent had never discharged him, he was still on the government payroll. In March 1869 he hastily penned a note to Superintendent Murphy, complaining that he had still not received his pay:

> I have written to Col. Wynkoop several times but I have not receive no [sic] answer yet from him. I understand that other Interpreter have received their pay. You will do me a great favor if you let me know how I will get my pay, and also assist me all you can to get my pay.[44]

By now, he depended solely on the "courtesy and kindness" of others to feed his two families, an embarrassment to a Cheyenne warrior and a Bent. Uncle John Smith, who was on the army's payroll as interpreter, made certain that George and his family could draw government rations. Even during this difficult time, he continued to interpret whenever asked by army officers, agency officials, and post traders. The Cheyennes needed him, and he enjoyed being in demand and the center of attention.[45]

In the first few months of 1869, Camp Supply was a bustling military post. Because it was located in the heart of Indian country and the center of Sheridan's operations against the southern plains tribes, the army fortified the camp's perimeter. A log stockade, 15 feet high and 126 feet square, protected storehouses and great stacks of equipment, food, and ammunition. In fact, there was no room in the fort to house the troops, who quartered in tent camps outside the stockade. Cheyenne and Arapaho lodges also dotted the surrounding landscape. Enterprising traders, W. M. D. Lee and Albert E. Reynolds, set up a store and saloon outside the encampment and did a brisk business with soldiers, teamsters, and Indians.[46]

Lee and Reynolds desperately needed a reliable interpreter to carry on trade with the Cheyennes. Reynolds, who was the sutler at Fort Lyon, knew the Bent name and its influence and power among all the tribes of the southern plains. And here was George Bent looking for a job. Reynolds eagerly struck a deal, for George would offer the firm instant credibility. His duties would not be confined to interpreting. Lee and Reynolds saw the mixed blood as the perfect representative of their firm. He was fluent in Cheyenne and English, knew all the chiefs, had established good relations with army officers and officials of the Bureau of Indian Affairs, and was an experienced trader—and he possessed the Bent name. With his help, Lee and Reynolds soon outstripped all other traders and realized profits far beyond their expectations.[47]

Although business boomed at Camp Supply, there was still a war going on. Sheridan and Custer were in the field, seeking the surrender of the various bands that had scattered after Washita. Military pressure was not effective in bringing the Indians into Camp Supply, and the Cheyennes themselves were divided over the best course of action. At a meeting of council chiefs held in May 1869, the Dog Soldiers, led by Tall Bull and White Horse, argued for continued resistance to white encroachment. They would live free or die and never give up their country. Little Robe and other peace chiefs urged surrender, for this was the only way to secure the release and return of the Cheyenne hostages taken by Custer on the Washita. Little Robe told the Dog Men that if they would not join the Southern Cheyennes and surrender at Camp Supply as Sheridan had demanded, they should get out of the country. Their presence and incessant raiding threatened the lives of the hostages and caused the soldiers to attack peaceful Cheyenne villages. Tall Bull and White Horse saw that Little Robe and the southern bands lacked the resolve to continue the war. Soon after the council ended, the Dog Men struck their lodges and taking only essential supplies with them, headed north to join their Lakota allies on the Republican River.[48]

George heard of the Tall Bull–Little Robe conference through John Smith's Cheyenne wife, *Na-to-mah*. He agreed with Little Robe. In the past, the chief had been sympathetic to the Dog Soldiers and at times even joined them in war on the whites. But George knew the Dog Men often caused trouble. He said that "the young men of this band were very wild and reckless...and would make a raid and get out of the way and the troops would come and stumble across some other band of Cheyennes and punish them for what the Dog Soldiers had done."[49] Little Robe had been right to send the Dog Soldiers north. Not only were the Washita prisoners at risk, but just recently Custer had taken more hostages, this time three Cheyenne elders named Lean Face, Fat Bear, and Curly Hair. These men surely would be executed unless Little Robe and the other southern band leaders surrendered.

By mid-May, Little Robe and Eagle Head began moving their people into Camp Supply, where George helped agency officials issue rations and supplies. Lee and Reynolds's demand on his time increased, too, as the Cheyennes sought to barter at the traders' store.

Then sad new reached the Cheyenne camps. William Bent—Grey Beard—was dead at the age of sixty. The news hit George hard. His father had always seemed indestructible; now he was dead, a victim of pneumonia. At the Purgatoire ranch, Mary had done all she could for the old man, but he had slipped away on May 19, 1869.[50] Cheyennes, and army officers too, talked about his death, for no man on the southern plains was better known or more influential. Whites saw him as the last of the great mountain men and western traders, while the Cheyennes regarded him as a trusted tribal advisor and the only white man who truly understood them. With his death came the end of an era. When William had first ventured into the mountains and plains, the Indians roamed free following the great herds and suffered white men only on tribes' own terms. Now the buffalo were almost gone and the Cheyennes and other southern plains people faced utter defeat, their lands reduced to small reservations defined by the white intruders.[51]

Yet, George decided not to leave Camp Supply while the trading was good. His father would have understood—business was business. Besides, the old man was already in the ground and there was little he could do to help Mary and Robert. At the same time, Sheridan's columns were still in the field crushing pockets of Indian resistance.

The Dog Soldiers were raiding white settlements as they moved north toward the Republican. Tall Bull was determined to strike the whites one last blow as the Cheyennes left their homeland to join the Lakotas. On June 21, Sheridan made good on his promise to free the Washita hostages, releasing them to Little Robe at Camp Supply. Agency officials relied on George to translate for the chiefs as the captives were finally returned to their families.[52]

Tall Bull and White Horse swept through settlements on the Smoky Hill and Solomon Rivers, plundering and taking captives as they went. All the way, they decoyed Carr's Fifth Cavalry away from the main village, protecting the women and children. Even Carr's chief of scouts Buffalo Bill Cody and the Pawnee Scouts, led by Major Frank North, were fooled by the false trails left by the Dog Men. But on July 10, 1869, after an exhausting five-hundred-mile flight from the army and relentless Pawnees, Tall Bull allowed his people to rest at a place called White Buttes—Summit Springs to the whites—just south of the Platte River in northeastern Colorado. Here, the women erected their lodges for the first time in days. The people refreshed in the cool waters of the springs and put the horses out to graze on the rolling grasslands surrounding the chalky buttes.

The following day, just after noon as the village slept, a herder shouted a warning: "People are coming!" In an instant, Pawnee scouts and soldiers crashed through the camp. The surprise was complete. Tall Bull called out: "All of you who are on foot and cannot get away, follow me!" He led the people to a deep ravine in the buttes, half a mile from his lodge, where fighting men soon joined him. Here they made their stand, the soldiers firing on them from all sides. Singing their death songs, the warriors fought with their guns, their knives, and their bare hands. Wolf With Plenty of Hair fought to the death staked to the ground by his rawhide Dog Rope. Tall Bull, fighting next to his wives and children, was killed by a bullet through his brain, fired by Buffalo Bill.[53] With Tall Bull died fifty-one other Cheyenne men. The power of the Dog Soldiers was forever broken. No longer would they be an independent fighting force; no longer could the Cheyenne people turn to the Dog Men for leadership in their war for freedom and survival.[54]

George knew these men—he had ridden with them in those glory days of revenge following Sand Creek. Yes, they had caused grief to the tribe, with their wild and warlike ways, but they were Cheyenne warriors who had resisted white encroachment and fought to the death to preserve their freedom. He admired them for this, even though he now followed the road of accommodation.

And he could not help but wonder if he had chosen the right road.

Chapter 10

WALKING THE
WHITE MAN'S ROAD

Midsummer in the Upper Arkansas River country is almost always hot, but the afternoons usually are cooled by towering thunderheads and, sometimes, pounding rains. When the Bent boys, George and Bob, along with sisters Mary Moore and Julia Guerrier, gathered at their father's Purgatoire ranch, sounds of thunder rolled across the valley. They were all together, and the time had finally come to settle William Bent's estate. No one—not even Bob, William's partner in the trade business—knew what the old man was worth. But all expected to inherit a small fortune in real estate, trade goods, and other property.

Today, July 16, 1869, the estate administrator Alfred P. Warfield, all the way from Independence, Missouri, intended to make a preliminary distribution of William's ranch holdings, especially the livestock, which needed immediate attention. William provided in his last will and testament, dated May 10, 1866, that each of the children would receive "an equal undivided share of my estate, share and share alike." A special provision for Mary, however, stipulated that Silas Bent, William's St. Louis brother and sole executor, would hold Mary's share in trust, "free from the control of her . . . husband, Robert [*sic*] Moore, so long as she shall live."[1] William, it seemed, never really trusted the former bartender.

Warfield believed the estate's monetary value could easily exceed $50,000; for now, he simply wanted to dispose of personal and perishable property associated with the ranch. Mary and Julia claimed the house furnishings and personal effects, including the family bible. To Bob went two pairs of mules, a small wagon, and all the remaining merchandise of the "R[obert] & W[illiam] Bent" trading company, valued at $1,943.35. George received seventy-eight head of cattle, a pair of matched gray mules, and a small wagon complete with harness, worth $3,255.00. The brothers agreed the value of these goods would be deducted from their shares of the final estate settlement—"share and share alike," as provided in the will.[2]

But in July 1869 none of the Bents knew there would be no further property distribution. For in truth, at his death the old man was not only broke but deeply in debt. Although he was the first permanent white settler in Colorado Territory, he had never legally owned any land. He had tried to sell his forts on the Arkansas—old Bent's Fort and the new stone fort overlooking Fort Lyon—to the War Department, but the government never recognized his title to the land and refused to buy. Even on his Purgatoire ranch he was nothing more than a squatter. He had little collateral, other than his rolling stock and the Westport property.

William W. Bent spoke five Indian languages and kept the peace between the tribes on the Arkansas, negotiated treaties, and successfully lobbied congressional leaders and U.S. presidents. But as a bookkeeper he had been an abject failure. Old fur trade partner Robert Campbell said he was "not very systematic in business. . . . He declines to make out a formal bill for services in detail—for he never keeps accounts."[3] Within the year, the Bent children would learn that creditors claimed $32,000 of the estate. True, the house in Westport was worth $15,000, but their father's child bride, Adaline, occupied it with her newborn baby girl, arguing that the property belonged to her as Bent's lawful wife, will or no will. Although the court evicted Adaline from the house and sold the property at public auction, it permitted her to keep $2,214.00 from the sale of three of William's Westport lots.[4] In the end, the court took control of the estate, liquidated the assets, and paid off the creditors.

The Bent heirs received nothing more. Nothing, despite William's forty years in the Rocky Mountain West. He had brought the Cheyennes to the Arkansas River and helped shape the Cheyenne nation itself. He had brought the warring tribes together at Bent's Fort and helped negotiate a lasting peace among the southern plains tribes. He had influenced U.S. Indian policy and had pledged his life to preserve peace between Indians and whites. He had pulled the Santa Fe Trail through Bent's Old Fort and over Raton Pass, and no man more powerfully influenced commerce in the Southwest. And yet, in the end, he had nothing to give his children other than his name—no small gift, but not the fortune that everyone expected.

But for now, George felt flush with his newfound wealth, more wealth, in fact, than he had ever known. The day after the distribution he rode over to Boggsville to see rancher John Prowers, his father's old friend who had married Amache, the daughter of the one-eyed Cheyenne chief Lone Bear.[5] George met up with Prowers at the rancher's busy general store and while there bought canned oysters, a rare delicacy that cost him $1.50.[6] No doubt the men talked about George's cattle, for Prowers was always on the lookout for good beef stock. George had no way of driving the animals back to Camp Supply, Indian Territory, so he agreed to sell the herd at $35 a head.[7] Prowers and George also discussed the Arkansas River lands of the mixed-bloods, who had been granted land by Article V of the 1865 Treaty of the Little Arkansas as reparation for the Sand Creek Massacre. George had already sold his 640-acre holding to Prowers. Although it was prime land located on the north bank of the Arkansas between Big Timbers and Big Sandy Creek, George had no need for Colorado land, for he was sure there would be plenty of land and money coming his way from his father's estate. He gave little thought, if indeed he knew at all, how his father had struggled to acquire land for his children and the other Cheyenne mixed-bloods, for he believed they were a breed apart, not Indian, not white, deserving of special protection under the law. In an uncertain world, the land would sustain them when Indians and whites inevitably turned on them and took advantage of their precarious position between two peoples. Only the land was forever, and only through land would they have a chance to support themselves and their families. Land ownership had always eluded William, but he fought to his dying day to make landowners of his sons and daughters. George never understood his father's passion for land. In his Cheyenne way, while he appreciated the white man's concept of land as a commodity, something to be bought and sold, he never quite grasped the reality that it also brought power and prestige and security. Naïvely, he viewed his treaty lands as a windfall, selling his Arkansas holdings to Prowers and staking his future on the dream of his father's estate.

Prowers, however, knew the power of land. He was even now building a huge cattle operation anchored on the Arkansas River and wanted all the lands and accompanying water rights held by the mixed-bloods. George agreed to assist Prowers in acquiring not only Julia's property but also those sections belonging to the Guerriers, Poisals, Fitzpatricks, and Smiths. Within a year, with George's help, Prowers absorbed the mixed-blood lands and built one of the largest cattle empires in the Southwest.[8]

There was nothing to hold George in Colorado now. He made up his mind to return to Indian Territory and his Cheyenne kinfolk. The new Cheyenne and Arapaho agent, Brinton Darlington, had asked George to be his first official Cheyenne interpreter. Also pulling him back to Camp Supply was the prospect of a good-paying job with the traders Lee and Reynolds. He had already established a close friendship with Albert Reynolds, who urged him to return and resume his position as Indian trader. But most of all, he wanted to return to Magpie and Kiowa Woman and his children.

Bob was destined for a traders' life as well. It was the only life he knew; William had groomed him to take over the family business, and he was savvy enough to realize that the trade as he knew it existed only in the fast-moving Indian camps close to the ranging buffalo herds. The days of fixed trading posts like Bent's Old Fort or even the Purgatoire ranch were gone. He packed up his remaining trade merchandise and joined George on the journey back to Camp Supply.

Julia had made her choice when she cast her lot with mixed-blood Ed Guerrier, who served both the army and the Department of the Interior as an interpreter. Following her husband and brothers, Julia also returned to the Cheyennes in Indian Territory.

Of the Bent children, Mary alone chose to live in the white world. Her husband, R. M. Moore, was a successful rancher and had played an active role in the organization of Bent County, Colorado. In time, he served as superintendent of schools and county judge, and along with John Prowers and Tom Boggs, he influenced every aspect of community affairs. Mary raised her children in the Episcopal Church and enrolled them in the public schools. She dressed them in the latest eastern fashions, gave the girls piano lessons, and instructed them in proper Victorian domestic skills, just as Aunt Dorcas had taught her when she was a girl growing up in St. Louis. She knew Dorcas loved her, but in her aunt's house the white way was the right way. Although her dark skin and Cheyenne features never left any doubt of her Indian ancestry, her bustles and petticoats and other white-society trappings gave evidence of Aunt Dorcas's influence. Mary had learned well—neither she nor her children ever returned to the Cheyenne camps.[9]

When George arrived at Camp Supply and the Cheyenne and Arapaho Agency, Brinton Darlington was already on the job. Darlington represented a great change in U.S. Indian policy. President Ulysses S. Grant, inaugurated in March 1869, appointed his former aide-de-camp, Colonel Ely S. Parker, as commissioner of Indian Affairs.

As one of Grant's first official acts, the appointment drew considerable public attention, for Parker, a New Yorker, was a full-blood Iroquois Indian descended from a long line of Seneca chiefs but thoroughly acculturated through his white education and his military service. Grant and Parker devised a grand plan that they believed would save American Indians from extinction and bring them into mainstream American life. Under the new plan, the agencies would be administered not by political appointees but by missionaries dedicated to converting their charges to Christianity. Presumably, men of the cloth would not abuse their office or engage in the corrupt business practices that characterized the Bureau of Indian Affairs. Parker directed Indian agents to treat their charges as individuals—not as members of tribes—and prepare them for American citizenship through educational and cultural programs that would strip them of their "savagery" and replace it with Christianity. In short, the policy aimed to "kill the Indian and save the man."[10]

Parker thought Darlington the ideal choice to implement the new policy. The sixty-five-year-old Quaker, with his bald head, snowy white beard, and bushy eyebrows, impressed the Indians with his kindly ways, for he genuinely cared for the Cheyenne and Arapaho people and was determined to demonstrate that the "Quaker policy"—as Grant's program became known—of peaceful assimilation was superior to military coercion.

But missionary zeal and good intentions soon confronted the reality of agency conditions. Darlington established his headquarters at Pond Creek, one hundred miles east of Camp Supply. There, he erected two log buildings and dug a well. But these improvements did not draw the Indians into the agency. For in truth, Darlington spoke not a word of Cheyenne. Raphael Romero—an interpreter on loan from the army—helped out when he could, but not until George returned from the Arkansas did Darlington have someone he could rely on. Through George, the agent learned that the Cheyennes and Arapahos did not like the land selected for them, complaining that the reserve's brackish waters made the region unfit for man or beast. Further, the Dog Soldier refugees from Summit Springs stayed away from the new agency, suspicious of any government authority.[11]

Darlington hardly knew what to do and turned to his interpreter for advice. George suggested the agent hold a council with the Arrow Keeper, Rock Forehead, who still exerted a strong influence over all the Cheyenne bands, including the renegade Dog Soldiers. Darlington agreed, but the old man was not up to the hundred-mile journey to the Cheyenne village near Camp Supply, and the Cheyennes refused to travel to distant Pond Creek. So, in his stead, Darlington sent George to Camp Supply to read a letter of instructions addressed to the Cheyenne leaders.

At the conference on September 2, 1869, the Arrow Keeper was not in good humor. After George read Darlington's patronizing letter, Rock Forehead dictated an angry reply. He complained about making a thirty-mile trek in the hot sun, only to have a letter read to him by Darlington's interpreter. Although the Arrow Keeper loved George like a son, he thought the agent showed disrespect by not coming in person. Adding to the insult, the Indian leaders were not provided with food—not even coffee or sugar. Was this the way the government treated a Cheyenne leader? Rock Forehead went on to outline his concerns. Surely the military knew the Cheyennes wanted peace, for the tribes had waited patiently for "four moons" to receive the food and clothing promised by General Sheridan last winter. Because the supplies had not been delivered, the bands now must leave Camp Supply in search of buffalo. The Cheyennes cared little for Darlington's remote agency, with its useless buildings and brackish waters. They wanted, instead, the arms and ammunition necessary to carry out a successful buffalo hunt. As for the corn the agent proposed to issue, the Arrow Keeper said it was worthless, for "even our ponies will not eat it. If you can change this corn for sugar & coffee you will please do so." George drafted the letter in his finest hand, and signed Rock Forehead with the impressive title of "Medicine Arrow, Chief of the Cheyenne Nation."[12] This was nonsense of course. There never was or ever would be a single chief of the Cheyennes, but George felt this exaggeration would help Rock Forehead in future negotiations with the agent.

Darlington was pleased with George's performance on his first official mission. He had demonstrated tact and diplomacy in dealing with the Indians, but he brought back a troubling message from the conference. Winning over the disaffected tribes would be more difficult than the old Quaker had imagined.[13]

In fact, Darlington never succeeded in luring the Cheyennes to his Pond Creek agency. No matter. On August 10, 1869, President Grant signed an executive order creating a new Cheyenne and Arapaho reservation. Although no one consulted the Indians or even informed them of the change, the president and Commissioner Parker believed the new reserve would be more to the liking of the tribes. Bounded by the Texas Panhandle on the west, the Kiowa-Comanche reservation on the south, the Cherokee Strip on the north, and the ninety-eighth meridian on the east, the new reservation comprised more than four million acres of rolling grassland. On the advice of army officers and to place himself in the center of the new reserve, Darlington relocated his headquarters to the North Canadian River, ninety miles south of Pond Creek.

In early May 1870 he completed the move. On rich bottomlands near a bubbling spring, he built several structures fashioned from cottonwood logs, topped with dirt roofs. Only a few trees along the river and a sandy ridge to the north broke the featureless expanse of prairie—waves of grass that seemed to stretch forever in all directions. The nearest military posts were Fort Sill, 80 miles southwest, and Camp Supply, 140 miles northwest. The Kansas Pacific Railroad lay some 200 miles north. Supplies and annuities had to be freighted by wagons over nearly trackless plains, and cattle contractors had to drive herds out of Texas or from Kansas railheads. It soon became apparent that the new agency was far from practically anywhere.[14]

Problems continued for the well-meaning agent. The Indians only came into the agency headquarters when buffalo were scarce and the people faced starvation. But in April, just when the tribes arrived to receive rations, Darlington had none to give. "This is the darkest hour I have experienced in Indian Affairs," he wrote. "We are nearly out of every kind of subsistence. The worst of all is the want of beef."[15]

At the same time, rumors persisted that the Cheyennes would join the Kiowas and Comanches in raids on white settlements in Texas. Darlington sent George to the camps to find out the truth. In Big Jake's village he smoked with Red Moon, Black White Man, Big Man, and young Whirlwind. From these leaders, he learned that the threat was real and a breakout was likely early in the spring. George urged the chiefs to restrain their young men, while he would see what he could do about improving the conditions that caused the discontent. First, however, he would reassure Darlington that peace prevailed in the camps and no troops were necessary. His strategy worked. Darlington reported to his superiors, "George Bent thinks they are disposed to be peaceable, at least has learned nothing to the contrary and he has taken considerable pains to ascertain the true state of their feelings and intentions."[16] By mid-May, Agent Darlington recommended that peace medals be awarded to Big Jake, Little Robe, Red Moon, Stone Calf, young Whirlwind, Lean Bear, and Eagle Head.[17]

Darlington now determined to send Uncle John Smith and Philip McCusker to Washington, D.C., to accompany a delegation of Cheyenne and Arapaho chiefs. Ed Guerrier, on detached service from the army, would join them, while George would remain in the camps as Darlington's eyes and ears. Of course, George would have preferred to join the Washington delegation, but yielding to Darlington's gentle persuasion, he agreed to stay behind.

The government hoped to impress upon the chiefs—particularly Little Robe, Stone Calf, and Little Raven—the expanse and might of the United States. During May and June 1871, in the great seaboard cities of Philadelphia, Washington, Boston, and New York, the Indian leaders rode streetcars, visited zoos and icehouses, experienced indoor plumbing, looked down from the dizzying heights of tall buildings, heard the roar of great cannons, toured factories, and lectured to standing-room-only crowds. Through it all, the chiefs handled the attention they received with grace and good humor, winning admirers and supporters everywhere. In Washington they posed for a photograph with superintendent of Indian Affairs, Mahlon Stubbs. Seated on straight-backed chairs, the Indians showed off newly acquired vests and frock coats, Little Raven even affecting the use of a fancy, carved ivory cane. The interpreters looked chummy, Uncle John draping an arm around Phil McCusker, and behind Little Raven stood dapper Ed Guerrier with shoulder-length hair and a floppy silk cravat.[18] ·

When the tribal leaders returned to Darlington in mid-July, George heard their fantastic tales with growing resentment. He felt he should have been there, but he was relieved that the delegation got back safely, for sometimes traveling chiefs "disappeared" in the East, victims of the white man's sicknesses.

The arduous journey had in fact taken a toll. Within days of the delegation's return, old John Smith was dead. Smith had been a fixture on the plains since the 1830s, when he gave up a tailor's apprenticeship in Kentucky to become a Rocky Mountain trapper. After living with the Blackfeet for a few years—the Cheyennes always knew him as "Blackfoot Smith"—he married a succession of Cheyenne women and for the rest of his life identified himself with that tribe. George knew him as "Uncle John," for the Bent children had grown up with his son Jack, the same Jack Smith murdered at Sand Creek in 1864. But he held mixed feelings for the old trader. William Bent had often criticized him for cheating the Cheyennes and Arapahos out of their annuity goods. And Uncle John had a dangerous side to him. Even his friends watched their backs when he was around. Yet, he was a survivor. As a young man he had killed seven Blackfeet warriors by trickery and lived to tell the tale. In later years, he had sidestepped Denver vigilantes who took exception to his wife-beating ways. And at Sand Creek he had almost shared the fate of his son when soldiers shot at him, thinking him "no better than an Indian." But he always came through with his hide intact; actually, when he died he had little else. Before his wife placed his body on a scaffold in a tree near Darlington

Agency, authorities reported that the old man's estate consisted of a pair of horses, a saddle, and a gun.[19]

Smith's death aside, the return of the interpreters caused a major headache for Darlington, who was still trying to find his way through the mind-numbing bureaucracy of the Indian department. From what fund—army or agency—should he pay interpreter Guerrier? Technically, Ed was on the army's payroll, but he had been in Washington on agency business. After a back-and-forth flurry of correspondence with his superiors at the Central Superintendency, Darlington resolved the matter and Guerrier received his pay.[20]

This was but one of several worries afflicting the agent. He worked long hours to feed, educate, and Christianize his Cheyenne and Arapaho wards. By spring 1872 the frail old man was used up. The Arapahos, who had expressed an interest in giving up the hunt for farming, petitioned for permission to split off from, in Darlington's words, the "more turbulent Cheyennes." The agent endured constant bickering between the two tribes.[21] Moreover, many of the Cheyenne chiefs still refused to come into the agency, and when they did venture in, Darlington often could not feed them. Unreliable and fraudulent contractors tormented him and undermined the efficient operation of the agency.

On May 1, 1872, Brinton Darlington died. George heard that the agent had died from an attack of "brain fever." Bent attended his funeral and, along with hundreds of Cheyennes, filed by his open casket. Many wept openly, their tears wetting the dusty, wooden floor of the meetinghouse where his body lay in state. George rarely had seen such a open display of affection, especially for a white man. The Cheyennes always regarded Darlington as their best agent, a rare white man who could be trusted. At the missionary's own request, he was buried atop a sand hill just west of the agency buildings.[22]

Shortly after the funeral, chiefs Big Jake, Bull Bear, Heap of Birds, and Whirlwind met with the acting agent, John A. Covington. The new man warned the chiefs that unless they began farming now, there would be no crops to harvest in the fall. But the chiefs gathered their blankets about them and let the agent know that although the Arapahos might farm, the Cheyennes were not yet "ready for the corn road of the whites." Besides, in recent months buffalo had been seen in great numbers beyond the reservation's boundaries. The hunters ranged far, filling the meat pots, and the people enjoyed prosperous times. Indeed, during the previous winter and current spring the Cheyennes had dressed nearly ten thousand robes for trade.[23]

When Agent John D. Miles took over the Cheyenne-Arapaho agency in June 1872, he was a troubled man. His first order of business was to inform the Cheyennes and Arapahos of Grant's 1869 executive order creating the new tribal reservation in Indian Territory, thus nullifying the 1867 Treaty of Medicine Lodge. Knowing the sensitivity of the subject, especially among the Dog Soldiers, Darlington had been afraid to broach the matter. But Enoch Hoag, Superintendent of Indian Affairs for the Upper Arkansas Agency, had insisted that Miles meet the leaders in council and explain how President Grant had unilaterally abrogated the old treaty and assigned the Cheyennes and Arapahos a new reservation far from their traditional lands. Further, this executive order forbade them to hunt between the Arkansas and Platte Rivers as promised by the peace commissioners at Medicine Lodge.

In short, with the stroke of the Great Father's pen and without consultation, the Cheyennes were now prisoners on a reservation practically barren of buffalo.

When Miles asked for his interpreter's help in breaking the news, George flatly refused. More than any other man, he was responsible for the Dog Soldiers' acceptance of the Medicine Lodge Treaty. At the council he had walked with the chiefs and given his word that if they signed the treaty they would retain the right to hunt buffalo on their traditional lands between the Arkansas and Platte for as long as the herds lasted. Of course, there was no such provision written into the treaty itself, but the commissioners, through George, had made a promise. If he went to the chiefs now and told them it had all been a lie, not only would his reputation suffer but his life might be forfeit. Miles understood this and agreed, for the present, to postpone the discussion until a more propitious time.[24]

George and Miles had assessed the mood of the Cheyennes correctly, for conditions on the reservation were rapidly deteriorating. Whiskey peddlers made the rounds of the Indian camps, trading cheap rotgut for valuable ponies and buffalo robes. George confessed to A. E. Reynolds that the liquor addiction was so powerful Cheyenne men would trade a pony for ten gallons of whiskey. In turn, Reynolds warned Agent Miles that if the whiskey trade continued "the tribes will be naked and left on foot."[25] Cheyenne women increasingly refused to tan the hides brought in by their husbands lest the men exchange them for whiskey instead of food and supplies. Miles himself saw more than a thousand Cheyennes in camp near the agency "drunk as loons." He lamented in his reports that drunken brawling had resulted in serious injuries, even death. This kind of behavior had occurred only rarely before the Cheyennes' confinement on the reservation. Now the combination of cheap liquor and boredom were more of a threat to the tribe than the white soldiers were.[26]

When buffalo became scarce, food shortages also threatened the peace. Miles, like Darlington before him, seldom had enough beef on hand to feed his wards. He asked his superiors repeatedly for an increase in the daily beef allowance. At the same time, he thought the flour ration should be reduced, for the Indians would not eat the stuff. To make matters worse, white hide-hunters, with their long-range rifles, trespassed on the reservation, decimating the already dwindling buffalo herds.[27] The whites stripped the valuable hides and left the carcasses to rot at the same time Indian hunters were trying to feed hungry villages.

Incredibly, as the food shortages became critical, the paternalistic Bureau of Indian Affairs encouraged Miles to withhold annuities to ensure good behavior. If the Cheyennes wanted food and essential supplies, they would have to send their children to school and begin farming.[28]

Adding to these difficulties, horse thieves from Kansas and Texas operated with impunity on the reservation. Agent Miles hired stock detectives, but they were too few to protect the scattered Indian herds. The army refused to help police the agency, claiming that it had no jurisdiction on the reservation.

On April 22, 1874, white horse thieves struck George Bent's herd at his camp just two miles from Darlington and made off with four mules and five ponies worth more than a thousand dollars. The outlaw gang, nine in number, included William Martin, alias "Hurricane Bill";

Robert Hollis, alias "Texas Bob"; and Jack Gallagher—all well known in the district. George seethed when told that the army refused to help track down the desperadoes and recover his stock. He wrote a letter to Miles demanding that the agent either take action or pay him for his lost stock. He warned that "the Indians . . . tried to persuade me to raise a party of young men to follow the thieves and capture the property and punish the offenders." Though sorely tempted, George had declined the offer and prevented the Cheyennes from taking the law into their own hands. He feared that once the warriors set out, there would be no way to control them.[29] Enough innocents—white and Indian—had already died. A month earlier, the same thieves ran off forty-three horses belonging to Little Robe's and Stone Calf's bands. Miles's stock detectives finally arrested Hurricane Bill, but not before Cheyenne war parties—one led by Little Robe's son—set out on raids of their own.[30]

The war that Grant's peace policy had been designed to prevent was now at hand. Kiowa and Comanche warriors, riled by a charismatic holy man named *Isatai*, carried their war pipes to the Cheyennes.[31] To counteract their influence, Miles sent George to the camps of White Shield, Whirlwind, and Little Robe.[32] Several days later the three chiefs brought their bands into the safety of the Cheyenne-Arapaho agency.

But on the North Canadian River in the Texas Panhandle, Indian warriors descended on Adobe Walls, the isolated trading post once operated by Bent and St. Vrain. The cluster of run-down adobe and sod buildings now served as a hunting camp and way station. At dawn, on June 27, 1874, two hundred Cheyennes, Comanches, and Kiowas, led by *Isatai*, attacked twenty-eight buffalo hunters and wagoners. The warriors charged the buildings, then backed their horses against the doors in an unsuccessful attempt to force their way in. Armed only with bows and arrows and short-range pistols and carbines, the Indians had hoped to take the whites by surprise and fight them at close quarters. But the hunters were awake and well protected by the thick adobe walls. When the shooting started, the whites poked their long-barreled buffalo guns through the windows and killed more than a score of the attackers—some at a distance of nearly a mile—and wounded many more. The Indians slaughtered the hunters' horses and killed three men who had been caught outside the compound, but it had been a bad day for the allied tribes—and especially for *Isatai*, whose medicine had failed. Unable to get at the whites in their stronghold, the Indians scattered and sought revenge on ranches, wagon trains, and mail carriers in Kansas and Texas.[33]

George had seen trouble coming. On the evening of May 21, just a month after Hurricane Bill had run off his stock, two young Arapahos, their carbines resting across their saddles, rode up to the house of an agency employee at Darlington. Without warning one of the Arapahos fired through the window, killing Frank Holloway, the son of agency physician Dr. Jason Holloway. Panic seized the settlement as white employees armed themselves and slept behind bolted doors. A few days after the shooting, George spoke to a Cheyenne who identified the killers as renegade Arapahos. He also learned that these same Arapahos had warned Miles that the Cheyennes were plotting war and had even offered their services as a special police force. Competition for limited resources had turned the once allied tribes against one another. Given the conditions, George knew the restless young men would soon lash out at any white target. He believed the army needed to come onto the reservations with a strong force; otherwise, full-scale war was likely.[34]

When Miles learned of the Adobe Walls affair, he realized that the Quaker peace policy was doomed. The agency now required military protection. Gathering as many armed men as he could spare without leaving the agency helpless, he set out for Lawrence, Kansas, to persuade his superiors to authorize the army to enter the reservation. George remained with his people, doing all he could to calm and reassure them. As Miles traveled north he observed firsthand the horrors of an Indian war: dead and mutilated bodies of white herders and freighters, abandoned ranches, and, thirty-five miles north of Darlington, the still smoking wreckage of Patrick Hennessey's wagon train. Three freighters lay dead, two of them scalped, while Hennessey himself was found tied spread-eagle to the lead wagon's rear wheel. Burned alive, he was identified only by his hands and feet.[35]

Thoroughly frightened, Miles hurried on to Lawrence, Kansas, and there, in an impassioned appeal, told his Quaker superiors that unless the military intervened the agency would be burned and its employees massacred. The Quaker executive committee thought the panicked agent was overreacting, and some members even called for his resignation. But Enoch Hoag supported Miles, and the two men won over the elders and convinced generals Sherman and Sheridan to unleash the army.[36]

On July 20, 1874, the army received permission to hunt down the raiders and drive the warring bands back to their agencies. The Red River War had begun. By late summer, five strong columns converged on the hostile Cheyenne, Kiowa, and Comanche camps scattered in Indian Territory and the Texas Panhandle.

At George's urging, White Shield, Little Robe, and Whirlwind, along with fewer than three hundred of their followers, had remained at Darlington. The decision for Little Robe had been particularly difficult. Not only had his son recently been wounded in a fight with the Sixth Cavalry, but in his own camp, when the chief announced his intention to move over to the agency and surrender, Dog Soldier society men had rounded up his horses and shot them down. Little Robe had lost control of his own village. He and his few remaining followers slipped away by night, leaving behind lodges, food, and camp equipment.

After the defeat at Summit Springs in July 1869, many of the Dog Soldiers had gone north to join Lakota and Northern Cheyenne villages. But by winter most had returned south and quietly mingled with the Southern Cheyennes without challenge by the army. Their numbers may have been reduced, but their fighting spirit had not diminished. Dog Soldier chiefs White Horse and Bull Bear—supported by Rock Forehead, the Arrow Keeper—still exerted a powerful influence, even though they could no longer lead an independent fighting force.

Now, in 1874, the main village of nearly two thousand Cheyennes acted under the influence of the war faction, including Big Jake, Red Moon, Grey Beard, Eagle Head, Heap of Birds, Sand Hill, Medicine Water, and Stone Calf. Through the summer and fall, war parties eluded army patrols, striking deep into Texas and Kansas. On September 11, 1874, a war party led by Medicine Water attacked a lone wagon on the Smoky Hill Trail near Fort Wallace, in western Kansas. The warriors killed John German, his wife, and three of their seven children. They took captive four girls: Catherine, age seventeen; Sophia, twelve; Julia, seven; and Adelaide, five. The attack on the emigrant family and the capture of the four German sisters caused a national outcry. From Boston to Denver, newspapers sensationalized the attack, and mothers everywhere prayed for the girls' rescue. The army redoubled its efforts to bring the war to a speedy conclusion.[37]

At first light on the morning of September 28, 1874, Colonel Ranald Mackenzie's Fourth Cavalry surprised a combined Cheyenne, Kiowa, and Comanche village of nearly three hundred lodges in Palo Duro Canyon in the Texas Panhandle, two hundred miles west of Darlington. The Indians fled as the soldiers scrambled down the canyon's walls. The people left everything—even their horses—behind. Although only three warriors were killed in the fight, Mackenzie's men completely destroyed the village, burning all the lodges and the winter's supply of dried meat. Then they turned their carbines on the captured horse herd, slaughtering nearly a thousand animals. The attack at Palo Duro Canyon shattered Cheyenne resistance. Without their lodges, food, clothing, and horses, survival on the Staked Plains was impossible. Coupled with the mounting pressure of the other four columns—Colonel Nelson Miles from the north, lieutenant colonels John W. Davidson and George P. Buell from the east, and Major William R. Price from the west—this destruction drove the Cheyennes back toward the safety of the reservation and the Darlington Agency.[38]

On the North Canadian at Darlington, George sent a runner to Rock Forehead's camp on the Cimarron River. He knew that it was only a question of time before the converging columns found the fleeing bands. He reasoned that if the Arrow Keeper came into the agency, others would follow. Rock Forehead responded to George's peace overture, but as he moved toward Darlington the Dog Men told him that the whites only wished to capture his Sacred Arrows and steal their power. Abruptly, the chief turned north, crossed the Platte, and headed for the Lakota and Northern Cheyenne villages in Montana and the Dakotas.[39]

Even as George carried on negotiations with the Arrow Keeper, his friend Howling Wolf was leading a large party of warriors into Mexico in search of horses and provisions, hoping to hold out against the soldiers for as long as possible. George warned Miles that it would not be easy to bring the bands back to the agency. The agent, in turn, informed authorities that in Bent's view the "Cheyennes are not yet whipped . . . and the majority of the fighting element would prefer to die rather than submit to prison life."[40]

A short time later, however, five of Howling Wolf's raiders surrendered at Darlington. From them George learned that Stone Calf had expressed a willingness to give up the two oldest German sisters, Catherine and Sophia, in exchange for a promise that his people would be well treated when they surrendered.

Stone Calf, with Catherine and Sophia German, arrived at the agency on March 1, 1875. Already there were the two younger sisters, who had been rescued from Grey Beard's camp four months earlier. As George translated, Catherine began pointing out the Cheyenne men who had raped and mistreated them during their captivity, including Medicine Water and three others. Sophia also identified Calf Woman, the wife of Medicine Water, whom she claimed "chopped my mother's head open with an ax."[41] Tension mounted, but to George's relief all were arrested without incident. The rape of the white girls had brought much trouble to the Cheyennes. Although this sort of behavior by war parties was not unheard of, it certainly was not sanctioned. Those guilty of such excesses usually felt shame and suffered the disapproval of the village. George felt that the pent-up resentment of confinement had bred in the warriors a hatred of the whites that he had not seen before.[42]

By March 6, more than eight hundred Cheyennes had surrendered, including chiefs Grey Beard, Heap of Birds, Lean Bear, High Back Wolf, Red Moon, Bull Bear, Eagle Head, Bear Shield, Bear Tongue, Medicine Water, Long Back, and Wolf Robe.

Army and agency officials assigned George the onerous duty of identifying other Cheyennes guilty of committing "criminal acts." The ugly mood among the whites at the agency made his assignment even more difficult. While George interrogated the Indians, Mrs. Miles interviewed Catherine German, who had just turned eighteen. The agent's wife learned the details of Catherine's treatment during her captivity. She had been traded three times and repeatedly raped, or "put on the prairie," *noha' se westan* (literally, "any man's wife"). Rumors of her treatment had already swept the agency, and soldiers and civilians believed the worst. George knew that the whites wanted revenge, and now it would be difficult to protect the innocent.[43]

Immediately after the surrender, Lieutenant Colonel Thomas H. Neill of the Sixth Cavalry lined up all 240 Cheyenne men who had come in with Stone Calf. Raphael Romero acted as Neill's interpreter. With Miles on leave, George translated for acting agent Covington. As the four men walked down the line, Neill stumbled and seemed unable to walk. Romero told George that the officer was drunk, for he had been drinking hard all morning. Reading from a list of thirty-three names, Neill slurred his words as he shouted out the names of those he believed guilty of criminal acts. It soon became clear that only chiefs and headmen had been called out. George was shocked. He had personally interviewed more than 80 Cheyenne families and knew the worst offenders were not even present.

Night was fast approaching, but Neill had identified and arrested only fifteen men, including Eagle Head and his son, Howling Wolf. To finish off the work before dark, the officer ordered the guards to "cut off eighteen from the right of the line."[44] Neill offered no evidence or explanation as the guards arbitrarily pulled eighteen men from the line and marched them off at bayonet point with the others. George could not stop this vigilante-style roundup.

A few days later, as an army blacksmith began shackling the thirty-three prisoners, Cheyenne women gathered a short distance away, shouting encouragement and singing war songs. Black Horse, a powerful warrior, stirred to action by the strong-heart songs, knocked the smithy down and broke toward the canvas tipis of White Horse's camp clearly visible on the north side of the Canadian River. Bullets riddled him before he reached the water. The affair might have ended there, but stray shots tore through the nearby village, wounding several people. Panicked women and children abandoned their lodges and ran in every direction.

George was riding through the village when he heard the shots. He reined his horse to a stop in front of Big Shell's lodge. Just then, as his friend emerged from the tipi, the soldiers fired a volley and Big Shell fell dead with a bullet in his head. It was like Sand Creek all over again. Bullets thudded through the taut canvas lodge covers, terrified women and children screamed, and mothers clutched their babies, holding them tight against their breasts. George again saw the whites as enemies. But despite his rage, he knew he had to get back to the agency and help stop the killing. In his white-man garb, he felt shame as he spurred his horse through the camp.

The Cheyennes splashed across the river and ran for the protection of the sand hills, where the warriors had cached weapons. Now the women used knives and axes—anything they could find—to dig protective trenches in the soft sand. Here, the warriors held off three companies of cavalry, armed with a rapid-fire gatling gun. Although completely surrounded, when night fell the Cheyennes slipped away without being seen by the troops.[45]

The people had escaped, but Neill's prisoners were still shackled in the guardhouse. Two days later, the army, under cover of darkness, shipped them off to Fort Sill, and then to imprisonment at Fort Marion, Florida, two thousand miles away.

Chapter 11

LOST IN A NEW WORLD

At least Magpie and the children were all right, safe on Wolf Creek with the hunting party sanctioned by Agent John D. Miles. Miles had told Bent that Nathan Davis, the hunt boss, had personally seen them in the camp. Ada, now eight, helped Magpie look after young William and baby Mary. All were hungry but out of harm's way. Miles, too, was glad to hear they were safe, for he wanted the undivided attention of his top interpreter.[1] Together the two men had been constant companions, working day and night to reassure the survivors of Sand Hill's band that the fight at White Horse's village had all been a terrible misunderstanding. Bent convinced many that they should not be afraid. The army, he said, was interested only in their peaceful resettlement on the reservation—they could even keep their horses and firearms, which, he had convinced Miles, they would need for hunting buffalo. But every day, as more refugees returned to the agency, it became more apparent that food supplies were dangerously low. Anyone could see there was not enough to go around. Hollow-eyed and gaunt children lay listlessly about the villages, and many people sickened and died. Hunger threatened the peace even more than the Fort Marion deportation and the government's policy to confine the Cheyennes on reservation lands stolen from the Kiowas and Comanches.

As much as he hated to admit it, Miles now realized that the supply of beef coming to him from government contractors was so inadequate that the Indians would have to fend for themselves and find their own meat to supplement the prescribed ration. He feared, however, that Indians out hunting would never learn to farm. And this would inevitably delay their conversion to Christianity and an agricultural life. Further, Bent relayed reports from warriors who had

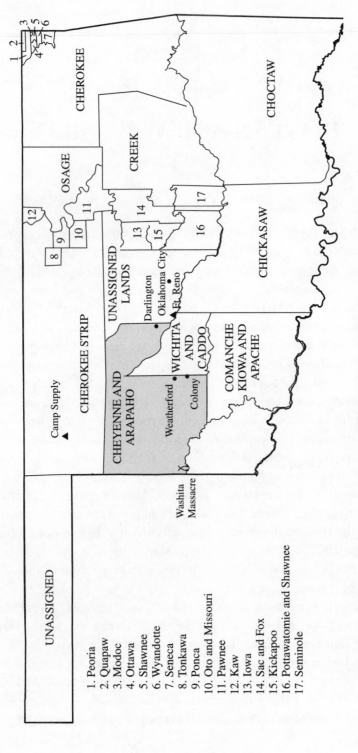

George Bent's Oklahoma

recently come in from the Central Plains that the great buffalo herds normally found between the Platte and Arkansas Rivers were virtually gone, shot down by Indian and white hide hunters.

But Cheyenne scouts had spotted buffalo along the Washita River, only one hundred miles from the agency. Bent urged Miles to allow the Cheyennes to hunt. The agent nervously agreed but selected trusted white men to watch over the camps and manage the hunting parties. But the chiefs quickly grew restless under their white overseers, for it was their duty to lead hunts and distribute meat. Only a chief should decide which families were most needy and which hunters deserved the greatest share. The people chafed under the restrictive orders of their arrogant white hunt bosses, who insisted that the Cheyennes and Arapahos should stay together in a large group during the expedition. Banding together, of course, made it harder to find game, but the whites found it easier to guard and control the larger group.[2]

Miles would not trust the chiefs to manage their bands without white men looking over their shoulders—the gun smoke from the Red River War had hardly cleared—but George helped him understand that hunt bosses chosen from among the mixed-bloods might be more acceptable to the Indians. George could not go himself, for the agent needed him at agency headquarters. Miles had come to depend on his interpreting skills and counsel. So in June 1875 the agent appointed George's brother Robert to guide Little Robe's band of 203 men, 289 women, and 133 children on a twenty-day hunt. The experiment succeeded beyond expectation, and the agent soon authorized more hunts to be led by mixed-bloods, including Ed Guerrier.[3]

Although the hunts temporarily filled the meat kettles, tensions again mounted in the summer of 1876, for startling news came down from the north. Cheyennes and Lakotas had defeated Lieutenant Colonel George Armstrong Custer and the Seventh Cavalry on the high bluffs overlooking the Little Bighorn River in Montana. News of the stunning victory shot through the camps. The warriors had killed Custer and wiped out all the men under his immediate command. Remnants of the shattered Seventh had huddled behind dead horses or in shallow holes hastily scraped in the dirt until finally rescued by a relief column. The army soon sent more troops to Montana, forcing the united tribes to disperse. Families from the north, some who had fled with Sand Hill's band, as well as Northern Cheyennes looking to stay out of the way, filtered into the agency camps at Darlington. The northern tribesmen boasted of Custer's defeat and proudly displayed trophies—scalps, carbines, and horses—as evidence of the victory. The southern men resented the implication that the northerners were somehow bolder and more skilled fighters. Yet this much was true: the southerners had known only defeat in their battles against the troops, and some of their best warriors had been shackled and packed off in boxcars for imprisonment in Florida, an unknown land far to the east.[4] By October 1876, Miles believed that most of Sand Hill's people, along with other scattered bands, had quietly slipped back onto the reservation.

Bent had performed his agency duties well, and finally Miles offered him an opportunity to lead a hunt. He jumped at the chance. Of course, he understood he was treading a treacherous path, for he was taking on the responsibilities of a chief. Although there was nothing he would rather do than ride and hunt with his people—recapturing if only for a moment the taste of the old free life rather than living behind an agency desk, counting heads, doling out rations, and acting as the middleman between the agent and the chiefs—taking on chiefly duties would likely cause trouble, especially for a mixed-blood. There would be jealousies, perhaps even open resistance. He would be the "white man's chief." But he was drawn to leadership, the power of it, the prestige of it—the honor of it. His white father had ruled Bent's Fort and the Santa Fe trade, and his Cheyenne grandfather had been Keeper of the Arrows. Leadership was in his mixed blood.

But he was a halfbreed. That was the rub.

Neither Indians nor whites would ever accept him except as a mixed-blood, a man apart from both Indian and white worlds. His father had tried to make him understand the special place that he and his brothers and sisters occupied between two worlds. They would never fully be of one or the other. William always believed the mixed-bloods needed special protection, and he fought doggedly to secure for them government land grants and recognition of their unique status. As U.S. Indian agent to the Cheyennes and Arapahos in 1859, he had written to the superintendent of Indian Affairs that "there are in each of these tribes a few halfbreeds, the children of white men intermarried with the Cheyennes and Arapahoes, for whom these tribes desire to make suitable reservations and provisions."[5] Believing that the halfbreeds would fall through the government's bureaucratic cracks and not receive the land and annuities guaranteed the full-bloods, William used his influence to amend the 1861 Fort Wise Treaty to include large land grants to his son Robert and young Jack Smith, the son of trader John Smith. In the treaty's postscript, endorsed by Black Kettle, White Antelope, Lean Bear, and other Cheyenne and Arapaho leaders, William maneuvered the treaty commissioners into believing that this provision was "the particular request and wish of the Chiefs" for the protection of their "halfbreed tribe."[6] William's power of persuasion was not solely responsible for this political coup, considering that Albert G. Boone, the one-time guardian of his children, had just assumed William's place as Indian agent.

After Sand Creek, William again returned to the plight of the mixed-bloods. In the 1865 Treaty of the Little Arkansas, he made certain with Article V, that they each received 640 acres of land, more than that set aside for each of the chiefs victimized at Sand Creek. William told the secretary of the interior this was necessary because "I am satisfied that unscrupulous parties will not hesitate to enter upon the Reservation of the Cheyenne & Arapahoe and make settlements to the prejudice of the rights of the Halfbreeds."[7]

Despite his father's efforts, George still did not understand the special place of halfbreeds in Indian and white worlds. George thought himself Cheyenne and believed he had earned the respect of the people. He was, after all, a Crooked Lance warrior and veteran of twenty-seven war parties. He was wealthy enough to support two wives—Magpie and Kiowa Woman—and two separate families. He had stood beside the chiefs at Medicine Lodge as they negotiated a great treaty. He was the scion of great Cheyenne leaders and had married into Chief Black Kettle's family.

And yet, because he was a halfbreed, the Cheyenne people would never—could never—accept him as a traditional chief. Could they accept him as a friend? Yes. As a respected warrior? Yes. As family? Yes. As a chief? No.

The truth of this would dawn on him during this hunt, and he would struggle with it for the rest of his life. For the rest of his life he would throw himself against the invisible barrier that separated a halfbreed from the rest of the world.

This struggle to find his place would define him as a man.

On October 11, 1876, Bent set out at the head of more than twenty-four hundred Cheyennes and Arapahos in search of the buffalo herds.[8] It was a huge camp, fully two-thirds of the two tribes living in the south and one of the largest hunting parties ever mounted in Indian Territory. He took his job seriously, determined to prove to Miles that he could boss a hunt as well as any white man. His first reports were formal and written in his best hand:

Cheyenne Camp on Wolf River
Nov. 4th. 1876
John D. Miles
U.S. Indian Agt.

Sir:
I have the honor to report our present situation. We are camped on Wolf River thirty (30) miles west of Camp Supply. We got buffalo on the 23rd of last month, and made only one days hunt since, on the 2nd of this month. The both tribes killed some 800 buffalo on one run. The hides of course are not good, only for lodge skins. Both hunts have been made with success and satisfaction to both tribes.

I shall remain at this place waiting your orders. Plenty of buffalo 12 miles of here, north, south and west. I hear of no [white] buffalo hunters near here. Two northern Arapahoes came down from north on 10th last month, but brought no news of any importance.

The Indians of both tribes are doing nicely and had no trouble with each other of whatever. The Arapahoes are very anxious for you to send some one to take charge of them. They want to pull off by themselves. I think it would be a good plan to do so when the robes gets to be good. The Cheyennes also wish to split up in small camps so that they can get more robes when the robes get good. Very little sickness among the Indians now. The both tribes are better satisfied on this hunt than I have ever seen them before.

Yours Respectfully
Geo Bent

Agent—The Cheyennes killed 12 or 15 of our cattle on the way up from Agency but I did not make any fuss about it because they were in need of something to eat.

Geo Bent
Nov. 4th 1876[9]

At first, everything went well. The Indians found buffalo, the people were healthy, Cheyennes and Arapahoes were getting along, and white horse thieves and buffalo hunters were keeping their distance. But quickly the happy hunt devolved into intertribal bickering and tensions born of command and leadership. Who was really in charge? Traditional chiefs? Or the white man's chief? People were coming to Bent with problems, and increasingly he found himself turning to the chiefs for solutions.

A week after his first glowing report, he wrote Miles again:

Camp on Wolf Creek
Nov. 10th 76.
Jon. D. Miles
U.S. Indian Agent

Sir:

I received your letter yesterday, and called all the chiefs of both tribes together to have a talk [with] them. I read your letter to them. Scabby was present. I told him he had to go right away and said he would start right off. Little Robe's son is going to go with him to see that he gets there all right. Limpy [George had identified him as one of the warriors involved in the killing of the German family] has no ponies at all. He tried to sell his little daughter's dress made of Elk teeth but nobody would buy it of him. He says [he] found the pony. I cannot make him give up any pony for he has none to give up.

We are camped 35 miles from Camp Supply. When I wrote you before, I said there was plenty of buffalo all around. But now the buffalo is all going west very fast, so we will have to move up the stream until we strike buffalo. The Arapahoes & Cheyennes are all going together except White Horses [band]. They are going to move over on to Canadian. I wrote to you that I would wait here for your orders. When White Bear's party got here they brought news that the Osages, Pawnees, Wichitas & Caddoes were coming out on big hunt. The Cheyennes & Arapahoes got restless when they heard this. They wanted to move right away to get head those other Indians where the buffalo is plenty. I can say this much: both tribes are on good terms now.

I understand that Dutch Henry party horse thieves are at Mouth Creek. They send word [to] Camp Supply they were going to steal ponies from these Indians. We will have to look out for them. I will write to you again when we get to where there is plenty buffalo.

Yours Respectfully
Geo. Bent[10]

So now the buffalo had run off; neighboring tribes threatened to beat the Cheyenne hunters to the dwindling herds; ponies were in short supply, forcing some Cheyenne men to trade their most prized possessions; and white horse thieves stalked the tribes.

By now, George was beginning to feel the weight of his responsibility. Acting the chief was harder than it looked. Miles wanted him to keep the village together, but the chiefs demanded that each band hunt for itself. They would split up whether Bent liked it or not. His authority had lasted as long as meat boiled in the kettles. With the return of hunger the chiefs took charge of their own bands, scattering in all directions to hunt. Bent had no choice but to allow the breakup of the camp, and he tried to put the best possible face on the situation. He wrote to Miles:

Camp on Wolf River
Nov 15th 1876
John D. Miles
U.S. Indian Agent

Sir:
I have the honor to report again so as to let you know that the Cheyennes have scattered in small camps. You know it is best to let them camp in small camps. They can kill more buffalos by doing so. Some of them are so poor off for ponies they will have to hunt the

buffalo on foot. I thought it was best to let some of them camp by themselves those that were worst off for ponies.

Whirlwind's band and all the Arapahoes have moved up on this stream (Wolf Creek). White Horse's band have gone over on to Canadian near the mouth of Elk Creek. About 30 lodges will stop here. Buffalo has all gone west of here. I [hear] the buffalo is plenty on Beaver Creek. Dave Tramp is over on Beaver with five or six lodges. Dave had some mules stolen from him by Butch Henry's party. I have been telling the Indians that they had better not to go over on Beaver Creek. If they did they would lose some ponies, but they would not listen to me. So you can not blame me if they lose any stock over there. I will report again soon.

Respectfully
Geo Bent[11]

Traditional chiefs derived their authority from hard-earned respect. Bent's authority came from the agent and by doling out precious supplies of coffee, sugar, and bacon. Without this he was just another white man's chief—without power or stature.[12] Even when the hunters stumbled on fresh herds, Bent realized that his power was in name only. Miles sensed that Bent was losing control and sent A. E. Reynolds out to the camps to help.[13]

In August 1877 Bent's influence on agency affairs was temporarily weakened by the infusion into the reservation population of nearly a thousand Northern Cheyennes, who had been ordered by General Phil Sheridan to leave their Montana home and forever live side by side with their southern kin. Sheridan feared these northern warriors above all others. He held them responsible for Custer's defeat and believed them to be fiercely independent and always ready for a fight. He had taken the Cheyennes' measure as early as 1868 when he and Chief Stone Calf had verbally sparred. He never forgot the warrior's words, which Bent had interpreted, "Let your soldiers grow long hair, so that we can have some honor in killing them."[14] Sheridan knew it would take time to crush the fiery spirit of these free people, but he was determined to neutralize them by moving them south and merging them with the reservation bands in Indian Territory.[15]

Led by Dull Knife, Little Wolf, Wild Hog, Turkey Legs, Standing Elk, and Broken Dish, these Northerners had surrendered to Colonel Nelson A. Miles and his Custer-avenging army earlier that spring. After an uneventful seventy-day journey, they arrived at Fort Reno on August 5, escorted by Lieutenant H. W. Lawton of the Fourth U.S. Cavalry.

As agency interpreter and the principal liaison between the Cheyennes and the government, George helped the lieutenant process the newcomers. He later recalled, "Lawton had men, women, and children [stand] in line and counted them before turning them over to agent Miles." Nearly 950 of the refugees needed to be fed, clothed, and otherwise provisioned, a big job that took, Bent remembered, almost three days. When the bands settled in, Bent had dinner with William Rowland, who in 1850 had married into the Northern Cheyenne tribe and now acted as their interpreter, and Rowland's mixed-blood sons Jim and Bill. The mixed-blood boys wore black mustaches and white man's suits—just like the Bent brothers—and they all agreed that the transition for these newly surrendered bands would not be easy, that the sedentary life in a land without buffalo would likely cause unrest, especially among the warrior society men. The steady presence of whites and the contrasting lifestyle of their southern cousins who had been forced to yield to agency directives would touch off a tribal culture clash that would dispirit and divide the people.[16]

Miles again entrusted Bent with the management of the 1877 winter hunt. But the joy had now gone out of it, and he felt burdened by the responsibility of command. By late December he gave up all pretense of being in charge. Writing to Miles on December 20, 1877, Bent confessed that the "Indians had scattered all over the country. They can't find nothing but few old bulls and not enough to live on. I do not know what they will do." As for himself, he was ready to go home. He would stay near Camp Supply and do what he could to protect the straggling Indian ponies from horse thieves, but he told Miles he was sending Magpie and Kiowa Woman with the children back to the agency, where he hoped they might draw government rations. He was plainly fed up. "I see no chance of any buffalo for this winter's hunt. I don't wish to lose my ponies this winter for nothing. . . . Let me know what you want me to do and what to say to the Indians."[17]

George was plainly frustrated by his failure to control his charges. But he had much on his mind. "I don't wish to lose my ponies this winter for nothing," he had written. Horses. Like all Cheyennes, he judged his personal wealth by the number of horses and mules in his herd. At the same time that he was leading the hunts, white desperadoes were raiding his stock. Nothing angered him more than the thought of his best animals racing for the Texas or Kansas borders, whipped and driven by a scruffy band of white horse thieves. He had complained before and had received some satisfaction when the army captured the Martin gang, but law enforcement seemed incapable of ridding the reservation of these misfits. Their continuing presence threatened the peace as much as the slow starvation that seemed government policy now.

Agent Miles said as much when he wrote to Superintendent William Nicholson requesting funding for the recapture of stolen stock. "There is a stolen pony in almost every stable from the Cimarron to the Platte." The Cheyennes and Arapahos had lost nearly four thousand dollars' worth of their "very best animals," and Miles admitted it would be "criminal negligence on my part or that of the Gov't" if agency and military authorities did not expend the necessary funds to bring the gangs to justice.[18] Nicholson agreed and fired off a heated letter to the commissioner of Indian Affairs, invoking the frightening specter of an Indian war to make his point. "There is not cause of vexation and disturbance to these Indian tribes so fruitful as this," he said, "and unless some decided efforts are made to break up these heavy robberies we shall reap the fruits in the blood, and wastage of another Indian war."[19] A. E. Reynolds took immediate action by personally offering cash rewards for the recapture of stolen stock, including a three hundred dollar reward for the return of Bent's ponies and mules—deemed the most valuable of all the animals recently run off.[20]

As Bent fumed and dispatched letters of his own, stock detective and tribal herder William Malaley and Dog Soldier leader Stone Calf tracked down one of the horse thieves. But the crime spree continued.

So George had lost his ponies and he had lost control of the hunting camps, all the while he was holding down two jobs—agency interpreter at Darlington and representative for A. E. Reynolds, the dominant white trader on the reservation—trying to feed and clothe his two growing families. He had been under enormous pressure struggling to please the agent and the chiefs, a nearly impossible course in this time of change. No one knew whether the Cheyennes would agree to settle on the reservation, take the white man's road of Christianity and farming, send their children to school, and give up their sun dances.

In fact, Dull Knife, Wild Hog, and Little Wolf had had enough of southern life. Their people were sick and dying, and the chiefs decided to go home—with or without government permission. On September 9, 1878, in the dead of night, they stole the horses and equipment they needed, and leaving their tipis standing, headed for Powder River country and freedom. Three hundred fifty-three people left, but 650 had stayed behind.[21]

Bent understood why they had bolted—they were dying by the dozens, and their chiefs had warned him that if the government tried to stop them they would fight. He did not betray their confidence, but he did not agree with their decision. The buffalo were gone, and he had come to believe, as his father had years before, that the people must either plow or perish.

Bent knew that the old ways were strong and that the chiefs retained their power as long as tradition prevailed. Nowhere was this more obvious than on beef distribution days when George would stand beside the agent as the food was parceled out. To many Cheyennes it appeared that he had taken on chiefly responsibilities. He was always there, sitting or standing behind a big desk, making marks on paper as the people received their beef rations. And like a chief, rumor had it, he received more than his share of meat—two beeves a week and up to twenty-five pounds of meat at Reynold's butcher shop. But, it was whispered, he kept it all for himself and his own family instead of giving it to those in greatest need.[22] No one questioned that he was the gatekeeper to Agent Miles and the trader Reynolds, who now held the lives of the people in their hands. Wherever the Cheyennes looked, they saw Bent, on ration days in the stockade, in the trading post, or at agency headquarters. Clearly, he was an important man, more than just a go-between, more than just a translator, but a man of power and influence.

And then, in December 1878, just after Dull Knife and Little Wolf bolted from Darlington, Little Chief and his northern band of thirty families arrived from Montana. They had been on the trail for thirty days, pulling their worldly possessions and children in willow baskets attached to travois.

Among these newcomers was a young woman who stood out from the rest. She had always made her own way, even as a child. Her parents named her Standing Out Woman, a traditional name in her family. Now, as a twenty-year-old, she still stood out. She turned heads wherever she went, her black braids, thick and shining, outlining an extraordinary face with large, expressive eyes. She carried herself with regal dignity that some might have thought haughty were it not for her pleasing laugh and ready smile. When she sang, people stopped and listened. Even the way she clothed herself drew attention. The finest quillwork—of her own making—graced her white buckskin dress and moccasins.[23]

It was this beauty who boldly followed Little Chief and the band's headmen into the large tipi that served as the ration tent at Darlington. And there she saw Bent for the first time, standing before the chiefs, a commanding presence. He dressed as a white man, with coat and vest—and shoes. Buckled suspenders held up his trousers, and a broad-brimmed hat shaded his Cheyenne features. He hardly looked at her, but she watched his every move. And she resolved to marry him.

George had seen her—he had an eye for beauty—and in the weeks and months that followed he sought her out, talking with her, meeting her friends and family. She was an exotic Northern Cheyenne woman. In 1865, up in Powder River country, he had been drawn to the "wild" and free Northerners and was struck by the contrast with the Southern Cheyennes on the Arkansas River, who had long since given up buckskins for white man's cloth. Standing Out was fun loving and strong willed. She loved the traditional life, the taste of freshly killed buffalo, the stirring wolf songs of the society men, the scalp dances, the healing ceremonies and herbal cures. She loved being who she was and was proud of being Cheyenne. She had no use for the white man's beef, patent remedies, and doctors. When she first saw silver dollars at the trader's store, she thought them playthings, pretty decorations for her hair or belt. She had much to learn in this new world of the reservation, and Bent was willing to teach her.[24]

In fact, he courted her.

Yet, what of his other wives and families? What did Magpie Woman make of all this? And Kiowa Woman, how did she feel?

Ever since Kiowa Woman had come into his life in 1868, Magpie had lived with her mother, taking baby Ada with her. Though George and Magpie lived apart, they were still intimate. Magpie bore George a son, Robert, in 1870. Two other children, William and Mary, followed, but both died in infancy by 1875. Now, Magpie was pregnant with their fifth child, whom George was determined to name for his brother Charley.

As for Kiowa Woman, she and George never enjoyed a loving relationship. She was an orphaned child when they met—Custer's troopers had massacred her parents at the Washita—and she looked on George more as a protector than a lover. She bore him two children, Julia in 1871, and George W.—known as "Junior"—in 1877. But by 1878 she had left Bent and moved into the lodge of a Cheyenne man named Bird. She would not formally divorce George until five years later, when Bird died and she married an old warrior named Buffalo Thigh.[25]

Even though Kiowa Woman had moved out, Bent continued to provide for her family, as well as Magpie's. This obligation included not just the children but also extended relations. In all he fed and clothed six men, eight women, and ten children. No wonder he needed so much agency beef as well as provisions from the trader's store.[26]

Yet it seemed he could please no one. Magpie objected to his insistence that they send eleven-year-old Ada to the agency school. Agent Miles had decreed that Cheyenne children must attend school and was willing to starve the Indian families into submission by withholding beef rations. He expected Bent, his best interpreter, to set an example for other Cheyennes, but George really did not need to be convinced.

He already knew the advantages that a white education would give his children. Still, it was hard convincing Magpie—she was the daughter of a chief, and the old traditions ran deep.

Kiowa Woman had always felt like a second-class wife, claiming that Bent never cared for her children as he did for Magpie's. The bickering between the two families and their competition for his attention wore him down. By the time he met Standing Out he was looking for a supportive relationship, someone who would take him as he was. And in Standing Out he found the perfect mate. From the first, she adored him and never found fault—even with his drinking.

For by this time, Bent's drinking was the talk of the reservation.

Whiskey could be gotten almost anywhere, legally or illegally. At Fort Reno the post trader served liquor to officers and white travelers; enlisted men needed an order from the commanding officer if they wanted more than an ordinary drink. But for Indians and halfbreeds, the law was clear. No liquor, except on written order from the agent, and only for patent medicines and food extracts containing trace amounts of alcohol. Yet whiskey peddlers followed the camps like predators, hawking their stores of rotgut everywhere and at every opportunity.[27]

Despite the strict prohibition against liquor on the reservation, Indian country was awash in whiskey. Indians and whites alike drank their fill, and in the general lawlessness of the territory, public drunkenness was an accepted way of life. It was almost a running joke. The Pan Handle Stage Company, the agency mail contractor, conducted its business in an alcoholic haze. Miles received this alarming report:

Our able "Pan Handle" (stage Co) arrived much the worse for the wear night before last. Williamson [the contractor] was drunk—the driver was drunk—and even the mules felt the effect of the spree. They started from here (north) about nine oclock and some time about midnight here come the stage back again—everybody sound asleep—when they awoke and found themselves here [Red Fork Ranch] they were the most "sheepish" lot of "Pan Handlers" you ever saw.[28]

Miles complained to the commissioner of Indians Affairs that "beastly drunkenness" was epidemic:

Whiskey has frequently found its way into this country over this line and I have frequently had to request of Mr. Williamson the discharge of drivers on account of drunkenness—and mails have often been detained on account of drunkenness. . . . How can we expect anything else than a free flow of whiskey through this country so long as the worm extends through the Pan handle.[29]

All around him people were drinking, in the camps, at the forts, on the trails—everywhere. As a halfbreed, Bent was prohibited from drinking. But he had access. When he first arrived at the agency, he had the privileges of a white man, often purchasing ale by the bottle and keg from Lee and Reynolds's trading post. In December 1870 he had run up a tab of $98.60 in his "Ale Account." The following year he purchased one thousand cases of beer.[30] Of course, these quantities were not entirely for him—he was trading to the Indians. But eventually, the authorities shut down his liquor operations and his personal access to spirits. In short, they stopped treating him as a white man. Now, recognized as a halfbreed, he had to satisfy his thirst in other ways. Major J. K. Mizner of the Fourth U.S. Cavalry commanding Fort Reno described Bent as "a halfbreed who has had the benefit of a good education but has been addicted to intemperance for a number of years. . . . I know he has given Agent Miles a great deal of trouble and being unable to satisfy his appetite for strong drink, he has like many other inebriates, resorted to the use of Bay Rum Cologne, Jamaica Ginger and various extracts containing any traces of alcohol."[31] When George did get ahold of a bottle of whiskey, he got drunk and stayed drunk as long as it lasted.

The first time he got into trouble with binge drinking was in the spring of 1876. The army interpreter at Fort Reno, Phil McCusker—Bent's long-time friend—gave him a bottle of whiskey. Bent promptly got drunk. Agent Miles was furious and banned McCusker from the Cheyenne and Arapaho Agency. He then shot off a letter to Major Mizner at Fort Reno, denouncing McCusker for "Furnishing my Interpreter, Geo. Bent, with whiskey."[32]

302

George was caught in a complicated, three-way crossfire between the agency, the army, and competing rogue whiskey peddlers. When Miles decided to crack down on McCusker, he threw the book at him, charging him with everything from prostitution to whiskey selling.

His habits are so very objectionable, and consequently his influence for evil so great, I cannot consent to his return to this agency, and reservation, and will stand ready to prevent his return by lawful measures. The most aggravated case of prostitution that I have known McCusker to be guilty of came to my knowledge a few days since wherein it appears that during the past winter while out with the Cheyenne hunting party, and while he already had one or two of his women "as his wives," he induced the wife of Heap of Birds, now a prisoner in Florida, to believe he had influence with high officials, and for certain consideration would bring this influence to bear, to secure the release of her husband, the consideration was the surrender of her young and beautiful daughter a victim to his gross, sensual desires. I do not say without any hesitation that the man, if he is worthy of the name, who would take such advantage of a poor, helpless Indian wife, and mother, is not safe to run at large in a country where law is so scarce, and then look at the fearful consequences entailed upon his victim, the daughter. The immoral habits and influence of McCusker have been well known to the Dept for years, but as time progresses matters grow worse, and must be checked, or the consequences will rest upon the shoulders of those in authority.[33]

McCusker was the army's man. Miles's assault on his character was calculated to rid the agency of a competitor who threatened the agent's Indian trade monopoly. McCusker's incursion on the reservation wasn't just bad for business—it was personal. Miles based his case against McCusker on three main charges: "1st. Prostitution of Indian Women of this agency. 2nd. Drunkenness in this agency. 3rd. Furnishing my Interpreter, Geo Bent, with whiskey and also to other Indians of this agency."[34]

McCusker retaliated in kind, loosing a salvo of countercharges that echoed in Washington. Writing to commissioner of Indian Affairs E. A. Hayt, McCusker laid out his case against Miles. First, he reminded the commissioner that he had served the government for more than twenty years as an interpreter, a scout, and just recently a special agent to spy on Miles's reservation activities. Miles, he said, was jealous of his close relationship with the commissioner—and with the Indians, who admired him and often regarded him as one of their own, a rare honor for a white man. Second, he accused Miles of conspiring with Lee and Reynolds to establish a virtual monopoly over the reservation trade. Third, he implied that Miles had turned a blind eye to the ongoing reservation liquor trade and shared in the profits. Four, he charged the agent with stealing cattle from the tribal herd to augment his own herd, which was then sold back to the Indians. In response to Miles's prostitution charge, McCusker suggested that the agent opposed interracial marriage. "If I choose to marry an Indian woman and take her for a wife agt. Miles calls it prostitution. This is merely his opinion. My reputation does not depend on what agt. Miles chooses to say." He challenged Miles to prove his "opinions," confident that army officers, government officials, and the Indians would come forward to vouch for his character. Finally, he directly attacked George Bent, "a halfbreed Cheyenne, [who] has been employed by Miles for six years as interpreter for the [Cheyenne and Arapaho] tribes against the repeated protests of the Arapahoe, who desire an interpreter of their own. Miles allows them to furnish their own interpreter but Geo. Bent gets the pay, another name being called upon to sign the rolls for him. All this with Miles knowledge and consent. Bent is also an employee of the Indian trader Reynolds at a salary of $100 per month. His first services are given to the trader in direct violation of sec[tion] 2078 Rev[ised] Statutes. The Indian trader runs the Indians and their agent through this man Bent. At the very time that Indians are actually suffering for food, agt Miles issues to Bent two beeves a week, beside the amt of beef he gets at the butcher shop."[35]

Miles successfully defended his interpreter against McCusker's charges. In Washington the commissioner of Indian Affairs agreed that Bent's relationship with Reynolds did not constitute a conflict of interest and ruled that he could continue in government service.[36] But Bent's reputation had been damaged among Cheyenne leaders—and the people. It was widely believed that he received more than his fair share through his inside dealings with the agent. He was after all, *vehoe*—a spider, a white man. The shadow of envy and distrust would haunt him. The people saw his loyalty divided between the whites and the Cheyennes. He could not be both white and Indian—he had to choose.

But Bent chose escape instead—through the bottle. When he could get no whiskey he would get drunk on Jamaica Ginger. In October 1878, his friend Jack Martin bought him a bottle from the post trader at Fort Reno. George's drunk caused such a stink that Colonel Mizner ordered Martin arrested. The affair reached the desks of the both the secretary of war and the commissioner of Indian Affairs. Finally, the authorities released Martin, recognizing that he had purchased the extract innocently, not fully understanding Bent's addiction to alcohol.[37]

In fact, Miles had his hands full keeping his chief interpreter sober. Straight on the heels of the Martin affair, Miles charged another liquor peddler in Cantonment with a violation of the Indian whiskey prohibition. "My interpreter George Bent, a halfbreed Cheyenne, was furnished with liquor within an hour or two of his arrival at the post and in quantities sufficient to keep him intoxicated for five or six days."[38]

But Bent was not an idle reservation drunk. Not only did he continue to interpret for Miles and work for Reynolds and other agency traders, he bought and sold racehorses, partnered with brother Bob in a cattle ranch on the South Canadian, attended cowboy balls, made pleasure excursions to Colorado and Kansas, and lived in high style, full of himself, spending lavishly, and confident of his power and influence on the reservation.

On one of his off-reservation jaunts to Arkansas City, a wild Kansas cow town, he stopped in at the newspaper office. The editor of the *Arkansas City Traveler* was mighty impressed by the man who stood before him. He saw not a drunken halfbreed, but rather a Cheyenne leader of distinction.

We had the pleasure of meeting Geo. Bent yesterday, one of the most remarkable Indians now living in the territory. Mr. Bent is a son of old Col. Bent, who married a Cheyenne woman and for years held Bent's Fort on the Arkansas River, at a time when Kansas as a state was not known. Bent County, Colorado, is also named in honor of the old colonel. At the present time George is chief of the Cheyennes, and as government interpreter he probably has more influence among his people than has any other man in the tribe. He is a fine specimen of physical manhood, weighing 200 pounds, and well proportioned. His complexion is of the swarthy hue peculiar to halfbreeds, and with his heavy jet black hair gives a striking appearance. This is his first visit since there has been anything of a town to mark the place. About fifteen years ago he camped on the Shilocco [sic], and hunted buffalo on the divide between the Arkansas and Salt Fork Rivers.[39]

Surprisingly, Phil McCusker accompanied George to Arkansas City. The editor noted that McCusker was another of the "celebrities of the Indian country." He also observed that McCusker "had been with the Indians for thirty years, and no doubt will die among them." When the editor effused about their role as old-time frontiersmen and government scouts, George—who always enjoyed a good story—did not set him straight. Bent had only served the government as an interpreter, never as an army scout. But the editor went on, saying that "they met at this place several friends who knew them years ago, and one or two who had been with them on many of their scouts and hunts."[40]

In 1882 he traveled in style to Denver with his drinking buddy, William Frass. It was rumored that the men had hired a private railroad car for the journey and enjoyed a nonstop party over the same ground Bent once rode with the Cheyenne Dog Soldiers. He paused only long enough to visit his sister Mary's children at their home on the Arkansas near the site of Bent's Old Fort. Mary had died in 1878, and he had not visited the children or their father, Robison Moore, since her death.[41]

On his return to the reservation, Bent's binge drinking did not seem to interfere with business. In May 1883, the commissioner of Indian Affairs saw fit to approve the application of licensed traders, Hamphill and Moy, to hire Bent as "interpreter and salesman."[42] He was flush now, paying as much as five hundred dollars for a team of horses and spending large sums gambling and horse racing.

In October of 1884, Bent told everyone who would listen that he was going to Caldwell, Kansas, to watch the state's first Spanish bullfight. He got to Caldwell all right, but he never saw the bullfight. Before the matador appeared, George was dead drunk. He was still dead drunk when Samuel Rogers brought him home in the back of his buckboard.[43]

These sprees did not help Bent's tarnished reputation on the reservation. The chiefs frowned, the agent tired of writing in defense of his behavior, and Kiowa Woman cut him no slack at all. Even though she had divorced and remarried, she still felt her high-flying ex-husband had abandoned his children who were, after all, still Bents.

Everyone seemed angry with him just now. He may have told people he wanted to see the bullfight in Caldwell, but he really wanted to join the delegation of Cheyenne leaders who had been invited to Washington, D.C., to see the president and tour the capital city. Not only would they see the white Father, but they would also stop off in Carlisle, Pennsylvania, to visit their children at the newly opened Indian school. They would continue on to Gettysburg, where they would tour the greatest battlefield of the Civil War. Of course George wanted to go. Guerrier had been invited, as had brother Bob. But George's reputation as a drunk had finally caught up with him. No one trusted him to be on the train or in a hotel and not find a bottle.[44]

The Cheyennes may have been angry with him, but he still had friends. White cattlemen liked him—and for good reason. They came in droves to take advantage of his influence with the Indians. They needed him to get to the chiefs, who controlled the reservation grasslands and ultimately the leases that would allow them to graze and fatten their cattle prior to driving their herds north to the railheads in Kansas and then on to eastern markets. George was dealing fast and loose in this high-stakes cattle scheme. Both Bent and Miles had rationalized that leasing Indian lands to white cattlemen was good business. The rich grassland was just lying there, unused. The Cheyennes desperately needed cash to supplement their meager government rations and to invest in building their own cattle herds, which Bent believed was their only hope for the future. He knew in his heart that the Cheyennes would never become farmers. He had tried farming himself, hoping to set an example for the chiefs, but he simply could not do it. The brutally hard work of breaking sod in the hot Oklahoma sun and the miserably low crop yields discouraged all but the most determined farmers. Bent ended up leasing his farm to white men and turned his attention to ranching with Bob.[45] The Bents and other mixed-bloods— Edmund Guerrier, the Poisal brothers John and Robert, Jack Fitzpatrick, Mary Keith—encouraged the Cheyenne and Arapaho chiefs to lease the tribal lands to white cattlemen until the Indians themselves could build herds large enough to supplement government rations and earn a profit. George led the effort to convince Indian leaders to lease their lands to white cattlemen for up to ten years.

But it was a risky proposition, and in the end it brought trouble to the reservation and drove a wedge of mistrust between Bent and the chiefs of the still influential Dog Soldiers.

To be sure, George's motives were not entirely selfless. He was paid well for his influence peddling. His good friend George Reynolds, Albert's brother, gained huge profits by leasing for two cents an acre more than seventy thousand acres of prime grassland, nearly a quarter of all the leased lands on the reservation.[46] The cattlemen crisscrossed the rolling prairie with hundreds of miles of barbed wire fences, preventing not only the free movement of tribal horse and cattle herds but also of the people themselves. Conflict between white drovers and Indians was inevitable. Cheyenne leaders complained that the whites' herds ran over Indian garden plots, trampled crops, spoiled waterholes, and mixed indiscriminately with Indian herds. Indians and whites exchanged charges of rustling, and heated confrontation soon turned bloody.

As it did on May 4, 1884.

On that day, E. M. Horton, a Texas stockman, was driving four hundred ponies to Caldwell, Kansas. When he found the water too high at the usual crossing of the North Canadian, he diverted his herd across the Cheyenne and Arapaho Reservation directly through the land occupied by Running Buffalo, a leading Dog Soldier warrior. As Horton's herd galloped toward Running Buffalo's family garden plot, the Dog Man himself intercepted it and demanded the cowboys pay him a dollar a head, the prevailing toll for passing herds. Horton's sneered refusal caused Running Buffalo to ride to the front of the herd, where he fired two pistol shots, hoping to turn the horses before they ran over his crops. Horton spurred his horse and came face to face with Running Buffalo. The enraged Texan drew his revolver and fired at the Indian's pony. The bullet struck the animal's forehead and glanced upward, lodging in Running Buffalo's neck. Man and horse tumbled into the dust. As blood gushed from the fallen Cheyenne, Horton leveled his pistol and fired another shot. But the Dog Man would not die. Horton's brother now came up, pulled his pistol, and fired a third shot, killing Running Buffalo.

As Horton looked at the body, he knew he was in big trouble. The killing would not go unavenged. The cowboys whipped their horses and hurried the herd toward Cantonment, some five miles away. There they tried to buy ammunition at the trader's store, but there was none to be had. So they rode to the nearby military telegraph station and signaled for help, only to learn that troops would not arrive until the next day. In the meantime, angry Cheyennes surrounded the stockmen, with only the Mennonite missionary S. S. Haury and an army interpreter, Amos Chapman, standing between them and death.

Horton called Chapman over for a talk. Looking nervously over his shoulder toward the armed Indians, he said, "Chapman, I am in a bad fix. Is there anyway you can fix it that I can get out of it."

Chapman replied, "I do not know."

Horton knew the Indians had a high regard for Chapman, who had married Chief Stone Calf's daughter. "Do what you can for me. I can give horses but I have got no money."

Chapman went over to the Cheyennes to negotiate for Horton's life. "The man that killed Buffalo requested me to ask you if there is any way he can settle this difficulty, he has not got any money, but is willing to give horses."

At first the Indians refused to negotiate. "We want the man, when we see the killer of Buffalo, cold, we will be satisfied."

Chapman reasoned, "You cannot get the prisoner as he is now in the hands of the U.S. authorities and it is foolish for you to talk that way. The prisoner is willing to go to Darlington, Reno, or any other place for trial, but for the inconvenience he has put you to, he is willing to pay you in ponies and stand his trial afterwards." Chapman concluded his appeal by asking, "How many ponies do you want?"

The Indians shot back: "All."

Chapman walked back to Horton and told him of the Cheyennes' demand. "No, I cannot do that," said Horton, "everything I have got in the world is in them ponies, but I am willing to give half."

Chapman convinced the Indians that half was better than none. Besides, the army would soon take Horton away, and now was the time to strike a deal. Reluctantly, the chiefs agreed. They would take half the herd and await white man's justice, but they were not happy about it. They wanted Horton dead—the sooner the better.[47]

Agent John D. Miles, who had staked his reputation on the efficacy of the cattle-lease program and other ventures that would promote Indian self-sufficiency, had resigned under pressure only a few weeks before. The new agent, D. B. Dyer, had only just arrived. When word got to him of the killing of Running Buffalo, he underestimated the importance of the incident and the terrible tension building on the reservation. Many Cheyennes were ready to fight over the murder, and war seemed inevitable. Incredibly, Dyer minimized the affair and even took Horton's side. He also supported the white cattlemen who continued to press for leases and access to reservation lands. The agent branded Stone Calf, Little Robe, and the Dog Soldiers as an outlaw element determined to take advantage of the situation by openly defying government authority.

Where was George? Why didn't he advise the new agent? Was he on a spree? Or was he so in league with the cattlemen that he had no choice but to remain silent? Certainly, he did not handle the situation well. In fact, his actions only made matters worse. To show his support of Dyer's new administration and the land-lease program, he confronted Stone Calf and threatened to personally lead white soldiers against any Cheyenne who did not accept the authority of the government and abide by the lease arrangements.

Drunk or sober he had made a choice—a dramatic departure from his long-standing policy of never, ever, taking the army's side against his own people. Perhaps he had come to believe the newspaper nonsense about being the "Chief of the Cheyennes" and the most influential man on the reservation. In any case, he alienated Stone Calf, the Southern Cheyennes' most respected leader. The old chief had complained that "white men are like wolves, they have come on to the Washita and are trying to force us out of that country." He directly attacked Bent and other mixed-bloods when he charged that "all of the Indians who have taken the money are no good, they live at the agency and can be bought for a handful of Chuck."[48] And to be sure, George and the agent had used food as a weapon to force the chiefs to accept land-lease money and send their children to school. By threatening to lead white troops against Stone Calf, Bent confirmed the traditional chiefs' worst fears that he could not be trusted, that he was in fact *vehoe* and not truly one of the people.[49]

George was no longer certain of his place in the Cheyenne world. He sent his children to school, stayed away from Sun Dances, stood up to Dog Soldier enforcers, and, perhaps most telling, wore a broadbrimmed white Stetson, wool suits, and leather boots. He had become the model of assimilation. Other mixed-bloods had bucked the traditional chiefs—and paid the price. Robert Poisal had quarreled with the chiefs, and soon after his body was found along a deserted reservation road.[50] Indian police from the Cheyenne and Arapaho Agency—urged by the agent and the promise of a five hundred dollars bounty—quickly tracked the killer down, but the incident chilled the mixedblood community. Soon after, William Minn, a white employee on the Bent ranch, was also murdered. Though George himself was appointed to the coroner's jury, no charges were ever filed. The chiefs denied any involvement in these terror tactics, but they had openly criticized the Bents and mixed-bloods generally for their support of the cattle leases. Stone Calf and Whirlwind centered their anger on George, whom they accused of misleading and bullying Cheyennes into accepting lease payments. The chiefs wanted Bent and other mixed-bloods along with Agent Dyer, banned from the reservation.[51]

Then, just as open warfare seemed inevitable, Phil Sheridan, newly appointed commander of the army, arrived on the reservation. Sheridan quickly took control, interviewing chiefs, cattlemen, and agency officials. Within a week the general had made up his mind. He would remove the insensitive agent and place the agency under army control. At the same time, he recommended to President Grover Cleveland that the lease system be abolished and the cattlemen banished from the reservation. Though he recognized Bent's role in the land-lease scheme, he did not call for his ejection. Bent stayed on as U.S. interpreter to Captain Jesse Lee, Dyer's replacement.

Just when it seemed things couldn't get any worse, Bent received word that Magpie Woman, the love of his life, was dead. Though they had been apart for some years, they had married during the old days when the Cheyennes lived free—a time that now seemed only a dream—and Bent doted on their surviving children, Ada and Charley. He never forgot how Magpie had presented baby Ada to General Harney at Medicine Lodge in 1867, how he courted her in Chief Black Kettle's lodge, and how they married according to traditional Cheyenne customs. How proudly they had posed in their wedding dress for the photographer at Camp Supply, George in his broadcloth suit but moccasins on his feet, Magpie in the finest elk-tooth dress. Now she was gone, and with her, part of him. All that remained was her photograph, taken so long ago. But the photographer's lens did not capture her smile, or the light in her eyes.

As for Kiowa Woman, for years she had poisoned her children against their father. Now Julia, the oldest, who had been away to eastern boarding schools, came home for the summer and laid into him for stealing the cattle that she claimed had been provided by the government to children attending agency schools. "He has never done right by us. If he was an uneducated Indian it would be different, but as he is educated there is no excuse. Family troubles have something to do with [it]. He has not lived with my mother for a number of years as drink [h]as made him what he is."[52]

Even his long-time friend Howling Wolf was mad at him. When Howling Wolf returned from his imprisonment at Fort Marion in 1878, he seemed a new man. In Florida, he had been a model prisoner, devoted to Captain Richard H. Pratt, who in turn had encouraged the young Cheyenne's artistic talents. Pratt firmly believed in the principle that to "save the man" white teachers must "kill the Indian." Pratt seemed to have done his work well, for back on the reservation, Howling Wolf adopted white ways and convinced twenty other Indian youths to cut their hair and wear suits and shoes. His father, who had also been interned at Fort Marion, had encouraged the young man to follow the white man's road, but when Eagle Head died in 1881,

Howling Wolf reverted to traditional ways and became an outspoken critic of George's leading role in the cattle-lease scheme. The strong bond between the two men, forged in the fires of Sand Creek, was not strong enough to survive the reservation schism between the Cheyenne traditionalists and assimilators.[53]

The cattlemen were gone—Sheridan had seen to that—but the reservation was still under siege, now by well-intentioned Eastern reformers and land-hungry sodbusters, who circled Indian country like so many vultures.

In 1887 humanitarians, many of them former abolitionists, united to push through Congress legislation they believed would save the Indians from themselves. Senator Henry L. Dawes of Massachusetts, chairman of the Committee on Indian Affairs, sponsored the act that would bear his name and bring sweeping change to the Cheyenne world. The Dawes Act was intended to wipe away the concept of tribal ownership of land by allotting to each individual family its own property. By owning—and working—their own agricultural and grazing land, the Indians, according to the theory, would become yeoman farmers and ranchers, and once they had been completely assimilated, the government would reward them with full citizenship.

Such was the theory—and the hope.

There was never any question that the Dawes Act would be applied to the Cheyenne and Arapaho Reservation. The reservation system had proved a failure, as the reformers were quick to point out. Only a quarter of the Cheyennes had abandoned their blankets and traditional ways. Few could speak English, and even fewer could read. Among those who could speak English, only a quarter had any formal education. The power of the chiefs still prevailed, but with the stroke of a pen reformers believed the Dawes Act would destroy the tribal way of life by substituting private ownership for communal.[54]

The reservation would be dismantled, as would a way of life.

George embraced the new thinking. He was already at odds with the chiefs, but there was more to his acceptance than that. He believed in private ownership, at least for himself if not for all Indians. Why shouldn't Cheyennes have the rights of white men? Why shouldn't they enjoy the privilege of citizenship? It made plain sense to him.

But he knew the chiefs would resist. He knew the people would not understand the benefits of throwing away the old and trusted ways for the uncertainties of the new. Many would question how the earth could be owned and bartered like a commodity. Only the earth was forever, they would say. How could one buy and sell such a sacred thing?

Soon, a host of government officials and white speculators descended on the reservation, quickly beating a path to Bent's door, eager to get his support and counsel. Most of all, they wanted him to go among the Cheyennes and explain the new legislation and persuade heads of families to sign the agreement that would cede to the government President Grant's 1869 Cheyenne and Arapaho Reservation. In exchange for the cession, the tribes would receive $1.5 million, and each man, woman, and child would be allotted 160 acres of land of their own choosing. Once the Cheyennes had selected their allotments, the government would open the surplus lands to white settlement.

But before the Dawes Act could be implemented, two white men came to Darlington and knocked on Bent's door. George knew them well—they were former agent John D. Miles and ex-Kansas governor Samuel J. Crawford. What they had to say very much interested him. In their opinion, and they were both lawyers, the Cheyennes had never ceded the Medicine Lodge Treaty reservation, a part of which was now known as the Cherokee Strip, located at the top of Oklahoma north of the Cheyenne and Arapaho Reservation.

Medicine Lodge, the treaty that George himself had negotiated in 1867.

Miles and Crawford believed that President Grant's 1869 reservation in no way wiped out the earlier reservation. The Cheyennes, they declared, still owned it, and there was big money to be made—for George and for the Cheyennes—if the Indians could make a valid claim. But the tribes would need expert legal representation, for the government and the Cherokees would surely contest the claim. Miles and Crawford offered their services, but they needed George to help them get the consent of the chiefs. They knew that Bent was the key to the entire plan. No one was better connected, and he, after all, was the very man who had convinced the chiefs and the Dog Soldiers to sign the Medicine Lodge treaty in the first place.

The lawyers promised George a fee of ten thousand dollars for his help. More money than his father could have gotten for Bent's Old Fort. More money than he would make in ten years as a government interpreter—enough to erase his gambling debts, save the ranch from creditors, and smooth things over with Kiowa Woman and the children. He would be set for life, beholding to no man. He would be free to go where he pleased, when he pleased.

It seemed too good to be true, but he signed on immediately.

On May 21, 1889, Bent, Miles, and Crawford gathered a delegation of chiefs. These men, they claimed, fairly represented the Cheyennes and Arapahos, and hurried them off to Oklahoma City, a raw, red gash in rolling hills of grass some thirty miles east of the reservation. Exactly one month earlier, with President Benjamin Harrison's blessing, fifty thousand Boomers rushed into the territory's unassigned lands nestled in the heart of Indian country. More than ten thousand Sooners—those who jumped the noon signal cannon and sneaked in the day before—and Boomers staked claims in and around Oklahoma Station, now renamed Oklahoma City. If any place could be called an instant city, this was it. Around the clock thousands of men pounded nails, erecting buildings and homes overnight. The sight of so many white people gathered in one place shocked and bewildered the chiefs. Where did they all come from? Would the Cheyenne reservation be overrun next?

It was time to make a deal.

With Bent interpreting, Little Chief, Cloud Chief, Cut Nose, Starving Elk, Wolf Face, Leonard Tyler, Little Bear, and Wolf Robe of the Cheyennes and Left Hand, Row of Lodges, White-eyed Antelope, and Heap of Bears of the Arapahos concluded contracts with Miles and Crawford. The lawyers, however, were still not sure of the legality of their contract to represent the Indians. Would the Indian commissioner and the Department of the Interior accept these hastily negotiated agreements? A week later they amended their primary contract to include Matt Reynolds of St. Louis. For a one-third interest in the profits, Reynolds would deliver the support of his good friend Interior Secretary John W. Noble.[55]

Agent Ashley validated the Oklahoma City proceedings by attesting before a federal judge that "resolutions and enactments of the Cheyenne and Arapahoe Tribes of Indians were duly declared and enacted in my presence in a full and duly represented majority of the said Tribes, and was free and voluntary upon their part."[56]

All the while the chiefs were in Oklahoma City, George constantly assured them that the selling of the Cherokee Strip claim was "like finding so much money in the road." There would be plenty of money for everyone—so much money in fact that the chiefs need not worry about the 10 percent set aside for lawyers' fees.[57]

Meanwhile, other sharp-eyed lawyers also saw the "money in the road" and began their own efforts to represent the tribes in the Cherokee Strip dispute. To head them off, Miles asked Ashley to move against former agent Gilbert B. Williams and his partner, Wichita lawyer T. F. McMechan, by banning them from the reservation before they could draw up their own contract with a "duly appointed" delegation of "chiefs." But another lawyer, ex-agent Daniel B. Dyer, was not run off so easily. Rather than carry on a long, messy battle with him, Miles, Crawford, and Reynolds brought him into the syndicate as a partner.

Still, Miles and his cronies remained nervous, so they reconvened the chiefs in Arkansas City, Kansas, on August 20, 1889. They revised the original agreement with uncontestable language that would allow them to represent the tribes not just on the Cherokee Strip, but on all lands claimed by the Cheyennes, including the 1869 reservation.

George supported Miles and company, for he desperately needed the money. His brother Bob, who had handled most of his financial affairs, had died suddenly on the Bent Canadian River ranch just weeks before the lawyers offered him that ten thousand-dollar windfall. Since Bob's funeral in April, George had suffered a severe bout of what he called the blues. He and his brother had always been close, and though Bob was only three years older, George had looked upon him as the leader of the Bent clan and a rock of stability. While George was still in school, Bob was bossing freight wagons on the Santa Fe Trail. And although Bob never fought in the Civil War, even hard-eyed frontiersmen considered him a pretty tough customer. George remembered how his brother had saved him from Gratiot Street Prison in

1862. The memory of Sand Creek, where he had been forced to lead the soldiers to Black Kettle's camp, had haunted Bob all his life. But at great risk in 1865 he had testified about the horrors of the massacre before a congressional committee. When their father died in 1869, Bob gave up the Arkansas River ranch in Colorado determined to build a new Bent empire in Indian Territory. When government officials needed a reliable interpreter to go to Washington, D.C., they went to Bob first. When army officers needed someone to watch over the abandoned military buildings at Cantonment, they chose Bob to "hold the fort." And everyone considered him a model Cheyenne rancher.

But there was a wild side to him, too. Everyone knew the story of when Bob rode into a Cantonment saloon, guns blazing, shouting a Cheyenne war whoop. He had overheard a bunch of cowboys bragging of their prowess as Indian fighters and decided to test their nerve. One eyewitness reported, "These brave Indian killers did not wait to go through the door but jumped through the windows, taking the sash and all with them. The last we saw of them they were on their way to Texas, not waiting to say 'Goodbye.'" That was Bob.[58]

When the chiefs arrived in Arkansas City to meet the lawyers, George had his brother's oldest son Jesse in tow. Jesse loved his uncle—he had named his first son after him—but Uncle George was not the best mentor. By the time the lawyers convened the meeting, neither Bent nor his nephew was fit to interpret. As the *Arkansas City Traveler* reported, "Ever since the Cheyenne and Arrapahoe council arrived in the city the interpreters, Jesse Bent and [George Bent], have been drunk. They were of no use to the council." Miles summed up the condition of his two interpreters: "Both drunk."[59]

But George and Jesse had not just gone in search of a bar and gotten drunk. In fact, Dyer provided them with drinking money to keep them out of the way. Without the two official interpreters, the Indians could be easily manipulated.[60]

So the lawyers turned to Leonard Tyler, an eastern-educated Cheyenne, to read the revised contract aloud. Then Miles thought better of it and instructed Tyler to just say to the chiefs that this second agreement was the same as the first. Re-signing was just a formality. Tyler got the chiefs to make their marks.

Miles had gotten what he wanted. And he no longer needed Bent. If it all came through for them, the lawyers stood to gain hundreds of thousands of dollars in legal fees.

When Bent sobered up, he learned that he had been cut out of the syndicate and the ten thousand-dollar windfall he was banking on. His spree in Arkansas City had not only shattered his relationship with Miles and teetotalling Ashley but with the chiefs as well.

Back in Darlington, Bent fumed. How could Miles and the others cut him out? He had delivered the chiefs. He had selected them himself. But he knew they were not a council of chiefs, as Miles and Ashley now pretended, but leaders over whom George had influence. They were not council-approved representatives of the Cheyenne and Arapaho tribes. How dare Miles discard him like some hired hand. He knew the lawyers could not by themselves hold together the loose coalition that George had assembled. Without his steadying hand, the whole thing would fall apart.

Then, in late August, Bent happened to run into T. F. McMechan in Darlington, the same lawyer Ashley had earlier banned from the reservation. The two men talked, even though Ashley had warned Bent away from Wichita lawyers, especially McMechan. But George could not hold back and poured out his anger. Miles had offered him ten thousand dollars "for his influence in getting a contract signed." Besides, they were playing fast and loose with the truth when they claimed to have the full support of the tribes.[61]

McMechan listened carefully and sensed opportunity—and revenge—in what Bent had to say. After all, McMechan had been the first to go among the Indians in hope of becoming their legal representative for land claims. Bent agreed to meet the lawyer again in Wichita in mid-September while the federal district court was in session.[62]

Wichita. Once it had been a cattle boomtown on the old Chisholm Trail, but now it was an established trade and agricultural center. It was no gash in the earth like raw and untamed Oklahoma City, but a substantial western metropolis on the main line of the Santa Fe Railroad, with tall buildings, electric lights, telephones, and an impressive street railway system.

And saloons. Hundreds of saloons. When George arrived on September 10, he had no trouble finding them. But he managed to stay sober long enough to find the lawyer McMechan. On September 17, he met McMechan on the steps of the federal courthouse. The crafty lawyer persuaded George to go with him to the nearby office of his law partner, Fred W. Bentley, another outspoken critic of Miles and his cohorts. Bentley officed in the Sedgwick Block, Wichita's sensational new skyscraper—a bastion for attorneys, who occupied the fourth and fifth floors. The five-story red brick building located at First and Market was elaborately ornamented with stone lintels, and a magnificent turret atop the corner. Skylights illuminated the spacious main floor, and the entire building boasted gas-lit chandeliers. Every appointment was calculated to impress visitors with Wichita's progress and productivity. A sign over a large railroad map shouted the city's slogan: "Harmony, Unity, Strength." Everything—brass, glass, imported wood—was of the highest quality. Bent gawked like a tourist as McMechan ushered him into the elevator, Wichita's first and Bent's first ride. An unseen operator hauled on the ropes threaded through multiple pulleys, raising the cage noiselessly to the fifth floor, where Bentley and a stenographer seemed to be expecting them.[63]

It was afternoon and George had already had a few drinks—enough to loosen his tongue. McMechan and Bentley treated him like an honored quest. They asked him about the old days on the plains and his life among the Cheyennes. As he began telling stories, McMechan quietly brought in his associates and a public notary. Bent enjoyed having an appreciative audience and assumed the air of an expert witness testifying before a sympathetic jury. He was enjoying himself.

He told the clutch of important-looking men, dressed in their starched white collars, silk cravats, and pinstripes, that he was the son of Colonel William Bent and his Cheyenne wife, Owl Woman. He and his brothers and sisters had been raised among the Cheyennes, but he told them proudly that he had attended white schools in St. Louis, had a college education, and was knowledgeable in the ways of the white world. He had hobnobbed with the likes of Buffalo Bill Cody, Wild Bill Hickok, George Armstrong Custer, and their Indian counterparts, Tall Bull, Roman Nose, Red Cloud, and Crazy Horse. The lawyers nodded their approval and sucked their cigars.

Bent grew expansive. He told them about Cheyenne history and customs and recounted the lineage of chiefs and headmen. He told them about Henry M. Stanley, the African explorer, who was the only white man he knew who could pronounce difficult Cheyenne names. Without breaking the mood or appearing to change the subject, Bentley deftly maneuvered him to the heart of the matter. What about those chiefs who signed the agreement with Miles and Crawford in Arkansas City? They weren't chiefs nor did they represent the tribes, Bent answered. They represented only themselves. No official Indian council had selected them. Usually, he explained, "whenever there is any voting to be done by the tribe the war chiefs and the tribe meet and the head chief makes a speech and a pipe is passed around among the war chiefs and all in favor of the proposition made by the head chief smoke the pipe, and all against it pass it along and refuse to smoke, and if a majority of the war chiefs smoke the proposition is adopted by the tribe, if not it is rejected, such meetings are called a 'council.'" But he assured his listeners that "no such council has ever been held which approved or ratified any such contracts as the ones made at Arkansas City and Oklahoma City."[64]

Bent further offered that the majority of tribesmen would oppose any dealings with the white men named in the contract. Dyer, he said, was a "bad man" who "made a great deal of money out of the Indians while Indian Agent" at Darlington. He also accused ex-governor Crawford of being a crook because he had "made so much money out of the Creeks." As for Miles, he was "worse than Dyer, while agent, and made much money out of the Indians." Urged on by McMechan and Bentley, Bent now hit his stride, as did the alcohol he had consumed earlier in the day. He moved on to criticize his friend Charles Ashley, detailing how the agent had threatened to arrest McMechan if the lawyer attempted to talk with Whirlwind, the "real and hereditary chief of the Cheyennes." Bent admitted that he and Whirlwind did not always agree, but he asserted that no legitimate tribal council could be convened without the chief.

Bent's impromptu remarks demonstrated his vast knowledge of Cheyenne tribal history, relationships, and politics. Altogether a tour de force—and one that pulled the rug out from under Miles and company, all to the delight of McMechan and Bentley.

The lawyers placed a pen in Bent's hand and asked him to read over his remarks, which they now called an "affidavit." His eyes refused to focus. He asked the stenographer to read the document aloud. The words sounded fine, so he obligingly signed the paper in a bold hand. The meeting quickly ended. Bent shook hands with everyone, then, physically supported by his new friend McMechan, he shuffled to the new-fangled elevator. The car's motion this time seemed not so gentle. He lurched against the cage. McMechan shouted to the operator, "Let it go down slow!" Even so, Bent felt woozy and nearly lost his footing. By the time the elevator hit bottom, he wasn't feeling quite so full of himself. He felt sick to his stomach. As he entered the brightness of the street, a mule-drawn streetcar rumbled past, but not even the stunning white mules captured his attention. He looked for McMechan, but the attorney had vanished. His head throbbed, and he stumbled to the alley. And in the rear of magnificent Sedgwick Block, Bent gagged and vomited until there was nothing left to expel.[65]

The snow stung his face as Bent rode toward the dimly lit agency buildings at Darlington. It was January 7, 1890, not a good way to begin the new year, but he had no choice but to testify before government officials who had come to the reservation. His performance in Wichita back in September had loosed a storm of its own. Before the ink was dry on Bent's affidavit, Bentley had alerted the Secretary of the Interior that Miles and company were frauds, the Indians had been duped, and Bent was part of the conspiracy.[66] Within days the commissioner of Indian Affairs called for Bent's immediate dismissal as U.S. interpreter, citing as cause his public drunkenness at Arkansas City. Miles and company realized Bent could blow their whole scheme. It was in their best interest to protect him, but only if he agreed to recant his Wichita statement. Miles urged Agent Ashley to write a strong letter of support for his interpreter. The agent knew that he, too, might be a target of the government's investigation, so he held nothing back in his defense of Bent: "[He] has been the interpreter at this agency the past eighteen years. He is thoroughly competent, and his services cannot be equaled. His knowledge of and extensive personal acquaintance with individual Indians makes his services indispensable." Ashley freely admitted that

George had a drinking problem, but "he promised me he would not drink anymore, and I believe he has not to any perceptible extent since. He is in the office every day and I would certainly notice if he had. . . . He feels very badly about it, says he has made up his mind to leave intoxicating liquors alone and asks that his discharge be held in abeyance pending his good behavior." Ashley added his own plea for George's retention, confident that this time his interpreter would be true to his word. Bent had learned a hard lesson in Arkansas City.[67]

Ashley's letter failed. On December 19, 1889, the commissioner of Indian Affairs confirmed Bent's dismissal. Two days later he sent off Special Indian Agent Robert S. Gardner to investigate the charges leveled by Bentley and McMechan.

Ever since Bent had returned to the reservation he had been under intense pressure. Whirlwind and the traditional leaders had been furious with him for his role in appointing the fraudulent council that supported the Miles scheme. But Bent had made amends with his Wichita statement, which confirmed Whirlwind's leadership. On the other hand, he had acquired powerful new enemies in Ashley and Miles, who could not let the Wichita affidavit stand unchallenged. Ashley had written his letter of support but only because Bent had promised he would recant.

As he approached Darlington, Bent could see through the blur of snow many carriages and hacks lined up outside the agency office. Then he saw the Indian ponies tethered nearby, among them the fine warhorse of Chief Whirlwind. This was not going to be an easy day.

Knocking the snow off his coat, he entered the office. People crowded the anteroom—clerks, Indians wrapped in blankets who had been called to testify, and government officials. Whirlwind, surrounded by chiefs and soldier society men, stood tall at the end of the room. The chief had just finished his testimony to Special Agent Gardner, interpreted by Bent's old friend Ben Clark. George was glad that Gardner had hired Clark to interpret, along with nephew Jesse Bent and his new son-in-law Robert Burns, Ada's husband. He knew better than anyone how interpreters could influence and manipulate a translation, and Ben, Bob, and Jesse might soften the chiefs' harsh words about George's role in the whole affair. Bent had known Whirlwind a long time. He still remembered the day at Julesburg back in 1865 when Whirlwind, then a Dog Soldier, carried his bear-paw shield and shouted his war cry as he chased the soldiers back into Fort Sedgwick.[68] He was older now and a chief, but he was still a formidable presence. Bent feared him more than all the lawyers in Wichita. After all, he had to live on the reservation. It would be tricky business finding a path between Whirlwind, Miles, McMechan, and Ashley. It was impossible to please them all. And he needed a drink.

Special Agent Gardner wasted no time. He motioned for Bent to follow him into the deposition room, where Ashley and McMechan were waiting for them. A clerk recorded every word. Gardner quickly got to the legitimacy of the delegation that had signed the Miles contract:

Q. Was this delegation, on the part of the Cheyennes regularly and legitimately appointed or chosen, if so by whom.
A. I was not present at the council where these delegates were appointed or selected and don't know. They had frequent councils among themselves regarding this matter, and how, or where they appointed these delegates I don't know.

Q. From your knowledge and frequent talks with the agency Indians, are you prepared to state whether or not they understood fully and thoroughly the nature and purport of this agreement.
A. Yes Sir.

Q. What is it.
A. They all understand it.

Q. Who went with the Indians from here to Arkansas [City].
A. Col. D. B. Dyer. We got there on Sunday and on Tuesday, Mr. Miles came and then the papers were signed.

Q. When you say the Indians understand it, what Indians did you mean.

A. I mean the more intelligent and progressive ones, those who are around farming & working.

Q. Were you in Wichita in September 1889.
A. Yes Sir.

Q. Whilst there did you make an affidavit or deposition regarding this agreement, or any matter connected with it, or agency affairs.
A. I guess I did.

Q. Look at this paper marked Exhibit "G," and state whether you signed it or not.
A. I must have signed it, but I don't recollect.

Q. Why do you not recollect.
A. I was drunk when I signed it. I was drunk before I went there and whilst I was there.

Q. Where do you mean when you say there.
A. In the office of Mr. McMechan. I supposed it was his office. I don't know. This was in Wichita. I drank nothing in his office, none offered me.

Q. Were the statements you made and swore to, at this time, as appears in Exhibit "G" true or false.
A. Think they are false. They were made whilst I was under the influence of liquor, towards the last I was very stupid. I could hardly stand on my feet, when I got up. I recollect that. And when going down in the elevator, the motion of it pretty near throwed me off of my feet, as I was under the influence of liquor. Mr. McMechan told the elevator man to let it go down slow. After getting down, we went down the street together, and I went into the rear of a building and threw up. I did not see him any more in Wichita.

Furious at Bent's recantation of Exhibit G, McMechan jumped into the questioning, but George answered in vague generalities. Ashley then pitched in, hoping to clear himself:

Q. Did I ever instruct you to hold no conversation with Mr. McMechan in any matter whatever.

A. I do not recollect, but it is in the statement I made at Wichita. I did tell Mr. McMechan that the agent understood that he was councilling with Whirlwind in his camp.

Certain that Bent had been influenced by the Miles cabal, MeMechan fired off another round of questions:

Q. Have you had any talk with Jno D. Miles about your affidavit since you made it.

A. No Sir.

Q. Were there any persons present in Mr. Bentley's office in Wichita when you made the affidavit, other than myself and Mr. Bentley.

A. I don't recollect, only when I got up to go out I met two or three gentlemen and was introduced to them. Don't know them, & don't recollect their names.[69]

Bent's testimony was a masterpiece of obfuscation. At once, he admitted he was drunk in Wichita but did not cast blame on McMechan and Bentley; he recanted Exhibit G to please Ashley and Miles but recognized the authority of Whirlwind; and he admitted he signed the document but did not recollect its contents. By the end of the day, no one in the room, including Bent, understood what was plain truth or liquored invention.

Bent left the building relieved. He had somehow survived the interrogation, but he was still jobless and his reputation among the Cheyennes had never been lower. In the weeks and months to come, government commissioners would descend on Darlington and bureaucrats would oversee the dismantlement of the reservation. In this effort, Bent accepted whatever work came his way—mostly acting as an interpreter and a go-between—and he received money for services rendered. Some called these payments bribes; others saw them as fees for work honestly performed. Captain Jesse Lee, former Cheyenne and Arapaho agent, knew George played a critical role in gaining tribal support for the sale and breakup of the reservation into individual allotments. And he knew that George received money for this. "I heard that my friend George Bent got either five hundred or a thousand dollars." But Lee was sympathetic. "I am not blaming George, now, for taking that money. I am not scolding him about it for maybe he was a little hard up and was needing money, you know. If there was anything wrong in this business it was the men who gave this money."[70]

Though Bent may have fallen out of favor with the commissioner of Indian Affairs and some powerful Cheyenne chiefs, both the government and the tribe recognized him as the official interpreter for the most important agreement ever negotiated between the U.S. government and the Southern Cheyennes. On November 14, 1890, Bent certified that three-quarters of the adult males approved the relinquishment "of all their right, claim, and interest in and to lands in Indian Territory."[71] This allowed Congress in March 1891 to apply the Dawes General Allotment Act to the Cheyenne and Arapaho Reservation, thus opening it for allotment and sale. Once, the Cheyennes and Arapahos freely roamed the Central Plains—now carved up into the states of Colorado, Wyoming, Montana, Kansas, and Oklahoma Territory. Now a government map showed 3,329 allotments of 160 acres each along the Canadian and Washita Rivers. The rest of the reservation—considered surplus—was opened for sale and white settlement.

But no one really believed that Bent had gotten three-quarters of the adult males to approve the cession. The final agreement included names of many who had not consented to selling the land. Ineligible names of school children and women also appeared on the roll. All this would have happened without Bent. Still, many Cheyennes remembered him with the timeless gesture of sign language—a hand darting outward from the mouth with two fingers spread wide, the unmistakable description of a man who talked out of both sides of his mouth.[72]

Chapter 12

NOTHING LIVES FOREVER

A hard, driving rain beat down on the small, wood-frame house. Bent stood on the porch, looking out anxiously. He worried about Porcupine Bull and his wife, Medicine Woman. The old warrior must be close to eighty now, and they had a rough fifty rough miles to travel from their camp to Colony, Oklahoma. The storm might delay them. But Grinnell was here, his wife too, waiting with his notepad, impatient to begin. Then, out of the torrent, came an uncovered wagon. Bent ran out to meet it and found Porcupine Bull and Medicine Woman huddled under their soaking blankets. But they did not complain and quietly stepped onto the porch and entered the house. George had told them that Grinnell, the "Indian authority," would be here and would pay them for their stories. But it was not the money that brought them through the rain to Colony—they came because Bent had asked them.[1]

George Bird Grinnell and his wife Elizabeth greeted Porcupine Bull and Medicine Woman in the front room of the modest three-room cottage. Bent had not revealed to the Cheyenne elders everything he knew about Grinnell or how famous the man really was: how he had been groomed to be a New York stockbroker but had turned his back on Wall Street for a career in the "wild and wooly West," how he had been trained as a paleontologist, and, later, how he had recorded the history of Indians, the "Vanishing Americans."[2] They would never understand all this. But Bent knew that Grinnell had accompanied Custer's 1874 Black Hills exploring expedition and had been struck by the manly qualities of the Pawnee scouts who guided the troops. Unlike many other whites who encountered Indians for the first time, he saw them not as savages but as human beings worthy of respect—

and study. He thought them, however, a doomed people and had made it his life's mission to preserve their memory, before it was too late. In his own way, Bent had come to the same conclusion. If the story of his people was not written down, it would be lost forever. For the last eleven years, ever since their first meeting in 1901 when Grinnell had hired him on as interpreter, Bent had shared with the ethnographer stories of the Cheyennes—from the exploits of war parties to the mysteries of the Sacred Arrows and the Sun Dance.

Soon after that first meeting, Grinnell realized that Bent was much more than an interpreter. He was a gold mine of information, and, even more, he was literate. He could write out his own stories as well as those of others. Bent became Grinnell's eyes and ears among the Southern Cheyennes and the key to unlocking the secrets of their culture.[3] Before coming to Oklahoma, Grinnell had feared that any interpreter he hired would require a lot of training. But his confidence in Bent jumped when he witnessed the blessing of the mixed-blood's new lodge. All the tribal leaders were there, and Grinnell recorded the ceremony in detail. Little Bear, an old warrior who had killed men in battle, recounted his bravest coup, then struck the lodge with a small branch and stepped inside, followed by Little Chief, Man Above, Long Neck, Man on the Cloud, Horse Rode, "and other brave men." Bent instructed Grinnell and other spectators to sit in silence until the coup had been counted. Only then could they enter the tipi. The whole blessing ceremony astonished the New Yorker. Bent so far exceeded his expectations that he instantly engaged him at two dollars a day plus all the "grub" he could eat.[4]

Now, in June 1912, the ethnographer completely depended on him. Only Bent could consistently bring in the chiefs and elders for long interviews. No one else had the power or tribal connections to do that. The informants were Bent's friends and family. He had lived with them, fought beside them, and shared their sorrows and hardships as the free life came to an end. They would tell him stories that a white man, by himself, could never hope to uncover. Bent learned to trust Grinnell. He was a good listener, took careful notes, and usually got the story straight, unlike the Smithsonian scholar James Mooney, who had been haunting the Cheyenne and Arapaho Reservation since 1890.

Grinnell, though, had his faults. To Bent, he seemed unable to complete his Cheyenne book, always making excuses. He had been working on it for eleven years, and George had helped every step of the way, in the early years mainly for the money—fifty cents for a short story and up to five dollars for a longer tale.[5] But now Bent was driven to preserve the history of his people before the old ones were gone, and he grew impatient at Grinnell's slowness. Every year the Colony Indian cemetery held more scaffolds and fresh graves. Soon there would be no one left who knew the old ways. The students at Colony's Seger Indian School, where Bent now served as clerk and interpreter, read from white man's books. Classes were conducted in English, not Cheyenne, and many youngsters spoke only broken phrases of their parents' language, hardly able to put together a complete thought. Even worse, most of the children seemed to care little about the history of their people. The days of the buffalo were gone, they said, and there was no use in remembering a dead past.[6]

It was for this reason that Porcupine Bull and Medicine Woman were here. They knew those long-ago days, knew the names of all the bands and where they camped in the great village circle, knew how many times the Sacred Arrows had been moved and against which enemies, knew about the Sacred Hat of the Northern people and about clans and how they shaped Cheyenne life, and Porcupine Bull also knew about the battles with the whites, from the first clash with saber-slashing dragoons on the Solomon to the fight at Summit Springs where Tall Bull's Dog Soldiers had been destroyed. Together they remembered these things, and Bent wanted Grinnell to write it all down, *now*, before they died and the stories were lost forever.

Today, Grinnell seemed indifferent of the opportunity presented him. And Bent seethed with indignation when the "Indian authority" offered the old couple only fifty cents apiece for their trouble. He did not seem to understand the importance of what they had told him. They were giving him priceless insights into the very center of Cheyenne life, and Grinnell tossed them four bits and sent them on their way. It wasn't right. *Damn* it wasn't right. For all his supposed sensitivity toward Indians, he treated Porcupine Bull and Medicine Woman like hirelings, like he was doing them a favor.[7]

Never had Bent been so angry with Grinnell, but he held his temper. This was not the time to confront him. The Grinnells stayed with him for two more weeks, and during that time George treated them with appropriate courtesy. He needed Grinnell. There was no one else who possessed the skills or the New York connections to publish a book on the Cheyennes. Besides, Grinnell's visit enhanced Bent's own stature among both tribal leaders and agency officials. He had learned the value of self-promotion and good press. For years he had written anonymous columns for both the *Colony Courier* and Darlington's *Carrier Pigeon*, noting in one that he was the "son of the famous Indian trader of early days, Col. Bent, [and] reads from one to two dailies and about fourteen weekly papers regularly."[8] Somehow Bent found time to slip away from the intense interview sessions to file stories announcing Grinnell's stay in Colony: "Mr. and Mrs. George B. Grinnell of New York City have been spending a few weeks with George Bent and Family. Mr. Grinnell is a writer of fame and is authority on Indian life. During his visit he interviewed some of the older Indians, among them Two Crows and Porcupine Bull. He was gleaning facts for his future writings."[9]

Despite the growing strain between Bent and Grinnell, they enjoyed some pleasant moments during the visit. Elizabeth got along well with Standing Out, admiring her beadwork and singing; in turn Standing Out called Elizabeth "my little daughter."[10] The two women had little trouble communicating, even though Standing Out spoke only Cheyenne. Elizabeth's close relationship with Bent's wife seemed to smooth the edges off the stuffy historian, and she encouraged Bent to talk about himself. Grinnell listened with interest as George recalled his childhood at Bent's Old Fort. He paid special attention to the story of the graveyard outside the fort's adobe walls. An old red-haired Irishman, whose toes had been frozen off by a sudden spring blizzard, had been assigned to drive a two-wheeled cart, a Mexican *carreta*, to dig up prickly pear cactus, roots and all, and transplant them on the graves of George's uncles to keep away scavenging wolves. As usual Bent remembered every detail, although the event had taken place nearly sixty years before. On June 7, 1912, Grinnell scribbled in his red-lined stenographer's pad, "The children used to go out to the dump and wait there for the cart and then ride back. The mule was a big old sorrel mule."[11]

Still, George and Standing Out felt relief when the Grinnells finally left for Denver on June 20. It had been a stressful visit. Now the Bents looked forward to seeing daughter Lucy and her new husband Otto Little Man, who married in Clinton, Oklahoma, just six months ago. Bent saw to it that a white minister conducted the ceremony "according to the laws and customs of white men" and made certain that the Darlington newspaper covered the event in detail. A week later, he hosted an even larger wedding ceremony in a beautiful grove of trees at the Seger Indian School in Colony, but this one according to Indian custom. The *Colony Courier* reported on the extravagant affair:

> The bride's relatives and friends presented three regular Indian lodges, one being especially provided with a fine Indian-style bed with fancy painted willow head and foot-pieces, with beautiful beaded hide pillow-shams and beaded bedspread to ornament the bed during the day, and ten wall tents. The groom's relatives presented eight head of horses, two carriages and two top-buggies, with the harness. And then the shawls and Indian robes! There were fifty-seven, worth up to fifteen dollars each, and hundreds of pounds of coffee, flour, rice, prunes, etc., and nearly a wagon-load of fine granite kitchen war [*sic*]; altogether there being four wagon-loads of presents. A part of the presents consisted of beads which different ones of the Indian women present volunteered to take, each selecting the color she desired, to be put on moccasins which she would make for the groom. The mother of the bride presented portions of coffee, sugar, flour, etc., to numerous friends present, dipping out a small kettle of sugar, one of coffee, one of rice, etc., as each person came up just before the leaving time.[12]

Bent presided over the whole proceeding like a chief. Indeed, those who had attended, Indian and white, treated him with the respect generally reserved for a great leader. The large turnout and lavish gifts honored Bent as much as they did the newlyweds.

He had come a long way since those terrible days following his humiliation at Darlington, when the lawyers forced him to admit he was a drunk and the commissioner fired him for it. The chiefs supported the government's action—and hard times followed. Without steady employment as a U.S. interpreter, he turned to odd jobs, eking out a living by accepting anything that came his way. He had a large family to feed, the children of his three wives and some of their dependents. It helped that at annuity time licensed traders sought him out to help them take advantage of agency Indians who were flush with ready cash. But mostly he got by, leasing his land on the South Canadian to white farmers, selling his best horses and wagons, even part of his allotment, to cover debts and put food on the table.[13]

And he had stopped drinking.

Even so, stories about his drunkenness followed him. His critics were quick to throw it in his face, especially when he sought work at the agency. In the fractured politics of the Southern Cheyenne and Arapaho world, Bent was an easy target. No matter the issue—white versus traditional education, land ownership and leases, the outlawed Ghost Dance and the use of peyote, traditional religious ceremonies such as the Sun Dance, tribal allotments—if Bent was involved, either as an interpreter or as an advocate, his enemies could use his past to discredit him. Some even accused him of supplying liquor to schoolboys home from Carlisle. Nothing came of it, but for many Indians, rumor and innuendo became fact. In one heated council meeting, called to discuss Indian allotments, Cloud Chief objected to Bent's presence as interpreter, saying he was "full" and at one point ordered him to "sit down."[14]

These rebukes stung. Even worse, they forced Bent away from agency affairs and the mainstream of Cheyenne life. Once he had stood beside the chiefs and guided them, once he had sat next to the agent and distributed food rations, now he was marginalized, without power in either world.[15]

With creditors close on his heels he retreated, sold his large house at Darlington, and holed up on his ranch on the South Canadian, thirty-five miles from Bridgeport, the nearest post office.[16] One of those in pursuit was his own daughter, Julia, now living with her mother, Kiowa Woman. The headstrong girl had just returned from Carlisle and had moved in with Little Hawk, a traditional Cheyenne who had "thrown away" his first wife and married Julia "Indian Custom." The Indian agent considered her behavior immoral and illegal but offered her a good-paying job—provided she leave Little Hawk. This she would not do and now was desperate for money.

Bent could offer her nothing, not a dowry, not even a loan. He was flat broke. Estranged from her father for years—he had not been invited to the wedding—she accused him of stealing her land and cattle, which she claimed had been issued to her by the government. Although the commissioner of Indian Affairs ruled in George's favor, the affair publicly held up Bent's poverty for everyone to see. He could not even pay for his own daughter's wedding.[17]

When he did appear in public, he wore an old suit, the seat of the trousers nearly worn through and the cuffs frayed. Soon after Christmas 1896 he pulled out his best stationery and carefully penned a letter to his former employer, A. E. Reynolds, who now lived in Denver:

> My dear friend, I thought of asking a few favors of you for an old friendship, as I am hard up and have been for some time and no more work in stores to get any thing. First of all, I like to have you to send me overcoat size 50 in[ches] as I weigh 250 lbs now. Suit of clothes: coat 48 in, vest 48 in., pants 46 in waist, 33 in legs, and if you can stand it I would like have shotgun, gauge 10 heavy gun.[18]

He needed the gun badly. The truth was his table was bare, though geese were plentiful on the South Canadian this time of year. Bent had his pride, and it was hard asking for charity. But if anyone owed him, it was Reynolds. Now a mining king in Colorado, Reynolds had built his first fortune on Bent's influence with the Cheyennes. As Reynold's agent he had brought not only customers but negotiated the best deals possible—just as his trader father had years before. Reynolds understood that without Bent he could never have succeeded on the reservation. Within two weeks, Reynolds responded with an express package. Bent got his new suit and gun—and a box of supplies and gifts, including calico for the women and razors for the men.[19]

Through the lean years, as early as the 1880s, Bent came to realize that his unique understanding and memory of Cheyenne history and culture had value. He frequently corresponded with army officers, former Cheyenne captives, government scouts, and frontiersmen about battles fought between Indians and whites. Captives like Mary Fletcher, the girl he befriended in 1865 while she was held in the Cheyenne camps, wanted to know the real story behind abductions to help her in filing depredation claims against the U.S. government.[20] For his testimony in depredation cases, he was paid by the agency. The Cheyennes had much to gain by Bent's depositions, for successful claimants received payment deducted from the Cheyennes' annuities. Agency officials who deposed him invariably described him as a "very intelligent, half-blood Cheyenne" and praised his unerring memory.[21]

George especially enjoyed corresponding with army officers—men he had once held in his gunsights. Through these letters he relived the glory days of the Cheyennes at the height of their power. And he remembered everything. He amazed Edward Wynkoop and Samuel Tappan with his near-perfect memory. Tappan, who lived in Washington, D.C., told Smithsonian ethnographer James Mooney about this educated half-blood who seemed to know all about Cheyenne culture.

In 1890 Mooney journeyed to Oklahoma, where he met Bent for the first time. He was so impressed that he not only photographed the Bent family but made a portrait of Bent himself. The circular snapshot reveals Bent's commanding presence. Wearing a gray flannel suit, his eyes shaded by a broad-brimmed hat, he sits on the porch of the agency headquarters at Darlington, leaning imperially against a rough-hewn post as if it were the straight back of a throne. Behind him, arrayed like subjects, are Indians wrapped in blankets and uniformed tribal policemen. But it is Bent who dominates the picture. He exudes power and confidence, a man to be reckoned with.

Bent made a strong impression on Mooney, at the time considered the world's foremost Indian expert (the press had dubbed him the "Indian Man").[22] Year after year he returned to Oklahoma, interviewing old Cheyennes and snapping pictures with his Kodak box camera. But George never warmed to him and later remembered, "He always thought he was right in every thing . . . and wanted all his own way."[23]

At first Bent hoped to make some money from his stories, but the "Indian Man" paid little for artifacts and almost nothing for information. Yet when Mooney came to Cheyenne country, Bent was there, guiding him, introducing him to elders, getting him access to sacred ceremonies, even revealing the tortures of the Sun Dance.[24] In turn, Mooney gave Bent's name to Grinnell, the gifted amateur ethnographer who published the nation's leading magazine for outdoorsmen, *Forest and Stream*, and who had gained a reputation as a popularizer of Indian history.[25]

When Grinnell arrived on the scene in 1901, Bent drew away from Mooney in favor of a man who would pay for his services. And Grinnell, unlike Mooney, would listen. Bent had tried to explain to Mooney the Cheyenne clan system, but the Indian Man dismissed the idea as humbug, arguing that no true clan system existed. Grinnell accepted Mooney's thesis and, at first, rejected Bent's assertion that clans were a major force in Cheyenne life. But Bent insisted that the clans were strong until the 1849 cholera epidemic and the 1864 Sand Creek Massacre. After these disasters, the old rules prohibiting marriage within a clan fell by the way as men and women sought relationships among the survivors. As Bent told it, the Southern Cheyennes "boldly violated the law and began to marry cousins."[26] Clans now existed only in memory. When Grinnell questioned elders, again and again they confirmed what Bent had told him. It was Mooney, the Indian Man, who was confused, not Bent the halfbreed interpreter.

Grinnell's respect for his new associate soared. He could use this man. Bent had exposed Mooney's errors, and now Grinnell would exploit the opportunity and become the Indian Authority.[27]

Once again, Bent was caught in a crossfire, this time between dueling anthropologists. Mooney stewed as Grinnell filled his western notebooks with stories recounted by Bent and the elders he brought to Grinnell's field desk.

In Omaha, Nebraska, a Crachit-like little man hunched over his desk stacked high with papers and books. In his hand he clutched a large magnifying glass, moving it rhythmically across lines of type, his nose pressed against the glass. George Hyde, just twenty-three-years old, lived with his mother and loved Indians—he had loved them ever since he met real live Indians when the Trans-Mississippi Exposition came to town in 1898. As a boy, an attack of scarlet fever left him deaf and nearly blind. He was old before his time, a savant gnome of a man, earnest, impatient, and short-tempered with those who were not his intellectual equal. With little formal education, he had taught himself. He read voraciously everything about Indians, everything his mother could find on the shelves of the Omaha Public Library.[28]

By 1904 the housebound scholar tirelessly penned letters and shotgunned them across the country, seeking from old scouts and frontiersmen the untold stories of pioneer life and the Indian wars. One stray letter found George Bent in Colony, Oklahoma, and the two struck up a correspondence. Hyde wanted to know all about the Cheyennes, everything Bent could tell him about customs, battles, skirmishes, and war parties. What impressed George most about this unusual recluse was his genuine desire to know these things from the Indian point of view. The boy asked the right questions, and Bent responded with an avalanche of letters detailing specific people, places, and events. If he had no personal knowledge, he found people who did.

Hyde immediately saw the importance of Bent's Cheyenne memories—through him Hyde had a direct connection to the past. Not that Bent's letters were easy reading. His stream-of-consciousness writing was, at first, difficult to decipher. He would begin a story, digress without warning, then return to it. And Bent's style defied all known rules of capitalization, punctuation, and grammar. He wrote as he spoke—Indian style, with a Cheyenne cadence.[29] On February 23, 1904, in one of his first letters to Hyde, he wrote:

George E. Hyde
1816 Chicago Street
Omaha Nebraska

Sir
I reply to your letter in regard to the fight Genl Forsyth had with Cheyennes Dog Soldiers and. Spotted Tail's band of Siouxs on

Arickaree Fork. Cheyennes and Aricakarees had fight on this Crick some years ago and therefore it was called Arickaree Crick. Tall Bull. Bull Bear. White Horse were leaders of the Dog Soldiers. Roman Nose was only war chief and belong to company or society called Bone Scrapers or Crooked Lances. in this fight 6 Cheyennes and 3 Siouxs were killed white Horse's son and his bro.in.law were among the killed in this fight great many Cheyennes are still living that were in this fight at Cantonment 60 Miles west of Darlington. Dog Soldiers are band or Society it was big society and were always together in large Village to themselves. there are Dog Soldiers among Arapahoes and also among the Kiowas head men of all these Tribes wore sashs made of buffalo skin worked with porcupine quills as bead work. only head men and brave men could wear this sash it called Dog Rope. one End of these is sharp pin or Picket pin 8 inches long. in fight these head men supposed to stick this pin in ground. and not run of. any one could pull this pin out and handed to the owner. at same time person pulling this pin must hit him with whip to make him leave. at the fight Genl Carr had with them. the time that Tall Bull was killed Heap of Wolf Hair. they say perced himself and was killed or shot down by Pawnee Scouts Wm Cody. Buffalo Bill was there at the time soon as I see Two Crows who was at Forsyths fight I will write you the names of those killed at this fight
George Bent[30]

Other letters followed in rapid succession. Hyde marveled at the rich detail and knew he was getting something special. Bent's stories had never before been published. This was original material coming straight from an Indian source. In turn, Bent was encouraged by Hyde's eagerness to write history from the Cheyenne point of view.

Soon the two men came to an understanding. Bent would write his stories out long hand, and Hyde would edit them for publication. "I will write Book," Bent said, "if you will help me out on it. I know every fight that took place among the Whites and the Indians. What I do not know I can find out from Old Indians."[31] His interest in writing a book was not just about setting the historical record straight or preserving the memory of his people. Right now, his family needed food and clothing, and the tax man was calling. He felt certain a book would make big money.[32] Then he discovered that the boy scholar in Omaha still lived with his mother and was as poor as he was. Further, Bent found out that Hyde had little experience in the publishing world. In fact, he had never actually written a book, but he had successfully placed articles in a few popular journals. When a new magazine in Colorado Springs, *The Frontier—A Journal of Early Days and Their Thrilling Events*, offered to pay for a serialized version of Bent's autobiography, the partners jumped at the chance. Bent redoubled his efforts to supply Hyde with stories that could be quickly reworked into articles.

The back cover of the October 1905 issue featured a full-page advertisement:

FROM THE INDIAN'S STANDPOINT
By GEORGE BENT, Pioneer and Scout

BEGINNING with the October Frontier, we will publish an interesting history of early days in the West from the Indian's standpoint.

We have read the other side of the story. Let us see what the red man has to say about it.

These articles were written beside the Indian Camp-Fire. Written by one who witnessed the scenes described. Written without color or varnish by the white man's brush.

Wars between Indian tribes and between white and red men. Wars to the death.

Habits, legends, customs and real life of the men of the plains.

Frontier titled the Bent-Hyde collaboration "Forty Years with the Cheyennes," and for four issues running it was the magazine's lead article. The first focused on Bent's early life, the second on Cheyenne history and the Sand Creek Massacre, and the third and fourth on the great raids of 1865 along the Platte River and up into Montana.

But the promised money never came. Bent was happy to see his stories in print—the Cheyenne view of the Indian wars had never been published before—but he railed against *Frontier* for its failure to pay. The magazine had only a small circulation in Colorado Springs and the Rocky Mountain West, and no one was surprised when it suddenly folded shortly after the Bent articles appeared.

But enough copies circulated in Denver to catch the attention of some old soldiers there. In 1905 Denver was a bustling city of well over one hundred thousand people. The mile-high city boasted all the appurtenances of "civilization." Tall buildings sprang up where once there were rude shacks and mud streets, and horse-drawn wagons made way for electric trolleys and motorcars. But Denver was also home to a ruling elite, a proud pioneer caste unreconstructed in its hatred of Indians. Many of the city fathers had skeletons in their closets and Cheyenne scalps above their mantles—mementos they would rather not see dragged into the light of day, as they themselves had willingly done in 1864 on the stage of a Denver playhouse.[33] Bent's article on Sand Creek ripped open old wounds and unleashed Chivington's war dogs, including the respected attorney Jacob Downing, a die-hard Indian hater and lifelong apologist for the Colorado veterans and their preacher colonel. Chivington himself had been dead and buried for more than a decade, his funeral the largest in the city's history. So Downing rose to speak for the Sand Creek veterans. In the *Denver Times*, he lashed out at Bent, calling him a "cutthroat, and a thief, a liar and a scoundrel, but worst of all a halfbreed." Downing continued his tirade. "Bent's father, Col. Bent, for whom one of our counties was disgracefully named, was a renegade. Bent's mother was a squaw. Bent's father was too much of an outcast to marry a white woman." He concluded his harangue by contending that Sand Creek was no massacre, for only a handful of Indians were killed and "only one squaw and only one papoose in the lot."[34] Even with his pale blue eyes, well-groomed gray hair, and affected gentility, he could not mask his hate. Deep inside beat the heart of a killer. He had mercilessly butchered Cheyenne women and children, and then without shame, his men had adorned their hats and saddle bows with trophies made from body parts and rode laughing back to Denver, hoping to be home for Christmas. No one was laughing now. Not after Bent's articles and the newspaper flap that followed. The reputation of the Queen City, it seemed, was on trial.[35]

Milo Slater of the local Grand Army of the Republic chapter and spokesman for the Colorado veterans, even now engaged in an effort to erect a monument on the grounds of the state capitol to glorify Colorado's Civil War volunteers. Beneath the heroic figure of a cavalryman, battle honors would be cast in bronze. Among the victories, the "battle" of Sand Creek.[36]

When the aging Thirdsters attacked, only one friend came to Bent's defense. A. E. Reynolds took on Major Downing and the angry veterans in a letter to the editor of the *Denver Times*. This prompted Milo Slater to write a private letter, a veiled threat, to Reynolds:

> I do not know whether George Bent was present at the (so called) "Sand Creek Massacre" or not, but in the article named there are statements, given as facts, which are absolutely false; this I say from my own personal knowledge. . . . Fearing that you may have been misled, and not knowing where this discussion may lead, I tell you this now, as a personal friend.[37]

Incensed by the "gross assault upon George Bent," Reynolds shot back a reply. "I stand by what I said. . . . Whatever George Bent writes on the subject, or dictates to somebody else who publishes it, if they follow his statements, they will get a perfectly accurate and truthful statement of the other side of the controversy."[38]

Denver's explosion of racial hatred hardly surprised Bent. He had known of Slater's efforts to erect the soldiers' monument, and he knew he had few friends in Denver, but the controversy served only to strengthen his resolve to tell the Cheyenne story.

Just as the newspaper clippings arrived in his mail, Bent was meeting with Grinnell's longtime hunting pal and now research assistant, John J. White. Grinnell had written that he himself could not make the trip this year but assured Bent that White was a "good fellow" and George should treat him as he would Grinnell himself.[39] But White was not Grinnell. He was insufferable, arrogant, and impatient with the unpredictable tempo of Indian country. "Supper is over," he grumbled to Grinnell, "& I have been talking with Bent. The lodge (promised for last summer) is not up yet but will be 'in a day or two.' Meanwhile I am to have a tent." He complained further that the Indian informants

· promised by Bent were nowhere to be found. "Bent is to telephone them. Isn't that about the end of romance. Summoning an Indian by telephone!"[40]

From the beginning White's patronizing attitude grated on Bent. This was not the man he wanted to record Cheyenne history, and he would be damned if he would bring in the elders for interviews, only for them to be subjected to this whining white man.

So he slowed things down. White considered the maddening delays as clear evidence of Bent's laziness. He again complained to Grinnell:

> There is no use of wasting my time & feeding Bent's family & all the tribe of Southern Cheyennes & getting no results. I have got some fair stories; but only 2 I would really call good, & I am tired of having stories promised me only to find they don't or will not tell them to me. Bent is so sympathetic I would like to knock him on the head with an axe. He agrees cordially that it is a shame & is perfectly content to sit & have me chop my firewood & buy meat for the Indians, which means for the Bent family (with a big B.). I would not kick if I could accomplish any thing but it seems to be N.G. [no good]. I know what you want & if I can't get it I might as well quit. I know when I am whipped & I am whipped now.[41]

White would not do. As long as he was in Indian country, Bent would treat him with treacly courtesy but would work with him only on his own terms. White left Colony, frustrated and worn down by Bent's passive resistance. Next time, Grinnell would have to come himself.

In the meantime Bent would stick with Hyde. The two explored various publishing options, including the *Saturday Evening Post*, but found no takers.[42]

Still, Bent wanted his book—even if there was no money in it. The *Frontier* articles had brought him recognition, and he had seen his name in print for the first time. The nastiness and hoopla in Denver notwithstanding, what mattered most was to get his story—the true story of the Cheyennes—told. And so he kept the pressure on Hyde, bombarding him with yet more stories, always urging him to hurry and finish the book.[43]

For a time, Hyde kept up with him, even outlining a plan for the book. It would be written in four parts:

1. An account of Bent's childhood at the old fort, with some account of his father, mother, brothers, his uncle Chas. Bent, the Mexican campaign, events and life at the fort. 2. A description of his life in Missouri and in the Confederate service. 3. His life in the hostile camps, 1863–5. 4. His life in Kansas during the campaigns of 1867–9.[44]

But Bent's pressure overwhelmed Hyde. He simply could not summon up the strength or the research resources or the money to continue the project, and he told Bent so. More, he had no clear idea where to go with the Bent stories or where to end them. His deafness and failing eyesight, he said, prevented him from vigorously pursing the completion of the book. Bent's pestering had even brought on a nervous attack.[45]

Bent thought perhaps Grinnell might take up where Hyde left off but worried that Grinnell was too busy with other Indian writing interests. For years Grinnell had been collecting Cheyenne material, yet he had done nothing with it. But it was worth a try—Grinnell was after all the Indian Authority. Perhaps Hyde could convince Grinnell to complete the book.

At Bent's urging, Hyde wrote to Grinnell:

As to Bent's book, I wrote [Bent] a few days ago that I could not help him with it any father on account of my deafness, but I suggested that he try to get some one else to take it up; so I believe he would be glad to have you do it. I certainly should be very glad to have you undertake it, for I hate to see such good material lie unused.[46]

Hyde went on to explain his difficulty with his Indian work and the Bent collaboration:

When I took up Bent's story I had hopes of doing something in historical work, but the libraries here are so deficient in books on Indians and Civil War (the two subjects I was studying) that I could do nothing—everything I took up was brought to a stand thro' lack of proper reference books on the subject; so I have taken refuge in fiction work but it is very slow and hard going, tho' like the mule (emblem of hope) with the bundle of hay tied before his nose I always think I see success just ahead and plod on.[47]

Grinnell wrote a carefully guarded response to Hyde's offer to share the Bent material. He knew, of course, the two had been working together on a Cheyenne book based on Bent's life, and he had read the *Frontier* articles. When he learned that Hyde had collected hundreds of additional stories, all written by Bent, he could hardly contain his excitement. His own Cheyenne book was really two books—one on the "Fighting Cheyennes," and another larger work on "Cheyenne lifeways." Knowing the quality of the Bent material he had already extracted, he knew Hyde must be sitting on a treasure trove of Cheyenne history. He wanted to see it badly, but he kept his cool:

> It would be impossible to say, without looking at the manuscript, what if anything could be done with the Bent matter. I should suppose that possibly there might be in it a great deal that is interesting, and yet I have very little notion that the Forest and Stream would want to print the whole matter as a book. You understand, of course, that these things are commercial propositions, and while all Bent's writings would be of great interest to me personally, the Forest and Stream would look at the matter from a cold blooded point of view, as to whether they would get their money back.
>
> I should be glad to see the matter whenever you feel inclined to send it on, and would have it looked over and pronounced upon as soon as possible.[48]

His letter was as disingenuous as Hyde's was naïve. The painfully honest Hyde had loosed a fox in the henhouse. Grinnell was *Forest and Stream*; he owned and controlled it. The "cold blooded point of view" was his. He had no intention of doing a Bent biography. Instead, he would incorporate the rich new material into his own book on Cheyenne wars. After he received the Bent manuscript from Hyde, he co-opted the budding young historian by offering him a job as an assistant to edit and organize more than a hundred of the Bent-Hyde letters for Grinnell's use. Hyde indicated a willingness to accept Grinnell's assignment: "I've been thinking the matter over and I do not see that it would be of any great use to send you the letters at any rate, because I have put *all* the details they contain into the narrative I prepared, and if I send you that it will save you a great deal of bother as well as saving me the time it would require to put his letters into type."[49]

In short, Hyde offered to write Grinnell's book for him. His pay? Twenty cents an hour. The impoverished Hyde, nearly blind and totally deaf, still lived in his mother's house, along with his sister and her young children. Times were tough, and the family scrambled for every cent they could get. While his sister scoured the libraries for obscure Indian war references, Hyde minded the children, frantically trying to keep them away from his carefully stacked notes and letters. No wonder his nerves were frayed. Handing the Bent material over to Grinnell would be a relief. Besides, he was honored to be an assistant to the famed writer and publisher.[50]

In April 1908 they struck a deal. Hyde would write the book, and the Indian Authority would polish it off with his unique Grinnellian touch.

But the Hyde-Grinnell collaboration was not the *Bent* book. Though it was largely based on George's material, references to his participation in events, battles, and war parties vanished from the edited copy. Grinnell finally published his book in 1915, titled *The Fighting Cheyennes*, but he buried Bent in the acknowledgments as just one of a number of "eyewitnesses."[51]

When Grinnell had said he would consider publishing the Bent-Hyde book, George believed him and supplied the ethnographer all he needed for his Cheyenne wars book. At the same time, he sent additional Cheyenne stories that he expected Grinnell to incorporate into the Bent-Hyde book. Grinnell took advantage of Bent's eternal hope, wringing more stories out of him through correspondence and using him as the entrée to elders during visits to Oklahoma.

Shamelessly, he led Bent on.

For the next seven years, George waited. And he waited.

Through those years, slowly, Bent changed. The book no longer was for money or glory, nor was it just his own life story. He now believed that his book, written from the Cheyenne point of view, was the only way to preserve the memory of his people. It had become his mission, and he felt passionate about it. No one else could do it, not Grinnell, not Hyde, not even the chiefs. If it was to be done, he would have to do it. But he needed help, and Grinnell seemed to be his best bet. "I am in hopes Grinnell will get out the Book soon," he told Hyde in June 1909.[52]

But he heard nothing.

In 1911 Grinnell again dangled hope, and Bent grabbed at it. He happily confided to Hyde, "I just got letter from Grinnell saying he was going to get his Indian stuff now together . . . and it would not take long to finish the work."[53]

But disappointment followed. A year later, he sadly told Hyde, "I got letter from Grinnell few days ago. He doesn't seem to be doing any thing at least he doesn't say so."[54]

By 1913, Bent knew the Indian authority had been stringing him along. "I got letter from Grinnell asking me for some Stuff. I am getting tired of him. He does not seam [sic] to go ahead with what he has already."[55]

Fed up, he lashed out at Grinnell, telling Hyde, "He is too slow on his work. He takes and lays aside his stuff and forgets." Worse still, Grinnell never gave "any Credit to any body only himself as he is Called by whites Authority on Indians."[56]

Although he vented his frustration privately to Hyde, he continued his correspondence with Grinnell and graciously acted as host when the anthropologist visited Colony. His father had taught him to temper his anger and not burn bridges. But he gave up any hope of collaborating with Grinnell on the book. Instead he once again turned to the overwrought Hyde, now housebound for weeks at a time by panic attacks and ill-defined illnesses.

Hyde simply could not refuse his old friend's pleadings. He would take the book on again but only if he could find a writing partner who could help finish the manuscript and push it through publication. B. W. Butler of Washington, D.C., seemed to be the right man. He had access to archives in Washington, appeared to have publishing connections, and talked a good game.[57]

Almost immediately, however, Hyde regretted the association, for Butler took the book off on unexpected tangents. He particularly wanted to include the history of the Northern Cheyennes and their fights, events beyond Bent's personal experience. Hyde thought the work could be completed quickly. He had already finished his portion—Bent's life through Sand Creek and its aftermath—but Butler's digressions had complicated things. Bent blamed Hyde. As Hyde plaintively explained to Grinnell, "Bent hasn't written for some time. I suppose he is sulking again because I cannot work faster."[58] Bent knew enough not to place all his trust in Hyde. He corresponded directly with Butler, even sending him gifts, including a fine pipe with beaded bag, to spur him to greater efforts.[59]

In fact, Bent was writing to journalists, historians, anthropologists—anyone who would listen, hoping against hope that someone would take up the Cheyenne story. Jerome Smiley of the Colorado Historical Society; Walter M. Camp, the noted Custer historian and researcher; Joseph Thoburn at the Oklahoma Historical Society; Hamlin Garland, the famed short-story writer; Walter Campbell, who wrote about Plains Indians and mountain men under the pen name Stanley Vestal; and F. W. Cragin, who was so enchanted by Bent's Cheyenne stories that he quit his teaching job in Colorado Springs to work full-time on his western notebooks, which he hoped to turn into a magnum opus on the American West.

Still, Bent devoted most of his attention to Hyde and Butler. They held hundreds of his letters—the story of his life and the history of the Cheyennes—in their hands. By March 1916, Hyde announced to Grinnell, "I finished my part of the Bent book last week, but perhaps my partner will wish me to help with his part now. God Forbid!" He lamented that "my partner [Butler] was in New York, 'peddling' the Bent book, the last I heard of him. I am afraid he will not be able to find a publisher." Exhausted and at the end of his rope, Hyde admitted, "I do not think the book will ever see print."[60]

But there was more to Bent's life than "the book." He still clerked and interpreted at the Seger Indian School in Colony, enrolling students, organizing parent-teacher meetings and holiday dinners, reading mail to elders. He also assisted the agency superintendent with annuity payrolls and census-taking. Mostly, he loved telling stories to children about the old free life of the fighting Cheyennes. When the big man came round, swinging his "fine umbrella" with its "fine handle," the children flocked to him, laughing.[61] He never had a coin for them, but he had treats—and he always left them with a story. His favorite young follower, daughter Mary's five-year-old son, worshipped him, even imitated his swagger. They were inseparable. Then the boy died, suddenly, in February 1915. Bent took it hard. It was one thing to bury the old ones in the cemetery on the hill, but this was different. He was so young, so like George when he was boy at Bent's Old Fort. This child listened and remembered everything. Now, who would be the memory of the Cheyennes?[62]

Life went on. Standing Out supplemented their meager income by making and selling fine beaded moccasins, buckskin dresses, and even a skin lodge made in the traditional way. Mary, Daisy, William, and Lucy visited their parents often, bringing with them their children. The Bents, with grandchildren in tow, attended traditional dances and ceremonies, but they also took in the Ringling Brothers Circus when it came to town. The 1917 Oklahoma State Fair featured the Bent women, who proudly displayed their elk-teeth dresses and beaded buckskin finery. A company of French infantry, fresh from the battlefields of the Great War in Europe, posed for photographs with three generations of Bents. George kept abreast of world events, reading more than a dozen newspapers and magazines every week. The concept of aerial combat and mechanized warfare intrigued him. Telephones, skyscrapers, automobiles, safety razors, moving pictures, medical advances—the world had changed so much from the world he had known. He found it hard, sometimes, to believe he had been born in a buffalo-hide lodge.

And it saddened him that no one would remember those days. He had tried his best to tell the story of his people, the Cheyennes, to Hyde and Grinnell and Mooney, and all the others who came to him. But he had failed. His years of letter writing, storytelling, and interpreting had come to almost nothing, only a handful of articles in obscure publications.

In May 1918 the global influenza epidemic found its way to remote Colony, Oklahoma. on May 19, one week after he fell ill, George Bent was dead.

Halfbreed

With the help of friends, Standing Out buried her husband in the old Indian cemetery east of town. She had no money for a stone, only a rough-sawn board marked the grave, "George Bent, 1843–1918." In the valley echoed the Cheyenne death song:

Nothing Lives Forever
Only the Earth and the Mountains

EPILOGUE

In 1915, George Bird Grinnell published *The Fighting Cheyennes*, a landmark book on the Plains wars from the Cheyenne perspective, based on the interviews and letters of George Bent.

In 1916, George E. Hyde finished his manuscript, *Life of George Bent,* based entirely on Bent's letters. Hyde's manuscript went unpublished and forgotten for over fifty years until Savoie Lottinville, a University of Oklahoma professor, discovered the long-lost manuscript, complete with Bent's own handwritten edits, and published the book in 1968.

In 1923, Grinnell published *The Cheyenne Indians* in two volumes, to this day the standard source on Cheyenne history and culture, based on the interviews and letters of George Bent.

In 2000, the United States Congress passed a bill establishing the Sand Creek Massacre site. George Bent's letters and maps inspired the search for the exact location of Sand Creek and the movement to create the National Historic Site.

George Bent saved the memory of the *Tsistsistas*, the Cheyenne people.

Nothing lives forever . . . but memory.

Notes

Prologue

1. Grinnell Fieldnotes, 6/3/1912, Folder 351, and 6/26/1902, Folder 338, *George Bird Grinnell Papers*, Southwest Museum; Bent to George E. Hyde, 8/21/1914, *George Bent Letters*, Coe Collection, Yale. For Bent's description of the cemetery, see *Colony Courrier*, 1/6/1916.

2. Bent to Reynolds, 1/3/1897, 11/6/1906, *A.E. Reynolds Papers*, Colorado Historical Society.

3. Bent to Hyde, 3/2/1904, 3/6/1913, 8/2/1913, 10/26/1916, *George Bent Letters*, Coe Collection, Yale; Bent to Hyde, 9/11/1905, *George Bent Papers*, Colorado Historical Society; Bent to Hyde, 10/17/1913, *George Bent Papers*, Western History Collection, Denver Public Library; Bent to Thoburn, 4/23/1918, *Joseph B. Thoburn Collection*, Oklahoma Historical Society; Grinnell to Hyde, 5/20/1908, Folder 389, and Bent to Grinnell, 2/12/1912, Folder 56.2, *George Bird Grinnell Papers*, Southwest Museum.

4. Grinnell to Robert M. Peck, 5/26/1908, Folder 389, and Robert M. Peck to Grinnell, 6/5/1908, Folder 50.1, *George Bird Grinnell Papers*, Southwest Museum; Bent to Hyde, 7/6/1917, *George Bent Letters*, Coe Collection, Yale.

5. Bent to Hyde, 2/19/1913, 9/23/1913, *George Bent Letters*, Coe Collection, Yale; Hyde to Grinnell, 9/14/1914, Folder 51a, 3/15/1915, Folder 51b, 1/27/1917, Folder 51c, *George Bird Grinnell Papers*, Grinnell to F. W. Hodge, 8/4/1926, *F. W. Hodge Papers*, Southwest Museum.

Chapter 1

1. William Waldo, "Recollections of a Septuagenarian," in Missouri Historical Society, *Glimpses of the Past 5* (April–June 1938): 62. See also William W. Bent, "Last Will and Testament," *Bent Family Genealogy*, Kansas City Public Library.

2. Dale L. Morgan, *Jedediah Smith and the Opening of the West* (Indianapolis and New York: The Bobbs-Merrill Company, Inc., 1953), 299; David Lavender, *Bent's Fort* (Garden City, N.Y.: Doubleday & Company, Inc., 1954), 77; Harold H. Dunham, "Charles Bent," in LeRoy R. Hafen, ed., *The Mountain Men and the Fur Trade of the Far West*, 10 vols. (Glendale, Calif.: Arthur H. Clark Co., 1965–72), 2:32–34.

3. Sylvia Van Kirk, *Many Tender Ties: Women in Fur-Trade Society, 1670–1870* (Norman: University of Oklahoma Press, 1980), passim.

4. Thomas D. Bonner, *The Life and Adventures of James P. Beckwourth*, introduction, notes, and epilogue by Delmont R. Oswald (Lincoln: University of Nebraska Press, 1972), 102.

5. Ibid., 105–6; Morgan, *Jedediah Smith*, 297; Cecil J. Alter, *James Bridger* (Norman: University of Oklahoma Press, 1962), 102–5.

6. Bonner, *Life and Adventures of James P. Beckwourth*, 106.

7. Ibid., 107.

8. Joshua Pilcher report to the Secretary of War, "Message From the President of the United States, In answer to a resolution of the Senate relative to the British establishments on the Columbia, and the state of the fur trade, &c," January 24, 1831, 21 Cong., 2 sess, S.D. No. 39, 7–8. See also John E. Sunder, *Joshua Pilcher: Fur Trader and Indian Agent* (Norman: University of Oklahoma Press, 1968), 68–69.

9. Warren Ferris, *Life in the Rocky Mountains: Diary of Wanderings on the Sources of the Rivers Missouri, Columbia, and Colorado from February, 1830, to November, 1835*, ed. Paul C. Phillips (Denver: Old West Publishing Co., 1940), 30–31.

10. Waldo, "Recollections of a Septuagenarian," 72.

11. Ibid.

12. Otis E. Young, *First Military Escort on the Santa Fe Trail, 1829* (Glendale, Calif.: Arthur H. Clark Co., 1952), 75; "Military Affairs," *American State Papers* 4 (Washington, D.C.: Gales & Seaton, 1860), 277; Philip St. George Cooke, *Scenes and Adventures in the Army: or Romance of Military Life* (Philadelphia: Lindsay & Blakiston, 1857), 46.

13. Waldo, "Recollections of a Septuagenarian," 73–74.

14. Lavender, *Bent's Fort*, 102.

15. Cooke, *Scenes and Adventures in the Army*, 47.

16. Ibid., 48–49.

17. Waldo, "Recollections of a Septuagenarian," 75; Harvey L. Carter, *"Dear Old Kit": The Historical Christopher Carson* (Norman: University of Oklahoma Press, 1968), 42.

18. George Bent to A. E. Reynolds, 11/6/1906, *A.E. Reynolds Papers*, Colorado Historical Society.

19. George Bent to George E. Hyde, 3/6/1905, 4/10/1905, 4/14/1906, 2/4/1913, 2/20/1914, 6/5/1914, 6/11/1914, 5/13/1914, 5/22/1914, *George Bent Letters*, Coe Collection, Yale. See also Grinnell, "Bent's Old Fort and Its Builders," 31; George E. Hyde, *Life of George Bent Written from His Letters* (Norman: University of Oklahoma Press, 1968), 40–46; Grinnell, *Beyond the Old Frontier*, 130; Samuel P. Arnold, "William W. Bent," in LeRoy R. Hafen, ed., *Mountain Men and the Fur Trade of the Far West*, 10 vols. (Glendale, Calif.: Arthur H. Clark Co.,

1965–72), 6:66–7; Harold H. Dunham, "Charles Bent," in ibid., 2:35–37; Lavender, *Bent's Fort*, 128–29.

20. LeRoy R. Hafen, ed., "W. M. Boggs Manuscript About Bent's Fort, Kit Carson, the Far West and Life Among the Indians," *Colorado Magazine* 7 (March 1930): 49.

21. Dunham, "Charles Bent," in Hafen, *Mountain Men*, 2:38–39; Lavender, *Bent's Fort*, 128–32.

22. George Bent to George E. Hyde, 4/10/1905, 4/14/1906, 2/4/1913, 6/11/1914, 2/20/1914, 5/13/1914, 5/22/1914, *George Bent Letters*, Coe Collection, Yale. See also Grinnell, "Bent's Old Fort and Its Builders," 31.

23. James Mooney, *Miscellaneous notes on the Cheyenne, 1903–1906*, No. 2213, Cheyenne Folder, National Anthropological Archives, Smithsonian Institution. George Bent to George E. Hyde, 2/20/1914, 5/13/1914, 4/14/1906, *George Bent Letters*, Coe Collection, Yale.

24. Matthew C. Field, *Matt Field on the Santa Fe Trail*, ed. John E. Sunder (Norman and London: University of Oklahoma Press, 1995), 143–44.

25. Thomas J. Farnham, *Travels in the Great Western Prairie, the Anahuac and Rocky Mountains, and in the Oregon Territory [1839–40]*, 2 vols (London: Richard Bentley, 1843), in Reuben Gold Thwaites, ed., *Early Western Travels* (Cleveland: Arthur H. Clark Co., 1906), 28:171.

26. George Bent to George E. Hyde, [n.d.], 2/6/1905, *George Bent Letters*, Coe Collection, Yale; George Bent to George Bird Grinnell, 9/24/1912, Folder 56.2, *George Bird Grinnell Papers*, Southwest Museum. Hyde, *Life of George Bent*, 49–52. Grinnell and Father Peter John Powell place the date of the Cheyenne-Pawnee fight in 1830. See Powell, *People of Sacred Mountain: A History of the Northern Cheyenne Chiefs and Warrior Societies, 1830–1879, With an Epilogue, 1969–1974*, 2 vols. (San Francisco: Harper & Row, 1981), 1:3–15; Grinnell, *The Fighting Cheyennes* (Norman: University of Oklahoma Press, 1915), 72.

27. George Bent to Thoburn, undated questionnaire, *Joseph B. Thoburn Papers*, Oklahoma Historical Society. Father Peter John Powell renders the spelling *Vohpe-Nonoma'e*, which he translates literally as "Thunder Painted With White Clay." See Powell, *People of Sacred Mountain*, 1:622, n. 3.

28. *Tsistsistas* is the Cheyenne word for "Our People." The word *Cheyenne* comes from a Sioux word, *Sha-hi-ye-na*, meaning "Red Talkers," or those people of alien speech. See Grinnell, *The Cheyenne Indians: Their History and Ways of Life*, 2 vols. (Lincoln and London: University of Nebraska Press, 1972), 1:2.

29. Powell, *People of Sacred Mountain*, 1:4. See also Powell, *Sweet Medicine: The Continuing Role of the Sacred Arrows, the Sun Dance, and the Sacred Buffalo Hat in Northern Cheyenne History*, 2 vols. (Norman: University of Oklahoma Press, 1969), 1:43.

30. When up in the Powder River Country of Montana during the Patrick E. Connor 1865 campaign, George Bent recalled viewing Bear Butte or Sacred

Mountain for the first time. "We could see Pipe Mountain looming up plain southwest of us. 25 of us stood on knoll looking at Pipe Mountain. Bear Tail, the leader of our party, told us as he was older: 'My men this is the Medicine Mountain (Pipe Mountain) that Sweet Root Medicine Man brought the medicine Arrows from that the Cheyennes have now." George Bent to George E. Hyde, 12/20/1915, *George Bent Letters*, Coe Collection, Yale. Bent also called the mountain "Medicine Pipe Mountain." Bent to Hyde, 11/5/1913, ibid.; and Bent to Grinnell, 2/1/1907, Folder 41, *George Bird Grinnell Papers*, Southwest Museum.

31. Laird Cometsevah, a chief of the Council of Forty-four and president of the Southern Cheyenne Sand Creek Descendants, is speaker for the Arrow Keeper. He states that the arrow quiver is made from coyote skin. Interview, authors-Cometsevah, 4/14/1998. Bent says the quiver is of wolf skin. See George Bent to Grinnell, 2/[n.d.]/1907, Folder 41, *George Bird Grinnell Papers*, Southwest Museum. Powell says the quiver was of kit fox skin. See Powell, *People of Sacred Mountain*, 1:4. Powell also identifies the quiver as coyote skin. See *Sweet Medicine*, 2:464.

32. The story of Sweet Root and the Medicine Arrows can be followed in George Bent to George E. Hyde, [n.d.], 2/20/1905, 4/12/1906, 8/5/1911, 2/23/1912, 12/18/1913, 2/19/1914, 6/2/1914, 6/26/1914, 7/6/1914, *George Bent Letters*, Coe Collection, Yale; George Bent to Thoburn, [n.d.], *Joseph B. Thoburn Papers*, Oklahoma Historical Society; George Bent to Grinnell, 5/21/1906, 2/1/1907, Folder 41, Grinnell Fieldnotes #335 (11/4–5/1901), 157, 168, 140, Grinnell Fieldnotes, #351 (6/18/1912), 60, "Medicine Arrows," Folder 459, *George Bird Grinnell Papers*, Southwest Museum. See also Grinnell, *Cheyenne Indians*, 2:337ff.; Grinnell, *By Cheyenne Campfires* (New Haven, Conn.: Yale University Press, 1926), 263ff.; Karl N. Llewellyn and E. Adamson Hoebel, *The Cheyenne Way: Conflict and Case Law in Primitive Jurisprudence* (Norman: University of Oklahoma Press, 1952), 74ff.; John H. Moore, *The Cheyenne Nation: A Social and Demographic History* (Lincoln and London: University of Nebraska Press, 1987), 102–5, as well as his *The Cheyennes*, 216–27; Powell, *People of Sacred Mountain*, 2:3–6; Powell, *Sweet Medicine*, passim. Powell believes that Sweet Medicine received the arrows through *Maheo*, the Creator himself.

33. The origins of the Cheyennes can be followed in George Bent to Grinnell, 2/1/1907, Folder 41, and Bent to Grinnell, 10/4/1902, Folder 10, *George Bird Grinnell Papers*, Southwest Museum; Bent to Hyde, 4/25/1906, 12/20/1912, 11/7/1914, *George Bent Letters*, Coe Collection, Yale; Grinnell, *Cheyenne Indians*, 1:2–3. Hyde, *Life of George Bent*, 13–14; Moore, *The Cheyennes*, 146ff.; Moore, *Cheyenne Nation*, passim; E. Adamson Hoebel, *The Cheyennes: Indians of the Great Plains* (Fort Worth: Harcourt Brace Jovanovich, 1978), 4–11; Powell, *Sweet Medicine*, 18–30.

34. Moore, *The Cheyennes*, 13–29; Donald J. Berthrong, *The Southern Cheyennes* (Norman: University of Oklahoma Press, 1963), 3–26; Hyde, *Life of George Bent*, 3–30; Hoebel, *The Cheyennes*, 4–25; Powell, *People of Sacred Mountain*, 1:xvii.

Notes

35. Bent to Grinnell, 2/1/1907, Folder 41, and Grinnell Fieldbook #335 (11/5/1901), 168, *George Bird Grinnell Papers,* Southwest Museum; Bent to Hyde, 8/5/1911, *George Bent Letters,* Coe Collection, Yale; James Mooney, "Miscellaneous Notes on the Cheyennes, 1903–1906," Field notes #2213, Smithsonian Institution, Washington, D.C.; Elliott West, "Called Out People: The Cheyennes and the Central Plains," *The Magazine of Western History* 48 (Summer 1998): 2–15; Joseph Jablow, *The Cheyenne in Plains Indian Trade Relations 1795–1840* (New York: American Ethnological Society Monograph 19, 1951), *passim*; Moore, *The Cheyenne,* 70ff.; Moore, *Cheyenne Nation,* 127–204; Hoebel, *The Cheyennes,* 4–13 43–53; Hyde, *Life of George Bent,* 3–30; Donald J. Berthrong, *The Southern Cheyennes* (Norman: University of Oklahoma Press, 1963), 3–26; Grinnell, *Cheyenne Indians,* 1:1–46; Powell, *People of Sacred Mountain,* 1:3–10; Powell, *Sweet Medicine,* 1:3–30, and 2:859–60; Grinnell, *Fighting Cheyennes,* 3–11. See also Virginia Cole Trenholm, *The Arapahoes, Our People* (Norman: University of Oklahoma Press, 1970), 33ff.; Stanley Noyes, *Los Comanches: The Horse People, 1751–1845* (Albuquerque: University of New Mexico Press, 1993), 106; Mildred P. Mayhall, *The Kiowas* (Norman: University of Oklahoma Press, 1962), 4–17; James Mooney, *The Cheyenne Indians,* American Anthropological Association Memoirs, vol. 1, Part 6 (Lancaster, Pa.: The New Era Printing Company, 1907), *passim.*

36. Bent to Hyde, 2/6/1905, [n.d.], 2/20/1905, 4/10/1905, 6/2/1914, *George Bent Letters,* Coe Collection, Yale; Bent to Grinnell, 2/1/1907, Folder 41, *George Bird Grinnell Papers,* Southwest Museum; George Bent, "The Battle of the Medicine Arrows," *The Frontier* 4 (November 1905): 3–4; George A. Dorsey, "How the Pawnees Captured the Cheyenne Medicine Arrows," *American Anthropologist,* n.s. 5 (October–December 1903): 644–58; Powell, *People of Sacred Mountain,* 1:7–10; Powell, *Sweet Medicine,* 1:3–41; Hyde, *Life of George Bent,* 31–57; Grinnell, *Fighting Cheyennes,* 72–73; Moore, *The Cheyennes,* 133–34; Moore, *Cheyenne Nation,* 102–5; Berthrong, *Southern Cheyennes,* 58–59.

37. James Mooney, "Miscellaneous notes on the Cheyenne, 1903–1906," Fieldnotes #2213, National Anthropological Archives, Smithsonian Institution. It is clear from Mooney's 1903 interview with George Bent, herein cited, that White Thunder was *Suhtai.* Bent reported to Mooney that some Cheyennes objected to his selection as Arrow Keeper; indeed, that the Arrows were taken from him but later returned. Further, Bent said that White Thunder's wife, Tail Woman, was *Tsistsistas.* Thus, their children, including Bent's mother, Owl Woman, and his stepmother, Yellow Woman, were half Cheyenne, half *Suhtai.* In his many letters to Grinnell and Hyde, Bent demonstrates his sensitivity to the *Suhtai-Tsistsistas* division and rivalry. He married into a *Suhtai* family, for Black Kettle himself was *Suhtai,* and Bent's first wife, Magpie Woman, was Black Kettle's niece. Still, it is strange that nowhere else does Bent refer to White Thunder's *Suhtai* ancestry.

38. Moore, *The Cheyennes,* 216–17; Laird Cometsevah, interview with authors, 4/14/98.

39. Laird Cometsevah interview with authors, 4/14/1998.

40. Hyde, *Life of George Bent*, 51–52.

41. Powell, in *Sweet Medicine*, 1:38, gives the date as "about 1835." However, in *People of Sacred Mountain*, 1:13, he gives the date as summer 1835. Bent gives the date as 1835 in Hyde, *Life of George Bent*, 52. Hyde gives the date as winter 1833–34 in *Pawnee Indians* (Denver: J. Van Male, 1951), 139.

42. Powell identifies Old Bark as Bear Feather. See his *People of Sacred Mountain*, 1:13 and *Sweet Medicine*, 1:38. Powell identifies the village as on Republican River. See *People of Sacred Mountain*, 1:13. Hyde, *Life of George Bent*, 52, says it was on the Loup River. In his own letters Bent says the village was on the Platte River. See Bent to Hyde, 2/6/1905, 2/23/1912, *George Bent Letters*, Coe Collection, Yale.

43. Hyde, *Pawnee Indians*, 132–33. Powell says the Pawnee chief was Big Spotted Horse or Big Eagle. See *People of Sacred Mountain*, 1:13. Contemporary sources list both men as the Skidi chief. See Hyde, *Pawnee Indians*, 133.

44. Powell, *People of Sacred Mountain*, 1:13. Bent to Hyde, 2/6/1905, 12/18/1913, 2/23/1912, *George Bent Letters*, Coe Collection, Yale.

45. Powell, *People of Sacred Mountain*, 1:15.

46. "Military Affairs," American State Papers, vol. 6 (Washington, D.C.: Gales & Seaton, 1861), 141.

47. Ibid., 142–43.

48. Ibid., 143.

49. See American State Papers, vol. 4, 140. See Lavender, *Bent's Fort*, 186–89; Grinnell, *Cheyenne Indians*, 1:127–58. The special beauty of Cheyenne women is mentioned by almost every white observer who went among them.

50. John Gavin, ed., *Through the Country of The Comanche Indians in the Fall of the Year 1845: The Journal of a U.S. Army Expedition led by Lieutenant James W. Abert of the Topographical Engineers* (San Francisco: John Howell Books, 1970), 3.

51. Bent to Hyde, 6/27/1914, *George Bent Letters*, Coe Collection, Yale; Hyde, *Life of George Bent*, 68; Lavender, *Bent's Fort*, 188–89.

52. Grinnell, *Cheyenne Indians*, 1:137–45; Grinnell Fieldbook #341 (1905), *George Bird Grinnell Papers*, Southwest Museum; Mooney, "Miscellaneous Notes on the Cheyenne, 1903–06," Fieldbook #2213, National Anthropological Archives, Smithsonian; Sylvia Van Kirk, *Many Tender Ties: Women in Fur-Trade Society, 1670–1870* (Norman: University of Oklahoma Press, 1980), 28–52; Lavender, *Bent's Fort*, 185–89; Moore, *The Cheyenne*, 151–52, 238–39.

53. "Medicine Arrows," Folder 459, *George Bird Grinnell Papers*, Southwest Museum; George E. Hyde, *Life of George Bent, as Written from His Letters* (Norman: University of Oklahoma Press, 1968), 71–72; Bent to Cragin, 10/5/1905, F. W. *Cragin Collection*, Pioneer Museum, Colorado Springs.

54. George Bent to George Bird Grinnell, 5/21/1906, Folder #41, *Grinnell Papers*, Southwest Museum; Peter Powell, *Sweet Medicine: The Continuing Role*

of the Sacred Arrows, the Sun Dance, and the Sacred Buffalo Hat in Northern Cheyenne History, 2 vols. (Norman: University of Oklahoma Press, 1969), 1:43–45; Hyde, *Life of George Bent*, 72–73.

55. For the Bowstrings–White Thunder encounter and the annihilation of the Bowstrings, see Bent to Hyde, 6/[n.d.]/1914, 1/23/1905, 6/11/1914, *George Bent Letters*, Coe Collection, Yale; Bent to Grinnell, 10/23/1908, Folder 56.2, *George Bird Grinnell Papers*, Southwest Museum; Hyde, *Life of George Bent*, 72; Grinnell, *The Fighting Cheyennes* (Norman: University of Oklahoma Press, 1955), 45–46; Powell, *People of Sacred Mountain*, 1:38–41; Powell, *Sweet Medicine*, 1:44–45; Donald J. Berthrong, *The Southern Cheyennes* (Norman: University of Oklahoma Press, 1963), 81; Karl N. Llewellyn and E. Adamson Hoebel, *The Cheyenne Way: Conflict and Case Law in Primitive Jurisprudence* (Norman: University of Oklahoma Press, 1941), 146.

56. Bent to Hyde, 2/6/1905, *George Bent Letters*, Coe Collection, Yale; Powell, *Sweet Medicine*, 1:39.

57. George Bent states emphatically that Porcupine Bear was his uncle. White Thunder and Tail Woman had no sons. It seems logical to conclude that Porcupine Bear was the husband of one of the Arrow Keeper's daughters and, therefore, Bent's uncle. See Bent to Hyde, 6/2/1914, *George Bent Letters*, Coe Collection, Yale.

58. Powell, *Sweet Medicine*, 2:861–62; Powell, *People of Sacred Mountain*, 1:622; Bent to Hyde, 5/20/1905, *George Bent Letters*, Coe Collection, Yale.

59. Bent to Hyde, 6/2/1914, *George Bent Letters*, Coe Collection, Yale; Grinnell, *Fighting Cheyennes*, 49.

60. Bent to Hyde, 6/2/1914, 6/11/1914, *George Bent Letters*, Coe Collection, Yale; Hyde, *Life of George Bent*, 75–5; Grinnell, *Fighting Cheyennes*, 49.

61. Powell, *People of Sacred Mountain*, 1:46; Hyde, *Life of George Bent*, 75.

62. It is not entirely certain which tribes and bands participated in the move against the Kiowas. George Bird Grinnell believes that at least some northern Cheyennes came, bringing with them the Sacred Hat, *Esevone*. See Grinnell, *Fighting Cheyennes*, 57. However, George Bent in his detailed accounts to George Hyde makes no mention of the presence of the hat at Wolf Creek. See, for example, Bent to Hyde, 6/[n.d.]/1914, *George Bent Letters*, Coe Collection, Yale; and Hyde, *Life of George Bent*, 76–82.

63. Grinnell, *Fighting Cheyennes*, 52.

64. Grinnell, *Fighting Cheyennes*, 55; Hyde, *Life of George Bent*, 77; Bent to Hyde, 6/[n.d.]/1914, *George Bent Letters*, Coe Collection, Yale.

65. George Bent, himself a veteran of twenty-seven war parties, told Grinnell that war parties of seven almost always brought bad luck. Howling Wolf led the only successful war party of seven in 1850. For seven days, the Cheyennes tracked seven Pawnees who had stolen seven horses. Bent says this is the only time the Cheyennes had overcome the misfortune associated with the number 7. Grinnell Fieldbook, Folder 341 (November 10, 1905), *George Bird Grinnell Papers*, Southwest Museum.

66. Grinnell, *Fighting Cheyennes*, 56.

67. Ibid., 59.

68. Grinnell, *Cheyenne Indians*, 1:355–57; Berthrong, *Southern Cheyennes*, 82–83.

69. The battle of Wolf Creek can be followed most importantly in George Bent to Hyde, [n.d.], June [n.d.] 1914, 1/23/1905, 2/20/1905, 6/2/1914, 2/6/1905, 6/5/1909, 5/2/1914, 4/12/1906, 8/7/1914, 6/26/1914, 6/11/1914, *George Bent Letters*, Coe Collection, Yale. See also Grinnell, *Fighting Cheyennes*, 45–62; Hyde, *Life of George Bent*, 78–82; Powell, *People of Sacred Mountain*, 1:51–66; Berthrong, *Southern Cheyennes*, 82–83; Moore, *The Cheyennes*, 130, 134.

70. For the Carson–Bent connection, see Harvey Carter and M. Morgan Estergreen, *Kit Carson: A Portrait in Courage* (Norman: University of Oklahoma, 1962), 76–80; Lavender, *Bent's Fort*, 197.

71. Bent to Hyde, 6/[n.d.]/1914, *George Bent Letters*, Coe Collection, Yale; James Mooney, "Miscellaneous Notes on Cheyennes," 1903–1906, Fieldnote #2213, *Mooney Papers*, National Anthropological Archives, Smithsonian; Powell, *Sweet Medicine*, 2:860; Powell, *People of Sacred Mountain*, 1:65–66.

72. Grinnell, *Fighting Cheyennes*, 64.

73. Ibid., 65.

74. Ibid., 67.

75. Ibid., 65–67.

76. Ibid., 68–69.

77. Bent to Hyde, [n.d.], *George Bent Letters*, Coe Collection, Yale; Lavender, *Bent's Fort*, 201–3, Grinnell, *Fighting Cheyennes*, 67–69; James Hobbs, *Wild Life in the Far West; Personal Adventures of a Border Mountain Man*, 40–45.

78. For the peace negotiations and great celebration, see Bent to Hyde, 6/2/1914, 6/[n.d.]/1914, [n.d.], 2/19/1914, *George Bent Letters*, Coe Collection, Yale; Grinnell Fieldbook #335 (11/5/1901) and Fieldbook #351 (6/12/1912) *George Bird Grinnell Papers*, Southwest Museum; Hobbs, *Wild Life in the Far West*, 39–48; Grinnell, *Fighting Cheyennes*, 63–69; Lavender, *Bent's Fort*, 201–3; Powell, *People of Sacred Mountain*, 1:72–73; Berthrong, *Southern Cheyennes*, 82–84.

Chapter 2

1. See Bent to George E. Hyde, 2/26/1906, *George Bent Letters*, Coe Collection, Yale. Bent also gave July 7, 1842, as his date of birth. See James Mooney, "Miscellaneous Notes on Cheyennes, 1903–1906," Fieldnote #2213, National Anthropological Archives, Smithsonian Institution. Bent's grave monument in the Indian cemetery at Colony, Oklahoma, however, gives July 7, 1843, as his date of birth.

2. William married Island and Yellow Woman before Owl Woman died in 1847, but George was vague on this subject and may have tried to mask the fact

that his father had entered into a plural marriage. Charley must have been much closer in age to his brother than George allowed in his letters to historians and anthropologists. For the birth of the Bent children, see Bent family genealogical chart, F. W. *Cragin Papers*, Pioneer Museum, Colorado Springs; Bent to George E. Hyde, 2/26/1906, 3/9/1905, *George Bent Letters*, Coe Collection, Yale; Bent to Hyde, 10/17/1913, *George E. Hyde Papers*, Western History Collections of Denver Public Library; Bent to George Bird Grinnell, 1/23/1912, Folder 56.2, and "Bent's Fort," Folder 32.2, *Grinnell Papers*, Southwest Museum; Bent to Thoburn, 11/2/1910, *Joseph B. Thoburn Papers*, Oklahoma Historical Society; George Bird Grinnell, *Beyond the Old Frontier: Adventures of Indian-Fighters, Hunters, and Fur-Traders* (New York: Charles Scribner's Sons, 1913), 130; Grinnell, "Bent's Old Fort and Its Builders," *Kansas Historical Collections* 15 (1919–22): 20; LeRoy R. Hafen, ed., "The W. M. Boggs Manuscript About Bent's Fort, Kit Carson, the Far West and Life Among the Indians," *Colorado Magazine* 7 (March 1930):48; H. L. Lubers, "William Bent's Family and the Indians of the Plains," 13 *Colorado Magazine* (January 1936): 19; Quantrille D. McClung, comp., *Carson-Bent-Boggs Genealogy: Line of William Carson, Ancestor of "Kit Carson" Famous Scout and Pioneer of the Rocky Mountain Area with the Western Branches of the Bent and Boggs Families with Whom "Kit" was Associated and the Line of Samuel Carson Supposed to be a Brother of William Carson* (Denver: Denver Public Library, 1962), 100–1; David Fridtjof Halaas, "'All the Camp was Weeping': George Bent & the Sand Creek Massacre," *Colorado Heritage* (Summer 1995): 2–3; Jean Afton, David Fridtjof Halaas, and Andrew E. Masich, *Cheyenne Dog Soldiers: A Ledgerbook History of Coups and Combat* (Niwot and Denver: University Press of Colorado and Colorado Historical Society, 1997), 98–101; David Fridtjof Halaas and Andrew E. Masich, "'You Could Hear the Drums for Miles": A Cheyenne Ledgerbook History," *Colorado Heritage* (Autumn 1996): 36; David Lavender, *Bent's Fort* (Garden City, N.Y.: Doubleday & Company, Inc., 1954), 323; George E. Hyde, *Life of George Bent, Written from His Letters* (Norman: University of Oklahoma Press, 1968), passim.

3. See John H. Moore, *The Cheyenne* (Cambridge, Mass.: Blackwell Publishers, 1996), 42. See also Andrew E. Masich, "Cheyennes and Horses: A Transportation Revolution on the Great Plains," *History News* 52 (Autumn 1997): 10–13.

4. See Masich, "Cheyennes and Horses," 10–13. See also Frank Gilbert Roe, *The Indian and the Horse* (Norman: University of Oklahoma Press, 1955), passim; Robert West Howard, *The Horse in America* (Chicago and New York: Follett Publishing Company, 1965); Richard E. Ahlborn, ed., *Man Made Mobile: Early Saddles of Western North America* (Washington, D.C.: Smithsonian Institution Press, 1980); Clark Wissler, *North American Indians of the Plains*, American Museum of Natural History Handbook Series No. 1 (New York: American Museum of Natural History, 1927), passim; John Ewers, *The Horse in Blackfoot Indian Culture; With Comparative Material from Other Western Tribes*, Bureau

of American Ethnology Bulletin 159 (Washington, D.C.: Government Printing Office, 1955): 68, 78–79, 130–31.

5. Bent to Hyde, 2/19/1913, *George Bent Letters*, Coe Collection, Yale; Hyde, *Life of George Bent*, 84; Grinnell, *Beyond the Old Frontier*, 182–83; and Grinnell, "Bent's Old Fort and Its Builders," 33. See also Masich, "Cheyennes and Horses," 12–13.

6. Lewis H. Garrard, *Wah-to-Yah & the Taos Trail*, With an Introduction by Carl I. Wheat, and Illustrations by Mallette Dean (Palo Alto, Calif.: American West Publishing Company, 1968), 52.

7. See Bent to Hyde, 10/17/1913, *George Bent Papers*, Western History Department, Denver Public Library; Hyde, *Life of George Bent*, 84; Lavender, *Bent's Fort*, 323.

8. Grinnell, *Cheyenne Indians*, 1:102–26; Hyde, *Life of George Bent*, 84.

9. Hafen, "W. M. Boggs Manuscript About Bent's Fort," 48.

10. Garrard, *Wah-to-Yah*, 41, 105.

11. John Galvin, ed., *Through the Country of the Comanche Indians in the Fall of the Year 1845: The Journal of a U.S. Army Expedition Led by Lieutenant James W. Abert of the Topographical Engineers, Artist Extraordinary whose Paintings of Indians and Their Wild West Illustrate This Book* (San Francisco: John Howell-Books, 1970), 3; Grinnell, *Cheyenne Indians*, 1:109, 131.

12. "To Go in Suhtai," Folder 5, *Grinnell Papers*, Southwest Museum; Hyde, *Life of George Bent*, 4, 14. See also Grinnell, *Cheyenne Indians*, 1:48–49, 87, 113–14, 247, 308–10.

13. Herman J. Viola, *Warrior Artists: Historic Cheyenne and Kiowa Indian Ledger Art, Drawn by Making Medicine and Zotom* (Washington, D.C.: National Geographic Society, 1998), 30–31.

14. Bent to Grinnell, 11/1/1917, 12/5/1917, Folder 56.2, *George Bird Grinnell Papers*, Southwest Museum; Bent to Hyde, 10/12/1917, *George Bent Letters*, Coe Collection, Yale. For Cheyenne fondness for gambling and games, see Grinnell, *Cheyenne Indians*, 1:326–28, 2:215.

15. Hafen, "W. M. Boggs Manuscript About Bent's Fort," 68–69. See also "Historic Bent's Fort and Its Founders," *Denver Post*, January 11, 1920, and "William Bent's Life Saved by 'Lawyer' A Cheyenne Doctor," *Denver Post*, January 25, 1920. The Cheyenne doctor One Eye was also known as Lawyer. See Bent to Hyde, 10/12/1917, *George Bent Letters*, Coe Collection, Yale.

16. Bent to Hyde, 10/12/1917, *George Bent Letters*, Coe Collection, Yale; Budd Boggs to Dr. J. O. Boggs, 4/21/1857, *Boggs Papers*, Missouri Historical Society; Bent to Grinnell, 12/13/1912, Folder 56.2, *George Bird Grinnell Papers*, Southwest Museum.

17. Stella M. Drumm, ed., *Down the Santa Fe Trail and Into Mexico: Diary of Susan Shelby Magoffin, 1846–1847* (New Haven and London: Yale University Press, 1962), 60–61; Grinnell, *Beyond the Old Frontier*, 187; Lavender, *Bent's Fort*, 177.

18. Grinnell, *Beyond the Old Frontier*, 186–87.

19. Ibid.

20. Grinnell, *Beyond the Old Frontier*, 137, 184–85; Grinnell, "Bent's Old Fort and Its Builders," 34. Andrew Green, "Black Whiteman," was William's cook; Dick, known to the Cheyennes as "Turtle Shell," was the servant of Charles Bent. For the Green brothers, see Grinnell Fieldbook #351 (6/7/1912), 21–25, *George Bird Grinnell Papers*, Southwest Museum; Bent to Hyde, 3/19/1906, *George Bent Letters*, Coe Collection, Yale.

21. Grinnell, *Beyond the Old Frontier*, 185.

22. Ibid.

23. Galvin, *Through the Country of the Comanche Indians*, 2.

24. Bent to Hyde, 3/10/1916, *George Bent Letters*, Coe Collection, Yale; Bent to Grinnell, 7/12/1905, Folder 10, and [n.d.], Folder 41, *Grinnell Papers*, Southwest Museum; Galvin, *Through the Country of the Comanche Indians*, 2.

25. Grinnell, *Beyond the Old Frontier*, 171.

26. George Frederick Ruxton, *Life in the Far West*, LeRoy R. Hafen ed., with Introduction by Mae Reed Porter (Norman: University of Oklahoma Press, 1951), 181.

27. See Hyde, *Life of George Bent*, 85; Ruxton, *Life in the Far West*, 179–181; Grinnell, *Beyond the Old Frontier*, 161.

28. Drumm, *Down the Santa Fe Trail and Into Mexico*, 67.

29. See Bent to Hyde, 2/26/1906, *George Bent Letters*, Coe Collection, Yale; Hyde, *Life of George Bent*, 85–6.

30. Lavender, *Bent's Fort*, 284–87; Harold H. Dunham, "Charles Bent," in Hafen, ed., *The Mountain Men and the Fur Trade of the Far West*, 10 vols. (Glendale, Calif.: Arthur H. Clark Co., 1965–72) 2:47–48; Hyde, *Life of George Bent*, 85–7; James Hobbs, *Wild Life in the Far West: Personal Adventures of a Border Mountain Man* (Hartford, Conn.: Wiley, Waterman & Eaton, 1873), 137–41; LeRoy R. Hafen, ed., *Ruxton of the Rockies* (Norman: University of Oklahoma Press, 1950), 191–92.

31. *Denver Post*, February 1, 1920; Lavender, *Bent's Fort*, 301–3.

32. Bent to Hyde, 2/19/1913, *George Bent Letters*, Coe Collection, Yale; Bent to Grinnell, 10/20/1902, Folder 10, *Grinnell Papers*, Southwest Museum. See also Hafen, "W. M. Boggs Manuscript About Bent's Fort," 59–60; Lavender, *Bent's Fort*, 298–99, 310.

33. Garrard, *Wah-to-Yah*, 113.

34. Bent to Grinnell, 10/15/1913, Folder 56.2, *George Bird Grinnell Papers*, Southwest Museum.

35. Garrard, *Wah-to-Yah*, 164–91; Lavender, *Bent's Fort*, 304–18.

36. *Missouri Republican*, 12/23/1847; Bent to Hyde, 9/3/1913, 9/12/1913, *George Bent Letters*, Coe Collection, Yale; James Mooney, "Miscellaneous Notes on Cheyennes, 1903–6," Fieldnotes #2213, National Anthropological Archives, Smithsonian Institution; Grinnell, *Cheyenne Indians*, 2:104; Lavender, *Bent's Fort*, 325–26; and Grinnell, "Bent's Old Fort and Its Builders," 31.

Notes

37. George Bird Grinnell fieldnotes, Folder #351, 6/7/1912, 21–25, *Grinnell Papers*, Southwest Museum. For Cheyenne burial practices, see Grinnell, *Cheyenne Indians*, 2:160–64.

38. Grinnell, *Cheyenne Indians*, 2:380.

39. Photographs of William reveal the scars. See also Grinnell, *Beyond the Old Frontier*, 132; and Lavender, *Bent's Fort*, 148.

40. Bent to Hyde, 3/16/1915, 3/29/1917, *George Bent Letters*, Coe Collection, Yale.

41. Grinnell, *Cheyenne Indians*, 2:164–65; Bent to Hyde, 3/16/1915, 10/17/1916, *George Bent Letters*, Coe Collection, Yale.

42. Hyde, *Life of George Bent*, n. 97; Bent to Hyde, 4/3/1915, 10/6/1916, 1/23/1905, 9/15/1914, 2/10/1915, 10/26/1916, 3/29/1917, 3/16/1915, 3/30/1915, 10/17/1916, *George Bent Letters*, Coe Collection, Yale; Grinnell "Bent's Old Fort and Its Builders," 47.

43. Now Kiowa Creek, a tributary of the South Platte River. This site is just east of present Denver.

44. George Bent to George E. Hyde, [n.d.], 4/13/1914, and 2/15/1912, *George Bent Letters*, Coe Collection, Yale. See also, George Bird Grinnell, *The Fighting Cheyennes* (Norman: University of Oklahoma Press, 1956), 43–44; George E. Hyde, *Life of George Bent Written From His Letters*, Savoie Lottinville, ed., (Norman: University of Oklahoma Press, 1968), 55–56; and Donald J. Berthrong, *The Southern Cheyennes* (Norman: University of Oklahoma Press, 1963), 81–82.

45. George Bent to F. W. Cragin, 10/5/1905, *Cragin Papers*, Pioneer Museum, Colorado Springs.

46. Bent to Hyde, 5/8/1918, 6/2/1917, 4/10/1905, *George Bent Letters*, Coe Collection, Yale; Lewis Garrard, *Wah-to-Yah & the Taos Trail*, introduction by Carl I. Wheat (Palo Alto, Calif.: American West Publishing Company, 1968), 6–7.

47. Lavender, *Bent's Fort,* 333. Red eventually gave up on Marcellin and married a white man named Bill Bransford. She converted to Catholicism and bore Bransford seven children. Red died in Trinidad, Colorado, in 1885.

48. Bent to Hyde, 7/29/1914, *George Bent Letters*, Coe Collection, Yale.

49. See LeRoy R. Hafen, *Broken Hand: The Life of Thomas Fitzpatrick: Mountain Man, Guide and Indian Agent* (Denver: Old West Publishing Company, 1973, rev. ed.), 241.

50. Lavender, *Bent's Fort*, 321.

51. Hiram Martin Chittenden and Alfred Talbot Richardson, *Life, Letters and Travels of Father Pierre-Jean De Smet, S.J., 1841–1873*, 4 vols. (New York: Francis P. Harper, 1905), 2:677.

52. Ibid., 679. George Bird Grinnell, *The Cheyenne Indians: Their History and Ways of Life*, 2 vols. (Lincoln and London: University of Nebraska Press, 1972), 1:105–7, 2:276–77.

53. Grinnell, *Cheyenne Indians*, 1:61–2, 105–7. Photographs of the Bent family and the letters of George Bent indicate that the Bent children never participated

in the ear piercing ceremony. Moreover, in a Cheyenne ledgerbook at the Colorado Historical Society, one of the drawings depicts George Bent riding with the Dog Soldiers in 1865. In the drawing, details of dress and adornment are clearly visible. But Bent does not display eardrops, commonly seen on the other warriors depicted in the book. See Jean Afton, David Fridtjof Halaas, and Andrew E. Masich, *Cheyenne Dog Soldiers: A Ledgerbook History of Coups and Combat* (Niwot and Denver: University Press of Colorado and Colorado Historical Society, 1997), 98–100.

54. Bent to Hyde, 7/29/1914, *George Bent Letters*, Coe Collection, Yale.

55. John Dunbar visited the fort just before its final abandonment in 1852. He remembered that the "bastions were then looking pretty old, much adobe washed down at the base of them and timbers of cedar bare in places." F. W. Cragin to George Bent, 9/30/1905, *Cragin Papers*, Pioneer Museum, Colorado Springs.

56. Bent to Hyde, 2/19/1913, *George Bent Letters*, Coe Collection, Yale. A. E. Reynolds, a trader at Fort Lyon, and many others reported that the fort still stood in the 1860s when it was a stage stop. These travelers saw no evidence of an explosion, although they mentioned that the walls were weathered and in disrepair. See *Denver Post*, February 8, 1920. In any case, the black smoke, which George Bent reported seeing, could not have been caused by black powder, which produces clouds of white smoke. See also F. W. Cragin to George Bent, 9/39/1905, *F. W. Cragin Papers*, Pioneer Museum, Colorado Springs. According to George Bent, in 1852 the government offered his father twelve thousand dollars for the fort, a price William thought insulting. See Bent to Hyde, 2/26/1906, 6/2/1917, 3/19/1906, 6/29/1914, 8/18/1814, *George Bent Letters*, Coe Collection, Yale. However, George E. Hyde researched H. H. Bancroft's notes and found a scrap indicating that Agent Calhoun in Santa Fe was told by Ceran St. Vrain that one of the partners had removed the goods from Bent's Fort "on the Arkansas and burned the place—that this action was taken because of Indian hostility. I suppose this was a Mexican rumor, but I've asked [George] Bent about it." The rumor of a fort's burning may not have referenced Bent's Arkansas River establishment, but rather Fort Adobe on the Canadian, which Bent blew up with gunpowder in the spring of 1849. See Hyde to Grinnell, 4/6/1917, Folder 51C, *George Bird Grinnell Papers*, Southwest Museum; and Lavender, *Bent's Fort*, 332.

57. Bent to Hyde, 6/2/1917, *George Bent Letters*, Coe Collection, Yale; Donald Jackson and Mary Lee Spence, eds., *The Expeditions of John Charles Fremont* (Urbana: University of Illinois Press, 1970), 3:419.

58. Bent to Hyde, 6/2/1917, *George Bent Letters*, Coe Collection, Yale.

59. Bent to Hyde, 2/19/1913, *George Bent Letters*, Coe Collection, Yale. For the traders, see Grinnell, *Beyond the Old Frontier*, 179–80, and Grinnell, "Bent's Fort and Its Builders," 56–57, 65; Lavender, *Bent's Fort*, passim.

60. Bent to Hyde, 2/19/1913, *George Bent Letters*, Coe Collection, Yale.

61. Bent family genealogical chart, F. W. *Cragin Papers*, Pioneer Museum, Colorado Springs. See also Lincoln B. Faller, "Making Medicine against 'White Man's

Side of Story': George Bent's Letters to George Hyde, " *American Indian Quarterly* 24 (Winter 2000): 65–66.

62. James Larkin, 10/13/1856, *Memorandum Book, 1856*, Bent's Old Fort National Historic Site.

63. Mark J. Stegmaier and David H. Miller, eds., *James F. Milligan: His Journal of Fremont's Fifth Expedition, 1853–1854: His Adventurous Life on Land and Sea* (Glendale, Calif.: The Arthur H. Clark Company, 1988), 139–68.

64. Ibid., 145.

65. William contracted gonorrhea at this time. See "Dr. John W. Parker's Professional Services to William Bent and Family in Westport, 1856–1862," vertical file, Missouri Valley Room, Kansas City, Missouri Public Library.

66. Grinnell, "Bent's Old Fort and Its Builders," 84–85.

67. Ibid., 167–68.

68. Stegmaier and Miller, *James F. Milligan*, 168; Bent to Hyde, 6/29/1914, *George Bent Letters*, Coe Collection, Yale.

69. Stegmaier and Miller, *James F. Milligan*, 172.

70. Bent to Hyde, 5/8/1918, *George Bent Letters*, Coe Collection, Yale.

71. Ibid., 181.

Chapter 3

1. George Bent to George E. Hyde, 5/8/1918, *George Bent Letters*, Coe Collection, Yale.

2. George Bent to George E. Hyde, 3/19/1906, *George Bent Letters*, Coe Collection, Yale.

3. See George A. Root, "William Darnell," *Collections of the Kansas State Historical Society, 1926–28*, 17:509; Percival G. Lowe, *Five Years a Dragoon ('49 to '54), and Other Adventures on the Great Plains*, Introduction and notes by Don Russell (1906; reprint, Norman: University of Oklahoma Press, 1965), 301; George Bird Grinnell, *Beyond the Old Frontier: Adventures of Indian-Fighters, Hunters, and Fur-Traders* (New York: Charles Scribner's Sons, 1913), 172–76.

4. Grinnell, *Beyond the Old Frontier*, 175–76.

5. George Bird Grinnell, "Bent's Old Fort and Its Builders," *Collections of the Kansas State Historical Society, 1919–22*, 15:58–59.

6. Bent to Hyde, 9/1/1917, *George Bent Letters*, Coe Collection, Yale.

7. Bound volume 2, x, p. 21, and Bound volume 4, xx, pp. 1–6, 11, 22–23, F. W. *Cragin Papers*, Western History Department, Denver Public Library.

8. L. S. Bolling to A. G. Brown, 3/12/1860, *Colorado Appointment Papers*, Record Group 48, National Archives Record Administration, Washington, D.C.

9. William R. Bernard, "Westport and the Santa Fe Trade," *Collections of the Kansas State Historical Society, 1905–06*, 9: 557–58, 564–65. See also George Bent to George E. Hyde, 5/13/1912, *George Bent Letters*, Coe Collection, Yale.

10. William R. Bernard, "Westport and the Santa Fe Trade," 9: 557–58. See also *History of Jackson County, Missouri, Containing A History of the County, Its Cities, Towns, Etc.* (Kansas City, Mo.: Union Historical Company, 1881), 350–52.

11. George Bent to George Bird Grinnell, 10/12/1913, Folder 56.2, *George Bird Grinnell Papers*, Southwest Museum.

12. *William Bent Vertical File*, Missouri Valley Room, Kansas City Public Library, Kansas City, Missouri; Mrs. Sam Ray, "Sunset Hill House Link to Fur Trade Days," *Kansas City Times* [Missouri], July 30, 1965.

13. Donald J. Berthrong, *The Southern Cheyennes* (Norman: University of Oklahoma Press, 1963), 154.

14. "Dr John W. Parker's Professional Services to William Bent and Family in Westport," *Seth Ward Vertical File*, Missouri Valley Room, Kansas City Public Library, Kansas City, Missouri.

15. Rodney Staab, "The Mission's Cross-Town Rival, The (First) Westport High School, 1853-Circa 1862," New Views of Shawnee Mission, No. 18 in *Friends Newsletter* (Fairway, Kans.: Shawnee Indian Mission, 1998). Information on the academy appears also in *Border Star* [Westport, Missouri], August 25, 1860; Reverend Nathan Scarritt, "Reminiscences of the Methodist Shawnee Mission: And Religious Work Among that Tribe," *Annals of Kansas City* (1924): 434; Col. Milton Moore, "An Incident on the Upper Arkansas in 1864," *Collections of the Kansas State Historical Society, 1907–1908*, 10:417; Rev. J. J. Lutz, "The Methodist Missions among the Indian Tribes in Kansas," *Collections of the Kansas State Historical Society, 1905–1906*, 9:180–81; Stephen C. Ragan, "Notes on the Pioneer School of Kansas City," 1 *Annals of Kansas City* (December 1922): 169–70.

16. J. J. Lutz, "The Methodist Missions among the Indian Tribes in Kansas," 9:181.

17. Nellie McCoy, "Memories of Old Westport," *Annals of Kansas City* (October 1924).

18. For descriptions of Bent's New Fort see *O. A. Nixon Journals*, Miscellaneous Collections, Kansas State Historical Society, Topeka, Kansas; Robert Morris Peck, "Early Times in Kansas Territory," *Collections of the Kansas State Historical Society, 1903–1904*, 8:491; "J. E. B. Stuart's Journal, 1860," in LeRoy R. Hafen, ed., *Relations with the Indians of the Plains, 1857–61: A Documentary Account of the Military Campaigns, and Negotiations of Indian Agents—with Reports and Journals of P. G. Lowe, R. M. Peck, J. E. B. Stuart, S. D. Sturgis, and Other Official Papers* (Glendale, Calif.: Arthur H. Clark Co., 1959), 231–32; Mark J. Stegmaier and David H. Miller, *James F. Milligan: His Journal of Fremont's Fifth Expedition, 1853–1854: His Adventurous Life on Land and Sea* (Glendale, Calif.: Arthur H. Clark Co., 1988), 164; Grinnell, "Bent's Old Fort and Its Builders," 15:84–85; David Lavender, *Bent's Fort* (New York: Doubleday &

Company, Inc., 1954), 324, 415. See also Bent to Hyde, 4/10/1905, 2/26/1906, 3/19/1906, 11/3/1910, 8/18/1914, *George Bent Letters*, Coe Collection, Yale.

19. *O. A. Nixon Journal*, August 5, 1855, 10.

20. Ibid, July 14, 1855, 10.

21. "Private Journal of Robert Campbell," *Bulletin of the Missouri Historical Society* 20 (October 1963–July 1964): 3; Stephen F. Huss to authors, 2/17/98, original in authors' possession.

22. Bent to Hyde, 9/1/1917, 4/25/1918, *George Bent Letters*, Coe Collection, Yale.

23. *Daily Missouri Democrat* [St. Louis], 1/26/1857. Although a slave state, Missouri possessed a large French population noted for its tradition of slave emancipation. Campbell's act was not unheard of in St. Louis but still would have been newsworthy. There is a further point: Eliza's children may have been his own.

24. U.S. Census Bureau, 1860; Perry McCandless, *A History of Missouri, Vol. 2, 1820–1860* (Columbia: University of Missouri Press, 1972), 39–58; William B. Faherty, *The Saint Louis Portrait* (Tulsa, Ok.: Continental Heritage, Inc., 1978), 51; Clement Eaton, *The Growth of Southern Civilization, 1790–1860* (New York: Harper & Row, 1961), 249–50.

25. Bud Boggs to Dr. J. O. Boggs, 4/21/1857, *Boggs Family Papers*, Missouri Historical Society, St. Louis. See also Bent to Grinnell, 12/13/1917, Folder 56.2, *George Bird Grinnell Papers*, Southwest Museum.

26. "The Brothers of the Christian Schools in the Mid-West, 1849–1949," in *Mississippi Vista* (Winona, Minn.: Saint Mary's College Press, 1948), 101–5. Stephen Huss personal communication to authors, 2/19/1998, copy in possession of the authors. See also *C&A Patents*, Indian Archives, Oklahoma Historical Society; Nelson A. Miles, *Personal Recollections and Observations of General Nelson A. Miles, Embracing a Brief View of the Civil War; Or, From New England to the Golden Gate, and the Story of His Indian Campaigns, with Comments on the Exploration, Development and Progress of Our Great Western Empire*, 2 vols., Introduction by Robert Wooster (1896; reprint, Lincoln and London: University of Nebraska Press, Bison Book Edition, 1992), 1:140.

27. *Missouri Presbyterian Recorder*, 1 (September 1855): 146–49. Joseph K. Bent fathered a son named George, who was two years older than William's son George. This George Bent was listed as a nineteen-year-old farmer in the 1860 U.S. Census. He was credited with ten thousand dollars in real estate, and possessed at least four personal servants. See U.S. Census Bureau, Population for Saint Louis County, Missouri, 1860. His father, Joseph, also of Saint Louis County, was listed in the 1850 U.S. Census as a thirty-four-year-old carpenter, born in Massachusetts. His worth was assessed at forty-five hundred dollars. See U.S. Census Bureau, Population for Saint Louis County, Missouri, 1850. George, son of Joseph, causes confusion for historians attempting to track the William Bent family, for this George attempted to join Major General Sterling Price's Confederate division in 1861 but was intercepted by Union patrols and forced to sign an oath

of allegiance to the United States. See *Miscellaneous Unfiled Papers and Slips Belonging in Confederate Compiled Service Records—George Bent*, Record Group 109, Microcopy M347, National Archives Record Administration, Washington, D.C.; and *Union Provost Marshal's File, One Name Papers Re Citizens—Charles Lewis*, Record Group 109, M345, National Archives Record Administration, Washington, D.C.

28. *Catalogue of the Officers and Students of Webster College Family Boarding School for Boys, for the Annual Session, 1858-9* (St. Louis: Webster College, 1859), passim. See also *Missouri Presbyterian Recorder* 1 (September 1855): 146–49; and Webster Groves, "Webster College for Boys," *Mrs. Charles Hiram Wood Papers*, Missouri Historical Society, St. Louis.

29. "Webster College for Boys," *Mrs. Charles Hiram Wood Papers*, Missouri Historical Society, St. Louis.

30. H. L. Lubers, "William Bent's Family and the Indians of the Plains," *The Colorado Magazine* 13 (January 1936): 19–21; F. W. Cragin, "Early Far West Notebooks," VI, 11, Western History Department, Denver Public Library; Camille N. Dry and Richard J. Compton, *Pictorial St. Louis* (1875), 94; Theodore R. Davis, "A Summer on the Plains," *Harper's New Monthly Magazine* 36 (February 1868): 305–6; Robert Morris Peck to Grinnell, 6/5/1908, "Peck Correspondence," Folder 50.1, *George Bird Grinnell Papers*, Southwest Museum; Henry M. Stanley, *My Early Travels and Adventures in America*, Foreword by Dee Brown (1895; reprint, Lincoln & London: University of Nebraska Press, 1982), 161; Thoburn to Standing Out Bent [Mrs. George Bent], 11/5/1930, George Bent to Thoburn, 11/2/1910, Bent to Thoburn, 9/29/1910, *Joseph Thoburn Papers*, Indian Archives, Oklahoma Historical Society; *C&A Patents*, Indian Archives, Oklahoma Historical Society; "Miscellaneous Notes on Cheyennes, 1903–1906," *James Mooney Papers*, Smithsonian National Anthropological Archives. See also Bent to Hyde, 4/25/1918, 5/8/1918, 12/5/1913, 5/29/1906, 9/1/1917, 2/26/1906, *George Bent Letters*, Coe Collection, Yale; *Denver Post*, 1/11/1920 and 1/18/1920; Lavender, *Bent's Fort*, 325, 335; *Catalogue of the Officers and Students of Webster College Family Boarding School for Boys for the Annual Session, 1858–59* (St. Louis, 1859), 6–7, Missouri Historical Society, St. Louis; Allen H. Bent, *The Bent Family in America, Being Mainly a Genealogy of the Descendants of John Bent* (Boston: David Clapp & Son, 1900), 124.

31. Allen H. Bent, *The Bent Family in America*, 126.

32. At the time of the census, George was listed as a fifteen-year-old male Indian; Robert [*sic*] M. Moore was identified as an Ohio-born farmer worth one thousand dollars; and Mary A. Moore was listed a twenty-three-year-old female Indian. See U.S. Census Bureau Population for Jackson County, Missouri, 1860. See also Lavender, *Bent's Fort*, 344. "Early Far West Notebooks," Notebook 20, 1–5, 39, *Francis W. Cragin Papers*, Western History Collections, Denver Public Library.

33. L. S. Bolling to A. G. Brown, 3/12/1860, *Colorado Appointment Papers*, Record Group 48, Roll 13, M808, National Archives Record Administration,

Notes

Washington, D.C.; William W. Bent to Jacob Thompson (Sec. of Int.), 9/19/1860, *Colorado Appointment Papers*, Record Group 48, Roll 13, M808, National Archives Record Administration, Washington, D.C.; William R. Bernard, "Westport and the Santa Fe Trade," 9:565; Lavender, *Bent's Fort*, 340.

34. As quoted in Jay Monaghan, *Civil War on the Western Border, 1854–1854* (Lincoln and London: University of Nebraska Press, 1955), 129.

35. Bent to Hyde, 2/26/1906, 3/9/1905, *George Bent Letters*, Coe Collection, Yale; Bent to Thoburn, 3/17/1915, 11/2/1910, Thoburn to Standing Out Bent [Mrs. George Bent], 11/5/1930, George E. Hyde to Thoburn, 11/15/1930, *Joseph B. Thoburn Papers*, Indian Archives, Oklahoma Historical Society; "Bent's Fort," Folder 32.2, 16–17, *George Bird Grinnell Papers*, Southwest Museum; William R. Bernard, "Westport and the Santa Fe Trade," 9:54; "Miscellaneous Notes on Cheyennes, 1903–06," *James Mooney Papers*, National Anthropological Archives, Smithsonian Institution; George E. Hyde, *Life of George Bent Written from His Letters*, Savoie Lottinville, ed. (Norman: University of Oklahoma Press, 1968), 110–11. For weapons and organization, see Richard C. Peterson et al., *Sterling Price's Lieutenants: A Guide to the Officers and Organization of the Missouri State Guard, 1861–1865* (Shawnee Mission Kansas: Two Trails Publishing, 1995), 7.

36. Peterson, et al., *Sterling Price's Lieutenants*, 26; Jean Afton, David Fridtjof Halaas, and Andrew E. Masich, *Cheyenne Dog Soldiers: A Ledgerbook History of Coups and Combat* (Niwot and Denver: University Press of Colorado and the Colorado Historical Society, 1997), 44–45; Philip St. George Cooke, *Cavalry Tactics, or Regulations for the Instruction, Formations, and Movements of the Cavalry of the Army and Volunteers of the United States.* Prepared under the Direction of . . . the Secretary of War (Philadelphia: J. B. Lippincott & Co., 1862), passim.

37. Cooke, *Cavalry Tactics*.

38. Jay Monaghan, *Civil War on the Western Border, 1854–1865* (1955; reprint, Lincoln and London: University of Nebraska Press, Bison Book Edition, 1984), 170–81; Peterson et al., *Sterling Price's Lieutenants*, 7–8; William Garrett Piston and Richard W. Hatcher III, *Wilson's Creek: The Second Battle of the Civil War and the Men Who Fought It* (Chapel Hill: University of North Carolina Press, 2000).

39. George E. Hyde to Thoburn, 11/15/1930, *Joseph B. Thoburn Papers*, Indian Archives, Oklahoma Historical Society; Ephraim McD. Anderson, *Memoirs: Historical and Personal; including the Campaigns of the First Missouri Confederate Brigade* (St. Louis: Times Printing Co., 1868), 200–2; "Missouri Troops in the Civil War," *57th Congress, Senate Document No. 412*, 282, National Archives Records Administration, XXXXXXX; John F. Walter, *Capsule Histories of Missouri Units*, 4 vols. (Middle Village, N.Y.: Privately printed, n.d.), 1:passim; Janet B. Hewett, ed., *Supplement to the Official Records of the Union and Confederate Armies, Part II—Record of Events*, (Wilmington, N.C.: Broadfoot Publishing Company, 1996), 38:passim; Janet B. Hewett, ed., *Roster of Confederate*

Soldiers, 1861–1865 (Wilmington, N.C.: Broadfoot Publishing Company, 1995), 1:passim. See also Phillip Thomas Tucker, *The South's Finest: The First Missouri Confederate Brigade from Pea Ridge to Vicksburg* (Skippensburg, Pa.: White Mane Publishing Company, Inc., 1993); Joseph H. Crute, Jr., *Units of the Confederate States Army* (Midlothian, Va.: Derwent Books, 1987); Stewart Sifakis, *Compendium of the Confederate Armies: Kentucky, Maryland, Missouri, the Confederate Units and the Indian Units* (New York: Facts on File, 1995); Phil Gottschalk, *In Deadly Earnest: The Missouri Brigade* (Columbia: Missouri River Press, 1991); William L. Shea and Earl J. Hess, *Pea Ridge: Civil War Campaign in the West* (Chapel Hill and London: University of North Carolina Press, 1992); Carolyn Bartels, ed., *The Forgotten Men: Missouri State Guard* (Independence, Mo.: Two Trails Publishing Co., 1995).

40. Ephraim McD. Anderson, *Memoirs: Historical and Personal; Including the Campaigns of the First Confederate Brigade* (St. Louis: Times Printing Co., 1868), 200–2; Phillip Thomas Tucker, *The South's Finest: The First Missouri Confederate Brigade from Pea Ridge to Vicksburg* (Skippensburg, Pa.: White Mane Publishing Co., Inc., 1993), 95. In latter life George recounted with pride his service under Beauregard and even affected a Beauregardian mustache. Bent's wife, Standing Out, in an interview described her husband as part Spanish and Indian. See "Mrs. Standing Out Bent Interview, 1938," Indian Pioneer History, vol. 90, 241–44, Grant Foreman Collection, Oklahoma History Society. Beauregard's life can best be followed in T. Harry Williams, *P. G. T. Beauregard: Napoleon in Gray* (Baton Rouge: Louisiana State University Press, 1995).

41. Bent to Hyde, 2/26/1906, *George Bent Letters*, Coe Collection, Yale; Hyde, *Life of George Bent*, 110–11; "Bent's Fort," 16–17, Folder 32.2, *George Bird Grinnell Papers*, Southwest Museum; James Mooney Papers, "Miscellaneous Notes on Cheyenne, 1903–1906," National Anthropological Archives, Smithsonian. On Landis's battery see Crute, *Units of the Confederate States Army*, 209.

42. *Consolidated Index to Compiled Service Records of Confederate Soldiers*, National Archives Records Administration.

43. Ibid.

44. *Daily Missouri Democrat*, 9/5/1862.

45. Griffin Frost, *Camp and Prison Journal* (Quincy, Ill., 1867), entries for January 8 and March 2, 1863; Brother Hubert Gerard, ed., *Mississippi Vista: The Brothers of the Christian Schools in the Mid-West, 1849–1949* (Winona, Minn.: Saint Mary's College Press, 1948), 105. See also Lonnie R. Speer, "A Hell On Earth," *Civil War Times Illustrated* (July/August 1995): 58–65.

46. *Daily Missouri Democrat*, 9/2/1862.

47. Ibid., 9/5/1862.

48. Hyde, *Life of George Bent*, 111. See also Bent to George E. Hyde, 2/26/1906, *George Bent Letters*, Coe Collection, Yale.

49. Bent to Hyde, 4/25/1918, *George Bent Letters*, Coe Collection, Yale. See also Bent to Thoburn, 3/17/1915, *Joseph B. Thoburn Papers*, Indian Archives,

Oklahoma Historical Society; "Private Journal of Robert Campbell," *Bulletin of the Missouri Historical Society* 20 (October 1963-July 1964): 3.

50. *Compiled Service Records of Confederate Soldiers for State of Missouri*, Roll 88, M332, National Archives Records Administration. George also thought Major General Fremont may have played a role in his release. Shortly before he died, Bent wrote: "[Campbell] and Gen. Fremont sent me out west as both of them good friends of my father." Later in his life, George gave conflicting accounts of his capture and release from Gratiot Street prison. Of his release from prison, for example, he told George Bird Grinnell that "Robert went to several officers of the old regular army who knew my father and our family well, and through the aid of these officers I was released under the condition that I should return home with Robert and not join the Confederates again." See "Bent's Fort," Folder 32.2, *George Bird Grinnell Papers*, Southwest Museum. However, in 1915, he confided to Joseph B. Thoburn, curator at the Oklahoma Historical Society, "I was captured down in Miss. and was taken with other prisoners to St. Louis Mo and was *paroled* [italics added] there on account every old army officer knew my father at that time." Bent to Thoburn, 3/17/1915, *Joseph B. Thoburn Papers*, Indian Archives, Oklahoma Historical Society. Burdened with this information, Thoburn thought that George was eligible for a government pension because he had honorably served in the Confederate army and had been paroled. In fact, he had deserted and taken an oath of allegiance to the United States. This disqualified him for a Confederate pension. See George Bent to George E. Hyde, 4/25/1918, *George Bent Letters*, Coe Collection, Yale; Hyde to Thoburn, 11/15/1930, Major General C. H. Bridges to Confederate Pension Department, State of Oklahoma, 5/25/1931, B. W. Butler to Jesse Stovall, 2/29/1932, and Pension Commissioner to Jesse Stovall, 3/7/1932, *Joseph B. Thoburn Papers Indian Archives*, Oklahoma Historical Society; William R. Bernard, "Westport and the Santa Fe Trade," 9:564. Farrar's service record can be conveniently followed in Mark Mayo Boatner III, *The Civil War Dictionary* (New York: David McKay Company, Inc., 1959), 276.

51. Frost, *Camp and Prison Journal*, entry for January 5, 1863.

52. Martin Abernethy to Walter Campbell, 11/9/1929, *Walter Campbell Papers*, University of Oklahoma. The day after George's release, September 6, Bernard Farrar resigned as provost marshal and began service as major in the 30th Missouri Infantry. See *Daily Missouri Democrat*, 9/6/1862. Later in the war, Farrar became colonel of the 2nd Mississippi Artillery, African Descent, a black artillery unit. See *Compiled Service Records, Missouri*, Record Group Roll M390, National Archives Records Administration. For the biographical sketches of both Farrars, see *Encyclopedia of the History of St. Louis* (1899), 730.

Chapter 4

1. For George's return to Colorado, see George Bent to George E. Hyde, 3/9/1905, 1/12/1906, 2/26/1906, *George Bent Letters*, Coe Collection, Yale.

Notes

2. For a description of Fort Lyon in 1862, see Albert B. Sanford (ed.), "Life at Camp Weld and Fort Lyon in 1861–62: An Extract from the Diary of Mrs. Byron N. Sanford," *The Colorado Magazine* 7 (July 1930): 135.

3. According to Article III of the agreement, "the Government shall have entire control over the said 'Bent's Fort.' . . . Lieutenant James B. McIntyre, Regimental Quartermaster, 1st Cavalry, for and on behalf of the United States, agrees to turn the same over to William Bent, his heirs, executors, assignees, or administrators, in as good repair as when received." Sedgwick to Quartermaster General, 9/8/1860, Sedgwick to Assistant Adjutant General, 9/12/1860,, and "Articles of Agreement . . . with William W. Bent, 9/9/1860 in BENT, William file, Record Group 109, M-345, National Archives Record Administration.

4. Colonel H. L. Scott, *Military Dictionary: Comprising Technical Definitions* . . . *and Law, Government, Regulations, and Administration Relating to Land Forces* (New York: D. Van Nostrand, 1864), 282–83.

5. See Sedgwick's letters to Sister and Asst. Adjutant General, Head Quarters, Department of the West, in LeRoy R. Hafen and Ann W. Hafen, eds., *Relations with the Indians of the Plains, 1857–1861* (Glendale, Calif.: Arthur H. Clark Company, 1959), 161–63, 260–63, 270, 272–74, 276; see also "General Orders No. 8," 6/30/1860, "R. M. Peck's Account of the Sedgwick Division," and "Lieutenant J.E.B. Stuart's Journal," in ibid., 259–60, 108 (fn.15), 321–32.

6. Bent to Hyde, 4/10/1905, 3/19/1906, 2/19/1913, 8/2/1913, 5/22/1914, 8/18/1914, *George Bent Letters*, Coe Collection, Yale. See also George Bird Grinnell, *Beyond the Old Frontier: Adventures of Indian-Fighters, Hunters, and Trappers* (New York: Charles Scribner's Sons, 1913), 158; David Lavender, *Bent's Fort* (Garden City, N.Y.: Doubleday & Company, Inc., 1954), 346.

7. Bent to Hyde, 11/14/1912, *George Bent Letters*, Coe Collection, Yale.

8. Bent to Hyde, 8/28/1915, *George Bent Letters*, Coe Collection, Yale.

9. Bent to Hyde, 8/28/1915, *George Bent Letters*, Coe Collection, Yale.

10. Agent Robert C. Miller to John Haverty, Superintendent of Indian Affairs, 10/14/1857, *Report of the Commissioner of Indian Affairs, 1857*, 145. See also Hafen and Hafen, *Relations with the Indians of the Plains*, 34–35.

11. Robert C. Miller to John Haverty, 10/14/1857, *Report of the Commissioner of Indian Affairs, 1857*, 147.

12. George E. Hyde, *Life of George Bent Written from His Letters*, Savoie Lottinville, ed. (Norman: University of Oklahoma Press, 1968), 103–4. E. V. Sumner to Adjutant General, 8/9/1857, "Report of the Killed and Wounded," in Hafen and Hafen, *Relations with the Plains Indians*, 29–30.

13. Bent to Hyde, 3/19/1906, 11/14/1912, 8/28/1915, 9/22/1915, 2/11/1916, *George Bent Letters*, Coe Collection, Yale. See also Robert C. Miller to John Haverty, 10/14/1857, *Report of the Commissioner of Indian Affairs, 1857*, 141–48; Hafen and Hafen, *Relations with the Plains Indians*, 15–156; George Bird Grinnell, *The Fighting Cheyennes* (Norman: University of Oklahoma Press, 1956), 111–123, Hyde, *Life of George Bent*, 102–3; Lavender, *Bent's Fort*,

331–33; Donald J. Berthrong, *Southern Cheyennes* (Norman: University of Oklahoma Press, 1963), 139–41; Elliott West, *Contested Plains: Indians, Goldseekers, & the Rush to Colorado* (Lawrence: University of Kansas Press, 1998), 1–14. For the complete history of the Solomon Fork's fight, see William Y. Chalfant, *Cheyennes and Horse Soldiers: The 1857 Expedition and the Battle of Solomon's Fork*, foreword by Robert M. Utley (Norman and London: University of Oklahoma Press, 1989).

14. Lavender, *Bent's Fort*, 333.

15. Bent to A. M. Robinson, Superintendent of Indian Affairs, as quoted in Lavender, *Bent's Fort*, 341–42.

16. William W. Bent to Superintendent of Indian Affairs, 10/5/1859, *Report of the Commissioner of Indian Affairs, 1859*, 137–39.

17. Ibid., 138.

18. Fort Wise Treaty, February 18, 1861, in Hafen and Hafen, *Relations with the Plains Indians*, 298–99.

19. See *Report of the Commissioner of Indian Affairs, 1860*, 228–29; Francis Paul Prucha, *The Great Father: The United States Government and the American Indians* (Lincoln and London: University of Nebraska Press, 1984), 460–61; Berthrong, *Southern Cheyennes*, 150–51; Hafen and Hafen, *Relations with the Plains Indians*, 298–99.

20. For the formation of the First Colorado Regiment of Volunteers and the battle of Glorieta Pass, see William C. Whitford, *Colorado Volunteers in the Civil War: The New Mexico Campaign in 1862* (Denver: State Historical and Natural History Society, 1906); Don E. Alberts, *The Battle of Glorieta: Union Victory in the West* (College Station: Texas A&M University Press, 1998); and Thomas S. Edringnton and John Taylor, *The Battle of Glorieta Pass: A Gettysburg in the West, March 26–28, 1862* (Albuquerque: University of New Mexico Press, 1998).

21. Bent to Hyde, 5/4/1906, 9/23/1913, *George Bent Letters*, Coe Collection, Yale.

22. George told George E. Hyde that "after he was paroled and returned to his father's ranch in Colorado, as an ex-Confederate, he was suspected and mistreated by the union soldiers at Ft. Lyon, and in the following spring he went out and joined his mother's tribe, the S. Cheyennes, mainly because of this prejudice against him as a rebel." Hyde to Thoburn, 11/15/1930, *Joseph B. Thoburn Papers*, Indian Archives, Oklahoma Historical Society. See also Acting Assistant Adjutant-General J. S. Maynard to Maj. E. W. Wynkoop, 5/16/1864, *The War of the Rebellion: A Compilation of the Official Records of the Union and Confederate Armies*, 70 vols. (Washington, D.C.: Government Printing Office, 1880–1901), I, vol. 34, pt. 3, 630 [hereafter cited as *Official Records*]; and Maj. B. S. Henning to Maj. C. S. Charlot, 12/7/1864, *Official Records*, I, vol. 41, pt. 4, 796–97. Henning was correct in identifying George as an ex-Confederate, but his reference to the Missouri farming George Bent is in error.

23. Cheyenne males normally adopted new names when they reached adulthood, especially after combat. George's Cheyenne name was *Ho-my-ike*, or Beaver, until he returned from the Civil War. Then he was called *"Tejano,"* *"Tejanoi,"* *"Do-hah-en-no,"* *"Tohanoi,"* even *"Tex."* See Bent to Hyde, 4/12/1906, *George Bent Letters*, Coe Collection, Yale; C&A Patents, Indian Archives, Oklahoma Historical Society; James Mooney, "Miscellaneous Notes on the Cheyenne, 1903–06, National Anthropological Archives, Smithsonian; Father Peter John Powell, *People of the Sacred Mountain: A History of the Northern Cheyenne Chiefs and Warriors Societies 1830–1879, Withan Epilogue, 1969–1974*, 2 vols. (San Francisco: Harper and Row, 1981) 1:259; Hyde to Thoburn, 11/15/1930, *Joseph B. Thoburn Papers*, Indian Archives, Oklahoma Historical Society; and Southern Cheyenne Chief Laird Cometsevah personal communication to authors, 4/13/1996.

24. Bent to Hyde, 10/12/1905, 5/11/1906, 5/15/1906, *George Bent Letters*, Coe Collection, Yale; George Bent to Thoburn, 9/29/1910, *Joseph B. Thoburn Papers*, Indian Archives, Oklahoma Historical Society; Bent to Hyde, 6/20/1904, *George Bent Papers*, Colorado Historical Society; George Bent to Grinnell, 3/1905, Folder 10, *Georege Bird Grinnell Papers*, Southwest Museum. George Bird Grinnell, *The Cheyenne Indians: Their History and Ways of Life*, 2 vols. (Lincoln: University of Nebraska Press, 1972) 2:48–86; Hyde, *Life of George Bent*, 7, 22–23, 200–1, 213, 335–40; Grinnell, *Fighting Cheyennes*, passim.

25. Bent to Hyde, 7/14/1913, *George Bent Papers*, Western History Department, Denver Public Library. Even in old age, the fall affected him: "I have hard time to get shaved. I cannot shave myself as I have crippled arm." Ibid.

26. Bent to Hyde, 4/30/1906, *George Bent Letters*, Coe Collection, Yale.

27. Bent to Hyde, 4/30/1906, 7/21/1915, *George Bent Letters*, Coe Collection, Yale; Bent to Grinnell, 4/8/1914, Folder 56.2, and Bent to Grinnell, 11/4/1901, Grinnell Fieldnotes, Folder 335, *George Bird Grinnell Papers*, Southwest Museum. For a full description of the Medicine Lodge ceremony, see Grinnell, *Cheyenne Indians*, 2:211–84.

28. *Report of the Commissioner of Indian Affairs, 1863*, 129–30.

29. Bent to Hyde, 4/17/1906, *George Bent Letters*, Coe Collection, Yale.

30. Bent to Hyde, 11/16/1906, *George Bent Papers*, Colorado Historical Society; George Bent, "Forty Years with the Cheyennes, Part 1," George E. Hyde, ed., *Frontier* (October 1905): 3; Hyde, *Life of George Bent*, 115–17.

31. Bent to Hyde, 4/17/1906, *George Bent Letters*, Coe Collection, Yale, Grinnell Fieldnotes 11/4/1901, Folder 335, "Life of Black Kettle by Wolf Chief," Folder 69, "Medicine Arrows," Folder 471, *George Bird Grinnell Papers*, Southwest Museum.

32. Grinnell, *Cheyenne Indians*, 2:58. See also George Bent to George E. Hyde, 5/11/1906, 10/12/1905, 5/15/1906, *George Bent Letters*, Coe Collection, Yale; Bent to Grinnell, ca. 3/1905, Folder 10, *George Bird Grinnell Papers*, Southwest

Notes

Museum; Bent to Thoburn, 9/29/1910, *Joseph B. Thoburn Papers*, Oklahoma Historical Society; Bent to Hyde, 6/20/1904, *George Bent Papers*, Colorado Historical Society; Bent to Prof. Holmes, ca. January 1907, #3275, National Anthropological Archives, Smithsonian.

33. Grinnell Fieldnotes, 11/10/1905, Folder 341, *George Bird Grinnell Papers*, Southwest Museum..

34. Hyde, *Life of George Bent*, 112; Bent to Hyde, 4/30/1906, *George Bent Letters*, Coe Collection.

35. Bent to Hyde, 4/30/1906, *George Bent Letters*, Coe Collection, Yale; Hyde, *Life of George Bent*, 112; D. S. Rees, "An Indian Fight on the Solomon," *Collections of the Kansas State Historical Society, 1901–1902*, 7:471–72.

Chapter 5

1. On April 12, 1864, at Fremont Orchard, Colorado Territory, Lt. Clark Dunn with a detachment of fifteen men of the First Colorado Cavalry posted at nearby Camp Sanborn responded to civilian W. D. Ripley's report of stolen stock from the firm of Irwin and Jackman and confronted a party of Dog Soldiers. Cheyenne and army accounts of the incident differ in the particulars, but Dunn reported two soldiers killed and two wounded; Cheyenne killed he reported at eight or ten. See *The War of the Rebellion: A Compilation of the Official Records of the Union and Confederate Armies*, 70 vols. (Washington, D.C.: Government Printing Office, 1880–1901), series 1, vol. 34, pt. 1, 884–85 [hereafter cited as *Official Records*]; *Report of the Commissioner of Indian Affairs, 1864*, 239. For Cheyenne accounts see George Bent to George E. Hyde, 3/6/1905, 3/26/1906, 11/22/1908, 3/19/1912, 3/5/1913, 9/17/1914, *George Bent Letters*, Coe Collection, Yale; and George Bent to George E. Hyde, September 1905, *George Bent Papers*, Colorado Historical Society. See also George E. Hyde, *Life of George Bent Written From His Letters*, Savoie Lottinville, ed. (Norman: University of Oklahoma Press, 1968), 122–23; George Bird Grinnell, *The Fighting Cheyennes* (Norman: University of Oklahoma Press, 1915), 141–42; Captain Eugene F. Ware, *The Indian War of 1864*, Introduction by John D. McDermott, Notes by Clyde C. Walton, (1911; reprint, Lincoln and London: University of Nebraska Press, Bison Book Edition, 1994), 194; Peter John Powell, *People of the Sacred Mountain: A History of the Northern Cheyenne Chiefs and Warrior Societies, 1830–1879, With an Epilogue 1969–1974*, 2 vols. (San Francisco: Harper & Row, 1981), 1:258–59. Jean Afton, David Fridtjof Halaas, and Andrew E. Masich, *Cheyenne Dog Soldiers: A Ledgerbook History of Coups and Combat* (Niwot and Denver: University Press of Colorado and Colorado Historical Society, 1997), 288; Donald J. Berthrong, *The Southern Cheyennes* (Norman: University of Oklahoma Press, 1963), 179–80; Gary Roberts, "Sand Creek: Tragedy and Symbol," 2 vols. (Ph.D. dissertation, University of Oklahoma, 1984), 1:218–19.

2. Bent to Hyde, 3/26/1906, *George Bent Letters*, Coe Collection, Yale.

3. Powell, *People of the Sacred Mountain*, 1:259.

4. John W. Prowers testimony, 3/24/1865, in John M. Carroll, ed., *The Sand Creek Massacre: A Documentary History* (New York: Sol Lewis, 1973), p. 293–94.

5. Bent to Hyde, 4/12/1906, 3/5/1913, *George Bent Letters*, Coe Collection, Yale.

6. Hyde, *Life of George Bent*, 133; Powell, *People of the Sacred Mountain*, 1:262–64.

7. Bent to Hyde, 3/26/1906, 3/6/1905, 4/12/1906, 3/5/1913, 11/22/1908, 4/2/1912, *George Bent Letters*, Coe Collection, Yale. See also *Daily Rocky Mountain News* (Denver), 4/20/1864; Hyde, *Life of George Bent*, 131–33; Powell, *People of the Sacred Mountain*, 1:263–65; Grinnell, *Fighting Cheyennes*, 145–46; Berthrong, *Southern Cheyennes*, 185–87; Roberts, "Sand Creek," 236–38.

8. Bent to Hyde, 2/28/1906, 3/26/1906, 4/30/1906, 3/20/1913, *George Bent Letters*, Coe Collection, Yale; Hyde, *Life of George Bent*, 133–35; Grinnell, *Fighting Cheyennes*, 152–53; Roberts, "Sand Creek," 238–39; Berthrong, *Southern Cheyennes*, 185–87.

9. Afton, Halaas, and Masich, *Cheyenne Dog Soldiers*, passim.

10. George said that his father told him Lieutenant Eayre had been arrested for exceeding his orders. See Bent to Hyde, 4/30/1906, *George Bent Letters*, Coe Collection, Yale.

11. Testimony of William Bent in Carroll, *Sand Creek Massacre*, 182–83; David Lavender, *Bent's Fort* (Garden City, N.Y.: Doubleday and Company, 1954) 352–53; Grinnell, *Fighting Cheyennes*, 152; Roberts, "Sand Creek," 1:241; Berthrong, *Southern Cheyennes*, 186–87.

12. John M. Chivington to Rev. Hugh D. Fisher, 6/25/1862, *John M. Chivington Papers*, Western History Department, Denver Public Library.

13. In his rush to assume command of the First Colorado, Major Chivington not only forced Colonel Slough's resignation but "overslaughed," or leapfrogged, Lieutenant Colonel Samuel Tappan, who was senior to Chivington and by rights next in line to command the regiment. At the Battle of Glorieta, Chivington supporters may have even shot at Slough, who expected assassination at any moment. With these acts, Chivington gained the enmity of Tappan and other officers. See *Samuel F. Tappan Papers*, Colorado Historical Society; *John M. Chivington Papers*, Western History Department, Denver Public Library; Gary L. Roberts, *Death Comes to the Chief Justice: The Slough-Rynerson Quarrel and Political Violence in New Mexico* (Niwot: University Press of Colorado, 1990), 11–12; Roberts, "Sand Creek," 2:655–70; Don E. Alberts, *Battle of Glorieta: Union Victory in the West* (College Station: Texas A&M University Press, 1998), 163; Thomas S. Edrington and John Taylor, *The Battle of Glorieta Pass: A Gettysburg in the West, March 26–28, 1862* (Albuquerque: University of New Mexico Press, 1998), 107; William C. Whitford, *The Battle of Glorieta Pass: The Colorado Volunteers in the Civil War, March 26, 27, 28, 1862, With a Factual Analysis of the*

Military Strategy of Both Sides, Illustrated with Explanatory Maps Compiled and Drawn by Burt Schmitz (Glorieta, N.M.: Rio Grande Press, Inc., 1991), 130.

14. Chivington to Rev. Hugh D. Fisher, 6/25/1862, *John M. Chivington Papers*, Western History Department, Denver Public Library.

15. William Bent sworn statement, [n.d.], in Carroll, *Sand Creek Massacre*, 182–83.

16. John M. Chivington testimony, 4/26/1865, in Carroll, *Sand Creek Massacre*, 112. See also Lavender, *Bent's Fort*, 352–53.

17. Chivington's tirades were often punctuated with biblical phrases and the emphatic "So Mote It Be." See, for example, Chivington to Rev. Hugh D. Fisher, 6/25/1862, *John M. Chivington Papers*, Western History Department, Denver Public Library.

18. Lavender, *Bent's Fort*, 350.

19. William Bent sworn statement, [n.d.], 184; Robert Bent sworn statement, [n.d.], 185, in Carroll, *Sand Creek Massacre*. See also Lavender, *Bent's Fort*, 352–53.

20. *Report of the Commissioner of Indian Affairs, 1864*, 218–19.

21. At the Camp Weld conference in September 1864, territorial officials learned that a party of Arapahos led by Roman Nose was responsible for the Hungate killing. See Berthrong, *Southern Cheyennes*, 191.

22. For contemporary newspaper coverage, see the *Commonwealth* [Denver], 6/15/1864. For accounts of the Hungate killings, see Berthrong, *Southern Cheyennes*, 190–91; Roberts, "Sand Creek," 244–45; Robert L. Perkin, *First Hundred Years: An Informal History of Denver and the Rocky Mountain News* (Garden City, N.Y.: Doubleday & Company, Inc., 1959), 265; Jerome C. Smiley, *History of Denver: With Outlines of the Earlier History of the Rocky Mountain Country* (Denver: Denver Times-Sun Publishing Company, 1901), 404, 410; Stan Hoig, *The Sand Creek Massacre* (Norman: University of Oklahoma Press, 1961), 58–59, 118, 164; Elliott West, *Contested Plains: Indians, Goldseekers, and the Rush to Colorado* (Lawrence: University Press of Kansas, 1998), 290; Grinnell, *Fighting Cheyennes*, 150; Elmer R. Burkey, "The Site of the Murder of the Hungate Family by Indians in 1864," *Colorado Magazine* 12 (1935): 135–42; Harry Kelsey, "Background to Sand Creek," *Colorado Magazine* 45 (Fall 1968): 280–87.

23. Testimony of Agent Samuel G. Colley, 3/7/1865, 116, and 3/14/1865, 36, testimony of William Bent, [n.d.], 183, in Carroll, *Sand Creek Massacre*. For George Bent's movements, see "Sand Creek Massacre of the Cheyennes," Folder 17, *George Bird Grinnell* Papers, Southwest Museum. See also Roberts, "Sand Creek," 247; Nathaniel P. Hill, "Nathaniel P. Hill Inspects Colorado: Letters Written in 1864," *Colorado Magazine* 33 (October 1956): 246; Grinnell, *Fighting Cheyennes*, 150.

24. Lt. R. M. Fish to Governor Thomas Carney, 6/6/1864; Carney to Curtis, 6/17/1864; "Charges and Specifications against Capt. James W. Parmetar, 12th

Regt. Kan. Vols.," James W. Parmetar, CMSR AGO, NARS, RG 94,. as quoted in Roberts, "Sand Creek," 264.

25. Testimony of William Bent, [n.d.], in Carroll, *Sand Creek Massacre*, 183. Bent to Hyde, 4/30/1906, *George Bent Letters*, Coe Collection, Yale; Hyde, *Life of George Bent*, 133.

26. *Official Records*, Series I, vol. 41, pt. 2, 735.

27. Ibid.

28. Bent to Hyde, 2/28/1906, 3/20/1913, *George Bent Letters*, Coe Collection, Yale; Hyde, *Life of George Bent*, 140–41.

29. The great raids can be followed in Ronald Becher, *Massacre along the Medicine Road: A Social History of the Indian War of 1864 in Nebraska Territory* (Caldwell, Idaho: Caxton Press, 1999); Russ Czaplewski, *Captive of the Cheyenne: The Story of Nancy Jane Morton and the Plum Creek Massacre* (Kearney, Nebr.: Dawson County Historical Society, 1993); and John G. Ellenbecker, *Tragedy at the Little Blue: The Oak Grove Massacre and the Captivity of Lucinda Eubank and Laura Roper*, With Introduction, Maps, Photos, Annotations and References by Lyn Ryder (Niwot: Prairie Lark Publications, 2d rev. ed., 1993). For contemporary coverage see *Daily Rocky Mountain News*, August 9, 1864.

30. *Thomas F. Dawson Scrapbooks*, 8:101, 109, and 9:237, Colorado Historical Society.

31. Ellenbecker, *Tragedy at the Little Blue*, 22.

32. Ibid., 23.

33. Ibid., 13; see also Becher, *Massacre along the Medicine Road*, 315.

34. Czaplewski, *Captive of the Cheyenne*, 129; Becher, *Massacre along the Medicine Road*, 258.

35. Czaplewski, *Captive of the Cheyenne*, 129; 15.

36. Czaplewski, *Captive of the Cheyenne*, 130, 15; Becher, *Massacre along the Medicine Road*, 259.

37. Czaplewski, *Captive of the Cheyenne*, 20.

38. Ibid., pt. 2:20–22.

39. Ibid., 22.

40. Berthrong, *Southern Cheyennes*, 191.

41. *Daily Rocky Mountain News*, 8/1/1864.

42. *Report of the Commissioner of Indian Affairs, 1864*, 218, 230–31, 240; *Daily Rocky Mountain News*, 8/13/1864.

43. Bent to Hyde, 9/26/1905, *George Bent Letters*, Coe Collection, Yale; Hyde, *Life of George Bent*, 140–41, 155–56; Berthrong, *Southern Cheyennes*, 203. A good summary of the Murphy fight is in Becher, *Massacre along the Medicine Road*, 192–205.

44. Colorado College Library, Colorado Springs. A photograph of the letter appears in Benjamin Capps, *The Indians* (New York: Time-Life Books, rev. ed., 1975), 183.

45. Roberts, "Sand Creek," 345–46; Berthrong, *Southern Cheyennes*, 207–8; Hyde, *Life of George Bent*, 142.

46. Christopher B. Gerboth, ed., *The Tall Chief: The Autobiography of Edward W. Wynkoop*. Monograph 9, *Essays and Monographs* (Denver: Colorado Historical Society, 1993), 89.

47. *Report of the Commissioner of Indian Affairs, 1864*, 234.

48. Capt. Silas S. Soule testimony, 2/17/1865, in Carroll, *Sand Creek Massacre*, 206

49. Lt. Joseph A. Cramer testimony, 3/2/1865, in Carroll, *Sand Creek Massacre*, 246; Roberts, "Sand Creek," 356.

50. Lt. Joseph A. Cramer testimony, 3/2/1865, in Carroll, *Sand Creek Massacre*, 246.

51. Lt. Joseph A. Cramer testimony, 2/23/1865, in Carroll, *Sand Creek Massacre*, 220.

52. Ibid., 221.

53. The Sioux released Nancy Morton at Fort Laramie in late January 1865. During her captivity, she had endured endless hardships but had not suffered sexual abuse. Lucinda Eubank, released at Fort Laramie in May 1865, experienced harsh treatment by the women and was passed among the warriors. Throughout her nine-month ordeal, she watched over her son, Willie, who was freed with her. The capture and release of both Morton and the Eubanks is best followed in Czaplewski, *Captive of the Cheyenne*; Ellenbecker, *Tragedy at the Little Blue*; and Becher, *Massacre along the Medicine Road*. See also, *Report of the Commissioner of Indian Affairs, 1864*, 234; and Roberts, "Sand Creek," 357–58.

54. Simeon Whiteley testimony, 5/16/1865, in Carroll, *Sand Creek Massacre*, 403.

55. Bent to Thoburn, 5/20/1912, *Joseph B. Thoburn Papers*, Indian Archives, Oklahoma Historical Society; Hyde, *Life of George Bent*, 145–46.

56. Powell, *People of Sacred Mountain*, 1:287; Hyde, *Life of George Bent*, 143.

57. "Fieldnotes 1905," Vol. 2, Folder 341, *George Bird Grinnell Papers*, Southwest Museum.

58. Bent to Hyde, 9/17/1914, 5/30/1906, 9/26/1905, 4/2/1906, 1/29/1913, 3/2/1904, *George Bent Letters*, Coe Collection, Yale; *Official Records*, Series I, Vol. 41, pt. 1, 818; Maj. Scott J. Anthony testimony, 3/14/1865, in Carroll, *Sand Creek Massacre*, 32, 29–30; Hyde, *Life of George Bent*, 145–46; Berthrong, *Southern Cheyennes*, 209–10; Grinnell, *Fighting Cheyennes*, 163–64; Powell, *People of Sacred Mountain*, 1:287–88; Afton, Halaas, and Masich, *Cheyenne Dog Soldiers*, 291, 122.

59. Simeon Whiteley, United States Agent of the Grand River and Uinta Utes, took notes of the Camp Weld Conference in Denver, September 28, 1864. He marked as present: "Governor John Evans; Colonel Chivington, commanding district of Colorado; Colonel George L. Shoup, Third Colorado volunteer cavalry;

Major E. Wynkoop, Colorado First; S. Whiteley, United States Indian agent; Black Kettle, leading Cheyenne chief; White Antelope, chief central Cheyenne bank; Bull bear, lead of Dog soldiers (Cheyenne;) *Neva,* sub Arapahoe chief, was in Washington, *Bosse,* sub Arapahoe chief; Heaps-of-Buffalo, Arapahoe chief; *No-ta-nee,* Arapahoe chief; the Arapahoes are all relatives of Left Hand, chief of the Arapahoes, and are sent by him in his stead; John Smith interpreter to Upper Arkansas agency; and many other citizens and officers." Simeon Whiteley testimony, 5/16/1865, in Carroll, *Sand Creek Massacre,* 403.

60. "Of Council with Cheyenne and Arapahoe Chiefs and Warriors, Brought to Denver by Major Wynkoop; Taken Down by U.S. Indian Agent Simeon Whiteley as it Progressed," 9/28/1864, in Carroll, *Sand Creek Massacre,* vii.

61. Camp Weld Conference, 9/28/1864, in Carroll, *Sand Creek Massacre,* 403.

62. Camp Weld Conference, 9/28/1864, in Carroll, *Sand Creek Massacre,* 407.

63. Berthrong, *Southern Cheyennes,* 215; Roberts, "Sand Creek, 396.

64. Maj. Scott J. Anthony testimony, 3/14/1865, in Carroll, *Sand Creek Massacre,* 24; Roberts, "Sand Creek," 402.

65. Maj. Scott J. Anthony testimony, 3/14/1865, in Carroll, *Sand Creek Massacre,* 24; Berthrong, *Southern Cheyennes,* 214–15; Roberts, "Sand Creek," 402.

66. Bent to Hyde, 11/7/1914, *George Bent Letters,* Coe Collection, Yale; Grinnell, *Fighting Cheyennes,* 176; Hyde, *Life of George Bent,* 147.

67. George Bent, untitled map of Sand Creek village site, Cheyenne and Arapaho Agency file, "Warfare, 1864–1885," Microfilm Roll #24, Indian Archives, Oklahoma Historical Society; George Bent maps of "Arapaho [Cheyenne] Positions at Sand Creek," Folder 1, map of "Arkansas River Area," Folder 2, "Sand Creek Area," Folder 10, "Arkansas River, Sand Creek, and Western Kansas [Sand Creek Massacre located below junction of Sand and Rush creeks], "Camp after Sand Creek & Trail," Folder 4, "Arkansas River Valley and Yellow's Trail in Red-1828," *Bent-Hyde Collection,* Western History Collections, University of Colorado Library, Boulder; Samuel W. Bonsall, "Map Accompanying Journal of the march of a detachment of the men belonging to the Garrison of Fort Lyon, C.T., under the command of Lieut. S. W. Bonsall, 3rd Infantry, from Old Fort Lyon C.T., to Cheyenne Wells, pursuant to S.O. No. 66 Hdqrs., Fort Lyon C.T., June 12, 1868," Record Group 177, National Archives Record Administration, Chicago Branch Office; Lt. Joseph A. Cramer testimony, 3/4/1865, 253, Pvt. Naman D. Snyder testimony, 3/8/1865, 267–68, Pvt. George M. Roan testimony, 4/1/1865, 333, in Carroll, *Sand Creek Massacre;* Frank Murray Wynkoop, "Data Concerning Col. Edward W. Wynkoop," Tutt Library, Special Collections and Archives, Colorado College, Colorado Springs; C. E. Van Loan, "Veterans of 1864 Revisit Scene of Indian Battle on the Banks of Sand Creek, Colo.," *Denver Post,* 7/26/1908; Josiah M. Ward, "Chivington at the Battle of Sand Creek," *Denver Post,* 2/6/1921; "Reunion of Indian Fighters, Veterans Who Participated in Sand Creek Battle Will Congregate on Scene July 14," *Colorado Springs Gazette,* 6/25/1908; Cornelius J. Ballou, "The Sand Creek Affair," *National Tribune*

Notes

(Washington, D.C.), 11/23/1905; "To Visit Scene of Massacre, Veterans to Hold Reunion," *Colorado Springs Gazette*, 11/8/1904.

The Colorado Historical Society funded a search for the Sand Creek Massacre site in 1995. See Douglas C. Scott et al., "Archeological Reconnaissance of Two Possible Sites of the Sand Creek Massacre of 1864," unpublished report, April 1998, Department of Southwest Studies, Fort Lewis College, Durango, Colorado.

Congress passed legislation in October 1998 authorizing the National Park Service, in cooperation with the Colorado Historical Society, the Northern Cheyenne Tribe, the Northern Arapaho Tribe, and the Cheyenne and Arapaho Tribes of Oklahoma, to make its own search for the massacre site. See Gary L. Roberts, "The Sand Creek Massacre Site: A Report on Washington Sources," unpublished report, January 1998, Intermountain Support Office, National Park Service, Denver; Jerome A. Greene, "Report on the Historical Documentation of the Location and Extent of the Sand Creek Massacre Site," unpublished report, May 1999, Intermountain Support Office, National Park Service, Denver; Lysa Wegman-French and Christine Whitacre, "Interim Report No. 2: Historical Research on the Location of the Sand Creek Massacre Site," unpublished report, January 29, 1999, Intermountain Support Office, National Park Service, Denver.

In June 1999, the National Park Service located a portion of the village site on the north bank of Big Sandy Creek in the South Bend area.

68. Many soldiers saw the flag above Black Kettle's lodge on the morning of the attack. For a sampling, see Pvt. Naman D. Snyder testimony, 3/8–9/1865, 268, 270, John Smith testimony, 1/15/1865, 318, Pvt. George M. Roan testimony, 4/1/1865, 332, in Carroll, *Sand Creek Massacre*.

69. Based on Cheyenne oral histories and more than forty years of research, Laird Cometsevah, president of the Traditional Sand Creek Descendants and a Southern Cheyenne chief of the Council of Forty-four, differs from this description. According to Cometsevah, the following clans were present at the Sand Creek village: *Heviksnipahis*—Sand Hill Clan; *Wotapio*—Black Kettle Clan—Aka, *Hestol da nil*; *Hesiometanio*—White Antelope Clan; *Nako vi tan*—Bear Tongue Clan; *Oiuimana*—War Bonnet Clan; *Oh ki nie*—One Eye Clan; *Na Mos*—Left Hand Clan [Cheyenne]; *Ta ne vo*—Arapaho/Buffalo Shedding Clan; *Nak Nogis*—Lone Bear Clan; *Suhtai*—Southern Clan. "Sand Creek Massacre—Nov.29, 1864: Cheyenne Clans," handwritten communication to the authors, June 4, 1999.

70. Bent to Hyde, 10/23/1914, 11/7/1914, *George Bent Letters*, Coe Collection, Yale; George Hyde to Grinnell, 1/22/1915, Folder 51A, *George Bird Grinnell Papers*, Southwest Museum. The Arapaho presence at Sand Creek is controversial. Contemporary military and civilian accounts consistently place Left Hand's Arapahos in the village. John Smith reported six to eight lodges; Major Edward Wynkoop put the number at eight; Benjamin Wade's Congressional Committee on the Conduct of the War concluded that there were ten Arapaho lodges; Chivington reported the Arapaho presence, as did Cramer, Anthony, Shoup, and Soule. The Bent family—William, Robert, and George—indicated that Arapahos

were camped near Lone Bear at the upper end of the village. James Beckwourth, who helped guide Chivington to Sand Creek, also reported the Arapaho's presence. Samuel Colley, agent to the Cheyennes and Arapahos, said they were there, as did Ed Guerrier, who said Left Hand had been mortally wounded. Little Raven, the Arapaho chief, confirmed this at the negotiations at the Little Arkansas River in October 1865. Eugene Ridgley, Sr., of the Northern Arapaho Tribe believes that the Arapahos would have camped apart from the main Cheyenne village but fell victim to the surprise attack. However, the oral tradition of Cheyenne Sand Creek Massacre descendants strongly argues against the Arapaho presence, at least within the Cheyenne camp circle. Laird Cometsevah, a Cheyenne chief of the Council of Forty-four and president of the Traditional Southern Cheyenne Sand Creek Descendants, points out that it was not customary for Arapahos to camp within the Cheyenne camp circle. He also notes that of the 112 names listed on the reparation schedule authorized by the 1865 Treaty of the Little Arkansas, no Arapaho names appear. Steve Brady, chairman of the Northern Cheyenne Band of Cheyenne Massacre Descendants and headman of the Crazy Dog Society, supports this view. Despite this strong evidence, the authors feel compelled to follow George Bent's perspective: the Arapahos suffered grievous losses, with only three or four surviving the attack and Chief Left Hand mortally wounded. See Bent to Hyde, 4/17/1905, 1/20/1915, 3/5/1905, 4/30/1913, *George Bent Letters*, Coe Collection, Yale; and Bent to Tappan, 11/15/1889, 3/15/1889, *Samuel F. Tappan Papers*, Colorado Historical Society. See also for the Arapaho presence *Report of the Commissioner of Indian Affairs, 1865*, 517–27; and soldier and civilian testimony in Carroll, *Sand Creek Massacre*: Report of Benjamin F. Wade, chairman of the Joint Committee on the Conduct of the War, 5/4/1865, 5; Jesse H. Leavenworth testimony, 3/13/1865, 9; John S. Smith testimony, 3/13–14/1865, 12, 14; Maj. Scott J. Anthony testimony, 3/14/1865, 22, 26, 27–9, 31; Maj. S. G. Colley testimony, 3/14/1865, 37, 38; William Bent testimony, [n.d.], 183; James P. Beckwith [*sic*] testimony, 3/6/1865, 259. Secondary accounts include Hyde, *Life of George Bent*, 149; Grinnell, *Fighting Cheyennes*, 170–72. Berthrong, *Southern Cheyennes*, 216; Powell, *People of Sacred Mountain*, 1:299, 310; and Margaret Coel, *Chief Left Hand: Southern Arapaho* (Norman: University of Oklahoma Press, 1981), passim; Hoig, *Sand Creek Massacre*, 149–53; Roberts, "Sand Creek," 421; West, *Contested Plains*, 302

71. Major Scot J. Anthony testimony, 3/14/1865, in Carroll, *Sand Creek Massacre*, 29.

72. John Smith testimony, 3/14/1865, in Carroll, *Sand Creek Massacre*, 11.

73. John S. Smith testimony, 3/14/1865, 17, David H. Louderback testimony, 3/30/1865, 325, in Carroll, *Sand Creek Massacre*.

74. "Sand Creek Massacre of the Cheyennes," Folder 17, 2, *George Bird Grinnell Papers*, Southwest Museum; Bent to Hyde, 3/15/1905, *George Bent Letters*, Coe Collection, Yale; Tablet #20, 83–88, E. S. Ricker Papers, Western History Department, Denver Public Library; Vol. 4, 20–21, *F. W. Cragin Papers*, Western

Notes

History Department, Denver Public Library; Hyde, *Life of George Bent*, 151–54; Grinnell, *Fighting Cheyennes*, 177.

75. Lt. Joseph Cramer to Maj. Edward Wynkoop, 12/19/1864, Colorado Historical Society.

76. Bent to Hyde, 4/25/1906, *George Bent Letters*, Coe Collection, Yale.

77. Hyde, *Life of George Bent*, 154–55; Grinnell, *Fighting Cheyennes*, 177–78.

78. Cramer opposed Chivington's attack on the Sand Creek village. The night before at Fort Lyon, Chivington told him that it was "honorable to use any means under God's heaven to kill Indians; that he would kill women and children, and 'damn any man that was in sympathy with Indians.'" See Cramer's testimony, 3/1/1865, in Carroll, *Sand Creek Massacre*, 237–39. For a graphic description of the incident, see Lt. Joseph A. Cramer to Maj. Edward Wynkoop, 12/19/1864, Colorado Historical Society.

79. Testimony of John S. Smith, 3/14/1865, 11, and David H. Louderback, 3/30/1865, 325, in Carroll, *Sand Creek Massacre*.

80. Edmund G. Guerrier sworn statement, Fort Riley, 5/25/1865, in Carroll, *Sand Creek Massacre*, 155.

81. Personal communication from Blanche White Shield, June 2, 1999, Clinton, Oklahoma.

82. John S. Smith testimony, 3/14/1865, in Carroll, *Sand Creek Massacre*, 16.

83. Bent to Tappan, 2/23/1889, *Samuel F. Tappan Papers*, Colorado Historical Society.

84. In fact, all were killed with the exception of one of the brave man's daughters, who survived and later was adopted by Colonel Samuel Tappan. Taken to Boston, she was a great favorite of New England literati and spiritualists. See Bent to Tappan, 2/23/1889, *Samuel F. Tappan Papers*, Colorado Historical Society.

85. Bent to Tappan, 2/23/1889, 3/15/1889, *Samuel F. Tappan Papers*, Colorado Historical Society; Bent to Hyde, 4/30/1913, 3/15/1905, *George Bent Letters*, Coe Collection, Yale; "Sand Creek Massacre of the Cheyennes," Folder 17, 9, *George Bird Grinnell Papers*, Southwest Museum; Hyde, *Life of George Bent*, 152–53; Grinnell, *Fighting Cheyennes*, 178–79.

86. Robert Bent sworn statement, [n.d.], in Carroll, *Sand Creek Massacre*, 185.

87. Bent to Hyde, 3/9/1905, *George Bent Letters*, Coe Collection, Yale; William Bent sworn statement, [n.d.], 183, Robert Bent sworn statement, [n.d.], 184–85, Lt. Joseph A. Cramer testimony, 3/1/1865, 241, James P. Beckwith [*sic*] sworn statement, 3/7/1865, in Carroll, *Sand Creek Massacre*; Bent to Thoburn, undated [(ca. 1910)], *Joseph Thoburn Papers*, Indian Archives, Oklahoma Historical Society; Hyde, *Life of George Bent*, 148–49; Grinnell, *Fighting Cheyennes*, 168–69; Lavender, *Bent's Fort*, 358; Hoig, *Sand Creek Massacre*, 144.

88. Robert Bent sworn testimony, [n.d.], in Carroll, *Sand Creek Massacre*, 185.

89. Held captive were one Arapaho boy named White Shirt and three Cheyenne children. Also in the lodge were John Smith's wife and his youngest child. See Roberts, "Sand Creek," 1:431–32.

90. Capt. Silas S. Soule to Maj. Edward Wynkoop, 12/14/1864, Colorado Historical Society.

91. Bent to Hyde, 3/9/1905, *George Bent Letters*, Coe Collection, Yale; Bent to Tappan, 3/15/1889, *Samuel F. Tappan Papers*, Colorado Historical Society. See also Capt. Luther Wilson sworn statement, [n.d.], 156; William Bent sworn statement, [n.d.], 183; Robert Bent sworn statement, [n.d.], 185; Capt. Silas S. Soule testimony, 2/17/1865, 205, 212; Lt. Joseph A. Cramer, 3/1/1865, 241; James P. Beckwith testimony, 3/6/1865, 261; Pvt. Naman D. Snyder testimony, 3/8/1865, 367, in Carroll, *Sand Creek Massacre*. Also see, Roberts, "Sand Creek," 1:431–32.

Although Soule reported to his family that he himself did not kill any Indians at Sand Creek and held his command back from the fighting, his men expended 2,220 rounds of Sharps carbine ammunition and an equal number of cartridges from the Colt Army revolvers. In his testimony in the army hearings, Soule admitted "he done some firing" and that "we opened fire from the south or southeast." See Soule to Mother, 12/18/1864 and 1/8/1865, *Silas S. Soule Papers*, Western History Department, Denver Public Library. See also Capt. Silas S. Soule testimony, 2/16/1865, in Carroll, *Sand Creek Massacre*, 201–3; and "Abstract of Material Expended or Consumed by Company D, First Colorado Cavalry for the Fourth Quarter of 1864," *Silas S. Soule Papers*, Denver Public Library.

92. Pvt. David H. Louderback testimony, 3/30/1865, in Carroll, *Sand Creek Massacre*, 326.

93. John S. Smith testimony, 3/14/1865, in Carroll, *Sand Creek Massacre*, 16.

94. James P. Beckwith [*sic*] testimony, 3/6/1865, in Carroll, *Sand Creek Massacre*, 261–62.

95. Pvt. David H. Louderback testimony, 3/30/1865, in Carroll, *Sand Creek Massacre*, 326.

96. R. W. Clark to George Bird Grinnell, 4/10/1929, Folder 92b, *George Bird Grinnell Papers*, Southwest Museum.

97. Sayre later recalled the circumstances of Jack's death with macabre humor and sarcasm. "Jack was sitting across from [his family] and was an attentive onlooker of an inspection of guns which was being made by [John] Smith and the Colorado soldiers. Accidentally, or other wise, the weapon which was in the hands of one of our men was discharged when pointed directly at Jack. The shot was fatal, and of course his mother and other squaws set up a great howl." See Hal Sayre, "Early Central City Theatrical and Other Reminiscences," *Colorado Magazine* 6 (March 1929): 52–53. In his diary, however, Sayre makes no mention of the incident. See Lynn I. Perrigo, "Major Hal Sayr's [*sic*] Diary of the Sand Creek Campaign, *The Colorado Magazine* 15 (March 1938): 54–55. For another account of the killing, see Stan Hoig, *The Western Odyssey of John Simpson Smith: Frontiersman, Trapper, Trader, and Interpreter* (Glendale, Calif.: Arthur H. Clark Company, 1974), 159–61.

98. Hyde, *Life of George Bent*, 154. See Little Bear's direct account, which differs slightly from Hyde's reworked version, in Bent to Hyde, 4/2/1906,

4/14/1906, *George Bent Letters*, Coe Collection, Yale. Little Bear had started his run to the pits with Big Head, Crow Neck, Smoker, and Cut Lip Bear. The latter named was the father of Magpie Woman, George Bent's first wife's. All these warriors were killed on the bluffs west of Sand Creek.

99. Stephen Decatur testimony, 5/6/1865, in Carroll, *Sand Creek Massacre*, 385. See also Morse Coffin, *Colorado Sun* [Greeley, Colo.], December 1878–February 1879.

100. Afton, Halaas, and Masich, *Cheyenne Dog Soldiers*, 74–76, n.353; *Ordnance Manual for the Use of the Officers of the United States Army, 1860* (Philadelphia: J. B. Lippincott & Co., 1861), passim; David F. Halaas and Andrew E. Masich, "'You Could Hear the Drums for Miles': A Cheyenne Ledgerbook History," *Colorado Heritage* (Autumn 1996): 26–27.

101. Bent to Tappan, 3/15/1889, *Samuel F. Tappan Papers*, Colorado Historical Society.

102. Roberts, "Sand Creek," 1:439. See Hoig, *Sand Creek Massacre*, 186.

103. Bent to Hyde, 4/25/1906, *George Bent Letters*, Coe Collection, Yale; Bent to Tappan, 2/23/1889, *Samuel F. Tappan Papers*, Colorado Historical Society; Hyde, *Life of George Bent*, 155; Grinnell, *Fighting Cheyennes*, 178.

104. See, for example, Luella Shaw, *True History of Some of the Pioneers of Colorado* (Hotchkiss, Colo.: W. S. Coburn, John Patterson, A. K. Shaw, 1909), 83–85.

105. Hyde, *Life of George Bent*, 157–58; Grinnell, *Fighting Cheyennes*, 179–80; Bent to Hyde, 12/21/1905, *George Bent Letters*, Coe Collection, Yale.

106. Hyde, *Life of George Bent*, 158.

107. Ibid.

108. Ibid., 158–59; Bent to Hyde, 12/21/1905, *George Bent Letters*, Coe Collection, Yale.

Chapter 6

1. George Bent to George E. Hyde, 4/30/1913, *George Bent Letters*, Coe Collection, Yale. Sand Creek casualties have been the subject of heated debate, starting from Chivington's inflated and self-serving reports, which put the number of dead at "500 warriors." Lt. Col. Samuel F. Tappan says 37 warriors and old men and about 100 women and children. Tappan also noted that the army board of inquiry was "of the opinion that not over 40 warriors and 100 women and children were killed." See Tappan Diary transcription, January 1865, 14, 17, 18, 20, 21, 23, Colorado Historical Society.

2. Bent to Hyde, 3/15/1905, *George Bent Letters*, Coe Collection, Yale.

3. Bent to Hyde, 10/23/1914, *George Bent Letters*, Coe Collection, Yale; George E. Hyde to George Bird Grinnell, 1/22/1915 [enclosure], Folder 51A, *George Bird Grinnell Papers*, Southwest Museum; George E. Hyde, *Life of George Bent, Written from His Letters*, Savoie Lottinville, ed. (Norman: Univer-

sity of Oklahoma Press, 1968), 159–62. For the presence of the Arapahos at Sand Creek and the number killed, see Bent to Hyde, 3/15/1905, 4/17/1905, 4/30/1913, 1/20/1915, *George Bent Letters*, Coe Collection, Yale; Bent to Samuel F. Tappan, 3/15/1889, *Samuel F. Tappan Papers*, Colorado Historical Society; and Commissioner Report of 1865, 517–27; Beckwith testimony, 3/6/1865, 259; William Bent testimony, 183; S. G. Colley testimony, 3/14/1865, 37–38; Maj. Scott J. Anthony testimony, 3/14/1865, 22, 26–27; John S. Smith testimony, 3/14/1865, 12–14, all in John M. Carroll, ed. *The Sand Creek Massacre: A Documentary History*, With an Introduction by John M. Carroll (New York: Sol Lewis, 1973).

4. George E. Hyde, "Manscript based on letters of George Bent (working copy)," *George Bent Collection*, WH 1704, Box 1, Western History Department, Denver Public Library.

5. Joyce M. Szabo, *Howling Wolf and the History of Ledger Art* (Albuquerque: University of New Mexico Press, 1994), 177.

6. Lt. Joseph A. Cramer testimony, 3/1/65, 241; Capt. Silas Soule testimony, 2/17/1865, 205; Col. George Shoup testimony, 2/3/1865, 367; in Carroll, *Sand Creek Massacre*.

7. Silas Soule to Edward Wynkoop, December 14, 1864, in Gary L. Roberts and David Fridtjog Halaas, "Written in Blood—The Soule–Cramer Sand Creek Massacre Letters," *Colorado Heritage* (Winter 2001): 25–26.

8. Ibid., 28.

9. Bent to Hyde, 3/15/1905, *George Bent Letters*, Coe Collection, Yale; George Bird Grinnell, *The Fighting Cheyennes* (Norman: University of Oklahoma Press, 1956), 181–82; George E. Hyde, *Life of George Bent*, 164–65.

10. Jean Afton, David Fridtjof Halaas, and Andrew E. Masich, *Cheyenne Dog Soldiers: A Ledgerbook History of Coups and Combat* (Niwot and Denver: University of Colorado Press and Colorado Historical Society, 1997), passim.

11. Afton, Halaas, and Masich, *Cheyenne Dog Soldiers*, passim; David F. Halaas and Andrew E. Masich, "'You Could Hear the Drums for Miles': A Cheyenne Ledgerbook History," *Colorado Heritage* (Autumn 1996): 2–44.

12. Bent to Hyde, 5/7/1906, *George Bent Letters*, Coe Collection, Yale.

13. Bent to Hyde, 5/7/1906, *George Bent Letters*, Coe Collection, Yale; Hyde, *Life of George Bent*, 170; "Cheyenne Escapades Recalled by Scout," unidentified newspaper clipping, ca. 1914, *Fred S. Barde Collection*, Oklahoma Historical Society.

14. Grinnell, *Fighting Cheyennes*, 182; Hyde, *Life of George Bent*, 170–71.

15. Bent to Hyde, 5/10/1906, *George Bent Letters*, Coe, Yale; Afton, Halaas, and Masich, *Cheyenne Dog Soldiers*, passim.

16. "Dog Soldier Ledgerbook," 134, Ms #614, Manuscript Collections, Colorado Historical Society; Bent to Hyde, 10/27/1914, *George Bent Letters*, Coe Collection, Yale; Grinnell, *Fighting Cheyennes*, 185; Hyde, *Life of George Bent*, 171; Afton, Halaas, and Masich, *Cheyenne Dog Soldiers*, 266; Halaas and Masich, "'You Could Hear the Drums for Miles,'" *Colorado Heritage*, 21–26.

17. "Dog Soldier Ledgerbook," 81, Colorado Historical Society; Afton, Halaas, and Masich, *Cheyenne Dog Soldiers,* 164–66; Halaas and Masich, "'You Could Hear the Drums for Miles,'" *Colorado Heritage,* 18–19.

18. "Dog Soldier Ledgerbook," 113, Ms. #614, Manuscript Collections, Colorado Historical Society; Bent to Hyde, 10/18/1906, 5/3/1906, 4/24/1905, *George Bent Letters,* Coe Collection, Yale; Afton, Halaas, and Masich, *Cheyenne Dog Soldiers,* 232–34; Halaas and Masich, "'You Could Hear the Drums for Miles,'" *Colorado Heritage,* 20–22. See also Dallas W. Williams, *Fort Sedgwick, Colorado Territory: Hell Hole on the Platte* (Julesburg: Fort Sedgwick Historical Society, 1993, rev. ed. 1996), 1–28.

19. Hyde, *Life of George Bent,* 172; Grinnell, *Fighting Cheyennes,* 186.

20. Bent to Hyde, 5/3/1906, *George Bent Letters,* Coe Collection, Yale; Grinnell, *Fighting Cheyennes,* 186; Hyde, *Life of George Bent,* 172.

21. Bent to Hyde, 5/7/1906, *George Bent Letters,* Coe Collection, Yale; Hyde, *Life of George Bent,* 173; Afton, Halaas, and Masich, *Cheyenne Dog Soldiers,* 354, n. 6.

22. Hyde, *Life of George Bent,* 173; Bent to Hyde, 10/12/1905, 10/18/1906, 5/3/1906, 4/24/1905, *George Bent Letters,* Coe Collection, Yale; Grinnell to Adjutant General, 4/13/1909, *George Bird Grinnell Papers,* Southwest Museum; Donald J. Berthrong, *The Southern Cheyennes* (Norman: University of Oklahoma Press, 1963), 225–26. Afton, Halaas, and Masich, *Cheyenne Dog Soldiers,* 232–35; Halaas and Masich, "'You Could Hear the Drums for Miles,'" *Colorado Heritage,* 20–22.

23. Halaas and Masich, "'You Could Hear the Drums for Miles,'" *Colorado Heritage,* 20–22.

24. *Grit-Advocate* (Julesburg, Colo.), 10/21/1920. See Afton, Halaas, and Masich, *Cheyenne Dog Soldiers,* 266–68; Halaas and Masich, "'You Could Hear the Drums for Miles,'" *Colorado Heritage,* 23–25.

25. Hyde, *Life of George Bent,* 173.

26. Ibid., 175; Bent to Hyde, 5/3/1906, *George Bent Letters,* Coe Collection, Yale.

27. Bent to Hyde, 5/3/1906, *George Bent Letters,* Coe Collection, Yale; George E. Hyde, *Spotted Tail's Folk: A History of the Brule Sioux* (Norman: University of Oklahoma Press, 1961), 96; Hyde, *Life of George Bent,* 175; Grinnell, *Fighting Cheyennes,* 191; Stephen E. Ambrose, *Crazy Horse and Custer: The Parallel Lives of Two American Warriors* (New York: Doubleday & Co., 1975), 152.

28. Hyde, *Life of George Bent,* 176; Grinnell, *Fighting Cheyennes,* 189 n.; Eugene F. Ware, *The Indian War of 1864,* Introduction by John D. McDermott (Lincoln and London: University of Nebraska Press, Bison Book Edition, 1994), 353–55.

29. Bent to Hyde, 1/12/1906, *George Bent Letters,* Coe Collection, Yale; Grinnell, *Fighting Cheyennes,* 188–89; Hyde, *Life of George Bent,* 177.

30. Bent to Hyde, 1/12/1906, *George Bent Letters,* Coe Collection, Yale.

31. Ibid.

32. Hyde, *Life of George Bent*, 178.

33. Bent to Hyde, 5/3/1906, *George Bent Letters*, Coe Collection, Yale; Hyde, *Life of George Bent*, 181.

34. Hyde, *Life of George Bent*, 179; Grinnell, *Fighting Cheyennes*, 189–90.

35. Bent to Hyde, 5/3/1906, 3/9/1905, 10/12/1905, *George Bent Letters*, Coe Collection, Yale; Bent to Grinnell, 12/15/1913, Folder 56.2, *George Bird Grinnell Papers*, Southwest Museum; Hyde, *Life of George Bent*, 181; Grinnell, *Fighting Cheyennes*, 192; Afton, Halaas, and Masich, *Cheyenne Dog Soldiers*, 168–70. Army reports and newspaper items only account for two Sand Creek veterans suffering such a fate. However, Little Bear and Touching Cloud, who were both present, confirm George's version of the affair. For newspaper accounts, see *Daily Rocky Mountain News* (Denver), 4/28/1865, 1/16/1865.

36. Bent to Hyde, 5/3/1906, *George Bent Letters*, Coe Collection, Yale; Hyde, *Life of George Bent*, 179; Grinnell, *Fighting Cheyennes*, 191.

37. Ware, *Indian War of 1864*, 377.

38. Bent to Hyde, 5/3/1905, 5/3/1906, *George Bent Letters*, Coe Collection, Yale; Hyde, *Life of George Bent*, 186; Grinnell, *Fighting Cheyennes*, 190–91.

39. Ware, *Indian War of 1864*, 362–63. It is not certain that Captain Ware encountered George Bent, but George is the only mixed-blood known to have been in the area at the time.

40. Bent to Hyde, 5/4/1906, *George Bent Letters*, Coe Collection, Yale; Hyde, *Life of George Bent*, 189; Grinnell, *Fighting Cheyennes*, 196; *Dog Soldier Ledgerbook*, 63, Ms. #614, Manuscript Collections, Colorado Historical Society; Afton, Halaas, and Masich, *Cheyenne Dog Soldiers*, 138–40. See also John D. McDermott, "'We Had a Terribly Hard Time Letting Them Go': The Battle of Mud Springs and Rush Creek, February 1865," *Nebraska History* 77 (Summer 1996): 78–88.

41. Bent to Hyde, 5/4/1906, *George Bent Letters*, Coe Collection, Yale; Hyde, *Life of George Bent*, 190; Grinnell, *Fighting Cheyennes*, 197.

42. *Dog Soldier Ledgerbook*, 20, Ms. #614, Colorado Historical Society; Afton, Halaas, and Masich, *Cheyenne Dog Soldiers*, 36–43.

43. Hyde, *Life of George Bent*, 192.

44. Hyde, *Life of George Bent*, 193. See also Bent to Hyde, 5/3/1906, *George Bent Letters*, Coe Collection, Yale. Collins never mentioned this dispatch in his official report. See Grinnell, *Fighting Cheyennes*, 210. For the best account of the Rush Creek fight, see McDermott, "'We Had a Terribly Hard Time Letting Them Go,'" *Nebraska History*, 82–86.

45. Bent to Hyde, 5/4/1906, *George Bent Letters*, Coe Collection, Yale; Hyde, *Life of George Bent*, 194–95; Grinnell, *Fighting Cheyennes*, 202.

46. Bent to Hyde, 5/14/1914, *George Bent Letters*, Coe Collection, Yale; Hyde, *Life of George Bent*, 195–97.

47. Hyde, *Life of George Bent*, 198. "Dog Soldier Ledgerbook," Manuscript Collections, Colorado Historical Society, 127; Afton, Halaas, and Masich, *Cheyenne Dog Soldiers*, 246–48.

48. Hyde, *Life of George Bent*, 199.

49. Bent to Hyde, 10/12/1905, *George Bent Letters*, Coe Collection, Yale; Hyde, *Life of George Bent*, 200–1. Peter John Powell, *People of Sacred Mountain: A History of the Northern Cheyenne Chiefs and Warrior Societies, 1830–1879, Withan Epilogue, 1969–1974*, 2 vols. (San Francisco: Harper & Row, 1961), 1:336.

50. *The War of the Rebellion: A Compilation of the Official Records of the Union and Confederate Armies*, 10 vols. (Washington, D.C.: Government Printing Office, 1880–1901), Series I, vol. 48, pt. 1, 277–88. Hereafter cited as *Official Records*.

51. Bent to Hyde, 10/12/1905, *George Bent Letters*, Coe Collection, Yale.

52. Bent to Hyde, 5/22/1906, *George Bent Letters*, Coe collection, Yale.

53. Bent to Hyde, 5/22/1906, *George Bent Letters*, Coe collection, Yale; Dee Brown, *The Galvanized Yankees* (Urbana: University of Illnois Press, 1963), passim. Hyde, *Life of George Bent*, 217, Grinnell, *Fighting Cheyennes*, 221.

54. J. W. Vaughn, *The Battle of Platte Bridge* (Norman: University of Oklahoma Press, 1963), 66.

55. Bent to Hyde, 5/22/1906, *George Bent Letters*, Coe Collection, Yale; Bent to Hyde, 11/10/1915, *George Bent Collection*, Western History Collections, Denver Public Library; Bent to Hyde, 5/10/1905, *George Bent Papers*, Colorado Historical Society; Hyde, *Life of George Bent*, 218–19; Vaughn, *Battle of Platte Bridge*, 59–62; S. H. Fairfield, "The Eleventh Kansas Regiment at Platte Bridge," *Transactions of the Kansas State Historical Society*, 8: 357–60.

56. Bent to Hyde, 5/22/1906, *George Bent Letters*, Coe Collection, Yale.

57. Hyde, *Life of George Bent*, 221.

58. Bent to Hyde, 5/22/1906, 10/12/1905, *George Bent Letters*, Coe Collection, Yale; Bent to Hyde, 11/10/1915, *George Bent Papers*, Western History Collections, Denver Public Library; Bent to Hyde, 5/3/1905, 12/31/1906, *George Bent Papers*, Colorado Historical Society; Grinnell, *Fighting Cheyennes*, 228–29; Hyde, *Life of George Bent*, 220–22; Vaughn, *Battle of Platte Bridge*, 77–89, 94–99; *Official Records*, Series I, vol. 48, pt. 2, 1132; Fairfield, "Eleventh Kansas Regiment at Platte Bridge," Kansas Historical Society Collections 8 (1903–1904), 357–60; Berthrong, *Southern Cheyennes*, 248–49, Powell, *People of Sacred Mountain*, 1:336–42; Afton, Halaas, and Masich, *Cheyenne Dog Soldiers*, 278–80.

59. Bent to Hyde, 5/22/1906, 11/17/1915, *George Bent Letters*, Coe Collection, Yale; Hyde, *Life of George Bent*, 226.

60. Bent to Hyde, 11/17/1915, *George Bent Letters*, Coe Collection, Yale; Grinnell, *The Cheyenne Indians*, 2:39–44.

Notes

61. Grinnell Fieldnotes, 11/10/1905, Folder 341, *George Bird Grinnell Papers*, Southwest Museum; Bent to Hyde, 11/17/1915, *George Bent Letters*, Coe Collection, Yale. Careful to guard his reputation in the white world, George would never admit to killing or scalping any enemy.

62. Grinnell, *Cheyenne Indians*, 1:91, 156.

63. For Bent's account of his stepmother's death, see Bent to Hyde, 5/[16]/1906, 7/[n.d.]/1908, 9/23/1913, *George Bent Letters*, Coe Collection, Yale; Hyde, *Life of George Bent*, 227–28. See also Connor's report in *Official Records*, Series I, vol. 48, pt. 1, 356, which indicates that twenty-four Cheyennes were in the war party and all of them were killed. George Bird Grinnell, in his *Two Great Scouts and Their Pawnee Battalion: The Experiences of Frank J. North and Luther H. North, Pioneers in the Great West, 1856–1882, and the Defence of the Building of the Union Pacific Railroad*, Foreword by James T. King. (Lincoln: University of Nebraska Press, 1973), 89–92, says the Pawnees killed twenty-six men and one woman. Henry E. Palmer, who was acting quartermaster and commissary at Camp Connor when North's command returned, reported that twenty-four scalps including a woman's were taken but that he never counted them himself. See "Capt. H. E. Palmer's Account of the Connor Expedition," in LeRoy R. Hafen, *Powder River Campaigns and Sawyers Expedition of 1865: A Documentary Account Comprising Official Reports, Diaries, Contemporary Newspaper Accounts, and Personal Narratives* (Glendale, Calif.: Arthur H. Clark Company, 1961), 118. Capt. B. F. Rockafellow of the Sixth Michigan met the Pawnees on their return at 3 p.m. on August 17. He counted only ten scalps, raising the possibility that the scalps had been split and only five Cheyennes killed, as Bent and other Cheyenne survivors insisted. See "Diary of Capt. B. F. Rockafellow Sixth Michigan Cavalry," 8/17/1865, in Hafen, *Powder River Campaigns*, 181. George Bird Grinnell rejected Bent's account in favor of Luther North's. Grinnell explains the discrepancy in scalp counts by arguing that there were no Cheyenne survivors of this fight and therefore the Southern Cheyennes could know nothing of it. See Grinnell, *Fighting Cheyennes*, 207. Berthrong, *Southern Cheyennes*, 251; Powell, *People of Sacred Mountain*, 1:378–79.

64. "Official Report of James A Sawyers," in Hafen, *Powder River Campaigns*, 224–28.

65. Bent to Hyde, 9/21/1905, *George Bent Letters*, Coe Collection, Yale; Hyde, *Life of George Bent*, 231–32; Grinnell, *Fighting Cheyennes*, 208–9. See also Berthrong, *Southern Cheyennes*, 253.

66. "A. M. Holman's Reminiscent Account," in Hafen, *Powder River Campaigns*, 307–9.

67. Robert W. Larson, *Red Cloud: Warrior-Statesman of the Lakota Sioux* (Norman and London: University of Oklahoma Press, 1997), 90; R. Eli Paul, ed., *Autobiography of Red Cloud: War Leader of the Oglalas* (Helena: Montana Historical Society Press, 1997), 5.

68. *Official Records*, Series 1, vol. 48, pt. 2 (B), 1229.

69. Major General G. M. Dodge to Major General John Pope, 9/15/1865, in Hafen, *Powder River Campaigns*, 51–52; Capt. Rockafellow, 8/24/1865, in ibid., 185; Holman's Reminiscent Account, in ibid., 311; *Official Records*, Series 1, vol. 48, Pt. 2 (B), 1229.

70. Bent to Hyde, 5/10/1905, *George Bent Papers*, Colorado Historical Society.

71. The Sawyers negotiations and fight can be followed in Bent to Hyde, 4/24/1905, 9/21/1905, 5/[16]/1906, 9/24/1913, 11/17/1915, *George Bent Letters*, Coe Collection, Yale; Bent to Hyde, 5/10/1905, *George Bent Papers*, Colorado Historical Society; *Official Records*, Series 1, vol. 48, pt. 2 (B), 1229; Grinnell, *Fighting Cheyennes*, 209; Hyde, *Life of George Bent*, 232–33; Hafen, *Powder River Campaigns*, passim.

72. Capt. Rockafellow Diary, 8/17/1865, in Hafen, *Powder River Campaigns*, 182.

73. Bent to Hyde, 1/12/1906, *George Bent Letters*, Coe Collection, Yale; Bent to Hyde, 5/3/1905, 10/3/1905, *George Bent Papers*, Colorado Historical Society; Hyde, *Life of George Bent*, 251.

74. Afton, Halaas, and Masich, *Cheyenne Dog Soldiers*, 59–60, 165.

75. Bent to Hyde, 5/30/1906, *George Bent Letters*, Coe Collection, Yale; Afton, Halaas, and Masich, *Cheyenne Dog Soldiers*, 98–100.

76. Afton, Halaas, and Masich, *Cheyenne Dog Soldiers*, 258; Halaas and Masich, "'You Could Hear the Drums for Miles,'" *Colorado Heritage*, 9; Hyde, *Life of George Bent*, 235; Holman's Reminiscent Account, in Hafen, *Powder River Campaigns*, 307, 311.

77. Hyde, *Life of George Bent*, 228.

78. Hafen, *Powder River Campaigns*, 25–26, 40–41; Hyde, *Life of George Bent*, 223–26; Grinnell, *Fighting Cheyennes*, 204–7; Robert M. Utley, *Frontiersmen in Blue: The United States Army and the Indian, 1848–1865* (Lincoln and London: University of Nebraska Press, Bison Book Edition, 1981), 323–25.

79. Hafen, *Powder River Campaigns*, 35–36, 42–43. Although Major General Pope rescinded the order on August 11, 1865, it is clear that Connor meant to kill Indians wherever he found them. See *Official Records*, Series 1, vol. 48, pt. 1, 356.

80. Hyde, *Life of George Bent*, 235.

81. *Official Records*, Series 1, vol. 48, pt. 1, 375–76.

82. Hyde, *Life of George Bent*, 238.

83. Ibid., 239.

84. Ibid., 239–40; Grinnell, *Fighting Cheyennes*, 214. See also Bent to Hyde, 4/24/1905, 5/10,1906, 5/24/1906, 10/27/1913, *George Bent Letters*, Coe Collection, Yale.

85. Grinnell, *Fighting Cheyennes*, 214; Hyde, *Life of George Bent*, 240.

86. Bent to Hyde, 4/24/1905, 5/24/1906, *George Bent Letters*, Coe Collection, Yale; Hyde, *Life of George Bent*, 240; Grinnell, *Fighting Cheyennes*, 214.

Notes

87. Bent to Hyde, 11/5/1913, 12/20/1915, *George Bent Letters*, Coe Collection, Yale.
88. Hyde, *Life of George Bent*, 242–43; Berthrong, *Southern Cheyennes*, 256.
89. Bent to Hyde, 5/16/1905, *George Bent Papers*, Colorado Historical Society; Hyde, *Life of George Bent*, 243; Berthrong, *Southern Cheyennes*, 256.
90. Bent to Hyde, 5/16/1906, *George Bent Papers*, Colorado Historical Society; *Daily Rocky Mountain News* (Denver), 12/1/1865; Theodore R. Davis, "Stage Ride to Colorado," *Harpers New Monthly Magazine*, 143–45; Hyde, *Life of George Bent*, 243; Berthrong, *Southern Cheyennes*, 256; Lavender, *Bent's Fort*, 363. The evidence supports the presence of both Charley and George at Downer station.

Chapter 7

1. George Bent to George E. Hyde, 5/29/1906, *George Bent Letters*, Coe Collection, Yale; George E. Hyde, *The Life of George Bent, Written from His Letters* (Norman: University of Oklahoma Press, 1968), 250; Donald J. Berthrong, *The Southern Cheyennes* (Norman: University of Oklahoma Press, 1963), 256–57.
2. I. C. Taylor to Thomas Murphy, 12/26/1865, Record Group 48, Colorado Appointment Papers, M808, Roll 13, National Archives Record Administration, Washington, D.C.; Hyde, *Life of George Bent*, 250. The other white traders in the camp were Charles Rath and Charles P. Dodds.
3. Berthrong, *Southern Cheyennes*, 240–41; Richard N. Ellis, *General Pope and U.S. Indian Policy* (Albuquerque:University of New Mexico Press, 1970), 108; *Report of the Commissioner of Indian Affairs, 1865*, 515–16; William Bent to D. N. Cooley, 5/29/1866, Letters Received, Office of Indian Affairs, Upper Arkansas Agency, 1865–67, Microfilm #234, Roll 879, National Archives Record Administration, Washington, D.C.; Robert Campbell to D. N. Cooley, 5/22/1866, Letters Received, Office of Indian Affairs, Upper Arkansas Agency, 1865–67, Microfilm #234, Roll 879, National Archives Record Administration, Washington, D.C.; J.W. Barnes to Murphy, 9/8/1865, Record Group 75, Field Office Records, Records of Central Superintendency of Indian Affairs, M856, Roll 18, National Archives Record Administration, Washington, D.C.
4. *Report of the Commissioner of Indian Affairs, 1865*, 516–17.
5. Ibid., 520.
6. Ibid., 522.
7. Ibid., 522–23.
8. Ibid., 523.
9. Ibid., 524.
10. William Bent to James Harlan, 6/4/1866, Letters Received, Office of Indian Affairs, Upper Arkansas Agency, 1865–67, Microfilm #234, Roll #879, National Archives Record Administration, Washington, D.C.; William Bent Memoir, 6/7/1866, Letters Received, Office of Indian Affairs, Upper Arkansas Agency,

1865–67, Microfilm #234, Roll #879, National Archives Record Administration, Washington, D.C.

11. *Report of the Commissioner of Indian Affairs, 1865*, 525.

12. Ibid.

13. Soule to Mother, 12/18/1864, 1/8/1865, *Silas S. Soule Papers*, Western History Collection, Denver Public Library; Tappan Diary, 4/27/1865, 5/2/1865, 5/13/1865, *Samuel F. Tappan Papers*, Colorado Historical Society.

14. *Report of the Commissioner of Indian Affairs, 1865*, 517. Chiefs would receive 320 acres of land, while widows and orphans would receive 160 acres. Further, families who suffered loss would be paid in "United States securities, animals, goods, provisions, or such other useful articles." See also D. N. Cooley to O. H. Browning, *Report of the Commissioner of Indian Affairs, 1866*, 3.

15. George estimated the value of his horses at $200, the Navaho blankets at $100 each, and other personal effects at $150. See "Abstract of property . . . ," 1865 Treaty of Little Arkansas, Record Group 75, "Documents Relating to the Negotiation of Ratified and Unratified Treaties with Various Indian Tribes, 1801–69," T494, Roll 7, National Archives Record Administration, Washington, D.C.

16. *Report of the Commissioner of Indian Affairs, 1867*, 3–4.

17. I. C. Taylor to Thomas Murphy, 121/26/1865, Record Group 48, Colorado Appointment Papers, M808, Roll 13, National Archives Record Administration, Washington, D.C.; Cheyenne and Arapaho chiefs to Thomas Murphy, 10/14/1865, Record Group 75, Field Office Records, Central Superintendency of Indian Affairs, M856, Roll 18, National Archives Record Administration, Washington, D.C.

18. Christopher B. Gerboth, ed., *The Tall Chief: The Autobiography of Edward W. Wynkoop*, Monograph 9 (Denver: Colorado Historical Society, 1993), 114–15.

19. Berthrong, *Southern Cheyennes*, 257–58; Hyde, *Life of George Bent*, 250–51.

20. Bent to Hyde, 5/29/1906, 4/18/1914, 11/9/1916, *George Bent Letters*, Coe Collection, Yale; Bent to Hyde, 5/3/1905, *George Bent Papers*, Colorado Historical Society.

21. Gerboth, *Tall Chief*, 116.

22. Ibid., 117–18. See also Berthrong, *Southern Cheyennes*, 258–63.

23. G. M. Dodge to John Pope, 3/15/1866, Letters Received, Office of Indian Affairs, Upper Arkansas Agency, 1865–67, Microfilm #234, Roll #879, National Archives Record Administration, Washington, D.C.; Bent to Hyde, 5/29/1906, *George Bent Letters*, Coe Collection, Yale; Hyde, *Life of George Bent*, 250–51; Berthrong, *Southern Cheyennes*, 258–59.

24. Hyde, *Life of George Bent*, 252; Berthrong, *Southern Cheyennes*, 259.

25. See, for example, Bayard Taylor, *Colorado: A Summer Trip*, ed. William W. Savage, Jr., and James H. Lazalier, (Niwot:University Press of Colorado, 1980), 23.

26. See Taylor, *Colorado*, 22–23, 31; Elizabeth Keyes, "Across the Plains in a Prairie Schooner," *Colorado Magazine* 10 (March 1933): 76–77; A. W. Hoyt, "Over the Plains to Colorado," *Harper's New Monthly Magazine* 35 (June 1867): 5.

27. "Bent Family Genealogy Chart," *F. W. Cragin Collection*, Pioneer Museum, Colorado Springs.

28. George Bird Ginnell, *The Cheyenne Indians: Their History and Ways of Life*, 2 vols. (Lincoln and London: University of Nebraska Press, 1972), 1:132ff.; Joyce M. Szabo, *Howling Wolf and the History of Ledger Art* (Albuquerque: University of New Mexico Press, 1994), 150; Janet Catherine Berlo, ed., *Plains Indian Drawings: Pages from a Visual History* (New York: Harry N. Abrams, 1996), 26–29.

29. Folder 7, Bent to Grinnell, 3/21/1907, Folder 41, "Life of Black Kettle by Wolf Chief," Folder 69, *George Bird Grinnell Papers*, Southwest Museum; Bent to Hyde, 4/17/1906, 4/25/1906, *George Bent Letters*, Coe Collection, Yale; Bent to Thoburn, 1/19/1912, Box 1, *Joseph B. Thoburn Papers*, Oklahoma Historical Society; Hyde, *Life of George Bent*, 253.

30. Grinnell Fieldnotes, 11/10/1905, Folder 341, *George Bird Grinnell Papers*, Southwest Museum; *Report of the Commissioner of Indian Affairs, 1865*, 525.

31. See David Fridtjof Halaas, "'All the Camp was Weeping': George Bent and the Sand Creek Massacre," *Colorado Heritage* (Summer 1995): 3.

32. Grinnell Fieldnotes, 11/10/1905, 68–74, Folder 341, *George Bird Grinnell Papers*, Southwest Museum.

33. Bent to Cooley, 5/29/1866, Letters Received, Office of Indian Affairs, Upper Arkansas Agency, 1865–67, Microfilm #234, Roll #879, NARA; Bent to Gen. John Pope, 8/28/1866, Letters Received, Office of Indian Affairs, Upper Arkansas Agency, 1865–67, Microfilm #234, Roll #879, National Archives Record Administration, Washington, D.C.

34. Berthrong, *Southern Cheyennes*, 260–61.

35. Bent to James Harlan, 6/4/1866, Letters Received, Office of Indian Affairs, Upper Arkansas Agency, 1865–67, Microfilm #234, Roll 879, National Archives Record Administration, Washington, D.C.; William W. Bent Memoir, 6/7/1866, ibid.

36. Berthrong, *Southern Cheyennes*, 264; Hyde, *Life of George Bent*, 252–53. Butterfield was the former operator of the Overland Despatch Stage Company.

37. W. R. Irwin to Lewis V. Bogy, 11/3/1866, Letters Received, Office of Indian Affairs, Upper Arkansas Agency, 1865–67, Microfilm #234, Roll 879, National Archives Record Administration, Washington, D.C.; Berthrong, *Southern Cheyennes*, 263–64; David Lavender, *Bent's Fort* (Garden City, N.Y.: Doubleday & Company, Inc., 1954), 363.

38. The 1866 Fort Zarah proceedings can be followed in John Thompson to Acting Ass't Adjt General, District Upper Arkansas, 12/21/1866, Letters Received, Office of Indian Affairs, Upper Arkansas Agency, 1865–67, Microfilm #234, Roll 879, National Archives Record Administration, Washington, D.C., and W. R.

Irwin to Lewis V. Bogy, 11/3/1866, ibid.; "Report of Council held at Fort Zarah, Kansas, 11/10/1866, 11/13/1866 with the Cheyenne Indians," Record Group 75, Ratified and Unratified Treaties, T494, Roll 7, National Archives Record Administration, Washington, D.C., and Charles Bogy and W. R. Irwin to Louis V. Bogy, 12/8/1866, ibid.

39. Grinnell Fieldnotes, 11/9/1905, pp. 33–36, 73–74, 78, Folder 341, *George Bird Grinnell Papers*, Southwest Museum. Nine months after his return from this war party, George and Magpie's first child, Ada Bent, was born. See *Cheyenne and Arapaho Carrier Pigeon* (Darlington, Okla.), 8/15/1910. For scalp dances and sexuality, see Grinnell, *Cheyenne Indians*, 2:39–44.

Chapter 8

1. Dan Flores, "Bison Ecology and Bison Diplomacy: The Southern Plains from 1800 to 1850," *Journal of American History* 78 (September 1991): 465–85.

2. George Bent to George E. Hyde, 12/17/1913, *George Bent Letters*, Coe Collection, Yale; George E. Hyde, *Life of George Bent, Written from His Letters* (Norman: University of Oklahoma Press, 1968), 267–68.

3. Bent to Hyde, 12/17/1913, *George Bent Letters*, Coe Collection, Yale; Hyde, *Life of George Bent*, 268.

4. Bent to Hyde, 12/17/1913, *George Bent Letters*, Coe Collection, Yale; Hyde, *Life of George Bent*, 268–69.

5. Article V of the October 1865 Treaty of the Little Arkansas is the first document that identifies Julia Bent as the wife of Ed Guerrier.

6. W. J. D. Kennedy, ed., *On the Plains with Custer and Hancock: The Journal of Isaac Coates, Army Surgeon*, With an Introduction by Jerome A. Greene (Boulder: Johnson Books, 1997), 56–57.

7. Henry M. Stanley, *My Early Travels and Adventures in America*, Foreword by Dee Brown (Lincoln: University of Nebraska Press, Bison Books Edition, 1982), 29–35; Robert M. Utley, ed., *Life in Custer's Cavalry: Diaries and Letters of Albert and Jennie Barnitz, 1867–1868* (Lincoln: University of Nebraska Press, Bison Books Edition, 1987), 24. At the council, the Arapahos recognized the boy, Tom Wilson (White Shirt), as the son of one of their tribesmen, Red Bull. Later, the government turned Tom over to George Bent, who returned him to his family. George received a horse from the grateful family at the Medicine Lodge treaty council in October 1867. See George Bent to Grinnell, 10/9/1916, Folder 82, *George Bird Grinnell Papers*, Southwest Museum; Bent to Hyde, 6/5/1906, *George Bent Letters*, Coe Collection, Yale; Hyde, *Life of George Bent*, 257.

8. Bent to Hyde, 6/12/1906, *George Bent Letters*, Coe Collection, Yale; Hyde, *Life of George Bent*, 259.

9. Theodore R. Davis, "Summer on the Plains," *Harper's New Monthly Magazine* 36 (February 1868): 295. See also George Bird Grinnell, *The Fighting Cheyennes* (Norman: University of Oklahoma Press, 1955), 250–51; Donald J.

Notes

Berthrong, *The Southern Cheyennes* (Norman: University of Oklahoma Press, 1963), 276.

10. Hyde, *Life of George Bent*, 260.

11. George Bent to Thoburn, 9/29/1910, *Joseph B. Thoburn Papers*, Indian Archives, Oklahoma Historical Society; Bent to Hyde, 5/20/1913, *George Bent Letters*, Coe Collection, Yale; Berthrong, *Southern Cheyennes*, 276; Hyde, *Life of George Bent*, 259; Grinnell, *Fighting Cheyennes*, 251–52. See also Robert M. Utley, *Frontier Regulars: The United States Army and the Indian, 1866–1891* (New York: Macmillan Publishing Co., Inc., 1973), 118.

12. Statement of Fred Fleshman, 8/18/1907, Notebook 3, 32, *Francis W. Cragin Papers*, Western History Department, Denver Public Library.

13. Bent to Hyde, 5/20/1913, George Bent Letters, Coe Collection, Yale; George Armstrong Custer, *My Life on the Plains*, Edited and with an Introduction by Milo Milton Quaife (New York: Promontory Press, 1995), 44–45; Hyde, *Life of George Bent*, 261–62.

14. Custer, *My Life on the Plains*, 35.

15. Bent to Hyde, 12/17/1913, 6/5/1906, *George Bent Letters*, Coe Collection, Yale; Hyde, *Life of George Bent*, 270–71.

16. Berthrong, *Southern Cheyennes*, 283.

17. Utley, *Life in Custer's Cavalry*, 70.

18. *Report of the Commissioner of Indian Affairs, 1868*, 9.

19. Utley, *Frontier Regulars*, 122–23; Berthrong, *Southern Cheyennes*, 281–83; Afton, et al., *Cheyenne Dog Soldiers*, passim.

20. Bent to Hyde, 12/17/1913, 5/22/1917, 6/5/1906, *George Bent Letters*, Coe Collection, Yale; Hyde, *Life of George Bent*, 278–79; Grinnell, *Fighting Cheyennes*, 270–71.

21. Hyde, *Life of George Bent*, 280–81.

22. Bent to Hyde, 6/9/1905, *George Bent Letters*, Coe Collection, Yale; Hyde, *Life of George Bent*, 279–80.

23. Bent to Hyde, 12/17/1913, 6/5/1906, 5/29/1906, *George Bent Letters*, Coe Collection, Yale; George Bent to George E. Hyde, 6/9/1905, *George Bent Papers*, Colorado Historical Society; Hyde, *Life of George Bent*, 278–82; Grinnell, *Fighting Cheyennes*, 270–73; Peter John Powell, *People of the Sacred Mountain: A History of the Northern Cheyenne Chiefs and Warrior Societies, 1830–1879, With an Epilogue, 1969–1974*, 2 vols. (San Francisco: Harper & Row Publishers, 1981), 1:502–8.

24. George Bent to Charles E. Snell, 5/7/1907, C&A Patents, Cheyenne and Arapaho Agency Records, Indian Archives, Oklahoma Historical Society.

25. George Bird Grinnell, *The Cheyenne Indians: Their History and Ways of Life*, 2 vols. (Lincoln and London: University of Nebraska Press, 1972), 1:351–53; Grinnell, *Fighting Cheyennes*, 70–71; Stanley, *My Early Travels*, 258–62; Berthrong, *Southern Cheyennes*, 297; *Report of the Commissioner of Indian Affairs, 1868*, 30.

26. Bent to Hyde, 7/8/1905, *George Bent Letters*, Coe Collection, Yale; Bent to Thoburn, 3/3/1914, *Joseph P. Thoburn Papers*, Indian Archives, Oklahoma Historical Society; Hyde, *Life of George Bent*, 283–84, 322; Grinnell, *Fighting Cheyennes*, 273–74; Stanley, *My Early Travels*, 227; Douglas C. Jones, *The Treaty of Medicine Lodge: The Story of the Great Treaty Council as Told by Eyewitnesses* (Norman: University of Oklahoma Press, 1966), 72.

27. Berthrong, *Southern Cheyennes*, 295–96.

28. Berthrong, *Southern Cheyennes*, 294. See also Bent to Hyde, 7/8/1905, *George Bent Papers*, Colorado Historical Society.

29. Berthrong, *Southern Cheyennes*, 294; Hyde, *Life of George Bent*, 284, Bent to Hyde, 7/8/1905, *George Bent Papers*, Colorado Historical Society.

30. Newspaper correspondents made much of the confrontation between Wynkoop and Roman Nose, but George Bent denied that Roman Nose ever drew a pistol on the agent. See Berthrong, *Southern Cheyennes*, 296; Hyde, *Life of George Bent*, 284; Powell, *People of Sacred Mountain*, 1:673.

31. Jones, *Treaty of Medicine Lodge*, 141.

32. Bent to Grinnell, 10/9/1916, Folder 82, *George Bird Grinnell Papers*, Southwest Museum.

33. Jones, *Treaty of Medicine Lodge*, 17–8, 229–30; Berthrong, *Southern Cheyennes*, 289, 295.

34. Jones, *Treaty of Medicine Lodge*, 82.

35. Dan L. Thrapp, *Encyclopedia of Frontier Biography*, 3 vols. (Lincoln: University of Nebraska Bison Books, 1991), 618; William Y. Chalfant, *Cheyennes and Horse Soldiers: The 1857 Expedition and the Battle of Solomon's Fork*, Foreword by Robert M. Utley (Norman: University of Oklahoma Press, 1989), 181ff.

36. Jones, *Treaty of Medicine Lodge*, 85.

37. Powell, *People of Sacred Mountain*, 1:514–15; Jones, *Treaty of Medicine Lodge*, 98; Berthrong, *Southern Cheyennes*, 297.

38. The sequence and timing of Black Kettle's trip to the Cimarron is open to interpretation. See Powell, *People of Sacred Mountain*, 1:521–53; and Berthrong, *Southern Cheyennes*, 297.

39. Stanley, *My Early Travels*, 230–31.

40. John R. Elting and Michael J. McAfee, eds., "Long Endure: The Civil War Period, 1852–1867," in *Military Uniforms in America* (Novato, Calif.: Presidio Press, 1982) 3:4–5; *Leslie's Illustrated Newspaper*, 11/16/1867; Afton et al., *Cheyenne Dog Soldiers*, passim.

41. Jones, *Treaty of Medicine Lodge*, 111–12.

42. Stanley, "A British Journalist Reports," *Kansas Historical Quarterly* 33 (Autumn 1967): 269.

43. Powell, *People of Sacred Mountain*, 1:515; Jones, *Treaty of Medicine Lodge*, 112.

44. *Cheyenne and Arapaho Carrier Pigeon* (Darling, Oklahoma), 8/15/1910.

45. Jones, *Treaty of Medicine Lodge*, 113.

46. Ibid., 138.

47. Stanley, "A British Journalist Reports," *Kansas Historical Quarterly* 33 (Autumn 1967): 290–91; Powell, *People of Sacred Mountain*, 1:523.

48. Powell, *People of Sacred Mountain*, 1:523; Stanley, "A British Journalist Reports," *Kansas Historical Quarterly*, 33 (Autumn 1967): 291.

49. Powell, *People of Sacred Mountain*, 1:521–52; Jones, *Treaty of Medicine Lodge*, 139–41.

50. George Bent to Robert M. Peck, 12/1907–08, in James Albert Hadley, "The Nineteenth Kansas Cavalry and the Conquest of the Plains Indians," *Kansas Collections* 5:441–42; Hyde, *Life of George Bent*, 322; Bent to Thoburn, 3/3/1914, *Joseph P. Thoburn Papers*, Indian Archives, Oklahoma Historical Society.

51. Jones, *Treaty of Medicine Lodge*, 159–60; Powell, *People of Sacred Mountain*, 1:524; Stan Hoig, *The Battle of the Washita: The Sheridan-Custer Indian Campaign of 1867–69* (Lincoln: University of Nebraska Bison Books, 1979), 32–33.

52. Utley, *Life in Custer's Cavalry*, 114. For a stirring description of the charge, see Jones, *Treaty of Medicine Lodge*, 164–67.

53. Jones, *Treaty of Medicine Lodge*, 168; *Missouri Democrat*, 11/2/67; *Missouri Republican*, 11/2/67, Hyde, *Life of George Bent*, 248.

54. Bent to Thoburn, 3/3/1914, *Joseph P. Thoburn Papers*, Indian Archives, Oklahoma Historical Society.

55. Charles K. Kappler, *Indian Affairs: Laws and Treaties*, vol. 2 (Washington, D.C.: Government Printing Office); Berthrong, *Southern Cheyennes*, 298.

56. For the identity of the enigmatic Cheyenne leader, see Powell, *People of Sacred Mountain*, 1:675–76.

57. Jones, *Treaty of Medicine Lodge*, 173.

58. Ibid., 176.

59. Kappler, *Indian Affairs; Laws and Treaties*; Jones, *Treaty of Medicine Lodge*, 177–78; Hoig, *Battle of the Washita*, 36; Powell, *People of Sacred Mountain*, 1:530–31.

60. Bent to Hyde, 5/20/1913, *George Bent Letters*, Coe Collection, Yale; Jones, *Treaty of Medicine Lodge*, 179–80; *Missouri Republican*, 11/2/1867; Berthrong, *Southern Cheyennes*, 299.

Chapter 9

1. Grinnell Fieldnotes, 6/28/1902, Folder 338, *George Bird Grinnell Papers*, Southwest Museum.

2. George Bent to Thoburn, 9/29/1910, *Joseph B. Thoburn Collection*, Indian Archives, Oklahoma Historical Society; Michael Lansing, "Plains Indian Women and Interracial Marriage in the Upper Missouri Trade, 1804–1868," 31 *Western Historical Quarterly* (Winter 2000): 414, 418.

3. *Sunday Oklahoman* [Oklahoma City], 10/2/1910, *Fred S. Barde Collection*, Oklahoma Historical Society; George W. Bent to Cragin, 6/21/1902, Reel 7,

Correspondence File, *Francis W. Cragin Papers*, Western History Department, Denver Public Library; George Bent to George E. Hyde, 1/12/1906, 7/6/1914, *George Bent Letters*, Coe Collection, Yale; Bent to Thoburn, 9/23/1910, *Joseph B. Thoburn Papers*, Indian Archives, Oklahoma Historical Society; Genealogical Chart, Bent Family file, *Francis W. Cragin Collection*, Pioneer Museum, Colorado Springs; David Lavender, *Bent's Fort* (Garden City, N.Y.: Double Day & Co., 1954), 364; Donald J. Berthrong, *The Southern Cheyennes* (Norman: University of Oklahoma Press, 1963), 299. The circumstances of Charley's death are shrouded in mystery. George rarely spoke of it. On various occasions he said Charley died November 10, 1867, "with fever and not with wound." But George Bent's son, George W. Bent, elaborated, saying his uncle had died from the "effects of a wound received in fight with Kaw Indians near mouth of Walnut Creek in Kansas," and a family genealogical chart lists the death as occurring on November 20, 1867. Lavender wrote that Charley was "severely wounded in a fight with Pawnees, caught malaria, and died in an Indian camp." However, he does not cite a source. All these accounts may be partially correct. Charley was out with the Dog Soldiers, who were raiding against the Kaws at about the time of his death. Most likely he succumbed to pneumonia or other complications several weeks after suffering a gunshot wound. While McGinley's memory may have faded over the years, the details of his account have the ring of truth. In addition, the major knew and respected George Bent, and, at the time the story ran in the *Sunday Oklahoman*, he lived near him in Oklahoma. Neither George E. Hyde, *Life of George Bent, Written From His Letters* (Norman: University of Oklahoma Press, 1968), nor George Bird Grinnell, *The Fighting Cheyennes* (Norman: University of Oklahoma Press, 1955), mentions Charley's death.

4. See for example, Theodore R. Davis, "A Summer on the Plains [1867]," *Harper's New Monthly Magazine* 36 (February 1868): 305–6; William A. Bell, *New Tracks in North America: A Journal of Travel and Adventure Whilst Engaged in the Survey for a Southern Railroad to the Pacific Ocean during 1867–1868* (1870; reprint, Albuquerque: Horn and Wallace, 1965), 81–2; Henry M. Stanley, *My Early Travels and Adventures in America*, Foreword by Dee Brown (1895; reprint, Lincoln: University of Nebraska Press, Bison Books Edition, 1982), 161; Mrs. Frank C. Montgomery, "Ft. Wallace and Its Relation to the Frontier," *Kansas State Historical Society Collections* 17 (1926–1928): 207; General Nelson A. Miles, *Personal Recollections and Observations of General Nelson A. Miles, Embracing a Brief View of the Civil War*, Introduction by Robert Wooster, 2 vols. (Lincoln: University of Nebraska Press, Bison Books Edition, 1972), 1:140–41; W. R. Irwin to Lewis V. Bogy, 11/3/1866, Letters Received, Office of Indian Affairs, Upper Arkansas Agency, 1865–67, Microfilm #234, Roll 879, National Archives Record Administration, Washington, D.C., Oklahoma Historical Society. See also Colin G. Calloway, "Neither White Nor Red: White Renegades on the American Indian Frontier," *Western Historical Quarterly* 17 (January 1986): 43–66.

5. Stanley, *My Early Travels*, 161; Grinnell, *Fighting Cheyennes*, 267–68; Hyde, *Life of George Bent*, 276–77; Berthrong, *Southern Cheyennes*, 282; John H. Monnett, *The Battle of Beecher Island and the Indian War of 1867–1869* (Niwot: University Press of Colorado, 1992), 93–99.

6. Bell, *New Tracks in North American*, 62–65; Robert M. Utley, ed., *Life in Custer's Cavalry: Diaries and Letters of Albert and Jennie Barnitz, 1867–1868* (Lincoln and London: University of Nebraska Press, 1987), 74–79.

7. Davis, "Summer on the Plains," *Harper's New Monthly Magazine*, 305–6; Bell, *New Tracks in North American*, 54; H. L. Lubers, "William Bent's Family and the Indians of the Plains," *The Colorado Magazine* 13 (January 1936): 21; W. R. Irwin to Lewis V. Bogy, 11/3/1866, Letters Received, Office of Indian Affairs, Upper Arkansas Agency, 1865–67, Microfilm #234, Roll 879, National Archives Record Administration, Washington, D.C.

8. John H. Moore, *The Cheyenne* (Oxford, UK: Blackwell Publishers, 1996), 157; *Sunday Oklahoman* [Oklahoma City], 10/1/1910, *Fred S. Barde Collection*, Oklahoma Historical Society; Bell, *New Tracks in North America*, 54.

9. Edward Wynkoop to Thomas Murphy, 2/1/1868, Thomas Murphy to Charles E. Mix, 1/15/1868, Murphy to N. G. Taylor, 2/20/1868, Murphy to Mix, 8/29/1868, Letters Received, Office of Indian Affairs, Upper Arkansas Agency, 1868–70, Microfilm roll 880, National Archives Record Administration, Washington, D.C.; Berthrong, *Southern Cheyennes*, 300.

10. Berthrong, *Southern Cheyennes*, 299–301.

11. E. B. Dennison to Wynkoop, 4/30/1868, Letters Received, Office of Indian Affairs, Upper Arkansas Agency, 1868–70, Roll 880, National Archives Record Administration, Washington, D.C.; Berthrong, *Southern Cheyennes*, 302.

12. William W. Bent probate records, Court of Common Pleas, Jackson County, Missouri, Estate #327, Bent Family Genealogy File, Missouri Valley Room, Kansas City Public Library; "Early Far West Notebooks," 1:38–39, 3:33–36, transcription of *Francis W. Cragin Collection*, Western History Department, Denver Public Library; William W. Bent Will, 5/10/1866, Vertical File, Missouri Valley Room, Kansas City Public Library; Quantrille D. McClung, ed., *Carson-Bent-Boggs Genealogy* (Denver: Denver Public Library, 1962), 99; GB to Hyde, 2/11/1916, *George Bent Letters*, Coe Collection, Yale; Grinnell Fieldnotes, 6/28/1902, Folder 338, *George Bird Grinnell Papers*, Southwest Museum; *The War of the Rebellion: A Compilation of the Official Records of the Union and Confederate Armies*, 70 vols. (Washington, D.C.: Government Printing Office, 1880–1901), Series 1, vol. 41, pt. 2, 735; Berthrong, *Southern Cheyennes*, 199.

13. Virginia McConnell Simmons, *The Ute Indians of Utah, Colorado, and New Mexico* (Boulder: University Press of Colorado, 2000), 131.

14. Bent to Hyde, 3/19/1906, 5/13/1914, 5/19/1914, 12/13/1905, 4/17/1906, 5/2/1917, *George Bent Letters*, Coe Collection, Yale; Bent to Cragin, 10/5/1905, *Francis W. Cragin Collection*, Pioneer Museum, Colorado Springs; Harvey Lewis

Carter, *'Dear Old Kit,'* *The Historical Christopher Carson* (Norman: University of Oklahoma Press, 1968), 218; Hyde, *Life of George Bent*, 292.

15. *Report of the Commissioner of Indian Affairs, 1868*, 64–67; Hyde, *Life of George Bent*, 288. See also Berthrong, *Southern Cheyennes*, 303; Afton, Halaas, and Masich, *Cheyenne Dog Soldiers*, 52–55; Father Peter John Powell, *People of the Sacred Mountain: A History of the Northern Cheyenne Chiefs and Warrior Societies, 1830–1879, With an Epilogue 1969–1974*, 2 vols. (New York: Harper & Row, 1981), 1:567.

16. Paul Andrew Hutton, *Phil Sheridan and His Army*, Foreword by Robert M. Utley, (Norman: University of Oklahoma Press, 1999), 89–9.

17. Bent to Hyde, 6/12/1906, *George Bent Letters*, Coe Collection, Yale; Bent to Thoburn, 1/19/1912, *Joseph B. Thoburn Papers*, Indian Archives, Oklahoma Historical Society; Hyde, *Life of George Bent*, 290; Hutton, *Phil Sheridan and His Army*, 35.

18. Frederick Beecher to Sheridan, 6/13/1868, 7/22/1868, *Philip Sheridan Papers*, Containers 91–93, Reel 91, Library of Congress; Berthrong, *Southern Cheyennes*, 304.

19. *Report of the Commissioner of Indian Affairs*, 1868, 73; Sheridan to Sherman, 11/1/1869, Report of Operations, 1868–69, Reel 75, Containers 70–71, and Statement of Ed Guerrier to J. Schuyler Crosby, 2/9/1869, Containers. 72–73, Reel 76, *Philip Sheridan Papers*, Library of Congress; Hyde, *Life of George Bent*, 288–89; Powell, *People of Sacred Mountain*, 1:568; David Dixon, *Hero of Beecher Island: The Life and Military Career of George A. Forsyth* (Lincoln: University of Nebraska Press, 1994), 67; Berthrong, *Southern Cheyennes*, 306; Robert M. Utley, *Frontier Regulars: The United States Army and the Indian, 1866–1891* (New York: Macmillan Publishing Co., Inc., 1973), 143.

20. *Report of the Commissioner of Indian Affairs, 1868*, 71–73; Philip Sheridan to William T. Sherman, 9/26/1868, "Report of Operations against Indians in the Department of the Missouri in the Winter of 1868–1869," and "List of Murders, Outrages, and Depredations Committed by Indians from 3rd August to 24th October, 1868," Reel 75, Containers. 70–71, *Philip Sheridan Papers*, Library of Congress; Hyde, *Life of George Bent*, 288–89; Bent to Hyde, 6/9/1905, *George Bent Papers*, Colorado Historical Society; Bent to Thoburn, 1/9/1912, 1/19/1912, *Joseph B. Thoburn Papers*, Indian Archives, Oklahoma Historical Society. See also, Dixon, *Hero of Beecher Island*, 67–69; Stan Hoig, *The Battle of the Washita: The Sheridan-Custer Indian Campaign of 1867–69* (Lincoln: University of Nebraska Press, Bison Books Edition, 1979), 47.

21. Bent to Thoburn, 1/9/1912, 1/19/1912, *Joseph B. Thoburn Papers*, Indian Archives, Oklahoma Historical Society; Bent to Hyde, 6/9/1905, *George Bent Papers*, Colorado Historical Society; Afton, Halaas, and Masich, *Cheyenne Dog Soldiers*, 312; Hyde, *Life of George Bent*, 288–89; Berthrong, *Southern Cheyennes*, 305–7.

22. *Report of the Commissioner of Indian Affairs, 1868*, 72.

23. Sheridan to Sherman, 11/1/1869, Report of Operations, 1868–69, Reel 75, Containers 70–71, *Philip Sheridan Papers*, Library of Congress; Bent to Thoburn, 12/27/1911, *Joseph B. Thoburn Papers*, Indian Archives, Oklahoma Historical Society; Bent to Hyde, 6/10/1904, 9/11/1905, *George Bent Papers*, Colorado Historical Society; Bent to Hyde, 4/17/1906, *George Bent Letters*, Coe Collection, Yale; Hyde, *Life of George Bent*, 289–90.

24. H. L. Lubers, "William Bent's Family and the Indians of the Plains," *Colorado Magazine* 13 (January 1936): 19–21; McClung, *Carson-Bent-Boggs Genealogy*, 99.

25. Bent to Hyde, 6/9/1905, *George Bent Papers*, Colorado Historical Society; Hyde, *Life of George Bent*, 289.

26. Berthrong, *Southern Cheyennes*, 307.

27. Col. George A. Armes, *Ups and Downs of an Army Officer* (Washington, D.C., 1900), 282–85.

28. For the Beecher Island fight, see George A. Forsyth, *Thrilling Days in Army Life* (Lincoln: University of Nebraska Press, Bison Books Edition, 1994), 3–75); Cyrus T. Brady, *Indian Fights and Fighters* (Lincoln: University of Nebraska Press, 1971), 97–122; Orvel A. Criqui, *Fifty Fearless Men: The Forsyth Scouts and Beecher Island* (Marceling, Mo.: Walsworth Publishing Company), passim; Monnett, *Battle of Beecher Island*, passim; Dixon, *Hero of Beecher Island*, passim.

29. Hyde, *Life of George Bent*, 286–312; Grinnell, *Fighting Cheyennes*, 277–97; Bent to Hyde, 12/11/1905, *George Bent Letters*, Coe Collection, Yale; Brady, *Indian Fights and Fighters*, 123–42; Berthrong, *Southern Cheyennes*, 315; Monnett, *Battle of Beecher Island*, passim.

30. Bent to Hyde, 9/11/1905, *George Bent Papers*, Colorado Historical Society; Joseph G. Rosa, *They Called Him Wild Bill: The Life and Adventures of James Butler Hickok* (Norman: University of Oklahoma Press, 1964), 84–86; Hyde, *Life of George Bent*, 291.

31. Hyde, *Life of George Bent*, 312.

32. Hutton, *Phil Sheridan and His Army*, 180–200; Louise Barnett, *Touched by Fire: The Life, Death, and Mythic Afterlife of George Armstrong Custer* (New York: Henry Holt and Company, 1996), 109, 438, fn. 43.

33. Douglas C. McChristian, "Plainsman—or Showman? George A Custer's Buckskins," *Military Collector & Historian* 52 (Spring 2000): 2–13.

34. Bent to Hyde, 8/1/1913, 4/17/1906, *George Bent Letters*, Coe Collection, Yale; Bent to Tappan, 4/16/1889, 11/15/1889, *Samuel Tappan Papers*, Colorado Historical Society; Bent to Thoburn, 12/27/1911, *Joseph B. Thoburn Papers*, Indian Archives, Oklahoma Historical Society; Hyde, *Life of George Bent*, 316–17.

35. Bent to Tappan, 3/15/1889, *Samuel Tappan Papers*, Colorado Historical Society.

36. President Johnson to Adjutant General Office, 1/21/1869, Wynkoop to N. G. Taylor, 1/11/1869, W. A. Nichols to Chauncey McKeever, 1/29/1869, Sherman to Bvt. Major General E. D. Townsend, 1/28/1869, O. H. Browning to President Johnson, 1/16/1869, Taylor to O. H. Browning, 1/15/1869, Letters Received, Office of Indian Affairs, Upper Arkansas Agency, 1868–70, Microfilm Roll 880; Bent to Tappan, 3/15/1889, *Samuel Tappan Papers*, Colorado Historical Society. Adding to the confusion of the Black Kettle "widow/sister" story, Custer identified a woman named *Mah-wis-sa* (Red Hair) as Black Kettle's sister. Custer used *Mah-wis-sa* as an emissary to the Cheyennes; she was reunited with Little Robe's band in December 1868. See George A. Custer, *My Life on the Plains*, ed. Milo Milton Quaife, (New York: Promontory Press, 1995), 205; personal communication form Colleen Cometsevah, genealogist for Southern Cheyenne Sand Creek Descendants, to authors, 6/12/2000; Powell, *People of Sacred Mountain*, 2:696–97, 701, 708.

37. Bent to Hyde, 8/28/1913, 1/15/1906, *George Bent Letters*, Coe Collection, Yale; Bent to Grinnell, 10/2/1913, 10/12/1913, Folder 56.2, *George Bird Grinnell Papers*, Southwest Museum; Leonard Tyler notebook, 106–7 (A. S. Gatschet), National Anthropological Archives, Smithsonian Institution, Washington, D.C.; Hyde, *Life of George Bent*, 322.

38. Bent to Robert M. Peck, December 1907, in James Albert Hadley, "The Nineteenth Kansas Cavalry and the Conquest of the Plains Indians," *Kansas State Historical Collections* 10 (1907–1908): 441–42; Bent to Hyde, 9/11/1905, *George Bent Papers*, Colorado Historical Society; Hyde, *Life of George Bent*, 321–22; Grinnell, *Fighting Cheyennes*, 300–5. For the Washita battle, see also Hoig, *Battle of Washita*, 153–60; Powell, *People of Sacred Mountain*, 1:602–19; Berthrong, *Southern Cheyennes*, 318–44; Brady, *Indian Fights and Fighters*, 146–70.

39. The relationship between Custer and *Mo-nah-see-tah* is not known with certainty. Army officers who supported the sexual liaison thesis were generally Custerphobes. But scout Ben Clark, a Custer supporter, and Cheyenne oral tradition also confirmed the affair. See Custer, *My Life on the Plains*, 237–40. See also Berthrong, *Southern Cheyennes*, 336; Barnett, *Touched by Fire*, 194–97; Robert M. Utley, *Cavalier in Buckskin: George Armstrong Custer and the Western Military Frontier* (Norman: University of Oklahoma Press, 1988), 107; Powell, *People of Sacred Mountain*, 2:1327–28.

40. "Estate of Kiowa Woman (Bent), Report on Heirship" as collected by Theresa Bear of El Reno, Oklahoma [Probably from C&A records, Department of the Interior, United States Indian Service, Indian Archives, Oklahoma Historical Society], in possession of authors.

41. Grinnell Fieldnotes, 11/3/1901, 134, Folder 335, *George Bird Grinnell Papers*, Southwest Museum; George Bird Grinnell, *The Cheyenne Indians: Their History and Ways of Life*, 2 vols. (Lincoln and London: University of Nebraska Press, 1972), 1:149; Julia Bent to Commissioner of Indian Affairs, 7/22/1892, Bureau of Indian Affairs, Letters Received 1881–1907, Box 914, RG 75, NARA.

Notes

42. Army regulations entitled George to eleven hundred dollars in back pay and rations. See H. L. Scott, *Military Dictionary* (New York: D. Van Nostrand, 1864), 453–56, and 487.

43. Murphy to Taylor, 1/25/1869, Letters Received, Office of Indian Affairs, Upper Arkansas Agency 1868–70, microfilm Roll 880, National Archives Record Administration, Washington, D.C.

44. Bent to Murphy, 3/20/1869, Letters Received, Office of Indian Affairs, Upper Arkansas Agency 1868–70, Microfilm Roll 880, National Archives Record Administration, Washington, D.C.

45. Brinton Darlington to E. Hoag, 8/27/1869, Letters Received, Office of Indian Affairs, Upper Arkansas Agency 1868–70, Microfilm Roll 880, National Archives Record Administration, Washington, D.C.; Lee Scamehorn, *Albert Eugene Reynolds: Colorado's Mining King* (Norman: University of Oklahoma Press, 1995), 48.

46. Hoig, *Battle of Washita*, 80–81; Scamehorn, *Albert Eugene Reynolds*, 38–62.

47. Bent to Hyde, 8/25/1914, *George Bent Letters*, Coe Collection, Yale; Scamehorn, *Albert Eugene Reynolds*, 41–42.

48. Lt. Henry Jackson to McKeever, 6/6/1869, Microfilm Roll 76, Container 72–73, *Philip Sheridan Papers*, Library of Congress; Hyde, *Life of George Bent*, 325; Berthrong, *Southern Cheyennes*, 339–40.

49. Hyde, *Life of George Bent*, 339, 326.

50. Lavender, *Bent's Fort*, 366.

51. In an issue reporting William's death, one newspaper also carried news of the completion of the transcontinental railroad at Promontory Point, Utah Territory, May 10, 1869. See *Missouri Republican* [Saint Louis], 5/24/1869.

52. Hyde, *Life of George Bent*, 324–25; Berthrong, *Southern Cheyennes*, 344.

53. Historians still debate the question of who actually shot Tall Bull. Strong evidence points to Major Frank North, commander of the Pawnee Scout battalion, who may have fired the fatal shot as the chief peered over the crest of the ravine. Other evidence supports Buffalo Bill's claim. For a full discussion see Don Russell, *The Lives and Legends of Buffalo Bill* (Norman: University of Oklahoma Press, 1960), 129–48; James King, *War Eagle: The Life of General Eugene A. Carr* (Lincoln: University of Nebraska Press, 1963), 94–119; Clarence Reckmeyer, "The Battle of Summit Springs," *Colorado Magazine* 6 (November 1929): 211–20. The Pawnees later told George Bent that everyone was shooting at the Dog Soldier chief and that it was impossible to know who killed him. See Hyde, *Life of George Bent*, 334.

54. Afton, Halaas, and Masich, *Cheyenne Dog Soldiers*, passim; Halaas and Masich, "'You Could Hear the Drums for Miles': A Cheyenne Ledgerbook History," *Colorado Heritage* (Autumn 1996): 2–15; Hyde, *Life of George Bent*, 328–40; Grinnell, *Fighting Cheyennes*, 310–18; Jack D. Filipiak, "The Battle of Summit Springs," *Colorado Magazine* 41 (Fall 1964): 343–54.

Chapter 10

1. William W. Bent Probate Records, Jackson Country, Missouri, in Bent Family Genealogy File, Missouri Valley Room, Kansas City Public Library.

2. William W. Bent personal property distribution in George Bent, To All Whom It May Concern, 7/26/1869, and Robert Bent, To All Whom It May Concern, 7/26/1869, File #18, *Bent's Fort Collection*, Colorado Historical Society.

3. Robert Campbell to D. N. Cooley, 5/22/1866, Letter Received, Office of Indian Affairs, Upper Arkansas Agency, 1865–67, National Archives Records Administration, Washington, D.C.

4. "William W. Bent Will and Sale," Missouri Valley Special Collections, Kansas City (Mo.) Public Library, Vertical File; Pauline S. Fowler, "Historical Review of 1032 West 55th Street [Kansas City, Mo.]," personal communication to authors, July 11, 1999; U.S. Census Bureau, Westport, Missouri, 1870. Adaline died February 26, 1905, in Pueblo, Colorado, and was buried in the city's Riverview Cemetery. See State of Colorado Death Certificate, Mrs. Adalaide V. Bent; *Pueblo* [Colorado] *Chieftain*, 2/28/1905. For Adaline's marriage to William W. Bent, see Jackson County Marriages, 1868–1878, 4, Missouri Valley Room Special Collections, Kansas City (Mo.) Library.

5. See Bent to George E. Hyde, 3/15/1905, *George Bent Letters*, Coe Collection, Yale.

6. *Las Animas* [Colorado] *Leader*, 8/1/1933.

7. William W. Bent personal property distribution in George Bent, To Whom It May Concern, 7/26/1869, File #18, *Bent's Fort Collection*, Colorado Historical Society.

8. Prowers also enlisted the aid of A. E. Reynolds's to acquire the land and convince Brinton Darlington that he was not attempting to defraud the mixed-bloods. See William Bent to Secretary of the Interior James Harlan, 6/4/1866, Letters Received, Office of Indian Affairs, Upper Arkansas Agency, 1865–67, Microfilm #234, Roll 879, National Archives Records Administration, Washington, D.C.; James MacDonald to Brinton Darlington, 9/25/1871, Commissioner letter, 10/5/1870, John W. Prowers to George Bent, 10/15/1870, Prowers to Darlington, 10/15/1870, C&A Patents, Indian Archives, Oklahoma Historical Society; Bent to Grinnell, 10/29/1912, Folder 56.2, *George Bird Grinnell Papers*, Southwest Museum; Cyrus Beede to Edward P. Smith, 5/2/1873, Letters Received, Office of Indian Affairs, Upper Arkansas Agency, 1871–73, Roll 881, National Archives Records Administration, Washington, D.C. See also Lee Scamehorn, *Albert Eugene Reynolds: Colorado's Mining King* (Norman and London: University of Oklahoma Press, 1995), 187.

9. In Memoriam, "Robison Malory Moore: A Tribute From His Family," 12–13; "Early Far West Notebooks," 1:iii, 39, transcription of *Francis W. Cragin Collection*, Western History Department, Denver Public Library.

10. For excellent overviews of the so-called Quaker Policy, see William S. Mcfeely, *Grant: A Biography* (New York: W. W. Norton & Company, 1981), 308–9; and Francis Paul Prucha, *The Great Father: The United States Government and the American Indians*, Vols. 1 and 2 (Lincoln and London: University of Nebraska Press, 1995), 479–608.

11. Donald J. Berthrong, *The Southern Cheyennes* (Norman: University of Oklahoma Press, 1963), 345–46.

12. Medicine Arrow to Brinton Darlington, 9/2/1869, Letters Received, Office of Indian Affairs, Upper Arkansas Agency, 1868–1870, Microfilm Roll #880, National Archives Records Administration, Washington, D.C.

13. Bent to Thoburn, 9/29/1910, *Joseph B. Thoburn Papers*, Indian Archives, Oklahoma Historical Society; Bent to Hyde, 9/25/1904, *George Bent Papers*, Colorado Historical Society.

14. William D. Welge, "Colonial Experience on Cobb Creek: A Modest Attempt of Indian Acculturation" (M.A. thesis, Central State University, Oklahoma, 1988), 28.

15. Brinton Darlington to Enoch Hoag, 4/25/1871, Field Office Records, Central Superintendency, Record Group 75, M856, Roll 35, National Archives Records Administration, Washington, D.C.

16. Brinton Darlington to Enoch Hoag, 6/10/1871, 2/6/1871, 2/9/1871, 4/6/1871, 5/22/1871, Field Office Records, Central Superintendency, Record Group 75, M856, Roll 35, National Archives Records Administration, Washington, D.C.

17. Brinton Darlington to Cyrus Beede, 5/15/1871, Field Office Records, Central Superintency, Record Group 75, M856, Roll 35, National Archives Records Administration, Washington, D.C.

18. *Report of the Commissioner of Indian Affairs, 1871*, 13–40.

19. Stan Hoig, *The Western Odyssey of John Simpson Smith* (Glendale, Calif.: Arthur H. Clark Company, 1974). For Smith's estate, see Darlington to Hoag, 7/20/1871, Field Office Records, Central Superintendency of Indian Affairs, Record Group 75, M856, Roll 35, National Archives Records Administration, Washington, D.C.

20. Darlington to Hoag, 7/15/1871, Field Office Records, Central Superintendency of Indian Affairs, Record Group 75, M856, Roll 35, National Archives Records Administration, Washington, D.C.

21. *Report of the Commissioner of Indian Affairs, 1872*, 42.

22. George C. Reynolds, "Darlington: The Man and Place," in the Archive Room, El Reno Carnegie Library. See also Hoag to F. A. Walker, 5/9/1872, Letters Received, Office of Indian Affairs, Upper Arkansas Agency, 1871–73, Roll 881, National Archives Records Administration, Washington, D.C.; Berthrong, *Southern Cheyennes*, 367.

23. Berthrong, *Southern Cheyennes*, 367–68.

24. Ibid., 370.

25. Lee & Reynolds to Miles, 10/27/1873, Letters Received, Office of Indian Affairs, Upper Arkansas Agency, 1871–73, Roll 881, National Archives Records Administration, Washington, D.C.

26. Berthrong, *Southern Cheyennes*, 363, 374, 377.

27. Bent to Hyde, 9/3/1913, *George Bent Letters*, Coe Collection, Yale. See, for example, *Report of the Commissioner of Indian Affairs, 1873*, 223; ibid., *1874*, 235–36.

28. *Report of the Commissioner of Indian Affairs, 1872*, 136.

29. Bent to Miles, 5/6/1874, Letters Received, Office of Indian Affairs, Upper Arkansas Agency, 1874, Roll 882, National Archives Records Administration, Washington, D.C.; Bent to Hyde, 9/3/1913, *George Bent Letters*, Coe Collection, Yale.

30. Miles to "Commanding Officer at Camp Supply," 4/25/1874, Lt. John R. Brooke to Miles, 4/30/1874, Deputy Marshal E.C. Lefebore to Miles, 5/5/1874, Miles to Edward P. Smith, 7/22/1874, Letters Received, Office of Indian Affairs, Upper Arkansas Agency 1874, Roll 882, National Archives Records Administration, Washington, D.C.; George E. Hyde, *The Life of George Bent, Written from His Letters*, ed. Savoie Lottinville (Norman: University of Oklahoma Press, 1968), 355, Berthrong, *Southern Cheyennes*, 383. Little Robe's son was seriously wounded in an encounter with troops of the Sixth Cavalry.

31. Bent to Hyde, 1/15/1906, *George Bent Letters*, Coe Collection, Yale.

32. Hyde, *Life of George Bent*, 357; Berthrong, *Southern Cheyennes*, 370; Robert M. Utley, *Frontier Regulars: The United States Army and the Indian, 1866–1891* (New York: Macmillan Publishing Co., 1973), 220.

33. Olive K. Dixon, *Life of "Billy" Dixon* (Austin, Tex.: State House Press, 1987), 131–98; Nelson A. Miles, *Personal Recollections and Observations of General Nelson A. Miles* (Lincoln: University of Nebraska, Bison Books Edition, 1992), 1:160; Hyde, *Life of George Bent*, 353–69; Utley, *Frontier Regulars*, 220–21; Berthrong, *Southern Cheyennes*, 385–87.

34. *Report of the Commissioner of Indian Affairs, 1874*, 233; Jason Holloway to Orland and Fannie Holloway, 6/3/1874, 7/21/1874, typescript copies in Cheyenne and Arapaho Files, Indian Archives, Oklahoma Historical Society.

35. Hyde, *Life of George Bent*, 360–61; Berthrong, *Southern Cheyennes*, 387.

36. Berthrong, *Southern Cheyennes*, 388–89; Hyde, *Life of George Bent*, 361; Paul Andrew Hutton, *Phil Sheridan and His Army*, Foreword by Robert M. Utley (Norman: University of Oklahoma Press, 1999), 245–61.

37. Hyde, *Life of George Bent*, 363; Dixon, *Life of "Billy" Dixon*, 226–27; Berthrong, *Southern Cheyennes*, 392, 400; Peter John Powell, *People of Sacred Mountain: A History of the Northern Cheyenne Chiefs and Warrior Societies, 1830–1879, With an Epilogue, 1969–1974* (San Francisco: Harper & Row, 1981), 2:868.

38. Utley, *Frontier Regulars*, 226; Hutton, *Phil Sheridan and His Army*, 246–51.

39. Bent to Hyde, 5/11/1915, *George Bent Letters*, Coe Collection, Yale.

40. Miles to E. P. Smith, 1/20/1875, Field Office Records, Central Superintendency, Record Group 75, M856, Roll 61, National Archives Records Administration, Washington, D.C.; Berthrong, *Southern Cheyennes*, 399.

41. Miles to E. P. Smith, 3/15/1875, Field Office Records, Central Superintendency, Record Group 75, M856, Roll 61, National Archives Records Administration, Washington, D.C.

42. E. Adamson Hoebel, *The Cheyennes: Indians of the Great Plains* (New York: Holt, Rinehart, Winston, 1978), 101; Grinnell, *Cheyenne Indians* 1:131.

43. Miles to E. P. Smith, 3/9/1875, Field Office Records, Central Superintendency, Record Group 75, Microfilm 856, Roll 61, National Archives Records Administration, Washington, D.C.; Dixon, *Life of "Billy" Dixon*, 227–35; *Report of the Commissioner of Indian Affairs, 1875*, 269.

44. *Report of the Commissioner of Indian Affairs, 1875*, 49.

45. Hyde, *Life of George Bent*, 366–67; Miles to E. P. Smith, 5/1/1875, Field Office Records, Central Superintendency, Record Group 75, M856, Roll 61, National Archives Records Administration, Washington, D.C.; J. A. Covington to E. P. Smith, ibid.; *Report of the Commissioner of Indian Affairs, 1875*, 49–50; George Bird Grinnell, *The Fighting Cheyennes* (Norman: University of Oklahoma Press, 1956), 326. See also John H. Monnett, *Massacre at Cheyenne Hole: Lieutenant Austin Henely and the Sappa Creek Controversy* (Niwot: University Press of Colorado, 1999), 40–42.

Chapter 11

1. N. Davis to J. D. Miles 2/16/1875, "Camp on Wolf Creek," Record Group 75, Letters Received OIA, M234, Roll 119, National Archives Records Administration, Washington, D.C.

2. George Bent to George Hyde, 7/?/1908, *George Bent Letters*, Coe Collection, Yale; Benjamin Williams to John D. Miles, 7/5/1875, Record Group 75, Field Office Records, Central Superintendency of Indian Affairs, M856, Roll 61, National Archives Records Administration, Washington, D.C.

3. William Nicholson, to Commissioner of Indian Affairs, 6/20/1876, Record Group 75, Letters Received OIA, M234, Roll 121, National Archives Records Administration, Washington, D.C.

4. Donald J. Berthrong, *The Cheyenne and Arapaho Ordeal: Reservation and Agency Life in the Indian Territory, 1875–1907* (Norman: University of Oklahoma Press, 1976), 27–31.

5. William Bent to Superintendent of Indian Affairs, 10/5/1859, in LeRoy R. Hafen and Ann W. Hafen, eds., *Relations with the Indians of the Plains, 1857–1861* (Glendale, Calif.: Arthur H. Clark Company, 1959), p. 186.

6. Fort Wise Treaty, February 18, 1861, in Hafen and Hafen, *Relations with the Indians of the Plains*, 298–99.

7. William Bent to James Harlan, Secretary of the Interior, 6/4/1866, in Hafen and Hafen, *Relations with the Indians of the Plains*, p. 298.

8. B. Miles to William Nicholson, 10/12/1876, CAA, 8, Oklahoma Historical Society, Indian Archives.

9. George Bent to John D. Miles, 11/4/1876, CAA 51, George Bent File, Oklahoma Historical Society, Indian Archives.

10. George Bent to John D. Miles, 11/10/1876, George Bent File, Indian Archives, Oklahoma Historical Society.

11. George Bent to John D. Miles, 11/15/1876, ibid.

12. George Bent to John D. Miles, 11/17/1876, ibid.

13. George Bent to John D. Miles, 11/26/1876, ibid.

14. George E. Hyde, *Life of George Bent, Written From His Letters*, (Norman: University of Oklahoma Press,1968), 290.

15. Paul A. Hutton, *Phil Sheridan and His Army* (Norman: University of Oklahoma Press, 1999), 334.

16. George Bent to George E. Hyde, 10/16/1906, 2/22/1912, 2/24/1913, *George Bent Letters*, Coe Collection, Yale.

17. George Bent to John D. Miles, 12/20/1877, George Bent File, Indian Archives, Oklahoma Historical Society.

18. John D. Miles to William Nicholson, 3/28/1877, Record Group 75, Letters Received OIA, M234, Roll 122, National Archives Records Administration, Washington, D.C.

19. William Nicholson to Commissioner J. Q. Smith, 4/2/1877, Record Group 75, Letters Received, OIA, M234, Roll 122, National Archives Records Administration, Washington, D.C.

20. J. D. Miles to William Nicholson, 3/28/1877, Record Group 75, Letters Received OIA, M234, Roll 122, National Archives Records Administration, Washington, D.C.

21. Bent to Hyde, 10/16/1906, George Bent Letters, Coe Collection, Yale. Berthrong, *Cheyenne and Arapaho Ordeal*, 33. For the Cheyenne breakout, see also George Bird Grinnell, *The Fighting Cheyennes* (Norman: University of Oklahoma Press, 1956), 398–427; Ramon Powers, "Why the Northern Cheyenne Left Indian Territory in 1878: A Cultural Analysis," *Kansas Quarterly* 3 (Fall 1971): 72–81; and idem, "The Northern Cheyenne Trek through Western Kansas in 1878: Frontiersmen, Indians and Cultural Conflict," *Trail Guide*, 17 (September/December 1972): 2–23; and John H. Monnett, *Tell Them We Are Going Home: The Odyssey of the Northern Cheyennes* (Norman: University of Oklahoma, 2001).

22. Philip McCusker to E. A. Haigt, 3/3/1878, Record Group 75, Letters Received, Cheyenne and Arapaho Agency, 1878, National Archives Records Administration, Washington, D.C.

23. *Colony* [Oklahoma] *Courier*, 8/24/1911, 4/5/1915, 1/4/1917.

24. Frances Densmore, *Cheyenne and Arapaho Music*, Southwest Museum Papers 10 (Los Angeles: Southwest Museum, 1936); "Standing Out Bent Interview," 3/29/1938, Indian Pioneer History, vol. 90, 241–44, Grant Foreman Collection, Indian Archives, Oklahoma Historical Society.

25. Kiowa Woman had two children of Buffalo Thigh—yet she insisted that Nellie (Crooked Nose Woman) and Neal (Lee Big Eagle) bear the Bent name, perhaps in recognition of its power and influence. For Kiowa Woman's marriage record and children, see Estate of Kiowa Woman (Bent) Transmitting Record, including Report on Heirship, Kiowa Woman (Bent), 6/23/1914, W. D. Goodwin to Commissioner of Indian Affairs, 6/23/1914, Collected by Theresa Bear, in the possession of authors.

26. J. D. Miles to William Nicholson, 7/14/1877, Cheyenne Family Enrollment, 7/1/1877, Record Group 78, Letters Received OIA, M234, Roll 122, National Archives Records Administration, Washington, D.C.

27. For the liquor trade in Indian country, see William E. Unrau, *White Man's Wicked Water: The Alcohol Trade and Prohibition in Indian Country, 1802–1892* (Lawrence: University Press of Kansas, 1996), passim; and Francis Paul Prucha, *The Great Father: The United States Government and the American Indians* (Lincoln and London: University of Nebraska Press, Bison Books Edition, 1995), 98–103.

28. G. M. Russell to J. D. Miles 5/27/1875, Record Group 75, Letters Received, OIA, M234, Roll 119, National Archives Records Administration, Washington, D.C.

29. Miles to Commissioner of Indian Affairs, 6/3/1875, Record Group 75, Letters Received, Office of Indian Affairs, M234, Kroll 119, National Archives Records Administration, Washington, D.C.

30. Journal, January 1, 1870–December 31, 1871, vol. 9, A. E. Reyonolds Collection, Colorado Historical Society.

31. Brevet Lt. Col. J. K. Mizner to War Department, 11/12/1878, Record Group 75, Letters Received, C&A, 1878, National Archives Records Administration, Washington, D.C.

32. J. D. Miles to Col. J. K. Mizner, 5/30/1876, Record Group 75, Letters Received, Office of Indian Affairs, M234, Roll 121, National Archives Records Administration, Washington, D.C.

33. J. D. Miles to William Nicholson, 2/6/1876, Record Group 75, Letters Received OIA, M234, Roll 121, National Archives Records Administration, Washington, D.C.

34. J. D. Miles to Col. J. K. Mizner, 5/30/1876, Record Group 75, Letters Received OIA, M234, Roll 121, National Archives Records Administration, Washington, D.C.

35. Phil McCusker to E. A. Hayt, 3/3/1878, Record Group 75, Letters Received, C&A, 1878, National Archives Records Administration, Washington, D.C. See also McCusker to A. C. Williams, 5/29/1877, ibid.

36. Miles to H. Price, 12/17/1883, Record Group 75, Letters Received 1881–1907, BIA, National Archives Records Administration, Washington, D.C.

37. Col. J. K. Mizner to Secretary of War George McCrary, 11/12/1878, Record Group 75, Letters Received, C&A, 1878, National Archives Records Administration, Washington, D.C.

38. Miles to Commissioner of Indian Affairs, 1/19/1880, Record Group 75, Letters Received, OIA, M234, Roll 126, National Archives Records Administration, Washington, D.C.

39. *Arkansas City Traveler*, 8/29/1883.

40. Ibid.

41. Walter Campbell [Stanley Vestal] to Dorothy Gardiner, 12/5/1939, *Walter Campbell Papers*, University of Oklahoma.

42. Miles to Hamphill & Moy, 5/29/1883, C&A Letter Book, vol. 6, 424, Indian Archives, Oklahoma Historical Society.

43. *Cheyenne Transporter* [Darlington, Indian Territory], 9/15/1884, 10/10/1884.

44. *Arkansas City Traveler* [Caldwell, Kansas], 11/26/1884.

45. *Cheyenne Transporter*, 4/15/1885, 6/30/1885, 7/12/1886.

46. *Report of the Commissioner of Indian Affair, 1886*, p. 114, 123. See also Brief of Papers, Sheridan Report, 7/24/1885, Record Group 94, Letters Received, AGO, M689, Roll 362, 24–25, National Archives Records Administration, Washington, D.C.; Lt. W. L. Clarke to Commanding Officer at Cantonment, 6/18/1880, Record Group 75, Letters Received, OIA, M234, Roll 126, National Archives Records Administration, Washington, D.C.

47. Amos Chapman to Col. J. H. Potter, 1/25/1885, Record Group 94, Letters Received, AGO, M689, Roll 275, National Archives Records Administration, Washington, D.C.; Col. J. A. Potter to General C. C. Augur, 1/26/1885, ibid.; Brief of Papers, Sheridan Report, 7/24/1885, ibid. See also Berthrong, *Cheyenne and Arapaho Ordeal*, 100–1.

48. Stone Calf to Senator Vest, 12/23/1884, Record Group 94, Letters Received, AGO, 1881–1889, M689, Roll 275, National Archives Records Administration, Washington, D.C.

49. Berthrong, *Cheyenne and Arapaho Ordeal*, 109.

50. *Arkansas City Traveler*, 10/18/1882.

51. *Arkansas City Traveler*, 9/27/1882, 10/18/1882; *Cheyenne Transporter* [Darlington], 1/28/1884. Berthrong, *Cheyenne and Arapaho Ordeal*, 109–10.

52. Julia Bent to Commissioner of Indian Affairs, 7/22/1892, Record Group 75, Letters Received, 1881–1907, BIA, Box 914, #36573, National Archives Records Administration, Washington, D.C. The cattle dispute between Julia and her father continued until 1892, when Agent Charles Ashley in a letter to the com-

Notes

missioner of Indian Affair denied her allegations, stating that the government in 1879 had issued cattle to heads of families with children in school but that the stock was not the property of the children. Ashley concluded that the hungry Bents had long since consumed the small herd. See Ashley's letter to the commissioner dated 7/22/1892 in ibid.

53. Berthrong, *Cheyenne and Arapaho Ordeal*, 81, 108, 127. See Joyce M. Szabo, *Howling Wolf and the History of Ledger Art* (Albuquerque: University of New Mexico Press, 1994), 129.

54. Prucha, *Great Father*, 667–70.

55. C. C. Painter, *Cheyennes and Arapahoes Revisited and a Statement of Their Agreement and Contract with Attorneys* (Philadelphia: Indian Rights Association, 1893), 53–62; see also Berthrong, *Cheyenne and Arapaho Ordeal*, 149.

56. Painter, *Cheyennes and Arapahoes Revisted*, 57.

57. Ibid., 37.

58. Henry C. Keeling, "The Indians: My Experience with the Cheyenne Indians," *Kansas Historical Society Collections*, 11 (1909–1910), 311.

59. *Arkansas City Traveler*, 8/21/1889; Painter, *Cheyennes and Arapahoes Revisited*, 44.

60. Painter, *Cheyennes and Arapahoes Revisited*, 43.

61. T. F. McMechan Affidavit 1/11/1890, S. J. Crawford-Cheyenne-Arapaho Contract Case, Record Group 75, Office of Indian Affairs, Letters Received. NARA.

62. Ibid.

63. Photo archives and vertical files, Wichita-Sedgwick Country Historical Museum; personal communication from Susan and Craig Miner, 6/3/2003, Wichita, Kansas.

64. George Bent Testimony, Exhibit "G," 9/17/1889. S. J. Crawford-Cheyenne-Arapaho Contract Case, RG75, OIA, Letters Received, NARA.

65. Crawford Case, George Bent Testimony, Exhibit 13, 1/7/1890, National Archives Records Administration, Washington, D.C.

66. Painter, *Cheyennes and Arapahoes Revisited*, 50.

67. Charles F. Ashley to Commissioner of Indian Affairs, 10/3/1889, CAA 30, Indian Archives, Oklahoma Historical Society.

68. Jean Afton, David Fridtjof Halaas, and Andrew E. Masich, *Cheyenne Dog Soldiers: A Ledgerbook History of Coups and Combat* (Niwot: University Press of Colorado, 1997), 164–67.

69. Crawford Case, George Bent deposition, Exhibit 13, National Archives Records Administration, Washington, D.C.

70. Cheyenne and Arapaho Council Minutes, 5/9/92, C&A Letterbook, vol. 33, 428, Indian Archives, Oklahoma Historical Society.

71. George E. Fay, ed., *Treaties, Land Cessions, and Other U.S. Congressional Documents Relative to American Indian Tribes, Cheyenne and Arapaho, 1825–1900* (Greeley: Museum of Anthropology, University of Northern Colorado, 1977), 100; Berthrong, *Cheyenne and Arapaho Ordeal*, xvi.

72. Painter, *Cheyennes and Arapahoes Revisited*, 4–5; Berthrong, *Cheyenne and Arapaho Ordeal*, 168–69.

Chapter 12

1. Grinnell Fieldnotes, 6/13/1912, MS.5, Folder 351, *George Bird Grinnell Papers*, Southwest Museum.

2. Sherry L. Smith, "George Bird Grinnell and the 'Vanishing' Plains Indians," *Montana The Magazine of Western History* 50 (Autumn 2000): 20.

3. Bent to Grinnell, 2/12/1912, 4/27/1912, 1/23/1912, MS. 5, Folder 56.2, *George Bird Grinnell Papers*, Southwest Museum.

4. Grinnell Fieldnotes, 11/2/1901, MS. 5, Folder 335, *George Bird Grinnell Papers*, Southwest Museum; Grinnell to Major G. W. H. Stouch, 5/11/1901, 9/26/1901, *George Bird Grinnell Letters*, Yale.

5. George Bird Grinnell to George Bent, 8/11/1904, 5/9/1905, 3/27/1905, *George Bird Grinnell Letters*, Box 9, Folder 14, Yale.

6. George Bent to Grinnell, 5/24/1910, MS. 5, Folder 56.2, *George Bird Grinnell Papers*, Southwest Museum.

7. Bent to George E. Hyde, 11/29/1912, 6/27/1912, 7/12/1912, *George Bent Letters*, Coe Collection, Yale.

8. *Colony Courier*, 5/30/1912.

9. *Carrier Pigeon* [Darlington, Oklahoma], 7/1/1912; *Colony Courier*, 6/6/1912.

10. Bent to Grinnell, 12/17/1916, 1/13/1917, MS. 5, Folder 56.2, *George Bird Grinnell Papers*, Southwest Museum.

11. Grinnell Fieldnotes, 6/7/1912, MS. 5, Folder 351, *George Bird Grinnell Papers*, Southwest Museum.

12. *Carrier Pigeon*, 11/1/1911.

13. Martin Abernethy to Walter Campbell [Stanley Vestal], 11/9/1929, Walter Campbell Papers, University of Oklahoma; Bent to Charles E. Shell, 5/7/1907, Cheyenne and Arapaho Agency Records, C&A Patents, Indian Archives, Oklahoma Historical Society.

14. Proceedings of Council, 5/3/1892, 5/9/1892, Cheyenne and Arapaho Agency Records, Letterbooks, vol. 33, 388, 438, Indian Archives, Oklahoma Historical Society.

15. Donald J. Berthrong, *The Cheyenne and Arapaho Ordeal: Reservation and Agency Life in the Indian Territory, 1875–1907* (Norman: University of Oklahoma Press, 1976), 225.

16. Bent to Reynolds, 1/13/1897, George Bent Letters, Colorado Historical Society.

17. Julia Bent to Commissioner of Indian Affairs, 7/22/1892, Record Group 75, BIA, Letters Received, Box 914, #36573, National Archives Record Administration, Washington, D.C.; Charles Ashley to Commissioner of Indian Affairs,

10/7/1892, ibid.; Ashley to Commissioner of Indian Affairs, Cheyenne and Arapaho Agency Records, Letterbook vol. 34, 157–58, Indian Archives, Oklahoma Historical Society; Berthrong, *Cheyenne and Arapaho Ordeal*, 190, 220–21.

18. Bent to Reynolds, 1/13/1897, *A. E. Reynolds Papers*, Colorado Historical Society.

19. Reynolds to Bent, 1/27/1897, 11/6/1906, ibid. See also *Colony Currier*, 5/3/1917. A Reynold's Christmas box containing hundreds of dollars of gifts came annually hereafter.

20. Bent to Hyde, 1/12/1906, *George Bent Letters*, Coe Collection, Yale.

21. G. B. Williams to Commissioner of Indian Affairs, 4/27/1887, 5/24/1887, 9/28/1887, 12/17/1887, Cheyenne and Arapaho Agency Records, Letterbooks, vol. 20, 105–6, 151, 309, 351, Indian Archives, Oklahoma Historical Society; Ashley to Commissioner of Indian Affairs, CAA Records, Letterbooks, vol. 27, 236, ibid.

22. L. G. Moses, *The Indian Man: A Biography of James Mooney* (Urbana and Chicago: University of Illinois Press, 1984), xii.

23. Bent to George E. Hyde, 9/22/1915, *George Bent Letters*, Coe Collection, Yale.

24. Moses, *Indian Man*, 140–41. In 1903, Mooney paid Bent to induce a Cheyenne man to undergo the tortures of the Sun Dance. Mooney was widely criticized for his role in the incident and for taking graphic photographs of the ceremony.

25. Smith, "George Bird Grinnell and the 'Vanishing' Plans Indians," 24.

26. Grinnell Fieldnotes, 11/3/1901, MS. 5, Folder 335, *George Bird Grinnell Papers*, Southwest Museum.

27. For the Grinnell-Mooney clash over clans, see Bent to Grinnell, 2/10/1902, 8/7/1902, 10/4/1902, 10/20/1902, 4/4/1905, 5/21/1906, 6/4/1909, 9/6/1912, 9/24/1912, 10/2/1913, 12/15/1913, MS. 5, *George Bird Grinnell Papers*, Southwest Museum; Grinnell Fieldnotes, 5/29/1908, Folder 348; 6/14/1912, Folder 351, *George Bird Grinnell Papers*, Southwest Museum. See also Smith, "George Bird Grinnell and the 'Vanishing' Plains Indians," 27; Moses, *Indian Man*, 161.

28. Hyde to Grinnell, 3/12/1909, MS. 5, Folder 37, *George Bird Grinnell Papers*, Southwest Museum; Grinnell to Joseph B. Thoburn, 10/22/1919, Thoburn Collection, Indian Archives, Oklahoma Historical Society.

29. Hyde to Grinnell, 3/12/1909, MS. 5, Folder 37, *George Bird Grinnell Papers*, Southwest Museum.

30. Bent to Hyde, 2/23/1904, [Lincoln B. Faller transcription], *George Bent Letters*, Coe Collection, Yale.

31. Bent to Hyde, 1/19/1905, *George Bent Letters*, Coe Collection, Yale.

32. Hyde to Grinnell, 4/27/1917, MS. 5, Folder 51.1, *George Bird Grinnell Papers*, Southwest Museum.

33. Cheyenne skeletal remains housed at the Smithsonian Institution were recently repatriated and buried at Concho, Oklahoma. The widow of Major Hal

Sayre, a veteran of the Third Colorado, donated to the Colorado Historical society Cheyenne scalps that her husband had proudly displayed over the mantle of their Denver home. One of these scalps may be found today in the material culture collection of the Colorado Historical Society, Denver.

34. *Denver Times*, November 5, 1905.

35. Hyde to Grinnell, 5/11/1908, MS. 5, Folder 51.1, *George Bird Grinnell Papers*, Southwest Museum.

36. The Civil War monument, flanked by two bronze cannons, still dominates the west side of the state capitol. In the year 2002 the authors worked with Cheyenne leaders Laird Cometsevah (Clinton, Oklahoma) and Steve Brady (Lame Deer, Montana) to install an interpretive marker that put the offensive wording of the monument into historical perspective.

37. Milo H. Slater to A. E. Reynods, 11/10/1905, *A. E. Reynolds Papers*, Colorado Historical Society.

38. Reynolds to Slater, 11/11/1905, ibid. See also Lee Scamehorn, *Albert Eugene Reynolds: Colorado's Mining King* (Norman: University of Oklahoma Press, 1995), 60–61.

39. Grinnell to Bent, 7/5/1905, 7/14/1905, *George Bird Grinnell Letters*, Yale.

40. John J. White to Grinnell, 10/31/1905, *George Bird Grinnell Letters*, Yale.

41. J. J. White to Grinnell, 11/7/1905, 11/9/1905, 11/11/1905, *George Bird Grinnell Letters*, Yale.

42. Bent to Hyde, 12/18/1905, *George Bent Letters*, Coe Collection, Yale.

43. Hyde to Grinnell, 11/5/1907, MS. 5, Folder 51.1, *George Bird Grinnell Papers*, Southwest Museum.

44. Hyde to Grinnell, 3/22/1908, MS. 5, Folder 37, *George Bird Grinnell Papers*, Southwest Museum.

45. Hyde to Grinnell, 3/12/1909, ibid.

46. Hyde to Grinnell, 10/30/1907, MS. 5, Folder 51.1, *George Bird Grinnel Papers*, Southwest Museum..

47. Hyde to Grinnell, 3/12/1909, MS. 5, Folder 37, *George Bird Grinnel Papers*, Southwest Museum.

48. Grinnell to Hyde, 1/29/1907, *George Bird Grinnell Letters*, Yale.

49. Hyde to Grinnell, 3/12/1909, MS. 5, Folder 37, *George Bird Grinnell Papers*, Southwest Museum.

50. Hyde to Grinnell, 3/22/1908, ibid.

51. George Bird Grinnell, *Fighting Cheyennes* (New York: Charles Scribner's Sons, 1915); Bent to Hyde, 1/29/1913, *George Bent Letters*, Coe Collection, Yale.

52. Bent to Hyde, 6/5/1909, *George Bent Letters*, Coe Collection, Yale.

53. Bent to Hyde, 12/26/1911, *George Bent Papers*, Denver Public Library.

54. Bent to Hyde, 3/4/1912, Bent Letters, Coe Collection, Yale.

55. Bent to Hyde, 2/19/1913, ibid.

56. Bent to Hyde, 1/29/1913, 6/3/1909, 6/5/1909, 8/31/1910, 5/12/1911, 12/18/1911, 2/22/1912, 11/26/1912, 12/20/1912, 1/13/1913, 1/29/1913,

2/19/1913, 3/3/1915, ibid. See also Bent to Hyde, 1/15/1909, 11/13/1909, 1/5/1911, 6/6/1911, 11/29/1911, 12/26/1911, 7/115/1913, 9/9/1913, 4/2/1914, 9/22/1914, 11/10/1915, 3/30/1916, 12/6/1917, *George Bent Papers*, Western History Department, Denver Public Library; and Bent to Joseph B. Thoburn, 10/22/1919, *Jason B. Thoburn Collection*, Indian Archives, Oklahoma Historical Society.

57. Hyde to Grinnell, 3/23/1915, MS. 5, Folder 51.b, *George Bird Grinnell Papers*, Southwest Museum.

58. Hyde to Grinnell, 12/9/1915, ibid.

59. Hyde to Grinnell, 2/5/1918, MS. 5, Folder 51.1, *George Bird Grinnel Papers*, Southwest Museum.

60. Hyde to Grinnell, 3/12/1916, MS. 5, Folder 51.b, and Hyde to Grinnell, 10/1/1916, Folder 51.c, *George Bird Grinnell Papers*, Southwest Museum.

61. *Colony Courier*, 6/25/1914. George said he was very proud of his umbrella and always carried it because he thought "every day it might rain."

62. Ibid.; Bent to Hyde, 3/3/1915, *George Bent Letters*, Coe Collection, Yale; Hyde to Grinnell, 3/15/1915, MS. 5, Folder 51b, *George Bird Grinnell Papers*, Southwest Museum.

Bibliography

Unpublished Sources

Bent's Old Fort National Historic Site
James Larkin Memorandum Book, 1856.
Berthrong, Donald. "The Bent Descendants and the World They Knew."
Colorado College, Tutt Library, Special Collections and Archives
George Bent Letter.
Frank Murray Wynkoop Papers.
Colorado Historical Society, Books and Manuscripts Department, Denver
Scott Anthony Papers.
Bent Family Bible
Bent's Fort Collection.
George Bent Papers.
John M. Chivington Papers.
Joseph Cramer-Silas S. Soule Letters.
Thomas F. Dawson Scrapbooks.
Dog Soldier Ledgerbook.
A. E. Reynolds Papers.
Samuel F. Tappan Papers.
Colorado State Archives, Denver
"Documents Concerning the Battle of Sand Creek, November 29, 1864."
Cometsevah, Colleen. Communication to authors, June 12, 2000.
Cometsevah, Laird. Interview with authors, April 13–14, 1998.
———. "Sand Creek Massacre-Nov. 29." Communication to authors, June 4, 1999.
Denver Public Library, Western History Department
George Bent Papers.
John M. Chivington Papers.
William O. Collins Papers
F. W. Cragin Notebooks.
George E. Hyde Papers.
E. S. Ricker Papers.
Silas S. Soule Papers.

Bibliography

El Reno Carnegie Library [Oklahoma], Archive Room
   George C. Reynolds, "Darlington: The Man and Place."
"Estate of Kiowa Woman (Bent), Report on Heirship." Collected by Theresa Bear, in the possession of authors.
Fowler, Pauline E.. "Historical Review of 1032 West 55th Street [Kansas City, Mo.]." Communication to authors, July 11, 1999.
Greene, Jerome C. "Report on the Historical Documentation of the Location and Extent of the Sand Creek Massacre Site." Denver: Intermountain Support Office, National Park Service, May 1999.
Goertner, Thomas Grenville. "Reflections of a Frontier Soldier on the Sand Creek Affair as Revealed in the Diary of Samuel F. Tappan." M.A. thesis, University of Denver, 1959.
Huss, Stephen F. Letter to authors, February 17, 19, 1998.
Kansas City [Missouri] Public Library, Missouri Valley Room
   William W. Bent, Last Will and Testament.
   Jackson County Marriages, 1868–1878.
   John W. Parker, "Professional Services."
   In Memoriam, "Robinson Malory Moore: A Tribute from his Family"
Kansas Historical Society, Topeka
   Indian Clipping File, 1899–1938.
   O. A. Nixon Journals. Miscellaneous Collections.
   Nathan Scarritt File.
Library of Congress
   Philip Sheridan Papers.
Marlatt, Gene R. "Edward W. Wynkoop: An Investigation of His Role in the Sand Creek Controversy and Other Indian Affairs, 1863–1868." M.A. thesis, University of Denver, 1961.
Masich, Andrew E. "Arizona during the Civil War: The Impact of the California Volunteers, 1861–1866." M.A. thesis, University of Arizona, 1984.
Missouri Historical Society, St. Louis
   Bent Family Bible.
   Bent Family Papers.
   Boggs Family Papers.
   Indian Collection.
   Missouri Presbyterian Recorder.
   Mrs. Charles Hiram Wood Papers.
National Anthropological Archives, Smithsonian Institution, Washington, D.C.
   No. 3275, George Bent to Prof. Holmes, January 1907.
   James Mooney Papers. "Miscellaneous Notes on the Cheyenne, 1903–1906."
   Leonard Tyler Notebook.
National Archives Record Administration, Chicago
   Record Group 177. Samuel W. Bonsall Map.
National Archives Records Administration, Washington, D.C.

Bibliography

Compiled Service Records of Confederate Soldiers.

Compiled Service Records, Missouri.

Office of Indian Affairs, Upper Arkansas Agency. Letters Received.

Consolidated Index to Compiled Service Records of Confederate Soldiers

Record Group 48. Colorado Appointment Papers.

———. Records of the Office of Secretary of Interior.

Record Group 75.

———. Office of Indian Affairs, Letters Received.

———. Central Superintendency of Indian Affairs.

———. Ratified and Unratified Treaties, 1801–1869.

Record Group 78. Office of Indian Affairs. Letters Received.

Record Group 94. Adjutant General Office. Letters Received.

———. Eugene A. Carr Papers.

———. Department of the Platte. Letters Received.

Record Group 109. Bent, William, M-345 Confederate Service Records—
George Bent.

———. Provost Marshal File—Charles Lewis.

Record Group 123. U.S. Court of Claims. Indian Depredation Files.

Record Group 156. Ordnance Returns, Cavalry, 1861–1865.

Record Group 205. U.S. Court of Claims, Indian Depredation Files (College
Park).

Oklahoma Historical Society, Indian Archives, Oklahoma City

Fred S. Barde Collection.

George Bent File.

Cheyenne and Arapaho Agency Records.

———. C&A Patents.

———. Lawlessness File

———. Letterbooks. Microfilm and letterpress books.

———. Vices File.

———. Warfare, 1864–1885.

Grant Foreman Collection. "Standing Out," Indian Pioneer History, vol. 90.

Joseph B. Thoburn *Collection.*

Pioneer Museum, Colorado Springs

F. W. Cragin Collection.

Roberts, Gary. "Sand Creek: Tragedy and Symbol." 2 vols. Ph.D. diss., University of Oklahoma, 1984.

———. "The Sand Creek Massacre Site." Denver: Intermountain Support Office,
National Park Service, January 1998.

Scott, Douglas C., et al. "Archaeological Reconnaissance of Two Possible Sites of
the Sand Creek Massacre of 1864." Department of Southwest Studies, Fort
Lewis College, Durango, Colorado.

Southwest Museum, Los Angeles

George Bird Grinnell Papers.

Bibliography

F. W. Hodge Papers.
State Historical Society of Missouri, Kansas City
George Bent Letters.
State of Colorado
Adalaide V. Bent Death Certificate.
University of Colorado Libraries, Boulder
Bent-Hyde Collection.
University of Oklahoma
Walter Campbell Papers.
Wegman-French, Lysa, and Christine Whitacre. "Interim Report No. 1: Historical Research on the Location of the Sand Creek Massacre Site." Denver: Intermountain Support Office, National Park Service, September 11, 1998.
———. "Interim Report No. 2: Historical Research on the Location of the Sand Creek Massacre Site." Denver: Intermountain Support Office, National Park Service, January 29, 1999.
———. "Interim Report No. 3: Historical Research on the Location of the Sand Creek Massacre Site. Denver: Intermountain Support Office, National Park Service, April 27, 1999.
Welge, William D. "Colonial Experience on Cobb Creek: A Modest Attempt of Indian Acculturation." M.A. thesis, Central State University [Oklahoma], 1988.
White Shield, Blanche. Communication to authors, June 2, 1999.
Yale University, Beinecke Library
George Bent Letters.
George Bird Grinnell Letters.

Government Documents

Kappler, Charles K. Indian Affairs: Law and Treaties. Vol. 2. Washington, D.C.: Government Printing Office, 1904.
Record of Engagements with Hostile Indians within the Military Division of the Missouri, from 1866 to 1882, Lieutenant General P.H. Sheridan, Commanding. Washington, D.C.: Government Printing Office, 1882.
Report of the Commissioner of Indian Affairs, 1857.
———, 1859.
———, 1860.
———, 1864.
———, 1865.
———, 1866.
———. 1867.
———. 1868.
———. 1871.
———. 1874.

Bibliography

———. *1886.*

Senate Executive Document No. 13. 40th Cong., 1st Session. *Report to the Senate on the Origins and Progress of Indian Hostilities on the Frontier.* Washington, D.C.: Government Printing Office, 1867.

Senate Executive Document No. 26. 39th Cong., 2nd Session. *Report of the Secretary of War, Communicating . . . a Copy of the Evidence Taken at Denver and Fort Lyon, Colorado Territory, by a Military Commission Ordered to Inquire into the Sand Creek Massacre, November, 1864.* Washington, D.C.: Government Printing Office, 1867.

Senate Report No. 142. 38th Cong., 2nd Session. *Report of the Joint Committee on the Conduct of the War.* 3 vols. Washington, D.C.: Government Printing Office, 1865.

U.S. Cenus Bureau. Population for Saint Louis County, Missouri, 1850.

———. Population for Saint Louis County, Missouri,1860.

———. Population for Jackson Country, Missouri, 1860.

———. Population for Westport, Missoura, 1870.

U.S. Congress, Senate. "Testimony as to the Claim of Ben Holliday." Sen. Mis. Doc. No. 19, 46th Congress, 2nd Session, 1879.

War of the Rebellion, The: A Compilation of the Official Records of the Union and Confederate Armies. 70 vols. Washington, D.C.: Government Printing Office, 1880–1901.

Published Sources

Afton, Jean, and David Fridtjof Halaas, and Andrew E. Masich. *Cheyenne Dog Soldiers: A Ledgerbook History of Coups and Combat.* Niwot, Colo., and Denver: University Press of Colorado and the Colorado Historical Society, 1997.

Ahlborn, Richard E., ed. *Man Made Mobile: Early Saddles of Western North America.* Washington, D.C.: Smithsonian Institution Press, 1980.

Alberts, Don E. *The Battle of Glorieta: Union Victory in the West.* College Station: Texas A&M University Press, 1998.

Alter, Cecil J. *James Bridger.* Norman: University of Oklahoma Press, 1962.

Ambrose, Stephen E. *Crazy Horse and Custer: The Parallel Lives of Two American Warriors.* New York: Doubleday & Company, 1975.

Anderson, Ephraim McD. *Memoirs: Historical and Personal; Including the Campaigns of the First Missouri Confederate Brigade.* St. Louis: Times Printing Company, 1868.

Anderson, Harry H. "Stand at the Arikaree." *Colorado Magazine* 41 (Fall 1964).

Armes, Col. George A. *Ups and Downs of an Army Officer.* Washington, D.C., 1900.

Athearn, Robert G. *William Tecumseh Sherman and the Settlement of the West.* Norman: University of Oklahoma Press, 1956.

Bibliography

Ballou, Cornelius J. "The Sand Creek Affair." *National Tribune* [Washington, D.C.] (November 23, 1905).

Barnett, Louise. *Touched By Fire: The Life, Death, and Mythic Afterlife of George Armstrong Custer.* New York: Henry Holt and Company, 1996.

Bartels, Carolyn, ed. *The forgotten Men: Missouri State Guard,* (Independence, Mo.: Two Trails Publishing Company, 1995).

Becher, Ronald. *Massacre along the Medicine Road: A Social History of the Indian War of 1864 in Nebraska Territory.* Caldwell, Idaho: Caxton Press, 1999.

Bell, William A. *New Tracks in North America: A Journal of Travel and Adventure Whilst Engaged in the Survey for a Southern Railroad to the Pacific Ocean during 1867–1868.* London: Chapman and Hall, 1870.

Bent, Allen H. *The Bent Family in America, Being Mainly a Genealogy of the Descendants of John Bent.* Boston: David Clapp & Son, 1900.

Bent, George. "The Battle of the Medicine Arrows." *Frontier* 4 (November 1905).

———. "Forty Years with the Cheyennes, Part 1." Edited by George E. Hyde. *The Frontier* 4 (October 1905).

———. "Forty Years with the Cheyennes, Part 2: Battles Beyond the Border." Edited by George E. Hyde. *The Frontier* 4 (November 1905).

———. "Forty Years with the Cheyennes, Part 3." Edited by George E. Hyde. *The Frontier* 4 (December 1905).

———. "Forty Years with the Cheyennes, Part 4." Edited by George E. Hyde. *The Frontier* 4 (January 1905).

Berlo, Janet Catherine, ed. *Plains Indian Drawings: Pages from a Visual History.* New York: Harry N. Abrams, 1996.

Bernard, William R. "Westport and the Santa Fe Trade." *Kansas Historical Society Collections* 9 (1905–1906).

Berthrong, Donald J. *The Cheyenne and Arapaho Ordeal: Reservation and Agency Life in the Indian Territory, 1875–1907.* Norman: University of Oklahoma Press, 1963.

———. *The Southern Cheyennes.* Norman: University of Oklahoma Press, 1963.

Billon, Frederic L., comp. *Annals of St. Louis in its Early Days under the French and Spanish Dominations.* St. Louis: Privately printed, 1886.

Boatner, Mark Mayo, III. *The Civil War Dictionary.* New York: David McKay Company, Inc., 1959.

Bonner, Thomas D. *The Life and Adventures of James P. Beckwourth.* Introduction, Notes, and Epilogue by Delmont R. Oswald. Lincoln: University of Nebraska Press, 1972.

Bowles, Samuel. *Across the Continent: A Summer's Journey to the Rocky Mountains, the Mormons, and the Pacific States, With Speaker Colfax.* Springfield, Mass., and New York: Samuel Bowles & Company and Hurd & Houghton, 1865.

Brady, Cyrus Townsend. *Indian Fights and Fighters.* Introduction by James T. King. Lincoln: University of Nebraska Press, 1971.

Bibliography

Brown, Dee. *The Galvanized Yankees*. Urbana: University of Illinois Press, 1963.

Burke, John M. "Buffalo Bill, the Scout." *Trail* 11 (September 1918).

Burkey, Elmer R. "The Site of the Murder of the Hungate Family by Indians in 1864." *Colorado Magazine* 12 (1935).

Cahill, Luke. "Unwritten Scraps of History." *Trail* 18 (September 1925).

Campbell, Charles E. "Down Among the Red Men." *Kansas Historical Society Collections* 17 (1926–1928).

Campbell, Robert. "Private Journal of Robert Campbell." *Missouri Historical Society Bulletin* 20 (October 1963-July 1964).

Campbell, Walter S. "The Cheyenne Dog Soldiers." *Chronicles of Oklahoma* 1 (January 1921).

Capps, Benjamin. *The Indians*, rev. ed. New York: Time-Life Books, 1975.

Carey, Raymond. "The 'Bloodless Third' Regiment, Colorado Volunteer Cavalry." *Colorado Magazine* 38 (October 1961).

———"The Puzzle of Sand Creek." *Colorado Magazine* 41 (Fall 1964).

Carroll, John M., ed. *The Sand Creek Massacre: A Documentary History*. Introduction by John M. Carroll. New York: Sol Lewis, 1973.

Carter, Harvey Lewis. *'Dear Old Kit': The Historical Christopher Carson*. Norman: University of Oklahoma Press, 1990.

———, and M. Morgan Estergreen. *Kit Carson: A Portrait in Courage*. Norman: University of Oklahoma Press, 1962.

Case, Frank M. "Experiences on the Platte River Route in the Sixties." *Colorado Magazine* 5 (August 1928).

Catalogue of the Officers and Students of Webster College Family Boarding School for Boys, for the Annual Session, 1858–1859. St. Louis: Webster College, 1859.

Chalfant, William Y. *Cheyenne and Horse Soldiers: The 1857 Expedition and the Battle of Solomon's Fork*. Norman: University of Oklahoma Press, 1989.

———. *Cheyennes at Dark Water Creek: The Last Fight of the Red River War*. Foreword by Father Peter John Powell. Norman: University of Oklahoma Press, 1997.

Chittenden, Hiram Martin, and Alfred Talbot Richardson. *Life, Letters and Travels of Father Pierre-Jean De Smet, S.J., 1841–1873*. 4 vols. New York: Francis P. Harper, 1905.

Clark, Mrs. Olive A. "Early Days along the Solomon Valley." *Kansas Historical Society Collections* 17 (1926–1928).

Coel, Margaret. *Chief Left Hand: Southern Arapaho*. Norman: University of Oklahoma Press, 1981.

Collins, Hubert E. *Storm and Stampede on the Chisholm*. Foreword by Hamlin Garland. Introduction by Robert R. Dykstra. Lincoln: University of Nebraska Press, 1998.

Cooke, Philip St. George. *Calvary Tactics, or Regulations for the Instruction, Formations, and Movements of the Calvary of the Army and Volunteers of the*

United States. Prepared under the direction of the Secretary of War (Philadelphia: J.B. Lippincott & Co., 1862).

——. *Scenes and Adventures in the Army: Or Romance of Military Life*. Philadelphia: Lindsay & Blakiston, 1857.

Crawford, Samuel J. *Kansas in the Sixties*. Chicago: A. C. McClurg & Company, 1911.

Criqui, Orvel A. *Fifty Fearless Men: The Forsyth Scouts and Beecher Island*. Marceling, Mo.: Walsworth Publishing Company, 1995.

Crute, Joseph H., Jr. *Units of the Confederate States Army*. Midlothian, Va.: Derwent Books, 1987.

Custer, George Armstrong. *My Life on the Plains*. Edited and Introduction by Milo Milton Quaife. New York: Promontory Press, 1995.

Czaplewski, Russ. *Captive of the Cheyenne: The Story of Nancy Jane Morton and the Plum Creek Massacre*. Kearney, Nebr.: Dawson County Historical Society, 1993.

Danker, Donald F., ed. "The Journal of an Indian Fighter: The 1869 Diary of Major Frank J. North." *Nebraska History* 39 (June 1958).

——, ed. *Man of the Plains: Recollections of Luther North, 1856–1882*. Lincoln: University of Nebraska Press, 1961.

——. "The North Brothers and the Pawnee Scouts." *Nebraska History* 42 (September 1961).

Davis, Theodore R. "A Stage Ride to Colorado." *Harper's New Monthly Magazine* 35 (July 1867).

——. "A Summer on the Plains." *Harper's New Monthly Magazine* 36 (February 1868).

DeVoto, Bernard. *The Year of Decision*. Boston: Little, Brown & Company, 1943.

Densmore, Frances. *Cheyenne and Arapaho Music*. Southwest Museum Papers, 10. Los Angeles: Southwest Museum, 1936.

Dixon, David. *Hero of Beecher Island: The Life and Military Career of George A. Forsyth*. Lincoln: University of Nebraska Press, 1994.

Dixon, Olive K. *Life of 'Billy' Dixon*. Austin: State House Press, 1987.

Dorsey, George A. *The Cheyenne: Ceremonial Organization*. Anthropological Series, *Field Columbian Museum Publication* 99 9 (1905).

——. "How the Pawnees Captured the Cheyenne Medicine Arrows." *American Anthropologist*, n.s. 5 (October–December 1903).

Drumm, Stell M., ed. *Down the Santa Fe Trail and Into Mexico: The Diary of Susan Shelby Magoffin, 1846–1847*. Foreword by Howard R. Lamar. New Haven, Conn.: Yale University Press, 1962.

Dunlay, Tom. *Kit Carson and the Indians*. Lincoln: University of Nebraska Press, 2000.

Eaton, Clement. *The Growth of Southern Civilization, 1790–1860*. New York: Harper & Row, 1961.

Bibliography

Edrington, Thomas S., and John Taylor. *The Battle of Glorieta Pass: A Gettysburg in the West, March 26–28, 1862.* Albuquerque: University of New Mexico Press, 1998.

Ellenbecker, John G. *Tragedy at the Little Blue: The Oak Grove Massacre and the Captivity of Lucinda Eubank and Laura Roper.* Introduction, Maps, Photos, Annotations, and Reference by Lyn Ryder. 2d rev. ed. Niwot, Colo.: Prairie Lark Publications, 1993.

Ellis, Richard N. *General Pope and U.S. Indian Policy.* Albuquerque: University of New Mexico Press, 1970.

Elting, John R., and Michael J. McAfee, eds. "Long Endure: The Civil War Period 1852–1867," in *Military Uniforms in America.* Novato, Calif.: Presidio Press, 1982.

Encyclopedia of the History of St. Louis. 1899.

Ewers, John C. *The Horse in Blackfoot Indian Culture, With Comparative Material from Other Western Tribes.* Bureau of American Ethnology Bulletin 159. Washington, D.C.: Government Printing Office, 1955.

Faherty, William B. *The Saint Louis Portrait.* Tulsa: Continental Heritage, Inc., 1978.

———. "St. Louis College: First Community School." *Missouri Historical Society Bulletin* 2 (1968).

Fairfield, S. H. "The Eleventh Kansas Regiment at Platte Bridge." *Kansas Historical Society Collections* 8 (1903–1904).

Faller, Lincoln B. "Making Medicine against 'White Man's Side of Story': George Bent's Letters to George Hyde." *American Indian Quarterly* 24 (Winter 2000).

Farnham, Thomas J. "Travel in the Great Western Prairies, the Anahuac and Rocky Mountain, and in the Oregon Territory," in Reuben Gold Thwaites, *Early Western Travels*, vol. 28. Cleveland: Arthur H. Clark Company, 1906.

Fay, George E., ed. *Treaties, Land Cessions, and Other U.S. Congressional Documents Relative to American Indian Tribes, Cheyenne and Arapaho, 1825–1900.* Greeley: Museum of Anthropology, University of Northern Colorado, 1977.

Ferris, Warren. *Life in the Rocky Mountains: Diary of Wanderings on the Sources of the Rivers Missouri, Columbia, and Colorado from February 1830 to November 1835*, ed. Paul C. Phillips. Denver: Old West Publishing Company, 1940.

Field, Matthew C. *Matt Field on the Santa Fe Trail.* Edited and Introduction by John E. Sunder. Foreword by Mark L. Gardner. Norman: University of Oklahoma Press, 1995.

Filpiak, Jack D. "The Battle of Summit Springs." *Colorado Magazine* 41 (Fall 1964).

Flores, Dan. "Bison Ecology and Bison Diplomacy: The Southern Plains from 1800 to 1850." *Journal of American History* 78 (September 1991).

Bibliography

Forsyth, George A. *Thrilling Days in Army Life*. Lincoln: University of Nebraska Press, 1994.

Frost, Griffin. *Camp and Prison Journal*. Quincy, Ill., 1867.

Galvin, John, ed. *Through the Country of the Comanche Indians in the Fall of the Year 1845: The Journal of a U.S. Army Expedition Led by Lieutenant James W. Abert of the Topographical Engineers, Artist Extraordinary Whose Paintings of Indians and Their Wild West Illustrate This Book*. San Francisco: John Howell-Books, 1970.

Garrard, Lewis H. *Wah-to-Yah and the Taos Trail*. Introduction by Carl I. Wheat. Palo Alto, Calif.: American West Publishing Company, 1968.

Gerard, Hubert, ed. *Mississippi Vista: The Brothers of the Christian Schools in the Mid-West, 1849–1949*. Winona, Minn.: Saint Mary's College Press, 1948.

Gerboth, Christopher B., ed. *The Tall Chief: The Autobiography of Edward W. Wynkoop*. Denver: Colorado Historical Society, 1993.

Gill, Helen G. "The Establishment of Counties in Kansas." *Kansas Historical Society Collections* 8 (1903–1904).

Gottschalk, Phil. *In Deadly Earnest: The Missouri Brigade*. Columbia: Missouri River Press, 1991.

Grinnell, George Bird. "Bent's Old Fort and Its Builders." *Kansas Historical Society Collections* 15 (1919–1922).

———. *Beyond the Old Frontier: Adventures of Indian-Fighters, Hunters, and Fur-Traders*. New York: Charles Scribner's Sons, 1913.

———. *By Cheyenne Campfires*. New Haven: Yale University Press, 1962.

———. *The Cheyenne Indians: Their History and Ways of Life*. 2 vols. Lincoln: University of Oklahoma Press, 1972.

———. *The Fighting Cheyennes*. Norman: University of Oklahoma Press, 1956.

———. *Pawnee Hero Stories and Folk-Tales, with Notes on the Origin, Customs and Character of the Pawnee People*. Lincoln: University of Nebraska Press, 1961.

———. *Two Great Scouts and Their Pawnee Battalion: The Experiences of Frank J. North and Luther H. North, Pioneers in the Great West, 1856–1882, and the Defence of the Building of the Union Pacific Railroad*. Foreword by James T. King. Lincoln: University of Nebraska Press, 1973.

———. "When Beaver Skins Were Money." *Forest and Stream* (January 1, 1910).

Hadley, James Albert. "The Nineteenth Kansas Cavalry and the Conquest of the Plains Indians." *Kansas Historical Society Collections* 10 (1907–1908).

Hafen, LeRoy R. *Broken Hand: The Life of Thomas Fitzpatrick, Mountain Man, Guide and Indian Agent*. Denver: Old West Publishing Company, 1973.

Hafen, LeRoy R., ed. *Life in the Far West*. Norman: University of Oklahoma Press, 1951.

———, ed. *The Mountain Men and the Fur Trade of the Far West*. 10 vols. Glendale, Calif.: Arthur H. Clark Company, 1965–1972.

Bibliography

Hafen, Leory R., and Ann W. Hafen, eds. *Relations with the Indians of the Plains, 1857–1861: A Documentary Account of the Military Campaigns, and Negotiations of Indian Agents—With Reports and Journals of P. G. Lowe, R. M. Peck, J. E. B. Stuart, S. D. Sturgis, and Other Official Papers.* Glendale, Calif.: Arthur H. Clark Company, 1959.

———. *Ruxton of the Rockies.* Foreword by Mae Reed Porter. Norman: University of Oklahoma Press, 1951.

———, ed. "The W. M. Boggs Manuscript about Bent's Fort, Kit Carson, the Far West and Life among the Indians." *Colorado Magazine* 7 (March 1930).

Halaas, David Fridtjof. "'All the Camp was Weeping': George Bent and the Sand Creek Massacre." *Colorado Heritage* (Summer 1995).

———. *Boom Town Newspapers: Journalism on the Rocky Mountain Mining Frontier, 1859–1881.* Albuquerque: University of New Mexico Press, 1981.

———. *Worlds Apart: Indians and Whites in Nineteenth-Century Colorado.* Denver: Colorado Historical Society, 1984.

———, and Andrew E. Masich. "'You Could Hear the Drums for Miles': A Cheyenne Ledgerbook History." *Colorado Heritage* (Autumn 1996).

Hall, Frank. *History of the State of Colorado.* 4 vols. Chicago: Blakely Printing Company, 1889.

Harvey, J. R. "Pioneer Experiences in Colorado: Interview with Elizabeth J. Tallman." *Colorado Magazine* 13 (July 1936).

Hauptman, Laurence M. *Between Two Fires: American Indians in the Civil War.* New York: Free Press Paperbacks, 1996.

Hewett, Janet B., ed. *Supplement to the Official Records of the Union and Confederate Armies, Part II—Record of Events.* Wilmington, N.C.: Broadfoot Publishing Company, 1996.

———, ed. *Roster of Confederate Soldiers, 1861–1865.* Wilmington, N.C.: Broadfoot Publishing Company, 1995.

Hill, Nathaniel P. "Nathaniel P. Hill Inspects Colorado: Letters Written in 1864." *Colorado Magazine* 33 (October 1956).

"Historic Bent's Fort and Its Founders," *Denver Post* (January 11, 1920).

History of the Arkansas Valley, Colorado. Chicago: O. L. Baskin and Company, 1881.

History of Jackson County, Missouri, Containing A History of the County, Its Cities, Towns, Etc. Kansas City, MO.: Union Historical Company, 1881.

Hobbs, James. *Wild Life in the Far West: Personal Adventures of a Border Mountain Man.* Hartford, Conn.: Wiley, Waterman & Eaton, 1873.

Hodder, Halie Riley. "Crossing the Plains in War Times." *Colorado Magazine* 10 (July 1933).

Hoebel, E. Adamson. *The Cheyennes: Indians of the Great Plains.* Fort Worth: Harcourt Brace Jovanovich, 1978.

Hoig, Stan. *The Battle of the Washita: The Sheridan-Custer Indian Campaign of 1867–69.* Lincoln: University of Nebraska Press, Bixon Books Edition, 1979.

——. *The Peace Chiefs of the Cheyennes.* Norman: University of Oklahoma Press, 1980.

——. *The Sand Creek Massacre.* Norman: University of Oklahoma Press, 1961.

——. *The Western Odyssey of John Simpson Smith: Frontiersman, Trapper, Trader and Interpreter.* Glendale, Calif.: Arthur H. Clark Company, 1974.

Holder, Preston. *The Hoe and the Horse on the Plains: A Study of Cultural Development Among the North American Indians.* Lincoln: University of Nebraska Press, 1970.

Howard, Robert West. *The Horse in America.* Chicago and New York: Follett Publishing Company, 1965.

Hoyt, A. W. "Over the Plains to Colorado." *Harper's New Monthly Magazine* 35 (June 1867).

Hudnall, Mary Prowers. "Early History of Bent County." *Colorado Magazine* 22 (November 1945).

Hutton, Paul Andrew. *Phil Sheridan and His Army.* With a Foreword by Robert M. Utley. Lincoln: University of Nebraska Press, 1985.

Hyde, George E. *Indians of the High Plains: From the Prehistoric Period to the Coming of the Europeans.* Norman: University of Oklahoma Press, 1959.

——. *The Life of George Bent, Written from His Letters.* Edited by Savoie Lottinville. Norman: University of Oklahoma Press, 1968.

——. *The Pawnee Indians.* Denver: J. Van Male, 1951.

——. *Red Cloud's Folk: A History of the Oglala Sioux Indians.* Norman: University of Oklahoma Press, 1957.

——. *Spotted Tail's Folk: A History of the Brule Sioux.* Norman: University of Oklahoma Press, 1961.

Ingersoll, Lurton Dunham. *Iowa and the Rebellion: A History of the Troops Furnished by the State of Iowa to the Volunteer Armies of the Union, which Conquered the Great Southern Rebellion of 1861–1865.* Philadelphia: J. B. Lippincott & Company, 1866.

Isern, Thomas. D. "The Controversial Career of Edward W. Wynkoop." *Colorado Magazine* 56 (Winter/Spring 1979).

Jablow, Joseph. *The Cheyenne in Plains Indian Trade Relations, 1795–1840.* Monographs of the American Ethnological Society, 19. New York: J. J. Augustin, 1951.

Jackson, Donald, and Mary Lee Spence, eds. *The Expeditions of John Charles Fremont.* Vol. 3. Urbana: University of Illinois Press, 1970.

Jauken, Arlene Feldmann. *The Moccasin Speaks: Living As Captives of the Dog Soldier Warriors, Red River War, 1874–1875.* Lincoln, Nebr.: Dageforde Publishing, Inc., 1998.

Jones, Douglas C. *The Treaty of Medicine Lodge: The Story of the Great Treaty Council as Told by Eyewitnesses.* Norman: University of Oklahoma Press, 1966.

Josephy, Alvin M., Jr. *The Civil War in the American West*. New York: Alfred A. Knopf, 1992.

Keeling, Henry C. "The Indians: My Experience with the Cheyenne Indians." *Kansas Historical Society Collections* 11 (1909–1910).

Keim, De B. Randolph. *Sheridan's Troopers on the Border: A Winter Campaign on the Plains*. Williamstown, Mass.: Corner House Publishers, 1973.

Kelsey, Harry. "Background to Sand Creek." *Colorado Magazine* 45 (Fall 1968).

Kennedy, W. J. D., ed. *On the Plains with Custer and Hancock: The Journal of Isaac Coates, Army Surgeon*. Foreword by Jerome A. Green. Boulder: Johnson Books, 1997.

Keyes, Elizabeth. "Across the Plains in a Prairie Schooner." *Colorado Magazine* 10 (March 1933).

King, James T. *War Eagle: A Life of General Eugene A. Carr*. Lincoln: University of Nebraska Press, 1963.

———. "The Republican River Expedition, June–July, 1869, I, On the March," and "The Republican River Expedition, June–July, 1869, II, The Battle of Summit Springs." *Nebraska History* 41 (September/December 1960).

Knight, Oliver. *Following the Indian Wars: The Story of the Newspaper Correspondents among the Indian Campaigners*. Norman: University of Oklahoma Press, 1960.

Lansing, Michael. "Plains Indian Women and Interracial Marriage in the Upper Missouri Trade, 1804–1868." *Western Historical Quarterly* 31 (Winter 2000).

Larson, Robert W. *Red Cloud: Warrior-Statesman of the Lakota Sioux*. Norman: University of Oklahoma Press, 1997.

Lavender, David. *Bent's Fort*. New York: Doubleday & Company, Inc., 1954.

Lecompte, Janet. "Sand Creek." *Colorado Magazine* 41 (Fall 1964).

Llewellyn, Karl N., and E. Adamson Hoebel. *The Cheyenne Way: Conflict and Case Law in Primitive Jurisprudence*. Norman: University of Oklahoma Press, 1952.

Long, Margaret. *The Smoky Hill Trail*. Denver: Kistler, 1947.

Lowe, Percival G. *Five Years a Dragoon ('49 to '54) and Other Adventures of the Great Plains*. 1906. Reprint, with an Introduction and Notes by Don Russell. Norman: University of Oklahoma Press, 1965.

Lubers, H. L. "William Bent's Family and the Indians of the Plains." *Colorado Magazine* 13 (January 1936).

Lutz, J. J. "The Methodist Missions among the Indian Tribes in Kansas." *Kansas Historical Society Collections* 9 (1905–1906).

McCandless, Perry. *A History of Missouri, Vol. 2, 1820–1860* (Columbia: University of Missouri Press, 1972).

McChristian, Douglas C. "Plainsman—or Showman? George A. Custer's Buckskins." *Military Collector & Historian* 52 (Spring 2000).

Bibliography

McCoy, Nellie. "Memories of Old Westport." *Annals of Kansas City* (October 1924).

McClung, Quantrille D. *Carson-Bent-Boggs Genealogy*. Denver: Denver Public Library, 1962.

McDermott, John D. "'We had a Terribly Hard Time Letting Them Go': The Battle of Mud Springs and Rush Creek, February 1865." *Nebraska History* 77 (Summer 1996).

McDonnell, Janet A. *The Dispossession of the American Indian, 1887–1934*. Bloomington and Indianapolis: Indiana University Press, 1991.

McFeely, William S. *Grant: A Biography*. New York: W. W. Norton & Company, 1981.

McGinnis, Anthony. *Counting Coup and Cutting Horses: Intertribal Warfare on the Northern Plains, 1738–1889*. Evergreen, Colo.: Cordillera Press, 1990.

Mann, Henrietta. *Cheyenne-Arapaho Education, 1871–1982*. Niwot: University Press of Colorado, 1997.

Marquis, Thomas B. *Wooden Leg: A Warrior Who Fought Custer*. Lincoln: University of Nebraska Press, 1957.

Masich, Andrew E. "Cheyennes and Horses: A Transportation Revolution on the Great Plains." *History News* 52 (Autumn 1997).

Mattes, Merrill J. *The Great Platte River Road: The Covered Wagon Mainline Via Fort Kearny to Fort Laramie*. Lincoln: University of Nebraska Press, 1987.

Mayhall, Mildred P. *The Kiowas*. Norman: University of Oklahoma Press, 1962.

Miles, General Nelson A. *Personal Recollections and Observations of General Nelson A. Miles, Embracing a Brief View of the Civil War; Or, From New England to the Golden Gate, and the Story of His Indian Campaigns, With Comments on the Exploration, Development and Progress of Our Great Western Empire*. Introduction by Robert Wooster. 2 vols. Lincoln: University of Nebraska Press, 1992.

"Military Affairs." *American State Papers*. Vol. 4. Washington, D.C.: Gales & Seaton, 1860.

"Military Affairs." *American State Papers*, Vol. 6. Washington, D.C.: Gales & Seaton, 1861.

Mishkin, Bernard. *Rank and Warfare among the Plains Indians*. Lincoln: University of Nebraska Press, 1992.

Monaghan, Jay. *Civil War on the Western Border, 1854–1865*. Lincoln: University of Nebraska Press, 1984.

Monahan, Doris. *Destination: Denver City, the South Platte Trail*. Athens: Swallow Press/Ohio University Press, 1985.

Monnett, John H. *The Battle of Beecher Island and the Indian War of 1867–1869*. Niwot: University Press of Colorado, 1992.

———. *Massacre at Cheyenne Hole: Lieutenant Austin Henely and the Sappa Creek Controversy*. Niwot: University Press of Colorado, 1999.

Bibliography

——. *Tell Them We Are Going Home: The Odyssey of the Northern Cheyennes*. Norman: University of Oklahoma Press, 2001.

Montgomery, Mrs. Frank C. "Fort Wallace and Its Relation to the Frontier." *Kansas Historical Society Collections* 17 (1926–1928).

Mooney, James. *The Cheyenne Indians*. American Anthropological Association Memoirs, Vol. 1, pt. 6. Lancaster, Pa.: The New Era Printing Company, 1907.

Moore, John H. *The Cheyenne Nation: A Social and Demographic History*. Lincoln: University of Nebraska Press, 1987.

——. *The Cheyenne*. Cambridge, Mass.: Blackwell Publishers, 1996.

Moore, Milton. "An Incident on the Upper Arkansas in 1864." *Kansas Historical Society Collections* 10 (1907–1908).

Morgan, Dale L. *Jedediah Smith and the Opening of the West*. Indianapolis and New York: Bobbs-Merrill Company, Inc., 1953.

Moses, L. G. *The Indian Man: A Biography of James Mooney*. Urbana and Chicago: University of Illinois Press, 1984.

North, Capt. L. H. "My Military Experiences in Colorado." *Colorado Magazine* 11 (March 1934).

Noyes, Stanley. *Los Comanches: The Horse People, 1751–1845*. Albuquerque: University of New Mexico Press, 1993.

O'Brien, Emily Boyton. "Army Life at Fort Sedgwick, Colorado." *Colorado Magazine* 6 (July 1929).

Ordnance Manual for the Use of the Officers of the United States Army, 1860. Philadelphia: J. B. Lippincott & Company, 1861.

Painter, C. C. *Cheyennes and Arapahoes Revisited and a Statement of Their Agreement and Contract with Attorneys*. Philadelphia: Indian Rights Association, 1893.

Palmer, H. E. "History of the Powder River Indian Expedition of 1865." *Transactions and Reports of the Nebraska State Historical Society* 2. Lincoln: State Journal Company, 1887.

Parker, Mrs. C. F. "Old Julesburg and Fort Sedgwick." *Colorado Magazine* 7 (July 1930).

Parkhill, Forbes. *The Law Goes West*. Denver: Sage Books, 1956.

Paul, R. Eli, ed. *Autobiography of Red Cloud: War Leader of the Oglalas*. Helena: Montana Historical Society Press, 1997.

Peabody, Frances Clelland. "Across the Plains DeLuxe in 1865." *Colorado Magazine* 18 (March 1941).

Peck, Robert Morris. "Recollections of Early Times in Kansas Territory." *Kansas Historical Society Collections* 8 (1903–1904).

Perkin, Robert L. *First Hundred Years: An Informal History of Denver and the Rocky Mountain News*. Garden City, N.Y.: Doubleday & Company, Inc., 1959.

Perrigo, Lynn I., ed. "Major Hal Sayr's Diary of the Sand Creek Campaign." *Colorado Magazine* 15 (March 1938).

Petersen, Karen Daniels. "Cheyenne Soldier Societies." *Plains Anthropologist* 9 (August 1964).

———. *Howling Wolf: A Cheyenne Warrior's Graphic Interpretation of His People*. Palo Alto, Calif.: American West Publishing Company, 1968.

Peterson, Richard C., et al. *Sterling Price's Lieutenants: A Guide to the Officers and Organization of the Missouri State Guard, 1861–1865*. Shawnee Mission, Kans.: Two Trails Publishing, 1995.

Piston, William Garrett, and Richard W. Hatcher III. *Wilson's Creek: The Second Battle of the Civil War and the Men Who Fought It*. Chapel Hill: University of North Carolina Press, 2000.

Powell, Peter John. *People of Sacred Mountain: A History of the Northern Cheyenne Chiefs and Warrior Societies, 1830–1879, With an Epilogue, 1969–1974*. 2 vols. San Francisco: Harper & Row, 1981.

———. *Sweet Medicine: The Continuing Role of the Sacred Arrows, the Sun Dance, and the Sacred Buffalo Hat in Northern Cheyenne History*. 2 vols. Norman: University of Oklahoma Press, 1969.

Powers, Ramon. "Why the Northern Cheyenne Left Indian Territory in 1878: A Cultural Analysis." *Kansas Quarterly* 3 (Fall 1971).

———. "The Northern Cheyenne Trek through Western Kansas in 1878: Frontiersmen, Indians and Cultural Conflict." *Trail Guide* 17 (September/December 1972).

Prince, George P., comp. *Across the Continent with the Fifth Cavalry*. New York: Antiquarian Press, Ltd., 1959.

Prucha, Francis Paul. *The Great Father: The United States Government and the American Indians*. Vols. 1 and 2 unabridged. Lincoln: University of Nebraska Press, 1995.

Ragan, Stephen C. "Notes on the Pioneer School of Kansas City." *Annals of Kansas City* (December 1922).

Ray, Mrs. Sam. "Sunset Hill House Link to Fur Trade Days." *Kansas City Times* [Missouri], July 30, 1965.

Reckmeyer, Clarence. "The Battle of Summit Springs." *Colorado Magazine* 6 (November 1929).

Rees, D. S. "An Indian Fight on the Solomon." *Kansas Historical Society Collections* 7 (1901–1902).

"Reunion of Indian Fighters, Veterans Who Participated in Sand Creek Battle Will Congregate on Scene July 14." *Colorado Springs Gazette* (June 25, 1908).

Richardson, Albert K. *Beyond the Mississippi: From the Great River to the Great Ocean*. Hartford, Conn.: American Publishing Company, 1867.

Roberts, Gary L. *Death Comes to the Chief Justice: The Slough-Rynerson Quarrel and Political Violence in New Mexico*. Niwot: University Press of Colorado, 1990.

———, and David Fridtjof Halaas, "Written in Blood: The Soule-Cramer Sand Creek Massacre Letters." *Colorado Heritage* (Winter 2001).

Bibliography

Roe, Frank Gilbert. *The Indian and the Horse*. Norman: University of Oklahoma Press, 1955.

Root, George A. "Reminiscences of William Darnell." *Kansas Historical Society Collections* 17 (1926–1928).

Rosa, Joseph G. *They Called Him Wild Bill: The Life and Adventures of James Butler Hickok*. Norman: University of Oklahoma Press, 1964.

Roster and Record of Iowa Soldiers in the War of the Rebellion. 4 vols. Des Moines: Emory H. English, State Printer, 1910.

Russell, Carl P. *Firearms, Traps, and Tools of the Mountain Men*. New York: Alfred A. Knopf, 1967.

Russell, Don. *The Lives and Legends of Buffalo Bill*. Norman: University of Oklahoma Press, 1960.

Ryder, Lyn. *John G. Ellenbecker: Tragedy at the Little Blue: The Oak Grove Massacre and the Captivity of Lucinda Eubank and Laura Roper*. Niwot, Colo.: Prairie Lark Publications, 1993.

Sabin, Edwin L. *Kit Carson Days, 1809–1868: Adventures in the Path of Empire*. Introduction by Marc Simmons. 2 vols. Lincoln: University of Nebraska Press, 1995.

Sand Creek Massacre Project. Site Location Study, Vol 1, and *Special Resource Study and Environmental Assessment, Vol. 2*. Denver: National Park Service, Intermountain Region, 2000.

Sanford, Albert B. "Early Colorado Days: An Interview with Thomas T. Cornforth." *Colorado Magazine* 1 (September 1924).

———. "Life at Camp Weld and Fort Lyon in 1861–1862: An Extract from the Diary of Mrs. Byron N. Sanford." *Colorado Magazine* 7 (July 1930).

Sayre, Hal. "Early Central City Theatrical and Other Reminiscences." *Colorado Magazine* 6 (March 1929).

Scamehorn, Lee. *Albert Eugene Reynolds: Colorado's Mining King*. Norman: University of Oklahoma Press, 1995.

Scarritt, Reverend Nathan. "Reminiscences of the Methodist Shawnee Mission: And Religious Work Among that Tribe." *Annals of Kansas City* (1924).

Scott, Colonel H. L. *Military Dictionary: Comprising Technical Definitions . . . and Law, Government, Regulations, and Administration Relating to Land Forces*. New York: D. Van Nostrand, 1864.

Secoy, Frank Raymond. *Changing Military Patterns of the Great Plains Indians*. Lincoln: University of Nebraska Press, 1992.

Seger, John H. *Early Days among the Cheyenne and Arapahoe Indians*. Edited and with an Introduction by Stanley Vestal. Norman: University of Oklahoma Press, 1934.

Shaw, Luell. *True History of Some of the Pioneers of Colorado*. Hotchkiss, Colo.: W. S. Coburn, John Patterson, A.K. Shaw, 1909.

Shea, William L., and Earl J. Hess. *Pea Ridge: Civil War Campaign in the West*. Chapel Hill & London: University of North Carolina Press, 1992.

Sievers, Michael A. "Sands of Sand Creek Historiography." *Colorado Magazine* 49 (Spring 1972).

Sifakis, Steward. *Compendium of the Confederate Armies: Kentucky, Maryland, Missouri, the Confederate Units and the Indian Units.* New York: Facts on File, 1995.

Simmons, Virginia McConnell. *The Ute Indians of Utah, Colorado, and New Mexico.* Boulder: University Press of Colorado, 2000.

Skogen, Larry C. *Indian Depredation Claims, 1796–1920.* Norman: University of Oklahoma Press, 1996.

Smith, Sherry L. "George Bird Grinnell and the 'Vanishing' Plains Indians." *Montana The Magazine of Western History* 50 (Autumn 2000).

Snell, Jopseph W., and Robert W. Richmond. "When the Union Pacific Built through Kansas," part 1. *Kansas Historical Quarterly* 32 (Summer 1966).

———. "When the Union Pacific Built through Kansas," part 2. *Kansas Historical Quarterly* 32 (Autumn 1966).

Speer, Lonnie R. "A Hell on Earth." *Civil War Times Illustrated* (July/August 1995).

Spring, Agnes Wright. *Caspar Collins: The Life and Exploits of an Indian Fighter of the Sixties.* New York: Columbia University Press, 1927.

Staab, Rodney. "The Mission's Cross-Town Rival, The (First) Westport High School, 1853-Circa 1862." *New Views of Shawnee Mission, No. 18,* in *Friends Newsletter.* Fairway, Kan.: Shawnee Indian Mission, 1998.

Stands in Timber, John and Margot Liberty. *Cheyenne Memories.* Lincoln: University of Nebraska Press, 1972.

Stanley, Hemry M. "A British Journalist Reports." *Kansas Historical Quarterly* 33 (Autumn 1967).

———. *My Early Travels and Adventures in America.* 1895. Reprint, with a foreword by Dee Brown. Lincoln: University of Nebraska Press, 1982.

Stegmaier, Mark J., and David H. Miller. *James F. Milligan: His Journal of Fremont's Fifth Expedition, 1853–1854: His Adventurous Life on Land and Sea.* Glendale, Calif.: Arthur H. Clark Company, 1988.

Stiles, T. J. *Jesse James: Last Rebel of the Civil War.* New York: Alfred A. Knopf, 2002.

Stobie, Charles Steward. "Crossing the Plains to Colorado in 1865." *Colorado Magazine* 10 (November 1933).

Sunder, John E. *Joshua Pilcher: Fur Trader and Indian Agent.* Norman: University of Oklahoma Press, 1968.

Svingen, Orlan J. *The Northern Cheyenne Indian Reservation, 1877–1900.* Niwot: University Press of Colorado, 1993.

Szabo, Joyce M. *Howling Wolf and the History of Ledger Art.* Albuquerque: University of New Mexico Press, 1994.

Szasz, Margaret Connell, ed. *Between Indian and White Worlds: The Cultural Broker.* Norman: University of Oklahoma Press, 1994.

Bibliography

Taylor, Bayard. *Colorado: A Summer Trip.* William W. Savage, Jr., and James H. Lazalier, eds. Niwot: University Press of Colorado, 1989.

Taylor, Colin, and William C. Sturtevant. *The Native Americans: The Indigenous People of North America.* New York: Smithmark Publishers, Inc., 1991.

Thompson, George W. "Experiences in the West." *Colorado Magazine* 4 (December 1927).

Thrapp, Dan L. *Encyclopedia of Frontier Biography.* 3 vols. Lincoln: University of Nebraska Press, 1991.

Trenholm, Virginia Cole. *The Arapahoes, Our People.* Norman: University of Oklahoma Press, 1970.

Tucker, Phillip Thomas. *The South's Finest: The First Missouri Confederate Brigade from Pea Ridge to Vicksburg.* Shippensburg, Pa.: White Mane Publishing Company, Inc., 1993.

Unrau, William E., "A Prelude to War." *Colorado Magazine* 41 (Fall 1964).

———., ed. *Tending the Talking Wire: A Buck Soldier's View of Indian Country, 1863–1866.* Salt Lake City: University of Utah Press, 1979.

———. *White Man's Wicked Water: The Alcohol Trade and Prohibition in Indian Country, 1802–1892.* Lawrence: University Press of Kansas, 1996.

Utley, Robert M. *Frontier Regulars: The United States Army and the Indian, 1866–1891.* New York: Macmillan, 1973.

———. *Frontiersmen in Blue: The United States Army and the Indian, 1848–1865.* New York: Macmillan, 1967.

———, ed. *Life in Custer's Cavalry: Diaries and Letters of Albert and Jennie Barnitz, 1867–1868.* New Haven, Conn.: Yale University Press, 1977.

Van Kirk, Sylvia. *Many Tender Ties: Women in Fur-trade Society, 1670–1870.* Norman: University of Oklahoma Press, 1983.

Van Loan, C. E. "Veterans of 1864 Revisit Scene of Indian Battle on the Banks of Sand Creek, Colo." *Denver Post* (July 26, 1908).

Vaughn, J. W. *The Battle of Platte Bridge.* Norman: University of Oklahoma Press, 1963.

Viola, Herman J. *Warrior Artists: Historic Cheyenne and Kiowa Indian Ledger Art, Drawn by Making Medicine and Zotom.* Washington, D.C.: National Geographic Society, 1998.

Waldo, William. "Recollections of a Septuagenarian." Missouri Historical Society, *Glimpses of the Past 5* (April–June 1938).

Walter, John F. *Capsuule Histories of Missouri Units.* 4 vols. Middle Village, N.Y.: Privately printed, n.d.

Ward, Josiah M. "Chivington at the Battle of Sand Creek." *The Denver Post* (February 6, 1921).

Ware, Eugene F. *The Indian War of 1864.* 1911. Reprint, with an introduction by John D. Mc Dermott and notes by Clyde C. Walton. Lincoln: University of Nebraska Press, Bison Books Edition, 1994.

Bibliography

Wessel, Thomas R. "George Bird Grinnell," in *Historians of the American Frontier*, John R. Wunder. New York: Greenwood Press, 1988.

West, Elliott. "Called Out People: The Cheyennes and the Central Plains." *Montana The Magazine of Western History* 48 (Summer 1998).

———. *Contested Plains: Indians, Goldseekers, and the Rush to Colorado.* Lawrence: University Press of Kansas, 1998.

Whitford, William C. *The Battle of Glorieta Pass: The Colorado Volunteers in the Civil War, March 26, 27, 28, 1862, With a Factual Analysis of the Military Strategy of Both Sides, Illustrated with Explanatory Maps, Compiled and Drawn by Burt Schmitz.* Glorieta, N.M.: Rio Grande Press, Inc., 1991.

———. *Colorado Volunteers in the Civil War: The New Mexico Campaign in 1862.* Denver: State Historical and Natural History Society, 1906.

"William Bent's Life Saved by 'Lawyer' A Cheyenne Doctor." *Denver Post* (January 11, 1920).

Williams, Dallas. *Fort Sedgwick, C.T.: Hell Hole on the Platte.* Sedgwick, Colo.: F.S.R. Trust, 1993.

Williams, T. Harry. *P. G. T. Beauregard: Napoleon in Gray.* Baton Rouge: Louisiana State University Press, 1995.

Wissler, Clark. *North American Indians of the Plains.* American Museum of Natural History Handbook Series No. 1. New York: American Museum of Natural History, 1927.

Woodward, Arthur. "Sidelights on Bent's Old Fort." *Colorado Magazine* 33 (October 1956).

Wright, Robert M. "Personal Reminiscences of Frontier Life in Southwest Kansas." *Kansas Historical Society Collections* 7 (1901–1902).

Young, Otis E. *First Military Escort on the Santa Fe Trail, 1829.* Glendale, Calif.: Arthur H. Clark Company, 1952.

Newspapers

Arkansas City Traveler [Kansas]
Cheyenne Transporter [Darlington, Oklahoma]
Colony Courrier [Oklahoma]
Colorado Springs Gazette
Colorado Sun [Greeley]
Daily Commonwealth [Denver]
Denver Post
Denver Times
Grit-Advocate [Julesburg, Colorado]
Kansas City Times
Las Animas Leader [Colorado]
Missouri Democrat

Missouri Republican
National Tribune [Washington, D.C.]
Pueblo Colorado Chieftain
Rocky Mountain News [Denver]
Sunday Oklahoman [Oklahoma City]
Westport Border Star [Missouri]

Index

Index

Index

Index

Index